Confucius and the *Analects*

Confucius

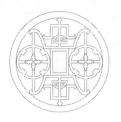 and the *Analects*

New Essays

EDITED BY
BRYAN W. VAN NORDEN

OXFORD
UNIVERSITY PRESS

2002

OXFORD

UNIVERSITY PRESS

Oxford   New York

Athens   Auckland   Bangkok   Bogotá   Buenos Aires   Cape Town
Chennai   Dar es Salaam   Delhi   Florence   Hong Kong   Istanbul   Karachi
Kolkata   Kuala Lumpur   Madrid   Melbourne   Mexico City   Mumbai   Nairobi
Paris   São Paulo   Shanghai   Singapore   Taipei   Tokyo   Toronto   Warsaw

and associated companies in
Berlin   Ibadan

Published by Oxford University Press, Inc.
198 Madison Avenue, New York, New York 10016

Oxford is a registered trademark of Oxford University Press

Library of Congress Cataloging-in-Publication Data
Confucius and the analects : new essays / edited by Bryan W. Van Norden.
p.   cm.
Includes bibliographical references and index.
ISBN 0-19-513395-1; ISBN 0-19-513396-X (pbk.)
1. Confucius. Lun Yè.   I. Van Norden, Bryan W. (Bryan William)
PL2471.Z7 C65   2000 2002
181'.112—dc21   00-025758

The publisher gratefully acknowledges the permission granted for the following:

Kwong-loi Shun, "Jen and Li in the Analects," Philosophy East and West 43:3 (July 1993), pp. 457–79.
Reprinted with permission from Philosophy East and West.

Stephen A. Wilson, "Conformity, Individuality, and the Nature of Virtue:
A Classical Confucian Contribution to Contemporary Ethical Reflection,"
Journal of Religious Ethics 23:2 (fall 1995): 263–89.

1 3 5 7 9 8 6 4 2

Printed in the United States of America
on acid–free paper

For my father,
Charles R. Van Norden Sr.

Contents

Contributors

E. Bruce Brooks and A. Taeko Brooks are the cofounders of the Warring States Project and e-mail list, and coauthors of *The Original Analects: Sayings of Confucius and His Successors*. E. Bruce Brooks is research professor of Chinese at the University of Massachusetts at Amherst and director of the Warring States Project. A. Taeko Brooks is a research associate of the Warring States Project. They are currently working on monographs that extend their methodology and the results of their research to other Warring States texts.

Mark Csikszentmihalyi is an assistant professor in both East Asian Languages and Literature and Religious Studies at the University of Wisconsin at Madison. He is a co-editor (with P. J. Ivanhoe) and contributor to *Religious and Philosophical Aspects of the Laozi*, and is the editor of the American Academy of Religion's Texts and Translations series. He is currently working on a book, *Material Virtue: Ethics and Natural Philosophy in Early China*.

Philip J. Ivanhoe is an associate professor in both the Department of Asian Languages and Cultures and the Philosophy Department at the University of Michigan. He has published on a range of topics in the fields of Religious Studies, Philosophy, and Asian Studies. He is the author of *Ethics in the Confucian Tradition: The Thought of Mencius and Wang Yang-ming* and *Confucian Moral Self Cultivation*. He has also contributed to and edited *Chinese Language, Thought and Culture*, *Essays on Skepticism, Relativism and Ethics in the Zhuangzi* (with Paul Kjellberg), *Religious and Philosophical Aspects of the Laozi* (with Mark Csikszentmihalyi), and *Readings in Classical Chinese Philosophy* (with Bryan W. Van Norden). He is currently at work on a translation of the writings of the Chinese philosophical historian, Zhang Xuecheng.

Joel J. Kupperman is a professor in the Philosophy Department at the University of Connecticut. He has published on both "mainstream" Anglo-American ethics and on comparative philosophy, including the books *Value . . . And What Comes After*, *Character*, and *Learning from Asian Philosophy*.

Robert B. Louden is a professor in the Philosophy Department at the University of Southern Maine. His research focuses primarily on Western ethics. He has written *Moral Theory: A Reappraisal and Reaffirmation* and *Kant's Impure Ethics: From Rational Beings to Human Beings*, is a coeditor and contributor to *The Greeks and Us: Essays in Honor of Arthur W. H. Adkins*, and is the translator of several of Kant's works on education and anthropology for the forthcoming *Cambridge Edition of the Works of Immanuel Kant*.

Lisa A. Raphals is an associate professor and director of program in Comparative and World Literature in the Department of Comparative Literature and Foreign Languages at the University of California at Riverside. She is the author of *Knowing Words: Wisdom* and Cunning in the Classical Traditions of China and Greece and Sharing the Light: Representations of Women and Virtue in Early China. She is currently working on a study of fate and fatalism in China and Greece, and also on a smaller-scale study of gnomon shadow measurements and their use in Chinese and Greek mathematical astronomy.

Joel Sahleen is a doctoral student in the Department of Asian Studies at Stanford University, where he is writing a thesis on the relationship between early Confucian theories of self-cultivation and politics. He has translated portions of the Han Feizi for Readings in Classical Chinese Philosophy.

Kwong-loi Shun is a professor of philosophy at the University of California at Berkeley. In addition to many articles, he has published Mencius and Early Chinese Thought, which is the first of a projected three-volume series on the textual and philosophical issues raised by the sayings attributed to Confucius, Mencius, and some of the major thinkers influenced by them.

Bryan W. Van Norden is an associate professor in both the Philosophy Department and the Asian Studies Program at Vassar College. He has published on many aspects of early Chinese philosophy, edited The Ways of Confucianism, and has coedited (with Philip J. Ivanhoe) and contributed to Readings in Classical Chinese Philosophy.

Stephen A. Wilson is an assistant professor of the humanities at Christ College, the honors college of Valparaiso University. His primary research interests lie in the history of Christian ethics, but he also has an abiding interest in comparative ethics and the cross-cultural implications of religious claims to universality. He is currently writing a book, The Virtue of the Saints: Reconsidering Jonathan Edwards' Ethics.

Lee H. Yearley is the Evans-Wentz Professor of Religious Studies at Stanford University. His research specializes in comparative religious ethics, virtue theory, selected Christian thinkers, and classical Chinese thought. He is the author of The Ideas of Newman: Christianity and Human Religiosity and Mencius and Aquinas: Theories of Virtue and Conceptions of Courage, as well as numerous journal articles.

Confucius and the *Analects*

Introduction

BRYAN W. VAN NORDEN

IMAGINE A PERSON WHO HAS AN INFLU-
ence on his native tradition comparable to the combined influence of Jesus
and Socrates on the Western tradition.
Such a person was Confucius.

The similarities continue. Although all three were literate, perhaps all highly so, neither Confucius, nor Jesus, nor Socrates left behind any of his own writings. We know each only through the later writings of his admirers and detractors. In addition, each had a distinctive, charismatic, and complex personality. These three common features have made each the object of love, hatred, admiration, denigration, and debate for over two millennia.[1]

Though Confucius is referred to in a variety of early Chinese texts, one of our most important sources of information about him is the *Analects*, a collection of sayings, brief discussions, and observations by and about Confucius, his disciples, and his contemporaries. Despite its great importance, prior to this volume there has never been a collection of secondary essays in English on the *Analects*. This volume is a collection of essays on the *Analects*, and on Confucius as seen (primarily) in that classic.

For the last two millennia, most scholars (whether Eastern or Western) have taken all twenty "books" of the *Analects* as an accurate record of what Confucius and his disciples have said. But scholarship in recent centuries has become more suspicious, investigating such issues as the historical composition of the text of the *Analects* and the sectarian motives behind various conceptions of Confucius. Consequently, the essays in this anthology are loosely grouped into two sections (based on an aphorism from *Analects* 2:11: "One who can keep warm the old, yet appreciate the new, is fit to be a teacher"). "Keeping Warm the Old" consists of essays that do not call into question the view that the received text of the *Analects* represents a coherent worldview. In contrast, the essays in "Appreciating the New" either call into question the integrity of the received text of the *Analects*, or explore aspects of the image of Confucius that have been neglected by some of the dominant interpretive traditions.

The remainder of this introduction provides background information to introduce the general reader to Confucius, his times, and the *Analects*.

China before and after Confucius

Confucius was born into an ancient and troubled culture.

The Yellow River valley in northern China is one of the great "cradles of civilization," with neolithic sites that date back to the fifth millenium B.C.E.[2] There is evidence that, already by the end of the Neolithic period, some of the characteristic features of later Chinese culture were in place, including social hierarchy connected with partilinial descent, the use of ritual objects, and elaborate burial procedures.[3] Some time after 2000 B.C.E., Bronze Age civilizations developed in the same region.[4] Distinctive of these civilizations was the use of bronze for weapons and for ritual objects, and eventually the use of early forms of Chinese characters.

Traditionally, Chinese history begins with the predynastic "sage kings" of antiquity, most notably kings Yáo 堯, Shùn 舜, and Yǔ 禹. There are two contemporary theories about the sage king traditions. One view is that they represent exaggerated hagiographic accounts of actual early Chinese rulers.[5] Another view is that such early accounts are a rationalization of the myths of the Shang people.[6]

Whatever the truth, the first "Three Dynasties" (*sān dài* 三代) of Chinese history are traditionally identified as the Xià 夏, the Shāng 商, and the Zhōu 周. The historicity of the Xià (which was allegedly founded by Sage King Yu) has not yet been verified, although many archaeologists believe that it is not mythical.[7] The Shāng is the earliest dynasty to have definitively emerged from the mists of prehistory. In the Shāng worldview, politics, ritual, and attitudes toward the dead were closely intertwined. When faced with uncertainty about the future, or a difficult decision, the Shāng rulers practiced "scapulimancy": the divination of the future through reading the cracks on heated "oracle bones."[8] Was the illness of the king's consort caused by such and such an ancestor? Would the ancestors look favorably upon our founding a new city in such and such a place? Would such and such a ritual appease the ancestors? These rituals typically involved giving sacrifices of food and wine to the ancestors using a wide variety of beautiful bronze vessels. K. C. Chang suggests that

> the possession of such sacred bronze vessels served to legitimize the king's rule. These vessels were clear and powerful symbols: they were symbols of wealth because they *were* wealth and possessed the aura of wealth; they were symbols of the all-important ritual that gave their owners access to the ancestors; and they were symbols of the control of metal, which meant control of exclusive access to the ancestors and to political authority.[9]

Consequently, already in Shāng civilzation, we see the characteristic Chinese joining of respect for ancestors, ritual activity, and political power.

Some time around 1040 B.C.E., the Shāng were defeated by their neighbors to the west, the Zhōu people.[10] Lacking the techniques or infrastructure of a strongly centralized state, the Zhōu rulers parceled out control of various regions to nobles, usually related by blood or marriage to the royal family, who administered their states in the name of the Zhōu king. (This has been described as a "feudal system," but the appropriateness of using the European term in a Chinese context has occasioned considerable debate.[11]) For our purposes, the most important Zhōu kings were Wén 文, his son Wǔ 武, who led the actual conquest of the Shāng but died soon after the conquest, and Chéng 成, who succeeded to the throne as a minor. Having a minor on the throne while still consolidating a recent conquest is a precarious situation. Fortunately for the Zhōu, there was Dàn 旦, better known to posterity as the Duke of Zhōu (Zhōu Gōng) 周公.

The Duke of Zhōu was a younger brother of King Wǔ, hence an uncle of young King Chéng. It would have been tempting for the duke to dispose of his nephew and assume the kingship himself. However, he chose to act as regent, and worked hard to solidify Zhōu rule.[12] For this, he has been admired by generations of Confucians for his loyalty. (Thus, centuries later, Confucius would remark, "How I have gone downhill! It has been such a long time since I dreamt of the Duke of Chou" [Lau 7:5].) But the Duke of Zhōu was apparently a very savvy and effective political and military leader, and he realized that it was better to rule than to reign. In addition to doing such things as taking decisive military action against rebellious nobles, the Duke of Zhōu apparently started a propaganda campaign, arguing that, because the last ruler of the Shāng was corrupt and cruel to his people, Heaven (tiān 天) had taken the mandate to rule (mìng 命) away from the Shāng king, and given it to the virtuous Zhōu rulers.[13] This doctrine became the basis of Chinese political thought for the next three millennia.[14]

The political system of the Zhōu apparently worked well for a period. (Indeed, the early Zhōu dynasty came to be thought of as a sort of utopia, to which later ages could only aspire.) Eventually, though, the local lords began to think of their own positions as hereditary, and their "fiefs" as their own states. The Zhōu ruler had less and less power, until in 771 B.C.E. a coalition of Chinese and "barbarian" soldiers attacked the Zhōu capital, killing the king. A member of the royal family survived, setting up a new capital, farther to the east, but it was now clear that the king was only a figurehead. Based on this watershed incident, the Zhōu dynasty is typically divided into the Western Zhōu (from about 1040 to 771 B.C.E.) and the Eastern Zhōu (from 770 to 221 B.C.E.).[15] The Eastern Zhou was characterized by increasingly brutal interstate and intrastate violence and warfare. In this fluid social context there was increased social mobility, as old nobility quickly fell from power, to be replaced by those more clever (or lucky) than they. For the first time in Chinese history, there arose a class of educated individuals who were not, from birth, in the employ of any particular nobility.[16] Confucius was one of these scholars.

Two subperiods within the Eastern Zhōu are especially important: the Spring and Autumn, and the Warring States eras. The former is named after the *Spring and Autumn Annals* (Chūn qiū 春秋), a cryptically terse historical work, which lists events correlated with the reigns of the dukes of Lǔ 魯 between 722 and 481 B.C.E.. Confucius lived during the later part of this "Spring and Autumn period."[17] There are three traditional commentaries on the *Spring and Autumn Annals*, the most famous of which is the Zuǒ zhuàn 左傳 (*The Commentary of Zuo*). The Zuǒ zhuàn provides a vivid and frightening picture of life before and during the time of Confucius.[18] Typical is the first extended narrative in the Zuǒ zhuàn, in which a mother plots with her younger son to murder her eldest son after he succeeds to his father's dukedom, forcing the older son to take military action against his brother and put his mother under "house arrest."[19] In the context of such unfamilial behavior, it is no wonder that, when asked about the way to govern a state, Confucius is reported to have simply said, "Let the prince be a prince, the minister a minister, the father a father and the son a son" (Waley 12:11).

One of the features of the Spring and Autumn era was the institution of the bà 霸 or "hegemon." The bà was a local lord who gained enough power to convince the other lords to accept his leadership. The power of a bà was intrinsically unstable, but the institution did manage to bring a degree of order to China during this period. The bà became a symbol of rule by force as opposed to rule by virtue.[20] The first official bà was Duke Huan of Qi (Qí Huán Gōng) 齊桓公, who gained the position with the assistance of his able (but somewhat unscrupulous) minister, Guǎn Zhòng 管仲. The *Analects* records apparently contradictory comments by Confucius about Guǎn Zhòng. At one point, Confucius denigrates Guǎn Zhòng for his pettiness, lack of frugality, and failure to understand ritual (3:22). Elsewhere, Confucius defends Guǎn Zhòng to two Confucian disciples (14:16–17). Although some have suggested that this reflects the complexity of Confucius' view of Guǎn Zhòng, I think it simply reflects the political agendas of different redactors of the *Analects*.[21] (In their contribution to this volume, E. Bruce Brooks and A. Taeko Brooks discuss some of the "political" issues that underlie the composition of the *Analects*.)

Eventually, the political and military situation decayed to the point that not even a bà could maintain order. Thus begins the "Warring States" (zhàn guó 戰國) era, the other subperiod in the Eastern Zhōu, which runs from 403 to 221 B.C.E.[22] In addition to being an era of intense interstate warfare, the Warring States is also a period of many changes (as summarized by Mark Lewis):

> the rise of private ownership of land, the development of water control
> and iron tools leading to expanding agricultural output, a probable
> increase in population, a massive upsurge in the scale and diversity of
> urban centers, the burgeoning of handicraft industries and trade, the
> increased use of money, and the introduction of hired labor. . . . the
> disappearance of the old [hereditary] aristocracy, the rise of a large class
> of land-owning peasants, and a substantial increase in the urban classes
> devoted to trade and handicraft production. . . . the creation of a
> government staffed entirely by appointed, salaried officials, the assertion
> of direct control over local governments by the court, the promulgation

of legal codes, and the comprehensive registration of the population.
. . . the introduction of cavalry, the invention of the crossbow, the
increased use of iron weapons, the rise of mass, infantry armies
[which, along with cavalry, replaced the chariot armies of the earlier
aristocracy], and the appearance of commanders who held office
through their mastery of the arts of generalship.[23]

The Warring States was also a period of flourishing philosophical debate.[24]
Although many people think of traditional Chinese culture as "Confucian," Confucianism was just one intellectual movement in Warring States period China.
(Hence, the period is sometimes known as the era of the "100 Schools," bǎi jiā
百家.[25]) Soon after Confucius died, Mohists (followers of the philosopher Mòzǐ
墨子) developed a consequentialist ethical system that was antitraditional and anti-
Confucian. (Confucius is subjected to a vicious personal attack in the Mohist essay,
"Against Confucians."[26]) Yáng Zhū 楊朱 criticized both Confucians and Mohists,
arguing that we should follow "human nature" (rén xìng 人性), which dictates
that we preserve our lives, rather than take part in governmental activity.[27] Angus
C. Graham has argued that Yáng Zhū made the notion of "human nature" central
to philosophical debate in China in a way that it had not been before, and we do
see later Confucians taking clear stands on the issue of whether human nature
is good (as argued in the fourth century B.C.E. by Mencius [Mèngzǐ] 孟子) or
bad (as argued in the third century B.C.E. by Xúnzǐ 荀子).[28] In addition, the
"Daoist" Zhuāngzǐ 莊子 rejected both the ethical self-cultivationism of the
Confucians and the consequentialism of the Mohists in favor of detached skillful
activity.[29]

The Warring States era came to an end in 221 B.C.E., when the state of Qín 秦
conquered all the other states, unified China, and reestablished order. The dominant ideology of Qín was Legalism, and the Qín ruler suppressed all other philosophies, including Confucianism.[30] He even ordered the mass murder of Confucian
scholars and the burning of Confucian and other books. Fortunately, the Qín
dynasty only survived until 207 B.C.E.[31]

The Hàn 漢 dynasty began in 202 B.C.E. and lasted (with a brief interregnum)
until C.E. 220. The Analects would always be an important text from this time on,[32]
although its influence varied with the vicissitudes of the Confucian movement.
Emperor Wǔ of the Hàn (Hàn Wǔ Dì 漢武帝, r. 141–87 B.C.E.) made Confucianism the official ideology of the state. This appears to signal the dominance of Confucianism, and in a sense it does. However, Han Confucianism was very eclectic,
combining elements of many non-Confucian philosophies. One scholar has
referred to the "content-free Confucianism" of this period, and it has even been
argued that the official biography of Confucius in the Shǐjì 史紀, "Records of the
Grand Historian," is a subtle Daoist attack on Confucius.[33] (Mark Csikszentmihalyi
discusses some of the interpretations of the figure of Confucius during the Hàn
in his contribution to this volume.)

One of the major intellectual events of the Hàn was the introduction of Buddhism to China, some time in the first century C.E. Buddhism (along with forms of Daoism) became (de facto) the dominant ideology in China after the fall of the Hàn. Centuries later, beginning in the Táng 唐 dynasty (C.E. 618–906), the so-called Neo-Confucian movement (in Chinese, *dào xué* 道學 or "study of the Way") reacted against the "barbarian" Buddhist religion.[34] The brilliant synthesizer Zhū Xī 朱熹 (C.E. 1130–1200) is considered by many to be the greatest philosopher and commentator of the Neo-Confucian tradition. Zhū Xī, who lived during the Southern Sòng 宋 dynasty (C.E. 1127–1279), held that each thing is a composite of lǐ 理 and qì 氣. Qì is the fundamental "stuff" out of which every physical object is composed. Lǐ is a metaphysical structuring principle fully present in each and every thing that exists, from a mote of dust, to a cat, to you or me. Although the lǐ is the same and complete in each thing, it manifests itself to different extents in different things because of the degree of clarity of the qì of which each thing is constituted. Zhū Xī also promoted a standard educational curriculum based on the "Four Books" (*sì shū* 四書): the *Great Learning*, the *Mean*, the *Mengzi*, and the *Analects*, and wrote commentaries that interpreted each book in terms of his metaphysics.[35] In C.E. 1313, during the Yuán 元 dynasty (C.E. 1280–1368), the Four Books and Zhū Xī's commentaries on them were made the basis of the civil service examinations, and remained so until the examinations were eliminated in 1905. Consequently, generations of Confucian scholars had to literally commit the *Analects* (and Zhū Xī's interpretation of it) to memory.[36] This colors many interpretations of Confucius and Confucianism, even today.[37] (In his contribution to this volume, P. J. Ivanhoe illustrates the influence of Neo-Confucianism and other Chinese intellectual movements by examining how interpretations of one line in the *Analects* have varied over two millennia under the influence of the interpreters' metaphysical views.)

Despite the fact that Neo-Confucianism is nominally anti-Buddhist, it is deeply influenced by Buddhism, especially Huáyán 華嚴 and Chán 禪.[38] Indeed, we might say that Neo-Confucians see their tradition through Buddhist lenses. As an illustration, consider the following quotations. The first is from the "Platform Sutra" of the Sixth Patriarch of Chan Buddhism:

> The purity of people's nature is comparable to the clear sky, their wisdom comparable to the sun, and sagacity comparable to the moon. Their sagacity and wisdom are always shining. It is only because externally people are attached to spheres of objects that erroneous thoughts, like floating clouds, cover the self-nature so that it is not clear.[39]

Now consider the following exchange between the great Neo-Confucian Wáng Yángmíng 王陽明 and one of his disciples:

> The Master [that is, Wáng Yángmíng] also said, "Pure knowing is within human beings. No matter what you do, you cannot deceive or destroy it. Even a thief knows he should not be a thief. If you call him a thief, he still will blush." Yü–chung said, "(He steals) only because

> (his pure knowing) is covered over and obscured by material desires.
> But pure knowing is within him; it can never be lost. It is like when
> clouds obscure the sun—how could the sun ever be lost!" The Master
> said, "How brilliant is Yü–chung! Others do not see it as clearly as he
> does."[40]

I submit that Confucius would find this language quite alien. Only someone who, like Wang, had been deeply influenced by Buddhist ideas, would speak in this way.

The influence of Confucius is not limited, of course, to East Asia. Confucius has been an influence, and a source of interest, in the West since at least the reports of early Jesuit missionaries in the seventeenth century. In his contribution to this volume, Robert B. Louden discusses the interpretation of Confucius in an infamous lecture by the early Enlightenment scholar Christian Wolff. And just as Wolff made Confucius a figure in the Enlightenment debate over the relationship between religion and ethics, so have more recent philosophers invoked Confucius as an ally in defense of behaviorism and postmodernism. Stephen A. Wilson takes issue with some of these more recent interpreters in his contribution to this volume.

The Life of Confucius

We owe to Jesuit missionaries the name "Confucius," which is a Latinization of the Chinese Kǒngfūzǐ 孔夫子, which means "Master Kong." However, if you actually use the expression "Kǒngfūzǐ" when talking to a native Chinese speaker, you will probably elicit only a puzzled stare, because contemporary Chinese speakers typically refer to Confucius simply as Kǒngzǐ 孔子, which also means "Master Kong."[41]

Confucius was born in either 552 or 551 B.C.E., in the village of Zōu 郰,[42] in the state of Lǔ 魯, which was located in what is now Shāndōng 山東 province in the People's Republic of China.[43] The state of Lǔ was established by the Zhōu rulers for the descendants of the Duke of Zhōu.[44] However, by the time of Confucius, Lu was a small state, harrassed by more powerful states on all sides. Officially, the ruler of Lǔ when Confucius was born was Duke Xiang (Xiāng Gōng 襄公). However, the real power in the state was divided between the so-called "Three Families": the Jì 季, the Mèng (孟), and the Shú (叔). The most powerful of the three was the Jì, so the position of "chief minister" in Lǔ, the most powerful position in the state, was always occupied by a member of this family. Although the duke of Lǔ had titular authority, the families usurped some of the ritual signs of the authority and prestige of the duke, and even of the king, such as having eight rows of dancers perform in their courtyard (3:1), performing the Yong ode during the removal of sacrificial vessels (3:2), and making a ritual offering on Mount Tai (3:6). Regarding one such abuse, Confucius moaned, "If this can be tolerated, what cannot be tolerated?" (Lau 3:1)

Of Confucius' life between birth and middle age we know little. However, he himself remarked, "I was of humble station when young. That is why I am skilled in many menial things" (Lau 9:6). According to one account, he was from a noble family that had fallen on hard times. It is possible that, as Creel has suggested,[45] Confucius' own rise from poverty and obscurity contributed to the meritocratic aspects of his thought: "I have never denied instruction to anyone who, of his own accord, has given me so much as a bundle of dried meat as a present" (Lau 7:7). Confucius' father is said to have died when he was young.[46] Perhaps significantly, Confucius stressed the importance of following the "Way of one's father" (1:11, 4:20). This is only speculation on my part, but I wonder whether the early death of his father contributed to Confucius' strong traditionalism. After all, it is easier to idealize a paternal figure when you have never actually interacted with him.

We know nothing for certain about Confucius' mother. However, to have, in such circumstances, raised a son who could aspire to high office was a considerable achievement. She is likely to have had an impressive character. He often mentions "fathers and mothers" together when discussing filial piety, so he obviously felt that she was due affection and respect (1:7; 2:6; 4:18, 19, 21; 11:5; 17:19). Typical is his comment that, "In serving your father and mother you ought to dissuade them from doing wrong in the gentlest way" (Lau 4:18).

It would be interesting to know more about Confucius' relationships with women, who are conspicious for their near absence from the *Analects*. The only women who is even named is Nánzĭ 南子, the politically influential but allegedly licentious wife of the duke of Wèi 衛.[47] Confucius had an audience with her, displeasing his disciple Zĭlù 子路. Confucius responded, "If I have done anything improper, may Heaven's curse be on me, may Heaven's curse be on me!" (Lau 6:28). The early Confucian attitude toward women is partly a response to the political problems of their era. As the Zuŏ Zhuàn indicates, affairs were a common source of intrigue in the Spring and Autumn era.[48] The Confucian solution was bié 別, "separation" or "distinction," between the genders.[49] This involved at least separation of functions (child rearing vs. political and educational activities). But more than that, women seem almost completely excluded from the life of Confucius and his disciples. I am struck by an incident in which Confucius, after almost dying from an illness, asks his disciples, "would I not rather die in your hands, my friends, than in the hands of retainers?" (Lau 9:12). Confucius makes no mention of wanting to be with his wife or daughter at the time of his death.[50] (In her contribution to this volume, Lisa Raphals examines Confucian attitudes toward women through some stories regarding a woman allegedly praised by Confucius, in texts other than the *Analects*, for her knowledge of the rites.)

In addition to his wife and daughter (5:1), the other members of Confucius' immediate family were an elder brother (5:2), about whom we know almost nothing (although he is reputed to have been disabled), and a son. His son did not outlive his father (11:8), and one disciple described their relationship while the son was alive as "distant" (16:13). (Interestingly, the disciple does not seem to regard this "distance" as regrettable.)

Sometime late in the sixth century (before 505 B.C.E.), Confucius visited the neigboring state of Qí 齊 (to the north and east of Lǔ, also in what is now Shandong province) and had some conversations with its ruler, Duke Jǐng (Jǐng Gōng) 景公 (12:11, 16:12). Confucius remarked, "At one stroke Qí can be made into Lǔ, and Lǔ, at one stroke, may be made to attain the Way" (Lau 6:24). Consequently, it is possible that he went to Qí because he believed that there were good opportunities for positive social change there, and hoped that he could bring such change about. It is also said that Confucius heard a certain type of classical Chinese music in Qí and was so deeply moved that "for three months [he] did not notice the taste of the meat he ate." Confucius remarked, "I never dreamt that the joys of music could reach such heights" (Lau 7:14). Duke Jing failed to give Confucius any official position, so he returned to Lǔ (18:3).

After he returned to Lǔ, someone named Gōngshān fúrǎo 公山弗擾 revolted against the Jì family in Lǔ and invited Confucius to join him. Confucius seriously considered the offer. This displeased his disciple Zǐlù, who asked, "We may have nowhere to go, but why must we go to Gongshan?" Confucius replied, "The man who summons me must have a purpose. If his purpose is to employ me, can I not, perhaps, create another Zhou in the east?" (Lau 17:5).

Confucius was appointed to an executive position, "minister of crime" (sī kòu 司寇), in his home state by Jìhuánzǐ 季桓子, who himself was chief minister of Lǔ between 505 and 492 B.C.E.[51] Confucius allegedly assisted in a diplomatic meeting between Duke Dìng (Dìng Gōng) 定公 of Lǔ and Duke Jǐng in 500 B.C.E.[52] Presumably, Confucius' experience with Duke Jǐng on his previous visit to Qí made him a useful assistant.

Confucius eventually resigned his position. It looks like, even at the time, there was uncertainty about Confucius' reason for resigning. According to the Analects, "The men of Qi made a present of singing and dancing girls [to Jihuanzi]. Jihuanzi accepted them and stayed away from court for three days." Confucius, presumably outraged that Jihuanzi would ignore his duties for so long, resigned (Lau 18:4). In contrast, according to the Mèngzǐ,

> Confucius was the police commissioner of Lu, but his advice was not followed. He took part in a sacrifice, but, afterwards, was not given a share of the meat of the sacrificial animal. He left the state without waiting to take off his ceremonial cap. Those who did not understand him thought he acted in this way because of the meat, but those who understood him realized that he left because Lu failed to observe the proper rites. For his part Confucius preferred to be slightly at fault in thus leaving rather than to leave with no reason at all. The doings of a gentleman are naturally above the understanding of the ordinary man. (Mèngzǐ 6B6)[53]

Confucius then traveled to a number of states over the course of about a decade, beginning with Wèi, where he had the interview with Nánzǐ that scandalized Zǐlù. Passing through Sòng 宋 on his way to Chen, someone named Huán Tuí 桓魋 tried to assassinate Confucius, for reasons that are not clear.[54] He then returned to Wèi, before being invited back to Lǔ in 484 B.C.E. by Jìkāngzǐ 季康子, who was high minister.

During the period before and during Confucius' travels, his disciples achieved a large measure of political sucess. Apparently on the strength of Confucius' recommendations (6:1, 6:8), Zǐlù, Rǎn Qiú 冉求, and Rǎn Yōng 冉雍 were each, at some point, steward of the Jì family (Jìshì zǎi 季氏 宰).[55] (Creel points out that the stewardship "was the most important post in Lu that could normally be attained in any manner other than inheritance."[56]) Zilu eventually either resigned or was discharged from his post, and went to serve the ruling family of Wei, whom he died defending.[57] Rǎn Qiú was apparently responsible for organizing Lǔ's defense against an invasion from Qí, even leading soldiers into combat.[58] As Creel suggests, Confucius' disciples were in high demand for several reasons. They were well trained in ritual, history, and literature. Rulers no doubt found irritating their penchant for moralizing, but precisely because of their ethical commitment, Confucian disciples could be trusted not to betray their rulers.[59]

Upon his return to Lǔ, Confucius was apparently given some low-ranking advisory position.[60] (Indeed, the position may have been merely honorary or ceremonial.) In 481 B.C.E., Chen Chengzi assasinated the ruler of the state of Qí, Duke Jian. Confucius encouraged the duke and ruling families of Lǔ to intervene militarily. They rejected his advice (14:21).

Confucius died in 479 B.C.E.

Confucius apparently did not intend to start an intellectual "school" or "movement." He said, "I transmit but do not innovate; I am truthful in what I say and devoted to antiquity" (Lau 7:1). However, he did found the movement known in English as "Confucianism", but as the rújiā 儒家 ("school of the ru"[61]) in Chinese. Every movement needs a founding god, saint, or at least sage. The near apotheosis of Confucius began soon after his death. A little more than a century later, Mencius asserted, "Ever since man came into this world, there has never been another Confucius" (Mèngzǐ 2A2).[62] However, although agreeing in their admiration for Confucius, later Confucians disagreed about much else. (Consider the debate, mentioned earlier, between Mencius and Xúnzǐ over the goodness of human nature.) There were apparently eight competing Confucian sects by the time of Hánfēizǐ 韓非子 (third century B.C.E.).[63] These divisions were already evident in the *Analects*.[64] Consequently, readers of the *Analects* should not assume that something one of Confucius' disciples is reported as saying would be accepted by all Confucians, let alone by Confucius himself. Readers should also be alert to the ways in which the political agendas of various Confucian sects have shaped the composition of the *Analects*.[65]

The *Analects*

I didn't say all the things I said.

—Yogi Berra

"Analects" is an obscure English word standardly used as a translation of the Chinese Lúnyŭ 論語, which probably means "selected sayings." The received text of the *Analects* is divided into twenty "books" (really the size of chapters), which are further divided into "chapters" (ranging in length from brief quotations to short dialogues). There is near-universal agreement among competent contemporary scholars that the present *Analects* is a work composed by many hands, with various agendas, over the course of many years. Disagreement begins when we try to sort out which parts are more likely to represent authentic Confucian dicta.[66]

At most, one pre-Hàn dynasty text quotes the *Analects* and identifies the Lúnyŭ as its source.[67] However, many pre-Hàn authors attribute to Confucius quotations found in our *Analects*. There are also a number of quotations attributed to Confucius in texts that date from before the Hàn that are not found in the present *Analects*, though. (It would be interesting to see what image of Confucius resulted if we focused only on the quotations attributed to Confucius in the writings of Mencius, or on those in the writings of Mencius' rival Xúnzǐ.) Consequently, we cannot be absolutely certain that anything like the current *Analects* existed prior to the Hàn.

It seems that there were three versions of the Lúnyŭ in existence during the Hàn dynasty. Our modern version is apparently a synthesis of these versions that evolved through the efforts of successive interpreters in the Hàn. (The Brookses and Csikszentmihalyi discuss the composition of the *Analects* in more detail in their contributions to this volume.)

Already in the Qīng 清 dynasty, Cuī Shù 崔述 (1740–1816) demonstrated, on linguistic grounds, that the last five books of the *Analects* are much later than the rest of the work.[68] In addition, several scholars, most notably Itō Jinsai 伊藤仁齋 (1627–1705), have argued that both linguistic and content distinctions allow us to distinguish an "upper *Analects*" (shàng lún 上論) of books 1–10, and a "lower *Analects*" (xià lún 下論) of books 11–20.[69] More recently, Arthur Waley suggested (without argument) that "Books III–IX represent the oldest stratum" of the *Analects*.[70] E. Bruce Brooks and A. Taeko Brooks have noted that these views can be combined to form what the Brookses call the "four-stratum theory" of the composition of the text:[71]

3 4 5 6 7 8 9

1 2   1 0

11 12 13 14 15

16 17 18 19 20

The Brookses suggest refining and modifying this theory to give the following order of composition for books 3–11: 4-5-6-7-8-9-10-11-3. Here I oversimplify, because they regard many chapters and even groups of chapters within these books as interpolations from other periods. In addition, their theory covers all twenty books, but I am only interested now in what they have to say about Waley's "core books," 3–9.

I have learned a great deal from the Brookses' work, and I agree with them that Waley's offhand suggestion requires further refinement. Furthermore, I shall make use of some of their key arguments (although not always to the same end as they). However, my position will end up, I think, much closer to Waley's view than to that of the Brookses.

It will be useful to begin by noting what stands out about books 3–9 that probably has led scholars like Waley to treat them as a unit. It is true (with exceptions that I shall discuss later), that the sayings grouped in a given book of 3–9 share some common features. This feature may be the topic, or it may have to do with the style of the sayings. Book 3 is organized by topic: it discusses ritual and music (two concepts that were closely associated in early Chinese thought). Book 4 is organized by style, consisting of aphorisms of general application (as opposed to statements about particular individuals or occasions). There is also some topical subdivision within this book, though: in the first part are grouped statements about the virtue of rén 仁. (Yearley discusses the organization of book 4 in his contribution to this volume.) Turning to book 5, we see that it consists of passages in which Confucius expresses judgments about other people. The first part of book 6 (chapters HY 1–16) consists of passages that are similarly "judgmental;" however, the focus in this part of book 6 seems to be the suitability of various individuals for office. Arguably, the next few chapters (HY 17–21 and possibly 22–23) are closely related, because they provide insight into how to make the kind of judgments Confucius has been making in the two previous books. The chapters at the end of this book, 24–30, seem harder to fit under this theme, though. The passages in book 7 are, in a broad sense, biographical with regard to Confucius. Book 8 seems less well organized than the other members of this group. However, there is a section (chapters HY 3–7) of quotations from Confucius' disciple Zēngzǐ 曾子 (meaning "Master Zeng"), and several (1 and 18–21) in which Confucius discusses sage kings, including Yao, Shun, and Yu. Interestingly, book 9 returns to the topic of biographical comments and stories about Confucius, until we get to chapters 22–30, which neither fit in with the rest of the book nor seem to have a common topic of their own.

What about the rest of the "Upper *Analects*"? The sayings in book 10 are also grouped according to topic, all being descriptions of someone's behavior. It is not surprising, given this fact, and the proximity of book 10 to book 9, that 10 has frequently been read as further comments about the behavior of Confucius. However, my impression is that Waley is right in seeing book 10 as largely "a compilation of maxims from works on ritual" that does not belong with the rest of the text.[72] The sayings in books 1–2 seem to me to lack any discernible overall unifying feature. They also include a suspiciously large number of sayings by disciples of Confucius.

So if we consider books 1–10 as a unit, we find that (with exceptions that I acknowledged above, and to which I shall return) books 3–9 seem to belong together in a way that books 1–2 and 10 do not. Consequently, (assuming that one accepts the division of the text into an "upper" and "lower" *Analects*) it seems a plausible hypothesis that books 3–9 are part of an early *Analects* core around which later books were added.

Careful readers of books 3–9 may object that the organization of books 3–9 is less rigid than my characterization so far suggests (even taking into account the exceptions I noted). For example, I have suggested that book 9 is biographical of Confucius. But consider Waley's 9:16 (HY 9:17): "Once when the Master was standing by a stream, he said, Could one but go on and on like this, never ceasing day or night!" This seems much more like a record of a saying, rather than what we might describe as a "biographical comment." Similarly, Waley's 9:17 (HY 9:18), says, "The Master said, I have never yet seen anyone whose desire to build up his moral power was as strong as sexual desire." Even if Confucius means to include himself in this generalization, it seems odd to insist that this comment is "autobiographical." One could multiply these examples in an effort to show that books 3–9 have a much looser structure than I have suggested.

My answer is that the organization of books 3–9 is tight, but that the criteria the editor or editors used is different from what we might have used. For example, what is most interesting for us about 9:17 (Waley numbering) is what it tells us about Confucius' view of human ethical capacity. However, I think that the editor of books 3–9 included it because it has the word wú 吾, "I," in a context where that pronoun obviously refers to Confucius.[73]

I have given a defense of the claim that books 3–9 are distinct because they show the evidence of some kind of editing, and suggested that the most plausible explanation of this is that they were edited together at about the same time. But in order for my suggestion to be persuasive, I should address the Brookses' alternative accretional hypothesis. As far as I have been able to tell, the Brookses really only have three firm pieces of evidence for their view. (1) There are some grammatical archaisms in book 4 that suggest an earlier date than the rest of the text.[74] (2) *Analects* 6:3 "uses the posthumous epithet of Aǐgūng (d 0469), and so must have been written after 0469." (3) *Analects* 8:3 "portrays the death of" Zēngzǐ "(d 0436); it cannot be earlier than, and was probably written in or shortly after 0436." These are powerful and important arguments. However, these arguments are far from demonstrating the truth of the particular compositional theory that the Brookses advocate. Indeed, the Brookses seem to assume that (as Edward Slingerland has suggested) the *Analects*, in general, accumulated like coral reefs or like rings in a tree. But this assumption seems unwarranted.[75]

Furthermore, the kinds of differences we find among books 3–9 are not what we would expect to find if they developed through historical accretion. Say that, as the Brookses suggest, book 4 is the earliest book, to which book 5 and then book 6 were appended at later dates. Why would those who fabricated these books have decided specifically to fabricate two books, all of whose sayings were about judging others? Or why would those who fabricated 7 and 9 have chosen to fabricate only sayings that were comments about Confucius? If books were appended to a pre-existing text by later redactors with various sectarian motives, we would not expect to find the style or topic of each book so rigidly regimented, but would instead expect to find different styles and topics in each book. (And this is what we do find in books 1–2.) The fact that each of books 3–9 is organized around either style or topic suggests, in my view, the work of some editor (whether individual or committee), who took a largely pre-existing body of sayings and anecdotes (whether oral or written), and grouped them under various headings.

Now, I am not suggesting that we can assume that everything in the received text of books 3–9 was edited into its current form at the same time. Indeed, I have argued at length (in my contribution to this volume) that *Analects* 4:15 is a very late interpolation placed in that book by the followers of Master Zeng. Likewise, the final quotation in this book, since it is attributed to the disciple Zǐyǒu 子游, also jumps out as a likely interpolation. (I agree with the Brookses on both these points.) There are also, I think, more extensive interpolations in books 3–9. I noted earlier that book 6, chapters 24–30, and book 9, chapters 22–30, do not seem to share the organizational feature of their respective books, so I suspect that each set of chapters is an interpolation. More significantly, book 8 as a whole is suspect. To begin with, there does not seem to be any overall organizing principle to this book. Furthermore, the Master Zeng "mini-analects" of chapters 3–7 is suspect because, as we can see from 4:15, the followers of Zeng were willing to insert interpolations into an already existing text in order to aggrandize their master. Next, consider the fact that the book closes with references to the sage kings Yao, Shun, and Yu. Notice that none of these three are referred to anywhere else in books 3–9, with the exception of 6:30, which is part of a section that we have already identified as suspicious on other grounds.[76] Finally, recall that book 8 is sandwiched between two books that contain biographical details about Confucius, almost as if book 8 interrupted what was originally one book (or perhaps a paired set of books on related topics, much like 5 and 6). Consequently, there are multiple reasons to think that book 8 does not belong with the rest of 3–9.

Seen in the light of my argument so far, the Brookses' observation regarding the death of Master Zeng (recorded in book 8) takes on new significance. I assume that some version of the *Analects* existed prior to Zengzi's death. (One piece of evidence for this is the simple fact that book 8 is located between two books that seem to share structural features not shared by book 8: this suggests interpolation.) I also think it is likely that the Zengzi "mini-analects" was recorded and inserted into the rest of the *Analects* soon after the death of Zengzi. Why? Within books 3–9, Zengzi appears only in book 8 and in 4:15, both of which we have identified as later interpolations. In other words, Zengzi was not even mentioned in the earliest version of the *Analects*. This would present severe rhetorical and theoretical problems for his followers after his death, who would be competing—for prestige, patronage, and even pupils—with other Confucian sects, whose founders *were* mentioned in the original *Analects*. Consequently, the motive to interpolate would appear soon and forcefully after Zengzi's death. I think it is likely, then, that book 8 was interpolated into the rest of the text soon after Zengzi's death in 436 B.C.E. But if that is right, then 436 B.C.E. becomes the approximate terminus ad quem for the formation of the earliest version of the *Analects*.

Do we have a corresponding terminus a quo? We do: 469 B.C.E. This is the year in which Aigong died, and as the Brookses remind us, he must have been dead when 6:3 was recorded. So it looks like we can date the editorial work done on books 3–7 and 9 to within a three- or four-decade period, from 469 to around 436 B.C.E. (that is, within about fifty years of Confucius' death).

I still have not dealt with the Brookses' challenging observations regarding grammatical archaisms in book 4, though. Recall that the aphorisms of book 4 seem to be of general applicability. (They are, to use a distinction from philosopher W. V. O. Quine, "standing sentences," as opposed to "occasion sentences.") Unlike (almost?) every other comment in books 3–7 and 9, they refer to no particular individuals or historical contexts. The presence of the archaisms and the general applicability of these sayings can be explained by the following hypothesis: book 4 represents something like Confucius' "catechism." In other words, during his lifetime, Confucius used these sayings repeatedly, while teaching and conversing with a variety of pupils. Perhaps he himself thought of these quotations as being part of a set. Or perhaps these are simply the ones he used over and over again in teaching his disciples. If this hypothesis is true, it would explain both why there are no references to particular individuals or events in the book (that is, they were intended for use with a variety of disciples with reference to a variety of occasions), and why they contain archaisms (that is, the students memorized them verbatim, including the Master's own quaint locutions and old-fashioned ways of talking). Thus, in a sense, book 4 does antedate all the other books (whether it was physically written down first or not).

The immediate disciples would also have remembered a lot of other things about the Master besides what was to be recorded in book 4: what he said on particular occasions about particular situations or individuals, how he acted, what he said about himself. They would presumably have shared these anecdotes with their own disciples and others. But at some later date (after 469 B.C.E.) one or more of the surviving disciples decided to write this additional information down in what became the core of the *Analects*. (At this point, book 4 may already have existed in some written form, or it may have been passed down only by memory, but it would be written down from here on.) The likely motives for the composition of this text were failing memories, disagreements about what the Master had said, and the death (either recent or impending) of the "first-generation" disciples who actually knew the Master. These factors would lead people to want some fixed (or so they thought it would be) record of what Confucius said and did. There probably was some uncertainty (and maybe some dispute) about how to organize the remembered stories and quotations. The solution (or compromise) is the topical and thematic organization of (most of) the current books 3–7 and 9. Then, soon after 436 B.C.E., book 8 was interpolated into the text, with later interpolations and then additions to follow.

There is one more objection I must address. On both my own and on the Brookses' hypothesis, book 4 has a sort of priviledged status. If books 3–7 and 9 date from the same period, why is book 3 positioned in front of book 4? Wouldn't it be natural to begin with the Master's "catechism" (that is, what is now book 4), and only then move on to the Master's "occasion statements" about ritual, other people, and himself?[77] The Brookses hold that book 3 is not coeval with books 4–7 and 9, but is later, and was prepositioned so that readers of the *Analects* would view ritual as much more central to the Master's original vision than it actually had been. This is a possible explanation. But there are explanations that are consistent with my interpretation and that seem at least as plausible to me as the Brookses'. For example, perhaps ritual *was* central to the Master's world-view, and so the redactors of the *Analects* collected all the Master's comments about ritual into one book and placed this book first precisely to make this fact clear.

Is my hypothesis correct? I think so, but on an issue where the evidence is so tenuous and the arguments on both sides so subtle, strong conviction can only be a sign of hubris. In any case, I shall refer to books 3–7 and 9 as "the core books" of the *Analects*.[78]

Among the best English translations of the *Analects* are those by James Legge (which, although dated, includes the Chinese text and extensive interpretive notes), Arthur Waley, D. C. Lau, and Raymond Dawson. "Chapter" divisions within books of the *Analects* differ slightly from edition to edition, so when citing a passage from the *Analects* one should always specify which translation or Chinese edition one is following. Contributors to this volume may cite the Legge, Waley, Lau, or Dawson translations simply by the translator's last name (for example, Lau 2:1). In addition, the frequently used Harvard-Yenching Institute edition of the *Analects* may be cited as "HY." Joel Sahleen's annotated bibliography in this volume lists other translations, as well as secondary studies in English, Chinese, and Japanese.

Key Concepts

The *Analects* often speaks in terms that will seem familiar to any educated person, but also says much that seems quite alien to the uninitiated. As David S. Nivison has noted, we see the alien and the familiar "in the same breath" in *Analects* 2:24, "To offer sacrifice to the spirit of an ancestor not one's own is obsequious. Faced with what is right, to leave it undone shows a lack of courage" (Lau).[79] Conse-quently, in order to achieve a full understanding of the *Analects*, we must investi-gate some concepts foreign to the Western philosophical tradition.

In the remainder of this introduction, I shall discuss some of these concepts.

My purpose will be to facilitate greater understanding of the *Analects* as a text, and of the papers in this volume, rather than to arrive at an accurate portrayal of the historical Confucius. Consequently, I shall refer to passages from all over the received text of the *Analects*, leaving aside for the moment issues of their historical provenance.

Confucius, as portrayed by the *Analects*, was neither a relativist nor a skeptic. He thought there is a proper way for humans to behave, and a proper way for society to be organized. And he thought we can know what this way is.[80] The term in Chinese for this "way" is *dào* 道, which originally meant "way" in the sense of "path" or "road."[81]

The proper way to organize society is determined by the *lǐ* 禮. Lǐ is typically translated as "rites" or "rituals." This is an acceptable translation, because the *lǐ* include things like sacrificial rites performed to one's ancestors. But the *lǐ* also include everything from matters of etiquette to almost the whole of one's way of life, or ethos. Thus, in 12:1, Confucius is reported to have advised one of his disciples, "Do not look at what is contrary to ritual, do not listen to what is contrary to ritual, do not speak what is contrary to ritual, and make no movement which is contrary to ritual" (Dawson).

The reason Confucius emphasized the *lǐ* is a matter of dispute. He himself seemed to think that the power of *lǐ* is a mystery: "Someone asked for an explanation of the Ancestral Sacrifice. The Master said, I do not know. Anyone who knew the explanation could deal with all things under Heaven as easily as I lay this here; and he laid his finger upon the palm of his hand" (Waley 3:11). One influential view is that the *lǐ* have a "magic influence" on spirits, human beings, and even the natural world.[82] Ritual is connected with magic in many cultures, and the magical view of ritual is undeniably part of the Confucian tradition in general. Already in the Shāng dynasty ritual sacrifices were performed to appease the ancestors. And even in the later Confucianism of the Hàn, we find the view that proper ritual behavior, especially by the king, was essential to ensure good crops and prevent disasters such as floods. However, it is striking that little if anything in the *Analects* requires us to attribute a magical effect to the *lǐ*.

Nonetheless, the *Analects* does attribute causal efficacy of a kind to the *lǐ*: "Guide them by edicts, keep them in line with punishments, and the common people will stay out of trouble but will have no sense of shame. Guide them by virtue, keep them in line with the rites, and they will, besides having a sense of shame, reform themselves" (Lau 2:3). Donald Munro has suggested that part of this is simply the effect (hardly magical, and well known to us today) of "model emulation": "In their teaching roles [the Confucians] taught the *lǐ*, and they served as virtuous models whose own behavior embodied the *lǐ*."[83]

The *lǐ* also seem to have an "expressive" or "symbolic" function. In one passage (admittedly far outside the core books), one of Confucius' disciples complains about the three-year mourning period required after the death of a parent, suggesting that one year of mourning is sufficient. Confucius asks the disciple whether he would be "at ease" if he were to return to eating and dressing normally after one year of mourning. When the disciple says that he would be at ease, Confucius replies, "If you would really feel at ease, then do so" (Waley 17:21). However, after the disciple has left, Confucius remarks, "How inhuman [he] is! Only when a child is three years old does it leave its parents' arms. The three years' mourning is the universal mourning everywhere under Heaven. And [as for the disciple]—was he not the darling of his father and mother for three years?" (Waley 17:21). Thus, the three-year mourning period is symbolic of the parents' nurturing of the child, and it is intended to express the child's sense of loss. (In his contribution to this volume, Lee Yearley suggests that passages like this represent a "demythologization" of earlier traditions regarding the rites.)

One weakness of the translation of lĭ as "rites" or "ritual" is that these terms often have negative connotations in English. "Ritual" is sometimes used almost as a synonym for "routine" and "mechanical." However, as the passage just quoted suggests, Confucius insists that the lĭ must not be performed in an unfeeling or mechanical way: "High office filled by men of narrow views, ritual performed without reverence, the forms of mourning observed without grief—these are things I cannot bear to see!" (Waley 3:26)

As the connection between ritual and the emotions suggests, Confucius was concerned with ethical character and the cultivation of virtue. One of the key terms in Confucius' ethical vocabulary is rén 仁. This is a term easy to misunderstand, because its meaning evolved after the time of Confucius. As Benjamin Schwartz observes, Confucius seems to have used it to refer to "an attainment of human excellence which—where it exists—is a whole embracing all the separate virtues."[84] However, after Confucius, the Mohists would use rén in a much more narrow sense to refer to "universal love." This influenced later Confucian usage, so that the Mencius, for example, uses rén to refer to a sort of benevolence.[85] This later, Mohist-influenced Confucian usage is reflected in parts of the *Analects*, such as 12:22, in which rén is characterized as "Loving others."

Confucius' focus on rén suggests his general interest in the cultivation of character. This focus is one of his enduring contributions to his tradition. It is also one of the most interesting aspects of his thought for contemporary Western philosophers, because there has been a recent resurgence of interest in issues of character and virtue. Consequently, several contributors to this volume discuss issues raised by Confucius' views on virtue. Among these authors are Joel Kupperman, who explores the notion of "naturalness" as an aspect of one's ethical style of life; Kwong-loi Shun, who discusses the relationship between ren and ritual; and Stephen Wilson and Lee Yearley, who situate Confucius' thought in relation to recent Western "virtue ethics."

Almost as important as rén in Confucius' ethics is yì 義, typically rendered, for want of a better translation, as "righteousness." D. C. Lau has correctly observed that rén "is basically a character of agents and its application to acts is only derivative." He goes on to say that "The reverse is true of rightness. Rightness is basically a character of acts and its application to agents is derivative."[86] One early definition of yì is as "appropriate" (yí 宜, Zhōngyōng 中庸 20:5), and in a society as role conscious as early China, what was appropriate was presumably determined not only by the circumstances of one's situations, but also by one's relevant social role (compare Lau 12:11: "Let the ruler be a ruler, the subject a subject, the father a father, the son a son"). However, in common with thinkers in other traditions who emphasize the cultivation of virtue, Confucius seems reluctant to provide general rules that would mechanically identify correct actions in each context: "In his dealings with the world the gentleman is not invariably for or against any-thing. He is on the side of what is right" (Lau 4:10, modified).

Although Confucius was very interested in the topic of human virtue, he did not have any term that we may translate without discomfort as "virtue." There is a crucial term in the *Analects*, dé 德, which is frequently rendered "virtue," but dé is not used in the *Analects* as the name of a type of disposition of which rén and yì are kinds.[87] Dé was from very early on (perhaps originally) a sort of charisma or power a king has over others, which causes them to willingly follow him, without the need for physical coercion. This charisma was associated with good charac-ter; hence, it can be thought of as almost a "moral force," which radiates out from a good ruler, ensuring obedience. Thus, the *Analects* says, "He who rules by moral force is like the pole-star, which remains in its place while all the lesser stars do homage to it" (Waley 2:1). By the time of Confucius, dé had come to be thought of as a quality of not only a good king, but of any truly good person. Thus, when threatened by Huan Tui (see above), Confucius is reported to have remarked, "Heaven begat the power [dé] that is in me. What have I to fear from such a one as [Huan Tui]?" (Waley 7:22).[88]

Confucius' faith that his Heaven-bestowed dé would protect him from Huan Tui raises the question of how his views on ritual and virtue relate to broader cos-mological and metaphysical issues. Certainly, Confucius had some cosmological views, as suggested by his references to Heaven, or tiān 天. This term can refer to the sky, hence its common translation as "Heaven." But tiān can also refer to a quasi-anthropomorphic entity. The conception of tiān in early Chinese thought varies between two poles. At one extreme, tiān can be almost a personal God (as in some of the Mohist writings). At the other extreme, tiān can be the impersonal and inexorable process of natural change (as in the later Confucian Xúnzǐ's "Essay on Heaven"). The conception of tiān in the *Analects* generally seems less anthropo-morphic than the Mohist usage, but more anthropomorphic than Xúnzǐ's usage.[89] (Robert Louden explores Confucius' view of tiān in his contribution to this volume.) The tiān of the *Analects* does seem somewhat providential, in the sense of having concern with virtue and the course of history. For example, in addition to his remark about Huan Tui, Confucius is said to have dismissed another threat to his safety, remarking, "With King Wen dead, is not culture invested here in me? . . . If Heaven does not intend this culture to be destroyed, then what can [those who threaten me] do?" (Lau 9:5).

The *Analects'* evocative comments about tiān raise many questions. But I submit that most of the questions we might raise about tiān or other aspects of Confucius' cosmology have no answers, because, based on the *Analects*, there is no evidence that Confucius had *detailed* theoretical views about cosmology. Furthermore, I think that many of the key theoretical concepts from later Chinese philosophy were either unknown to Confucius, or at least did not figure prominently in his thinking (among these terms are lǐ 理 and qì 氣, which became central to mature Neo-Confucian metaphysics, and xìng 性, nature, which was a central term of debate already within a century of Confucius' death). This claim will seem heretical to many. I think it is important both to see why it will seem heretical to suggest that Confucius did not have a detailed cosmology, and to see why this claim is really quite plausible.

In this volume, Ivanhoe's "Whose Confucius? Which *Analects*?" traces two millennia of commentary on one line from the *Analects*. In Lau's translation (5:13), the line reads, "Tzu-kung said, 'One can get to hear about the Master's accomplishments, but one cannot get to hear his views on human nature and the Way of Heaven.'" Why has this line proved so provocative to interpreters? As Ivanhoe demonstrates, for all the diversity within the commentarial tradition, there is agreement that Confucius *did* have views on human nature and the Way of Heaven.[90] So the question becomes why "one" (or perhaps why Confucius' disciple Zǐgòng 子貢 in particular) could not get to hear about them.

But there is an alternative interpretation that is ignored by every major traditional commentator. Perhaps one could not get to hear Confucius' views on human nature and the Way of Heaven simply because he had no such views. Indeed, perhaps Zǐgòng's comment is an effort to make this clear to a younger generation of Confucians (after the death of Confucius himself), among whom discussions of these topics had become trendy, and who had begun to recklessly speculate about what the Master's views on human nature and the Way of Heaven were.

If we are open to the possibility that Confucius did not have detailed cosmological views, we are more likely to notice the discrepancy between what we find in the *Analects* and what sorts of views later commentators claim to find there. For example, Neo-Confucians like Zhu Xi frequently invoke the metaphysics of lǐ 理 and qì 氣 to interpret Confucius' dicta. But the term lǐ 理 never once occurs in the text of the *Analects*.[91] The word qì does occur six times in the *Analects*, but two of those occurrences are in book 10, which (as I noted earlier) seems to be largely a manual on ritual that has gotten interpolated into the *Analects*, and three of the other occurrences are in book 16, which is in the historically late stratum identified by Cui Shu. The only remaining occurence of qì is in a quotation attributed to Confucius' disciple Zengzi, not Confucius.[92]

What about xìng 性, or nature? Zhu Xi suggested that we can conceive of human nature in two senses, as human nature in itself, which is pure lǐ 理, or as human nature as manifested, which is lǐ as it manifests itself through a particular individual's qì 氣. Human nature in itself is good, but it may manifest itself as either good or bad, depending upon one's native endowment of qì, and the social and self-cultivation that one undergoes. Zhu Xi's distinction is ingenious, for it allows him to systematically interpret two thousand years of discussion of human nature in terms of whether each speaker is emphasizing or ignoring one of the two senses of "human nature." (Thus, when Mencius says that human nature is good, Zhu Xi takes him to be referring to human nature in itself, whereas Xúnzǐ's claim that human nature is bad is interpreted as an overemphasis on weaknesses in human nature as manifested through impure qì.) But, again, Zhu Xi's interpretation seems to have no basis in the *Analects*. As we have seen, Zǐgòng said bluntly that one cannot get to hear Confucius' views on human nature. The only other occurrence of the term xìng in the *Analects* is in 17:2 (a late book), where we find, "By nature close to one another; by practice, far from one another." This statement is almost completely content free, so even if Confucius did say it, he was expressing no specific view about human nature.[93]

Defenders of a Neo-Confucian interpretation will sometimes suggest that, although the *Analects* does not explicitly endorse anything like Zhu Xi's interpretation, something like it is the most plausible development of Confucius' ideas. But I submit that this is false. Most empty spaces can be filled by a number of different items. Similarly, the empty space we perceive in Confucius' cosmology can be filled equally well by cosmologies very different from Zhu Xi's. Indeed, were I forced to pick a cosmology to accompany Confucius' view, the one that seems to fit best, all things considered, is that of Xúnzǐ, whose views, quite different from those of Zhu Xi, are frequently considered unorthodox. Although Zhu Xi is undeniably a great genius, I find his metaphysics baroque. Xúnzǐ's cosmology seems less extravagant, and more like something Confucius could have understood and endorsed. In addition, Xúnzǐ's emphasis on the need to reshape human nature seems to me more in line with Confucius' emphasis on study and on the difficulty of achieving good character.

Table 1.1 presents the senses of some key Confucian terms with illustrative examples.

Conclusion

Why has Confucius been, and why does he continue to be, such a source of fascination? One easy answer is that he has been a symbol for a variety of different (and often contrasting) things: meritocracy, aristocracy, traditionalism, rationalism, aestheticism, "feudalism," secularism, wisdom, ignorance, Chinese culture, virtue, hypocrisy, and "the Orient." On this explanation, Confucius is almost a cipher that functions to mediate our interest in other ideas and institutions. This explanation is not completely inadequate. All of us, at our worst, reduce Confucius to the father figure we either love or love to hate. However, I am enough of a traditionalist to believe that there is something about genuine classics that draws us to them, again and again, independently of accidents of historical association

TABLE 1.1
SOME KEY TERMS

ROMANIZATION AND CHARACTER	TRANSLATIONS	MEANINGS	ILLUSTRATIVE QUOTATIONS
dào (tao) 道	"way"	This word has several related senses. (1) The original sense may have been "way," in the sense of "path" or "road." It came to mean (2) "way," in the sense of "a way to do something," or "the right way to do something, or "the order that comes from doing things in the right way," (3) a "linguistic account" of a way to do something, or a verb, that means "to give a linguistic account," (4) a metaphysical entity responsible for the way things act.	(2) If, for three years, a man makes no changes to his father's ways, he can be said to be a good son. (*Analects* 4:20) Wealth and high station are what men desire but unless I got them in the right way I would not remain in them. (*Analects* 4:5) The empire has long been without the Way. (*Analects* 3:24) (3) The way can be spoken of,/But it will not be the constant way. (Lau, *Tao Te Ching* 45) (4) There was something featureless yet complete, born before heaven and earth. . . . We may regard it as the mother of heaven and earth. . . . I style it the "Way." (Mair, *Tao Te Ching* 69 (25))
dé (te) 德	"virtue," "character," "power" (Waley, *Tao Te Ching*), "integrity" (Mair, *Tao Te Ching*)	(1) The "moral charisma" of political leaders that enables them to rule others without the use of force. This is something one gets from tiān (q.v.), and is partly a result, and partly a cause, of (2) personal ethical excellence in general. The word later comes to refer to (3) the characteristic quality or power of something (which is not necessarily ethically good). Eventually, the term comes to mean (4) individual excellences of character. (Contrast this with sense (2), which does not refer to particular, numerically distinct, virtues.)	(1) The rule of virtue can be compared to the Pole Star which commands the homage of the multitude of stars without leaving its place. (*Analects* 2:1) The virtue of the gentleman (jūnzǐ, q.v.) is like wind; the virtue of the small man is like grass. Let the wind blow over the grass and it is sure to bend. (*Analects* 12:19) (1, 2) Heaven is the author of the virtue that is in me. (*Analects* 7:23) (2) It is these things that cause me concern: failure to cultivate virtue. (*Analects* 7:3) (3) Ran Qiu was steward of the Ji family, but was unable to alter their character. (BVN, *Mengzi* 4A14) (4) Wisdom, benevolence and courage— these three are the universal virtues of the world. (BVN, *The Mean* 20)

TABLE 1.1
CONTINUED

ROMANIZATION AND CHARACTER	TRANSLATIONS	MEANINGS	ILLUSTRATIVE QUOTATIONS
jūnzǐ (chün tzu) 君子	"gentleman," "noble" (BVN)	(1) Literally, this means "son of a lord," and refers to a male child of a noble family. (2) Confucius shifts the sense toward "a person of high moral character," whether of noble descent or not. The opposite of a jūnzǐ is a xiǎo rén, 小人 "small man" (Lau, Tao Te Ching).	(1) Those steeds so strong,/ That our lord (jūnzǐ) rides behind,/That lesser men (xiǎo rén) protect. (Waley, Songs, no. 131) (2) The gentleman never deserts benevolence (rén, q.v.), not even for as long as it takes to eat a meal. (Analects 4:5) The gentleman understands what is moral. The small man understands what is profitable. (Analects 4:16)
lǐ (li) 禮	"ritual," "rites," "etiquette" (Mair, Tao Te Ching)	(1) Religious rituals, such as sacrifices to ancestors. (2) Matters of etiquette and ceremony in general. (3) Proper behavior in general. (Almost synonymous with "ethics" in this last sense.)	(1, 3) When your parents are alive, comply with the rites in serving them; when they die, comply with the rites in burying them; comply with the rites in sacrificing to them. (Analects 2:5) (2) A ceremonial cap of linen is what is prescribed by the rites (Analects 9:3) (3) Do not look unless it is in accordance with the rites; do not listen unless it is in accordance with the rites; do not speak unless it is in accordance with the rites, do not move unless it is in accordance with the rites. (Analects 12:1)
lǐ (li) 理	"good order," "reason" (Mencius), "principle"	(1) In Warring States texts this term simply means "good order." (2) Hua-yan Buddhists adopt the term to refer to the web of causal relationships among aspects of existence. (3) Neo-Confucians use the term to refer to the pattern or principle of order that is manifested in different kinds of qì (q.v.).	(1) What do all hearts have in common? Good order and righteousness. (BVN, Mengzi 6A7; cf. Lau's translation) (2) [D]ust has the character of roundness and smallness. This is fact. Its nature is empty and nonexistent. This is principle. (Chan, p. 420, quoting a Buddhist text from around C.E. 700) (3) The reason why it is said that all things form one body is that all have this principle. (Chan, p. 533,

25

TABLE 1.1
CONTINUED

ROMANIZATION AND CHARACTER	TRANSLATIONS	MEANINGS	ILLUSTRATIVE QUOTATIONS
			quoting the Neo-Confucian philosopher Cheng Hao, eleventh century C.E.)
mìng (ming) 命	"mandate," "decree," "fate," "destiny," and others	(1) The mandate to rule given by tiān (q.v.) to the virtuous. Related to this are two other senses: (2) a command or order in general, and (3) what is beyond human control: hence, "fate."	(1) Heaven accordingly gave a grand charge to King Wen to exterminate the great dynasty Yin and grandly receive its appointment. (Shu ching, p. 147) (2) A man who . . . , when sent abroad, does not disgrace the commission of his lord can be said to be a Gentleman. (Analects 13:20) (3) Unfortunately his allotted span was a short one and he died. (Analects 6:3) It is Destiny if the Way (dào, q.v.) prevails; it is equally Destiny if the Way falls into disuse. (Analects 14:36)
qì (ch'i) 氣	qì, "mist," "spirit" (Chuang Tzu), "air" (Mencius), "vapors" (Mair, Tao Te Ching), "material force" (Chan), "ether" (Graham), "psychophysical stuff" (Gardner)	(1) This term may originally have referred to the vapor rising from heated sacrificial offerings. It soon came to mean (2) "mist" in general, and (3) a sort of fluid, found in the atmosphere and the human body, responsible for the intensity of one's emotional reactions, and the reactions of others to oneself. Later (perhaps beginning in the Han Dynasty), (4) qì came to be thought of as the primal "stuff" out of which the things in the universe congealed. (It is an anachronism to read this last sense back into Warring States period texts, though.)	(2) He doesn't eat the five grains, but sucks the wind, drinks the dew, climbs up on the clouds and mist. (Chuang Tzu, p. 27) (3) There are . . . things the gentleman should guard against. . . . In the prime of life when the blood and ch'i have become unyielding, he should guard against bellicosity. (Analects 16:7) What you do not get from your heart, do not seek for in the qì. (BVN, Mengzi 2A2) A man's surroundings transform his air just as the food he eats changes his body. (Mencius 7A36) [D]on't listen with your mind, but listen with your spirit. (Chuang Tzu, p. 54) (4) Material force of necessity integrates to become the myriad things. (Chan, p. 501, citing the eleventh-century C.E. philosopher Chang Tsai)

TABLE 1.1
CONTINUED

ROMANIZATION AND CHARACTER	TRANSLATIONS	MEANINGS	ILLUSTRATIVE QUOTATIONS
rén (jen) 仁	"benevolence," "humaneness" (Mair, *Tao Te Ching*), "Goodness" (Waley, *Analects*)	(1) In the *Analects*, this refers to the consummation of personal ethical excellence. (2) In later Confucian thinkers, *rén* is "graded compassion" (i.e., compassion that should be stronger for family members than for strangers). (3) For Mohists, *rén* is "universal love" (i.e., equal compassion for each human).	(1) A man who finds benevolence attractive cannot be surpassed. (*Analects* 4:6) (2) The feeling of compassion is the sprout of benevolence. (BVN, *Mengzi* 2A6) Loving one's parents is benevolence. . . . What is left to be done is simply the extension of [this] to the whole Empire. (*Mencius* 7A15) (3) It is the business of the benevolent man to try to promote what is beneficial to the world and to eliminate what is harmful. (*Mo Tzu*, p. 39)
tiān (t'ien) 天	"heaven"	(1) The sky or "the heavens," or (2) an entity, originally a high diety, sometimes later conceived of as more impersonal, even to the point of being thought of as (3) impersonal "fate" or "nature." Note: The expression "heaven and earth" refers to the entire natural world.	(1) There cannot be two kings for the people just as there cannot be two suns in the heavens. (*Mencius* 5A4) (2) In pretending that I had retainers when I had none, who would we be deceiving? Would we be deceiving Heaven? (*Analects* 9:12) If I am understood at all, it is, perhaps, by Heaven. (*Analects* 14:35) (3) What does Heaven ever say? Yet there are the four seasons going round and there are the hundred things coming into being. (*Analects* 17:19)
yì (i) 義	"right," "righteousness," "moral" (*Mencius*)	(1) The quality of an action that makes it "fitting" or "appropiate," or (2) the quality of a person disposed to perform such acts. This second sense is closely related to (3) Mencius's use of yì to refer to a disposition to feel shame or disdain toward certain actions.	(1) Faced with what is right, to leave it undone shows a lack of courage. (*Analects* 2:24) (2) To be trustworthy in word is close to being moral. (*Analects* 1:13) (3) The heart of disdain and dislike is the sprout of righteousness. (BVN, *Mengzi* 2A6)

TABLE 1.1
CONTINUED

ROMANIZATION AND CHARACTER	TRANSLATIONS	MEANINGS	ILLUSTRATIVE QUOTATIONS
		Note: Yì tends to refer to qualities of acts, whereas *ren* (q.v.) tends to refer to qualities of individuals: "Benevolence is the heart of man, and rightness his road." (*Mencius* 6A11)	

Notes: The first column gives the Pinyin romanization of each term, followed by the Wade-Giles romanization in parentheses, and the Chinese character. The second column gives translations, beginning with the standard translation (if there is one) followed by more idiosyncratic translations, with parenthetical references to the translators who use these translations (see the bottom of the table for the key to abbreviations). The third column gives various senses of the key terms. The fourth column presents examples of the various senses.

Sources:
Analects = D. C. Lau, trans., *Confucius: The Analects* (New York: Penguin Books, 1979).
BVN = translation by B. W. Van Norden.
Chan = Wing-tsit Chan, trans., *A Source Book in Chinese Philosophy* (Princeton: Princeton University Press, 1963).
Chuang Tzu = Burton Wason, trans., *Chuang Tzu: Basic Writings* (New York: Columbia University Press, 1964).
Gardner = Daniel K. Gardner, *Chu Hsi: Learning to Be a Sage* (Berkeley: University of California Press, 1990).
Graham = A. C. Graham, *Two Chinese Philosophers* (Chicago: Open Court Press, 1992).
Lau, *Tao Te Ching* = D. C. Lau, trans., *Lao-tzu: Tao Te Ching* (New York: Alfred A. Knopf, 1994).
Mair, *Tao Te Ching* = Victor Mair, trans., *Tao Te Ching* (New York: Bantam Books, 1990).
Mencius = D. C. Lau, trans., *Mencius* (New York: Penguin Books, 1970).
Mo Tzu = Burton Watson, trans., *Mo Tzu: Basic Writings* (New York: Columbia University Press, 1964).
Shu ching = James Legge and Clae Waltham, trans., *Shu ching* (Chicago: Henry Regnery, 1971).
Waley, *Analects* = Arthur Waley, *The Analects of Confucius* (New York: Vintage Books, 1989; originally published 1938).
Waley, *Songs* = Arthur Waley, *The Book of Songs* (New York: Grove Press, 1987).
Waley, *Tao Te Ching* = Arthur Waley, *The Way and Its Power* (New York: Grove Press, 1958).

or priviledging. Some texts and thinkers touch on central aspects of human life in a way that is elusive, yet unendingly evocative. Confucius was such a thinker, and the *Analects* is such a text.

ACKNOWLEDGMENTS

I am indebted to E. Bruce Brooks, Paul Rakita Goldin, Philip J. Ivanhoe, John Makeham, and several anonymous referees for helpful comments on this introduction.

NOTES

I want to stress that this introduction is intended for the general, educated reader; it is not a scholarly overview. My aim is only to make this volume, and Confucius, accessible to those who may lack background knowledge on this topic. Consequently, specialists will recognize that I have left out references to many interesting scholarly issues and debates. Citations of the *Analects* in this introduction follow the sectioning in the Harvard-Yenching Institute index, unless otherwise noted. Translations by James Legge, *Confucian Analects, Great Learning, and Doctrine of the Mean*, reprint (New York: Dover Books, 1971); Arthur Waley, *The Analects of Confucius*, reprint (New York: Vintage Books, 1989); D. C. Lau, *Confucius: The Analects* (New York: Penguin Books, 1979); and Raymond Dawson, *Confucius: The Analects* (New York: Oxford University Press, 1993), will be by the translator's last name and the book and chapter number according to the individual translator's sectioning. Other translations by James Legge are from his *The Chinese Classics*, 5 vols., reprint (Taibei, Taiwan: SMC Publishing, 1991).

1. I have obviously been influenced here by Karl Jaspers, *Socrates, Buddha, Confucius, Jesus* (New York: Harcourt Brace and Company, 1990; originally published 1957).

2. K. C. Chang, *The Archaeology of Ancient China*, 4th ed. (New Haven: Yale University Press, 1986), pp. 87–91. On this and many other topics the reader may also consult Michael Loewe and Edward Shaughnessy, eds., *The Cambridge History of Ancient China* (New York: Cambridge University Press, 1999).

3. K. C. Chang, *Art, Myth, and Ritual* (Cambridge, Mass.: Harvard University Press, 1983), pp. 114–20; and David N. Keightley, "Early Civilization in China: Reflections on How It Became Chinese," in Paul S. Ropp, ed., *Heritage of China* (Berkeley: University of California Press, 1990), pp. 21–28.

4. Chang, *The Archaeology of China*, p. 295. See also Keightley, "Early Civilization in China," pp. 28–32.

5. See David S. Nivison and K. D. Pang, "Astronomical Evidence for the *Bamboo Annals'* Chronicle of Early Xia," *Early China* 15 (1990), pp. 87–95; and Nivison, "Response," *Early China* 15 (1990), pp. 151–72.

6. This view is forcefully defended by Sarah Allan in her *Myth, Art, and Cosmos in Early China* (Albany, N.Y.: SUNY Press, 1991).

7. For an optimistic discussion of whether Xia is to be identified with the Èrlĭtóu (Erh-li-t'ou) 二里頭 culture, see Chang, *The Archaeology of China*, pp. 307–16. For a more skeptical discussion, see Robert L. Thorp, "Erlitou and the Search for the Xia," *Early China* 16 (1991), pp. 1–38.

8. They often carved their questions, their interpretations of the cracks, and even the actual outcomes on these bones, leaving us our earliest samples of Chinese characters. For a brief introduction to these bones and to the philosophical significance of their inscriptions, see David S. Nivison, " 'Virtue' in Bone and Bronze," in *The Ways of Confucianism* (La Salle, Ill.: Open Court Press, 1996), pp. 17–30. The standard scholarly work on oracle bones is David N. Keightely, *Sources of Shang History* (Berkeley: University of California Press, 1978). For a discussion of more recent reference works on oracle bone inscriptions, see David Keightley, "Graphs, Words, and Meanings: Three Reference Works for Shang Oracle-Bone Studies, with an Excursus on The Religious Role of the Day or Sun," *Journal of the American Oriental Society* 117:3 (1997), pp. 507–24.

9. Chang, *Art, Myth, and Ritual*, p. 97.

10. The precise date of the Zhou conquest is not known. The traditional date is 1122 B.C.E. Many alternative dates have been championed by various scholars. David S. Nivison has argued, on the basis of the "Bamboo Annals," that the conquest occurred some time soon after a conjunction of planets that occurred, and was recorded by the Chinese, in 1059 B.C.E. Many scholars find this hypothesis plausible, but there is much dispute over how long after the conjunction the conquest occurred. I shall use Nivison's proposed date, 1040 B.C.E. See Nivison, "1040 as the Date of the Chou Conquest," *Early China* 8 (1982/1983), pp. 76–78.

11. See, e.g., Derk Bodde, "Feudalism in China," in Bodde, *Essays on Chinese Civilization* (Princeton, NJ: Princeton University Press, 1981), pp. 85–131; and Jack L. Dull, "The Evolution of Government in China," in Ropp, pp. 59–60.

12. What I say here follows what became the traditional Confucian account. For some revisionist accounts, see Edward L. Shaughnessy, "The Duke of Zhou's Retirement in the East and the Beginnings of the Minister-Monarch Debate in Chinese Political Philosophy," in Shaughnessy, *Before Confucius: Studies in the Creation of the Chinese Classics* (Albany, N.Y.: SUNY Press, 1997), pp. 101–36, and David S. Nivison, "An Interpretation of the 'Shao Gao,' " *Early China* 20 (1995), pp. 177–93.

13. Even today, the word for "revolution" in Chinese is *gémìng* 革命, "change of mandate." See "Key Concepts," below, for more on *tian*.

14. Many scholars believe that the five "announcement" (*gào* 誥) sections of the *Book of Documents* (*Shū jīng* 書經) may actually date from the period soon after the Zhou conquest (although many other parts of the *Shū jīng* are certainly inauthentic). If they are authentic, these chapters give us an insight into Chinese ethical and political thought centuries before Confucius was born. For translations, see James Legge, *The Chinese Classics*, vol. 3, *The Shoo King*, sections 35, 37–38, and 40–41.

15. The last Zhou king actually stepped down in 256 B.C.E., but it is traditional to date the Eastern Zhou until the beginning of the next dynasty, the Qín 秦, in 221 B.C.E.

16. See Hsu Cho-yun, *Ancient China in Transition* (Stanford: Stanford University Press, 1965).

17. Traditionally, Confucius is said to have edited the *Chūn qiū*, but this is no longer accepted by scholars.

18. An elegant and readable translation of selections is Burton Watson, *The Tso Chuan* (New York: Columbia University Press, 1989). James Legge offers a complete translation of both the *Chun qiu* and the *Zuo zhuan*, although not in a very reader-friendly format (*The Chinese Classics*, vol. 5).

19. Watson, *The Tso Chuan*, pp. 1–4.

20. Even today, when the People's Republic of China accuses foreign powers like the United States of "hegemony," it uses the word *bàquánzhǔyì* 霸權主義 ("hegemonism").

21. See "The *Analects*," below.

22. This period began when the Zhōu king (who was, by this point, a mere figure-head) formally recognized the breakup of the state of Jìn 晉 into three separate states. The period ended only with the unification of China by the ruler of the state of Qín 秦 (discussed later in the body of this introduction).

23. Mark Edward Lewis, *Sanctioned Violence in Early China* (Albany, N.Y.: SUNY Press, 1990), p. 5. Despite its narrow title, Lewis's book is actually a fairly broad study of China in the Spring and Autumn and Warring States periods.

24. For good general philosophical histories of this era, see Benjamin Schwartz, *The World of Thought in Ancient China* (Cambridge, Mass.: Harvard University Press, 1985), and Angus C. Graham, *Disputers of the Tao* (Chicago: Open Court Press, 1989). In addition, Nivison, *The Ways of Confucianism*, contains many important essays on Confucianism in this era. For a selection of philosophical writings from this era, see Philip J. Ivanhoe and Bryan W. Van Norden, eds., *Readings in Classical Chinese Philosophy* (New York: Seven Bridges Press, 2001).

25. Máo Zédōng 毛澤東 was invoking this period when he said, "Let a hundred flowers bloom! Let a hundred schools of thought contend!" (Sadly, Mao did not live up to this dictum.)

26. For selected translations from the Mohist writings, see Ivanhoe and Van Norden, *Readings in Classical Chinese Philosophy*, and Burton Watson, trans., *Mo Tzu: Basic Writings* (New York:

Columbia University Press, 1963). The latter includes "Against Confucians." For secondary discussions, see Graham, *Disputers of the Tao*; Angus C. Graham, *Later Mohist Logic, Ethics, and Science* (Hong Kong: Chinese University Press, 1978); and Philip J. Ivanhoe, "Mohist Philosophy," in the *International Encyclopedia of Philosophy* (New York: Routledge Press, 1998), vol. 6, pp. 451–58.

27. Unfortunately, Yang Zhu's writings do not survive. Kwong-loi Shun summarizes recent efforts to reconstruct Yang Zhu's doctrines in his *Mencius and Early Chinese Thought* (Stanford: Stanford University Press, 1997), pp. 35–47.

28. On the debate between Mèngzǐ and Xúnzǐ, see Paul Rakita Goldin, *Rituals of the Way* (Chicago: Open Court Press, 1999), and B. W. Van Norden, "Mengzi and Xunzi: Two Views of Human Agency," reprinted in Thornton C. Kline and Philip J. Ivanhoe, eds., *Virtue, Nature and Agency in the Xunzi* (Indianapolis: Hackett Publishing, 2000). For an overview of recent English-language research on Confucianism, see B. W. Van Norden, "What Should Western Philosophy Learn from Chinese Philosophy?" in P. J. Ivanhoe, ed., *Chinese Language, Thought, and Culture* (Chicago: Open Court Press, 1996), pp. 224–49.

29. For discussions of the thought of Zhuangzi, see Victor Mair, ed., *Experimental Essays on Chuang-tzu* (Honolulu: University of Hawaii Press, 1983); Paul Kjellberg and Philip J. Ivanhoe, eds., *Skepticism, Relativism, and Ethics in the Zhuangzi* (Albany, N.Y.: SUNY Press, 1997); and Bryan W. Van Norden, "Competing Interpretations of the Inner Chapters," *Philosophy East and West* 46:2 (Apr. 1996), pp. 247–68. It is important to note that "Daoism" was not an organized school during the Warring States period, but only a (sometimes) useful label for grouping together certain thinkers. During the Han dynasty, however, a Daoist religion developed, which continues to have a popular influence in the Chinese cultural sphere.

30. One of the leading Legalist thinkers was Hánfēizǐ 韓非子. For selections from his writings, see Ivanhoe and Van Norden, *Readings in Classical Chinese Philosophy*, and Burton Watson, trans., *Han Fei Tzu: Basic Writings* (New York: Columbia University Press, 1964).

31. Although brief, the Qin Dynasty is very important in Chinese history. First, any texts written during the Zhōu dynasty could be transmitted to the present day only if they passed through the "bottleneck" of the Qín book burning. Second, two of the most famous Chinese monuments date from the Qín: the first version of the Great Wall and the first emperor of Qín's army of terracotta figurines. Third, because of early contacts with the West during this period, our name "China" comes from "Qin" (written "Ch'in" in Wade-Giles romanization). Fourth, the centralized bureacratic structures pioneered by the Legalists, although carried to draconian extremes under the Qin and later excoriated in theory by generations of Confucians, became the basis of Chinese political organization.

32. There were actually several versions of the *Analects* in existence at this time. See "The Analects," below.

33. For the phrase "content-free Confucianism," see Benjamin E. Wallacker, "Han Confucianism and Confucius in Han," in David T. Roy and Tsuen-hsuin Tsien, eds., *Ancient China: Studies in Early Civilization* (Hong Kong: Chinese University of Hong Kong Press, 1978), p. 227. For suspicions about the Shǐjì account of Confucius, see Herrlee G. Creel, *Confucius and the Chinese Way* (New York: Harper and Row, 1960; originally published. *Confucius: The Man and the Myth*, 1949), p. 244–48. For a different assessment of the Shiji account of Confucius, see Stephen W. Durrant, *The Cloudy Mirror: Tension and Conflict in the Writings of Sima Qian* (Albany, N.Y.: SUNY Press, 1995).

34. As Hoyt Cleveland Tillman has observed, the label "Neo-Confucianism" is sometimes used so loosely that it no longer has any specific content. See Tillman, "A New Direction in Confucian Scholarship: Approaches to Examining the Differences between Neo-Confucianism and Tao-Hsüeh," *Philosophy East and West* 42:3 (July 1992), pp. 455–74.

35. For a discussion, see Daniel K. Gardner, *Chu Hsi and the* Ta-hsüeh (Cambridge, Mass.: Harvard University Press, 1986), Chapter 1.

36. For excellent discussions of Neo-Confucianism, see A. C. Graham, *Two Chinese Philosophers* (Chicago: Open Court Press, 1992; originally published 1958), Philip J. Ivanhoe, *Ethics in the Confucian Tradition: The Thought of Mencius and Wang Yang-ming* (Atlanta, Ga.: Scholars Press, 1990); Ivanhoe, *Confucian Moral Self Cultivation*, reprint (Indianapolis: Hackett Publishing, 2000); Daniel K. Gardner, *Learning to Be a Sage* (Berkeley and Los Angeles: University of California Press, 1990); and David S. Nivison, *The Ways of Confucianism*, especially "The Philosophy of Wang Yangming," pp. 217–31.

37. Since the fall of imperial China, attitudes toward Confucius in the Chinese cultural sphere have varied with attitudes toward the Chinese tradition. For one survey, see Kam Louie, *Inheriting Tradition: Interpretations of the Classical Philosophers in Communist China, 1949–1966* (New York: Oxford University Press, 1986), especially Chapter 3. For a discussion of the influence of Confucian ideas on early Chinese Marxist philosophy, see David S. Nivison, "Communist Ethics and Chinese Tradition," *Journal of Asian Studies* 16:1 (Nov. 1956). Nowadays, Confucius is officially held in high regard in the Republic of China on Taiwan, and there are signs that the waning of Communism in the People's Republic of China is leading to a waxing of respect for Confucius. Confucius has also had an immense influence, which I do not have the space to even sketch here, on Japan, Korea, and Vietman. For an impressive survey of the influence of Confucianism on traditional civilizations in East Asia, see William Theodore de Bary, *East Asian Civilizations* (Cambridge, Mass.: Harvard University Press, 1988). For discussions of the extent of the influence of Confucianism on contemporary East Asian societies, see Wei-ming Tu, ed., *Confucian Traditions in East Asian Modernity* (Cambridge, Mass.: Harvard University Press, 1996).

38. On Huáyán, see Francis H. Cook, *Hua-yen Buddhism: The Jewel Net of Indra* (University Park, Pa.: Pennsylvania State University Press, 1977). On Chán (better known to Westerners by its Japanese name, "Zen"), see Heinrich Dumoulin, *Zen Buddhism: A History, Volume 1: India and China* (New York: Macmillan Publishing, 1994).

39. Wing-tsit Chan, *A Source Book in Chinese Philosophy* (Princeton: Princeton University Press, 1963), pp. 437–38.

40. Quoted in Ivanhoe, *Ethics in the Confucian Tradition*, pp. 40–41. (Glosses in parentheses are Ivanhoe's; glosses in brackets are my own.) Wang was a critic of Zhu Xi, but they shared many fundamental metaphysical beliefs, which link them both to the Buddhist tradition.

41. I would not be forgiven by traditional scholars if I did not mention that Confucius' family name is Kǒng 孔, his personal name is Qiū 丘, and his zì 字 ("style," i.e., the name those not intimate with him used) is Zhòngní 仲尼. Lionel Jensen has recently argued that Jesuit missionaries invented not only the Latinization "Confucius," but even fabricated the expression "Kongfuzi"! (See his *Manufacturing Confucianism* [Durham, N.C.: Duke University Press, 1997], especially pp. 81–86.) However, John Makeham has noted (on the Warring States Email List) that the term "Kongfuzi" occurs in the *Zhūzǐ yǔlèi* 朱子語類 (Beijing: Zhonghua shuju, 1986), 8:3256, [卷 137]. See also B. W. Van Norden, review of *Manufacturing Confucianism*, *Journal of Asian Studies* 58:1 (Feb. 1999), pp. 165–66.

42. The name of Confucius' birthplace is written in a dizzying variety of ways. In addition to the version given in the body of the text, there are 耶, 騶, 陬, and 鄒. E. G. Pulleyblank has suggested that this is because the word is a phonetic transcription of an originally non-Chinese name. See his "Zou 鄒 and Lu 魯 and the Sinification of Shandong," in Ivanhoe, *Chinese Language, Thought, and Culture*, p. 43.

43. Important studies of the life of Confucius in English include Lau, *Confucius: The Analects*, Appendix 1; Creel, *Confucius and the Chinese Way*; Lionel Jensen, "Wise Man of the

Wilds," *Early China* 20 (1995), pp. 407–37; and E. Bruce Brooks and A. Taeko Brooks, *The Original* Analects: *Sayings of Confucius and His Successors* (New York: Columbia University Press, 1998), appendix 4. Given the nature of our sources, any biography of Confucius must be speculative.

44. See Shījīng 詩經, Mao 300, and Shǐjì 史紀，卷 33.

45. Creel, *Confucius and the Chinese Way*, p. 26.

46. On this claim, see the biography of Confucius in the Shǐjì 史紀，卷 47.

47. See, e.g., Watson, *The Tso Chuan*, pp. 195–97. (Duke Ding, Year 14 and Duke Ai, Year 2.)

48. See, e.g., ibid., pp. 13–14. (Duke Huan, Year 16.)

49. See, e.g., *Mengzi* 3A4, where "distinction between husband and wife" is advocated. D. C. Lau, trans. *Mencius* (New York: Penguin Books, 1970), p 102.

50. There is an almost misogynistic comment attributed to Confucius in 17:23, but note that this is one of the books universally agreed to be historically late. (See the discussion of "The *Analects*," below.) See also 8:20 on Confucius' views on women.

51. *Zuo zhuan*, Duke Ding, Year 1. (Legge, 745.) *Mengzi* 6B6 (see later in the body of the text). Watson, *Mo Tzu*, p. 134, "Against Confucians." Creel (pp. 37–38) regards these accounts as apocryphal. However, I find it hard to ignore the testimony of three independent sources.

52. *Zuo zhuan*, Duke Ding, Year 10. (Legge, vol. 5, 776–77.) Creel (p. 37 and pp. 299–300, n. 14) regards this account as apocryphal. I am skeptical of the details of the *Zuo zhuan* account, but if Confucius was in the service of the state of Lu in 500 B.C.E., it seems unlikely he would not have been taken along on the mission, given his previous experience with Duke Jing.

53. Lau, *Mencius*, p. 176.

54. See Waley 7:22. Creel discusses this incident (pp. 44–45).

55. On Zilu, see *Zuo zhuan*, Duke Ding, Year 12. (Legge, 781.) On Rǎn Yōng, see *Analects* 13:2.

56. Creel, p. 31.

57. See Watson, *The Tso Chuan*, pp. 198–99 for an account of Zilu's death. (Duke Ai, Year 15.)

58. See ibid., pp. 192–94 for an account of Ran Qiu's actions. (Duke Ai, Year 11.)

59. Creel, pp. 32–33.

60. Confucius describes himself as "following after the Counsellors" (Lau, *Analects*, 11:8; 14:21). This may be a polite way of referring to himself as a "Counsellor" (Creel, p. 39), or it may indicate that his position was just beneath that of the Counsellors (Waley, *The Analects of Confucius*, p. 15, thinks this made Confucius "Leader of the Knights"). But the precise title and rank makes little difference. His position was advisory, and carried no executive authority.

61. On the meaning of ru, see Robert Eno, *The Confucian Creation of Heaven* (Albany, N.Y.: SUNY Press, 1990), Appendix B, pp. 190–97; and Lionel Jensen, *Manufacturing Confucianism*, Part 2.

62. Translation by Lau, *Mencius*, p. 79.

63. Burton Watson, trans., *Han Fei Tzu*, p. 118. (*Hanfeizi* § 50.)

64. For a brief, readable, and reliable introduction to the great variety within the Confucian tradition, see Ivanhoe, *Confucian Moral Self Cultivation*.

65. There is an outstanding discussion of these issues in Stephen Van Zoeren, *Poetry and Personality* (Stanford: Stanford University Press, 1991), pp. 19–28.

66. Other important English language textual studies of the *Analects* include (in historical order) Creel (Appendix); Waley, *The Analects of Confucius* (pp. 21–26); Lau, *Confucius:*

The Analects (Appendix 3); John Makeham, "The Formation of *Lunyu* as a Book," *Monumenta Serica* 44 (1996), pp. 1–24; and Brooks and Brooks, *The Original* Analects.

67. Waley, *The Analects of Confucius*, notes (pp. 22–23) that the *Fang ji* chapter of the *Li ji* (chapter 27) quotes 1:11 (which is the same as the end of 4:20), and argues that the *Fangji* is a pre-Hàn text, although this is by no means uncontroversial. (Strangely, Waley misidentifies the *Analects* passage quoted by the *Fangji* in its reference to the *Lunyu*.) Wáng Chōng 王充 (first century C.E.) claims that the title "Lunyu" was first used by someone in the Hàn dynasty.

68. Cuī Shù, *Kǎoxìn lù* 考信錄.

69. Itō Jinsai, *Rongo kogi* 論語古義. My argument below depends on the assumptions that the "Upper" and "Lower" *Analects* are significantly different, and date from different historical periods. For a defense of these claims, see Hú Zhìkuī 胡志奎, *Lúnyǔ biànzhèng* 論語辯證 (Taibei: Lianjing chuban shiye gongsi, 1978). For powerful criticisms of these claims, see Makeham, "The Formation of *Lunyu* as a Book."

70. Waley, *The Analects of Confucius*, p. 21. However, Waley also pessimistically remarked that "we are justified in supposing that the book does not contain many authentic sayings, and may possibly contain none at all." Ibid., p. 25.

71. E. Bruce Brooks, "The Present State and Future Prospects of Pre-Han Text Studies," *Sino-Platonic Papers*, no. 46 (July 1994), especially pp. 31–43 and 69–74 passim. See also Brooks and Brooks, *The Original* Analects, pp. 201–2.

72. Waley, *The Analects of Confucius*, p. 21. This was not recognized by many traditional interpreters, who regarded the directions in Book 10 (e.g., "He did not sit, unless his mat was straight," Lau 10:12) as observations on Confucius' own manner. For a defense of the traditional interpretation of book 10, see Edward Slingerland, "Why Philosophy Is Not 'Extra' in Understanding the *Analects*," *Philosophy East and West* 50:1 (Jan. 2000), p. 141, n. 3.

73. I recognize that this is speculative, but allow me to pile one more speculation on top. The fact that the editor chose such an uninsightful way of organizing the quotations suggests one of two possibilities. Perhaps the editor of Books 3–9 was a single person who was simply uninsightful. (But then how did he obtain the authority to edit together the sayings?) Or perhaps the editing of books 3–9 was the work of something like a committee, composed of disciples with differing personalities and views of the Master. The diversity of opinions among such a group of disciples would create significant obstacles to achieving agreement on any organizational scheme that showed flexibility or insight. Consequently, the result was likely to be some plodding, lockstep, organizational scheme, that (for instance) forces everything that seems at least superficially like a comment about Confucius into either book 7 or book 9.

74. Indeed, there is one more archaism than they note (in 4:10): yì zhī yǔ bǐ 義之與比. On this construction, see Edwin G. Pulleyblank, *Outline of Classical Chinese Grammar* (Vancouver: University of British Columbia Press, 1995), pp. 70–71.

75. Brooks and Brooks, *The Original Analects*, p. 205, and Edward Slingerland, "Why Philosophy Is Not 'Extra,'" p. 138. But see E. Bruce Brooks and A. Taeko Brooks, "Response to the Review by Edward Slingerland," *Philosophy East and West* 50:1 (Jan. 2000), pp. 141–46. In addition, the Brookses respond to some criticisms of their views in their contribution to this volume.

76. David S. Nivison has suggested (see David S. Nivison and Kevin D. Pang, "Astronomical Evidence for the *Bamboo Annals'* Chronicle of Early Xia," *Early China* 15 [1990], p. 93 and p. 93n.18) that Confucius had never heard of "Yao," "Shun," and "Yu" under those descriptions. These names, he thinks, came into use after the time of Confucius. In addition, Nivison argues that the view that these rulers, under whatever name, were "sage kings" only developed in the late fifth century B.C.E. If this hypothesis is correct, it provides further support for regarding book 8 as a later interpolation.

77. Steve Angle has raised this question forcefully in correspondence.

78. Of course, contributors to this anthology are not bound by the editor's views on this or other topics.

79. David S. Nivison, "Comment on Bryan Van Norden, 'What Should Western Philosophy Learn from Chinese Philosophy?'" in Ivanhoe, *Chinese Language, Thought, and Culture*, p. 333.

80. For a very different interpretation of Confucius than the one I present here, see David L. Hall and Roger T. Ames, *Thinking Through Confucius* (Albany, N.Y.: SUNY Press, 1987). But see also the review of that book by Philip J. Ivanhoe, *Philosophy East and West* 41:2 (Apr. 1991), pp. 241–54.

81. For a discussion of the etymology of the term *dào*, see Robert Eno, "Cook Ding's Dao and the Limits of Philosophy," in Kjellberg and Ivanhoe, *Skepticism, Relativism, and Ethics in the Zhuangzi*, pp. 145–46, nn. 9–11.

82. Waley, *The Analects of Confucius*, p 64. Cf. Herbert Fingarette, *Confucius—the Secular as Sacred* (New York: Harper and Row, 1972).

83. Donald J. Munro, *The Concept of Man in Early China* (Stanford: Stanford University Press, 1969), p. 111.

84. Schwartz, *World of Thought*, p. 75. See also Waley, *The Analects of Confucius*, pp. 27–29.

85. Mencian benevolence is importantly different from the Mohist universal love, though, in that Mencius believed we should have greater concern for kin than for strangers. See, e.g., *Mengzi* 3A5 and 7A45, and David Nivison's discussion of these passages in *The Ways of Confucianism*, pp. 133–48 and pp. 196–97, respectively.

86. Lau, *Confucius: The Analects*, p. 27.

87. Some time after Confucius, though, *dé* did come to be used in a sense much like the English "virtue." Consider Zhōngyōng 中庸 20: "Wisdom, benevolence, and courage— these three are the universal virtues (*dé*) of the world."

88. *Dé* can also refer to the specific character of a given thing, in which case it can have a morally neutral or even negative sense. David Nivison discusses the evolution of the concept of *dé* in more detail in "'Virtue' in Bone and Bronze," and "The Paradox of 'Virtue,'" in his *The Ways of Confucianism*.

89. For a discussion of the etymology of the character 天, see Eno, *The Confucian Creation of Heaven*, Appendix A, pp. 181–89. Eno's conclusion is that we do not really know what the precise original sense of *tian* was: it may have been "the sky, the dead who lived there, the victims who were burnt and sent there, or an altar where they were burnt" (p. 188).

90. One common view is that Confucius' opinions on these topics were recorded in the Great Appendix to the Yì jīng 易經, but contemporary scholars know that the Yì jīng appendices date from centuries after Confucius was dead. An excellent introduction to the Yijing is Kidder Smith et al., *Sung Dynasty Uses of the I Ching* (Princeton, N.J.: Princeton University Press, 1990).

91. The Qing Dynasty philologist-philosopher Dài Zhèn 戴震 argued (I think persuasively) that even when the term *lǐ* 理 does occur in early Chinese philosophy, it has a sense very different from the sense it has for the Song and Ming dynasty Neo-Confucians. See the translation of Dai Zhen's *Mèngzǐ zìyì shùzhèng* 孟子字義疏證 by John Ewell, "Re-inventing the Way: Dai Zhen's *Evidential Commentary on the Meaning of Terms in Mencius* (1777)," Ph.D. dissertation, History, University of California at Berkeley (1990), UMI Order No. 9126550. See also the chapter on Dai Zhen in Ivanhoe, *Confucian Moral Self Cultivation*.

92. Furthermore, none of these passages suggests that *qì* is being used in the sense characteristic of later Chinese cosmology, in which *qì* is the fundamental "stuff" out of which everything else condenses. I suspect that, at least until the third century B.C.E., *qì* was always conceived of as just one physical component of the universe, rather than in the sense of "primal stuff." So, if Confucius thought about *qì* at all, he thought of it as

something that was *present* in the atmosphere, soil, and the human body, but not as something that *constitutes* the atmosphere, soil, and the human body. (Obviously, this claim requires a textual defense, which I do not have the space to offer here.)

93. Raymond Dawson notes that this statement "was accepted as the essential truth with regard to human nature and racial differences by a group of international experts in the UNESCO 'Statement on Race' " (*Confucius* [New York: Hill and Wang, 1981], pp. 43–44). But the fact that a group of international "experts" assembled by the UN could agree on *any* statement on as controversial a topic as human nature merely suggests its fundamental vacuity.

Part I 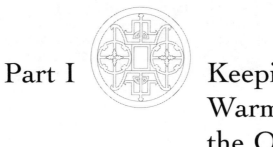 Keeping Warm the Old

2

Naturalness Revisited:
Why Western
Philosophers Should
Study Confucius

JOEL J. KUPPERMAN

To BEGIN ON A PERSONAL NOTE: MY interest in Chinese philosophy began when (in 1954–55) I wandered into H. G. Creel's seminar on Chinese philosophy at the University of Chicago. Creel was as fine a teacher as I have ever seen: clear, highly insightful, memorable, and responsive to his students. His book on Confucius (*Confucius: The Man and the Myth* [1949]), although out of print, remains useful and interesting. In a striking demonstration of the academic marketplace at work, two other students were registered for the seminar.

It seemed to me, and continued to seem to me during graduate study at Cambridge, that the fascinating philosophies presented by Creel offered things— principally views of everyday life that synthesized psychological observation with normative interpretation—that were largely neglected in contemporary Anglo-American philosophy, and that had never been developed so astutely anywhere else. At the center of ethics is the question, How do I develop as a person? This has not been treated as a major topic in the most influential recent ethical philosophy.

Perhaps there has been an element of rebellion, against the "normal" way of doing philosophy, in my continuing endeavor to work themes and insights native to China into what is after all a Western analytic kind of writing. This paper will revisit my first such attempt, "Confucius and the Problem of Naturalness" (1968). It will have two goals. One is to pursue the examination of naturalness as part of an ethical ideal. The other is to continue a subtext of the earlier paper: There are important gaps in contemporary Western philosophy, so that Western philosophers can learn a great deal from Confucius.

The Holes in the Emperor's New Clothes

It will immediately be said that Western ethical philosophy has broadened considerably in the years since 1968. There is closer attention to specific issues of justice and public policy, more ethical writing (especially within feminist philosophy) that gives special weight to personal relations, and a burgeoning school of "virtue" ethicists who take seriously the nature of the ethical agent (as well as of her or his action) in assessing decisions. (To get a good sense of the current state of feminist ethics and of virtue ethics, see Kittay and Meyers, *Women and Moral Theory* [1987], and Crisp and Slote, *Virtue Ethics* [1997], respectively.) Confucians must approve of the stronger sense that public policy issues are the business of philosophy. The special weight given to personal connections brings feminist philosophy, in important respects, close to Confucianism (see Li, "Confucian Concept of Jen and The Feminist Ethics of Care" [1994]). Virtue ethics, also, shares something important with Confucius, namely its focus on the agent's ethical development rather than on actions formulated impersonally. Does not all of this render the current state of Western ethical philosophy satisfactory from a perspective that is strongly sympathetic to Confucius?

The answer is "No." For one thing, it is still true that most contemporary Western ethical thinkers tend to ignore ethical problems that center on a style of life. Certainly "quality of life" issues are implicit in the European philosophies that are heavily influenced by Nietzsche; and one can argue that they are not very far from the surface of recent feminist ethics that emphasizes the importance of a person's special relationships and connectedness with others, or of recent virtue ethics (at least insofar as virtues have been thought of as personally advantageous). What seems largely absent from all of these philosophies, though, is any systematic account of how people could self-consciously attempt to integrate personal style, connectedness with others, and virtues into a way of life that would both be worth living on a minute-by-minute basis and also be civically useful. There is still no contemporary substitute for what Confucius has to offer. Whether there is any Western (or proto-Western) substitute at all is a more difficult question: some might suggest Aristotle. I will take this up shortly.

What is largely missing from contemporary Western philosophy can be explained in relation to what is most often there, at the center of philosophical ethics. The characteristic preoccupations of contemporary Anglo-American ethical philosophy, especially, begin with moral or social choice. Such choices in their nature involve a great deal at stake, and for most people will seem to occur infrequently. This focus leads to what I earlier spoke of as "big moment ethics," one of whose appealing features is that (by its emphasis on major choices at ethical crossroads) it in effect treats almost all of life apart from the big moments as an ethical free-play zone, in which one can do whatever one likes. This yields an ethics that does not make demands at all often, and certainly not continuously.

It should be said that this is a portrayal of the dominant tendency within contemporary (especially Anglo-American) ethical philosophy. One subversive movement that has been increasingly prominent since 1968 is the attempt of some philosophers (for example, Peter Singer and Shelly Kagan) to widen the scope of morality in such a way that moral choices occur (or at least are available) very frequently. There are some strong and interesting arguments for this, some of them having to do with the much increased ability of human beings to transform the lives of strangers far away. Whatever the merits of this movement, it scarcely covers the ground that Confucius covers, and thus it does not provide an objection to the argument that there are gaps in Western ethical philosophy that correspond to interesting and important lines of thought to be found in Confucius. It also does not challenge the dominant Western division between a high–pressure zone of moral and social choice and the low pressure area of the rest of life. Instead, it merely widens the high pressure zone so that it is almost all of life, thus greatly expanding the possibilities of guilt.

The combination of great pressure in a few moments (or many moments) of life and release of pressure in the remainder had been marked by the emergence of a specialized concept of morality to refer to the limited zone of high pressure. (For discussion of the limited nature of morality, see Kupperman, The Foundation of Morality [1983], chapter 1, and Williams, Ethics and the Limits of Philosophy [1985], chapter 10.) In Kant's ethics it is the zone in which the categorical imperative plays an active and decisive role, in which one cannot simply follow the hypothetical imperatives that tell us how to achieve happiness or whatever else one wants. In John Stuart Mill's Utilitarianism (chapter 5, para. 14) it is the zone—distinguished from "expediency"—in which a suboptimal choice is "wrong" and is subject to the pressure of either the law or public opinion or (at least) the agent's own feelings of guilt. Whether classical Greek or ancient Chinese ethics had any concept that closely corresponds to "morality" is debatable. Certainly what modern Western people would consider to be moral issues are discussed in both traditions, but both classical Greek and ancient Chinese ethics take seriously issues about the style and goals of life that concern the governance of all of the little moments of life between the big moments of what we would think of as moral decisions. There is no sharp division within the conduct of life comparable to Kant's between the categorical and hypothetical imperatives or Mill's between "expediency" and choices that are subject to punishment (either legal or stemming from other people's judgments or from personal conscience).

Two major figures in the West who clearly are not preoccupied with a division between the major moments of life (in which one must decide on universal principle, or that are specially subject to pressure) and the rest of life are Aristotle and Nietzsche. Aristotle's famous praise of the contemplative life establishes an ideal of the life most worth living that rivals Confucius'. Connectedness with others plays an important role in Aristotle's ideal, and he has many useful things to say about friendship. Anyone who has read Confucius will be struck by the lesser degree of attention in Aristotle to the role of nuances of style in personal connections—and in what we learn from others—and will be startled by Aristotle's emphasis (Nicomachean Ethics, book 10, 9, pp. 1864–65) on law in the formation of character. Clearly, also, Aristotle does not give family the ethical importance that Confucius does. Contemporary virtue ethics certainly has, by and large, shared Aristotle's relative inattention to the role of nuances of style in personal connections, and has largely failed to explore the ways in which personal style, connectedness with others, and virtues add up to a life worth living on a minute-to-minute basis. There is a comparable gap in recent feminist ethics.

Nietzsche might seem, among recent philosophers, closest to Confucius both in manner of presentation (that is, in fragments that the reader must synthesize for herself or himself) and in what he does. Nietzsche after all urged one "to 'give style' to one's character. . . . Here a large mass of second nature has been added; there a piece of original nature has been removed" (*The Gay Science* [1887/1970], section 290, p. 232). This similarity in areas of concern does not imply any closeness in outlook; indeed Nietzsche's disdain for the civic dimension of the good life is antithetical to Confucius' view, as is the great latitude in styles of good life that Nietzsche proclaims. But he shares with Confucius a tendency to think of a good life as a seamless web, rather than dividing big "moral" moments from the rest. Indeed, coming after the division of morality from the rest of life, Nietzsche is positively hostile to moralizing. Nietzsche also, like Confucius, clearly emphasizes the importance of personal style as manifest even in the quieter moments of life; there is room also for a sort of connectedness with others (albeit one that is very un-Confucian) in his idea of a good life, and for a similarly idiosyncratic set of virtues. Nietzsche however, I think, is more concerned with nuances of style in the mind-set and concerns of the strong, independent agent he requires than he is with nuances in the interactions with others. It is striking also that, whereas the ethical development of the Nietzsche *ubermensch*, like that of the best kind of Confucian, is never entirely finished (so that more growth or learning is always possible), the *ubermensch* (unlike his Confucian counterpart) is not pictured as learning from others. These elements that are largely missing in Nietzsche are largely missing also from the recent Continental philosophy influenced by Nietzsche with which I am acquainted.

Thus, neither Aristotle nor Nietzsche entirely supplies what can be found in Confucius. Each has his own strengths and absences, but Aristotle and Nietzsche share a lesser degree of attention to styles of interaction with others than Confucius provides. I have argued elsewhere that ethical decision is essentially a one-person game for Aristotle (as it clearly is also for Nietzsche) and that it is a multiperson game for Confucius (Kupperman, "Tradition and Community in the Formation of Self" [1999]). In what follows I will not pursue this point any further, but rather will focus on general issues of behavioral style, and especially on Confucius' emphasis on naturalness.

Naturalness, Harmony, and Personal Nature

My (1968) concern with naturalness was keyed to Soothill's use of the word in his translation of comments by the disciple You in *Analects* 1:12: "In the usages of decorum it is naturalness that is of value." Waley gives "In the usages of ritual it is harmony that is prized," and Lau has "Of things brought about by the rites, harmony is the most valuable." A relevant passage is 6:16. Soothill renders this as "When nature (zhì 質) exceeds training, you have the rustic. When training

exceeds nature, you have the clerk. It is only when nature and training are pro-
portionately blended that you have the higher type of man." Lau (for whom it is
6:18) has "When there is preponderance of native substance over acquired refinement, the result will be churlishness. When there is a preponderance of acquired
refinement over native substance, the result will be pedantry." Waley gives "When
natural substance prevails over ornamentation, you get the boorishness of the
rustic. When ornamentation prevails over natural substance, you get the pedantry
of the scribe."

In all of these versions, 6:16 is concerned with a contrast between something
original (nature or substance) and an addition to, or modification of, it. An ideal
balance between the two elements of the contrast is urged. It is not far-fetched
to see a connection between this ideal balance and the harmony or naturalness
(hé 和) of 1:12.

Clearly, when good translations differ we must think that the Chinese is to some
degree problematic. I am not equipped to comment on this. But it is worth pointing out that the English, too, must be taken as problematic: there are after all two
poles to the translator's art. What is meant by "harmony" or "naturalness"? What
is natural or native, "substance" or "nature"?

What complicates the discussion is that language changes over time, in ways
that reflect shifts in the surrounding culture. Even within relatively short periods
resonances can grow or dwindle. Naturalness and being natural had resonances
in the 1960s that are not strongly present in the same way thirty years later. These
were connected with two views: one that Confucius would have accepted, and
the other that he (in my view rightly) would have rejected. The first is the claim
(already emphasized in my discussion) that style of life or behavior is ethically
important: to put it crudely, even when the broad nature of what one does matters,
the style of how one does it also can be very important. The second is the view
that much of what would go under the heading of ritual (or of manners) represents a corruption or a warping of the essential goodness of human nature, and
that much traditional behavior (especially among elites) is so artificial as to be
unwholesome.

The appeal of Soothill's translation of 1:12, against this background, is that it
subverts the contrast between "natural" and "artificial." Like Bishop Butler's subversion of the contrast between altruism and self-interest, it appeals to a mixture
of logic and psychology in bringing together what an unthinking person might
view as opposite and conflicting. Ritual is by definition artificial, yet Confucius
clearly rejects any presumption that it is a questionable modification of what it is
to be a human being. (There is no logic that requires what is artificial to be unnatural.) Further, there is the psychological observation that ritual, if done right,
can be a fulfillment of what it is to be human. In effect, the passage grants that
ritual can be performed in such a way as to be unnatural, but insists that if the
ritual is done in the right spirit this will not be the case. Ritual and music, Confucius insists, are both more than the physical ingredients (Analects 17:11). He

would not, I think, have disagreed with Angela Zito's recent comment (Zito, "Silk and Skin: Significant Boundaries" [1994], p. 111) that "the participating ritualist himself—his faculties, senses, responses, clothing, and actions—is systematically included in that very set of signs called forth by the ritual."

What then is naturalness? The word implies a certain ease of behavior, an absence of strain: the agent is reasonably comfortable with her or his behavior, and there is no conflict between the behavior and what the agent normally is like. A simple current example would be the way in which a reasonably well brought-up person manages to say "thank you" for a favor done. In cases like this there is noticeable ease and fluency, and typically the agent does not miss a beat. Compare someone who has not been accustomed to express thanks, who in an extreme case might memorize the words, remind himself or herself of them when the occasion arises, and very likely does not say them in a relaxed and fluent way.

One needs to qualify this contrast, because there are a number of contexts in which good manners or ritual require that one not display ease and fluency: for example, in comforting a grieving friend, or in responding to a summons from the ruler (*Analects* 10:3), entering the Palace Gate (10:4), or carrying the ceremonial tablet of jade (10:5). Also, naturalness does not preclude reflectiveness or the ability to have second thoughts. Arguably, naturalness will rule out reflectiveness in some kinds of cases, the ones in which an accomplished person will find the best kind of behavior unproblematic: in these cases (to borrow a trademark phrase of Bernard Williams) to reflect may be to have "one thought too many." But it is impossible to read through the *Analects* without having a strong sense that in Confucius' view how one should behave sometimes is problematic—and requires reflection—even for a very good person. In particular, one is always able to learn from other people's reactions.

Even in the cases that call for reflection or hesitation, though, there is an important contrast between someone who can be "at home" in what is called for and someone who cannot. Some people find within themselves what is appropriate for the grieving friend, and mean it. Others do not.

The fact that thanking, in the right circumstances, comes naturally for most people (and arguably does not for most two-year-olds) suggests that what is natural evolves during a lifetime. "Second nature" is a familiar phrase, reminding us that the "nature" of most adults is not exactly the same as that of most two-year-olds. A riposte to the widespread 1960s idea that it is purifying to reject the artificial, thus returning to basic human nature, is the observation that much that is artificial becomes nature. This view is in broad outline shared by Confucius and Aristotle. Because of it, Soothill's translation of 6:16, which uses the phrase "original nature," fits nicely (in my opinion) with his rendering of 1:12.

What is "harmony" (Waley and Lau)? Teachers of philosophy are likely to think immediately of Plato's *Republic*, whose claims for the greater satisfactoriness of a rational and disciplined life are best explained by use of words like *harmony*. According to Plato, if some scope is allowed for appetites and spirited impulses but reason is in charge, then one can escape the inner conflicts that mark the lives of most people and that make the life of the tyrant (however glittering it may seem) a living hell. The word *harmony*, with its musical associations, is very much in place in explicating such a view, more especially because Plato presents to us discrete elements (of the soul) whose relation to one another should not be jarring. The word is also useful in relation to Confucius, because the Confucian ideal clearly requires a high degree of comfort with who one is, so that external disappointments will not destroy one's sense of well-being (compare *Analects* 12:4, 9:28, 7:36). This in turn requires absence of significant inner conflicts. However, we should note that the appropriateness in relation to Confucius is not quite as great as that for Plato because Confucius does not present us with discrete elements of the self in the way in which Plato does.

Note also that "harmony," explicated in this way, converges with "naturalness." Both require a lack of significant inner conflict, and an agent's ability to enter into what is represented by her or his behavior. Even though the two translations sound different, they point toward what are roughly the same set of ideas.

What about "substance" and "nature"? Substance has been problematic in Western philosophy since the time of John Locke. One worry is that all we know through perception is attribute, not substance. Thus, as in the Roman Catholic doctrine of transubstantiation, there could be a transformation of substance without any experiential clues. A secondary worry is whether it is meaningful to talk about substance at all, a point that Berkeley argued in relation to material substance and that others later extended to all substance.

"Substance" of course has meanings other than the technical one in metaphysics just discussed. To speak of someone's substance can suggest matter, which takes various forms, or something permanent to which other things are added. It might refer to genetic endowment as opposed to the influence of upbringing. Something like this could be part of the meaning of 6:16, especially if we think of the men who fall into pedantry as rather like those we might term "overachievers." One way of reading 6:16 is to see it as endorsing the view that some people, either because of early upbringing or heredity (or some combination of these) have greater capacity than others to be really good human beings, but that a balance between the refinements supplied by education and this early capacity is highly desirable. It is best not to be oafish or unrefined, but too much refinement can render a person "artificial" in the bad sense of the word.

It is plausible to see something like this as the meaning of 6:16, and Soothill's word "nature" seems to me to capture the contrast between what a person is before the educational progress is seriously underway and what then becomes second nature. Needless to say, this is different from "nature" as it would be understood when the contast is not between original and second nature, but rather between how something normally develops (or should develop) and what runs counter to this. Graham glosses this nature (hsing/xìng 性) as a thing's "proper course of development during its process of *shēng*" 生, having observed that *shēng* is commonly translated as "life" (Graham, "The Background of the Mencian Theory of Human Nature" [1990], pp. 10, 7). The word *substance*, which Waley and Lau use for 6:16, can be taken like Soothill's "nature" as capturing the contrast between what is original and what develops (in which case there is no significant difference between the translations). But it also can be taken as suggesting that there is *something* there, at the start of the educational process, which in some sense is permanent, so that it (perhaps with qualifications or subtractions) still exists after there has been considerable educational progress. This thought should not be disregarded. Folk psychology has sometimes held that the child is still present in the man (or woman), and if there is any truth in this, then this counts for "substance" (as opposed to "nature") in the translation of 6:16.

My primary interest, needless to say, is not in comparing translations, but rather in the philosophical lessons to be learned from Confucius. It should be clear by now that these include the thought that what many people might take to be artificial (ritual) can be performed in ways that do not run unwholesomely counter to human impulses and habits. Further, education that includes training in ritual can balance one's original substance or nature in such a way that training in ritual completes or perfects the education. More fundamentally, there is the lesson that style and attitude (as in how one performs the ritual) can be at least as important as the broad nature of what one does, so that ethical education should include education in style. If harmony or naturalness matters, then this education in style is in a way education in becoming a certain kind of person. This is a lesson that should refocus ethics.

Style and Responsibility to Family and Polity

Here we approach a large and complex subject. The lessons in the ethics of personal development to be learned from Confucius could hardly be explained in anything much shorter than the *Analects* itself. In what follows I will concentrate on the intersection between the development of personal style and of responsibility to others. Again the task is subversion, destroying an appearance of opposition. We associate emphasis on style with aesthetes like Oscar Wilde, one of whose sayings was "Democracy would take too many evenings." We may be tempted to associate responsibility to others, especially civic responsibility, with the worthy and dull. The two would hardly seem to go together. They do for Confucius, however, and what he has to say constitutes an important argument for the claim that they should.

To avoid misunderstanding, I should say that "style" includes anything distinctive in how something is done or said. The contrast is between the broad nature of what is done or said (its general category or what would be a prosaic rendering) and subtle features of how it appeared or what it conveyed that would be captured in a very fine-grained report but very possibly not in a prosaic general description. Oscar and Bloggs both tell a host or hostess that they have enjoyed the party (this is a prosaic general description); but Oscar does so with some unexpected turns of phrase that others later describe as "charming" or "witty," whereas Bloggs (exhibiting a style that is actually lack of style) says "I had a nice time" in a flat voice with utterly unaccented cadence. If style is how a thing is done or said, then (this is the point especially to be emphasized) much of what counts as style will include expression or revelation of attitudes. The same thing (more or less) can be done affectionately or coldly, in a dignified or a slovenly way, with diffidence or in a way that smacks of arrogance.

Some conceptual embarrassments should be noted before we move on. It is a truism in aesthetics that in fact there is no style (certainly none that can be exhibited) without content, and similarly no content without style. Style and content thus are not discrete elements. Rather they represent poles of our experience of objects of interest. What we might summarize prosaically as the action of the play or the subject of the painting counts as content; those subtle features of the treatment of different contents or subjects by the same (or similar) artists that may inspire a sense of recognition (the Corot painting recognized across the room, the Mozartean phrase) go under the heading of style. In short, style is not a precise concept, either in the arts or in life.

Nor do I mean to suggest that style always, or generally, includes expression or revelation of attitudes. This would be an excessively large claim in relation to Corot or Mozart. It might be argued that even here a general orientation toward life is expressed or revealed, but this claim will not concern us. The relevant claim rather is that *sometimes* style, in the words or actions of life, includes the expression or revelation of attitudes, and that this can make a great difference. We have already seen that, in Confucius' view, the harmony or naturalness revealed in the practice of ritual is important, although this perhaps can be viewed more as a matter of the general personal development of the agent than of specific attitudes. Something more specific is at stake when Confucius inveighes against "ritual performed without reverence, the forms of mourning observed without grief" (*Analects* 3:26, Waley). Here how the thing is done (and the attitudes that are expressed or revealed) is at least as important as what is done.

Some readers may object here that my account conflates personal attitudes with style. They are both matters of how things are done or said, it will be conceded, but there the connection ends. But why, one may reply, should one suppose this? Is it that one thinks of style as some kind of fancy dress for actions or words, which can be put on or discarded at will? This may be a plausible view of the style of inconsequential actions (for example, how one thanks the hostess), but it looks much less plausible in relation to cases in which a great deal is at stake (for example, what is said in tense moments in close personal relationships). It is in order to answer questions like "What was the style of his remarks?" by saying "arrogant" or "he sounded discouraged." The style of Mabel's response to the provocation, when she left the room and closed the door, may have been subdued or it may have been agitated.

Part of what we need to subvert is the kind of education in propriety that emphasizes compliance with the proper forms, leaving the impression that little else matters. This certainly was not Confucius' view, even in areas of life in which he was especially a stickler for form. Thus, when asked about proper treatment of parents, he replied, "It is the demeanour that is difficult. Filial piety does not consist merely in young people undertaking the hard work . . . or serving their elders first with wine and food. It is something much more than that" (*Analects* 2:8, Waley).

The difficulty in appreciating the ethical importance of style is hardly accidental: style, after all, is by definition what tends to get left out of the most prosaic, all-purpose summary of what was said or done. An ethics that centers on morality and also on the law is especially prone to disregard style. In the courts, comments on the style of someone's behavior are likely to be ruled out by lawyers and judges who insist on "sticking to the facts;" and our moral condemnation of actions will focus on broad categories like murder, rape, and theft, and at most peripherally on how they are done. Morality and the law are both blunt instruments, designed for the use of huge numbers of people with varying degrees of understanding and a wide variety of modes of experience. Style has at most a marginal role in them, and someone who thinks of morality as virtually the whole of ethics will have little interest in style.

In the flow of personal relationships, however, between the big moral moments that occasionally may occur within them, style counts enormously. What is said or done sends messages that influence people's attitudes to each other and their feelings about life; how it is said or done sends more messages, and often may have a deeper influence. One reason for the deeper influence may be connected, paradoxically, with the reason why we often are reluctant to blame people for the style of their behavior. We may feel that blame is appropriate only when what is blamed could have been controlled, and that style of behavior often cannot be controlled. If this is so, then it is not far-fetched to think of style of behavior as expressive of deep and relatively permanent attitudes, and this will make any encouraging (or discouraging) messages it sends seem especially encouraging (or discouraging).

Thus (to return to *Analects* 2:8), a son or daughter who simply does not love his or her parents can, out of a sense of duty, do all the right things, and still (in Confucius' view) fail. This seems very hard. Is this a new form of "moral luck"? Could someone be said to fail who never really (perhaps because the relationship was flawed from the start) had a chance to succeed? Perhaps Confucius' view was somewhat like Pascal's (on religious faith), that over time one could modify one's attitudes if one wished, by practice and by increments of the kind of style one wished to have. We can, to some degree and at least on some occasions, control demeanour, and if we can continue to do that, over time attitudes will evolve.

In any event, the style with which people behave can energize and encourage those who are nearest and dearest, or discourage them and make them feel hesitant and helpless. These are major consequences, and should be part of the concern of ethics, even if we hesitate to blame what we deplore. Any adequate account of what contributes to a good life must include the causal role played by the style of parents, teachers, friends, and partners.

The portraits of Confucius that emerge in the *Analects* are relevant to this. In his leisure hours his "manner was very free-and-easy, and his expression alert and cheerful." His "manner was affable yet firm, commanding but not harsh, polite but easy" (*Analects* 7:4, 7:37, Waley). It is tempting to read these quotations as bland, the philosophical counterparts of a travel brochure. We may begin to take them seriously, though, if we ask in whose company Confucius was "free-and-easy," "cheerful," and "polite but easy." This was not Confucius when he was absolutely by himself. He was interacting with other people, and there were unmentioned witnesses (in most cases probably the people he interacted with) who transmitted the portraits. By and large, these must have been his students, who were close to him and to whom he stood in loco parentis. It is fair to assume that their lives were heavily influenced by the style of his interactions with them, and that his ease and cheerfulness had an important role in this. (It is instructive to recall that one modern Western philosopher who resisted the division between morality and the rest of ethics, David Hume, considered cheerfulness a virtue; see Hume, *Treatise of Human Nature* [1739/1978], p. 611). Most of us are familiar with the ways in which, in the much more limited interactions of our educational system, some teachers bring out the best in their students and others do not. The qualities ascribed to Confucius in these seemingly casual portraits are very consequential. Indeed, the rise of Confucianism testifies to how consequential they were.

The case for the ethical importance of style, strong as it is, should not be overstated. The case is strongest in those areas of life (chiefly personal relationships) that are least likely to be viewed under the headings of "duty" or "justice" or possible "wickedness." It is far less strong in relation to the kinds of actions— such as murder, rape, torture, and theft—that are in the heartland of morality. Normally, the subtle features of how one of these actions is performed will matter far less than the broad nature of what is done.

A word should be said, though, about the importance of style in relation to that very public activity (normally contrasted with private personal relationships): politics. It is tempting here, as in the central territory of morality, to think that what matters is the broad nature of what is done, and that style is by and large inconsequential—except in winning popularity. But there is room for doubt.

There are two very different sources of doubt. One is that much of the business of politics, especially on the legislative level, does involves personal relationships that temper what is possible, so that the best (or the worst) outcome achievable may be the result of deals and compromises. There is no reason to assume that personal style cannot matter in this, and every reason to think that it sometimes might have consequences that are ethically significant.

The other source of doubt is that the style of leaders, above and beyond the broad nature of what they do, may inspire emulation and in other ways influence the mood and outlook of large numbers of people. Even if this is constructive, it arguably would not compensate for actions that, say, increase the incidence of desperate poverty within a country. Style is not everything. But there is room for a case that the effects of style, though subtle, can be quite considerable. If this is so, then an important part of the job of a political leader is that of exerting beneficial influence through a kind of personal projection. In this way, much might be accomplished at moments during which hardly anything is apparently being done. This would especially be the case if the moral force of a leader's attitudes inspired others to action, and would be analogous to the role of the polestar (see *Analects* 2:1).

My contention—to sum up this part of the argument—is that style has significant ethical importance, especially in what matters in personal relationships and, arguably, in much that matters in politics. If we care about what happens to our (and other people's) families, friends, students, and others, then we must regard style as within the realm of personal responsibility. Even if we are hesitant to blame those whose style is deleterious, there is no reason not to assign ethical importance to education in style—and no reason not to encourage people to move in the direction of constructive styles of personal interaction.

So emphases on the development of personal style and on responsibility for others converge rather than conflict. Why, then, would these emphases initially seem opposite, according to so many people? We already have seen two reasons. We can review these, and add a third.

One reason is that emphasis on style is most out of place in relation to the central subject matter of morality. A temptation that needs to be resisted, especially in philosophy, is that of fastening one's attention on a range of cases and then generalizing outward from it. Someone who is preoccupied with morality, to the exclusion of the values and goals of life that would not normally be placed under the heading of morality, may regard any emphasis on style as antithetical to the nature of ethics. Conversely, someone who is keenly aware of the importance of style in personal relationships, or preoccupied (as Nietzsche was) with the role of style in creating a life worth living, might be tempted to slight that part of ethics (that is, morality) in which style was least important.

A second reason is, as we have observed, that style in everyday life is most noticed when what actually happens is least consequential and relatively disconnnected from the rest of life (for example, when someone thanks a host or hostess, as opposed to, say, someone behaving in a harsh manner to a spouse, partner, or child). Style may seem most pure, as it were, in the disconnected, very small moments of life, when people can think about what they are doing rather than being carried forward simply by habit or the momentum of what they have done previously. This fact makes it tempting to associate style with the inconsequential. Reflection on the varieties of roles that style plays in human interactions, and in our sense of our own lives, should dispel this temptation, however.

A third source of the temptation to regard concern for style as antithetical to personal responsibility is related. Style—if one focuses on moments that are inconsequential and disconnected—appears to be something that can be adopted and discarded, so that different styles may be appropriate for different occasions. This impression is very different from the continuity and commitment that one associates with personal responsibility.

One corrective is to bear in mind *Analects* 1:12 and the importance of harmony or naturalness in ritual, as well as in much else. If, as I have argued, a style that is harmonious or natural is allied to second nature so that one does not merely put it on and take it off like an item of fancy dress, then an emphasis on style will translate itself in many cases into an emphasis on having become a certain sort of person. Clearly, a style of personal relationships is constructive only if it represents the person whose style it is, rather than being an artificial (in the bad sense of "artificial") and insincere affect of the moment. Thus, in important areas of life, personal responsibility converges with the development (and internalization) of style.

Again, a crucial point is that the truth of some cases may be highly misleading in relation to others. It would be priggish to criticize someone's variety of styles in thanking hosts or ending a letter. Variety of styles in the way one behaves toward a child, a partner, or a student, though, such that people "do not know where they stand," is another matter. The integration of a life also, arguably, demands some coherence of style. Absolute uniformity might well be excessive, but considerable continuity in things that matter (which include close personal relationships) can be important in allowing for a sense of personal integrity.

In short, the importance of style precludes what might be called an opportunism of style. Waley (1938, 91 n. 4) suggestively uses the word "opportunistic" in explicating *Analects* 2:16 ("He who sets to work on a different strand destroys the whole fabric"). There is no reason to read 2:16 as being merely about style, but no reason either to regard it as not subsuming many of the issues of what we have been discussing as style. Stability of style (see also *Analects* 13:22) matters.

Conclusion

Naturalness or harmony is important, not only in ritual but also as a feature of style in personal relationships and, arguably, in politics. If ethics is concerned, broadly, with what is most important in life, then it must devote considerable attention to the process of developing people for whom constructive styles of thought and action have become natural. Confucius is a major source of insight for this process. Recent Western philosophy, in contrast, has not devoted sufficient attention to this area of ethics, and its practitioners could benefit from the study of Confucius.

ACKNOWLEDGMENTS

I am indebted to Bryan Van Norden for a number of helpful suggestions and to Bonnie Smith for some useful e-mail discussion of ritual.

REFERENCES

Aristotle. Fourth c. B.C./1984. *Nicomachean Ethics*. In *The Complete Works of Aristotle* vol. 2, ed. Jonathan Barnes. Princeton: Princeton University Press.

Confucius. Sixth c. B.C./1910. *The Analects*, trans. W. E. Soothill. London: Oxford University Press.

———. Sixth c. B.C./1938. *The Analects*, trans. Arthur Waley. New York: Vintage Books.

———. Sixth c. B.C./1979. *The Analects*, trans. D. C. Lau. Harmondsworth, Eng.: Penguin Books.

Creel, Herrlee. 1949. *Confucius: The Man and the Myth*. New York: John Day. Reprinted as *Confucius and the Chinese Way* (New York: Harper and Row, 1960).

Crisp, Roger, and Michael Slote, eds. 1997. *Virtue Ethics*. Oxford: Oxford University Press.

Graham, A. C. 1990. "The Background of the Mencian Theory of Human Nature." In *Studies in Chinese Philosophy and Philosophical Literature*, pp. 7–66. Albany, N.Y.: SUNY Press.

Hume, David. 1739/1978. *Treatise of Human Nature*, ed. L. A. Selby-Bigge, rev. P. H. Nidditch. Oxford, Clarendon Press.

Kittay, Eva, and Diana Meyers, eds. 1987. *Women and Moral Theory*. Totowa, N.J.: Rowman and Littlefield.

Kupperman, J. J. 1968. "Confucius and the Problem of Naturalness." *Philosophy East and West* 18, no. 3 (July): 175–85.

———. 1983. *The Foundations of Morality*. London: Geo. Allen and Unwin.

———. 1999. "Tradition and Community in the Formation of Self." In Joel Kupperman, *Learning From Asian Philosophy*, 36–51. New York: Oxford University Press.

Li, Chenyang. 1994. "Confucian Concept of Jen and the Feminist Ethics of Care: A Comparative Study." *Hypatia* 9, no. 1 (winter): 70–89.

Mill, John Stuart. 1861. *Utilitarianism*, many editions.

Nietzsche, Friedrich. 1887/1970. *The Gay Science*, trans. Walter Kaufmann. New York: Vintage Books.

Williams, Bernard. 1985. *Ethics and the Limits of Philosophy*. London: Fontana Press.

Zito, Angela. 1994. "Silk and Skin: Significant Boundaries. In *Body, Subject and Power in China*, ed. Angela Zito and Tani E. Barlow, pp. 103–30. Chicago: University of Chicago Press.

3

Rén 仁 and Lǐ 禮

in the *Analects*

KWONG-LOI SHUN

Rén 仁 (humaneness, goodness) and lǐ 禮 (rites) are two concepts central to Confucius' ethical thinking as reported in the *Analects* (Lúnyǔ 論語). The former refers to the ethical ideal, and the latter to certain traditional norms that govern human conduct. It is generally agreed that Confucius regards the observance of lǐ as closely related to the ideal of rén, but there has been radical disagreement concerning the nature of the relation. In what follows, I will defend a certain interpretation of his conception of that relation.

There are at least two different views concerning the earlier meaning of the character "rén." According to one view, the character originally referred to the quality that makes someone a distinctive member of an aristocratic clan.[1] According to another view, it originally had the meaning of love, especially the kindness of rulers to their subjects.[2] For the purpose of my discussion, it is not necessary to adjudicate between these competing views. It suffices to note that, in the *Analects*, "rén" is used both more narrowly to refer to one desirable quality among others, and more broadly to refer to an all-encompassing ethical ideal that includes all the desirable qualities. That "rén" is used in both ways is seen from the fact that rén is both listed as one desirable quality among others, such as wisdom and courage (9.29, 14.28), and described as something that includes other desirable qualities such as courage (14.4).[3] In the narrower sense, it probably emphasizes affection for others; on one occasion (12.22), rén is explained in terms of love for fellow human beings. But the character is used more often in the *Analects* in the broader sense of an all-encompassing ethical ideal, and I will from now on use "rén" in this sense.

The character "lǐ" originally referred to rites of sacrifice but, even before the time of Confucius, its scope of application had expanded to include other things, such as norms governing polite behavior. For example in the Shījīng 詩經, which scholars generally agree to be datable to a time before Confucius, although the character is still used in connection with sacrifices (poems 279, 290), it is also related to yí 儀 (good form) (52) and used in contexts going beyond sacrifices (193/5).[4] In the Zuǒzhuàn 左傳, datable to a period that extends before and after the time of Confucius, "lǐ" is used in a much broader sense. Lǐ is distinguished from yí (good form); norms governing polite behavior such as ways of presenting a gift are described as a matter of yí (good form) but not lǐ (pp. 704/8–9; 601/8–12).⁵ Lǐ is related to norms of conduct that govern those in a higher and those in a lower position (704/16), to proper ways of governing a state (601/8–12; 521/10–12), and to the proper relation between rulers and ministers, fathers and sons, older and younger brothers, husbands and wives, and mothers and daughters-in-law (715/12–17). Proper observance of lǐ is supposed to be the basis for an orderly society (715/12–17) and the ideal basis for government (31/13). The broader use of "lǐ" is found in the Xúnzǐ 荀子, in which "lǐ" is at times used as if interchangeable with "lǐ-yì 禮義" (chap. 19/1–15), where "lǐ-yì" is often used to refer generally to social distinctions and norms that govern conduct appropriate to people by virtue of their social positions (for example, 4/72–77; 9/17–18; 9/64–75).⁶ What gives unity to the various things that have come to be included in the scope of lǐ is presumably jìng 敬 (reverence); as emphasized in various classical texts, one is supposed to have jìng toward spirits when performing rites of sacrifice, and toward other human beings when observing the norms of polite behavior and when observing the responsibilities that one has towards others by virtue of one's social position.

In the Analects, while it is clear that lǐ is regarded as ideally accompanied by jìng (for example, 3.26), it is not entirely clear what the scope of lǐ is. Many commentators on the Analects take lǐ to include all the rules that govern proper behavior in various kinds of social and political contexts, whereas some regard lǐ as still restricted to ceremonious behavior.⁷ The actual examples of lǐ found in the Analects have to do largely with ceremonious behavior (3.4, 3.15, 3.17, 9.3, 17.11), but it remains unclear how broad the scope of lǐ is when the text makes such general observations as that one has to learn lǐ to take a stand (8.8, 16.13, 20.3) or that lǐ is the ideal basis for government (2.3, 4.13). I will not attempt to determine the exact scope of application of "lǐ" as the character is used in the Analects. Whether we construe the scope more broadly or more narrowly, the question arises as to how the ideal of rén and the observance of lǐ are related.

One issue of disagreement concerning the relation between them is whether there are aspects of the rén ideal that bear no significant relation to lǐ.⁸ I will not address this issue of disagreement in my discussion. Instead, I will focus attention on that aspect of rén (whether it is the sole aspect or one of several aspects) that has to do with the observance of lǐ (whether construed more broadly or more narrowly), and discuss how the two are related. For convenience, I will continue to speak of the relation between rén and lǐ, but subsequent uses of "rén" are to be understood as a shorthand for referring to that aspect of rén having to do with the observance of lǐ.

In section II, I will distinguish between two opposed interpretations of Confucius' conception of the relation between rén and lǐ and indicate, for each interpretation, passages in the Analects that seem to fit in better with one interpretation than with the other. Because the two interpretations are opposed, this seems to reveal a conflict between different parts of the text. However, in section III, I will argue that the conflict is merely apparent, and that all the relevant passages can be accommodated by a third interpretation. That it can accommodate all the relevant passages in a way that the other two interpretations cannot counts in favor of this third interpretation. In section IV, I conclude with some general observations about the proposed interpretation.

Before proceeding to the main discussion, let me add some clarificatory observations concerning the use of certain terminology in the discussion and concerning methodology.[9] In the subsequent discussion, I will be using certain psychological locutions, such as the terms "emotion" and "attitude," in discussing Confucius. Some may be concerned that, in using such locutions, I might have thereby ascribed to Confucius a certain picture of the self which he does not have.[10] To address this concern, I will make explicit the presuppositions behind my use of such locutions.

I regard psychological locutions basically as locutions that people apply and regard as appropriate to apply to persons and perhaps certain other animals, but not (except in a derivative sense) to inanimate objects. I think the Analects does contain locutions, such as "jìng" (reverence), which are psychological in this sense, and my use of such psychological locutions as "emotion" and "attitude" is for the purpose of referring in a more general way to the phenomena referred to by the psychological locutions used in the Analects. In using such locutions, all I presuppose is that Confucius does use locutions that are psychological in the sense described. I have not thereby ascribed to him any reflective theory of the mind, whether Cartesian dualism or some form of behaviorism, nor have I ascribed to him more reflective thoughts about the phenomena referred to by his use of psychological locutions.

Some may also have methodological objections concerning the attempt to come up with an interpretation of Confucius' conception of the relation between rén and lǐ that can make sense of all the relevant passages, and the objections can take at least two forms. First, there is evidence that the Analects was compiled long after Confucius' death, by disciples with different views and a different understanding of Confucius' teachings. There is therefore reason to expect that parts of the Analects are not authentic reports of Confucius' teachings, and that the text as a whole does not present a single coherent account of the relation between rén and lǐ. So, it is misguided to attempt to come up with such an account.

In response to this objection, we may note that the fact that the Analects was compiled after Confucius' death by disciples with different views does not by itself show that some passages are not authentic. Philological studies may show this to be the case, but so far there is no general agreement on this issue. Until there is philological evidence for the inauthenticity of certain passages, it does not seem misguided to take the text as a whole, and to attempt to find an interpretation of Confucius' conception of the relation between rén and lǐ that can make sense of all the relevant passages. If the attempt fails, this will give reason to suspect either an inconsistency in Confucius' thinking or the inauthenticity of certain passages.

But there is no reason to regard the attempt as misguided and doomed to failure at the outset.

The second kind of methodological objection goes as follows. In the *Analects*, Confucius describes what the rén person is like, emphasizes the importance of observing lǐ, and sometimes relates rén to the observance of lǐ. He does not, however, put forward a reflective account of how rén and lǐ are related. So, reflective accounts of the relation between rén and lǐ, such as the ones to be discussed, cannot legitimately be regarded as interpretations of the text. To present the accounts as interpretations is to ascribe to Confucius a kind of reflectivity not supported by the text.

The objection raises difficult methodological issues that I cannot go into here. As a sketch of one possible response, we may observe that an attempt to interpret a thinker's position on a subject matter is an attempt to understand his position. Such understanding can be achieved by coming up with an account that meets two conditions: that it is intelligible to us, and that it can best explain the things the thinker has said in connection with the subject matter. An account that meets the first condition will employ conceptual apparatus familiar to us and foreign to that thinker, will have a systematic character not present in the relevant text, and will go beyond the text in various other ways. Although it will go beyond the text, it can still further our understanding of the text as long as it has the explanatory power described in the second condition. More specifically, an account may further our understanding of a thinker's position even if it exhibits a degree of reflectivity not present in the thinker himself. To present it as an interpretation is to ascribe to it the explanatory power described in the second condition, and does not commit us to ascribing to the thinker the same degree of reflectivity as exhibited in that account.

II

I now describe two opposed interpretations of Confucius' conception of the relation between rén and lǐ, which I will label the instrumentalist and the definitionalist interpretations. The distinction between them is intended as a heuristic device for highlighting certain apparently conflicting elements in the *Analects*, thereby preparing the ground for introducing my own interpretation. Given the heuristic nature of the distinction, I will set up the two interpretations in a way that is probably more elaborate and extreme than any of the interpretations actually proposed in the literature.

On the *instrumentalist interpretation*, Confucius regards the observance of lǐ as standing in a mere instrumental relation to the ideal of rén. By saying that two items stand in a mere instrumental relation, I mean that each of the two is distinct from and intelligible independently of the other, and may in principle obtain without the other obtaining. However, as a matter of fact, the two are related by causal relations that make one a means to the other. In so characterizing a mere instrumental relation, I leave it open that two items may be related in a way that warrants our speaking of one as a means to the other, but that relates the two in a more intimate manner than a mere instrumental relation.

Thus, on the instrumentalist interpretation, rén is supposed to be a state of the mind, comprising emotional dispositions and attitudes of certain kinds, which is distinct from and intelligible independently of the general observance of lǐ. It is in principle possible for rén to exist independently of the existence of lǐ, though, as a matter of fact, they are related by the following means-end relation. For someone who has approximated the rén ideal, observance of lǐ provides a means of expressing the emotional dispositions and attitudes that constitute the ideal. For example, the three-year period of mourning provides a means of expressing one's continuing love for and remembrance of a deceased parent. For someone who has not yet approximated the ideal, it provides a means of cultivating the appropriate emotional dispositions and attitudes. Participation in lǐ practices has a feedback effect on a person, and makes the person more susceptible to having emotional dispositions and attitudes of the ideal kind.

On this interpretation, the existence of elaborate lǐ practices in society is justified by the instrumental role they play with regard to rén. Rén has evaluative priority over lǐ in the following sense. It is rén alone that has ultimate value, and the value of the existence of lǐ practices in society, and of an individual's observing such practices, is derived from the instrumental role lǐ plays with regard to rén. Accordingly, rén also provides a standard against which one can assess the justifiability of revising or departing from a rule of lǐ. People may be justified in revising or occasionally departing from a rule of lǐ if observing the rule does not serve well its function with regard to the rén ideal, either generally or on particular occasions. And they may be justified in revising a rule of lǐ on other grounds such as economic grounds, if doing so does not affect the efficacy of the rule of lǐ in performing its function with regard to the rén ideal.

On the *definitionalist interpretation*, Confucius regards the rén ideal as defined in terms of the general observance of those lǐ rules actually existing in the Chinese society of his time. The claim is not just that to be a rén person is to be someone who generally observes the existing lǐ rules, whatever these may be. Rather, the claim is that to be a rén person is to be someone who generally observes those rules of lǐ that, as a matter of fact, actually existed in the Chinese society of Confucius' time. Moreover, this identity is supposed to follow from the concept of rén. Admittedly, the observance of lǐ has to be accompanied by the right spirit, however having the right spirit is to be interpreted. Still, unlike the instrumentalist interpretation, rén is no longer regarded as a state of mind distinct from and intelligible independently of the general observance of lǐ, and the observance of lǐ can no longer be regarded as a means to cultivating or expressing rén. Two consequences follow from the identity of rén with the general observance of the actually existing lǐ rules, distinguishing the definitionalist from the instrumentalist interpretation. First, rén no longer has an evaluative priority over lǐ. Indeed, since lǐ can be characterized independently of rén but not vice versa, one may even regard lǐ as having an evaluative priority over rén. That is, it is the observance of lǐ that has ultimate value, from which the value of being the kind of person who generally observes lǐ is derived. Second, rén no longer provides a standard against which one can assess the justifiability of revising or departing from a rule of lǐ, in the way just described for the instrumentalist interpretation. Furthermore, since the ideal is just generally to observe those rules of lǐ that actually exist, this conception of the relation between rén and lǐ is conservative in spirit in that it is opposed to any revision of or departure from the existing lǐ rules.

The distinction between the two interpretations is not intended as an exhaustive classification of interpretations found in the literature. In Section IV, I will consider other interpretations found in the literature that do not lie close to either of these two interpretations. For now, to show that these two interpretations are not totally unrelated to the literature, I will mention examples from the literature of ways of interpreting Confucius that lie close to one or the other of the two interpretations.

Something close to the instrumentalist interpretation is put forward by Xú Fùguān and Lin Yü-sheng. According to Xú Fùguān, one of the most important innovations of Confucius is the discovery of the ideal inner life, which he characterizes in terms of the rén ideal. Confucius gives the traditional lǐ rules a justification in terms of the rén ideal, thereby giving rén evaluative priority over lǐ.[11] And, according to Lin Yü-sheng, rén is an ideal inner life that has ultimate value, whereas lǐ derives its value from rén through the instrumental role it plays in the cultivation and development of rén. Accordingly, rén has evaluative priority over lǐ, and provides a perspective from which one can justify the revision of a lǐ rule.[12]

This way of interpreting Confucius contrasts sharply with that proposed by Zhào Jìbīn and Cāi Shàngsī, which lies close to the definitionalist interpretation. According to Zhào Jìbīn, Confucius regards the content of rén as determined by lǐ, and the observance of the lǐ practices of his time as providing the sole criterion for distinguishing between the possession and lack of rén. In doing so, Confucius has given lǐ a priority over rén. Furthermore, because the ideal is just to observe the existing lǐ practices, this conception of the relation between rén and lǐ is opposed to any revision of or departure from the existing lǐ practices.[13] Cāi Shàngsī proposes a similar interpretation. According to him, lǐ is the most important concept in Confucius' moral thinking, and it is lǐ that distinguishes human beings from other animals. Observance of lǐ is the criterion for the possession of rén, and Confucius' conception of the rén person is just the conception of someone who follows the existing lǐ rules in all areas of life.[14]

These two very different ways of interpreting Confucius are made possible by the fact that each seems to have some textual support. For each of the two interpretations, there are two observations about Confucius' conception of rén and lǐ that can apparently be more easily accommodated by one interpretation than by the other and, furthermore, the observations appear to have textual support. In what follows, I will state these observations and describe how certain passages can be read as supporting the observations. In doing so, I am not myself endorsing the proposed readings of the passages. Although I do regard them as possible and in some cases plausible readings, my sole purpose is to report how each passage can be read in a way that appears to provide support for something close to one of the two interpretations.

The first observation favoring the instrumentalist over the definitionalist interpretation is that there are passages in which Confucius seems to regard lǐ as playing an instrumental role with regard to rén. For example, in 3.3, he asks:

> A man who is not rén, what has he to do with li (rú lǐ hé 如禮何)?

This can be compared to 4.13, where he asks:

> If one is able to govern a state with li and deference, what difficulty
> will he have? If one is unable to govern a state with li and deference,
> what has he to do with li (ru li he)?

In 2.3, lǐ is described as having the function of keeping order among people and thereby governing the state. In 4.13, the query "what has he to do with li (ru li he)?" comes after the description of a situation in which lǐ fails to perform this function. In light of this, the instrumentalist would argue that, in 3.3, a man's not being rén is also regarded by Confucius as a situation in which lǐ does not perform its function. So, it seems that Confucius regards the observance of lǐ as a means to cultivate and express rén. As further support for regarding lǐ instrumentally, the instrumentalist may cite 15.18:

> The gentleman takes rightness (yì 義) as what is essential, and put
> rightness into practice by observing lǐ (lǐ yǐ xíng zhī 禮以行之).

Again, the instrumentalist would say, the observance of lǐ is here regarded as means to put rightness into practice.[15]

A second observation that favors the instrumentalist interpretation is that there are passages in which Confucius speaks as if there is a justification for the revision of or departure from an existing rule of lǐ. As mentioned earlier, a conception of rén as defined in terms of the observance of the existing lǐ practices is opposed to such revision or departure. In 2.23 and 3.9, Confucius describes changes in lǐ from the Xia to the Shang and then to the Zhou dynasty, and in 3.14 he advocates the lǐ practices of Zhou over those of Xia and Shang. These passages do not yet imply a justification for the changes or for Confucius' preference for Zhou lǐ. However, the instrumentalist would argue that a justification is implied in 9.3, where Confucius says: "Using a linen cap is lǐ. Today, black silk is used instead. This is more economical, and I follow the majority. Bowing before ascending the steps is lǐ. Today, people bow after ascending them. This is presumptuous and, although it is contrary to the majority, I follow the practice of bowing before ascending." According to the instrumentalist, Confucius is here not just advocating the retention of or departure from a rule of lǐ, but is also giving reasons for doing so. He cites economic consideration in favor of replacing the linen ceremonial cap used in rituals with one made of black silk. Economic consideration cannot be the only relevant consideration, because otherwise it would have justified the elimination of the ceremonial cap altogether. Presumably, it can justify departure from a lǐ rule only when the efficacy of the lǐ rule in serving its purpose remains unaffected. This explains why Confucius rejects departure from the traditional lǐ rule of bowing to the prince before ascending the steps to the upper hall. This lǐ rule serves as a means of paying homage to the prince, and to depart from the rule without good reason shows disrespect for the prince, thereby defeating the purpose of the rule. Following this line of thought, the instrumentalist would argue that Confucius regards lǐ rules as a means to express emotional dispositions and attitudes of certain kinds, and would accept revision of or departure from a lǐ rule on the basis of such considerations as economic consideration only if the efficacy of the rule in serving its purpose is unaffected.[16] As further evidence, the instrumentalist may cite 3.4: "Lin Fang asked about the basis of lǐ. The Master said, 'A great question indeed. With regard to lǐ, it is better to be economical than to be extravagant. With regard to mourning, it is better to have grief than to observe every formality.'" The instrumentalist would take the reference to a basis (běn 本) of lǐ to show that there is something with reference to which the existence of lǐ can be justified. And Confucius' observation that grief is what is important to mourning suggests that he regards grief as the basis to the lǐ rules that govern mourning—so long as such grief is present and appropriately expressed, it is not necessary to observe every formality, and we may depart from or revise lǐ rules in light of economic consideration.

Although the two observations described above seem to fit in better with the instrumentalist interpretation, there are two observations about Confucius' attitude toward lǐ that seem to fit in better with the definitionalist interpretation. The first is that, although Confucius sometimes speaks as if observing lǐ is a means to cultivate rén, he also speaks of it as constitutive of rén. Take, for example, the passage 12.1:

> Yan Yuan asked about rén.
> The Master said, "Kè jǐ fù lǐ 克己復禮 constitutes rén. If a person can for one day kè jǐ fù lǐ, all under Heaven will regard him as having rén. The attainment of rén comes from oneself, and not from others."
> Yan Yuan said, "May I ask about the items of this?"
> The Master said, "Do not look if it is contrary to li; do not listen if it is contrary to li; do not speak if it is contrary to li; do not act if it is contrary to li."

Depending on whether we take "kè 克" to mean "subdue" or "succeed in," and whether we take the object of "kè" to be "jǐ 己" (oneself) or "jǐ fù lǐ 己復禮" (aligning oneself with lǐ), the expression "kè jǐ fù lǐ" can be translated as "subduing oneself and returning to the observance of lǐ," or as "succeeding in aligning oneself with lǐ." However we read the expression, the definitionalist will take Confucius to be saying that the observance of lǐ is, at least in part, constitutive of rén. This reading the definitionalist will regard as supported by the rest of the passage, in which Confucius explains what he has in mind in terms of the general observance of lǐ in all areas of life.[17] As further evidence that Confucius regards the observance of lǐ as constitutive of rén, the definitionalist may also cite 12.2, in which Confucius explains rén in terms of lǐ-like behavior and attitudes. The definitionalist may also cite 1.2, where Youzi describes filial piety as a basis (běn 本), of rén, in the sense that it is an essential component of and a starting point for cultivating rén, along with 2.5, where Confucius explains filial piety in terms of the observance of lǐ. Taken together, the two passages are supposed to show that Confucius regards the observance of lǐ as standing to rén in a much closer relation than that of a mere instrumental relation.

A second observation that apparently favors the definitionalist interpretation is Confucius' generally conservative attitude toward lǐ as evidenced throughout the *Analects*. For example, he presents himself as an advocate of traditional Zhou lǐ (3.14) and as someone who loves and transmits ancient culture (7.1, 7.20). He emphasizes adherence to traditional lǐ practices (for example, 3.1, 3.17) showing that the departure from lǐ he occasionally advocates (for example, 9.3) is only a departure against the background of a general adherence to lǐ. Now, if participation in lǐ is a mere means for cultivating and expressing rén, we would expect more room for the revision of existing lǐ practices. On the other hand, if rén is defined in terms of the general observance of existing lǐ practices, this would explain why there is no room for such revision. So, Confucius' conservative attitude toward lǐ appears to support the definitionalist interpretation.

As mentioned earlier, although I think the ways of reading the relevant passages described above are possible reading, I am not myself endorsing these readings. A passage cited in support of one interpretation may be given an alternative reading on which it no longer supports that interpretation. For example, in 15.18, the expression "lǐ yǐ xíng zhī 禮以行之," which the instrumentalist takes to mean that observing lǐ is a means to put rightness into practice, can also be read as saying that observing lǐ is the manner in which (rather than the means by which) one puts rightness into practice, in which case the passage no longer provides support for the instrumentalist interpretation. Still, even if we take the possible alternative readings of the relevant passages into consideration, I believe it is not possible to come up with a way of reading *all* the relevant passages that is not artificial but that makes all the passages compatible with one of the two interpretations.

Consider, for example, how the instrumentalist may try to accommodate the passages usually cited in support of the definitionalist interpretation. The instrumentalist can account for Confucius' conservative attitude toward lǐ by appealing to Confucius' optimism that the existing lǐ practices do perform well the function of cultivating and expressing rén, and by citing the fact that some kind of stability is needed for them to perform this function.[18] Still, he will have difficulty making sense of 12.1 and the other passages cited in support of the observation that Confucius sometimes speaks as if observing lǐ is (at least in part) constitutive of rén.[19] On the other hand, although the definitionalist may dispute the reading of some of the passages cited in support of the instrumentalist interpretation, such as 15.18, which has just been considered, he will have difficulty accommodating all the passages. For example, it is difficult to see how the definitionalist can accommodate Confucius' endorsement in 9.3 of a departure from an existing rule of lǐ, without introducing an artificial reading of the passage.[20]

Suppose we grant that, for each of the two interpretations, there are passages that fit in better with that interpretation than with the other. This may seem to show that there is a conflict between different parts of the *Analects*, a conflict that may be explained in terms of either an inconsistency in Confucius' thinking or the inauthenticity of certain parts of the text.[21] However, I do not think we are yet justified in drawing this conclusion, because there remains the possibility that there is a third interpretation that can accommodate the apparently conflicting textual evidence. If we can find such an interpretation, the fact that it resolves the apparent conflict will count in its favor. In what follows, I will develop such an interpretation.

III

For this purpose, we need to introduce a kind of relation different from those in terms of which the instrumentalist and definitionalist interpretations have been characterized. Let us first consider a couple of example of such a relation. Imagine a community in which the only way of getting married is for the partners to perform certain motions, such as exchanging rings, on a ceremonious occasion of a certain kind. Now, within this community, two people's performing the appropriate motions on the appropriate occasion is both necessary and sufficient for their getting married. Moreover, performing these motions and getting married are not separate occurrences that happen to be causally related; rather, given the practice of the community, the former just constitutes the latter. So, the two do not stand in the mere instrumental relation in terms of which the instrumentalist interpretation is characterized. On the other hand, it is not the case that getting married is defined in terms of the performance of these particular motions on ceremonious occasions of this particular kind, for otherwise we would not have been able to make sense of people's getting married by some other ceremonial procedure in a different community. Rather, our conception of marriage is the conception of an institution in which partners undertake certain commitments to each other by following some appropriate ceremonial procedure, it being left open that different communities may have different ceremonial procedures for the undertaking of such commitments. So, getting married and performing the particular motions employed in this community for wedding ceremonies do not stand in the relation in terms of which the definitionalist interpretation is characterized.

The second example concerns the relation between the mastery of a concept and the mastery of a corresponding linguistic practice. Suppose we characterize the mastery of a concept as the capacity to have thoughts of a certain kind. For example, to master the concept of the past is to have the capacity to have the thoughts (to believe, doubt, conjecture, and so forth) that Socrates was a Greek, that Confucius had many disciples, and so forth. Also, suppose we understand language in the sense of a symbolism in which thoughts can be verbally expressed, allowing a language to be of varying scope. For example, just as we can speak of Chinese and English as different languages, we can also speak of different ways of talking about the past as different languages about the past. To master a linguistic practice is to have the capacity to use a language correctly in appropriate circumstances and to respond in appropriate ways to its use. Now, while it is a subject of controversy whether mastery of concepts is generally dependent on mastery of corresponding linguistic practices, it is much less controversial that such dependence relation obtains for some concepts, such as the concept of the past. Let us take a concept of this kind, and suppose that it is given verbal expression by a certain linguistic practice in a certain community. Within this community, mastery of the corresponding linguistic practice is not only necessary, but also sufficient, for the mastery of the concept; a person's ability to use correctly and respond appropriately to the use of the corresponding language will be sufficient for our attributing to the person the capacity to have thoughts of the relevant kind. Moreover, within this community, a person's mastery of the concept and mastery of the corresponding linguistic practice are not distinct capacities that happen to be causally related; given the linguistic practice of the community, we cannot make sense of a member of the community that has one but not the other of the two capacities. So, the two capacities do not stand in the mere instrumental relation in terms of which the instrumentalist interpretation is characterized. On the other hand, mastery of the concept is not defined in terms of mastery of the particular linguistic practice in use in this community, for otherwise we would not have been able to make sense of the concept's being shared by members of a different community with a different linguistic practice. So, the two do not stand in the relation in terms of which the definitionalist interpretation is characterized.

Our two examples illustrate a relation of the following kind between an item A (getting married, mastery of a concept), which can be instantiated in different communities, and an item B (performing certain motions on a ceremonious occasion of a certain kind, mastery of a certain linguistic practice), which concerns the observance of a certain conventional practice of a community. Within that community, instantiation of B is both necessary and sufficient for the instantiation of A, and this is not because A and B are related by some ordinary causal relation. Rather, given the conventional practice of that community, we cannot conceive of one of the two being instantiated without the other. So, A and B do not stand in a mere instrumental relation. On the other hand, neither is A defined in terms of B, for we can conceive of A's being instantiated in a different community with a practice different from but playing a role similar to B. Rather, our conception of A is the conception of something whose instantiation requires the observance of some appropriate conventional practice, this allowing for the possibility that different communities may have different practices that play the appropriate role.[22]

Let us return to the relation between rén and lǐ. We saw earlier that there appears to be a conflict between two pairs of observations that describe Confucius' attitude toward the relation, all of which appear to have some textual basis:

(1) that observance of lǐ is a means to cultivate and express rén;
(2) that revision of or departure from an actually existing lǐ rule can be justified by economic or some other consideration, as long as this does not affect its efficacy in performing the function described in (1);

and

(3) that the general observance of lǐ is, at least in part, constitutive of rén;
(4) a generally conservative attitude toward the existing lǐ practices.

The first pair of observations can be more easily accommodated on the instrumentalist than on the definitionalist interpretation, although the reverse is true of the second pair of observations. Because the two interpretations are opposed, this appears to show that the two pairs of observations are in conflict.

The apparent conflict can be resolved if we regard rén and lǐ as related by the kind of relation just described. The point can be illustrated by a comparison with the relation between mastery of a concept and mastery of a corresponding linguistic practice. Take a concept of the kind mastery of which is dependent on mastery of a corresponding linguistic practice, and suppose that the concept is expressed by a certain linguistic practice in a certain community. The following are four plausible observations concerning how mastery of the concept and mastery of the linguistic practice are related. First, within the community, the latter is both necessary and sufficient for the former, and it is inconceivable that a member of the community should have one but not the other of the two capacities. So, there is a sense in which the mastery of the linguistic practice is constitutive of mastery of the concept. Second, although mastery of the concept is constituted by mastery of the linguistic practice, it is not defined in terms of it because the concept can be shared by other linguistic communities. Because mastery of the concept transcends' mastery of the linguistic practice in this way, there is a sense in which observing the linguistic practice can be described as a means to acquire and later express that concept. Third, because mastery of the concept "transcends" mastery of the linguistic practice, it provides a perspective for assessing revision of the linguistic practice. Having mastered the concept through having been brought up in the linguistic practice, members of the community can propose revisions to simplify the existing practice as long as this does not affect its efficacy in expressing the concept. Fourth, although revisions may be justified by such considerations as simplicity, there is a constraint on the extent of the revision at any particular time. Because the concept itself is made available to members of the community by the existing linguistic practice, any revision has to proceed against the background of a general acceptance of the existing practice, thereby ruling out the possibility of a more comprehensive revision. This accounts for a generally conservative attitude toward the linguistic practice actually in existence.

These four observations parallel respectively the third, first, second, and fourth of the four observations about the relation between rén and lǐ. This shows that, if we regard the possession of rén and the general observance of lǐ as related in a similar manner, we will be able to resolve the apparent conflict between the four observations. To develop this suggestion, let us first try it out in the case of sacrificial rites, the kind of practices to which the character "lǐ" originally refers.

Such sacrifices can be directed toward other objects, but, to simplify discussion, let us confine our attention to sacrifices to ancestors. One may conduct such sacrifices with the belief that ancestral spirits literally exist as intelligent beings who are able to respond to sacrifices by bestowing good fortune. Although this may describe the way these sacrifices have been conducted in times earlier than that of Confucius, I take it that this is not the kind of rationale Confucius sees in such sacrifices. For him, the importance of such sacrifices derives from their association with a certain attitude toward ancestors. Roughly, the attitude can be described as a sense of dependence on or indebtedness to one's ancestors for one's present existence and the present conditions of one's existence, this sense of dependence or indebtedness leading to a reverential attitude.[23] Now, a similar attitude of indebtedness and reverence can be directed toward one's living parents. In this case, the attitude may admit of nonconventional expression, that is, expression in behavior the suitability of which for expressing the attitude is not dependent on the existence of appropriate conventional practices. For example, the attitude may be expressed in one's providing support for parents and in one's general obedience to their wishes. A similar attitude toward a recently deceased parent also admits of nonconventional expression. For example, one may continue to act in conformity with their wishes and avoid doing what would have been displeasing in their eyes if they were alive. However, in the case of long-deceased ancestors with whom one had no previous personal contact, no such nonconventional expression may be available, because one may have no idea of what their wishes may be. In this case, the only channel for expressing one's indebtedness and reverence may be through conventional practices such as rites of sacrifice.

Consider a member of a community in which there is no conventional practice associated with such an attitude or, if the community has such a practice, a member who does not engage in the practice. Because there is no nonconventional manifestation of the attitude, and because this individual does not engage in some appropriate conventional practice that manifests the attitude, there will be no basis for our ascribing to this person the attitude of indebtedness and reverence toward ancestors. That is, given that there is no nonconventional manifestation of the attitude under consideration, our conception of the attitude is the conception of something manifested in the observance of some appropriate conventional practice, and we cannot correctly ascribe the attitude to an individual unless that person belongs to a community in which some such practice exists and unless he or she is generally disposed to observe such a practice. This, however, leaves it open that the attitude may be manifested in the observance of different conventional practices in different communities.

In ancient Chinese society, there was an established practice of sacrifices to ancestors (to be conducted with the proper spirit) associated with such an attitude, a practice to which the character "lǐ" originally referred. If we look at the relation between the attitude and the corresponding practice in the manner just described, the following four observations follow. First, within the community, general participation in sacrificial rites (with the proper spirit) is both necessary and sufficient for one's having an attitude of indebtedness and reverence toward ancestors. Moreover, within the community, we cannot conceive of one of the two obtaining without the other, and so there is a sense in which general participation in sacrificial rites is constitutive of one's possessing the attitude under consideration. Second, the attitude is not defined in terms of general participation in the sacrificial rites that actually exist in this community, for it can be instantiated in other communities with different conventional practices associated with the attitudes. So, possession of the attitude "transcends" participation in the actually existing sacrificial rites, and thereby provides a sense in which participation in such rites is a means to cultivate and express the attitude. Third, given that possession of the attitude "transcends" participation in the rites, it provides a perspective from which revision of the existing ritual practices can be assessed. For example, having come to acquire the attitude through having been brought up to participate in such rites, members of the community can propose revisions in the rites on the basis of economic consideration, as long as this does not affect the efficacy of the revised practices in cultivating and expressing the attitude. Fourth, although revision can be justified in the manner described, it has to proceed against the background of a general acceptance of the existing practices, because it is the existing practices that make available to members of the community the attitude under consideration. There is reason to oppose any change initiated without good reason; the relevant practices have to be relatively stable to perform their function, and any arbitrary departure would demonstrate a lack of seriousness. This explains why, as long as the relevant attitude is regarded as desirable within the community, there will be a generally conservative attitude toward the existing ritual practices.

Although the character "lǐ" originally referred to sacrificial rites, its use has gradually expanded to include traditional norms that govern human conduct in other areas of life.[24] As the next step in working out our proposal, imagine that, along with the expansion of the scope of lǐ, the kind of emotional dispositions and attitudes associated with lǐ have also broadened to include not just the attitude of indebtedness and reverence toward ancestors, but also various emotional dispositions and attitudes (such as respect for elders) directed toward other people with whom one's relations are governed by traditional norms. What results is a cluster of emotional dispositions and attitudes that stand to the traditional norms in the same kind of relation in which the attitude of indebtedness and reverence originally stood to sacrificial rites. Rén comprises this cluster of emotional dispositions and attitudes, and lǐ, in the expanded sense, comprises the various norms that govern human conduct. We therefore see how rén and lǐ may be related in the way in which the relevant attitudes toward ancestors and sacrificial rites were related. Moreover, the four observations that concern the latter relation also hold true of the relation between rén and lǐ, and this shows how the apparent conflict between the two pairs of observations about the relation between rén and lǐ can be resolved on this interpretation of the relation. Its ability to resolve the apparent conflict provides support for this alternative interpretation, as against the instrumentalist and definitionalist interpretations.

IV

On the instrumentalist interpretation, rén is an ideal that is intelligible and can be shown to have a validity independent of lǐ; lǐ is a means to realize this ideal and is to be evaluated in terms of its efficacy in performing this function. On the definitionalist interpretation, a rén person is just someone who generally observes the actually existing lǐ practices, and advocacy of the rén ideal is linked to an extreme conservatism toward lǐ. My proposed interpretation lies between the two extremes. On this interpretation, the ideal of rén is shaped by the actually existing lǐ practices in that it is not intelligible and cannot be shown to have a validity independent of lǐ. However, it is not totally determined by lǐ because advocacy of the ideal allows room for departing from or revising an existing rule of lǐ.

Although Confucius does not advocate an unconditional observance of lǐ, it remains the case that he was a generally conservative attitude toward lǐ. On the proposed interpretation, this conservatism is not explained, as it is on the definitionalist interpretation, by the observation that Confucius regards rén as merely a matter of generally observing lǐ. Rather, it is explained by the observation that any departure from or revision of a rule of lǐ has to proceed against the background of a general acceptance of the existing lǐ practices and has to be based on good reasons, and probably also by Confucius' optimism that the existing lǐ practices do function well and that there is little basis for departure or revision.

That Confucius does not advocate an unconditional observance of lǐ is related to the use of the notion yì 義 in the *Analects*. It is likely that, in its earlier use, the notion yi is related to that of disgrace (rǔ 辱) not-yi is linked to disgrace in both the Mòzǐ 墨子 (3/6) and a Yangist chapter of the Lǚshì chūnqiū 呂氏春秋 (2/7b.5–9), and one typical example of behavior which is not-yi found in the *Mencius* (Mèngzǐ 孟子) is that of subjecting oneself to insulting treatment, such as accepting food given in an insulting manner (6A:10) or seeing a prince when the prince summons one in a manner inappropriate to one's status (5B:7).[25] Disgrace is something to which one has an aversion (wù 惡), and, to the extent that it reflects negatively on oneself in a way that other objects of aversion do not, it is also an object of shame (chǐ 恥). But because one may subscribe to standards concerning the things one does, or the kinds of situations one allows oneself to be in, which differ from ordinary standards concerning what is disgraceful, what is regarded as reflecting negatively on oneself, and hence the object of shame, need not be disgrace in the ordinary sense. For example, shame (chǐ) can be directed to such things as one's condition as an official in a state in which the Way does not prevail (*Analects* 14.1, *Mencius* 5B:5), one's words exceeding one's deeds (*Analects* 14.27), or one's reputation going beyond the way one actually is (*Mencius* 4B:18). This makes possible the linking of yì to standards that differ from ordinary standards of disgrace. One can, of course, still refer to disgrace as the falling short of the standards that define yi, but doing so will call for a distinction between two kinds of disgrace, such as the distinction in the Xúnzǐ 荀子 between disgrace linked to yi (yì rǔ 義辱) and ordinary or social disgrace (Shì rǔ 埶辱 18/104–111).

In the *Mencius*, although there are examples of yi behavior that are a matter of following lǐ, such as pouring wine first for certain individuals in ancestral temples (6A:5), there are also examples of yi behavior that are not a matter of following lǐ, such as not imposing heavy taxation (3B:8) or not taking from the common people in certain ways (5B:4). Also, although the text describes circumstances in which lǐ may be overridden by other considerations so that it is appropriate not to follow a rule of lǐ in some situations (4A:17, 6B:1), it is unlikely that yi is similarly viewed; rather, it is stated without qualification that yì is always more important than life (6A:10), and one is supposed always to abide by yì (4B:11). It seems that yì has to do with the appropriateness or rightness of one's behavior, which is not just a matter of following lǐ; rather, yì underlies both the observance of and departure from lǐ, and governs one's behavior in circumstances in which lǐ does not provide guidance.

The notion of yì is less prominent in the *Analects* than in the *Mencius*, but it is likely that the conception of yì and of the relation between yì and lǐ just described is already emerging in the *Analects*. On the proposed interpretation of Confucius' conception of the relation between rén and lǐ, there can be grounds for revising or departing from a rule of lǐ, and this calls for a notion of appropriateness or rightness that allows one to say that these grounds make it appropriate or right thus to revise or depart from the rule of lǐ. That there can be grounds for such revision or departure shows that, even when a rule of lǐ should be observed, one should observe the rule only because it is appropriate or right to do so. This notion of appropriateness or rightness is probably captured by the notion yì in the *Analects*, and this explains Confucius' observation that one's behavior should always be in accord with yì (4.10) and that yì is the substance that lǐ puts into practice (15.18).

Earlier, after setting up the distinction between the instrumentalist and the definitionalist interpretations, I discussed interpretations in the literature that lie close to one or the other of the two extremes. As I mentioned, the distinction is not intended as an exhaustive classification of interpretations actually found in the literature, but serves only as a heuristic device to prepare the ground for introducing my proposed interpretation. To give a more complete picture of the kinds of interpretations that have been proposed and of the relation of my proposed interpretation to them, I conclude by briefly considering some other interpretations found in the literature.

My proposed interpretation has two components. Unlike the instrumentalist interpretation, it acknowledges the role of lǐ in shaping the ethical ideal of rén, and, unlike the definitionalist interpretation, it allows for the possibility of departing from or revising an existing rule of lǐ if there is good reason for doing so. The second component, which is related to the conception of the relation between yì and lǐ just described, is highlighted not only by those interpretations in the literature that lie close to the instrumentalist interpretation, but also by other interpretations. For example, Chén Dàqí has observed that Confucius allows room for departing from or revising existing rules of lǐ if there are grounds for doing so, and Tu Wei-ming has observed that Confucius advocates a critical attitude toward existing lǐ.[26] Also, Antonio S. Cua has pointed out that Confucius regards yì as a sense of appropriateness that is important in applying rules of lǐ to particular cases, and D. C. Lau has likewise interpreted Confucius' conception of the relation between yì and lǐ in the way Cua describes.[27] Despite emphasizing the possibility of a critical assessment of lǐ, these authors have not presented their interpretations in a way that warrants ascribing to them anything close to the instrumentalist interpretation.

The first component of my proposed interpretation, that concerning the role of lǐ in shaping the rén ideal, has also been highlighted by interpretations in the literature that do not obviously lie close to the definitionalist interpretation. For example, Herbert Fingarette has emphasized the role of lǐ in shaping rén, for him, the rén person is someone "perfected in lǐ," and rén is "the shaping of oneself in lǐ."[28] Though these remarks may suggest something close to the definitionalist interpretation, Fingarette may have an interpretation closer to my proposed interpretation, because he also observes in other contexts that, for Confucius, lǐ is "reformable" and "corrigible," and one should "retain a certain critical independence" from lǐ.[29] Similarly, David L. Hall and Roger T. Ames have proposed an interpretation according to which Confucius stresses the contribution of lǐ in shaping the human ideal, an idea they expressed in terms of the "irreducibly social context of person making."[30] At the same time, they also observe that Confucius is not a rigid conservative, but emphasizes yì as a capacity to adapt inherited culture critically and creatively to one's own circumstances.[31]

So, there are interpretations in the literature that do not lie close to either the instrumentalist or the definitionalist interpretation, and some of these may even be close to my proposed interpretation. Although the kind of interpretation I propose is not entirely novel, what the discussion above has done is to spell out its nature in detail and in different terms, and to locate it in the literature by showing how it lies between two other kinds of interpretations. Furthermore, it shows how this kind of interpretation has an advantage over the other two in that it can make better sense of the relevant passages in the *Analects*.

NOTES

A slightly modified version of this essay was published in *Philosophy East and West* 43, no. 3 (July 1993): 457–79.

I have benefitted from comments by David S. Nivison on a much shorter version of this essay written in 1984, and from extensive written comments by Chad Hansen on a longer version, closer to its present form and written in 1987. The latter version was presented at the 1987 annual meeting of the Western Branch of the American Oriental Society, held in Berkeley on November 14, 1987, and I have benefitted from comments by the participants. In addition, I am indebted to an anonymous referee for *Philosophy East and West* for substantive suggestions, many of which I have incorporated. The whole of section IV is an expansion of a couple of footnotes in the submitted version, in response to the referee's suggestion that there is a need to discuss in detail the notion of yi and its relation to lǐ, and to discuss other interpretations in the literature going beyond those considered in section II.

1. Proponents of this view include Xú Fùguān 徐復觀, *Zhōngguó sīxiǎngshǐ lùn jí xùpiān* 中國思想史論集續篇 (臺北：時報文化出版事業有限公司, 1982), pp. 358–65; Lin Yü-sheng, "The Evolution of the Pre-Confucian Meaning of Jen and the Confucian Concept of Moral Autonomy," *Monumenta Serica (Journal of Oriental Studies)* 31 (1974–75): 172–83; Arthur Waley, trans., *The Analects of Confucius* (London: George Allen and Unwin, 1938), p. 27; and A. C. Graham, *Disputers of the Tao* (Chicago: Open Court, 1989), p. 19.

2. Proponents of this view include Táng Jūnyì 唐君毅, *Zhōngguó zhéxué yuánlùn: yuándàopiān* 中國哲學原論：原道篇, vol. 1, rev. ed. (臺北：臺灣學生書局, 1976), p. 71; Tu Wei-ming, *Confucian Thought: Selfhood as Creative Transformation* (Albany, N.Y.: SUNY Press, 1985), pp. 84–85, citing Fang Ying-hsien on p. 92 n. 23; and Wing-tsit Chan, "The Evolution of the Confucian Concept of Jen," in *Neo-Confucianism, Etc.: Essays by Wing-tsit Chan* (Hong Kong: Oriental Society, 1969), p. 2. Chan observes that "jen" has the connotation of the kindness of rulers to their subjects.

3. References to the *Analects* are by passage numbers, following the numbering of passages in Yáng Bójūn 楊伯峻, *Lúnyǔ yìzhù* 論語譯注, 2d. ed. (北京：中華書局, 1980).

4. References to the *Shī jīng* are by poem and (if applicable) stanza numbers.

5. References to the *Zuǒ zhuàn* are by page and line numbers, using the text in James Legge, trans., *The Chinese Classics*, vol. 5, *The Ch'un Ts'ew with The Tso Chuen* (Hong Kong: Hong Kong University Press, 1960).

6. References to the *Xúnzǐ* are by chapter and line numbers, using the text in the *Harvard-Yenching Institute Sinological Index Series: A Concordance to Hsün Tzu*.

7. "Li" as used in the *Analects* is regarded as referring to all rules of human conduct by Láo Sīguāng 勞思光, *Zhōngguó zhéxué shǐ* 中國哲學史, vol. 1, 2d. ed. (Hong Kong: Chung Chi College of the Chinese University of Hong Kong, 1974), p. 40; Cāi Shàngsī 蔡尚思, *Kǒngzǐ sīxiǎng tǐxì* 孔子思想體系 (上海：上海人民出版社, 1982), pp. 238, 240; Benjamin I. Schwartz, *The World of Thought in Ancient China* (Cambridge, Mass.: Harvard University Press, 1985), pp. 67–68. A. C. Graham (*Disputers of the Tao*, p. 11) seems to regard li as restricted to the ceremonious in the *Analects*.

8. For example, Benjamin I. Schwartz (*World of Thought*, pp. 80–81) argues against Herbert Fingarette that there are aspects of rén that have no obvious relation to lǐ.

9. I am indebted to Chad Hansen for pointing out the need to address these issues; the remainder of this section has been added in response to his comments.

10. Reservations about the use of psychological locutions have been expressed by Herbert Fingarette in his *Confucius: The Secular as Sacred* (Harper and Row, 1972), especially chap. 3. Fingarette's claims are still a subject of controversy; they have been challenged by Benjamin I. Schwartz (*World of Thought*, pp. 72–85), and defended by A. C. Graham (*Disputers of the Tao*, pp. 25–27), and in Graham's review of Schwartz's book in *Times Literary Supplement* (July 18, 1986).

11. Xú Fùguān 徐復觀, *Zhōngguó rénxìnglùn shǐ: xiān Qín piān* 中國人性論史：先秦篇 (臺北：臺灣商務印書館, 1975), pp. 69, 90.

12. Lin Yü-sheng, "Evolution," pp. 193–196. Charles Wei-hsun Fu gives a similar interpretation of Confucius in his "Fingarette and Munro on Early Confucianism: A Methodological Examination," in *Philosophy East and West* 28 (1978): 181–98, sect. II.

13. Zhào Jìbīn 趙紀彬, *Lúnyǔ xīntàn*, 論語新探 (北京：人民出版社, 1976), pp. 288–90, 307–9, 311–12. Zhao takes the further step of identifying lǐ with the feudal system of western Zhou, and regards Confucius' espousal of the rén ideal, understood in terms of the general observance of lǐ, as an attempt by Confucius to oppose the disintegration of the feudal system.

14. Cai Shangsi, *Kongzi sixiang tixi*, pp. 106–7, 238–40, 282–85.

15. For example, Xú Fùguān (*Zhōngguó rénxìnglùn shǐ*), p. 90, cites both 3.3 and 15.18 in support of his interpretation of Confucius.

16. For example, Lin Yü-sheng ("Evolution," p. 195) cites 9.3 in support of his interpretation of Confucius.

17. Zhào Jìbīn builds his interpretation of Confucius on an elaborate discussion of 12.1 (*Lúnyǔ xīntàn*, pp. 288–25), and Cāi Shàngsī likewise regards 12.1 as the key passage for understanding Confucius' conception of the relation between rén and li (*Kǒngzǐ sīxiǎng tǐxì*, pp. 106–7).

18. Cf. Lin Yü-sheng, "Evolution," p. 196.

19. Charles Wei-hsun Fu translates "kè jǐ fù lǐ" in 12.1 as "self-restraint and submission to li," and then claims that Confucius' emphasis is on self-restraint, the overcoming of selfish desire, rather than on lǐ ("Fingarette and Munro," p. 188). Lin Yü-sheng translates the phrase as "to master oneself and return to li," and takes Confucius to be saying that "to master the cultivation of a naturally endowed moral quality within the structure of the proper social and ritual norms is the way to achieve moral excellence" (ibid., p. 194). Taking 12.1 by itself, it is unclear why we should regard the passage as emphasizing self-restraint more than the observance of li and how the idea of a naturally endowed moral quality comes into the picture.

20. Zhào Jìbīn (*Lúnyǔ xīntàn*, p. 311) interprets 3.3 as emphasizing the priority of lǐ over rén, in the sense that lǐ can still exist even if people are not rén. This I find an artificial reading of the passage.

21. For example, Raymond Dawson, in his *Confucius* (New York: Hill and Wang, 1981), pp. 30–31, refers to a "conflict" between 3.3, which apparently gives priority to rén over

lǐ, and 12.1, which apparently gives priority to lǐ and defines rén in terms of the observance of lǐ.

22. An anonymous referee has observed that the kind of relation I am discussing has
been considered in contemporary writings in the philosophy of language, such as J. L.
Austin's work on performative utterances and John Searle's work on speech acts. The observation is plausible, and I think this kind of relation has also been considered in other subfields in philosophy, such as the philosophy of action. Since I am not relying on the work
of any particular philosopher in characterizing the relation, but am just spelling out the
nature of a phenomenon considered in various subfields of philosophy, I have not discussed the work of any particular philosopher in connection with the relation.

23. Arthur Waley (The Analects, p. 61) describes the attitude of reverence and love as the
prevailing attitude toward the dead among the upper classes of Confucius' time.

24. Earlier, I mentioned that it is not clear how broad the scope of application of lǐ is,
as the character is used in the Analects. The discussion in this paragraph does not require
our determining the actual scope of lǐ, because the proposal is that we should look at Confucius' conception of the relation between rén and lǐ in the manner described, whether we
construe the scope of lǐ more broadly to include all norms of conduct or more narrowly
to include only norms of ceremonious behavior.

25. References to the Mozi are by chapter and line numbers, using the text in the Harvard-
Yenching Institute Sinological Index Series: A Concordance to Mo Tzu. References to the Lüshi chunqiu are
by volume, page, and line numbers, using the text in Xǔ Wéiyù 許維遹, Lǚshì chūnqiū
jíshì 呂氏春秋集釋 (北京：中國書店, 1985). References to the Mencius (Mèngzǐ 孟子) are by
chapter and passage numbers, using the text in the Harvard-Yenching Institute Sinological Index
Series: A Concordance to Meng Tzu.

26. Chén Dàqí 陳大齊, Kǒngzǐ xuéshuō 孔子學説 (臺北：正中書局, 1964), pp. 150–52; and
Tu Wei-ming, Humanity and Self-Cultivation: Essays in Confucian Thought (Berkeley: Asian Humanities Press, 1979), pp. 22, 30.

27. Antonio S. Cua, "Confucian Vision and Human Community," Journal of Chinese
Philosophy 11 (1984): 230; and D. C. Lau, trans., Confucius: The Analects (Penguin Books, 1979),
pp. 37–39, 47–50.

28. Herbert Fingarette, Confucius: The Secular as Sacred, pp. 21, 48.

29. Herbert Fingarette, "Following the 'One Thread' of the Analects," Journal of the American Academy of Religion, Thematic Issue S, 47, no. 3 (1980): 390–91.

30. David L. Hall and Roger T. Ames, Thinking Through Confucius (Albany, N.Y.: SUNY Press,
1987), p. 84.

31. Ibid., pp. 84, 100, 108–11.

4

"What Does Heaven Say?": Christian Wolff and Western Interpretations of Confucian Ethics

ROBERT B. LOUDEN

> The Master said, I would prefer not to speak. Tzu-Kung said, If you did not speak, what would there be for us, your disciples, to transmit? The Master said, What does Heaven ever say? Yet there are the four seasons going round and there are the hundred things coming into being. What does Heaven ever say?
>
> Confucius, *Analects* 17:19[1]

Martyr of Reason

In the present age of multiculturalism, professors on most campuses are encouraged (and in some places even required) to include favorable coverage of non-Western cultures in their humanities and social science core courses. But in the not-too-distant-past one could get into serious trouble for pursuing this strategy. Consider the case of the German philosophy professor Christian Wolff, a man who, according to one recent study, has "influenced the philosophy of the German Enlightenment like hardly any other."[2]

On July 12, 1721, Wolff delivered a public lecture entitled *Oratio de Sinarum philosophia practica* (Discourse on the Practical Philosophy of the Chinese) at the conservative, Pietist University of Halle.[3] The official occasion for the lecture was Wolff's relinquishing of the university rectorship to his successor, Joachim Lange, a Pietist theologian. In this lecture (parts of which we will examine in more detail below) Wolff proclaimed that Confucius "is esteemed today by the Chinese just as much as Moses is by the Jews, Mohammed by the Turks; yes, just as much as Christ is by ourselves, to the extent that we regard him as a prophet or teacher, given to us by God."[4] This comparison of Christ to a mere Moses, Mohammed, or Confucius of course did not go over well, but what caused an even greater uproar was Wolff's insistent claim that Confucius somehow had been able to discover correct principles of morality without the aid of either revealed theology or even natural religion: "Since the ancient Chinese . . . did not know the creator of the world, they had no natural religion; still less did they know any witness of the divine revelation. That is why they could only count on the force of nature—

and indeed such as was free from all religion—in order to practice virtue" (26–27). The audience inferred here that Wolff was of the opinion that atheists and pagans were just as capable of being morally virtuous as were practicing Christians, and this proved to be too much.

The result? "On the day after Wolff delivered the lecture, Joachim Justus Breithaupt, the dean of the Halle theological faculty, preached openly against him and called upon the philosopher to turn his manuscript over to his colleagues for examination."[5] But Wolff refused the request, and so the theology faculty (led by Lange, who now also occupied Wolff's old rectorship position) intensified its attack, charging that Wolff was guilty of teaching subversive doctrine and demanding his dismissal from the university. After much academic hand waving and pamphlet publishing, they eventually took their case directly to Frederick William I, king of Prussia. By a secret royal edict of November 8, 1723, Wolff was formally accused of having advocated "in public writings and lectures a doctrine contrary to the religion which had been revealed by God's own words."[6] By means of this edict he was "not merely relieved of his position, but also forbidden, on penalty of death by hanging, of returning; and he was required to vacate all of the king's lands within forty-eight hours."[7]

This was more than even Wolff's conservative opponents had expected or wished for, though at least for the moment they had clearly won the battle. But the story does not end here. "Through his expulsion from Halle on November 8, 1723, an event that moved the minds of men like no other incident in university history, Wolff overnight became as it were the chief witness of the German Enlightenment."[8] Even more surprising is the fact that Wolff's instant martyrdom was not even particularly painful. On the contrary, he immediately accepted a previously offered position at the University of Marburg in Hesse, where he was welcomed with great enthusiasm by his new students—and given a very high salary. Meanwhile, the controversy over the grounds of his dismissal from Halle widened, taking on truly international proportions. The Swedish Royal Academy came out in support of his claims about Confucianism; the Universities of Leyden and Bologna also came to his defense. Russian tsar Peter the Great offered him the vice presidency of the St. Petersburg Academy. And new pamphlets on both sides of the debate appeared in ever increasing numbers. All told, it has been estimated that "Wolff's dismissal from Halle inspired the writing of two hundred polemical tracts, one hundred and thirty against Wolff and seventy for him."[9]

Finally, in 1726, Wolff himself responded by publishing the definitive version[10] of his Halle lecture along with an explanatory preface and copious notes in which he defended himself at length against his theological critics. In 1730, he delivered a second public lecture on ancient China at Marburg entitled *De rege philosophante et philosophoregnante*, this time focusing on Confucian political theory rather than ethics. In this second lecture he stressed that "the Chinese had a Custom, as appears in the Works of Confucius and Mencius, in Things of an arduous Nature to consult the Philosophers. . . . For the philosophers excelled, and far surpassed all others in political knowledge."[11]

Wolff was treated extremely well in Marburg, but during the late 1730s the political climate back in Prussia began to shift in his favor. Crown Prince Frederick II,[12] himself the author of a number of works in practical philosophy, including *Anti-Machiavel*, an idealistic refutation of Machiavelli, assumed the throne immediately after his father Frederick William I died on June 1, 1740. An "enthusiastic reader and admirer of Wolff's writings, Prince Frederick made it one of his first acts of office to make up for the injustice that had befallen Wolff earlier in Prussia."[13] And so Wolff finally returned to Halle, scene of his former defeat, in 1741—this time as vice chancellor of the university. Voltaire himself celebrated Wolff's landmark victory for academic freedom with the following verse:

> You whose virtue shines persecuted,
> You who proved the existence of a God yet was called an atheist,
> Martyr of reason, whom envy in its fury
> Chased out of his country by the hands of error,
> Come back, there is nothing now that a philosopher should fear;
> Socrates is on the throne, and truth reigns.[14]

German Philosophers and China

Wolff's strong admiration for Confucianism is a chapter within a much larger story of European Enlightenment interest in China, a story within which the travel reports and Latin translations of classic Chinese texts by Jesuit missionaries also play major roles.[15] Within philosophy, the earlier China writings of Leibniz—"the first European thinker of major stature to take a serious and substantial interest in China"[16]—are much better known than Wolff's, in part because English translations of them are more readily available.[17] But for those readers who are primarily interested in *moral* philosophy, Wolff's 1721 *Discourse* remains today the most influential appreciation of Confucian ethics by a major Enlightenment philosopher. And it is an effort that Anglo-American scholars have virtually ignored.[18]

It is also important to note that German philosophy's fascination with ancient China was definitely a fleeting phenomenon. By the late 1770s, by which time the upbeat accommodationist Jesuit reports on China had been seriously challenged on numerous fronts by more skeptical stories, "this enthusiastic rapture cleared the way for a strong disenchantment."[19] Kant, for instance, lectured frequently on Chinese moral philosophy and religion in his annual physical geography course. In an unpublished version of these lectures, he states:

> Philosophy is not to be met with in the entire orient. . . . Their teacher
> Confucius lectures in his writings on nothing but moral precepts for
> princes . . . and cites examples of previous Chinese princes. . . . [B]ut a
> concept of virtue and morality has never entered into the heads of the

Chinese. . . . This entire nation is incapable (*unfähig*) of rising to that which is noble and concerns duty, and the entire ethics of Confucius consists in moral maxims that are unbearable (*unerträglich*), because every individual can reel them off. Studies are required in order to arrive at the idea and incentive of the good, of which they know nothing.[20]

Clearly, Kant, like many of his contemporaries, has here "turned away from the earlier, heated interest in China and things Chinese. He dismissed the favorable reports of the Jesuit missionaries, sources from which Leibniz and Wolff derived their enthusiasm—as inspired propaganda."[21]

Hegel, in his *Lectures on the Philosophy of History*, is equally dismissive of Confucius. The teachings of Confucius, he notes,

> made a great sensation in Leibniz's time. . . . We have conversations between Confucius and his followers in which there is nothing definite further than a commonplace moral put in the form of good, sound doctrine, which may be found as well expressed and better, in every place and amongst every people. . . . He [Confucius] is hence only a man who has a certain amount of practical and worldly wisdom—one with whom there is no speculative philosophy. We may conclude from his original works that for reputation it would have been better had they never been translated.[22]

Given the revival of interest in Confucian ethics among contemporary Western scholars, it behooves us to take a closer look at Wolff's earlier enthusiasm. How well did Wolff actually understand Confucian ethics? Are there lessons to be learned from his interpretations, lessons from which we might benefit? In the remainder of this essay I shall focus on one crucial issue—the infamous "autonomy of morality" thesis that Wolff ascribes to Confucius. How exactly does Wolff understand this thesis? How good is his argument for attributing it to Confucius?

Tiān 天 in the *Analects*

> As to the question whether it is permitted for a
> Chinese Christian to say *Tien*—heaven—for
> God (which is done frequently in Europe) . . .
> is a matter, I think, for closer examination.
> Leibniz, "On the Civil Cult of Confucius," sect. 12

As is well known, the passages in the *Analects* that are most relevant to the religion question are those in which the term tiān (天, also romanized as t'ien, and normally translated as "Heaven") plays a prominent role. H. G. Creel, for instance, writes: "If we look for a firm and frankly stated conviction on the part of

Confucius as to things religious, we shall find it most clearly in connection with t'ien, Heaven."[23] More recently, Benjamin Schwartz, in his discussion of the religious dimension in Confucius's thought, echoes Creel's familiar assertion: "If there is any central religious term in the *Analects*, it is the term 'Heaven' "[24] The tiān passages form a frequently debated topic among interpreters of Confucius, and in the following brief discussion I cannot cover all aspects of it. Rather, my aim is simply to examine the main passages in the *Analects* in which the term tiān occurs, asking: (1) whether they support consistently the claim that Confucius espoused, in a noncontroversial sense, a fundamentally religious outlook; and (2), if so, how and to what extent this religious outlook affects his moral theory.

The tiān topic is also an extremely old one, and has plagued Western interpretations of Confucian texts since the time of Matteo Ricci (1552–1610), founder of the first Jesuit mission in China. Cook and Rosemont write:

> Theologically there were two burning questions which divided the
> missionaries to China, and the divisions quickly spread back to Europe.
> The first of these was whether the Chinese language did or did not
> contain a close lexical equivalent for the Christian "God." If not, it must
> follow that the Chinese were all atheists. The Jesuit founder of the
> mission in China, Matteo Ricci, allowed two terms from the Chinese:
> Shang Di [上帝]—"Supreme Ancestor"—and Tian—"Heaven"—as
> equivalents for "God."[25]

There are additional complications on the Chinese side. As a term within the Chinese language, tiān has multiple meanings—"a range of uses running from the most to the least anthropomorphic"; with more anthropomorphic meanings that dominated in the time before Confucius, and less anthropomorphic ones later.[26] And within the text of the *Analects* itself, many critics claim that the tiān passages contradict one another. Some of them are allegedly antireligious, portraying Confucius as "insincere, having no faith in anything extra-human, but following an opportunist's policy of conformity for the sake of attaining his objects"; others are religious, revealing a man who is "inspired by a profound sense of mission," that is, a mission to help human beings live in accord with "the guiding intelligence of the cosmos."[27]

Despite these and other problems, the tiān passages in the *Analects* are not the mystery that many critics have made them out to be. In what follows I shall argue against the view of Herbert Fingarette and others, who hold that although Confucius "did speak of Heaven, its role is not too clear and is unelaborated in the *Analects*."[28] On my view, the tiān passages do form a consistent whole, one from which we can reliably infer both that Confucius was a strong religious believer in a noncontroversial sense, and that his moral orientation was itself dependent upon his religious outlook.

Let me start with the "easy" passages: that is, those in which almost all commentators agree that a religious dimension is present. First are what might be called the "divine mission" passages—texts where Confucius asserts that Heaven is the source of the moral power within him and that Heaven has entrusted him with a sacred mission. For instance, when informed that Huan Tui, the Minister of War in Song, was attempting to kill him, Confucius replied: "T'ien is author of the virtue [dé 德] that is in me. What can Huan T'ui do to me?" (7:23). And when Confucius was surrounded in Kuang after being mistaken for Yang Huo, a scoundrel who had caused trouble there earlier, he repeated his conviction of a divine mission by stating that Heaven had now selected him as the champion and carrier of China's culture: "With King Wen dead, is not culture [wén 文] invested here in me? If Heaven intends culture to be destroyed, those who come after me will not be able to have any part of it. If Heaven does not intend this culture to be destroyed, then what can the men of K'uang do to me?" (9:5). Similarly, Confucius' student Zigong reports that tiān "set him [Confucius] on the path to sagehood" (9:6). Finally, a border official at Yi also expressed a similar view of Confucius' vocation to a group of the master's students: "The Empire has long been without the Way [dào 道]. Heaven is about to use your Master as the wooden tongue for a bell" (3:24)—that is, to rouse the Empire by "ringing out truth and justice."

Related to the divine mission passages are a group of darker statements in which Confucius despairs of achieving his goals of moral reform, but in which the overriding intention to follow Heaven is nevertheless present. For instance, at one point he complains to Zigong: "There is no one who understands me"—and then takes comfort in the thought that although human beings do not understand him, Heaven (perhaps) does: "I do not complain against Heaven, nor do I blame man. In my studies, I start from below[29] and get through to what is up above. If I am understood at all, it is, perhaps, by Heaven" (14:35). And when his favorite disciple Yan Yuan died, Confucius declared, "Alas! Heaven has bereft me! Heaven has bereft me!" (11:9). Similarly, on returning from a visit to Nanzi, "the notorious wife of Duke Ling of Wei," and hearing that his disciple Zilu was displeased, the "Master swore, 'If I have done anything improper, may Heaven's curse be on me, may Heaven's curse be on me!'" (6:28).

A third group of tiān passages, although not as dark in tone as the second group, repeat Confucius' underlying conviction that a good man must always try to model himself on, and seek moral guidance from, Heaven. On being asked by Wangsun Jia, commander in chief in the state of Wei, to explain a remark, Confucius replied, "The saying has got it wrong. When you have offended against Heaven there is nowhere you can turn to in your prayers" (3:13). Elsewhere Confucius eulogizes the legendary ruler Yao with the remark: "Great indeed was Yao as a ruler! How lofty! It is only Heaven that is great and it was only Yao who modeled himself upon it" (8:19). (That is, only Heaven is unqualifiedly great: it alone must therefore be our primary moral teacher.) Confucius also criticizes his disciple Zilu for ordering other followers to act as retainers for him when he was sick, out of office, and not in position to have retainers, by chiding: "In pretending that I had retainers when I had none, who would we be deceiving? Would we be deceiving Heaven?" (9:12). (That is, ultimately it is Heaven's judgment alone that counts—

not that of mere mortals.) Similarly, Confucius opens his litany of three things the gentleman (jūnzǐ 君子) fears by proclaiming: "He is in awe of the Decree of Heaven [tiān mìng 天命]. . . . The small man, being ignorant of the Decree of Heaven, does not stand in awe of it" (16:8). A second well-known passage in which the important phrase tiān mìng occurs is 2:4, where Confucius states: "at fifty I understood the Decree of Heaven." Here the difficulty of attaining such understanding is obviously stressed, but in both 16:8 and 2:4 the underlying message is that tiān mìng is a fundamental moral imperative to which individuals are subject.[30]

It may still be the case, as Creel noted back in 1932, "that if a poll of Western scholars must decide the matter, Confucius was beyond all doubt agnostic, or at least very, very skeptical."[31] However, if this is so it tells us more about the state of Western sinological scholarship (and/or the relevance of polls for deciding matters of textual interpretation) than it does about what Confucius meant.[32] The fundamental message that I see expressed in each of the above passages is a very strong conviction on the part of Confucius that tiān is the most important moral force in the universe and that human beings who wish to be morally good must therefore seek to discern and follow it. I believe that this faith in a more-than-human power that is believed to give moral values and obligations a deep grounding entitles us to call Confucius "religious" in a garden variety, noncontroversial sense. At the same time, I do not see any evidence that Confucius' tiān is anything like the "personal God" of the Western religions. I am thus essentially in agreement with Heiner Roetz, who writes that for Confucius "t'ien is clearly not a naturalistic concept but a religious one, . . . though it is not very much thought of anthropomorphically."[33] Confucius, we may say, is thus religious but not theistic.[34]

But the obligation to seek to discern tiān creates a special problem for Confucius, one that is highlighted in the passage chosen as an epigram for this essay, 17:19. Because tiān is not a personal being (much less an anthropomorphic personal being who commands us from on high), it does not speak. Consequently, it is extremely difficult for those of us who are verbally fixated to discern accurately the moral message of tiān. Still, despite Heaven's nonverbal modes of communication, the wise are able to discern tiān by examining "the four seasons going round and . . . the hundred things coming into being" (17:19). Confucius' point here is not simply that tiān is "the source of all phenomena and of the processes of natural change,"[35] or even that the "spirit of Heaven is still very much present in the regularities, routines, and generative processes of nature, even though Heaven does not speak."[36] Rather, he is implying that through the harmony, beauty, and sublimity of its natural processes Heaven communicates a great deal about how human beings ought to live and act,[37] at least to those who have learned to listen carefully to it.

What then of the allegedly antireligious tiān passages in the *Analects*? What do they tell us about Confucius' moral outlook? Given all the interpretive weight they have been asked to carry, they are surprisingly few in number. At 5:13 disciple

Zigong complains: "One can get to hear about the Master's accomplishments, but one cannot get to hear his views on human nature and the Way of Heaven (tiān dào 天道)." In Waley's note on this passage we are informed that what Zigong is getting at is that the "Tao taught by Confucius only concerned human behavior ('the ways of man'); he did not expound a corresponding Heavenly Tao, governing the conduct of unseen powers and divinities." But because 5:13 also states that Confucius allegedly declined to talk about his views "on human nature," it is not at all clear, based on this passage alone, how much teaching concerning "the ways of man" one could reasonably expect from him! Waley tries to finesse this conundrum by claiming that a distinction between human nature before and after "it has been embellished with 'culture'" is at work here, but it is extremely unlikely that Confucius could have believed that "the ways of man" were shaped completely by the embellishment of culture and not at all by natural forces.[38] A more sensible reading of 5:13, I suggest, is simply that Confucius was reticent to expound on speculative matters—human or divine—when he was not sure he knew exactly what he was talking about, and when he felt that such speculative chatter would only detract people's attention away from the more fundamental moral task of deciding how to live and act.[39]

A second passage often cited to show Confucius' supposedly strictly secular orientation is 6:22. When his student Fan Chi asked what constituted wisdom, Confucius replied: "To work for the things the common people have a right to and to keep one's distance from the gods and spirits while showing them reverence can be called wisdom." According to Creel, this passage, "more than any other, [has] given rise to the belief that Confucius was agnostic."[40] But why is a counsel of "keeping one's distance" from god and spirits necessarily an indication of religious skepticism? A more likely scenario (as both Creel and Schwartz emphasize) is simply that Confucius is reminding his audience that distance is a proper factor in the relationship between human beings and gods: indeed, not to respect this distance would itself be a sign of blasphemy. (Compare the story in Exodus that, when God spoke to Moses from the burning bush, he warned him, "Come no closer! . . . And Moses hid his face, for he was afraid to look at God" [NRSV 3:5–6].) A similar passage is 7:21: "The topics the Master did not speak of were prodigies, force, disorder and gods." Here too, from the report that Confucius "did not speak of" certain things we should not infer either that he did or did not believe in the existence of those things of which he did not speak. Rather, the point is that he was not given to speculation about such matters.

The last of the allegedly antireligious passages runs as follows:

> Chi-lu asked how the spirits of the dead and the gods should be served. The Master said, "You are not able even to serve man. How can you serve the spirits?"
>   "May I ask about death?"
>   "You do not even understand life. How can you understand death?"
> (11:12)

Here, too, I read this passage as evidence of Confucius' fundamentally practical (as opposed to speculative or metaphysical) orientation. His reluctance to engage in the latter tendency is not a sign of an antireligious attitude, but rather a reflection of his determination to adhere to what he feels is most important in human life.

When philosophers argue for or against "the autonomy of morality," they normally have in mind the thesis that moral principles are not dependent on religious belief—that we can attain accurate knowledge of correct moral norms without the assistance of any religious belief. A classic Enlightenment statement in defense of the thesis is the following, from Baron d'Holbach:

> To learn the true principles of morality, men have no need of theology,
> of revelation, or gods: They have need only of reason. They have only to
> enter into themselves, to reflect upon their own nature, consult their
> sensible interests, consider the object of society, and of the individuals,
> who compose it; and they will easily perceive, that virtue is the
> interest, and vice the unhappiness of beings of their kind.[41]

I do not see evidence of this outlook in the *Analects* of Confucius. Confucius does not advise human beings who wish to learn the true principles of morality "only to enter into themselves, to reflect upon their own nature." (Compare 5:13, where, as we have seen, Confucius declines even to present his views on human nature.) Nor does he console us by saying we "have need only of reason."[42] Rather, he urges us to look outward and upward to Heaven if we wish to find our true moral bearings. Confucius' moral outlook is religious (though again, not theistic) in the straightforward sense that he holds that moral standards are dependent on something outside of us, something bigger than human nature—or culture—that is much more than a human or even a rational construction. Additionally, to count as religious this source of value that is outside of us must be felt to be holy or sacred.[43] The sense of awe that Confucius experiences in contemplating *tiān* (compare 16:8) meets this basic description of religious experience.

Wolff's Confucius

In the previous section I argued, contra Wolff, as well as many others, that Confucius' basic moral outlook is in fact fundamentally religious rather than secular. In this last section, I wish to take a closer look at Wolff's argument against this claim.

The longest (nearly five full pages, in Albrecht's edition) of the 216 notes that Wolff published in 1726 along with the original text of his 1721 *Discourse* is number 54. The entire note concerns *tiān*/Heaven/God issues (it occurs immediately after his claim, cited earlier, that the ancient Chinese "did not know the creator of the world" [26–27]), and the mere fact that he devotes so much space to these problems shows us that they were of major importance to him. He begins by noting that "an intense conflict has reigned between the mission fathers of the Society of Jesus and the Dominican order over whether the ancient Chinese were atheists or whether they had some kind of knowledge of God" (N54, 144–45). The Jesuits, "following the example of Ricci, founder of the China mission," argued that "with the Chinese word 'tian,' which means 'Heaven,' was meant not the material Heaven, but God, the creator of Heaven" (N54, 146–47). Couplet, Wolff adds, argues "with body and soul" in the introductory explanation of his 1687 edition of Confucius' sayings (*Confucius Sinarum Philosophus*) "that the Chinese at their origin absolutely had knowledge and worship of the true divinity and probably maintained it for several centuries" (N54, 144–47).

On the next page Wolff confesses:

> I freely admit that when I prepared my lecture I had not yet seen
> Couplet's Introductory Explanation, much less read it. Of the China
> literature, only the classical texts of the Chinese empire that were
> translated into Latin by Noël were near at hand. Now in these texts God
> and the attributes of God are not mentioned, and because neither
> Confucius nor his interpreter clearly insists on duties toward God—for
> example, love, fear, trust, etc., I concluded that the ancient Chinese did
> not know the creator of the world. (N54, 148–49)

At the beginning of this passage it looks for a moment as though Wolff is about to declare a basic change of position. Couplet's argument for rendering tian as "God" (and more generally, for viewing the ancient Chinese as religious believers) was not available to him when he prepared his 1721 lecture. In Noël's translation, which Wolff had earlier relied on exclusively, tian is translated as "Heaven." However, in the following passage Wolff makes it clear that no such change of position is in store: "For although what Confucius describes as the law of Heaven is what we call the law of nature, it does not follow, and therefore I did not want to understand by this, that under 'Heaven' God, the Lord of Heaven, is meant." (N54, 148–49, compare N7, 86–87).[44] What was meant, Wolff claims, is that "the order of Heaven would be the guiding principle for the correct administration of the people and the state" (N54, 148–149, compare N7, 86–87).

This sense of Heaven as serving as the guiding principle for human moral and political conduct is in line with the interpretation of tian that I offered earlier, with one basic difference: Wolff does not see anything religious about it. His reasons are spelled out in the following passage:

> The main reason why I was persuaded by the claim that the ancient
> Chinese had no natural religion, since they did not know the creator of
> the world, was this: that in their classical texts . . . no duty toward God
> is mentioned, but only such duties as relate to custom in daily life. I
> also do not understand why I should allow myself to be dissuaded
> from this position. Natural religion consists in worship of the true

God, who is known through the light of reason as derived from His attributes and works. Therefore, where there is no proof for a knowledge of God; where love, fear, respect, and invocation of the divinity together with faith are not insisted on, there is no natural religion. (N54, 150–51)

Nevertheless, although the ancient Chinese allegedly "had no natural religion," Wolff—unlike many other critics—ascribes neither atheism nor agnosticism to them:

Still I concede gladly that neither the ancient Chinese nor Confucius were atheists. Because an atheist is someone who denies that there is a god; but one cannot deny God when one does not understand clearly what God is. . . . I do not doubt at all, that both the ancient Chinese and also Confucius knew that there is some kind of creator of this world; but I regard it as certain, that they did not know his attributes. They therefore had a confused concept of divinity, but not at all a clear one. However, for natural religion a clear concept of divinity is required. (N54, 152–53)

On Wolff's reading, Confucius's religious perspective is thus more or less the weak deistic one of Hume's Cleanthes:

In a word, *Cleanthes*, a man who follows your hypothesis is able, perhaps, to assert or conjecture that the universe sometime arose from something like design: But beyond that position he cannot ascertain one single circumstance, and is left afterwards to fix every point of his theology by the utmost license of fancy and hypothesis.[45]

Ultimately, the dominant force behind Wolff's interpretation of Confucius is not European vocabulary and assumptions but rather his own previously worked out ethical theory. Baldly put, Wolff reads the *Analects* through the lenses of his own influential text, *Vernünfftige Gedancken von der Menschen Thun und Lassen, zu Beförderung ihrer Glückseeligkeit* (often referred to as the "German Ethics"), interpreting the former (along with related texts concerning life in ancient China) as empirical confirmation for the theory contained in the latter.[46] The "German Ethics" was first published in 1720—one year before Wolff presented his lecture at Halle. Although it is a long and often repetitive work (over seven hundred pages in the Olms reprint edition), a quick look at some key claims made early on in the foreword to the second edition and in part 1 reveal some very strong parallels between ethical theory à la Wolff and Confucian ethics as interpreted by Wolff. In the foreword, for instance, Wolff informs readers that he has "shown conceptually that the actions of human beings are in themselves necessarily good or evil, but in no way do they first become good or evil through the command and prohibition of a superior."[47] Here we find a strong denial of the "divine command theory" of moral obligation, from which he derives a very radical conclusion later in part 1:

Because the free actions of human beings become good or bad through
their consequences . . . they are therefore in and of themselves good or
evil, and are not first made so through God's will. Thus if it were
possible that there were no God and that the present connection of
things could still subsist without Him, the free actions of human beings
would remain good or evil. (sect. 5)

Even in a godless world intelligent consequentialists could still ascertain their
moral obligations, for what makes actions morally good or evil on Wolff's view
is a function of consequences rather than divine commands. Indeed, God's own
commands only reiterate what smart consequentialists already know through the
light of reason alone: "God can give the human being no other law than the law
of nature, but in no way a law that conflicts with the law of nature" (sect. 29).
And since both "virtue can subsist simply with natural obligation" (4) and
"natural obligation is at once a divine obligation" (sect. 29), no knowledge of
God's commands is necessary to lead a virtuous life. Small wonder then, as Wolff
announces later in the Discourse, that Confucius and the ancient Chinese could
succeed in practicing virtue "free from all religion" (26–27).

But doesn't this radical preaching concerning the autonomy of morality render
God superfluous? No. In the Discourse, Wolff is careful to state that the Chinese had
only "the lowest grade of virtue" (26–27). This lowest grade is what Wolff calls
"philosophical virtue" (N51, 138–39), and consists in the ability to "judge one's
actions according to their consequences only through the guidance of reason"
(26–27). (Note the stress on the consequentialist dimension of philosophical
virtue, which also corresponds to the normative theory of the earlier "German
Ethics." Wolff's Confucius is therefore also a consequentialist.) Virtues at this
lowest grade are "attributed only to the force of nature" (26–27). (Here we see
an additional motive behind Wolff's nonreligious understanding of tiān. Any moral
value that comes from nature is by definition nonreligious.) The next grade is
dubbed "philosophical piety" (N52, 138–39), and consists in "a consideration of
God's attributes and divine providence supported only by the light of reason"
(26–27). Virtues at this second grade "arise from natural religion" (26–27).
Finally, there is the highest grade—"theological or Christian virtue" (N53,
138–39). Virtue here involves acting in accordance with "divine providence of
revealed truths, for which no natural evidence is in store." Such virtue comes from
"the power of grace" (26–27).

In the earlier "German Ethics" several additional doctrines are presented that
spell further trouble for Confucianism. Moral duties for Wolff are divided into
three classes: duties of the human being toward himself (part 2), of the human
being toward God (part 3), and of the human being toward others (part 4).[48]
"The main rule, according to which we have to judge all duties toward God is:
honor God" (sect. 652). Those who "did not know the creator of the world" or
who at most only perceived dimly that "there is some kind of creator of this

world" (see above, pp. 82, 83), are clearly unable to fulfill the main rule by which all duties in this second class are judged.

Also, Wolff's fundamental law of ethics is perfectionism: "Do what makes yourself and the condition of yourself and others more perfect; omit what makes them more imperfect" (sect. 12). Wolff believes he proves it "clear as the sun" that "included in the perfection of our nature" is "the honoring of God" (sect. 42) Here too, those who do not have a clear conception of the creator of the world are thus unable to fulfill a key aspect of this most basic Wolffian rule of ethics, one that he claims contains "the entire ground of all natural laws" (sect. 19). In his 1726 foreword to the *Discourse*, Wolff again reminds readers that "the first principle not only of natural law but also of decency itself is the performance of human actions toward the perfection of the microcosm, and consequently also toward that of the macrocosm itself" (6–7). He then adds: "When I studied the Chinese classical texts carefully, I was certain that the oldest Chinese, especially Confucius, had the same idea, even if it was confused and not at all clear" (6–7).[49] Confucius' ethics is perfectionist: Heaven is perfect, and our duty is to model our life and conduct on tiān. What Wolff undoubtedly means by the confused and unclear nature of Confucian perfectionism is its nontheistic orientation.

The above analysis shows, I believe, that Wolff's interpretation of Confucian ethics should not have upset his Pietist colleagues as much as it did. He clearly maintained that the ancient Chinese "had only the lowest grade of virtue," and that higher grades were not possible for them due to their ignorance of God. But I think my analysis also shows that Wolff cooked his data: he read his own ethical theory into Confucianism at nearly every available opportunity, and his resultant interpretations of what Confucius was up to are severely strained.

The lesson here is simple, but difficult: In our reach for otherness, we need to try harder to put our own philosophical agendas on hold. This is not easy to do, for as Donald Davidson notes, the attempt to understand others implies that charity "is forced on us; whether we like it or not, if we want to understand others, we must count them right in most matters."[50] To count others right in most matters, in the context of cross-cultural understanding, essentially means to assume that they hold the same basic beliefs that we hold. We cannot begin to make sense out of others unless we presuppose that we do indeed share a great many fundamental beliefs in common with each other. And since philosophical agendas themselves are about basic beliefs, this means that we will need to bring (at least the sturdier, less controversial parts of) them with us when we try to understand others. If we put our beliefs on hold at the very beginning, we rule out the possibility of understanding others. As a practical matter, the necessary presupposition of shared belief on most matters can only be realized by employing our normal concepts and theories when we attempt to understand others. Psychologically stated, a certain spirit of sympathy is needed right at the start in understanding others' beliefs. But sometimes sympathy itself contributes to misunderstanding. Sometimes our own conceptual baggage clearly does get in the way of cross-cultural understanding. Part of understanding others is also recognizing that they are indeed others. This recognition can only come after we allow that others might reject some of our prized concepts and theories. After charity comes the hard part.

NOTES

An earlier version of this essay was presented as an invited colloquium paper to the Philosophy Department at the University of Maine, Orono, in October 1997. I would like to thank my host Roger King, as well as the students and faculty present, for the thought-provoking discussion that followed my presentation. Thanks also to Bryan W. Van Norden, Craig Dietrich, and Philip J. Ivanhoe for their valuable criticisms of an earlier draft.

    1. In citing from the *Analects*, I use D. C. Lau's translation and chapter divisions in *Confucius: The Analects* (New York: Penguin Books, 1979).

    2. Norbert Hinske, "Wolffs Stellung in der deutschen Aufklärung," in Werner Schneiders, ed., *Christian Wolff 1679–1754: Interpretationen zu seiner Philosophie und deren Wirkung*, 2d ed. (Hamburg: Felix Meiner, 1986), p. 316. Kant, in the preface to the second edition of *Critique of Pure Reason*, also testifies to Wolff's importance in referring to "the celebrated Wolff, the greatest of all the dogmatic philosophers" (B xxxvi). For an overview of Wolff as a philosopher, see Lewis White Beck, *Early German Philosophy: Kant and His Predecessors* (Cambridge, Mass.: Harvard University Press, 1969; reprint, Bristol, England: Thoemmes Press, 1996), pp. 256–75. Paul Guyer's two entries on Wolff in Lawrence C. Becker and Charlotte B. Becker, eds., *Encyclopedia of Ethics* (New York: Garland, 1992), and Robert Audi, ed., *The Cambridge Dictionary of Philosophy* (New York: Cambridge University Press, 1995), are also helpful.

    3. German professors were still expected to lecture in Latin at this time, although a German translation of the *Oratio* did appear later in 1740. Part of Wolff's importance for German cultural life is due to his central role in developing "a special German conceptual language in the field of philosophy" (Hinske, "Wolffs Stellung," p. 310). As Beck notes, Wolff's "philosophy was the first comprehensive system to be published in German. . . . He was the principal author of the German philosophical vocabulary, and though, during the eighteenth century, much German philosophy continued to be written in Latin, German in his hands became an adequate vehicle for philosophical thought" (*Early German Philosophy*, p. 261).

    4. Christian Wolff, *Oratio de Sinarum philosophia practica. Rede über die praktische philosophie der Chinesen*, ed. Michael Albrecht (Hamburg: Felix Meiner, 1985), pp. 18–19. Future citations to Wolff's lecture are given in the body of the text, with page numbers to Albrecht's edition. (This edition includes Wolff's Latin original along with a new translation into German by Albrecht on facing pages.) Translations of the *Oratio* into English are my own. For discussion (in English) of Albrecht's edition, see David E. Mungello, review of *Oratio de Sinarum philosophia practica. Rede über die praktische philosophie der Chinesen*, by Christian Wolff, in *Studia Leibnitiana* 18 (1986), pp. 120–25.

    5. Donald F. Lach, "The Sinophilism of Christian Wolff," *Journal of the History of Ideas* 14 (1953), p. 564. Lach's account of the historical details that surrounded the controversy over Wolff's lecture is the best discussion in English that I have seen. I am indebted to it on a number of factual matters in this opening section. Julia Ching's short essay, "Christian Wolff and China: The Autonomy of Morality," *Synthesis Philosophica* 7 (1989), pp. 241–48, is also helpful, though (contrary to her opening statement in the abstract about concen-

trating "more on the use Wolff made of China and Chinese philosophy") she, too, tends to focus primarily on the historical issues that surround the *Oratio*.

6. Heinrich Wuttke, ed., *Christian Wolffs eigene Lebensbeschreibung* (Leipzig, 1841), p. 28 (as cited by Lach, "The Sinophilism of Christian Wolff," p. 565).

7. Eduard Zeller, "Wolff's Vetreibung aus Halle; der Kampf des Pietismus mit der Philosophie," *Preußische Jahrbücher* 10 (1862), p. 66.

8. Hinske, "Wolffs Stellung," p. 31.

9. Lach, "The Sinophilism of Christian Wolff," p. 567. (See Lach's documentation at n. 28.)

10. A bootleg version of the lecture was published in Rome in 1722, and reprinted in 1725 by Jesuits in Trévoux, France. These unauthorized publications strained Wolff's formerly cordial relations with the Jesuits. In his extensive notes to the 1726 edition Wolff refers often to the Jesuit Philip Couplet's Latin translation of *The Analects*—*Confucius Sinarum Philosophus* (Paris, 1687), the first complete Western-language version of Confucius' sayings. But Couplet's translation only came to Wolff's attention sometime after 1721. In the original 1721 *Oratio*, he relied on Jesuit missionary Francois Noël's 1711 translation—*Sinensis imperii libri classici sex* (Prague, 1711). Mungello, in his review of Albrecht's edition of Wolff's *Oratio*, argues that "Wolff treated these two Jesuit translations as separate works whereas they are, in the view of this writer, different manifestation[s] of the same long-term translation-project" (p. 122). In my view, Wolff's interpretation of Confucian ethics was driven primarily by his own preexisting ethical theory, rather than one or another Latin translation of the *Analects*. See the section on "Wolff's Confucius," below.

11. Lach, "The Sinophilism of Christian Wolff," p. 569. Lach is citing here from the 1750 English translation of Wolff's second China lecture, entitled *The Real Happiness of a People under a Philosophical King Demonstrated; Not only from the Nature of Things, but from the undoubted Experience of the Chinese under their first Founder Fohi, and his Illustrious Successors, Hoam Ti, and Xin Num* (London). As Lach also notes (p. 568, n. 35), many writers have unfortunately confused Wolff's original *Oratorio* with this second China lecture. H. G. Creel, for instance, on p. 256 of his influential study, *Confucius: The Man and the Myth* (New York: John Day, 1949), cites Wolff's remark that "in the Art of Governing, . . . [China] has ever surpassed all others without exception"; a quotation taken in turn from Arthur O. Lovejoy's essay, "The Chinese Origin of a Romanticism" (*Essays in the History of Ideas* [Baltimore: Johns Hopkins University Press, 1948], p. 108). Both authors state that the remark comes from Wolff's 1721 lecture at Halle, when in fact it comes from his 1730 lecture at Marburg.

12. Later to be known as Frederick the Great. Unlike his coarse father Frederick William I, Frederick II was extremely interested in contemporary intellectual developments, and corresponded frequently with Voltaire, d'Alembert, Wolff, and other leading figures in the Enlightenment. Kant, in his essay "An Answer to the Question: What Is Enlightenment?" pays tribute with the remark: "this age is the age of enlightenment or the century of *Frederick*" (Academy edition, vol. 8, p. 40).

13. Zeller, "Wolff's Vertreibung aus Halle," p. 71. Compare Albrecht, "Einleitung," *Rede über die praktische Philosophie der Chinesen*, p. 52.

14. François-Marie Arouet de Voltaire, *Oeuvres complètes de Voltaire*, ed. Louis Moland (Paris: Garnier, 1877–1885), vol. 10, p. 312; as cited by Ching, "Christian Wolff and China," p. 247; and Albrecht, "Einleitung," p. LIII. (I would like to thank Yves Dalvet for translating this passage for me.)

15. For overviews, see chap. 15 ("Confucianism and Western Democracy") of Creel, *Confucius: The Man and the Myth*; Donald F. Lach, "China in Western Thought and Culture," in Philip P. Wiener, ed., *Dictionary of the History of Ideas* (New York: Charles Scribner's Sons, 1968), vol. 1, pp. 353–73; and Johnathan Spence, "Western Perceptions of China from the Late Sixteenth Century to the Present," in Paul Ropp, ed., *Heritage of China: Contemporary Perspectives*

on *Chinese Civilization* (Berkeley: University of California Press, 1990), pp. 1–14. Detailed studies of the role of Jesuit missionary work in modern European understandings of China include Spence, *The Memory Palace of Matteo Ricci* (New York: Viking Penguin, 1984); and David E. Mungello, *Curious Land: Jesuit Accommodation and the Origins of Sinology* (Stuttgart: Franz Steiner, 1985).

16. David E. Mungello, "Some Recent Studies on the Confluence of Chinese and Western Intellectual History," *Journal of the History of Ideas* 40 (1979), p. 659. As a young man, Wolff corresponded frequently with Leibniz before the latter's death in 1716, and Leibniz's pioneering work on China undoubtedly did influence Wolff's own developing interest in this area to some extent. However, according to Albrecht, "so far it is unclear how extensive a direct influence Leibniz had on Wolff on detailed questions; indeed, whether Wolff actually read [Leibniz's] *Novissima Sinica*" ("Einleitung," p. XXII). Leibniz, like Wolff, praises Chinese practical philosophy very highly (indeed, even more highly than Wolff). For instance, in the preface to the *Novissima Sinica*, he states: "if we are their equals in the trial arts, and ahead of them in contemplative sciences, certainly they surpass us (though it is almost shameful to confess this) in practical philosophy, that is, in the precepts of ethics and politics adopted to the present life and use of mortals" (sect. 3, in Gottfried Wilhelm Leibniz, *Writings on China*, trans. Daniel J. Cook and Henry Rosemont Jr. [Chicago: Open Court, 1994]), p. 105. On the other hand, Leibniz and Wolff disagree strongly on the question of whether either natural religion or natural theology can be said to have existed in ancient China. Wolff, as we have already seen, denies this: "because the ancient Chinese did not know the creator of the world . . . they had no natural religion" (26–27). Similarly, in note 165 he adds: "there was no natural theology among them at all" (236–37, cf. N54, 145–55). But Leibniz, in his "Discourse on the Natural Theology of the Chinese," writes: "To offend Heaven is to act against reason, to ask pardon of Heaven is to reform oneself and to make a sincere return in word and deed in the submission one owes to this very law of reason. For me I find all this quite excellent and quite in accord with *natural theology*. . . . It is pure Christianity, insofar as it renews the natural law inscribed in our hearts" (sect. 31, trans. Cook and Rosemont), p. 105.

17. See in particular Cook and Rosemont's edition of Leibniz, *Writings on China*. This important collection includes translations of the following texts: (1) the preface to *Novissima Sinica* (1697/99—*Recent News from China*. An earlier English translation of and commentary on this text was also prepared by Donald F. Lach, *The Preface to Leibniz' Novissima Sinica* [Honolulu: University Press of Hawaii, 1957]); (2) "On the Civil Cult of Confucius" (1700); (3) "Remarks on Chinese Rites and Religion" (1708); and (4) "Discourse on the Natural Theology of the Chinese" (1716, the year of Leibniz's death). Cook and Rosemont also published this fourth translation separately under the title *G. W. Leibniz: Discourse on the Natural Theology of the Chinese* (Honolulu: University Press of Hawaii, 1977). Julia Ching and Willard G. Oxtoby, in their ambitious study, *Moral Enlightenment: Leibniz and Wolff on China*, Monumenta Serica Monograph Series, vol. 26 (Nettetal: Steyler Verlag, 1992), also include translations of "On the Civil Cult of Confucius" and the "Discourse," as well as the following Leibnizian texts on China: "Letter to Father Grimaldi" (1692), "The Secret of Creation: New Year's Letter to Duke Rudolph August" (1697), and "An Explanation of Binary Arithmetic" (1703). Additionally, they offer English translations both of Wolff's 1721 *Discourse* and of his 1730 Marburg lecture, "On the Philosopher King and the Ruling Philosopher." However, by their own admission, their translation of the *Discourse* is neither complete nor always accurate: "We decided therefore to edit the notes selectively. . . . These are frequently paraphrased from Wolff's original" (p. 7). (Unfortunately, occasional signs of this paraphrasing tendency are also evident in their translation of the main text.) I reject their view that Wolff's notes to the *Discourse* are not "of much service to the modern reader"

(p. 7). On the contrary, I believe that the notes are often more valuable than the original 1721 lecture. In my own analysis, I accordingly rely extensively on them.

18. For example, J. J. Clarke, in *Oriental Enlightenment: The Encounter between Asian and Western Thought* (New York: Routledge, 1997), a recent book which, judging from the title, might be expected to have at least one serious chapter on Wolff, offers only one short paragraph on him, which consists solely of points taken from Lach, "The Sinophilism of Christian Wolff" (p. 48).

19. Helmuth von Glasenapp, *Kant und die Religionen des Osten* (Kitzingen-Main: Holzner Verlag, 1954), p. 93.

20. Von Glasenapp, *Kant und die Religionen des Osten*, pp. 103–4. (Von Glasenapp is citing here from p. 305 of a manuscript he refers to as "Ms 2599.") Kant's remark that Confucius' maxims are "unbearable, because every individual can reel them off" seems odd, given his own commitment to building a normative theory reached through a descriptive analysis of what "common human reason (*die gemeine Menschenvernunft*)" holds to be true. For discussion, see my "*Gemeine Menschenvernunft* and *Ta Endoxa*," in Louden, *Morality and Moral Theory: A Reappraisal and Reaffirmation* (New York: Oxford University Press, 1992), pp. 116–20. The official version of Kant's physical geography lectures were edited by his former student Friedrich Theodor Rink in 1802, and appear in Academy vol. 9, pp. 151–436. In Rink's version there is a brief discussion of China (9:377–383), but not much on Confucius. In a superficial section on "Religion," which Kant begins by confessing that religion "will be treated here fairly coldly" (9:381), the only statement on Confucius is the following: "One also honors Confucius or Con-fu-tse, the Chinese Socrates" (9:382). An English translation of Rink's version of *Physical Geography* is forthcoming in Immanuel Kant, *Natural Science*, ed. H. B. Nisbet (New York: Cambridge University Press).

21. Julia Ching, "Chinese Ethics and Kant," *Philosophy East and West* 28 (1979), p. 168. See also Ching and Oxtoby, "Epilogue—A Reversal of Opinion: Kant and Hegel on China," in *Moral Enlightenment*, pp. 221–29.

22. Georg Wilhelm Friedrich Hegel, *Lectures on the History of Philosophy*, trans. E. S. Haldane (1892; reprint, New York: Humanities Press, 1963), vol. 1 pp. 120–21. Kant and Hegel both maintain in effect that Confucianism is insufficiently "philosophical"—there is not enough attention paid to foundational issues, matters of justification and argument, and so forth. For better or worse, this judgment is echoed by many later Western scholars of Chinese philosophy. See, e.g., Bryan W. Van Norden's references to and discussion of remarks by Donald Munro, Robert Eno, and Chad Hansen in "What Should Western Philosophy Learn from Chinese Philosophy?" in P. J. Ivanhoe, ed., *Chinese Language, Thought and Culture* (Chicago: Open Court, 1996), p. 230. My own view is that the *Analects* is less speculative and systematically ambitious than, for example, the canonical texts of German Idealism, but that its more practical intent certainly does not disqualify it from being philosophical. See also my interpretations of *Analects* 5:13 and 11:12, below.

23. Creel, *Confucius: The Man and the Myth*, p. 116.

24. Benjamin I. Schwartz, *The World of Thought in Ancient China* (Cambridge: Harvard University Press, 1985), p. 122.

25. Leibniz, *Writings on China*, p. 3. As Cook and Rosemont also note, many later missionaries—who eventually proved victorious—objected to Ricci's translations, claiming that both *shangdi* and *tian* had "connotations inconsistent with the Christian concept of deity" (p. 3). Albrecht, in his introduction to the *Oratio*, points out that Noël translated *tian* as "heaven," whereas Couplet rendered it as "God" (p. XXVII). Unfortunately, the underlying assumption in this debate (viz., that in order to have a *concept* of God one needs one or another specific *word* for God) seems clearly false. The same concept can be referred to by means of many different combinations of many different words.

26. Bryan W. Van Norden, s.v. "t'ien," *The Cambridge Dictionary of Philosophy*. See also Arthur Waley's and D. C. Lau's discussions of *t'ien* in their respective translations of the *Analects* (Arthur Waley, *The Analects of Confucius* [New York: Vintage Books, 1989; originally published 1938], pp. 41–43, and D. C. Lau, pp. 27–30) and David L. Hall and Roger T. Ames, *Thinking Through Confucius* (Albany, N.Y.: SUNY Press, 1987), pp. 201–16. For brief discussions of pre- and post-Confucius meanings of *tian*, see H. G. Creel, *Chinese Thought: From Confucius to Mao Tse-Tung* (New York: New American Library, 1960), pp. 21–23; C. K. Yang, "The Functional Relationship between Confucian Thought and Chinese Religion," in John K. Fairbank, ed., *Chinese Thought and Institutions* (Chicago: University of Chicago Press, 1957), p. 273; and Hans Küng and Julia Ching, *Christianity and Chinese Religions* (New York: Doubleday, 1989), pp. 16–17. See also Robert Eno's book-length study, *The Confucian Creation of Heaven: Philosophy and the Defense of Ritual Mastery* (Albany, N.Y.: SUNY Press, 1990), esp. his discussion, "The Origins of the Term 'T'ien,'" pp. 181–89. For critical discussion of Eno's approach, see Kwong-loi Shun's review in the *Harvard Journal of Asiatic Studies* 52 (1992), pp. 739–56.

27. Creel, "Was Confucius Agnostic?" *T'ung pao* 29 (1932), p. 64. Yet another complication concerns much-debated issues regarding the composition of the *Analects*, and how these might relate to determining Confucius's own views on *tian*. (Eno, for instance, draws a very strong distinction between the historical Confucius' views of *tian* and those we find in the text of the *Analects*. See "Confucius's Doctrinal Silence," in *The Confucian Creation of Heaven*, pp. 94–98.) However, because our primary concern in this paper is with Wolff's interpretation of Confucius, we need not concern ourselves with the details of this particular scholarly skirmish. Wolff treats the *Analects* as a whole and views the text as a trustworthy source of the historical Confucius' beliefs.

28. Herbert Fingarette, *Confucius—The Secular as Sacred* (New York: Harper and Row, 1972), p. 62. Similarly, Hall and Ames contend that "the *Analects* itself does not provide us with an altogether clear statement on *t'ien*" (*Thinking Through Confucius*, p. 208). On the other hand, Eno holds that "the portrait of *t'ien* that emerges [in the *Analects*] is remarkably consistent" (*The Confucian Creation of Heaven*, p. 84, cf. 94). Again, though, this picture of consistency seems to be fractured by Eno's own insistence that the historical Confucius' teaching about *tian* "might have been very different from that of *The Analects*" (p. 96).

29. Even this passage has been interpreted by some as implying a secular outlook on the part of Confucius. James Legge, for instance, translates the flagged sentence as "My studies lie low, and my penetration rises high," and then comments as follows: "the meaning appears to be that he [Confucius] contented himself with the study of men and things, common matters as more ambitious spirits would deem them" (James Legge, trans., *Confucian Analects, The Great Learning and The Doctrine of the Mean* [New York: Dover Publications, 1971], p. 289. This is a reprint edition of vol. 1 of Legge's *Chinese Classics* [Oxford: Clarendon Press, 1893].) But Lau's choice of "start" (which I follow) suggests merely that Confucius *begins* with "common matters"—not that "he contented himself with the study of men and things."

30. Compare Lau, "Introduction," *Analects*, p. 28.

31. Creel, "Was Confucius Agnostic?" p. 66. Certainly the opinion of Legge, "the formidable Scottish missionary-scholar" who published "what can be considered the archetype of all later scholarly editions of the Analects" (and who also "coined the title 'Analects'") would carry considerable weight in such a poll (Jonathan Spence, "What Confucius Said," *New York Review of Books*, April 10, 1997, p. 8). Legge's towering influence indicates a basic flaw in the poll scenario: some scholars' votes always count for more than others. In his discussion of Confucius' "Influence and Opinions," Legge notes: "Not once throughout the *Analects* does he use the personal name [God]. I would say that he was

unreligious rather than irreligious; yet by the coldness of his temperament and intellect in this matter, his influence is unfavorable to the development of ardent religious feeling among the Chinese people generally." (*Confucian Analects*, p. 99.)

32. A different kind of agnostic reading is present in the following remark: "T'ien is wholly immanent, having no existence independent of the calculus of phenomena that constitute it. . . . The meaning and value of t'ien is a function of the meaning and value of its many phenomena, and the order of t'ien is expressed in the harmony that obtains among its correlative parts" (Hall and Ames, *Thinking Through Confucius*, p. 207). When it is a question of the moral meaning and value of tiān, this assertion is false. Confucius looks to tiān for moral guidance, not vice versa. Confucius qua natural creature is one of the many phenomena that collectively constitute nature and physical reality, but Confucius nowhere suggests that human beings should get together and collectively calculate what their moral norms ought to be. Rather, the value and status of tiān as a moral norm is independent of such phenomena. Tiān qua moral norm is not simply a function of the value of its constituent parts.

33. Heiner Roetz, *Mensch und Natur im alten China* (New York: Peter Lang, 1984), p. 203, 203, n. 3. My one doubt here concerns Roetz's dualism between naturalism and religion. Why couldn't tiān for Confucius be both a naturalistic and religious concept? Tiān is not transcendent in the sense of being above or outside of nature, in the way that Western religions construe God. Rather, tiān is part of the cosmos itself and thus naturalistic. But tiān also serves as the ground of moral norms, and the wise feel a sense of awe in contemplating it. In this latter sense, tiān is both transcendent and religious.

34. I would like to thank Philip J. Ivanhoe for conversation on this point. It is true that in several of the passages cited above tiān is said to have intentions (9:5, perhaps 3:24); and in others to possess understanding (14:35, 9:12). These uses of language seem to me to be metaphorical. However, even if one thinks they are not, they do not add up to anything close to the "God-as-personal-being" that most mainstream believers within the major Western religions regard as being essential to their faith.

35. Contra Hall and Ames, *Thinking Through Confucius*, p. 206. Later, on p. 277, they offer a second reading of 17:19, stating that the point of the passage concerns the "harmony and meaning effected in the absence of the spoken word." On my reading, the point of 17:19 is not the romantic notion that language destroys meaning or that nonverbal communication is always to be preferred over verbal, but simply that Heaven does in fact communicate a great deal of moral meaning to the wise, albeit nonverbally.

36. Schwartz, *The World of Thought in Ancient China*, pp. 124–25. Schwartz's assertion that "the spirit of Heaven is still very much present" in the unspoken processes of nature heads in the right direction, but the normative content of this spirit needs to be articulated. What do the wise learn about how to live and act from the spirit of Heaven when they observe these processes of nature?

37. Compare Mencius: "Heaven does not speak but reveals itself through its acts and deeds" (D. C. Lau, trans., *Mencius*, [New York: Penguin Books, 1970], 5A5, p. 143). The vexing question of how exactly Heaven reveals its intentions is unfortunately not explored in detail in either the *Analects* or *Mencius*, and the hints that one finds in these two texts do not appear to be entirely compatible. (In the latter text, the ideas seem to be that Heaven reveals its intentions through the happiness of the people under virtuous rule. However, both texts agree that Heaven communicates nonverbally, and that its messages carry strong moral import.) The hypothesis I am proposing, based in part on *Analects* 17:19, is that the wise can discern moral norms in the regular patterns and interrelations of the natural world. At 2:1, for instance, we are told that the relationship between the Polestar and other stars provides us with a paradigm of "the rule of virtue [dé 德]." (For an Aristotelian

analogue here, see my "What is Moral Authority? *Euboulia, Sunesis,* and *Gnômê* vs. *Phronêsis,*" *Ancient Philosophy* 17 [1997], pp. 103–18). The idea of reading moral norms in nature is admittedly not elaborated on in great detail in the *Analects*, but I do believe it can be correctly attributed to Confucius. It is also a common thought that one finds expressed in many different cultural traditions.

38. Waley, *The Analects of Confucius,* p. 110, nn. 4 and 3 (respectively). See also Philip J. Ivanhoe's discussion of this passage in his contribution to this volume.

39. Compare Schwartz, *The World of Thought in Ancient China,* pp. 118–20. Here we find what is often referred to as Confucius' "pragmatic" orientation. On my view, his orientation is "pragmatic" only in the popular sense that it is fundamentally concerned with human practice rather than speculation. But Confucius' outlook is not what most philosophers mean by "pragmatic," because he does not espouse a doctrine of efficacy in practical application. Confucius does not argue that that which works out most effectively provides a standard of moral rightness. (Here I am also disagreeing with Wolff. As we shall see later, he reads Confucius as a consequentialist.) Rather, *tiān* itself provides us with this standard—regardless of whether it is or is not efficacious.

40. Creel, "Was Confucius Agnostic?" p. 82. Creel cites Legge's translation of this passage, in which wisdom is said to consist in keeping "aloof from" spiritual beings while also "respecting" them (cf. Legge, *Confucian Analects,* p. 191—in Legge's version this passage is numbered 6:20). Creel then suggests the following revision: "to respect spiritual beings, maintaining the proper distance in *relations* with them" (pp. 87–88).

41. Baron d'Holbach, *Common Sense, or Natural Ideas Opposed to Supernatural* (1772), in Isaac Kramnick, ed., *The Portable Enlightenment Reader* (New York: Penguin Books, 1995), p. 144.

42. I do not mean here that Confucius disavows reason. On the contrary, the goal is to *understand* the Decree of Heaven (cf. 2:4). However, I do not see evidence in the *Analects* for the strong rationalism that Wolff and others attribute to Confucius (see, e.g., *Discourse,* 24–25). Max Weber exaggerates when he claims that "Confucianism is more rationalist and sober, in the sense of the absence and the rejection of all non-utilitarian yardsticks, than any other ethical system, with the possible exception of J. Bentham's" ("The Social Psychology of the World Religions," *From Max Weber: Essays in Sociology,* eds. H. H. Gerth and C. Wright Mills [New York: Oxford University Press, 1946], p. 293).

43. For a classic discussion see Rudolf Otto, *The Idea of the Holy,* trans. John W. Harvey (London: Oxford University Press, 1923).

44. Mungello, in his review of Albrecht's edition of Wolff's *Oratio,* claims that "Noël, unlike Wolff[,] was aware of the ambiguity of meaning of T'ien. It could mean either physical sky or divine force—precisely the same ambiguity which the word 'heaven' carries in English today" (p. 124). I believe that several of Wolff's remarks in N54 (cited above) indicate clearly that he was well aware of the multiple meanings of *tiān.* But as I go on to argue, ultimately his reasons for interpreting the use of *tiān* in the *Analects* in the way that he does concern not so much the translation of either Noël or Couplet, but rather his own philosophical commitments in ethical theory.

45. David Hume, *Dialogues Concerning Natural Religion* (1779), ed. Richard H. Popkin (Indianapolis: Hackett, 1980), p. 37. These standard distinctions between atheism, agnosticism, and deism are important and should not be dissolved into one another, even if they do not map on perfectly to Confucianism (which again, on my reading, is religious without involving a concept of a personal God). It is odd, for instance, that Ching, in a section of her introductory essay to *Moral Enlightenment: Leibniz and Wolff on China* entitled "Wolff: The Chinese as Agnostics," writes: "it should be noted that Wolff, unlike Leibniz before him, regarded the Chinese to have been atheists" (p. 26). Again, because Wolff does not doubt at all, "that both the ancient Chinese and also Confucius knew that there is some kind of

creator of this world" (N54, 152–53), he regarded the Chinese as neither atheists nor agnostics. But odd, too, is the tension between Wolff's claim in the previous sentence and his assertion that the ancient Chinese "did not know the creator of the world" (26–27). Apparently, his considered view is that they had a fuzzy conception of "some kind of" creator, but lacked a clear conception of "the" creator. Roetz, in a brief discussion of these two passages, speculates that "after Wolff had to pay for the provocation in these lines [viz., 26–27] with his expulsion, he weakened his assertions in a later note"—viz., N54, 152–53 (*Mensch und Natur im alten China*, p. 9, n. 1). On my reading, Wolff neither softened his position in N54 nor changed his mind as a result of his expulsion from Halle.

46. Compare Albrecht, who writes that "in the *Discourse on the Chinese* Wolff tried to test experimentally [his] general practical philosophy. . . . The result of this experiment is: the truth of Wolff's general practical philosophy . . . is confirmed ("Einleitung," p. XLIII). However, Albrecht is assuming here that Wolff interpreted the data correctly, which I am denying.

47. Christian Wolff, *Vernünfftige Gedancken von der Menschen Thun und Lassen, zu Beförderung ihrer Glückseeligkeit*, Introduction by Hans Werner Arndt 4th ed. (1733; facsimile reprint, Hildesheim: Georg Olms, 1976), p. 2. J. B. Schneewind prepared a good English translation of selections from this text for his edited anthology, *Moral Philosophy from Montaigne to Kant* (New York: Cambridge University Press, 1990), vol. 1, pp. 333–48. Future references to the "German Ethics" are given in the body of the text with pagination (or section number) to the Olms edition.

48. As Paul Guyer notes, the primacy of duties to oneself is a key example of the strong influence that Wolff's ethics had on Kant's (s.v. "Wolff, Christian," in *Encyclopedia of Ethics*, p. 1325). (Perfectionism, discussed below, is another.) As is well known, in the *Metaphysics of Morals* Kant argues that without duties to oneself "there would be no duties whatsoever" (6:417). For discussion, see my "Morality and Oneself," in *Morality and Moral Theory*, pp. 13–26. But Kant also rejects Wolff's second category of duties. All so-called duties to God, Kant holds, are properly speaking duties to ourselves. They are not objective obligations "to perform certain services for another, but only subjective, for the sake of strengthening the moral incentive in our own lawgiving reason" (6:487, cf. 443–44).

49. In a later section entitled "The Highest Good of the Chinese" he makes essentially the same point: "That the highest good of the human being consists in unhindered and daily progress toward greater perfections has been proved by me in another place" (56–57). In an accompanying note (N71, 238–39, cf. Albrecht's own note on 296), he refers readers to sect. 44 of the "German Ethics," where we are told that the highest good the human being can attain is "an unhindered progress toward greater perfections" as opposed to actual attainment of perfection. The Chinese, he continues in the discussion of the highest good in the *Discourse*, "eagerly impress upon one" the same idea (56–57).

50. Donald Davidson, "On the Very Idea of a Conceptual Scheme," in Davidson, *Inquiries into Truth and Interpretation* (New York: Oxford University Press, 1984), p. 197.

5

1. Introduction

There can be no happy outcome in the contemporary debate that pits the priority of individual fulfillment against more traditional claims about the distinctive benisons of shared sources of meaning. This is, at least partly, because there are at least two different kinds of human flourishing, each one being raised up by one side or the other as the comprehensive human good. One kind of flourishing involves the distinctive development of what is unique to each individual agent as irreplicable subject. Although

Conformity, Individuality, and the Nature of Virtue: A Classical Confucian Contribution to Contemporary Ethical Reflection

STEPHEN A. WILSON

the total content of our identities may be ultimately unknowable,[1] most advocates of this view allow agents some substantive insights into their personalities—enough, in any case, to give determinate content to notions of self-interpretation. Another kind of flourishing stems from what given communities take human beings to be in some universal sense (given human nature, basic human capabilities, and so on). The successful formation of communally valued character traits is thought to enable participants to fulfill the highest possibilities afforded by that (or any) community's way of life. Both forms of flourishing represent very significant goods, and both are, in my judgment, indispensable to a nuanced understanding of the fullest human potential. To slight either, as both sides of the contemporary debate slight one or the other, is not only to impoverish ethical reflection but also to falsify human experience.

Common sense seems to counsel striking a balance between these sometimes competing goods, and there have been some very significant initiatives in this direction—most notably, Charles Taylor's *The Ethics of Authenticity*. A stable and persuasive "middle" position nevertheless remains elusive and difficult to specify in any detailed and convincing way. Moreover, advocates of the "middle" position all too often themselves end up going over too far to one side or the other.[2] The questions are perennial and powerful: How heavily can we weigh the values and claims of communal sources of meaning before we become advocates of oppressive regimes of conformity? How individualized can an agent's program of self-fulfillment be before it ceases to be, in any real sense, fulfilling?

I propose to bring the resources of comparative religious ethics to bear on these problems by considering the possibilities for a "middle" position suggested by classical Confucian ritual practice (see Van Norden 1996 and Yearley 1990 on the prospects of comparative study between Chinese and Western ethical sources). The *Analects* of Confucius (ca. 552–479 B.C.E.) serves as an interesting foil, for instance, to Taylor's diagnosis of the modern Western malaise (Taylor 1991, 1–12). For, at least on one reading, the *Analects* challenges the very possibility of a breach between universal and individual modalities of human flourishing.

Two influential interpretations of the *Analects*—*Confucius: The Secular as Sacred* by Herbert Fingarette and *Thinking through Confucius* by David L. Hall and Roger T. Ames—have made advances in bringing the rich heritage of classical Confucian thought into contemporary philosophical debates. The former points out that full ritual participation involves a high degree of personal investment. The latter points out that ritual also involves a certain degree of innovation: when new situations are confronted, the good person must imaginatively determine the most appropriate means of expressing himself or herself. Unfortunately, some of what these readings of the *Analects* have contributed to contemporary ethical reflection is obscured by the extreme character of the ethical positions they recommend. Fingarette, following a particular aspect of J. L. Austin's work on performative utterances (Austin 1961, 1962a, 1962b) and certain features of Gilbert Ryle's theory of the mind (Ryle 1949), allows almost no place for the "inner life" of the individual outside traditional social forms and so disregards the individual component of human flourishing. In Hall and Ames's account of ritual innovation, by contrast, individuals are almost completely free of the confines of tradition in their quest for personal significance; they thus disregard that aspect of human flourishing that stems from a substantive conception of basic human potentialities or human nature.[3] Both interpretations, by treating Confucian thought one-sidedly, fail to appreciate the delicate and impressive balance that the *Analects* puts before us.

Confucius's thought on ritual is subject to these two disparate readings for the simple reason that a commitment to the efficacy of tradition and a commitment to the activation of the individual agent's deepest and most personal motives are both necessary conditions for full ritual participation. Although it may be expedient to distinguish them for the purposes of philosophical clarity, they are integrally—albeit delicately—related in actual practice. For Confucius, the rites embody all of the virtues and trace out the proper place of human beings within their physical and/or metaphysical environment. Thus, one cannot express *anything* human, much less anything as complexly human as one's (unique) innermost aspirations, without recourse to them. On the other hand, no one springs from the womb either virtuous or ritually competent. Ritual appropriateness must be learned, and it takes root in a person gradually. The virtues, too, must be learned. Those that do bloom in us must (first) sprout and grow out of the uneven soil of each person's unique assemblage of dispositions, talents, sensitivities, and blind spots. Accordingly, we are moved to the rites' exemplification of true humanity by our deepest and most personal motives or not at all. Ritual participation allows us to express simultaneously what is most unique about us, as well as what is most human because it requires a correlation of the two.

As the focus of this essay shifts from the matter of interpreting the *Analects* to the broader implications of the ethical positions recommended by Fingarette and Hall and Ames, it will become clear that my analysis favors a virtue approach not only to Confucianism, but also to the good life as such. My aim is to use these two disparate readings of ritual self-cultivation to help articulate a plausible means of counterbalancing an overly restrictive conception of human flourishing with an overly indulgent one. The presentation of what I take to be a more balanced reading of the *Analects* will consequently be in the service of a broader affirmation of virtue ethics.[4] In defending my approach to classical Confucianism, I also seek (1) to defend virtue ethics from the objection that it is intrinsically conformist and oppressive and (2) to demonstrate that virtue ethics can, and indeed must, take seriously the individual aspect of human flourishing.

2. Fingarette's Reading of the *Analects*

In *Confucius: The Secular as Sacred*, Fingarette seeks first and foremost to impress upon us that ritual behavior is not simply following rules. Singing the national anthem at a public sporting event, for instance, amounts to more than raising one's right hand, placing it over one's heart, and singing the right words. It matters how one sings it, how one holds oneself, whether one faces the flag, whether or not one puts down one's hot dog. To a person up in the stands at such an event, with a contingent of elderly fans on one side and a brood of unruly children on the other, it is obvious that there are more and less serious ways of participating in this American ritual. Consider Fingarette's remarks concerning what a successful or correct ritual (lǐ 禮) entails:

> there are two contrasting kinds of failure in carrying out lǐ: the
> ceremony may be awkwardly performed for lack of learning and skill;
> or the ceremony may have a surface slickness but yet be dull,
> mechanical for lack of serious purpose and commitment. Beautiful and
> effective ceremony requires the personal "presence" to be fused with
> learned ceremonial skill. (1972, 8)

He uses the example of shaking hands to illustrate this point. When the ritual functions properly, both people stick out their hands at the same time, apply the same pressure to their grip, shake up and down with comparable vigor and for a comparable duration. They then let go at the same time. Neither person grimaces in pain from an overly firm grip. Neither is left hanging on when the other person begins to retract his or her palm. Moreover, there is a spirit of at least pleasantness, if not friendship, proper to this ritual. A limp and regretful intertwining of thumbs cannot convey what handshaking is supposed to convey: friendship, a greeting, an agreement.

If this seems neither new nor distinctive, Fingarette's characterization of the communal unity facilitated by ritual activity as the "consummation of humanity" is both (1972, 64–65). *Confucius: The Secular as Sacred* emphasizes the power and function of ritual as a means of shaping the members of a community to fit certain antecedently valued patterns of interaction. Although Confucius himself may have been a great cultural innovator, Fingarette does not think that the followers of Confucius are at liberty to change the lǐ.[5] Instead, they are guided in their imitation of these pre-established patterns of ritual interaction until they have incorporated into their own personalities the values that the rituals embody. Presumably, only sages fully internalize the lǐ.

We might grant all this, though, and still ask *why* Confucius does not encourage his disciples to interpret the rituals in whatever ways make the most sense to them. I think Fingarette would answer that this is because ritual is, at root, a communal phenomenon. In order for a handshake to be interpreted as a ritual greeting, as an expression of friendship, or as signifying a binding agreement of some kind, there has to be communal knowledge and acceptance that this is what clasping hands means.

> There is no power of lǐ if there is no learned and accepted convention, or if we utter the words and invoke the power of the convention in an inappropriate setting, or if the ceremony is not fully carried out, or if the persons carrying out the ceremonial roles are not those properly authorized. . . . In short, the peculiarly moral yet binding power of ceremonial gesture and word cannot be abstracted from or used in isolation from ceremony. (Fingarette 1972, 12)

Tradition and custom are part and parcel of what ritual is. According to Fingarette, lǐ is not like malleable wax, a vague and amorphous cultural form onto which one's novelty may be impressed; rather, it is a humane mold that directs and shapes the uncultivated person's desires (see Schofer 1993; Tu 1979a, 1985a, 1985b, 1985c; and Yearley n.d. for concurring arguments). Although Fingarette recognizes that a great deal of personal investment is required for successful or correct ritual, he argues that this must be supplemented by an emphasis on learning and the implementation of accepted conventions. More than shaping our raw impulses by any lǐ whatsoever, we become fully human when we participate in particularly those lǐ our culture(s) take(s) to be constitutive of the human.

This is all true and unobjectionable. We do not get at what is radical and dubious in Fingarette's position until we see that he presents tradition not simply as one important rationale for ritual, but as more or less the only rationale. In Fingarette's view, Confucius not only gives tradition primacy over "effective command" and "common agreement" (1972, 62), he gives it the "effective emotional-moral authority for lǐ, whatever other ideological, philosophical or religious frame might be added" (1972, 64). Tradition is the beginning and end of how the lǐ are justified for Fingarette, quite apart from beliefs about what human beings or the world are like. As he presents the case, we engage in ritual not because it embodies humaneness (rén 仁) but because (the other way around, if you will) it embodies what tradition says humaneness is. Without recourse to substantive views about human nature or basic human capacities, ritual is reduced to a narrow form of social conditioning or etiquette.

Fingarette arrives at this interpretation through a complicated series of reconstructions of the purpose behind Confucius's moral and political teachings. To a large degree, this reconstruction—which Fingarette regards as the most charitable reading of the *Analects*—is driven by his twofold assumption that Confucius *could* have conceived of a nontraditional alternative to his own position (1972, 57–59) and that he *would* have done so had he known as much about the diversity of cultures as we do today. Consider the following passage from *Confucius: The Secular as Sacred*:

> Confucius seems to take for granted . . . that there is one li and that it is
> in harmony with a greater, cosmic *Tao* [*Dào* 道]. He assumes that this li
> is the li of the land in which he lives (other lands being barbarian),
> that the Ancients of his tradition lived this li. He assumes that this li,
> and the cosmic *Tao* [*Dào*] in which it is rooted, are internally coherent
> and totally adequate, and that, finally, the only moral and social
> necessity is, therefore, to shape oneself and one's conduct in li. Each
> and every one of these interconnected and basic assumptions is initially
> placed in grave doubt when we take account of the now familiar facts
> of a plurality of great cultures each with its distinct history. (1972, 57)

Fingarette seems to assume that a great thinker could not possibly adopt an apologetic stance toward his or her own tradition when faced with a plurality of great cultures. Because he thinks it uncharitable to view the *Analects* in this light, however, he must find another explanation for Confucius's unremitting appeal to tradition. The explanation he settles on is that the *Analects* represents a calculated political maneuver to raise the traditional rites of Confucius's home state to a universal status. "Given the relative physical weakness of [the] tiny [state of] Lu," Fingarette writes, "it was a natural tactic for a man of Lu to turn attention not to military conquest but to cultural conquest as the primary basis for order and unity" (1972, 61).

Yet, if we take this to be the "real story" about Confucius, the ethics of the *Analects* becomes somewhat suspect. That is, if Fingarette is right, then Confucius is really advocating the rites just because he wants his own culture to be "on top" and not because he thinks the rites of Lu embody the culmination of human endeavor, the "consummation of humanity." I believe that there are strong reasons to reject this presumption. Although I do believe that, ultimately, it is interpretive charity that leads Fingarette to neglect the metaphysical underpinnings of the *Analects*, it remains a significant oversight to characterize the lǐ as only a modality of civilized social interaction. To think that the classical Chinese were only interested in maintaining their traditional rituals because they represent the way things were always done is to do them a great disservice indeed.[6] It seems much more charitable to think that Confucius was not recommending lǐ only on the basis of tradition, but because of a complex set of moral and political arguments ultimately supported by a coherent, if not wholly persuasive, picture of what human beings and the world are like.

In the final analysis, then, it is Fingarette's overstating of the case regarding Confucius's lack of interest in metaphysics that leads me to contend that he slights the individual side of full human flourishing. Although I agree that "[l]ooking at these 'ceremonies' through the image of lǐ, we realize that explicitly sacred rite can be seen as an . . . extension of everyday civilized intercourse" (1972, 11), I do not think this is *all* they are for Confucius. They also express a deeper relationship between optimally humane behavior and the picture of the world represented by the *Way of the Sage Kings of Old.*[7] What makes the particular way of life Confucius advocates optimally humane is its expressing perfectly the place of human beings within the context of society, societies within the context of the larger world, and the larger world within the context of what Fingarette calls the "Cosmic *Dao.*" That is to say, the consummation of humaneness is not merely "fitting in" or being a fully socialized, graceful, and avid participator in society. At least for Confucius, it is virtue, and virtue has everything to do with what one takes to be the nature of human beings and their proper place within their physical and/or metaphysical environment. By severing metaphysics from the traditional justificatory framework supporting the rites, Fingarette makes it impossible for ritual participants (in his model) to pursue virtue for anything but conformist (and so, instrumental) reasons. Again, Fingarette is right to draw out the way ritual practices depend on a communally shared interpretive framework, but he does not appreciate the extent to which it is individual ethical agents, judging the explanatory merits of a given framework within the context of their own experience, who either grant the practice a central place in their lives or not. I will endeavor to bring out the individual component of ritual participation more fully in my own reading of the *Analects* below.

3. Hall and Ames's Reading of the *Analects*

The underlying theme of *Thinking through Confucius* is that although self-cultivators are "counseled by [their] tradition" and its rituals, they must nevertheless "evaluate and alter this tradition in pursuit of appropriateness" (Hall and Ames 1987, 100). It is my contention that this reading of the *Analects* and the ethical views it recommends slights the communal side of full human flourishing. Ritual practice is not, as they would have us think, a modality of creatively adorning the already formed self; rather, it is a means whereby the self is shaped by pre-existing standards already valued by a community. There is, as we have seen, a certain amount of innovation we might apply to the cultural forms we inherit—minimally, this is a sensitivity to context in ritual settings—but in no way does this warrant Hall and Ames's vocabulary of authoring and creating. To their credit, they are forthright about the radical nature of the interpretation they are recommending, and I admire their attempt to disrupt the orthodox assumption that Confucius's thought represents a "conservative, order-imposing philosophical system" (1987, 100). Still, as we will see, significant objections can be lodged against their reading of the *Analects*—both as a textual interpretation and as a philosophical position.

In the section entitled "The Sage as Virtuoso" (1987, 275–83), Hall and Ames develop their notion of ritual qua creative innovation with regard to musical performance. Given their vision of the rituals as fluid and interchangeable according to the varying needs of personal meaningfulness, one can see why they were drawn to this metaphor for lǐ. Their view of music clearly implies their ideal for all ritual activity: "As with ritual action, music begins as a repository through which meaning can be transmitted and from which it can be appropriated. However . . . it further serves as a malleable apparatus for displaying one's own innovative contributions" (1987, 279). Two main points are made in this pivotal section of the book. The first is that personal investment is required for ritual or music to function properly. Hall and Ames write that "[r]itual action and music, without the sincerity and commitment of the particular person, are bald and trivial" (1987, 278–79). As we have seen, Fingarette also holds this view. However, Hall and Ames's second main point—that ritual appropriateness involves innovating or changing the rites—takes this concern further than any other recent commentary.

Hall and Ames's view of Confucian ritual practice may be likened to the improvisation of jazz musicians. According to this metaphor, self-cultivators participate in ritual much as jazz artists improvise on the songs and styles that engage their imaginations. Self-cultivators are not limited to the specific ritual forms they inherit, for, by definition, improvisation allows these to be changed according to the requirements of greater individual expression. Without depreciating the range of interpretive freedom accessible to virtuoso soloists in a classical orchestral performance, classical music—in contrast to jazz—is primarily a matter of presenting and re-presenting previously arranged compositions.[8]

A charitable way of looking at this account would be to suggest that behind Hall and Ames's radical reading lies the warranted concern that lǐ not be conceived as mechanistic rule-following. Beyond Fingarette's point that personal investment is required for proper ritual, they claim that the power of ritual is context specific, "qualified by a unique set of circumstances" (1987, 273). This is an extremely important component of Confucian ritual practice and one that Hall and Ames are very good at drawing out (see also Ivanhoe 1990). In order to inspire the kinds of attitudes that make for good or successful ritual, sages must know how to apply the *appropriate ritual appropriately to the appropriate situation.*

From these sound beginnings, however, Hall and Ames arrive at the unsound conclusion that "Confucius' social and political philosophy gives priority to aesthetic over rational ordering" (1987, 158). These terms of art are defined as follows:

> To the extent that our social interactions are limited by appeal to a preestablished pattern of relatedness, be it political or religious or cultural, and to the extent that we conform to and express this pattern as containing habits, customs, rules, or laws determinative of our conduct, we are constituted as a "rational" or "logical" order. . . . [T]o the degree that we interact without obligatory recourse to rule or ideal or principle, and to the extent that the various orders which characterize our modes of togetherness are functions of the insistent particularities whose uniqueness comprise the orders, we are authors of an "aesthetic" composition. (1987, 134)

Again, the metaphor of musical improvisation is a pivotal one in Hall and Ames's conception of ritual practice. Self-cultivators improvise on cultural themes much as jazz musicians improvise on musical themes. Giving pride of place to creative innovation in this manner, however, leaves open the possibility that innovators might make up new songs or rituals entirely—if, say, none of the traditional ones were to catch their fancy. Innovators might play traditional songs, but they are also at liberty to play them in new ways, choosing from among the melodies and refrains those that best reflect their quest for personal meaningfulness. The Taoist sage Zhuāngzǐ 莊子, in one striking example from the history of Chinese philosophy, may mourn for the death of his wife by banging on a tub with his legs splayed out (Graham 1986, 123) or, it would seem, by doing anything at all. For their part, Hall and Ames privilege "aesthetic ordering" to such a degree in the justification of the rites that (in ritual practice) "truth and reality are ultimately personal categories, unique for each participant" (1987, 159).

What Hall and Ames fail to appreciate is that one could not derive personal meaning from the rituals of one's culture without there being communal meanings already there for one's choosing. Although we certainly can pick from a tradition's rituals those we will participate in and those we will not, we cannot decide at will what a particular ritual means independent of what that tradition says it means. When and if we decide to participate in certain rituals, leaving others behind, what we are really choosing from are the meanings already assigned to them. However much we exercise whatever choice we have as to who we are— however "authentic" we may be—all of our possibilities are still given to us by our culture.[9] When we first awake to a degree of self-consciousness and survey what we can make out of our interpretive world, we see that we are already "thrown into" it (Heidegger 1927/1962, 188–224).

Taking a public ritual like handshaking and deciding that for oneself it will signify hostility and ill will rather than greeting or friendship—engaging in jazz-type, as opposed to classical-type, ritual activity—has two serious consequences for one's flourishing. First, it all but guarantees that no one will understand what one is seeking to convey in such a gesture. Everyone shakes hands with will think themselves liked when in actuality they are despised. Whether or not Zhuāngzǐ (in the instance cited above) intended his banging on the tub as a sort of mourning ritual, his friend Huìzǐ 惠子 could not have recognized it as such. Upon finding Zhuāngzǐ thus engaged, Huìzǐ exclaims, "When you have lived with someone . . . and brought up children, and grown old together, to refuse to bewail her death would be bad enough, but to drum on a pot and sing—could there be anything more shameful?" (Graham 1986, 123). A second consequence of substantially altering public rituals to fit one's private specifications is even more significant: to turn one's back on much of what one's culture deems human is to turn one's back on any possibility of a fully human life in that community. Granted, if one only changes a few rituals, one might still aspire to a good human life by participating in a whole host of others. Clearly, certain rituals are more central to a tradition or culture than others. Nevertheless, it would seem that a certain threshold of cultural participation or ritual proficiency would have to be crossed before one's innovations could even be recognized as a challenge to custom or tradition.

The power of communally accepted forms of cultural expression to shape and guide behavior largely hinges upon their communal acceptance. It is only under very specific conditions that traditional rituals can be changed without significantly dissipating this power. In this connection, it is notable that there are no examples in the *Analects* of Confucius changing a rite and only one example of his even slightly modifying one (Ivanhoe 1991b, 248). The interests of personal expression, although important, do not represent an exception to this general feature of ritual practice. The individual goods of personal expression and meaningfulness cannot be divorced from the normative goods of communally accepted beliefs and practices without a net loss in flourishing.

For all its insistence upon the personal investment of each individual participant, then, Confucian ritual practice is still more fruitfully compared to classical orchestral music than to jazz improvisation. Even supposing that a Confucian virtue like filial piety could be theoretically *generated* by the criterion of personal expression (which itself seems doubtful), it is unclear how it could be *sustained* as a motive in people's lives on such terms. How often would we be respectful and caring toward our parents if such responses were based solely on their fitting into our quest for personal meaning and if we did not believe that, in general, such responses represent more or less inherent goods? I submit that it would not be often enough. The Confucian requirement that full virtue be pursued for its own sake out of a sense of enjoyment offers a more balanced understanding of the relationship between these sometimes competing goods. I will endeavor to articulate this balance in my own reading of the *Analects* below.

4. An Alternative Reading of the *Analects*

There is much that is plausible about both Fingarette's and Hall and Ames's readings of the *Analects*. Fingarette rightly emphasizes the communal nature of ritual self-cultivation; Hall and Ames have gone a long way in showing that ritual self-cultivation can be an avenue for highly specific visions of the good life. Still, an alternative reading must be sought that better appreciates how values that are thought to stem from a substantive conception of human nature might be inculcated without undoing the individuality of ethical agents. Such an appreciation is as much for its own sake as it is for the purposes of coming to a truer understanding of the human situation (in conversation with Western ethical sources). I am convinced it is possible to interpret Confucius in such a way as to retain what is plausible in Fingarette and Hall and Ames without going to the extremes at which each, as we have seen, becomes implausible. The basis for my alternative reading is the manner in which the lǐ are justified in the *Analects*.

It is, first, important to recognize, contrary to Fingarette, that there is something inherently stable or determined in the picture of the world the *Analects* assumes and advocates. Confucius maintains the traditional ritual practices on a basis he and his predecessors, contemporaries, and followers would be likely to accept: namely, that they encapsulate what the *Sage Kings of Old* discovered to be the proper place of human beings within their physical and/or metaphysical environment. This involves at least two kinds of justification. On the one hand, the justification is practical. The *Way of the Sage Kings of Old* is the most efficacious means of organizing society. Confucius does not fear the uncouthness of the "barbarians," for instance, because he thinks that the example of true humanity is sufficient to transform and sustain the Empire (*Analects* 2:1, 4:25). For him, "The virtue of the gentleman is like the wind; the virtue of the small man is like grass. Let the wind blow over the grass and it is sure to bend" (Lau 1979, 115–16).

On the other hand, Confucius's justification of the rites is metaphysical (that is, it has recourse to metaphysics). Although I grant Fingarette's point that Confucius was uninterested in speculation about the nature of heaven or of the *Dao* (*Analects* 5:13, 7:21), this does not itself entail that Confucius had no views about the way the world is. He clearly did have such views. He is recorded in *Analects* 7:23, among other places, as claiming that "Heaven [tiān] is the author of the virtue that is in [him]" (Lau 1979, 89). Indeed, it is precisely because virtue, encapsulated in the lǐ, initiates and sustains a harmonious relationship between human nature and the larger world that the *Way of the Sage Kings of Old* is the most efficacious means of ordering society. As Yǒuzǐ 有子 remarks in *Analects* 1:12, "to aim always at harmony without regulating it by the rites simply because one knows only about harmony will not, in fact, work" (Lau 1979, 61). The very roots of "virtue" (dé 德) have, as Philip J. Ivanhoe notes, very strong metaphysical overtones (1993). Ivanhoe suggests that as early as the Shang Dynasty (ca. the twelfth century B.C.E.) this character conveyed "a kind of power which accrued to and resided within an individual who had acted favorably toward a spirit or another person" (1993, 1–2). Closely connected to *tiān* ("Heaven") and *mìng* 命 ("mandate," "decree," "command," or "fate"), *dé* alternately denoted a power granted to some by Heaven (especially rulers) and a power a person gradually accumulated through good acts (Ivanhoe 1993, 2). In either case, it refers to a character trait human beings may possess or lack according to the strength of their affiliation with "the order of things."

The normative thrust of the *Analects* comes out of what we can piece together of this twofold justificatory framework. Those seeking virtue practice the rites in order to inculcate the values they embody into their personalities. In the beginning stages, this would seem to entail following the rituals even though one's awareness of these values may be dim and imperfect. It may even involve the pursuit of virtue for instrumental reasons.[10] But at later stages of ethical development—when, for instance, the self-cultivator may be said to be a competent participant in ritual—the rites are pursued for their own sake and performed with optimum degrees of personal investment. What makes the life that embodies and expresses the Confucian virtues (especially *rén*) desirable for its own sake—the ultimate justification of Confucian self-cultivation—is its placing oneself (and others) into a harmonious relationship with the *Dào*.

The complex relationship between *lǐ* and *rén* culminates in the Confucian requirement that virtue be pursued for its own sake *with a sense of enjoyment.*[11] Just as high levels of personal investment must accompany formal ritual proficiency, an approbatory, affective disposition toward virtue must accompany formally good actions. This requirement is, I think, evident throughout the *Analects* (for example, 16:5, 4:16), but perhaps it finds its most eloquent expression in *Analects* 4:2: "The benevolent [*rén*] man is attracted to benevolence [*rén*] because he feels at home in it" (Lau 1979, 72). What does it mean to feel "at home" in virtue? Clearly, it is not just performing acts that most people would judge to be good if given a general description of them. Much more substantially, it is *hào dé* 好德, "to be fond of virtue";[12] *hào rén* 好仁, "to be fond of ren" (*Analects* 4:6); *hào lǐ* 好禮, "to be fond of ritual appropriateness" (1:15, 13:4, 14:41); *hào yì* 好義, "to be fond of ethical uprightness" (12:20, 13:4); *hào xìn* 好信, "to be fond of trustworthiness" (13:4); and *yù shàn* 欲善, "to desire excellence" (12:19, 15:10). Lacking the disposition to enjoy virtue, we fall short of full humanity regardless of the outward forms our actions take. As in *Analects* 2:7, to endeavor to care for one's parents without the proper reverence is to treat them like domestic animals or pets.

5. Conformity, Individuality, and the Nature of Virtue

I have argued that Hall and Ames's view of ritual as innovation does not do justice to the extent to which the quest for personal meaningfulness is shaped by pre-existing cultural forms. This is as far as I want to take a criticism of their reading of the *Analects*. It is Fingarette's reading that presents the greatest challenge to my own position and that it is most edifying to rebut at length. His downplaying of the extent to which Confucius's justification of the rites has recourse to substantive views about the nature of human beings and of the world—and here I move beyond the matter of interpreting the *Analects*—throws into relief a common objection to virtue ethics: namely, that the inculcation of community values is all social conditioning with little or no place for the "inner life" of the individual.

This objection to virtue ethics takes at least three different forms. The first is that a dispositional model of the self and the habitual model of ethical development that follows from it inherently undermine individuality. Critics suppose that someone who believes that good habits are a prerequisite of both "the that" and "the because" of the good life—employing the terms of M. F. Burnyeat's classic study of Aristotle's account of moral education (1980, 71–85)—must a fortiori hold that bad habits can only be corrected by oppressive paternalism or brute force. Neither, it is to be granted, is consistent with a respect for individual uniqueness.

Certain presentations of a virtue approach to ethics, more than others, seem to highlight what leads to the first sort of objection. One reading of Alasdair MacIntyre's *AfterVirtue*, for instance, seems to call for a return to the "narrative" models of the self evident in heroic societies (where there may be no such thing as an "individual" ethical agent apart from social roles). "In heroic society," MacIntyre writes, "there is no 'outside' except that of the stranger. A man who tried to withdraw himself from his given position in heroic society would be engaged in the enterprise of trying to make himself disappear" (1984, 126). MacIntyre thus laments as a loss what the (liberal) defenders of the Enlightenment see as decisive progress: namely, "the achievement by the self of its proper autonomy" wherein "[it] had been liberated from all those outmoded forms of social organization which had imprisoned it simultaneously within a belief in a theistic and teleological world order and within those hierarchical structures which attempted to legitimate themselves as part of such a world order" (1984, 60).

The second objection concerns the political implications of the first objection. Judith Shklar's work exemplifies the worry that a substantive conception of the good life, when enforced by the power of the state, leads to the worst kinds of political tyranny and cruelty. She argues that "the absolute prohibition against any efforts by government to impose disposition, not to mention motives of duty, upon citizens" ought to remain in full force because "[i]t is by keeping its hands off our characters that governments provide the setting and conditions in which we might begin our poor but epic battle against vice" (1984, 235). Kant's contribution to a liberal moral ideal that counters Aristotle's aristocratic "great-souled man" is praised in this connection.

The third objection is that whatever resources virtue theory does have for appreciating individuality pale in comparison to the resources of other approaches to ethics. Deontology has Kant's powerful advocacy of autonomy, the "right to make otherwise morally permissible decisions about matters deeply affecting one's own life without interference by controlling threats and bribes, manipulations, and willful distortion of relevant information" (Hill 1991, 48). To be sure, strong measures that protect agency are ready to hand in neo-Kantian ethics. Servility, for example, is denounced: "To the extent that a person gives even tacit consent to humiliations incompatible with this respect, he will be acting as if he waives a right which he cannot in fact give up" (Hill 1991, 16). Utilitarians have their staunch advocate of the individual in John Stuart Mill. For Mill, "It is not by wearing down into uniformity all that is individual in themselves, but by culti- vating it, and calling it forth, within the limits imposed by the rights and inter- ests of others, that human beings become a noble and beautiful object of contemplation." (1859/1975, 59). Insofar as contemporary virtue theory evolved in opposition to the exaggerated forms of individualism arising out of this kind of emphasis on personal development, its treatment of the ethical importance of individuality is muted at best.

I believe that the alternative reading of Confucian ritual practice sketched above yields at least a provisional answer to this objection in its several forms. Against Fingarette's reading of the *Analects*, I hope to show that there are resources within the discourse of Confucian ritual practice for the sustenance of, if not the encour- agement of, whatever part of human flourishing may reasonably be said to stem from a person's sense of his or her individual uniqueness.[13] My reasoning has two parts. I believe, first, that this form of individuality has a de facto validity in human flourishing. Second, I believe that it is integrally related to the reasons that moti- vate what Confucius (as well as Aristotle) takes to be true or full virtue.

One need be neither a neo-Kantian nor a utilitarian to appreciate the impor- tance of "the individual" for an ethical life or even for a minimally satisfying life. Kant and Mill do offer powerful ways of articulating this. However, there are other philosophical frameworks that might also be made to serve an ethical interest in individuality. We might, for example, come via Heidegger to the view that human beings are creatures with unique histories that enter into how they think, feel, and act (Taylor 1985a is one example of such an approach). Still, whether one's paradigm is Heideggerian or Humean, to suggest that human beings are only what their cultures make them—as I think Fingarette's position does when fol- lowed through to its logical extension—is to suggest a half-truth. Alongside the need to realize a vision of a good life for human beings generally (stemming from what is thought to be human nature or from a set of basic human capacities), there is a "need to possess a distinct history, which is one's own and not that of all mankind, and . . . to cultivate that which is particular and . . . believed to be the best of this time and of that place." (Hampshire 1983, 158). We are, decid- edly, what our cultures make us, but we are also what we make of ourselves.

Both the possibility of choosing one or another way of understanding one's identity and the subsequent possibility of choosing to act in conformity with that understanding seem to be given in each new moment of experience. This is the case even though the content of one's range of possible self-understandings is entirely determined by acculturation. A certain degree of individuality also retains a de facto validity in a sense pertaining to agency. Mill seems to be pointing to this when he insists that "[t]he same strong susceptibilities which make the personal impulses vivid and powerful, are also the source from whence are generated the passionate love of virtue, and the sternest self-control" (1859/1975, 57). Human beings act purposively. Moreover, our actions have motives, some of which must be seen to stem from our identities. We seek to realize ends which, at some level, it must be possible to say that we desire for ourselves. We act in one way rather than another, desire one thing rather than another, partly because of who we take ourselves (uniquely) to be and who we (uniquely) are. Stuart Hampshire brings out this connection well with regard to aesthetic experience:

> In cases where the imaginative response is especially strong, there will be no direct, traceable path from a set of original experiences to the highly specific visual or musical forms to which the person responds. Nor will there be any evident and generalizable relation between any set of experiences and the specific forms which convey this effect to the person's imagination. The memories involved are too many, too confused and too blurred by their past interactions, probably extending into the person's childhood, beyond the range of conscious recall and analysis. The vast capacity and scope of the art of Shakespeare or of Titian create a space into which a great variety of fused memories can enter: suggestions of happiness, of loss, of transience, of love, of innocence, and of old age. Into these inchoate and unparticularised suggestions, as into a vast, unfurnished cave, each person insinuates some highly specific version of these indefinite themes, which he finds sharply realized in the specific forms of the works before him. (1989, 126–27)

The diverse materials that make up the "wellsprings" of action are extremely complex and cannot be accommodated to universalizable maxims or laws, at least not fully.[14]

Granting individuality this kind of validity, however, need not lead to moral subjectivism, "the view that moral positions are not in any way grounded in reason or the nature of things but are ultimately just adopted by each of us because we find ourselves drawn to them" (Taylor 1991, 18). That it is only we ourselves (and those who have achieved a certain threshold of insight into our identities) who can navigate this vast and uneven terrain ought not to invalidate either the motives that are shaped in traveling it or the reasons we find (and give) along the way. We saw in the previous section that The Way of the Sage Kings of Old represents what is a more or less determined picture of the world implicit in

Confucian ritual self-cultivation. (Other examples of "determinedness" could be drawn from other ethical traditions.) Confucians inculcate into their personalities not whatever "rings true" for them, but the specific truths these sage kings are thought to have discovered about the proper place of human beings within nature and society. Taylor's account of the "inescapable" relationship between normative moral "sources" and human agency helps to pinpoint the significance of this difference.

Following Frankfurt (1971), Taylor argues that the capacity to form and cultivate "second-order desires" exemplifies the kind of agency we recognize as human (1985b, 16). Whereas all creatures (including human beings) exhibit desire *simpliciter* (for example, the desire for food, for sexual satisfaction, and for shelter), only human beings seem to exhibit the desire to have certain kinds of desires (and not others). Second-order desires represent our aspirations to exemplify or avoid character traits respectively valued or devalued by the communities in which we live. Above all, they have to do with the quality of our motivations, arising out of the twofold question, What sorts of people pursue a given activity and why would I want to be one of them? The answers we give make use of contrasting evaluative categories like "higher and lower, virtuous and vicious, more and less fulfilling, more and less refined, profound and superficial, noble and base" (Taylor 1985b, 16). Although this view is not without its formidable detractors, all we need draw from Taylor for our present purposes is the requirement that our ideal of humanity "stand independent of our own desires, inclinations, or choices, that it represent standards by which these desires and choices are judged" (1989, 20).[15] Within the context of Confucianism, it is the metaphysical, ontological, psychological, and cosmological standards implicit in the *Way of the Sage Kings of Old* that provide the normative framework in which evaluative distinctions become intelligible. Without them, the pursuit of virtue could only be instrumentally motivated and ritual practice would collapse into social adaptation: either the philistinism of the "village worthy" (*Analects* 17:13) or the Machiavellian posturing of the profiteer (*Analects* 4:16, 5:25, 17:17).

In the way that I have used it here, true or full virtue is made up of second-order rather than first-order desires. More than merely wanting to do what virtuous people do—to mimic the outward form their actions take or to reap whatever social advantages their states of character might afford them—the content of the complex desire to be virtuous is wanting to feel and judge the way virtuous people feel and judge. Pursuing virtue for its own sake is, accordingly, pursuing it as a life qualitatively different from, and significantly better than, all other forms of life. Insofar as true or full virtue must be pursued for its own sake, limiting ethical motivation to instrumental reasoning (in the manner implied by Fingarette's conception of ritual practice, for instance) ipso facto cuts ethical agents off from the highest states of virtue—instrumental reasons, by definition, are directed toward an end beyond a given activity itself. It is equally important to point out, however, that indiscriminately undercutting individuality cuts ethical agents off from the highest states of virtue as well. For in addition to being pursued for its own sake, true or full virtue must be pursued with a sense of enjoyment. However much traditions give ethical agents access to the kinds of practices, values, and justificatory frameworks that make it possible to pursue virtue for its own sake, at some deep level, it is still "individuals" who either enjoy it or not. The scope of "enjoyment," if you will, is individual. If it is to be said of a person that she enjoys virtue for its own sake, then virtue must not only be an end that she judges "in the light of her own experience, [to be] a specific picture of the best and most praiseworthy way of life which is accessible to her," it must also be one that, "more than any other, engages her imagination and her emotions" (Hampshire 1989, 115).

When parents and teachers make use of pronounced psychological force with the young people in their charge, they thus run the risk of damaging the delicate connections of reasons and desires that make up virtue. They run the risk of uprooting the sprouts of virtue (see Mencius 2A6) along with the sprouts of vice. Where the damage is moderate, perhaps a person retains some of his or her sense of individual uniqueness even in absently or despairingly conforming to the cultural forms incumbent upon him or her. But perhaps not. In cases of brutalization or trauma, where the damage is likely to be considerable, the connections of reasons and desires may be severed altogether. "[A]t the moment of trauma," Judith Herman writes,[16] "almost by definition, the individual's point of view counts for nothing. . . . The traumatic event thus destroys the belief that one can be oneself in relation to others" (1992, 53, italics original). In either case, there is "a loss and a waste, which can never be repaired, if we lead our lives always facing outward towards the shared and commonplace business of the world, and always turning our backs on the intimate emotions and perceptions, which are our own peculiar contributions to the sum of human experience" (Hampshire 1989, 128–29).

There are, then, two parts to true or full virtue within (and, I would argue, beyond) the classical Confucian context: (1) doing good things for their own sake and (2) doing good things out of a sense of enjoyment. Each is a necessary condition. Conjoined, they represent a sufficient condition. The Machiavellian profiteer falls short of true or full virtue on the first count. The gruff or reticent ritual participant falls short on the second count. Still, it is in the conformist and in the broken individual that virtue is most manifestly thwarted. For each falls short of true or full virtue on both counts. Neither can be said to choose or desire anything in a robust enough sense to count as choosing it for its own sake. Moreover, they lack a sense of personal uniqueness with respect to which the realization of individual aims and desires could be enjoyable or fulfilling. Accordingly, those in the business of inculcating virtues must respect and cultivate the agent's individuality lest the possibility be lost that he or she will be able to enjoy doing good things when that stage of ethical development is reached where instrumental reasons are left behind and virtue is pursued for its own sake.

6. Concluding Remarks

Fingarette and Hall and Ames all want to bring out what they take to be profound
and relevant aspects of Confucius's thought, but because they reduce the diverse
spectrum of human agency to one or the other of its extreme poles, their interpretive charity only obscures that in Confucius's powerful and enduring cultural
legacy which might help solve some of the problems raised by modern Western
conceptions of selfhood. Though I have not argued that Confucius is superior to
modern Westerners at critical junctures, as Bernard Williams (1993) does with
regard to the early Greeks,[17] I have offered a few examples of where such a case
might be made plausible. I do hope to have shown that Confucian ritual practice
need not be seen as either entirely a matter of innovation, where nothing is
antecedently determined, or as wholly determined, where nothing about the individual remains unique when communally shared values are internalized. Although
there is, of course, considerable diversity within and between the many traditions
of virtue thought—for example, classical Chinese, classical Greek, and Christian—
I also hope to have shown that a virtue approach to ethics need not be seen as
ipso facto entailing the dismantling of the individual. Further exploration into
this aspect of virtue theory is sorely needed.

It is, admittedly, both treacherous and laborious to inculcate virtues in the
manner I describe. To be sure, the interests of the community, which wants its
members to exemplify the character traits it values, are often in conflict with the
interests of individual uniqueness. However, if giving individuals ultimate say
over what constitutes humaneness leaves the door open to inhumane behaviors,
denying individual uniqueness a place in ethical development only serves to
diminish that humaneness. Moreover, even if the conflict between community
values and individual uniqueness is as intractable as Hampshire suggests (1983),
this does not necessarily reflect a defect in the account of ethical development I
have outlined. One can only be as exact, or as palliative, as one's subject matter
allows.

Aristotle thought, quite rightly, that it is possible to explain a phenomenon too
much. When formulating a description of human life, for instance, we might be
tempted to make it out to be better than it really is: more simple, more orderly,
more manageable, less tragic, and so on. Aristotle began his inquiry into the
human good with the testimony of "the many and wise" (as opposed to taking one
wise person's word for it) because he thought it was important to "save" certain
tensions, ambiguities, and puzzles (Nussbaum 1986, 240–63). What he was after
in inviting such a diversity of opinion (and thus such controversy) was the fullest
and most accurate description of human life. As Nussbaum points out, "over-
simplification and reduction will be deep and ever-present dangers. . . . In our
anxiety to control and grasp the uncontrolled . . . we may all too easily become
distant from the lives that we originally wished to control" (1986, 260). We need

accurate descriptions of what human beings are like before we can begin to give an account of what kinds of lives might be good (or best) for them. Where distortions in the former lead inexorably to distortions in the latter, the result is conception of the good more appropriate to gods or beasts than to human beings. Either is catastrophic for the prospects of ethical development outlined here. For god-like or beast-like virtues can only mutilate the humanity of those who seek to cultivate them (and those upon whom they are impressed). To borrow an image from the *Mencius* (a compilation of the teachings and ideas of the later Confucian thinker Mencius), it would be like making cups and bowls from the wood of a willow tree (6A1). Not only does cutting and beveling willow wood mutilate its unique qualities, it also does not yield very durable dishware.

NOTES

This essay, which was originally published with minor modifications in the *Journal of Religious Ethics* 23.2 (fall 1995): 263–89, has benefited from the diverse efforts of many. My discussion of individuality, for instance, owes much to conversations with Van Harvey. I would like to thank Mark Berkson, Arnold Eisen, Thomas Lewis, Derek Ling, John Reeder Jr., Mark Unno, Bryan Van Norden, Lee Yearley, and the JRE's anonymous referees for their generous comments and suggestions. My deepest gratitude, however, is to P. J. Ivanhoe, without whose inspiration, support, and tireless enthusiasm, this project would not have been possible. (Citations of the *Analects* follow the sectioning in Lau.)

1. See Hampshire 1989, 126–27, for an instance of the view that the ultimate sources of individuality are unknowable. That we value individuality at all is owing to the fact "[t]hat the sources of individuality are untraceable, and that we cannot in fact understand a person as a composition of influences" (1989, 123).

2. Taylor's proposed solution, for example, seems to favor a universalist account of human flourishing—one that hinges upon claims about human nature—whereas Hampshire seems to favor a more individualistic account. Hampshire's *Innocence and Experience* is, in part, an articulation of what he sees as detrimental about "well-roundedness" as an ethical ideal. His point of divergence with Aristotle is "precisely this picture of the good person or good human being as necessarily being the perfect human being, rounded and balanced, necessarily not eccentric or lopsided, and the consequent representation of the good for man as to be attained only in the fulfillment of the standard and normal potentialities of human beings in a complete life" (Hampshire 1989, 28). For Hampshire, "There seems to be no necessary connection between being an admirable human being and being a person who is the standard and normal and all-round and, in this sense, perfect human being" (1989, 28).

3. It is harder to trace Hall and Ames's philosophical assumptions to a single thinker or philosophical trend. Although they make some appeals to thinkers like Jacques Derrida and Michel Foucault, perhaps the more plausible source for their conception of the sage as authentic innovator is a certain reading of Friedrich Nietzsche together with elements of Martin Heidegger's thought.

4. My reading is supported by a number of Sinological reviews and studies: Kupperman 1989; Ivanhoe 1991b; Rosemont 1976, 1978; Schwartz 1985.

5. *Analects* 7:1 reveals that Confucius considered himself to be consistent with the *Way of the Sage Kings of Old*: "The Master said: "I transmit but do not innovate; I am truthful in what I say and devoted to antiquity'" (Lau 1979, 86).

6. Even more radically than Fingarette, Robert Eno has argued that the early (classical) Confucians made use of an ambiguity that surrounded the term tiān 天 ("heaven") to create an image of it consistent with their philosophical program, an image that would justify the conception of ritual activity they had already pieced together from various cultural sources: "The initial basis of Confucian claims is unclear. Universal axioms of logical or ontological necessity are not formulated, and direct statements describing empirical bases for Confucian commitments are regularly permeated by vagueness at critical junctures where a modern reader will feel most in need of clarity" (Eno 1990, 3; for reviews, see Ivanhoe 1991a; Shun 1992). Tu Wei-ming, in contrast, advances a view similar to mine: "Confucius may have insisted upon the importance of focusing our attention on life rather than death and on humans rather than gods, but to argue, accordingly, that Confucius was exclusively concerned about the living person here and now in a manner of secular humanism is a gross mistake" (1985d, 1).

7. This expression refers to a Golden Age in which the basic features of civilized human life were thought to have been discovered and instantiated in a perfect social, political, and ethical order. Yáo 堯, Shùn 舜, and Yǔ 禹 are the paradigmatic examples of these sage kings, the Golden Age being thought to have occurred during their respective reigns (2357–2198 B.C.E.). See Schwartz 1985, 16–136; Waley 1939.

8. I am indebted to Mark Berkson for this analogy.

9. *Analects* 2:4 tells us that for fifteen years Confucius did nothing but study the classics, that in the subsequent ten years he learned to identify himself with what they say about the place of human beings in the universe, and that ten more years were required before he had fully identified with the teachings of the classics. Not until he was fifty did he say he understood the *Decree of Heaven*. That is, only after thirty-five years of study and ritual practice did he fully understand the point behind the rituals. Ten additional years passed before he could see whether or not the true meaning of ritual was being carried out in different situations. Only when he was seventy could it be said of him that he embodied the meaning behind the rituals without self-consciously applying himself to their expression. It is ironic that Hall and Ames use these stages as the headings for the chapters in their book, because the image of Confucius undergoing rigorous training (in ritual and the classics) for fifty-five years is fundamentally at odds with their conception of the sage as a creative innovator.

10. Among classical Confucians, Xunzi is especially articulate with regard to the importance of instrumental reasons in the initial stages of self-cultivation.

11. Confucius shares this requirement with Aristotle. Aristotle writes that "no one is good unless they enjoy fine actions; for no one would call him just, e.g., if he did not enjoy doing just actions, or generous if he did not enjoy generous actions, and similarly for the other virtues" (1099a, 19–21). The good person or sage does not merely pursue virtue for instrumental reasons, but because it is inherently desirable and enjoyable.

12. See *Analects* 9:18 and 15:13. In *Analects* 6:20, there is a distinction made between hào 好 and lè 樂, which Lau translates as "being fond of" and "finding joy in," respectively. *Le* is said to be preferable or superior to *hao*. Although I do believe that this distinction is significant, I do not believe it invalidates my point that an approbatory, affective disposition toward virtue is required by true or full virtue. In any case, both being fond of something and taking joy in it are thought to be superior to having mere knowledge of it (zhī 知).

13. Tu Wei-ming calls attention to a similar point: "the road to sagehood is a 'narrow ridge' between spiritual individualism and ethical socialism. Nevertheless, nothing could be further from my intention than to suggest that the Confucian approach undermines either social collectivity or the individual self" (1979b, 22).

14. Even Kant, the advocate of universalizability *par excellence* (once) gave the desire for happiness a rational status and recognized the importance of connecting the requirements of rational morality with the wellsprings of action: "without a God and without a world invisible to us now but hoped for, the glorious ideas of morality are indeed objects of approval and admiration, but not springs of purpose and action. For they do not fulfill in its completeness that end which is natural to every rational being." (1787/1965, 640). Though Kant may very well have given up the idea of a necessary correlation of happiness and moral worth in the *Opus Postumum* (Förster 1992), at least in *Religion within the Limits of Reason Alone*, the question, "What is to result from this right conduct of ours? . . . cannot possibly be [a matter] of indifference to reason" (1793/1960, 4). Human beings cannot help but pursue happiness; but as rational and free, they must also seek to conform themselves to the Moral Law. The highest good is postulated so as to unite these ends (Kant 1788/1993, 113–14) and thus to prevent morality from becoming an "empty figment of the brain" (Kant 1787/1965, 639).

15. Both Flanagan 1990 and Weinstock 1994 deny that there is any inherent connection between Taylor's conception of strong evaluation and human agency per se.

16. For a compelling account of how selfhood may be lost (through rape, incest, and war) and how it might be recovered through therapy, see Herman 1992. For a discussion of attending to the subjective component of injustice in assessing its toll upon victims, see Shklar 1990.

17. The Fingarette and Hall and Ames readings of the *Analects* parallel the "progressivist" interpreters of the early Greek world discussed by Williams, though where the "progressivists" criticized by Williams make characters such as Oedipus and Eteocles overly strange, Fingarette and Hall and Ames have made Confucius too familiar.

REFERENCES

Aristotle. 1985. *Nicomachean Ethics*. 335–332 B.C.E. Translated by Terence Irwin. Indianapolis, Ind.: Hackett Publishing.
Austin, J. L. 1961. "Performative Utterances." In *Philosophical Papers*, 220–39. London: Oxford University Press.
———. 1962a. *How to Do Things with Words*. London: Oxford University Press.
———. 1962b. "Performatif-Constantif." In *La Philosophie Analytique*, 271–305. Cahiers de Royaumont, Phil. no. 5. Paris: Editions de Mincit.
Burnyeat, M. F. 1980. "Aristotle on Learning to Be Good." In *Essays on Aristotle's Ethics*, edited by Amelie Oksenberg Rorty, 69–92. Berkeley and Los Angeles, Calif.: University of California Press.
Eno, Robert. 1990. *The Confucian Creation of Heaven: Philosophy and the Defence of Ritual Mastery*. Albany, N.Y.: SUNY Press.
Fingarette, Herbert. 1972. *Confucius: The Secular as Sacred*. New York: Harper and Row.
Flanagan, Owen. 1990. "Identity and Strong and Weak Evaluation." In *Identity, Character, and Morality: Essays in Moral Psychology*, edited by Owen Flanagan and Amelie Oksenberg Rorty, 37–65. Cambridge, Mass.: M.I.T. Press.
Förster, Eckhart. 1992. " 'Was darf ich hoffen?' Zum Problem der Vereinbarkeit von theoretischer und praktischer Vernuft bei Immanuel Kant." *Zeitschrift für philosophische Forschung* 46:168–85.
Frankfurt, H. 1971. "Freedom of the Will and the Concept of a Person." *Journal of Philosophy* 67.1 (Jan.): 5–20.
Graham, A. C. 1986. *Chuang-Tzu: The Inner Chapters*. London: Unwin Paperbacks.

Hall, David L., and Roger T. Ames. 1987. *Thinking through Confucius*. Albany, N.Y.: SUNY Press.

Hampshire, Stuart. 1983. *Morality and Conflict*. Cambridge, Mass.: Harvard University Press.

————. 1989. *Innocence and Experience*. Cambridge, Mass.: Harvard University Press.

Heidegger, Martin. 1962. *Being and Time*. 1927. Translated by John Macquarrie and Edward Robinson. San Francisco, Calif.: Harper and Row.

Herman, Judith Lewis. 1992. *Trauma and Recovery*. New York: Basic Books.

Hill, Thomas E., Jr. 1991. *Autonomy and Self-Respect*. Cambridge, Eng.: Cambridge University Press.

Ivanhoe, Philip J. 1990. "Reweaving the 'One Thread' of the *Analects*." *Philosophy East and West* 40.1 (Jan.): 17–33.

————. 1991a. Review of *The Confucian Creation of Heaven*, by Robert Eno. *Journal of Asian Studies* 50.4 (Nov.): 907–8.

————. 1991b. Review of *Thinking through Confucius*, by David L. Hall and Roger T. Ames. *Philosophy East and West* 41.2 (Apr.): 241–54.

————. 1993. *Confucian Moral Self-Cultivation*. New York: Peter Lang.

Kant, Immanuel. 1960. *Religion within the Limits of Reason Alone*. 1793. Translated by Theodore M. Greene and Hoyt H. Hudson. New York: Harper and Row.

————. 1965. *Critique of Pure Reason*. 1787. Translated by Norman Kemp Smith. New York: St. Martin's Press.

————. 1993. *Critique of Practical Reason*. 3d ed. 1788. Edited and translated by Lewis White Beck. New York: Macmillan/Library of Liberal Arts.

Kupperman, Joel J. 1989. Review of *Thinking through Confucius*, by David L. Hall and Roger T. Ames. *Harvard Journal of Asiatic Studies* 49.1:251–59.

Lau, D. C., trans. 1979. *Confucius: The Analects*. New York: Penguin Books.

MacIntyre, Alasdair. 1984. *After Virtue*. 2d ed. Notre Dame, Ind.: Notre Dame University Press.

Mill, John Stuart. 1975. *On Liberty*. 1859. Edited by David Spitz. New York: W. W. Norton and Company.

Nussbaum, Martha C. 1986. *The Fragility of Goodness: Luck and Ethics in Greek Tragedy and Philosophy*. Cambridge, Eng.: Cambridge University Press.

Rosemont, Henry, Jr. 1976. Review of *Confucius: The Secular as Sacred*, by Herbert Fingarette. *Philosophy East and West* 26.4 (Oct.): 463–77.

————. 1978. "Reply to Professor Fingarette." *Philosophy East and West* 28.4:515–19.

Ryle, Gilbert. 1949. *The Concept of Mind*. Chicago: University of Chicago Press.

Schofer, Jonathan. 1993. "Virtues in Xunzi's Thought." *Journal of Religious Ethics* 21.1 (spring): 117–36.

Schwartz, Benjamin I. 1985. *The World of Thought in Ancient China*. Cambridge, Mass.: The Belknap Press of Harvard University Press.

Shklar, Judith N. 1984. *Ordinary Vices*. Cambridge, Mass.: The Belknap Press of Harvard University Press.

————. 1990. *The Faces of Injustice*. New Haven, Conn.: Yale University Press.

Shun, Kwong-loi. 1992. Review of *The Confucian Creation of Heaven*, by Robert Eno. *Harvard Journal of Asiatic Studies* 52.2 (Dec.): 739–56.

Taylor, Charles. 1985a. "Self-Interpreting Animals." In *Human Agency and Language: Philosophical Papers 1*, 45–76. Cambridge, Eng.: Cambridge University Press.

————. 1985b. "What Is Human Agency?" In *Human Agency and Language: Philosophical Papers 1*, 15–44. Cambridge: Cambridge University Press.

————. 1989. *Sources of the Self: The Making of Modern Identity*. Cambridge, Mass.: Harvard University Press.

————. 1991. *The Ethics of Authenticity*. Cambridge, Mass.: Harvard University Press.

Tu, Wei-ming. 1979a. "The Creative Tension between Jen and Li." In Humanity and Self-Cultivation: Essays in Confucian Thought, 5–16. Berkeley, Calif.: Asian Humanities Press.

———. 1979b. "Li as Process of Humanization." In Humanity and Self-Cultivation: Essays in Confucian Thought, 17–34. Berkeley, Calif.: Asian Humanities Press.

———. 1985a. "A Confucian Perspective on Learning to Be Human." In Confucian Thought: Selfhood as Creative Transformation, 51–66. Albany, N.Y.: SUNY Press.

———. 1985b. "Jen as Living Metaphor in the Confucian Analects." In Confucian Thought: Selfhood as Creative Transformation, 81–92. Albany, N.Y.: SUNY Press.

———. 1985c. "The Value of the Human in Classical Confucian Thought." In Confucian Thought: Selfhood as Creative Transformation, 67–80. Albany, N.Y.: SUNY Press.

———. 1985d. The Way, Learning and Politics in Classical Confucian Humanism. Occasional Paper and Monograph Series, no. 2. Singapore: The Institute of East Asian Philosophies.

Van Norden, Bryan W. 1996. "What Should Western Philosophy Learn from Chinese Philosophy?" In Chinese Language, Thought, and Culture: Essays in Honor of David S. Nivison, edited by Philip J. Ivanhoe. LaSalle, Ill.: Open Court.

Waley, Arthur. 1939. Three Ways of Thought in Ancient China. London: Allen and Unwin.

Weinstock, Daniel M. 1994. "The Political Theory of Strong Evaluation." In Philosophy in an Age of Pluralism: The Philosophy of Charles Taylor in Question, edited by James Tully, 171–93. Cambridge, Eng.: Cambridge University Press.

Williams, Bernard. 1993. Shame and Necessity. Sather Classical Lectures, vol. 57. Berkeley and Los Angeles, Calif.: University of California Press.

Yearley, Lee H. 1990. Mencius and Aquinas: Theories of Virtue and Conceptions of Courage. Albany, N.Y.: SUNY Press.

———. n.d. "Xunzi: Ritualization as Humanization." In Ritual and Religion in the Xunzi, edited by T. C. Kline. New York: Seven Bridges Press.

Part II  Appreciating the New

6

Whose Confucius? Which *Analects*?

PHILIP J. IVANHOE

FOR OVER TWO THOUSAND YEARS, CON-
fucian scholars have sought to
explicate the meaning of their sacred
texts, producing an extensive, rich,
and sophisticated commentarial tradi-
tion that is an indispensable aid to the modern interpreter.[1] In addition to writing
formal commentaries, Confucian thinkers regularly referred to and expounded
upon the meaning of classical passages in the course of their philosophizing. These
thinkers did much more than simply chant the words of their sages and provide
precise annotation and background information to these texts, they interpreted
the sayings of the ancients. We who study the classics today are in a significant
sense following their lead. Our modern interpretations may be the latest but surely
will not be the last word on what these texts mean.[2]

Like modern scholars, traditional Confucians did not always agree about the
meaning of the texts they studied. They shared a common language but only rarely
did they speak in a single voice. Traditional commentators have tended to argue
for one interpretation as definitive or orthodox or, on a more irenic note, have
sought to reconcile what they claim are only apparent differences among competing interpretations.[3]

This essay explores different interpretations of a single passage from the *Analects*
of Confucius. *Analects* 5.13 is important for a variety of reasons. It is one of only
two places in the text where the character human nature (xìng 性) is mentioned
(the other being 17.2) and it is the only passage that mentions the Way of Heaven
(tīandào 天道). Moreover, the text can be understood as implying that there are
esoteric as well as exoteric aspects to Confucius' teaching. Although this is only
one of several possibile readings, as we shall see, some version of this distinction
informs many of the interpretations we shall explore. It is also widely followed
by modern translators of the text.[4] This is only one of several issues raised in this
passage that had profound implications for how later Confucians came to think
about the teaching and practice of self-cultivation and that deeply influenced their
views concerning Confucius and the classics.

Analects 5.13 records the words of one of Confucius' disciples, a man named
Zǐgòng 子貢. It consists of two short sentences, twenty-eight characters in all, but
as we shall see it has generated many times this length in commentary. Although
the most interesting disagreements over interpretation reflect divergent philosophical assumptions or concerns, several involve different views that concern the

punctuation or grammar of these lines. It will help to have the Chinese text before us as we turn to the different commentaries.

子貢	曰	夫子	之	文章	可	得	而	聞	也。
Zǐgòng	yuē	fūzǐ	zhī	wénzhāng	kě	dé	ér	wén	yě
(name)	say	master's		culture	can	get	and	hear	(particle)

夫子	之	言	性	與	天道	不	可	得	而	聞
fūzǐ	zhī	yán	xìng	yǔ	tiāndào	bù	kě	dé	ér	wén
master's		talk	nature	and	Heaven's Way	no	can	get	and	hear

也。
yě
(particle)

We will trace the history of interpretation of *Analects* 5.13 from the earliest stages of the commentarial tradition, the Wei dynasty collection by Hé Yàn 何宴 (d. 249) and others,[5] through the Song dynasty thinkers Chéng Hào 程顥 (1032–85), Chéng Yì 程頤 (1033–1107), and Zhū Xī 朱喜 (1130–1200), down to the Qing dynasty scholars Dài Zhèn 戴震 (1723–77) and Zhāng Xúechéng 章學誠 (1738–1801). These are not the only interesting interpreters of this passage, nor are they in every case the originators of the hermeneutical innovations they employ. However, they are among the most developed and clear authors of profound readings of the passage and they are some of the finest and most influential thinkers within the Confucian tradition.

The Interpretations

The first commentary is a compilation associated with the third-century thinker Hé Yàn. Hé Yàn along with other contributors to this collection read and admired Daoist texts like the *Laozi* and *Zhuangzi*. But they were characteristically Confucian in their ethical, political, and social philosophy. The eclecticism and syncretism of this group of thinkers arose under the influence of the rich metaphysical speculation and grand philosophical system building that blossomed during the Hàn dynasty. Developing ideas that can be found in the *Laozi*, *Zhuangzi*, and *Yijing*, they devised comprehensive metaphysical schemes and used these as the foundation for largely Confucian ideals. For example, they elevated the notion of *non-being*, the formless and ineffable primordial state of the cosmos, to a preeminent position.[6] Because the world arose out of the common, undifferentiated state of "non-being," it provided the underlying unity of the cosmos and the justification for the universal concern of the fully virtuous individual. Hé Yàn in particular emphasized this idea, which figures prominently in his commentary on *Analects* 5.13.

According to the Hé Yàn commentary, *Analects* 5.13 says, "The culture of our master is evident and can be heard. But our master's teachings about human nature and the Way of Heaven cannot be heard." This interpretation relies first of all on a unique understanding of the characters *wénzhāng* in the first line. All the other commentaries we will discuss take both of these characters as nouns. But the Hé Yàn commentary takes *wén* as a noun and *zhāng* as a predicate adjective. Thus the first five characters of line one are read as a complete sentence. The commentary offers the following remarks on this line, "*Zhāng* means clear and bright. Pattern, color, form and substance are plainly manifest and can be followed with the ears and eyes." Regarding the second line, it says, "Human nature is what human beings receive at birth. The Way of Heaven is the original and pervasive Way which each day is renewed. These are deep and subtle issues; one cannot hear of them."

The commentary also sees considerable significance in the character *yán* (here rendered "teachings") in the second line.[7] According to the Hé Yàn commentary this character marks a distinction between concrete *observable phenomena* (which can be "talked about" and thereby "heard") and abstract *metaphysical entities* (which cannot be "talked about" and therefore "cannot be heard"). Echoing the language of the *Yijing* and the *Daodejing*,[8] the commentary explains that human nature and the Way of Heaven are mysterious, transcendental entities that are beyond our normal powers of comprehension. Such things are—like the original and unifying non-being of the universe—in principle ineffable. Because such things cannot be talked about, it follows a fortiori that they "cannot be heard."

By interpreting the passage in terms of a distinction between accessible and everyday phenomena and abstruse and distant metaphysical principles, the Hé Yàn commentary establishes a theme that, as noted above, greatly influenced later interpreters. Some later commentators softened the view we see here, claiming only that issues like human nature and the Way of Heaven are difficult—not in principle impossible—to hear about. Because the inherent subtlety and profundity of these topics makes them extremely hard to understand, such knowledge is of a different order. It takes a certain kind of person, one of profound intelligence, learning, or sensitivity to grasp these truths.

We now turn to the Song dynasty Neo-Confucian Chéng Hào. Chéng incorporated important aspects of the Hé Yàn commentary in his own interpretation of *Analects* 5.13, but he also introduced a number of new ideas. One of the first differences to note is his interpretation of the characters *wénzhāng* in line one.[9] Chéng took these characters as a compound noun that referred to Confucius' teachings about culture: "The *Book of Odes*, *Book of History*, and proper ritual observance—these were Confucius' regular topics."[10] "These were the things he often spoke about. As for human nature and the Way of Heaven even Zigong could not hear of these things. It seems that these are things that must be 'understood in silence.' "[11] Chéng Hào agreed with the Hé Yàn commentary in positing an esoteric versus exoteric division within Confucius' teachings. Chéng also followed the Hé Yàn commentary in seeing this division in terms of a contrast between the underlying metaphysical pattern of the world and its observable phenomena. He, too, invoked notions from the *Yijing*, specifically the well-known dichotomy between what is above form (*xíng ér shàng* 形而上) and what is within form (*xíng ér xià* 形而下). According to Chéng Hào, one cannot describe the immutable Dào, what is above form, in words, and so one cannot hear about the Dào itself. Although Chéng Hào believed that such knowledge was ineffable, he did not believe it beyond comprehension or even limited to the understanding of only a select few. However, it does require a special kind of understanding. One must employ the unique human faculty of moral understanding and develop an *intuitive grasp* of these things. Chéng takes the implications of the Hé Yàn commentary in a new direction when he says, "As for human nature and the Way of Heaven, if one does not 'attain a personal understanding of them'[12] then one does not understand. This is why Zigong said, 'One cannot hear of them.' "[13]

Chéng Hào believed that one cannot grasp the Way through the intellect alone and that over reliance upon the more intellectualist, academic style of learning advocated by other Neo-Confucians of his time could in fact become an impediment to one's understanding. Relying exclusively upon the "clever calculations" of one's intellect is an immature and ineffective approach. It cannot yield complete knowledge of the Way and is the mark of a beginner. Genuine understanding requires a deep personal insight, and those who experience such insights are transformed forever: "To know through clever calculation was something Zigong did in the early stages of his training. Saying 'one cannot hear our master talk about human nature and the Way of Heaven' was something he only achieved later on."[14] In another passage, Chéng Hào explicitly tells us that Zǐgòng was just beginning to achieve a genuine understanding of the master's teachings when he spoke the words recorded in *Analects* 5.13: "Zigong had at this point just begun to understand human nature and the Way of Heaven and sighed in admiration of these teachings. . . ."[15] From these and other of Chéng Hào's comments we see that he believed one could gauge a student's spiritual attainment by his command of these two types of knowledge: the exoteric, publicly available lessons Confucius taught, and the esoteric ineffable teachings that required a direct, personal insight. Chéng Hào thought he could diagnose Zǐgòng's level of attainment and know that his remarks were made as he first began to understand Confucius' higher teachings. This feature of Chéng Hào's commentary represents a remarkable shift in hermeneutical perspective. The earlier Hé Yàn commentary is essentially a description of the kinds of things Confucius taught. Chéng Hào understands the passage as describing an elaborate and nuanced process of learning. The former interprets the passage from a general point of view, whereas Chéng Hào understands the passage in terms of the personal spiritual narrative of Zǐgòng's life.

Chéng Yì's understanding of *Analects* 5.13 is similar in important respects to that of his elder brother. For example, he, too, believed in a fundamental distinction between an exoteric and an esoteric teaching and that the passage describes the personal spiritual development of Zǐgòng. But Chéng Yì added new features to this distinction that are characteristic of his own particular philosophical perspective. Whereas Chéng Hào said that the reason one "cannot hear" the teachings on human nature and the Way of Heaven is that these things in principle are beyond words and must be grasped intuitively by our special moral sense, Chéng Yì not only believed such things can be talked about, he also insisted that Confucius did not withhold these higher teachings from his disciples.[16]

> As for human nature and the Way of Heaven, these are things that in the early stages of his time with Confucius, Zigong did not yet comprehend. At this point, he was able to understand them, thus he spoke these lines, sighing in admiration of these teachings. It was not that Confucius did not explain them, but can people easily attain an understanding of topics as profound and subtle as these?[17]

In regard to Confucius' higher teachings, Chéng Hào talked of the need to "attain a personal understanding of them" and for a "silent understanding." He emphasized a personal, intuitive understanding. But Chéng Yì states explicitly that understanding these higher teachings was a matter of intellect—not intuition. These were inherently difficult concepts and represent the profound intelligence of the sage. "When Zigong spoke of the teachings on human nature and the Way of Heaven he was speaking of the master's *astute intelligence* (cōngmíng 聰明). When he spoke of how Confucius 'would make them (i.e. the people) happy and they would come to him; stimulate them and they would be harmonious,'[18] he was speaking of the master's virtuous nature."[19] For Chéng Yì, a critical part of the task of self-cultivation was using one's intellect to penetrate through to the underlying principles of different phenomena. Confucius' teachings captured the essential features of these principles in clear lessons and hence were an indispensable aid in self-cultivation. However, like most lessons, Confucius' teachings presented different degrees of difficulty. The most intelligent individuals readily were able to comprehend the principles behind his highest teachings: those concerning human nature and the Way of Heaven. But the majority of people found it exceedingly difficult to grasp such teachings; most were incapable of "hearing" them. According to Chéng Yì, this was the central point of Zǐgòng's remarks: "As for the line, 'One cannot hear our master talk about human nature and the Way of Heaven,' (among the disciples) only Zigong had grasped these principles. Thus he spoke this line, sighing in admiration of their beauty and saying that most people 'cannot hear them.'"[20] Chéng Yì further claimed that there is a complex hierarchical structure to Confucius' teachings, each level representing a higher degree of conceptual difficulty.[21] It would take time before those of less than exceptional ability could reach the highest levels and hear the teachings on human nature and the Way of Heaven.

Let us now turn to Zhū Xī, who was deeply influenced by both the Chéng brothers, especially Chéng Yì. In his interpretation of *Analects* 5.13, Zhū borrowed from both. He adopted their commonly held view that Zǐgòng spoke these words just as he began to understand Confucius' higher teachings, and he shared Chéng Yì's emphasis on the need for gradual intellectual progress in a distinctive, hierarchical program of learning. Zhū Xī introduced several of his own ideas, as well. For example, he understood Confucius' *wénzhāng* as the master's personal displays of virtue, things such as his speech, conduct, and bearing. Zhū also had a novel reading for the second line of the passage. Chéng Hào believed one cannot hear the teachings on human nature and the Way of Heaven because in principle these are beyond words. Chéng Yì argued that although the Master often discoursed on these topics, few could comprehend such complex and difficult teachings. Zhū directly contradicts Chéng Yì by claiming that Confucius "rarely spoke of these things." Zhū Xī could appeal to two types of evidence to support this interpretation. First, *Analects* 9.1 tells us that there were topics about which Confucius "rarely spoke."[22] Second, the case can be made from negative evidence: the *Analects* contains no significant passages that concern the topics of human nature or the Way of Heaven.[23] In this regard, Zhū Xī's interpretation recommends itself on the strength of both textual consistency and comprehensiveness. It is well attested, original, and ingenious.

> *Elegant displays* (*wénzhāng* 文章) are exterior, visible manifestations of virtue. A dignified bearing and refined speech are good examples. Human nature is Heavenly principle, which all receive. . . . When Zigong spoke of the master's elegant displays, he was referring to what each day could be seen on the outside. Without doubt, these were things about which all the students had heard. But as for human nature and the Way of Heaven, the master rarely spoke of these. And so there were some students who had not heard about them. Now, as for the sage's teachings, one cannot skip over any steps. At this point, Zigong had just begun to hear about these teachings and sighed in admiration of their beauty.[24]

An important feature of Zhū Xī's interpretation—one that he adopted from Chéng Yì—is the notion that Confucius' teachings consist of a number of discrete levels, each of which needs to be mastered before the next can be approached. According to this view, Zǐgòng's remarks provided a rough taxonomy of these stages. Elsewhere, for example in his introduction to the *Great Learning*, Zhū Xī tells us that these discrete levels of learning are keyed to specific texts and that there is a definite sequence to be followed in studying them.

> My master, the philosopher Cheng Yi, says, "The *Great Learning* is a book transmitted by the Confucian school. It forms the gate through which beginners enter into virtue. That we can now perceive the order in which the ancients pursued their learning is solely owing to the

preservation of this work, the *Analects* and the *Mencius* coming after it. Students must commence their course of study with this text; then it may be hoped that they will be kept from error."[25]

Zhū Xī argues that there is a proper sequence that one must follow in the course of one's studies, and he links different levels of Confucian teachings and specific topics to different texts. Our next commentator, the Qing dynasty thinker Dài Zhèn, perhaps influenced by this idea, identifies the *Yijing* as the text that contains Confucius' highest teachings: those on human nature and the Way of Heaven. Dài sees this as the key not only to *Analects* 5.13 but also to all of Confucius' thought.

Dài believed that Zǐgòng's distinction between what can and cannot be heard points to Confucius' unique contribution to the tradition of the sages. He argued that Confucius' teachings on human nature and the Way of Heaven could only be found in the *Yijing* and that in this text Confucius reveals the "source" (the under-lying principles) of the Way.[26] Earlier sages, who had held official positions and thus were responsible for the specific forms of culture, had produced the cultural ornamentations (wénzhāng 文章), that is, the regulations, customs, practices and institutions of the Golden Age. However, Confucius—who was destined not to secure an official position from which he could himself implement the Dào—accomplished something even more profound and marvelous: he described the theory behind these practices. Striking a bold and new interpretive path, Dài Zhèn insists that one could "hear about" the wénzhāng that Confucius followed from any number of people. After all, the classics, which recorded such matters, were available to everyone. But one could hear about human nature and the Way of Heaven only from the Master. Dài Zhèn completely inverts the traditional understanding of *Analects* 5.13. At the same time, he expands Zhū Xī's hermeneutical principles of consistency and comprehensiveness. For Dài, these criteria extend to the entire corpus of texts attributed to Confucius and specifically to the appendices of the *Yijing*.

Dài explains all of this in the preface to his magnum opus, "Attested Commentary on the Meaning of Terms in the *Mencius*."[27]

In my youth, I read in the *Analects* the words of Duanmu (Zigong):[28] "One can hear of our master's cultural ornamentations, but one cannot hear of our master's teachings on human nature and the Way of Heaven."[29] Only after I had read the *Yijing* did I realize that there is where his teachings on human nature and the Way of Heaven can be found!

When the Way of the Zhou declined, Yao, Shun, Yu, Tang, Wen, Wu and the Duke of Zhou's ideal method of government, which had shown forth brilliantly in their cultural ornamentations,[30] was abandoned and became a faded trace. Since Confucius did not secure an official position,[31] he could not pass down this method in institutions, rites and music.[32] Therefore, he set in order its basis and sought out its source, so that for countless generations the reasons for order and disorder and the proper standard for adopting or changing institutions, rites and music would be like a balance held up to determine light and heavy or like a compass, square or marking line are to the square, circular, level and straight. Though these teachings appear lofty and remote, he could not but teach them,[33] for when Confucius taught them, truly he taught what the former sages had yet to teach. Were it not for Confucius, from whom could we hear such things? This is why Zigong said, "these teachings cannot be heard."

Dài understood the term *wénzhāng* to refer to the classical cultural forms that Confucius had preserved, followed, and transmitted. However, Dài believed Confucius' unique contribution to learning went beyond preserving and transmitting these cultural forms. Confucius alone had discovered and made clear the underlying *principles* upon which these cultural forms were based. Dài understood the distinction Zǐgòng makes in *Analects* 5.13 as describing *practice* versus *theory*. Earlier sages had build glorious palaces but Confucius alone provided us—and all future generations—with the blueprints for such palaces. The early sages had developed the ideal cultural language, but Confucius' unique achievement was to describe the grammar of this language. The *Yijing* is the repository of Confucius' most sophisticated theoretical teachings. And although one can hear about the practices of former times from any number of people, apart from Confucius, the theoretical principles that underlie these practices "cannot be heard."

Dài was a master philologist and a great critic of "Song and Ming Confucians" (i.e., Neo-Confucians). What is less well understood is the relationship between his interest in philology and these criticisms. If we look carefully at the kind of books he wrote, this relationship and his philological interests in general become much easier to understand. This in turn can help us to appreciate more fully his unique interpretation of *Analects* 5.13.

Dài's complaint against Song and Ming Confucians was that they mistook their own subjective opinions for the objective and eternal values of the Way. He rejected their claim, made in various forms, that all people inherently possess and have access to moral knowledge. Instead, as mentioned above, Dài believed that the essential truths about the Way were inscribed by Confucius in a set of canonical texts, the classics. One made contact with this truth by coming to understand, in the most comprehensive and consistent manner, the *meaning* of these texts. In order to do this, one sought out and proved by example what each term in the text meant. In other words, one trained oneself to become a properly oriented, master philologist. The format of Dài's well-known essay, *On the Good* (*Yúan Shàn* 原善), and his masterpiece, "Attested Commentary on the Meaning of Terms in the *Mencius*," clearly manifest this orientation and demonstrate his method. For Dài Zhèn, then, philology was the method of philosophy.[34]

In regard to his understanding of *Analects* 5.13, this orientation meant that Dài must reject Zhū Xī's gloss on terms like *wénzhāng*, which is poorly attested in the classical sources. Instead, he must search out the most philologically sound sense, the one with the clearest historical precedents. However, above all else, the most important aspect of Dài's project was to attain a *comprehensive* and *consistent* explanation of *all* the classics.³⁵ This is precisely what he produced in his various philosophical works, and this approach is reflected clearly in his interpretation of *Analects* 5.13.

The last commentator we shall consider is Zhāng Xúechéng. Zhāng joined Dài Zhèn in criticizing Song and Ming Neo-Confucians for their "subjectivism" and for introducing notions not present in the classical sources, such as the dualism between principle (lǐ 理) and ether (qì 氣), into their interpretations of the classics.³⁶ He felt that such abstract metaphysical ideas tended to mislead people, causing them to turn away from the actual world (what is within form) and to seek for the Way in some insubstantial, metaphysical realm (what is above form) through regimens of meditation or speculation. As Dài had before, Zhāng pointed out that such notions were never a part of early Confucianism and in fact originated with the competing schools of Daoism and Buddhism. It was Zhāng's conviction that under the pernicious influence of these schools of thought, Neo-Confucians had radically misunderstood and misrepresented their own tradition.

Zhāng sought to eliminate these misunderstandings and return to the concrete, practical teachings of the Master. He insisted that Confucius himself *never* talked about obscure, abstract notions; he only discussed events in the observable, physical world, for this is where the Dào is—and nowhere else. Confucius would not even invoke examples from the real world unless they were solid and substantiated *facts*. Thus, although agreeing with Dài Zhèn in condemning the subjective and speculative notions of Song and Ming Confucians, Zhāng went a step beyond Dài by denying that Confucius *ever* engaged in devising an abstract theoretical system of his own. As a result of this philosophical orientation, Zhāng came to a very different understanding of *Analects* 5.13. He says,

> Zigong said, "One can hear about our master's cultural ornamentations, but one cannot hear our master talk about human nature and the Way of Heaven." Now of course *everything* the master talked about concerned human nature and the Way of Heaven. Yet he never indicated what these were in themselves by saying, "*This* is human nature or *This* is the Way of Heaven." That is why Zigong did not say, "One cannot hear about human nature and the Way of Heaven" but instead said, "One cannot hear our master *talk about* human nature and the Way of Heaven." *Everything* Confucius talked about concerned human nature and the Way of Heaven, but he never explicitly said what these were because he feared people would abandon the actual phenomena of the world in their search for the Way. Confucius could have talked about the rites of the Xia and the Yin dynasties but said that these were unsubstantiated and would not be trusted.³⁷ And so we see that in every case the master only talked about those things that could be substantiated in actual

phenomena. He never vainly employed *empty talk* (*kōngyán* 空言) in order to explain the Way.[38]

Zhāng claimed that everything Confucius taught concerned the issues of human nature and the Way of Heaven and yet he insisted that Confucius never directly *talked about* these issues. Confucius never tried to abstract the Way from its true arena: the actual, observable world. Apart from the actual world, there was no human nature or Way of Heaven.

However, if this is Zhāng's view, why should later Confucians regard Confucius and the classics he preserved as in any way normative or privileged? If Zhāng is correct, should they not just turn to a study of the world in which they live? Zhāng would say "no," but in order to see why we must consider briefly his particular view of the evolution of the Dào.

In certain respects, Zhāng's view bears a resemblance to Hegel's view of history, in which *geist* evolves through a series of necessary stages and reaches full form at a definite point in time. However, unlike Hegel, Zhāng saw this process culminating in the distant past, not in his own age, and understood subsequent history as the dissolution of this early grand unity. In these and other respects, he is more like the seventeenth-century historian George Horn than Hegel or even Vico. Zhāng had his own particular problems to solve. Whereas Hegel and Vico were looking for a comprehensive explanation of history, Zhāng also needed an account of the course of history that would justify the unique status of the classics and the preeminent position of Confucius.

According to Zhāng, the Dào evolved through necessary, successive stages and reached full flower in the culture of the Duke of Zhōu. Confucius, destined not to secure an official position from which he could implement the Dào, saw—as all sages do, according to Zhāng—his particular, historically conditioned imperative: to record precisely this unique moment in time and transmit his record to future generations. This, Zhāng tells us, is something Confucius "could not but do."[39] Confucius was unique, not for being a more insightful sage or, as Dài Zhèn would have it, because he was its greatest theoretician, but for being that sage who was at the proper historical moment to carry out this invaluable task. The classics could never be replaced because what they recorded would never occur again. The Dào evolved to perfection only *once*. Confucius was unique not in being qualitatively or quantitatively different from earlier sages, but for being on the scene at precisely the right moment to see, understand, preserve, and pass on the Dào when it reached the peak of perfection.

Zhāng used this view of the Confucian tradition to criticize the scholars of his own age for mistakenly doing what Confucius did instead of studying what Confucius studied. Zhāng's contemporaries believed that they, too, must write down and pass on some teaching about the Dào, just as they thought Confucius had done. But this was a mistake. This blindly imitated Confucius' unique historical task. Instead, Zhāng argued that his contemporaries should study what Confucius studied, that is, history. In order to understand and follow the Dào, one must understand how it came to be, how it has functioned through time, and thereby what it requires of one in the present age. One must avoid the empty talk of speculative philosophy and study the Dao as revealed in the process of history. For Zhāng, the right kind of history—not philology—was the master discipline, the method of philosophy. Several of these characteristic features of Zhāng's thought are reflected in his understanding of *Analects* 5.13. He believed that although human nature and the Way of Heaven were never topics for speculative theorizing, they were precisely what Confucius did discuss, in the concrete circumstances of his own life and times.

Conclusion

We have seen how some of the most eminent representatives of the Confucian tradition at times disagreed—often deeply—over the interpretation of an important passage from the *Analects*, a passage that seems innocent in its simplicity. These disagreements often reveal deep, complex, and subtle philosophical differences. This shows that although the Confucian tradition is formed around a sacred canon and certain central themes it is not a set of fixed ideas handed down unchanged through time. Rather, the tradition is the accumulated record of a series of individuals who struggled to interpret a shared set of texts[40] in light of their different circumstances and times.[41] In addition, this study serves to illustrate that an adequate understanding of Confucian philosophy requires that one understand the history of the tradition.

A sophisticated understanding of the depth and range of different interpretations within the commentarial tradition would enhance the work currently being done in the field of Confucian studies. First, it would raise important issues for the basic and profoundly undervalued task of translation. Many modern translations, both East and West, rely in an unsystematic way on a variety of different commentators.[42] If a translator has a clear and comprehensive theory about what a given text means, then relying on different commentaries may be warranted and effective. But in the absence of a guiding theory, such a practice tends to produce translations that are montages of unrelated views. This may well contribute to the mistaken impression that Chinese thought is strongly unsystematic.

A full appreciation of the commentarial tradition would also help to reveal the richness and diversity of Confucian philosophy and the broad interactions and mutual influence it has enjoyed with other East Asian traditions. A further related benefit would be greater sensitivity to the degree to which our present understanding of certain earlier figures in the tradition is overly informed by later interpretations of their thought. For example, the metaphysical views that inform even the relatively early Hé Yàn commentary are arguably largely of Daoist origin, whereas the complex metaphysics of the Song Neo-Confucian commentaries are deeply and fundamentally influenced by Buddhist philosophy. Such later views, and especially Neo-Confucian interpretations, often are read back into early texts and presented as the views of the tradition's founders in much the same way that Thomistic readings of Aristotle at one time colored and perhaps still distort our understanding. A more thorough appreciation of the tradition may also help contemporary interpreters avoid reading classical Confucian thinkers as if they were advocating or groping their way toward our view of things. Such work has little if any historical support, scant philosophical interest, and sometimes rather dubious intellectual motivation.[43]

We have just begun to distinguish clearly the challenging, distinct, and fascinating strata within the Confucian tradition. This essay is only one example of how such work can be done. Its primary point is that before we begin to read a text like the *Analects* we would do well to ask ourselves, Which *Analects* and Whose Confucius are we trying to understand?[44]

ACKNOWLEDGMENTS

Many thanks to Irene Bloom, Mark Csikszentmihalyi, T. C. "Jack" Kline III, David S. Nivison, Mark Setton, and Bryan W. Van Norden for helpful comments and suggestions on earlier drafts of this chapter.

NOTES

1. In can be argued that Confucius himself began the commentarial tradition by his remarks on the meaning of certain passages from the *Book of Odes*. Mencius offered quite sophisticated interpretations of classical texts. I discuss this issue in some detail in my *Ethics in the Confucian Tradition: The Thought of Mencius and Wang Yang-ming* (Atlanta, Ga.: Scholars Press, 1990): 96–99. For a fascinating study of commentarial traditions in both China and the West, see John B. Henderson, *Scripture, Canon and Commentary* (Princeton, N.J.: Princeton University Press, 1991).

2. For a remarkable view on how the work of modern interpreters might well require a form of commitment not wholly dissimilar to traditional commentators, see Charles Hallisey, "In Defense of Rather Fragile and Local Achievement: Reflections on the Work of Gurulogomi," in Frank E. Reynolds and David Tracy, eds., *Religion and Practical Reason*, (Albany, N.Y.: SUNY Press, 1994): 121–60.

3. Mengzi and Xunzi represent the first documented rift in the Confucian tradition. But perhaps the debate between the schools of Zhū Xī and Wang Yangming best represents the kind of disagreement I have in mind. Not only did the latter two argue over the meaning of individual passages and ideas, Wang also had radical doubts about the value of any classical text. For a brief discussion of this aspect of Wang's thought, see Ivanhoe, *Ethics*, pp. 102–12. Those who sought to reconcile disagreements within the tradition are also easy to find. Han thinkers such as Dong Zhongshu and Wang Bi are good examples, as is the Tang Confucian Han Yu.

4. For representative East Asian scholars see Lǐ Yǒulían 李友蓮 et al., trans., *Lúnyǔ xīnyì* 論語新義 (Tainan: Xinshiji chubanshe, 1969): 38; Yu Chong-ki 劉正基, trans., *Non-o* 論語, in *Sa-so sam-kyong* 四書三經 (Tong-a toso, 1980): 87; and Yoshida Kenkō (see note 7

below). For Western scholars, see Seraphin Couvreur, trans., *Liun Iu*, in *Les Quatre Livres* (Ho Kien Fou, 1895): 112; Arthur Waley, trans., *The Analects of Confucius* (George Allen and Unwin, 1938): 110; and D. C. Lau, trans., *The Analects* (New York: Dorset Press, 1986): 78.

5. *Lúnyǔ Héshìděng jíjiě* 論語何氏等集解 5.4a–b (SBBY).

6. Early Chinese thinkers tended to conceive of "non-being" as the primordial condition of the cosmos, a state in which things lacked definite and distinct qualities. It is not a state of nothingness but rather one of no-thingness. For a discussion of some of the important differences between early Chinese and Western views of being see Angus C. Graham, "Being in Western Philosophy Compared with SHIH/FEI (是非) and YU/WU (有無) in Chinese Philosophy," (reprint) in *Studies in Chinese Philosophy and Philosophical Literature* (Albany, N.Y.: SUNY Press, 1990): 322–59.

7. This distinction figures prominently in many of the commentators we will examine. One modern Japanese scholar, Yoshida Kenkō, suggests that the first line originally contained the character *yán*, as well. He argues that Confucius, who was interested primarily in practical moral education, regularly talked about issues of culture and only rarely discussed abstract philosophical notions such as human nature and the Way of Heaven. See Yoshida Kenkō, 吉田賢抗 , trans., *Rongo* 論語, in *Shinshaku Kanbun Taikei* 新釋漢文大系 (Tokyo: Meiji Shōin, 1965), vol. 1, p. 111.

8. Describing the Way of Heaven as "original and pervasive" echoes the opening lines of the *Yijing*. Saying that human nature and the Way of Heaven are "deep and subtle" recalls the description of the Daoist sage given in chapter fifteen of the *Daodejing*.

9. The exact meaning of the term *wénzhāng* is difficult to determine. It could refer to Confucius' personal displays of culture. One finds evidence for such an interpretation in a passage that follows closely (*Analects* 5.15). In this passage, Zǐgòng asks why an official named Kong was given the posthumous name the cultured (*wénzǐ* 文子). But equally plausible is the idea that *wén* refers to the cultural forms of the Zhōu dynasty. One finds support for this reading in *Analects* 9.5, and elsewhere. These two interpretations can be seen as mutually compatible: Confucius was the repository of knowledge about this culture and he displayed it in his personal conduct. The commentators we will examine show no clear consensus on this issue. Other plausible interpretations exist, as well. For example, Líu Xíe 劉勰 (465–522) in the second chapter of his *Wénxīn dīaolóng* 文心雕龍 says that Confucius' *wénzhāng* is his style of composition (*wéncí* 文辭). Húang Kǎn 皇侃 (488–545) in his commentary on the *Analects* identifies *wénzhāng* as the six classical works (*lìují* 六籍). See his *Lúnyǔ jíjiě yìshù* 論語集解義疏 3.10b.

10. From the *Yijing*, great appendix, sect. 1, chap. 12.

11. *Hénán Chéngshì yíshū* 河南程氏遺書 11.12a, in *Èr Chéng qúanshū* 二程全書 (SBBY). The phrase "understand in silence" is from *Analects* 7.2.

12. The expression *to attain a personal understanding of them* (*zìdézhī* 自得之) refers to a personal realization of the Way. The expresson is found in *Mencius* 4B13 and 3A4. Cheng Hao may be playing on the words to get (*dé* 得) in the line, cannot get to hear of them (*bùkědé ér wén* 不可得而聞) from *Analects* 5.13.

13. *Wàishū* 外書 2.1b, in *Èr Chéng qúanshū* 二程全書 (SBBY).

14. *Henan Chengshi yishu* 11.11b.

15. *Henan Chengshi yishu* 12.1b.

16. Confucius does seem to claim that he held nothing back from his disciples. See *Analects* 7.23. But Waley's interpretation is persuasive. See Waley, *Analects*, p. 128.

17. *Waishu* 1.2b. This passage is not explicitly attributed to Cheng Yi, but judging from its content it surely belongs to him.

18. Quoting *Analects* 19.25.

19. *Waishu* 6.9b.

20. *Waishu* 6.4a. Thus, Cheng Yi takes *wén* ("to hear") as a "success verb." I owe this way of putting the point to Bryan W. Van Norden.

21. One can find support for such a view in the *Analects*, e.g. 19.12.

22. The interpretation of this passage is quite problematic. For a discussion see Legge's footnotes in James Legge, trans., *Confucian Analects*, in *The Chinese Classics* (reprint) (Hong Kong: Hong Kong University Press, 1970), vol. 1, p. 216, n. 1. Also see note 16, above. For Zhu Xi's commentary, see *Lúnyǔ* 論語 5.1a, in *Sishū jízhù* 四書集注 (SBBY).

23. As mentioned earlier, except for Zǐgòng's remark in 5.13, the only other occurrence within the *Analects* of the character xìng is 17.2. The compound tiāndào is not found anywhere else in the text.

24. Zhū Xī, *Lúnyǔ* 3.4a–b.

25. Translation adapted from Legge, *Confucian Analects*, p. 355.

26. Dài Zhèn may have made this association after reading the He Yan commentary, which, as mentioned above, makes reference to the *Yijing*.

27. I have followed Hu Shih's punctuated text. See the appendix of *Dài Dōngyúan de zhéxúe* 戴東原的哲學 (Taiwan: Shangwu yinshuguan, 1960): 37–38.

28. Duanmu is the surname of the disciple whose style is Zǐgòng.

29. As will become clear, Dai (like Cheng Hao) believed wénzhāng refers to the classical culture of the past Golden Age and not, as Zhū Xī would have it, to Confucius' personal displays of virture. Dai argued that wénzhāng came from the sages of classical times and not from Confucius, who did not fashion culture because he did not have an opportunity to rule or advise a ruler in an official capacity. Confucius' unique contribution was to preserve and transmit this culture and discover its underlying principles—something no one before him had accomplished. Here Dai seems to be echoing and elaborating on the views of Mencius. See *Mencius* 2A2.

30. Paraphrasing *Analects* 8.19.

31. Cheng Yi invokes Confucius "not gaining an official position" as the explanation for why he "transmitted but did not create" (*Analects* 7.1; cf. *Doctrine of the Mean* 30.1). See *Henan Chengshi yishu* 22A12b. For interesting precedents for this notion, see *Analects* 8.14, 14.27, and *Doctrine of the Mean* chap. 28. David S. Nivison discusses this issue in regard to Zhang Xuecheng, who seems to have followed Cheng Yi. See *The Life and Thought of Chang Hsüeh-ch'eng* (Stanford, Calif.: Stanford University Press, 1966): 149–50.

32. Dài Zhèn probably had in mind *Doctrine of the Mean* 28.2–3, which specifically states that such matters are the exclusive prerogative of rulers. See also *Analects* 8.14, 14.27, etc.

33. Dài Zhèn insisted that Confucius' Way was not something abstract or abstruse, so he is at considerable pains to explain why Confucius taught such theoretical works.

34. Professor Yu Ying-shih argues that philosophy and philology were competing interests of Dài's and that, in the end, he chose to pursue or at least emphasize the former. See "Tai Chen's Choice between Philosophy and Philology," *Asia Major*, n.s., vol. 2, no. 1 (1989): 79–108. My own view is somewhat different. Because Dài believed the aim of philosophy was an understanding of the Dào that was in the classics, the right kind of philology is the very method of philosophy.

35. This point is made by Professor Yu in the course of his translation of Dài's writings. See "Tai Chen's Choice," p. 84.

36. For a thorough study of the history of the concept of li see Wing-tsit Chan, "The Evolution of the Neo-Confucian Concept Li as Principle," in *The Tsing Hua Journal of Chinese Studies*, n.s., vol. 4, no. 2 (1964): 123–49. As helpful as this study is in surveying the literature, it remains committed to the view that there is only one concept for terms of art like li. Thus the analysis often is different from my own understanding of the various uses of this term in the history of Chinese philosophy.

37. The reference is to *Analects* 3.9.

38. *Yúan Dào* 原道 2.12a, in *Zhāngshì yíshū* 章氏遺書, Líu Chénghàn 劉承幹 edition (Wuxing: Jiayetang, 1922).

39. Ibid.

40. Even on this issue there was notable variation. The set of canonical texts grew over time and the importance of individual works varied in different periods within the tradition.

41. Alasdair MacIntyre presents an insightful acount of how traditions are best understood as temporally extended dialogues. See chapter 15 of his *After Virtue* (rev. ed.) (Notre Dame, Ind.: University of Notre Dame Press, 1984), and *Three Rival Versions of Moral Enquiry* (Notre Dame, Ind.: University of Notre Dame Press, 1990).

42. In contrast to this unfortunate practice, ancient Indian texts, to this day, are almost always read according to a given commentary. (I owe this helpful point to an anonymous reader.)

43. An excellent discussion of this and related issues can be found in Richard Rorty, J. B. Schneewind, and Quentin Skinner, eds., *Philosophy in History* (reprint) (Cambridge, Eng.: Cambridge University Press, 1988), pp. 1–14.

44. The title of my work is taken from Alasdair MacIntyre's *Whose Justice? Which Rationality?* (Notre Dame, Ind.: University of Notre Dame Press, 1988). I share MacIntyre's conviction that even the most basic concepts of a given tradition can only be properly understood in terms of their historical context. However, I do not share what I call his "conquest model" of traditions: the belief that when different traditions come into conflict one will necessarily prove superior. This aspect of MacIntyre's analysis seems neither conceptually nor historically warranted. Ethical and religious traditions differ in this respect, at least from scientific traditions. In any case, it plays no role in my study. Although I believe that given an explicit interpretive goal (e.g. What was Zhū Xī's understanding of the text?) there are better and worse interpretations of the *Analects*, I am not arguing for any interpretation as definitive.

7

Confucius and the

Analects in the Hàn

MARK CSIKSZENTMIHALYI

Today, it is possible to read the *Analects* (Lúnyǔ 論語) and ignore the issue of who Confucius was and whether he even existed. Indeed, for some purposes, this might be the best approach to the text. Yet for millennia the *Analects* has been read not just as composed by a particular set of people at a particular time, but also as a guide to the exemplary lives of these people—readings in which the notion of authorship plays an important role. Even more, reverence for the figure of Confucius, imagined in various ways, has been a common element of the traditions today grouped under the rubric "Confucianism." For many of those who have read the *Analects*, the value of the text has been as a testimony to the sagacity of Confucius. For these reasons, the historical debate over the issue of who Confucius was and the impact of this debate on the development of East Asian traditions is a topic worth considering.

Attempting a reading of the *Analects* informed by a single "historical Confucius" is complicated by the diversity of images of Confucius accepted at different times. Those who think they know Confucius from the biographical details supplied in one or more of the works connected with him, from hagiographical accounts of his exemplary behavior learned at school in Taiwan or Singapore, or from the slightly nonsensical aphorisms attributed to him by patronizing Hollywood screenwriters, are at best only right in a partial sense. This is because, from the time of the earliest treatments of the Master, details in his biography have been added and subtracted, words and phrases attributed to Confucius have been interpreted according to the concerns of those who read them, and texts associated with the sage have gained or lost ascendancy, all to make Confucius conform to the needs of particular audiences. To be sure, few would disagree with the statement that at the end of the sixth century B.C.E., a man named Kǒng Qiū 孔丘 lived in China and his ideas and words were transcribed by those who studied with him. Some of these transcriptions probably survive today, but what makes the enterprise of "knowing" Confucius so puzzling is that unambiguous standards according to which one can definitively cull out his authentic words disappeared long ago. Although Kǒng Qiū was not mythical, Confucius—a Latinized named used here to denote persons that come to mind when the name Kǒng Qiū is invoked—most certainly is. This essay is concerned with the historical evolution of the mythic Confucius and not the recovery of the biography of the man named Kǒng Qiū.

The formation of this myth has been a continuous process, but the period from 206 B.C.E. to 220 C.E. was a particularly revealing phase.[1] The roughly four hundred years of the Hàn Dynasty were formative for narratives about Master Kǒng and the interpretation of works associated with him. Although some images of Confucius during the Hàn are easy to recognize because of their familial resemblance to their influential Late Imperial descendants, others contain evidence about a Confucius who has now largely disappeared. During the Hàn, as will be seen, Confucius was thought to have possessed superhuman abilities, have displayed visible marks placed by Heaven that proved his destiny to rule as king, have transmitted esoteric teachings and prophecies to his disciples, and have been sanguine about serving the ghosts and spirits. Because of these qualities, Confucius was seen and treated increasingly as a divinity. The disappearance or diminution of these divine features owed quite a bit to events of the Hàn, notably the adoption of the "Five Classics" associated with Confucius as the basis for attaining the academic position of erudit (bóshì 博士, literally "official of wide learning") in 136 B.C.E., the increasingly widespread distribution of the *Analects*, and the subsequent vogue that the text enjoyed with the politically reformist faction in the first half of the first century B.C.E.[2] The role played by the *Analects* in the Hàn was therefore tremendously important to the larger drama of the historical development of the image of Confucius.

By stealing a glimpse behind the traditional image of a unitary Master Kǒng whose utterances are collected in a Warring States *Analects*, it is possible to see the multitude of sometimes contradictory images and texts that more accurately describe the role Confucius and the *Analects* have historically played. It is this complex interplay between myth and text, identification and attribution, that is the key to a robust picture of Chinese Confucianism. As Lionel Jensen has noted, "our Confucius is a product fashioned by many hands, ecclesiastical and lay, Western and Chinese."[3]

A proper study of the "fashioning" of a Hàn Confucius is not simply an exercise in folklore, however, because the biography of Confucius has always been in an important sense a personification of particular texts associated with him. This essay will examine changing images of Confucius as a function of his association with particular texts, from the idea that the sage was marked by Heaven for his role as prophet and "uncrowned king," through his association with ritual and with childhood education, culminating in an examination of the social context in which the *Analects* became widely disseminated in the century from 155 to 55 B.C.E. The interplay between different texts, the social groups who promoted those texts, and the implicit image of Confucius associated with the texts reveals much about both the period and the early social role of the *Analects*. It also provides a look at images of Confucius that differ from those popular today, as well as a first look at a portrait of Confucius that was essentially scholastic and concerned with ritual.

Life of the Sage

Many attempts have been made to develop chronological accounts of the life of Confucius, starting with the Hàn dynasty portrayal of Confucius assembled around 100 B.C.E. by the historian Sīmǎ Qiān 司馬遷, in his *Records of the Grand Historian* (*Shǐjì* 史記). Many details of Confucius' life accepted today derive from that account, including his birthplace (Zōuyì 陬邑, near modern Qūfù 曲阜 in Shandong Province), given names (Kǒng Qīu, and his style name Zhòng Ní 仲尼), and dates (551 to 479 B.C.E.).[4] As Stephen Durrant has recently argued, Sīmǎ Qiān not only held Confucius in high esteem, but also aspired to be regarded as the successor to the sage.[5] Sīmǎ arranged the accounts available to him from both public and private sources in what he saw as chronological order, explaining the different locations of the stories by Confucius' movement from state to state in search of a ruler to influence. Although particular items in the *Records of the Grand Historian* are today rejected based on their disagreement with other sources, in particular the *Analects*, Sīmǎ Qiān's chronology was the first and most influential attempt to order the disparate accounts of events in the life of a figure that had already become one of the most revered in Hàn China.[6]

Confucius' importance during the Hàn is evident from the many extant works that contain narratives and sayings of Confucius not found in the later canonical assemblages of the Five Classics. Didactic stories about Confucius are to be found in the collections *New Preface* (*Xīnxù* 新序) and *Garden of Sayings* (*Shūoyuàn* 説苑) attributed to Líu Xiàng 劉向 (79–8 B.C.E.) in the last decades of the first century B.C.E. Collections devoted entirely to Confucius include the partially extant *Records of Confucius in the Three Courts* (*Kǒngzǐ sānchảo jì* 孔子三朝記),[7] and the *School Sayings of Confucius* (*Kǒngzǐ jiāyǔ* 孔子家語), attributed to Wáng Sù 王肅 (195–256 C.E.) Conversations between Confucius and his disciples appear in the Hàn portions of the *Record of Ritual* (*Lǐjì* 禮記), in the *Elder Dai's Record of Ritual* (*DàDài Lǐjì* 大戴禮記), and in newly excavated texts from Mǎwángduī 馬王堆. Yáng Xióng's 楊雄 (53 B.C.E.–18 C.E.) imitation of the *Analects*, the *Model Sayings* (*Fǎyán* 法言), was completed at the end of the Western Hàn and contains many references to Confucius. In these sources, Confucius often makes the equivalent of a cameo appearance at the end of a passage, providing a moral to a story that may actually have been much older. In other stories, probably attributable to the students or supporters of an intellectual lineage of one of his followers, he is there only to marvel at the wisdom of a statement made by one of his disciples. These two styles of appearance attest to the authority of Confucius during that period.

Although the narratives and text linked to Confucius were important during the Hàn, the reasons for this importance were largely dissimilar from the reasons that Confucius is studied today. Specifically, the importance of Confucius' life was due as much to his Heaven-endowed authority as to the ethical import of his writings. Anna Seidel has pointed out that a dominant Hàn dynasty motif is that of the earthly ruler and his heavenly teacher, and has argued that the pairing of Huángdì—the Yellow Emperor—and Lǎozǐ is an example of this motif.[8] Hàn portrayals of Confucius may be also divided into these two categories, those of a human sage and those of a supernatural teacher. Whereas the majority view of Confucius today is of a this-worldly philosopher along the lines of the former category, during the Hàn Confucius was just as often described as possessing supernatural insight and a special link with higher powers. This portrait of Confucius colored Hàn interpretations of Confucius' writings and accounts for examples from *The Analects*, to be examined below, that might strike a reader possessed of a contemporary portrait of Confucius as unduly otherworldly.

The Hàn image of Confucius displayed otherworldly qualities because during that period the sage was seen as extraordinary—different in kind from the common person. Although today Confucian moral self-cultivation is usually read against a background assumption of human perfectibility (an assumption arguably derived from the Mencius-influenced Confucius of the Sòng and later dynasties), many Hàn narratives concerning Confucius indicate that his achievement of sagehood was destined from birth. Sīmǎ Qiān gives ample indication of this fate, recording that Confucius was born with a sunken forehead[9] and grew to such a height that he was called "the tall man" and viewed as extraordinary (yì 異).[10] The most vivid description of the way his physical appearance showed his sagehood was his resemblance to a composite sketch of past sages: "a forehead like Yáo 堯, a neck like [Shùn's minister] Gāo Yáo 皋陶, shoulders like [former minister of the state of Zhèng] Zǐchǎn 子產, and only three inches shorter than Yǔ 禹 from the waist down."[11] Confucius' physical resemblance to sage kings and their worthy ministers was an omen of his future as a sage, capable of being read in the same way that Hàn specialists could evaluate or physiognomize animals, swords, and people through observation of their external characteristics.

One metaphor that speaks directly to the difference between such a sage and the ordinary person is that of the dragons in the field.[12] In some Hàn texts, Confucius's extraordinary qualities are explained by likening him to an entirely different species, and a fantastic one at that. A characteristically cryptic passage in the Xiàng 象, a text ancillary to the classic Changes (Yì 易), comments on the hexagram kūn 坤: "When dragons do battle in the fields, their blood is black and yellow."[13] A commentary buried in a tomb in south China at the beginning of the Hàn, assigned the title Questions of the Various Disciples (Èrsānzǐ wèn 二三子問), reads the original passage as a metaphor for the sage's encounter with the ordinary person. According to Liáo Míngchūn 廖名春, the Questions of the Various Disciples interprets the Xiàng text as "Dragons encounter [ordinary people] in the fields, their blood [as seen through the patterns of their scales] is black and gold."[14] When his disciples ask him what this means, Confucius answers that the image of the dragon is a metaphor for the sage:

Confucius said:

"These words refer to the great man's precious virtue and his imparting teachings to the people. Now, is it not the dragon that has the patterns (wén 文) of filial piety, and can suddenly show variegation through the display of different colors?[15] [Is it not] the sage whose virtue and righteousness are immense, who molds phenomena and perfects his devices?"

"The phrase 'dragons encounter in the fields,' refers to the great man's possessing tremendous virtue and meeting with the people. 'Their blood is black and gold' refers to seeing his patterns (wén). The sage's going out and guiding the people by molding and teaching, is also like the pattern (wén) of the dragons, and can be called 'black and gold', and so he is called a 'dragon.' Of having seen a dragon, it is said there is 'nothing greater.' "[16]

The key to this passage is the double meaning of the term wén, which refers to the patterns of the dragon and is also used to refer to the cultural pattern transmitted by the sage. It is the sage's virtue (dé 德) that separates him from the ordinary person, and is responsible for his physically distinguishing characteristics.[17] This saying of Confucius predates Sīmǎ Qiān's biography of Confucius by almost a century, but gives insight into what the biography means when it quotes Confucius marveling at the sage Lǎozǐ: "Today I have seen Lǎozǐ, and he is like a dragon!"[18] The metaphor, of course, implies that sages are a separate species from the ordinary person, and indeed Confucius' appearance implies he might well have been.

Confucius' exceptional virtue and status as a "heavenly teacher" is derived from a picture in which knowledge derives from Heaven. When the intellectual historian Féng Yǒulán 馮友蘭 observed of the Hàn view of Confucius that "if these views had prevailed, Confucius would have held in China a position similar to that of Jesus Christ, and Confucianism would have become a religion in the proper sense of the term,"[19] this aspect of Confucius was probably what he had in mind. The question of why these views did not prevail is a complex one, and one possible explanation is based on the ascendancy of the different texts associated with Confucius. The superhuman Confucius associated with the Changes or Spring and Autumn Annals is very different from the human Confucius of the Analects, the latter text being most closely associated with the sage today.

The "Uncrowned King" and the Spring and Autumn Annals

The Spring and Autumn Annals [Chūnqiū 春秋] was closely linked to Confucius during the Hàn because it was thought to have come from his own hand and not from those of his disciples, as had the Analects. The former text consists of a pithy chronicle of political events in Confucius' home state of Lu from the period 722 to 481 B.C.E. The attribution of the Spring and Autumn Annals to Confucius is first found in the fourth-century B.C.E. writings of Master Mèng 孟—Mencius. Mencius goes further than simply attributing the Annals to Confucius; he provides the reason that Confucius compiled it: "Confucius was anxious, and wrote the Spring and Autumn Annals. The writing of history is a matter for the Emperor, and so Confucius said: 'Those who understand me will do so on account of the Spring and Autumn Annals, and those who berate me will also do so on account of the Spring and Autumn Annals.' "[20] Mencius not only gives great weight to content of the text, but also states that it is the work that Confucius himself said he would be judged by. The question immediately arises, if history was "a matter for the Emperor," why would Confucius usurp that role? The compiler of the Mencius, Zhào Qí 趙岐 (d. 201 C.E.) did not see this as a problem: "Confucius feared the destruction of the kingly Way and so wrote the Spring and Autumn Annals. He based it on the historical records of the state of Lu, originating the method of the 'uncrowned king' (sùwáng 素王), and so it says 'a matter for the Emperor.' "[21] The Hàn commentator does not see any usurpation taking place because by the second century C.E. the tradition that Confucius was destined by Heaven to rule China was already well known. A theory that a true sage comes every five hundred years appears in the Mencius itself, which identifies Confucius as Heaven sent. More than two centuries before Zhào Qí edited the Mencius, Sīmǎ Qiān had recorded the physical characteristics, cataloged previously, that marked Confucius as a sage king. By Zhào's time, the doctrine that his method of ruling China was somehow encoded in the Spring and Autumn Annals, a fundamental tenet of what later scholars would call the "New Text" (jīnwén 今文) school of Confucianism, was also widespread.

One commentary to the Spring and Autumn Annals in particular was associated with this reading of the text. The Gōngyáng 公羊 commentary, supposedly written by Master Gōngyáng around 150 B.C.E. following centuries of esoteric transmission through the lineages of disciples of Confucius, elucidates the terse text of the classic by explaining why those who fared well in the text were deserving and why those who fared ill were blameworthy. An example of this style of explanation is the Gōngyáng commentary to the Spring and Autumn Annals entry for the fourteenth year of Duke Āi 哀, 481 B.C.E. The text reads simply: "In the spring, a unicorn (lín 麟) was captured on an imperial hunt in the west." The Gōngyáng commentary, in its characteristic question and answer style, dissects the hidden message:

Why was this written?
    To record an anomaly.
How was it an anomaly?
    [The unicorn] is not a beast indigenous to the Middle Kingdom.
If that is the case, then who captured it?
    Woodgatherers.

> If it was woodgatherers, then they were commoners. Why say "imperial hunt"?
> In order to magnify it.
> Why is it magnified?
> On account of the capture of the unicorn it is magnified.[22]

The *Gōngyáng* commentary is centrally concerned with Confucius' motive for making each entry, and often each word, in the *Spring and Autumn Annals*. That motive was almost never held to be apparent on the surface. Here, the beast's discovery by common woodgatherers, a fact that is not in the original text of the *Spring and Autumn Annals*, is introduced for the purpose of showing that Confucius exaggerated to emphasize the importance of the appearance of an omen. This extreme theory of author intentionality would not sound far-fetched to the reader of the commentary in the Hàn because Confucius was thought to have regularly used *wēiyán* 微言, subtle or secret words, in his teachings.

One Hàn view of Confucius was that he approved of a transmission of the Way that bypassed ordinary language. Even in the *Analects*, Confucius seeks to imitate Heaven by eschewing language: "I would like to go without words."[23] Confucius continues by saying that heaven's intent can be discerned through its creation and seasonal cycles, implying that heavenly communication takes place without words. This is perhaps the earliest reference to nonlinguistic communication by Confucius, a type of intercourse that those who were not conversant in the Way could not understand. In the third century B.C.E. *Spring and Autumn Annals of Master Lü* [*Lǜshì chūnqīu*], Confucius is shown to be able to communicate with another worthy without speaking. He explains: "If one is that sort of man, one's eyes meet and the Way is established in a way that cannot be conveyed by appearance or sound."[24] Confucius was also connected with the idea of esoteric transmission of text. One tradition preserved in a commentary to a poem in chapter twenty-nine of the medieval literary compendium *Wénxuǎn* 文選 implies that the *Analects* was written by the disciple Zǐ Xià 子夏 from the secret words of Confucius to make the case that Confucius was the "uncrowned king."[25] The archetypal example of this secret mode of transmission was the *Spring and Autumn Annals*.

Confucius' compilation of the *Spring and Autumn Annals* was seen as an exercise in recording the secret way of rulership, in effect an esoteric transmission, brought about in response to a sign from Heaven. The appearance of the unicorn examined just above, according to several Hàn sources, was the event in the life of Confucius that caused him to despair of becoming a ruler himself. Around 100 B.C.E., Sīmǎ Qiān picks up on the same narrative:

> In the Spring of the fourteenth year of Duke Āi of Lu, there was an imperial hunt in Dàyě 大野. Lord Shūsūn's 叔孫 chariot master Chú Shāng 鉏商 captured a unicorn, and it was taken to be an inauspicious sign. Zhòng Nǐ (i.e. Confucius) saw it and said:

> "It is a unicorn."
> He took possession of it, saying:
> "The Yellow River does not produce a chart, the
> Luo River does not produce its writings, and I am
> finished. . . . My Way is at an end."[26]

Confucius was able to interpret the omen of the unicorn, a sign sent by Heaven, and was not very happy with the message. Further, by speaking of the chart and writings, Confucius alludes to auspicious omens from great rivers that had presaged the rise of previous rulers. Their absence was seen as indicative of the fact that Heaven did not bestow its mandate (tiānmìng 天命) on Confucius. Sīmǎ Qiān has woven the accounts available to him together in such a way as to suggest that it was because of the untimely omen of the unicorn that Confucius became discouraged. Other texts relate this story in such a way as to imply that Confucius' own death was presaged by the appearance of the unicorn. The *Gōngyáng* commentary continues its version of the story with the following question and answer:

> What is accomplished by magnifying the capture of the unicorn?
> The unicorn is the beast of benevolence. It appears when a king
> arrives, but does not appear in the king's absence. Someone once
> told [Confucius] that there had appeared a deer with a horn.
> Confucius said: "Who is it that has come? Who is it that has come?"
> He brought his sleeves up to cover his face and cried into his robes.[27]

The parallel drawn here between the captured beast and the benevolent sage is made explicit in a passage from the later *Kong Family Masters' Anthology* [*Kǒngcóngzǐ* 孔叢子*], in which Confucius says: "I am to human beings what the unicorn is to other beasts. The unicorn appeared and immediately died, just as my Way is reaching its end."[28] The metaphorical use of the unicorn is of a kind with that of the "dragons in the field" examined above, setting Confucius apart from ordinary men.

During the Hàn period, the appearance of the unicorn was seen as the motivation for the production of the *Spring and Autumn Annals* as a manual for future sage kings. According to Sīmǎ Qiān, Confucius' response to the omen that he would not be able to rule the world before his death was to encode his Heaven-given knowledge in the *Spring and Autumn Annals*:

> [Confucius said:] "My Way has not been put into practice. How can I
> make myself known to future generations?"
> Thereupon, he wrote the *Spring and Autumn Annals* on the basis of
> historical records. . . . He was frugal with his language, but expressed
> profound meaning. Although the rulers of the states of Wú and Chǔ
> called themselves *wáng* 王 "king," in the *Spring and Autumn Annals* they are
> disparaged as *zǐ* 子 "barons." At the meeting at Jiàntǔ 踐土, to which the

Zhōu Emperor had really been summoned, the Spring and Autumn Annals
overstates the case by saying: "The Heavenly King [that is, the Zhōu
Emperor] was on an imperial hunt in Héyáng 河陽." The current
generation can be accurately measured by applying these [judgments]
to like categories. If at some point in the future a ruler can distinguish
and make clear [the text's] implications of disparagement and
belittlement, putting into practice the meaning of the Spring and Autumn
Annals, then chaotic ministers and thieving barons will fear them.[29]

Just as the Gōngyáng commentary contended that the phrase "imperial hunt" was
used to emphasize the importance of the omen of the unicorn's capture, here the
Zhōu Emperor's lack of power is disguised in order to castigate the feudal lord
who ordered him about. For Sīmǎ Qiān, in such details the Spring and Autumn Annals
contains the encoded Way of the true ruler. When Confucius realized that he lived
in an age that would not recognize his ability to rule, he used the historical records
available to him as a key, adding, deleting, and changing information so that when
a future ruler compared the product of his editing against original records, a blue-
print for government emerged. The method of reading the Spring and Autumn Annals,
seen above in the Gōngyáng commentary, pictures Confucius as a codemaker rather
than a historian. His intent was to pass on his method to future rulers—in order
to "to wait upon later sages," in the words of the Gōngyáng commentary.[30] As one
might expect, the reference to "later sages" was often read to be referring to the
house of Líu—the heriditary ruling clan of the Hàn dynasty.[31]

Confucius' Prophecies and Political Legitimation

During the Hàn dynasty, a tradition developed around a set of texts that were purported to be written by Confucius and contain his esoteric teachings and prophecies of future "legitimate" rulers. Although the commentaries on the Spring and
Autumn Annals were to some extent viewed as a "deciphering" of the sage's message,
these related texts were in some cases quite literally encoded. One example is a
lost text listed in the bibliographic survey in the History of the Hàn, the Charts and
Models of Confucius and His Disciples (Kǒngzǐ túrén túfǎ 孔子徒人圖法), the title indicating
encoded prophecies.[32] This text was probably an early example of what was to
become an important body of literature in the middle and later Hàn generally
known as the "weft texts" or "apocrypha" (wěishū 緯書). Like the commentaries
to the Spring and Autumn Annals, the apocrypha were to some extent based on what
has been called the "correlative cosmology" of the Hàn period, a system in which
the observable world was reduced to sets of natural categories, the elements of
like categories influencing each other according to subtle patterns. These correlations, expressed in categories like yīn and yáng or the five phases (wǔxíng 五行),
were applied both to the natural world and to human affairs, to the past and,
sometimes, to the prediction of the future.

By the end of the Western Hàn, these texts, closely associated with Confucius, already were taking on important political dimensions. The Japanese scholar Itano Chōhachi 板野長八 has argued that it was Emperor Guāngwǔ's 光武 (r. 25–57 C.E.) promotion of such texts as a means of legitimizing his rule that led to the establishment of Confucianism as a religious tradition. After the short-lived Xīn dynasty (9–23 C.E.) of Wáng Mǎng 王莽, the relegitimation of the Hàn was accomplished by recourse to the doctrine of "Red Governance" (chìzhì 赤制), which held that the Hàn, in common with the sage king Yáo, was associated with the virtue of fire (huǒdé 火德). Itano describes the central role that Confucius played in legitimizing this doctrine: "[B]ecause of the breakdown of the system of Rites and Music at the end of the three dynasties, Heaven made the Profoundly Holy Confucius put a system of learning together and help the Hàn[. I]t is obvious that these prophecies were regarded as classics, and it also seems clear that they were held to be connected with Confucius. That is to say, they were Confucian."[33] By establishing the "Red Governance," Confucius ensured that the Mandate of Heaven remained with the Hàn. That the doctrine itself was not attested until the first century was explained by its esoteric nature. According to Hàn loyalist Sū Jìng 蘇竟, the doctrine was contained in a text called *Kǒng Qīu's Secret Classic* [*Kǒng Qīu Mìjīng* 孔丘密經]: "Now, in *Kǒng Qīu's Secret Classic* [Confucius] established the 'Red Governance' for the Hàn, and mysteriously locked it away in a dark chamber. Although its language is hidden, the affairs it describes will become clear. Moreover, although the virtue of fire passed down from Yáo is dim, it will certainly become bright."[34] This esoteric tradition of Confucius was also accepted by the anti-Gūangwǔ cliques, but the tradition was interpreted to demonstrate a different thesis. According the Gōngsūn Shù 公孫述 (d. 39 C.E.), Heaven's Mandate had indeed been passed on to the Hàn, but the Hàn had gone through twelve rulers, the same number of Dukes of Lǔ chronicled by Confucius in the *Spring and Autumn Annals*. Hence their mandate had expired.[35] So it was that all sides accepted the role of Confucius' esoteric teachings in conferring political legitimacy.

These esoteric teachings were closely tied to omens, signs in the natural world that, interpreted in light of certain correlations based on the patterns that underlie the phenomenal world, revealed information about the present or future. In the above conflict between the supporters of Emperor Guāngwǔ and Gōngsūn Shù, numerous prodigies and freaks of nature that correlated with either fire or metal were adduced as evidence that their respective leaders fulfilled the prophecies of Confucius. This approach was similar to the way that the appearance of the unicorn was interpreted in Hàn apocryphal texts. According the one apocryphal text preserved in a Táng collection, the *Classic of Filial Piety's Right Half of the Wooden Tally* [*Xiàojīng yòuqì* 孝經右契], after Confucius correctly interpreted a dream in order to find the unicorn, the animal spat out three rolls of bound wooden text. Another fragment of that text says that the charts on these newly disgorged bundles contained the prophecy that the "Red Líu" house would arise.[36]

The image of Confucius as the last great sage emperor, albeit one who never got to rule, was an important one in the Hàn. Pivotal to the Hàn commentaries to the *Spring and Autumn Annals*, this image was behind the idea of the esoteric transmission of Confucius' method and prophecies, an idea popularized by several factions as a means to political legitimation. This is not the Confucius with whom most people in the twentieth century are familiar, however, because a competing Confucius was gaining currency during the Hàn. This other Confucius was less threatening to the newly unified empire because it was tied to a text understood to be concerned not with political legitimacy but with ritual self-cultivation within the existing structures of authority. This text was the *Analects*, and during the Hàn it was cast as an educational text to be used in training ritual officials and the Heir Apparent, a context that may even have influenced its formulation.

The Social Context of the Western Hàn Formation of the *Analects*

The *Analects* that circulates today was still being formed in the Hàn. Although the content of individual books may be dated back to the Warring States period, the paucity of references to and quotations from these books indicates that most were not widely available. Recent archaeological discoveries show that individual books also circulated independently well into the Hàn, but that a version very close to the received version existed by 55 B.C.E. Thus, although parts of the text undoubtedly were transmitted through master-disciple traditions perhaps all the way back to the time of Kǒng Qiū, the *Analects* itself was fixed as a text during the Hàn dynasty.

This state of affairs comes through clearly in light of *Analects*-related texts unearthed from tombs during the last few decades. These texts show that collections of narratives about Confucius circulated in rather fluid form during the first and second centuries B.C.E. Among the bundles of "miscellaneous quotations" buried around 300 B.C.E. and found in 1996 are at least two quotations now found in the *Analects*, neither of which are identified as such or otherwise distinguished from other quotations that surround them.[37] In 1977, the discovery of a list of the titles of forty-six narratives about Confucius at a grave site in Anhui Province that dates to 165 B.C.E. showed that individual stories were circulating independently, entering certain collections, and being omitted from others.[38] Four years earlier, a set of scattered bamboo slips that dated from 55 B.C.E. was discovered in a tomb in Ding county, Hebei Province. These slips contain snatches of narratives found in books three and fourteen of the *Analects*, stories about Confucius and his disciples that are included in other Hàn anthologies, and stories about noteworthy sages like Guǎnzǐ 管子, Yànzǐ 晏子, King Wén, the Duke of Zhōu, and the sage king Tàng 湯.[39] This last find is especially significant because these mixed narratives were found alongside a partial version of the *Analects*, which indicates that quotations found in the *Analects* continued to circulate as parts of other collections even after the *Analects* was formed. Although arguments from absence do not constitute proof, the lack of references to the title Lúnyǔ in pre-Hàn texts combined with recent archaeological evidence strongly indicates that the *Analects* was culled out of such isolated stories and sets of stories.[40]

In such a context, one function of the collection of the *Analects* was probably to isolate a particular set of narratives about Confucius from other such sets and from narratives that concerned other sages. In the middle of the second century B.C.E., Confucius enjoyed the kind of vogue that had made the Duke of Zhōu popular previously.[41] It is in this context that the "discovery" of the *Ancient [text] Analects* or *Gǔ Lúnyǔ* 古論語, traditionally dated 155 B.C.E., established an orthodox set of narratives about the sage. John Makeham argues that this was the point at which the disparate sets of narratives were first formed into a discrete "book:" "[The status of the *Ancient [text] Analects*] as a book was a product of being singled out for special attention in the Western Hàn precisely because it had been found in the wall of Confucius' house and the ascendancy of Confucianism at this time required that an orthodox and standard version of Confucius' recorded sayings be established."[42] This was the same type of selective valorization that historian Sīmǎ Qiān, in his *Records of the Grand Historian*, was engaged in around 100 B.C.E., when he assembled his biographical treatment of the sage.[43] During the second half of the second century, then, Confucius narratives existed in sets of narratives devoted to a number of ancient sages, as parts of smaller collections of Confucius narratives, and in the *Ancient [text] Analects*. Even a century after that version of the *Analects* came onto the scene, however, rival editions competed for attention.

An example of the individual redactions of the *Analects* that circulated during the first century B.C.E. was the one compiled by Zhāng Yǔ 張禹 (d. 5 B.C.E.). The marquis of Āncháng, Zhāng Yǔ had access to several versions of the Lúnyǔ around 45 B.C.E., although they exhibited different formal features. According to Bān Gù 班固 (32–92 C.E.), the discrepancies between these versions caused Zhāng to compile his own edition:

> When Zhāng Yǔ first became a tutor, he wrote and presented his *Sections and Sentences of the Analects* [Lúnyǔ zhāngjù 論語章句] because the crown prince questioned him repeatedly about the classic. Initially, Lǔ Fúqīng 魯扶卿, Marquis Shèng 勝 of Xià 夏, Wáng Yáng 王陽 [i.e., Wáng Jí 王吉], Xiāo Wàngzhī 蕭望之, and Wéi Xuánchéng 韋玄成 had all discussed the Lúnyǔ, but their book divisions and enumeration sometimes disagreed.[44]

Pedagogical motivations caused Zhāng to compile his edition, a work that attempted to reconcile the conflicting versions that other teachers of the text used. Zhāng's work did not survive, but Bān notes that Zhāng's reorganization of the text was followed by most later students of the text.

The example of Zhāng Yǔ highlights the connection between the profession of teaching during this period and the *Analects*. Zhāng Yǔ compiled his commentary during his time as imperial household grandee, when he was charged by the grand tutor to the Heir Apparent to teach the *Analects* to the Heir Apparent. Most other experts on the *Analects* mentioned by Bān Gù appear to have been engaged in similar enterprises. Perhaps the earliest text devoted exclusively to the *Analects* was the *Explanations of the Analects* [*Lúnyǔ shuō* 論語説], which Marquis Shèng of Xià wrote when he was grand tutor to the Heir Apparent around 73 B.C.E. Shèng received 100 catties of gold for his teaching and for a copy of his edition of the classic *Documents*, a text on which he was also an expert.[45] Xiāo Wàngzhī, an expert on the *Analects*, was from 59 to 49 B.C.E. the grand tutor to the Heir Apparent who employed Zhāng Yǔ.[46] Wéi Xuánchéng served as the next grand tutor to the Heir Apparent, from 49 to 43 B.C.E. (and later became chancellor from 42 until his death in 36 B.C.E.). Wáng Jí and Lǔ Fúqīng appear to have been the only experts who did not officially tutor the Heir Apparent. Wáng served in several offices in the middle of the first century and taught the *Analects* and the *Poetry* to private students, among them Zhāng Yǔ.[47] Nothing is known about Lǔ Fúqīng except for his connection with Kǒng Ān'guó 孔安國 (156–74 B.C.E.) and the text of the *Analects* that Kǒng is reputed to have presented to Emperor Wǔ.[48] The fact that both authors of commentaries to the *Analects* in the first century B.C.E. and four of the text's six experts served as grand tutors to the Heir Apparent shows that the text was closely associated with the education of minors.

The specific reasons for new or renewed interest in the *Analects* in the 50s and 40s may have been political events in the imperial court. With the accession of Emperor Xuān in 74 B.C.E., the succession of tutors to his son, then only two years old, were generally expert on the *Analects*. This continued after Emperor Xuān's death, when his son, Emperor Yuán, reigned from 49 to 33 B.C.E. This was exactly the period during which, in the analysis of historian Michael Loewe, the court began to move from a "modernist" to "reformist" ideology, wherein "statesmen now looked specifically to the example of the [Zhōu] rather than the [Qín]."[49] In the *Analects*, Confucius continually celebrates the example of the Zhōu, and passages such as *Analects* 2.3 are ideally tailored for use by Loewe's reformist in a debate against a modernist: "Lead them with government, unify their conduct with punishment, and the common people will avoid things without a sense of shame. Lead them with virtue, unify their conduct with ritual, and they will not only have a sense of shame but also discipline themselves."[50] The Qín described itself as ruling by law, and the Confucius of the *Analects* contrasts this to the Zhōu ideal of ruling by virtue. Whether or not this passage could have been spoken by Kǒng Qīu, anticipating as it does a fundamental debate in the third through first centuries B.C.E., its presence in the text that tutors connected with the rise of reformism taught to the prince is entirely consistent.

That editions of the *Analects* became standardized during this period of increased attention was attested in stunning fashion by the discovery of a partial bamboo slip version of the *Analects* in the Ding county tomb of Líu Xīu 劉脩, who died in 55 B.C.E. while serving as Prince Huài 懷 of Zhōngshān during the reign of Emperor Xuān 宣 (r. 7–49 B.C.E.).[51] Containing 7,576 characters, this version of the *Analects* reflects a self-conscious effort to amalgamate versions of the *Analects* later listed in Bān Gù's inventory of the editions of the *Analects* and collateral texts that circulated in the middle of the Hàn period.[52] The three versions of the *Analects* that Bān Gù listed are the *Ancient* [text] version in twenty-one books, the *State of Qí* 齊 version in twenty-two books, and the *State of Lǔ* 魯 version in twenty books, with an appended commentary in nineteen books.[53] The Ding county find shows that the versions listed by Bān Gù were already being reconciled as early as 55 B.C.E., two centuries before Zhèng Xuán 鄭玄 (127–200 C.E.) collated the current *Analects* with its twenty books. The text of the *Analects* found there has an extra section copied onto the end of book twenty, which attests to an attempt to reconcile the *Ancient* [text] version with the *State of Lǔ* version by copying the twenty-first book of the former onto to the end of the twentieth and final book of the latter in order to make the number of books coincide with each other.[54] This feature of the Ding country *Analects* confirms a suggestion by Zhái Hào 翟灝 (d. 1788) that the *Ancient* [text] version and the *State of Lǔ* version were formally differentiated by the division of the three sections of book twenty in the latter version into two parts, the second of which created a twenty-first book in the former version.[55] The recently discovered text appears to be the product of an anonymous copyist who worked before 55 B.C.E. to reconcile the formal differences between the competing versions of the *Analects* in exactly the way ascribed to figures like Zhāng Yǔ.

This new datum is consistent with some of Bān Gù's comments on the regional versions of the *Analects*. Bān Gù writes:

> At the beginning of the Hàn there were explanations [of the *Analects*] in the states of Qí and Lǔ. Those who transmitted the *State of Qí* [*Analects*] were the Commandant of the Capital of Chāngyì Wáng Jí, Privy Treasurer Sòng Jī 宋畸, Grandee Secretary Gòng Yǔ 貢禹, Prefect of the Masters of Writing Chōng Zōng 充宗 of Wubi and Yōng Shēng 庸生 of Liáodōng. Of these, only Wáng Yáng [i.e. Wáng Jí] is famous. Those who transmit the *State of Lǔ Analects* were the Chief Commandant of Changshan Gōng Jiù 龔舊, Chancellor Wéi Xián 韋賢, Lǔ Fúqīng, General of the Van Xiāo Wàngzhī, and the Marquis of Āncháng Zhāng Yǔ, who all have lineages named after them. Mr. Zhāng is the most recent to be known in this generation.[56]

The set of officials in this passage overlaps with the set mentioned by Bān Gù above, with this passage containing the additional names of several officials not specifically connected with the *Analects* in their biographies. The names added to the list are, as far as can be determined, officials who served in positions that required knowledge of ritual affairs rather than textual scholarship.[57] The fact that Zhāng Yǔ studied with the *State of Qí* [*Analects*] scholars Yōng Shēng and Wáng Jí, and yet is listed as a Lǔ text scholar, indicates that he was familiar with both Qí and Lǔ editions, and yet he was troubled only by the fact that "book divisions and enumeration sometimes disagreed." These statements about Zhāng suggest that the disagreements Zhāng Yǔ sought to reconcile were not based on content, but rather concerned the enumeration of books and sections, such as that of the sections of book twenty.

If, as this chronology suggests, the *Analects* was isolated and then standardized from various sets of collections of narratives about Confucius in the first two centuries B.C.E., this process would fit in well with literary trends of the time. The first two centuries of the Hàn saw tremendous changes in the role of books, changes that most certainly affected the maturation of the *Analects*. Recent archaeological discoveries confirm that texts on both wood and silk were often listed in grave inventories, which shows that the texts were assumed to have postmortem value to the grave occupant. This was also the period that saw the construction of imperial book repositories and attempts to take a census of all book titles.[58] In 26 B.C.E., a major effort was begun to catalog the books in circulation in the empire, which culminated in the bibliography included in Bān Gù's *History of the Hàn* and generated short descriptions of 13,269 bundles of text, according to one estimate.[59] Although books had economic value to individuals, the collection of books by the state likely reflected their increasing educational value as, among other things, textbooks for use in educating both the Heir Apparent and prospective civil servants.

The role of Confucian texts in the imperial examination system and the establishment of official positions devoted to their study was probably the most important single catalyst for consolidating and editing the texts associated with Confucius. In 136 B.C.E., the position of erudit in the Five Classics was established by Emperor Wǔ.[60] From 124 B.C.E. through 41 B.C.E., the number of disciples at the Tàixué 太學 or "Academy," went from zero to one thousand.[61] The classicists (rú 儒) who served as erudits were only secondarily expert on the *Analects*, but had to have a primary field of expertise in one of the Five Classics. Textual issues and matters of interpretation were the subject of major discussions at Stone Canal [Shíqú 石渠] Pavilion in 51 B.C.E.,[62] and at the White Tiger [Bóhǔ 白虎] Hall in 79 C.E.[63] The motives for the establishment of definitive editions of text during this period were bound up with career opportunities in teaching in general and in teaching these texts specifically to the imperial family and officials engaged in court ritual. The new legion of imperial text experts put much effort into standardizing and commenting upon the classics.

These developments may be summed up by saying that the popularization of the *Analects* in the Hàn served specific social and political ends. The context of the formation and reception of the *Analects* in the Hàn is therefore very different from the relatively private transmission of its precursors in the Warring States period.[64] Recent archaeological discoveries confirm that the start of the period saw the circulation of a wide variety of texts that contained narratives about Confucius, stories attributed to Confucius, and transcripts of his dialogues with disciples. Beginning with Emperor Xuān in 74 B.C.E., the title Lúnyǔ was used to refer to a selection of these texts used primarily in the education of the Heir Apparent and ritual officials. This subset of Confucius stories may have been culled out partly based on specific political objectives and pedagogical concerns of the tutors of the Heir Apparent, scholar-officials who were deeply concerned with matters of public policy and court ritual and with a particular reformist agenda. The formation of an edition by an anonymous copyist similar to that of Zhāng Yǔ around 45 B.C.E., characteristic of attempts during that period to standardize texts, prefigured the influential collation by Zhèng Xuán two centuries later.

Because the popularization of the *Analects* in the Hàn served specific social and political ends, the promotion of the image of Confucius that it puts forward might be explained, regardless of considerations about accuracy, as best serving these ends. The account given above about the promotion of the *Analects* as a set of Confucius narratives that centered on education and ritual and were selected for a specific use in politically sensitive circumstances explains why the *Analects* Confucius is so different from the image associated with his authorship of the *Spring and Autumn Annals*. Exactly when this selection took place is unclear, but it is clear that these narratives were closely associated with the office of grand tutor to the Heir Apparent for much of the Western Hàn period.

Eastern Hàn Commentaries and the "Demons and Spirits"

The ascendancy of the *Analects* during the first half of the first century B.C.E. may therefore be seen as the result of the advocacy of the text by court officials with a specific agenda. These circumstances did not continue into the second half of the dynasty, the "Eastern" Hàn (25–220 C.E.), but the *Analects* remained influential as an educational text.

During the Eastern Hàn, the *Analects* was the subject of much commentary and imitation as the life of Confucius became the subject of increased attention. Fragments of several Hàn commentaries to the *Analects* still exist. Comments attributed to Líu Xīn 劉歆 (45 B.C.E.–23 C.E.), Bāo Xián 包咸 (6 B.C.E.–65 C.E.), Hé Xīu 何休 (129–182 C.E.), Mǎ Róng 馬融 (77–166 C.E.), and a "Master Zhōu 周" appear in post-Hàn collections.[65] Zhèng Xuán's commentary was collected in Líu Bǎonán's 劉寶楠 Lúnyǔ zhèngyì 論語正義, and parts of Táng dynasty texts used for children's education have been discovered at Dūnhuáng.[66] Of these Hàn commentators, only Bāo fits the former image of a teacher to the Heir Apparent, the other commentators being private teachers and exegetes.[67] Mǎ commented on a dozen other books as did Zhèng.[68] Hé Xīu was a foremost expert on the various commentaries to the *Spring and Autumn Annals*, and "refined and researched the *Six Classics* and was unequaled by scholars in his generation."[69] Zhèng created an authoritative school of *Analects* interpretation. Once Confucius appeared to him in a dream, and his expertise on the sage was such that his students recorded his answers to questions on the classics and compiled an eight-chapter work, the lost Zhèngzhì 鄭志, on his answers to questions on the *Analects* alone.[70] When the *Analects* is referred to in works from the second half of the first century C.E., rarely are the disagreements between editions mentioned, and the type of scholars who worked on them indicate that the text had entered the commentarial mainstream.

Although each of these commentators doubtless had his own way of looking at the *Analects*, there are some ways in which Hàn readings of the text differed significantly as a group from later readings. To appreciate these differences, it is only necessary to examine one facet of the master's teachings as received today—the belief in demons and spirits (*guǐshén* 鬼神). Modern authority D. C. Lau has written that Confucius' attitude toward survival after death "can, at best, be described as agnostic."[71] Lau cites an important passage in the *Analects*, 11.12, to show that the Master was unwilling to commit himself on the subject of survival after death. Lau translates the Master's words thus: "You are not able even to serve man. How can you serve the spirits?"[72] This reading of the Master's attitude toward demons and spirits is characteristic of the modern reading of Confucius, described by Herbert Fingarette as "either as an empirical, humanist, this-worldly teaching or as a parallel to Platonist-rationalist doctrines."[73]

This is not the only possible reading of Confucius' attitude toward demons and spirits, and it was not the reading favored in the Hàn. A century ago, reformer and scholar Kāng Yǒuwéi 康有為 (1858–1937) wrote with characteristic dismissiveness: "Some contend that Confucius did not speak of the afterlife, but this is great stupidity." Kāng argued that the relationship between serving man and serving the spirits was a temporal one, that only after becoming a sage would access be gained to the afterlife, a view that he supported by citing *Analects* 4.8: "Having heard the Dào in the morning, it would be suitable to die that night."[74] He complained: "It is not that [he did not speak of] life, death, demons and spirits. . . . But rather that those who came after him censored it out on account of Buddhist doctrine."[75] Whether or not Kāng's interpretation is correct, there is little question that later commentaries on the *Analects* were generally very different from Hàn and Six Dynasties commentaries on the subject of the afterlife.

Confucius participates in ritual sacrifice at a number of points in the *Analects*, and even in an exorcism (10.14), but the interpretation of his attitude toward the propitiation of the "demons and spirits" in these passages changed significantly from the Hàn to the Sòng periods. One of the most famous lines in the *Analects* (6.22) is spoken by Confucius in response to a query about the nature of intelligence (*zhì* 知). The key, he says, is to serve the interests of the people and to revere the demons and spirits, keeping them distant. In the Hàn, commentaries focused on the imperative to "reverence," whereas in the Sòng they focused on maintaining "distance." Lau followed the second strategy by preposing the latter clause, translating it as: "keep one's distance from the gods and spirits while showing them reverence,"[76] and the line is often taken to be further proof of Confucius' reticence to be involved with demons and spirits. In the Sòng, for example, one of the Chéng 程 brothers explained it: "Most people trust in demons and spirits, and this is misguided. Yet some of those who do not trust in them are also incapable of being reverent. To be able to be reverent and distant at the same time—this truly may be called intelligent."[77] In other words, reverence is called for, but one does not put one's trust in demons and spirits—this would be succumbing to a common misconception. Zhū Xī 朱熹 (1130–1200 C.E.) agreed: "one must not be misguided by the unknowable affairs of the demons and spirits,"[78] but instead concentrate on the human Way. Surviving Hàn commentaries did not, however, see Confucius' words as a condemnation of such popular beliefs. The Later Hàn commentator Bāo Xián understood Confucius to advocate "revering the demons and spirits but not overindulging (dú 黷),"[79] whereas Zhèng Xuán interprets the term "distance" more literally: "Being 'distant from the demons and spirits' but 'close to people' refers to the ancestral temple being outside [the palace] and the court being inside it."[80] By sacrificing to the demons and spirits, the ruler administers to the spirit world in a way parallel to, but separate from, his administration of the human world. Not only is there no sense that concern with the demons and spirits is a waste of time or a popular superstition, but such concern is also considered one of the two primary foci of the ruler's ritual duties. Confucius was not perceived to proscribe these practices, especially in light of his approval of sage king Yǔ's filial attitude to the demons and spirits as expressed in *Analects* 8.21.

A similar contrast may been drawn between the Hàn and Sòng commentaries to *Analects* 5.18, in which a counsellor of the state of Lǔ is raised as an example by Confucius. Counsellor Zāng Wénzhòng 臧文仲 carved and painted ornate designs on the dwelling of his tortoise, something that Confucius implies casts doubt on his intelligence.[81] Zhèng Xuán's commentary from the Hàn describes the dwelling: "With mountains carved into the top and the beams painted in a duckweed pattern—the very decorations on the Emperor's temple, which were not suitable for Wénzhòng to have had."[82] This interpretation, that Zāng demonstrated lack of intelligence by usurping the ritual forms proper to those of higher rank, was standard during the Hàn. The modern scholar Chéng Shùdé 程樹德 writes: "The Hàn theory was that housing the tortoise was exceeding what was ritually correct for a feudal lord, and the mountains carved on top and duckweed painted on the beams was decorating the dwelling in a way that exceeded what was ritually correct for the ancestral temple of the Emperor. This is different from the commentary of Zhū [Xī]."[83] Indeed, the Sòng commentator Zhū Xī takes an entirely different tack, relating this passage to the one just examined about "keeping one's distance" from the demons and spirits. In his commentary on the *Analects*, Zhū Xī writes: "The people of the time thought Wénzhòng was intelligent, but Confucius said he did not 'serve the people's interests,' but instead fawningly indulged the demons and spirits in this way. How could he be called intelligent?"[84] The connection made here between the demons and spirits derives from the traditional use of tortoise shells for divination. Zhū Xī counters the Hàn reading by saying that even if Zāng usurped the ritual of those with higher status, this would not be unintelligent—but being obsessed by the realm of demons and spirits would be.[85] Again, the Sòng reading takes Confucius to be dismissive toward excessive concern with demons and spirits, whereas the Hàn reading does not.

During the Hàn, Confucius' association with divination practices was well established.[86] Confucius was also credited with the ordering and definitive interpretation of some of the commentaries to the *Changes*, and with the authorship of others. One of the texts he was thought to have written was the text ancillary to the *Changes* called Xìcí 繫辭, which relates mastery of the *Changes* to an understanding of the demons and spirits:

> The *Changes* follows Heaven and Earth, and so [with it] one is able to repair and discuss the Dào of the people of the world. [The *Changes*] looks up to observe the pattern of Heaven, down to examine the principle of Earth; this is how one may understand the causes of the imperceptible and the visible. [The *Changes*] observes the beginnings and relates this to endings; [this is how] one understands the explanations for life and death. Living things are made of essential qì 氣, and roaming hún 魂 spirits cause them to change; this is how one can understand the dispositions and circumstances of demons and spirits.[87]

If Confucius, late in life, was so interested in the *Changes* that he wrote about how they would help one understand matters not only of life and death, but also of demons and spirits, it is no wonder Hàn exegetes found it difficult to arrive at the same conclusion that Sòng literati did regarding the sage's agnosticism on such matters. Han writers like Wáng Fú 王符 (78–163 C.E.) quoted Confucius as advocating ascertaining the command of Heaven (words found in the Xìcí) before acting to make sure one's actions echo that mandate.[88] Images of Confucius in the Hàn depict him as a champion of divination, as long as it was used in its proper context.

Moreover, the *Records of the Grand Historian* attests to the Hàn Confucius' familiarity with the types of demons and spirits, a knowledge seen as akin to what we today would call historical knowledge. In one anecdote, a vessel that contains a creature like a sheep is unearthed. When Confucius is tested by being told that the animal was a dog, he politely disagrees. He enumerates the different types of oddity associated with forests and rocks, oceans, and the earth, the latter being an androgynous sheep.[89] Of course, he is right. In another story, a skeleton the size of a chariot is unearthed in Wú. The King of Wú sends an envoy to Confucius to ask about it, and Confucius uses his knowledge of spirit lore to answer. He recalls a previous instance of such a skeleton, that of the giant spirit (shén) named Fángfēng 防風, executed by the sage king Yǔ for being late to a meeting of the spirits.[90] The implication is that the skeleton is one of Fángfēng's descendants, then simply called the "big people." Confucius's knowledge of the supernatural is not seen as anything more than a detailed knowledge of the past, when the human and spirit world were not as strange to each other.

All this is not to say that Zhū Xī and other Sòng commentators were necessarily wrong about Master Kǒng's views about demons and spirits. It does, however, suggest that those who insist Master Kǒng "never spoke of . . . disorder and spirits (luàn shén 亂神)" (Analects 7.21) should realize they speak of an image constructed one and a half millennia after Confucius died. An earlier image of Confucius only failed to speak of "disorderly spirits (luànshén)"[91] because a sage was simply not ambivalent or agnostic about the "demons and spirits." The simple change from reading the two characters as a compound to reading them as two different objects captures nicely this change in Confucius' alleged worldview.

Although the Analects may have gained ascendancy because of the institutional and political circumstances of the first century B.C.E., the modern understanding of its content is not necessarily an expression of that period or the aims of its promoters. Even in the Analects, there are sections that seem to have come out of the mouth of the Confucius more closely associated with the Spring and Autumn Annals. This disparity makes sense when one considers the multiple concerns of Hàn writers, and is precisely the level of complexity that must characterize the examination of the interaction between myth and text and the early period.

Conclusion

This examination of images of Confucius and their relation to the formation and reception of the Analects in the Hàn has implications that go beyond the specific intellectual and historical contexts of the period. On the most basic level, it underscores an argument made earlier this century by Gù Jiégāng 顧頡剛: that each era has its own Confucius.[92] This is the level on which it is possible to differentiate the model of esoteric transmission of the Spring and Autumn Annals by a divine Confucius based on a way communicated to him by a quasi-anthropomorphic Heaven from the model of exoteric transmission of the Analects by a human Confucius interested in a way of developing certain potential that is intrinsic to every human being. In many ways, these contrasting models imply that Gù's thesis that the nature of Confucius changed from the Warring States period to the Hàn might be revised to note that different images of Confucius existed across different social groups during the same period.[93] On another level, however, these images of the sage are just poles of a dynamic continuum from which different social groups selected at different times. A more nuanced view must take into account the way that myth and text interacted at particular times and among particular groups. On this level, this essay argues that the Analects' initial connection with the education of the Heir Apparent and the career path of ritual officials perhaps accounts for the selection of narratives included in the Analects during the second century B.C.E. and its growing cultural influence in the first century B.C.E.

On either level, however, it is clear that the Hàn was a pivotal stage in the transformation of Master Kǒng into Confucius. It was in the Hàn that one sees both the Confucius closely associated with the legitimation of political authority and the Confucius associated with ritual self-cultivation. Confucius, fated to rule, was denied his fate. Intent on preserving his Heaven-endowed understanding of the Way, he created the *Spring and Autumn Annals* to accomplish this goal. At the same time, the *Analects* was being isolated from other sage-centered narratives for use in educational contexts to cultivate the virtues of the Heir-Apparent and others for whom knowledge of court ritual was imperative.[94] This paper does not seek to argue which Confucius is "right," but merely to suggest that both versions are possible, or at least have been viable historically.

ACKNOWLEDGMENTS

This chapter was written while the author was at the National Humanities Center supported by a grant from the Jesse Ball duPont Religious, Charitable, and Educational Fund. The author would like to thank Bryan W. Van Norden and John Makeham for their comments on this chapter.

NOTES

For some primary sources, the following conventions are used: (1) references to the Standard Histories are to the Zhonghua punctuated edition published in Beijing, either Shǐjì (1959), Hànshū (1962) or HòuHànshū (1965); (2) references to the Thirteen Classics refer to the Zhonghua reprint (1979) of the Qīng dynasty blockprint edition of Ruǎn Yuán's 阮元 (1764–1849) Shísānjīng zhùshū 十三經注疏; (3) other collections cited frequently are the 1983 Beijing Zhonghua edition of Zhūzǐ jíchéng 諸子集成 (ZZJC); and (4) Mǎ Guóhàn's 馬國翰 (1794–1857) collection of Confucian narratives published under the title Jiāyǔ děng 57 zhòng 家語等57種 in 1962 by Shijie in Taiwan. All official titles are translated according to Hans Bielenstein (1980). The numbering of the passages in the *Analects* follows D. C. Lau (1979).

    1. The Hàn is often divided into two sections: the Western Hàn from 206 B.C.E. to 23 C.E. (when the capital was in Cháng'ān) and the Eastern Hàn from 25 C.E. to 220 C.E. (when the capital moved east to Luòyáng). This division is sometimes altered to separate out the short intervening Xīn dynasty, which lasted from 9 C.E. to 23 C.E.

    2. For the adoption of the Five Classics (The *Changes*, *Poetry*, *Documents*, *Rites*, and *Spring and Autumn Annals*), see Hànshū 6.159. As Yáng Shùdá has pointed out, the post of erudit appears to have been conferred several decades earlier for selected scholars of the *Poetry* and the *Spring and Autumn Annals* (1984: 50). Other developments mentioned are treated in greater detail below.

    3. Jensen (1997: 5).

    4. D. C. Lau calls Sīmǎ Qiān's account of Confucius' life the "standard source" for his life (1979: 161), and, despite its inconsistencies, the account still provides most of the details in modern Chinese dictionaries for summaries of Confucius' life.

    5. Durrant (1995). See especially chapter two, "Sima Qian's Confucius."

    6. For a translation of relevant chapter of the *Records of the Grand Historian*, see Yang Hsien-yi and Gladys Yang, trans. (1979: 1–27).

    7. The three courts refer to the three separate places where the Zhōu court made policy. R. P. Kramers identifies chapters 67–70 and 74–76 of the DàDài Lǐjì as part of the *Records of Confucius in the Three Courts* (Loewe 1993: 258).

8. Seidel (1969).

9. Shǐjì 47.1905.

10. Shǐjì 47.1909.

11. Shǐjì 47.1921.

12. This is a metaphor used by the Hàn Confucius in the context of his editing the classic *Changes* and his authorship of some texts (or "wings") ancillary to it. This metaphor shows up in the purportedly ancient *Wényán* 文言 ancillary text, a work understood to have been composed by Confucius. Shǐjì 47.1938 n. 1, and 47.1939, n. 6.

13. *Shísānjīng zhùshū* 1.6, p. 18. The *Wényán* commentary to the hexagram explains the coloration in terms of the alteration of this most *yīn* hexagram by the rising of *yáng*. Because Heaven is associated with black and earth with yellow, the contest between *yīn* and *yáng* results in black and yellow (*Shísānjīng zhùshū* 1.7, p. 19).

14. See Liáo Míngchūn (1993: 192).

15. The comparison here is between the dragon's ability to change color and form at will (indeed, changing everything but its "pattern") and the Confucian's ability to bring about the differentiation of social categories by adornment with various colors of clothing or banner. For the compound *cǎiwù* 采物, see *Zuǒzhuàn* account of Duke Wén, year 6, *Shísānjīng zhùshū* 19a.142, p. 1844.

16. Chén Sōngcháng and Liáo Míngchūn (1993: 425). The phrase "nothing greater" does not come from the same source text, and appears to derive from the "Great Commentary." See *Shísānjīng zhùshū* 7.70, p. 82. Compare the translation of Shaughnessy (1996: 171).

17. Philip J. Ivanhoe has recently likened virtue in the *Laozi* to the Weberian concept of moral charisma ("The Concept of *De* in the *Laozi*," in Csikszentmihalyi and Ivanhoe, 1999). This intrinsic quality is also present in the received *Wényán* discussion of the hexagram, which prefaces the discussion of the dragons with the following description of the sage: "The gentleman, in the yellow center, understands principle, and corrects his position and deports his body. The beauty inside of him extends to his four limbs, and is emitted through his actions. This is ultimate beauty" (*Shísānjīng zhùshū* 1.7, p. 19).

18. Shǐjì 63.2140.

19. Féng (1948: 207). Here, of course, the definition of religion is consciously indexed to the example of Christianity.

20. *Mencius* 3b9. I follow Yáng Bójùn (1984: 154–58). See also Lau (1970: 113–15).

21. Jiāo (1987: 452). The Han critic Wáng Chōng 王充 (27–ca. 97 C.E.) uses the term "uncrowned king" in an earlier context: "It is by considering his employment of the empty spaces in the *Spring and Autumn Annals* that one can know Confucius had the virtue that makes one able to ruler as king. . . . Although Confucius did not rule as king, his employment as 'uncrowned king' lies in the *Spring and Autumn Annals*." *Lùnhéng* 論衡 79 (*Zhūzǐ jíchéng*, v. 7), p. 269.

22. *Shísānjīng zhùshū* 26:158, p. 2352.

23. *Analects* 17.19, Chéng (1990: 1227–29).

24. *Lǚshì chūnqiū* (*Zhūzǐ jíchéng*, v. 6) 18.222. A related example can be found in *Huáinánzǐ* (*Zhūzǐ jíchéng*, v. 7) 12.190.

25. Huáng Shì 黃奭 (1993, *Lúnyǔ wěi* 6).

26. There are several different lines of interpretation as to what the unicorn's appearance and its capture or death signified. Among the commentators, for example, Fú Qián 服虔 notes that the appearance of the beast is a bad omen because it is an anomaly, whereas Hé Xiu 何休 says it is "the same category as the sage" but its capture and killing were a sign from Heaven of Confucius' own impending death. Other Hàn sources indicate that animals like phoenixes and unicorns are attracted to the sage's virtue, e.g., *Kǒngzǐ jiāyǔ* 10. See Shǐjì 47.1942, nn. 3, 6. Note also the parallel to *Analects* 9.9.

27. *Shísānjīng zhùshū* 26:159, p. 2353.

28. Quoted by Ruǎn Yuán in *Shísānjīng zhùshū* 26:159, p. 2353, with the first sentence omitted. See Ariel (1989: 101).

29. *Shǐjì* 47. 1943.

30. *Shísānjīng zhùshū* 26:160, p. 2354.

31. See, for example, Hsiao Kung-chuan (1979: 130–31).

32. The phrase "*túfǎ* 圖法" also appears in the *Lǚshì chūnqiū* (*Zhūzǐ jíchéng*, v. 6) 16.179, where it is used in conjunction with the ministers of doomed states who are able to "read the writing on the wall."

33. Itano (1976: 53).

34. *HòuHànshū* 30a.1043.

35. *HòuHànshū* 13.538; Itano (1976: 56). Gōngsūn Shù was a contender with the future Emperor Guāngwǔ for the imperial throne, and claimed the association with the element metal.

36. Huáng Shì (1993: *Xiàojīng wěi* 6–7).

37. The third part of the group of bamboo slips found at Guōdiàn 郭店 in 1996, now labeled "Yǔcóng 語叢," contains two parallels to the *Analects*, which correspond closely to words attributed to Confucius in *Analects* 7.6 and 9.4. In the former case, the Guōdiàn text has no parallel to "The Master said," whereas in the latter case there is no parallel to the introductory phrase: "There were four things the Master would not do." The four are also presented in a different order. See Jīngménshì bówùguǎn (1998: 211–12).

38. See *Fùyáng Hànjiǎn zhěnglǐzǔ*, 1983, pp. 21–23. Only three titles were published: "The Master said: 'There is a beast to the north,'" "Confucius cried by the river," and "The men of the state of Wèi minced [the disciple] Zǐ Lù."

39. The transcription used is "*'Rújiāzhě yán' shìwén* 儒家者言釋文" *Wénwù* 1981.8, pp. 13–19. The words "Lín Fàng 林放 asked about the rites" (from *Analects* 3.4) were on a slip later destroyed in the 1976 earthquake, and the sequence *wèn* 問 "asked," an illegible character, and *gàoquè* 告朔 "the announcement of the new moon" (reminiscent of 3.17) were on another such destroyed slip. Three extant slips come from book 14: "... Zǐ Lù said: 'This is the case. I would like to hear about the complete man.' Confucius said ... ," "'... How is it possible [probably an error for: it is possible] to become a complete man?' Zǐ Lù said: 'By ... ,'" and "Confucius said: 'By this it is possible. ...'" The second slip (*héyǐ wéi chéngrén cái, Zǐ Lù yuē yóu* 何以為成人才子路曰由) is particularly interesting in its variant on the received text of 14.12 (*kěyǐ wéi chéngrén yì, yuē jīn* 可以為成人矣曰今) because it appears to indicate a change of speaker in the passage back to the disciple Zǐ Lù, which explains the presence of the *yuē* that had caused such a commentarial debate. These slips appear to have been in a different format than a partial *Analects* found at the same site, which will be discussed further on. Compare the Lín Fàng slip (p. 19) with the corresponding Dìngzhōu *Analects* slip (Héběishěng wénwù yánjiùsuǒ 1997c: 16).

40. See "The Name Lunyu," in Makeham (1996: 10–13). Note that attempts have been made to date particular chapters of the *Analects* to specific moments in time, notably by E. Bruce and Taeko Brooks. Although these attempts are suggestive, they are highly contingent, and will not be brought into this discussion.

41. The Duke of Zhōu enjoyed the type of acclaim from Confucius that later generations reserved for Confucius. See Lǐ Yùnfù (1996) for the discovery in Hénán Province of a set of speeches attributed to the Duke of Zhōu that perhaps date from the early fourth century B.C.E.

42. Makeham (1996: 14).

43. In that biography, Sīmǎ mentions the Five Classics by name, but not the *Lúnyǔ*. This shows that, although Sīmǎ traveled to the temple of Confucius, the practice at that time

was still to draw on the disparate narratives from many sources, rather than to privilege the *Analects* as orthodox.

44. Hànshū 81.3352.

45. Hànshū 75.3159. At the end of the first century C.E., Shèng's work was again used to tutor an eight-year-old emperor. See HòuHànshū 37.1255–6.

46. Hànshū 78.3271–3292. For specific offices, see the entries for these years in Hànshū 19b.

47. Hànshū 72.3066, 81.3347.

48. Shǐjì 30.1706.

49. Loewe (1986: 198).

50. Chéng (1990: 68–70).

51. Héběishěng wénwù yánjiùsuǒ (1997a and 1997c).

52. The bibliographic chapter of the Hànshū tabulates the results of a major effort, begun during the reign of the Emperor Chéng 成 (r. 32–7 B.C.E.), to catalog the books in the empire. As classified by Bān Gù, texts related to the *Analects* are listed in the same category as the "six pursuits (yì 藝)" of the gentleman, a canonical set of texts first defined by Sīma Qiān. Bān lists twelve texts that consist of 226 chapters (piān 篇), among them three versions of the text, five "explanations" (shuō 説), and the two collections of further dialogues. See Hànshū 30.1707–8.

53. It is interesting that neither Zhāng Yǔ's edition nor that of Marquis Shèng of Xià are listed, perhaps indicating that the changes they had made were incorporated into one or more of these three versions.

54. To appreciate this proof, it is necessary to note that book twenty of the received text is made up of three sections. Thirteen of the bamboo slips found at Dìngzhōu are inscribed with text that parallels the first two sections of the received book twenty, a total of 239 characters. The last of these slips *additionally* contains text parallel to the text of the third section of the received book twenty, squeezed in at half size on the bottom of the slip, separated from the second section by punctuation marks. The significance of this appended section would be debatable (e.g., the copyist might have simply been running out of bamboo) were it not for the content of a fourteenth slip: "[dot] In all, two sections, a total of 322 characters." This fourteenth slip is almost certainly a summary of the contents of book twenty, which indicates that the version being copied had only two sections. Because book twenty of the Dìngzhōu *Analects* had only two sections, and the number of characters on the summary slip almost exactly matches the number of characters that would have been on the bamboo slips for those two sections at burial, it is clear that the version originally copied onto the bamboo slips had twenty books, and that a twenty-first book (i.e., the third section of the received book twenty) was added from another source. Note here that the received version of the first two sections of book twenty has 343 characters, and compared to the sections of the received version that correspond to the 239 characters on the surviving slips, the same thing is said in thirteen more characters. We can estimate the number of characters in this way:

Slip version	*Corresponding received text*
239 characters survive/	252 received characters/
total slip characters	343 total received characters

This ratio allows us to estimate the number of characters in the slip version of the first two sections of the received text to be 325, so close to the figure in the summary slip that it is certainly the title slip for book 20.

55. Héběishěng wénwù yánjiùsuǒ (1997b: 59).

56. Hànshū 30.1717. Líu Láichéng 劉來成 notes that memorials of Xiāo Wàngzhī were

also found in the Ding county tomb, along with the partial bamboo slip *Analects*. He argues that the text is the *State of Lǔ Analects*, a conclusion with which Roger Ames and Henry Rosemont Jr. agree (1998: 276). Although this conclusion is possible, it must be remembered that the *original* numbering of the Ding county slips was consistent with the twenty-one books of the *Ancient [text]* version of the text. It is just as probable that the three texts mentioned by Bān Gù were representative of a much greater number of versions of the text that circulated in 55 B.C.E.

57. Specifically, Wéi Xián and Sòng Jī served as consecutive grand heralds (imperial receptionists) in the 70s B.C.E., both previously having served as supervisors of the household. Gòng Yǔ became grandee secretary in 44 B.C.E. (*Hànshū* 19b. 800–803.)

58. Emperor Wǔ 武 (r. 140–87 B.C.E.) had several different repositories, including the Tiānlùgé 天祿閣, Yángé 延閣, Guāngnèi 廣內, and the Mìshì 秘室. The imperial books were the responsibility of one of the "Three Excellencies," the grandee secretary or *yùshǐ dàifu* 御史大夫, delegated to the palace assistant secretary or *yùshǐ zhōngchéng* 御史中丞, who oversaw a staff of fifteen. See Bielenstein (1980: 9).

59. The Taiping publishing house edition of this chapter (Bān Gù, 1963, p. 1) calculates that these bundles are distributed among 596 titles arranged in 38 categories.

60. *Hànshū* 6.159. See also Wallacker (1978) on the limitations of this measure.

61. Bielenstein (1980: 138–39).

62. The Stone Canal Pavilion was a repository for books in the northern part of the Wèiyāng 未央 Palace. In 51 B.C.E. it was the location of one or more discussions on classical themes that included such luminaries as Bì Guāngdé 薛廣德, Bì Xiàng 辟向, Jiǎ Cāng 假倉, Lín Zūn 林尊, Oūyáng Shēng 歐陽生, Shī Chóu 施讎, Zhāng Cháng'ān 張長安, Zhāng Shānfù 張山拊, and Zhōu Kān 周堪. At the time they participated, almost all of these figures was an erudit, and the stated purpose of the discussions was to bring together scholars of the Five Classics to hold "miscellaneous discussions of their similarities and differences" (*Hànshū* 73. 3113). In the *Hànshū*, participation at the Stone Canal Pavilion is often mentioned in a scholar's bibliography alongside high offices attained, and participation clearly was seen as official recognition of high attainments. Gentleman of the Yellow Gates Liáng Qīuhè 梁丘賀 was said to have "received emissaries and questioned the various scholars at the Stone Canal [Pavilion]" (*Hànshū* 88.3600). The Commandant of the Capital of Huáiyáng 淮陽 Wéi Xuánchéng and the Tutor of the Grand Prince Xiāo Wàngzhī appear to have organized the event and edited the responses to become part of the official record (*Hànshū* 73.3113). Although the length and frequency of the discussions is not known, they generated a significant silk trail, which includes eighteen books on the *Analects*, the same number on the *Classic of Filial Piety* and on the *Record of Ritual*, thirty-nine chapters on the *Spring and Autumn Annals*, and forty-two chapters on the *Shàngshū* (*Hànshū* 30.1704–18).

63. See the discussion of this meeting and the translation of Bān Gù's account of it in Tjan (1949).

64. Eno (1990) is a good study of the text's early social context.

65. Fragments of Hé's commentary were collected by Yú Yuè 俞樾, and parts of Líu's commentary were incorporated into the Six Dynasties commentary of Huáng Kǎn 皇侃. The other early commentaries have been collected by Mǎ Guóhan in his *Yùhán shānfáng jíyìshū* 玉函山房輯佚書.

66. Ishizuka (1981). For Zhèng Xuán's commentary, see Makeham (1997).

67. Bāo Xián wrote his commentary during his time as the teacher of the crown prince, sometime between 25 and 56 C.E. *HòuHànshū* 79b.2570. Little is known about Master Zhōu.

68. *HòuHànshū* 60a.1972, 35.1212.

69. *HòuHànshū* 79b. 2582–83.

70. *HòuHànshū* 35.1211–12.

71. Lau (1979: 12).

72. Lau (1979: 107).

73. Fingarette (1972: 1). In his examination of *Analects* 11.12, the Qīng scholar Zhào Yòu 趙佑 attempts to differentiate the sacrifice to the spirits of the dead (*guǐ* and *shén*) from the sacrifice to one's parents or ancestors, arguing that the latter is subsumed under the category of "filial piety" and therefore part of "serving the living," see Chéng (1990: 761). It is interesting that, by and large, this categorization is accepted by modern scholars, who, in other contexts, tend to see all sacrifice to the dead as "otherworldy" and "religious."

74. Chéng (1990: 244–46). This interpretation is consistent with the analysis of Dài Cháofú 戴朝福 (1992), who argues that although Confucius was not interested in "spirit stories" (*shénhuà* 神話) that circulated at the time, he was deeply interested in a type of apotheosis that Dài terms "spirit nature" (*shénxìng* 神性).

75. Chéng (1990: 763). Whether or not Kāng is right about the influence of Buddhist apostasy, it is possible to see Confucius as having a view about death that is "gnostic" (that is, as believing in the continuation of the individual after death on the plane of "wisdom"). Projecting back the Hàn idea that the reuniting of the parts of the soul can only be influenced by proper postmortem burial and sacrifice by one's kin, the cultivation of filial piety may itself be seen as an attempt to gain postmortem advantage.

76. Lau (1979: 85).

77. Chéng (1990: 406–408).

78. Zhū (1982: 89).

79. Chéng (1990: 407). In the context of sacrifice, the term *dú* is often opposed to *jìng* 敬 "reverence," e.g., in the *Gōngyáng* commentary to the *Spring and Autumn Annals* account of year eight of Duke Huán. *Shísānjīng zhùshū* 5.2218.

80. Chéng (1990: 406).

81. Chéng (1990: 329–31). It is also possible to read the passage as saying that Zāng had a tortoise, and also had ornate carvings on his own home. Although Confucius simply asks: "What was his intelligence like?" the content of the *Analects'* next four sections all turn on the shortcomings of famous people, which also implies that Confucius' question is intended as criticism.

82. Chéng (1990: 330).

83. Chéng (1990: 330).

84. Zhū (1982: 80).

85. Chéng (1990: 331), citing *Zhūzǐ yǔlèi* 朱子語類.

86. Wáng Sù's *School Sayings of Confucius*, a text that contains narratives about the sage in circulation at the end of the Hàn, contains a narrative also found in the *Lǚshì chūnqiū*, a text that just predates the Hàn, that connects Confucius to the practice of divination using the hexagrams of the *Changes*. In it, Confucius uses milfoil stalks to obtain the hexagram bì 賁, which he interprets according to the *Xiàng* commentary. See *Kǒngzǐ jiāyǔ* 10.21 (*Jiāyǔ dēng* 57 *zhòng*) and *Lǚshì chūnqiū* 22.291 (*Zhūzǐ jíchéng*, v. 6). For a translation of the former, see Kramers (1950), 244–45 and 349.

87. Chén Sōngcháng (1993: 417). Compare the beginning of this Hàn version with the received text: "The *Changes* is a balance for Heaven and Earth, and has the ability to repair and enmesh the Dào of Heaven and Earth." *Shísānjīng zhùshū* 7.65, p. 77. Another variation is seen in treatise 10 of the *HòuHànshū*, p. 3213.

88. In his "Selections on divination" ("Bǔliè" 卜列), from section 25 of *Discourses of a Hidden Man* (*Qiánfūlùn* 潛夫論), Wáng Fú quotes Confucius as saying: "When a gentleman is about to act, he first enquires, and, based on what is said, he receives the mandate (*mìng* 命) and echoes it." See *Qiánfūlùn* (ZZJC, v. 8), p. 123.

89. *Shǐjì* 47.1912, following the comment of Táng Gù 唐固 on the meaning of *fén* 墳. Some commentators have assumed that such sheep must be clay burial objects.

90. *Shǐjì* 47.1913.

91. The Jìn writer Lǐ Chōng 李充 reads the passage as saying that Confucius never spoke of "disorderly spirits." See Chéng (1990: 480–82).

92. See Gù (1930) and Schneider (1965: 110).

93. Gù actually distinguished the Spring and Autumn Confucius from that of the Warring States, the Western Hàn, and the Eastern Hàn (Schneider 1965: 32). Although in sympathy with some aspects of Gù's approach, the recent work of Lionel Jensen might be used to point out Gù's deficiencies. Jensen argues that the equation of Confucius with Confucianism is a late invention, projected back onto periods like the Warring States and the Hàn. Gù's position assumes that "Confucius" evolved as a personification of a unitary but changing Confucian tradition, an entity and connection that Jensen correctly calls into question.

94. When the latter image overtook the former is the topic for another essay, but a cursory examination of the text's subsequent reception provides some hypotheses. The emphasis on self-cultivation in the post-Tang Dàoxué 道學 movement may well have favored texts, such as the *Analects, Mèngzi*, and the Hàn chapters of the classic *Ritual*, primarily interested in ritual self-cultivation. These texts, which emphasize teaching the means to attain Confucian "enlightenment," became the central texts of Confucianism a thousand years later.

REFERENCES

Ames, Roger, and Henry Rosemont Jr. 1998. *The Analects of Confucius: A Philosophical Translation.* New York: Ballantine.

Ariel, Yoav. 1989. *K'ung-Ts'ung-tzu: The K'ung Family Masters' Anthology.* Princeton, N.J.: Princeton University Press.

Asano Yūichi 淺野裕一. 1997. *Kôshi shinka* 孔子神話 [*The Myth of Master Kong*]. Tokyo: Iwanami shuten.

Bān Gù 班固. 1963. *Hànshū yìwénzhì* 漢書藝文志. Hong Kong: Taiping.

Bielenstein, Hans. 1980. *The Bureaucracy of Han Times.* Cambridge, Eng.: Cambridge University Press.

Chéng Shùdé 程術德. 1990. *Lùnyǔ jíshì* 論語集釋, 4 v. Beijing: Zhonghua shuju.

Chén Sōngcháng 陳松長. 1993. "Bóshū 'Xìcí' shìwén 帛書繫辭釋文 [An annotated transcription of the silk text 'Xicí']." *Dàojiā wénhuà yánjìu* 3, 416–23.

Chén Sōngcháng and Liáo Míngchūn 廖名春. 1993. "Bóshū 'Èrsānzǐ wèn,' 'Yì zhī yì,' 'Yào' Shìwén, 帛書二三子問易之義要釋文 [An annotated transcription of the silk text Èrsānzǐ wèn,' 'Yì zhī yì,' 'Yào']." *Dàojiā wénhuà yánjìu* 3, 424–35.

Csikszentmihalyi, Mark, and Philip J. Ivanhoe. 1999. *Religious and Philosophical Aspects of the Laozi.* Albany, N.Y.: SUNY Press.

Dài Cháofú 戴朝福. 1992. "Lùnyǔde zǒngjiào jīngshén yú zǒngjiào qíngdiào 論語的宗教精神 與宗教情調 [The religious spirit and religious atmosphere of the *Analects*]" in *KǒngMèng xuébào* 孔孟學報 63, 139–69.

Durrant, Stephen. 1995. *The Cloudy Mirror: Tension and Conflict in the Writings of Sima Qian.* Albany, N.Y.: SUNY Press.

Eno, Robert. 1990. *The Confucian Creation of Heaven: Philosophy and the Defense of Ritual Mastery.* Albany, N.Y.: SUNY Press.

Féng Yǒulán 馮友蘭 (trans. Derk Bodde). 1948. *A Short History of Chinese Philosophy.* New York: Free Press.

Fingarette, Herbert. 1972. *Confucius—the Secular as Sacred.* New York: Harper and Row.

Fùyáng Hànjiǎn zhěnglǐ zǔ 阜陽漢簡整理組, 1983. "Fùyáng Hànjiǎn jiǎnjiè [An Introduction to the Han Slips from Fuyang]," in Wéwù 文物 1983. 2, 21–23.

Gù Jiégāng 顧頡剛, ed. 1930. Gǔshǐbiàn 古史辨, v. 2. Shanghai: Kaiming.

Héběishěng wénwù yánjìusuǒ. 1997a. (Short for Héběishěng wénwù yánjìusuǒ Dìngzhōu Hànmù zhújiǎn zhěnglǐ xiǎozǔ 河北省文物研究所定州漢墓竹簡整理小組 [Hebei Province Archeological Research Institute Dingzhou Han Tomb Bamboo Slip Arrangement Group.]) "Dìngzhōu XīHàn Zhōngshān Huáiwángmù zhújiǎn Lúnyǔ shìwén xuǎn 定州西漢中山懷王墓竹簡論語釋文選 [Selections from the annotated text of the bamboo slip *Analects* from the Dìngzhōu tomb of the Western Hàn Prince Huài of Zhōngshān]." *Wenwu* no. 5, 49–54.

Héběishěng wénwù yánjìusuǒ. 1997b. "Dìngzhōu XīHàn Zhōngshān Huáiwángmù zhújiǎn Lúnyǔ jièshào 定州西漢中山懷王墓竹簡論語介紹 [Introduction to the annotated text of the bamboo slip *Analects* from the Dìngzhōu tomb of the Western Hàn Prince Huài of Zhōngshān]." *Wenwu* no. 5, 59–61.

Héběishěng wénwù yánjìusuǒ. 1997c. *Lúnyǔ: Dìngzhōu Hànmù zhújiǎn* 論語定州漢墓竹簡. Beijing: Wenwu.

Hsiao Kung-chuan. 1979. *A History of Chinese Political Thought*, vol. 1. Princeton, N.J.: Princeton University Press.

Huáng Shì 黃奭. 1993. *Chūnqiū wěi, Lúnyǔ wěi, Xiàojīng wěi* 春秋緯, 論語緯, 孝經緯 [*Weft texts of the Spring and Autumn Annals, Analects and Classic of Filial Piety*]. Shanghai: Guji.

Ishizuka Harumichi. 1981. "The texts of Lun yu, with commentaries by Cheng Hsüan, discovered in Tun-huang and Turfan." *Journal Asiatique* 269, 101–8.

Itano Chōhachi 板野長八. 1976–78. "The t'u-ch'an 圖讖 prophetic books and the establishment of Confucianism" in *Memoirs of the Research Department of the Toyo Bunko* 34 (1976): 47–111, 36 (1978): 85–107.

Ivanhoe, Philip J. "The Concept of *De* ("Virtue") in the *Laozi*" in Mark Csikszentmihalyi and Philip J. Ivanhoe (1999), pp. 239–58.

Jensen, Lionel. 1997. *Manufacturing Confucianism: Chinese Traditions and Universal Civilization*. Durham, N.C.: Duke University Press.

Jiāo Xún 焦循. 1987. *Mèngzǐ zhèngyì* 孟子正義. Beijing: Zhonghua.

Jīngménshì bówùguǎn 荊門市博物館. 1998. *Guōdiàn Chǔmù zhújiǎn* 郭店楚墓竹簡 [The Bamboo Slips from the Chu Tomb at Guodian]. Beijing: Wenwu.

Knapp, Keith. 1995. "The Ru Reinterpretation of Xiao." *Early China* 20, 195–222.

Kramers, R. P. 1950. *K'ung Tzu Chia Yü: The School Sayings of Confucius*. Leiden: E. J. Brill.

Lau, D. C., trans. 1970. *Mencius*. Harmondsworth, Eng.: Penguin.

———. 1979. *Analects*. Harmondsworth, Eng.: Penguin.

Lǐ Yùnfù 李運富. 1996. "Chǔguó jiǎnbó wénzì yánjìu gàiguān 楚國簡帛文字研究概觀 [A general overview of research into the language of Chǔ state slips and silk manuscripts]." *Jiānghàn kǎogǔ* no. 3, 60–65.

Liáo Míngchūn 廖名春. 1993." *Bóshū 'Èrsānzǐ wèn' jiǎnshūo* 帛書二三子問簡説 [An introductory discussion of the silk text 'Ersanzi wen']." *Dàojiā wénhuà yánjìu* no. 3, 190–95.

Loewe, Michael. 1986. "The Former Han Dynasty" in Denis Twitchett and Michael Loewe (1986), pp. 103–222.

———. 1993. *Early Chinese Texts: a Bibliographical Guide*. Berkeley, Society for the Study of Early China and Institute of East Asian Studies at the University of California, Berkeley.

Makeham, John. 1996. "The Formation of Lunyu as a Book." *Monumenta Serica* 44, 1–24.

———. 1997. "The Earliest Extant Commentary on Lunyu: Lunyu zheng shi zhu." *T'oung Pao* 83, 260–99.

Schneider, Laurence A., trans. 1965. "A translation of Ku Chieh-kang's essay 'The Confucius of the Spring and Autumn era and the Confucius of the Han Era'." *Phi Theta Papers* 10 (1965): 105–47.

Seidel, Anna. 1969. *La divinisation de Lao tseu dans le taoïsme des Han.* Paris: École Française d'Extreme-Orient.

Shaughnessy, Edward. 1996. *I Ching: The Classic of Changes.* New York: Ballantine.

Shyrock, John K. 1932. *The Origin and Development of the State Cult of Confucius.* New York: Century.

Tjoe Som Tjan, trans. 1949. *Po Hu T'ung; the Comprehensive Discussions in the White Tiger Hall.* Leiden: E. J. Brill.

Twitchett, Denis, and Michael Loewe, eds. 1986. *The Cambridge History of China,* vol. 1: *The Ch'in and Han Empires 221 B.C.–A.D. 220.* Cambridge, Eng.: Cambridge University Press.

Wallacker, Benjamin. 1978. "Han Confucianism and Confucius in the Han," in David T. Roy and Tsuen-hsuin Tsien, eds. *Ancient China: Studies in Early Civilization* (Hong Kong: Chinese University of Hong Kong Press), pp. 215–28.

Yáng Bójùn 楊伯峻. 1984. *Mèngzǐ yìzhù* 孟子意注. Beijing, Zhonghua.

Yang Hsien-yi and Gladys Yang, trans. 1979. *Selections from Records of the Historian.* Beijing: Foreign Languages Press.

Yáng Shùdá 楊樹達. 1984. *Hànshū kuīguǎn* 漢書窺管 [*Reading the Hànshū through a Straw*], 2 v. Shanghai: Guji.

Zhū Wéizhēng 朱維錚. 1986. "'Lúnyǔ' jiéjí cuòshuō 論語結集脞説 [Jottings on the collation of the *Analects*]." *Kǒngzǐ yánjìu* 孔子研究 1, 40–52.

Zhū Xī 朱熹. 1982. *Sìshū zhāngzhù jízhù* 四書章句集注 [*Collected Commentaries on Punctuated Edition of the Four Books*]. Beijing: Zhonghua.

8

Word Philology and Text Philology in *Analects* 9:1

E. BRUCE BROOKS AND
A. TAEKO BROOKS

SINOLOGICAL METHOD, OVER THE YEARS, has largely focused on the philology of the single word and its meanings. Its concern with a text has traditionally been to ask whether it is authentic or not. If it is, it counts as an area within which consistent word and concept usage may be expected to obtain. If it is not, it is generally not much discussed by scholars. The problems raised by compound or complex texts, which have an identity but are not homogeneous in the way that integral texts are homogeneous, have scarcely been noticed. This traditional lack has not been made good by the availability of modern Western textual expertise, whose principal model is also a presumed single compositional starting point, from which variant texts gradually diverge.[1] That the compositional integrity of a text may itself be the end result of a non-oral process is no more regularly recognized in the Homeric or Biblical fields than in the Chinese field. In a prolonged study of the Warring States, however, we have found that many texts of the period are best regarded as composite, and sometimes even as continuously accretional. Dealing with them on their own terms thus seems to require the recognition of new options of whole-text typology. To include these options in the conceptual tool kit of philology should then in principle give more fruitful results when one happens to be up against a text with a complicated rather than an authorially simple generation process. That is the general contribution which the present paper aspires to make.

More specifically, we will try to show how close examination of the *Analects*[2] might lead to a hypothesis of continuous *identity* and also continuous *growth* over time, and how that hypothesis can shed new light on previously intractable problems. As a problem on which it is narratively convenient to focus, we will attempt to demonstrate that this whole-text solution of the *Analects* makes possible a more convincing reading for the famous crux LY 9:1 than have earlier attempts to resolve its contradictions by the methods of single-word philology.

We will first (§1–3) consider what the 9:1 problem looks like from the traditional point of view, which assumes that the *Analects* is an integral text, and note that the problem remains effectively unsolved after two thousand years of work along these lines, then (§4–8) sketch a non-integral theory of the *Analects*, and finally (§9) return to 9:1 and (§10) another crux, 12:1, to see if the non-integral theory can rationalize points which the integral theory has clearly been unable to settle to the satisfaction of scholars generally.[3]

1. The Problem of 9:1

Analects 9:1 reads in its entirety: 子罕言利與命與仁. The meaning "The Master" for Dž 子 is ubiquitous at or near the beginning of *Analects* sayings, and appears in that sense in each of the adjacent sayings 9:2–5. Hǎn 罕 "rare, seldom" is unique in the *Analects* and rare in other Warring States texts, but none of its other occurrences invites an interpretation outside that semantic range. Yén 言 "spoke of/to" is common and unproblematic in the *Analects*. The sense "and" for yǔ 與 before a noun is well established in such phrases as 富與貴 "riches and honor" (4:5, conjunctive) and 父與君 "father [or] ruler" (11:22, disjunctive).[4] The natural reading of 9:1 would thus be "The Master seldom spoke of lì 利 ("profit") or mìng 命 ("fate; that which is ordained") or rŕn 仁." The problem arises because this grammatically natural reading is unacceptable to *Analects* readers, who note that the word rŕn 仁 occurs 109 times in the text[5] and that many of those occurrences are not casual but emphatic. LY 4:5 itself is very eloquent: "If the gentleman departs from rŕn, how shall he establish a name 君子去仁，惡乎成名?"[6] In the light of this and other passages, any solution of 9:1 which contradicts the impression that rŕn is a central Confucian value has been felt to be untenable. The problem has been seen as bringing 9:1 somehow into line with the agreed importance of rŕn in the text, by distinguishing it from lì and/or mìng. As an unstated assumption, the text itself has been assumed to be a whole. Let us for the moment accept that assumption, and see how the problem looks in those terms.[7]

We may first verify our impression that lì and/or mìng are antithetical to rŕn in the *Analects* as a whole.

As to lì 利 "profit, benefit, advantage," it is difficult for any *Analects* reader, who will tend also to be a Mencius reader, to take it in a positive sense. The question of the King of Lyáng to Mencius in MC 1A1, "You must surely have something with which to benefit my country 必有以利吾國乎" inspired the most famous explosion in the history of Chinese thought, in which Mencius shows how personal benefit (or profit) calculations will produce a society which is not only dysfunctional but self-destructive.[8] The sub-elite Micians speak openly of social utility in terms of lì, but the *Analects*, in which text the term occurs nine times (plus two times in the meaning "sharp," which are not relevant to the present discussion), is explicit in contrasting its own elite values with such vulgar ones. Thus 4:16, "The gentleman concentrates on what is right; the little man concentrates on advantage 君子喻於義，小人喻於利;" and as a further warning, 4:12, "Those who act with a view to their own personal advantage will arouse much resentment 放於利而行，多怨." Of the nine instances of lì as "profit" in the text, only the last, 20:2, seems to be positive: "To use what the people find profitable to profit them, is this not [to be] kindly but not extravagant 因民之所利而利之，斯不亦惠而不費乎？" Even here, a possible contrast exists between "what the people find profitable" and what the gentleman in his own sphere finds admirable, and though the difference from other instances of lì is certainly important, 20:2 does not decisively refute the impression that the *Analects* disallows lì *as an elite value*. The text as a whole thus seems to disapprove of the profit motive, and allows it as valid, if ever, only for the lower strata of society. On the *Analects* evidence, then, "The Master" might thus be said to have seldom spoken of profit *because he disapproved of it*.

Mìng "fate, command, mandate" occurs twenty-four times in the *Analects*, in various contexts such as "allotted span of life" (6:3 and 11:7, "Unfortunately his allotted span was short and he has died 不幸短命死矣"), or more generally, the aspects of existence which are beyond the power of individuals to change. There is also mìng in the everyday sense of a command given by one person to another (10:3, "he must return his charge 必復命"). None of these senses (together accounting for ten of the twenty-four occurrences) seems to fit 9:1. More relevant is mìng in the compound tyēn-mìng 天命, the "Will of Heaven," considered as the purpose of Heaven for individuals and for the course of history at large. None of the passages mentioning mìng in this sense either define or describe it, but it cannot be said that they disapprove of it. On the contrary, they seem to hold it in respect, as in the famous 2:4, "At forty I understood the commands of Heaven 四十而知天命," where an understanding of those commands is indisputably a stage in "Confucius's" progress toward moral perfection. The text speaks of mìng in this sense twelve times, comparable to the nine times for lì in the sense "profit." If the one usage is "seldom" for the purposes of 9:1, so is the other. But given the difference of approval, the nearest we can come to a statement for mìng parallel to that given above for lì is: "The Master" might be said to have seldom spoken of mìng *because he held it in awe*.

We then come to rýn, which, as noted above, is often, and always approvingly, spoken of in the *Analects*. No two of the three terms lì, mìng, and rýn can thus be said to be treated the same way elsewhere in the text. Lì and mìng are rare; mìng and rýn are positive. The riddle of 9:1 is that it seems to treat *all three* terms in the same way.

2. Philological Answers to the Problem of 9:1

One can simplify this three-way problem in one of two ways. First, by finessing the question of positive versus negative implication, and taking our guide from the hăn "seldom" in the text, we can argue that the key fact is that both lì and mìng are relatively rare in the text, whereas rýn is indisputably common. On this understanding, the riddle of 9:1 will be solved if we can find a reading which will group lì and mìng and separate them from rýn. We may call this a *Type A* solution. Second, focusing instead on the aspect of approval or disapproval, and remembering our finding that lì is largely pejorative, whereas mìng, though not common, is generally respectful, we can look for a way to separate lì from both mìng and rv́n. This we may call a Type B solution. Solutions of both types have been proposed. We here consider some of them, in order to see the problem as it has presented itself to traditional scholarship.[9]

The most influential of these solutions is the Type B one identified with Shř Shv́ng-dzǔ 史繩祖 but proposed earlier by Wáng Rwò-syw̄ 王若虛.[10] It proposes that yw̌ 與 is not here the coverb "and" but a full verb "allow," the gloss being syw̌ 許 "allow, permit" (與者，許也). This presumes an extension of the well-attested verbal sense of "give" for yw̌. Shř supports this extension with examples from the Analects, among them 7:29 與其進也, in Legge's version "I admit people's approach to me." Bodde suggests that this meaning can be further extended to "holding forth on (in the sense that an orator holds forth)." He renders 9:1 accordingly as "The Master rarely spoke of profit. (But) he gave forth (his ideas concerning) the appointments (of Heaven), (and also) gave forth (his ideas concerning) perfect virtue."[11] The freedom to supply "(his ideas concerning)" lets Bodde make yw̌ a virtual synonym of yén "spoke of." If this was the writer's intention, he could perhaps have realized it more clearly by a sentence in the form "The Master seldom spoke of lì, but often spoke of mìng and rv́n." Boltz, who also approves of the Wáng/Shř suggestion, paraphrases the latter part of 9:1 as "He allowed discussions of mìng and rv́n." This seems closer to the root idea of yw̌ = syw̌, but has its own problems: the implied meaning "The Master himself rarely spoke of lì, [but] allowed [others] to speak of mìng and rv́n" is not easy to visualize situationally, and the change within the sentence from prohibition to permission (symbolized by the bracketed "but" in both Bodde's and Boltz's renditions) is a difficulty in itself. No other Analects sentence reverses its tonality in this covert fashion. Of greatest comparative value for this point are some other third-person descriptions of the Master. These either list things the Master did do (7:13 子之所慎，齊，戰，疾, Legge "The things in reference to which the Master exercised the greatest caution were: fasting, war, and sickness," compare 7:18, 7:25), or things the Master did not do (7:21 子不語，怪，力，亂，神, Legge "The subjects on which the Master did not talk, were: extraordinary things, feats of strength, disorder, and spiritual beings," compare 9:4), or explicitly signal a transition from one type to the other (7:27 子釣而不網, Legge "The Master angled—but did not use a net"). None of these examply simply mixes the two types of statement, as the Wáng/Shř theory requires 9:1 to do.

Bodde, puzzling over the failure of that theory to win acceptance, remarks "[Shř] lived a little too late to have his researches adopted by [Jū Syī 朱熹, 1130–1200] and so receive the stamp of orthodox approval." Instead, Shř (mid-13c), and Wáng Rwò-syw̄ (1174–1243) before him, undoubtedly knew Jū Syī's commentary (1177). In dealing with several occurrences of yw̌, Jū Syī makes precisely the suggestion that it equals syw̌: 與，許也. One of these is at 5:9, where Confucius asks Dž-gùng how he thinks he compares to Yén Hwéɪ. Dž-gùng says that he would not dare compare himself with Hwéı. Confucius answers 弗如也，吾與女弗如也, which Legge, following Jū, translates "You are not equal to him. I *grant that* you are not equal to him." This may be orthodox, but it is not unassailable. Waley in particular has ridiculed several such interpretations in the following terms: "Again and again Confucius confesses to ignorance and imperfection. [Jū Syī] is at hand to tell us that this is only ritual modesty: 'How could a Sage really err, how could a sage truly not know?' or to construe the sentence differently, so that 'You and I are not equal to him'[5:9] becomes 'I grant you are not equal to him.' "[12] Waley thus construes yǔ in 5:9 as "and," and finds the "grant" interpretation unconvincing. Whether or not Wáng and Shř were inspired in their 9:1 suggestion by Jū's 5:9 gloss, we see that the gloss itself has impressed at least one careful modern scholar as unconvincing: a distortion rather than an explication of the text.

A variant of the Wáng/Shř theory (identified by most of its modern champions as the Shř theory) was proposed in Laufer, "LunYü," written in direct response to Bodde in the year after his paper appeared. Laufer argues for the sense "than" for yǔ; thus "The Master rarely discussed material gain compared with the will of Heaven and compared with humaneness (subjects he discussed frequently)", or "The Master discussed material gain *more rarely than* the will of Heaven and humaneness." For verbal yǔ 與 in the sense "than," Laufer refers to Hirth, *Notes* (no page reference given). In the 1981 preface to his republished 1933 paper, Bodde confirms what any reader might suspect, namely that Hirth's "than" is the coverb yǔ 於, which is the standard way of representing the idea "than" (along with other senses coming under the general rubric "in relation to"), and not the yǔ 與 of 9:1.[13]

Even if we waive the question of whether yǔ 與 means "than," and welcome the fact that Laufer's solution does seem to separate rźn from lì as desired, we must note that it does so at the cost of the implication "but he still discussed profit *now and then.*"Whether this picture of an *intermittently* profit-minded Confucius will fully satisfy the many puzzled readers of 9:1 (and of MC 1A1) is surely open to doubt.

AnotherType B solution is the 1970 suggestion ofWilliam Hung 洪業, strongly supported in a 1983 article by Boltz. This also separates lì as negative from mìng and rźn as positive, but does so through a different argument, that yǔ *as a coverb* means not "and" but rather "together with" or "in conjunction with."[14] Húng's translation is "lì *in connection with* mìng ['fate'] and lì *in connection with* rźn." This, as Boltz summarizes it, makes 9:1 "a straight-forward statement that Confucius rarely linked profit either to fate or to [rźn]. That is, when talking about matters of such moment as fate or rźn questions of profit were not proper considerations." This, if one reflects on it, has its own problems. Does it mean that it was only *in connection with* mìng or rźn that Confucius is said rarely to have rarely discussed profit? Did he discuss it more frequently *in other contexts*? Even in connection with mìng and rźn, why did he discuss lì *only* rarely? Why not *never*? As we have seen, the *Analects* as a whole gives no warrant for the idea that Confucius *ever* discussed lì in direct connection with mìng or rýn (it is perhaps a little hard to envision what a discussion of lì "in connection with" mìng would contain), or that he praised it in any connection. Why then this strangely limited statement in 9:1, when a much stronger one is available from the *Analects* as we have it? Whatever clumping or splitting one does among the three object terms, the fact remains that hăn "seldom" does not preclude Confucius's *sometimes* discussing whichever of them turn out, on a given theory, to be pejorative. The sensibilities of *Analects* readers would undoubtedly be shocked if any such proposal were made to them in direct terms. Hăn "seldom" in 9:1 is a riddle which no tinkering with yŭ can wholly dispel.

Boltz goes on to make and defend the statement that coverb yŭ *never* means simply "and," but always has the more precise meaning "together with, in conjunction with." There is no doubt that the corresponding full verb yŭ means, among other things "associate with," so that this claim has what might be called etymological plausibility. Boltz, like Bodde before him, makes much of the fact that the classical language can form a coordinate compound directly, simply by juxtaposing the two words, an example being fù/gwèi 富貴 "wealth and honor" in 12:5 (富貴在天, "Wealth and honor rest with Heaven"). From this fact he proposes to refute the idea that coverb yŭ can *ever* have a simple coordinative function. But a language may have more than one way of expressing a concept, and it seems hard to claim that the content of the phrase fù yŭ gwèi 富與貴 in 4:5, with the coverb, differs in any significant way from the same phrase *without* the coverb, namely fù/gwèi 富貴, in 12:5. Both are conventional expressions for the rewards of a successful career in state service. Nothing is very obviously clarified by assigning to either version a nuance of meaning that the other does not share. Additionally, Boltz's etymologically plausible claim that the true meaning of coverbal yŭ is not "and" or "with," but more precisely "in conjunction with" or "together with," breaks down if it is taken seriously. Most readers who try the experiment of substituting "together with" for "with" in *Analects* sentences containing coverb yŭ will find it not unacceptable; "together with" will seem to them merely a more cumbersome way of saying "with." But in Boltz's proposed solution of 9:1 it carries a more specific meaning ("only in conjunction with, and not otherwise"), and if precisely that logical relation is imported into other occurrences, it sometimes gives wrong readings. "In conjunction with" implies a close collaborative association. It does not solve 9:1 unless it means this. What would this do to the 2:9 sentence 吾與回言終日, Legge "I have talked with [Hwéı] for a whole day?" If it did anything, it could only enforce the sense "I together with Hwéı have talked all day [to other people]," that is, I have given a joint discourse *in collaboration with* Hwéı. But this is not what the sentence can mean in its 2:9 context. It can only mean "talked *with* Hwéı all day." The Master and Hwéı in 2:9 are not at the *same* end of the bench, speaking jointly to others, as the proposed sense requires; they are instead at *opposite* ends of the bench, speaking to each other, as the conventional understanding would have it.[15] The meaning "conjointly with" does indeed occur in some examples cited by Boltz. But in one of those cases, 19:16 難與並為

仁, Legge "It is difficult *along with him* to practice virtue," that meaning is carried not by yǔ 與, but by bìng 並. If yǔ already means "along with him," what is bìng "side by side" doing in this sentence? In at least this instance, the supporting evidence fails to support.[16]

The simple coordinate meanings "and/with" may well be semantic degradations of the probable prototype meaning "in association with," but to argue that these reduced meanings *never occur*, and that *only* the prototype meaning is present in the texts, is a methodological error. It reserves too much to etymology and allows too little to linguistic evolution, one of whose ubiquitous processes in all languages is precisely semantic degradation. The general principle thus seems to us perilous, and its application to the specific case of 9:1 ultimately unconvincing.

Type A glosses of 9:1, those that group lì and mìng together as against rŕn, are much rarer than Type B ones (despite the fact that the subjective reaction of most *Analects* readers is that it is rŕn which is out of place there). One was proposed in 1978 by Malmqvist, who argues that the first of the two yǔ is the conjunction "and," whereas the second has the Laufer sense "than." Malmqvist renders the whole passage as "The Master spoke more rarely of profit *and* of human destiny *than* of humanity." This has the merit of agreeing with the frequency data, and thus of making a statistically true statement. Malmqvist further cites 5:13 夫子之言性與天道，不可得而聞也, Legge "His discourses about man's nature, and the Way of Heaven, cannot be heard," as evidence of Confucius's reticence regarding mìng. For yǔ 與 in the sense "than," he cites 3:4 喪，與其易也, 寧戚, Legge "In ceremonies of mourning, it is better that there be deep sorrow than a minute attention to observances." As far as we know, the sense "than" for yǔ here is not resident in the word yǔ itself, but rather *in the phrase idiom* 與其。。。寧。, where part of the sense "than" is certainly carried by the coordinate adverb níng 寧 "rather." That *yǔ as a free coverb* can have this specific sense seems to us still without direct evidence.[17] Though Boltz characterizes Malmqvist's analysis as "of a sounder order" [than that of Fingarette, not here discussed], his final verdict is that "taking [yǔ] in two different senses in a single line of no more than eight characters is intuitively not especially satisfying." With this we can only concur.

3. Reception of the Conventional Answers to the Problem of 9:1

Whatever may be the force of the above objections to several proposals about the word yǔ in 9:1, the decisive point is that, for whatever reason, none of these proposals has found favor with scholarship in general. Commentators and translators from Hŕ Yèn 何晏 to Waley and beyond have overwhelmingly taken 9:1 as a coordinate statement,[18] and made their best peace with it as such. Waley, for example, translates as "The Master seldom spoke of profit or fate or Goodness," and adds: "We may expand: Seldom spoke of matters from the point of view of what would pay best, but only from the point of view of what was right. He did not discuss whether Heaven determines all human actions. . . . He refused to define Goodness[19] or accord the title Good to any of his contemporaries." The comments of Hv́ Yèn, Syíng Bǐn 刑昺 (832–1010), and Jū Syī (quoting the Chv́ng brothers), are all variants of this approach.[20] All these variants focus on the rarity of Confucius's statements, and not their collective import as a guide to action. They say nothing about 9:1 as a maxim. But to be a viable *Analects* statement, 9:1 must in the end work as a maxim. The problem is that there seems to be nothing which a reader, after deciphering 9:1 as directed, could confidently go and do in consequence of it. This marks it off from the other descriptive statements quoted above, where it is obvious that what Confucius taught we should learn, what Confucius forbore we should abjure, and what Confucius avoided we should shun. Having read 9:1, are we supposed to abjure lì only *most* of the time? While at the same time, ignoring this maxim and following the collective import of the other 108 occurrences of rv́n, striving to perfect ourselves in rv́n *all* of the time? The most ardent disciple could only hesitate before this question.

At the end, then, the passage remains admittedly puzzling to commentators. Nán Hwéi-jǐn 南懷瑾 ends three pages of commentary with the remark that the three central questions raised by the passage remain unanswered, and that "everyone can derive their own answer considering the *Analects* as a whole."[21] Durrant, explicitly declines to choose, and instead advises translators to warn readers that there is a problem; Dawson, implicitly accepting that advice, proposes no solution, and remarks in his note "This chapter has made commentators adopt all sorts of tortuous explanations. . . ." This abdication of normal commentarial function, by scholars both East and West, may without undue exaggeration be said to indicate an unsolved problem.

4. The Immediate Context

In this undoubted impasse, we suggest that another approach may be fruitful, which is not to scrutinize the words in the passage beyond the point where doing so yields convincing solutions, a point which we would seem to have passed in the case of 9:1, but instead to back off and consider 9:1 in its context. One of its contexts is undoubtedly the entire *Analects*, but as a first step let us begin by looking at its *immediate* context in the smallest formal unit defined by the text itself: the sayings in the rest of the chapter, LY 9.[22]

Of the first three sayings in LY 9, the first (our 9:1) is short as well as cryptic; 9:2–3 are moderately long, consisting of several sentences each. 9:1 is a third-person statement *about* the Master; 9:2–3 are quotations *from* the Master. In these basic ways, 9:2–3 pattern together against 9:1. This suggests that 9:2–3 may make a pair, that is, form a structure of which 9:1 is not a part. This suspicion can be verified by inspection. In content, 9:2–3 have nothing obvious in common: 9:2

is a sarcastic answer by Confucius to a no less sarcastic query by a villager, who accuses Confucius of not being good at anything in particular (Confucius replies wryly that he plans to take up chariot driving as a specialty), and 9:3 is a pronouncement on innovations in ritual costume (a cheaper kind of hat is approved of on grounds of economy) and deportment (a different place to make one's bow to the ruler is rejected as presumptuous). At the next higher level of abstraction, however, the two have a similar structure and a comparable horizon of reference. Both accept certain options and reject others. The options in both cases lie in the area of courtly practice, and are likely to have been created in the first place by social evolution. The issue of the generalist versus the specialist (9:2) presumably arises from the growth of the bureaucratic state, with its experts in finance and agronomy and indeed warfare, which in this period was undoubtedly replacing the older, more personalistic, less functionally differentiated state (where the ruler was in principle both the leader of the army and the chief officiant at the sacrifices). And the fact that silk is now cheaper than the older hemp-thread cloth (9:3) can only be due to systematic and widespread cultivation of sericulture. The second issue in 9:3, whether to bow at the foot or the top of the steps leading to the ruler's dais (obviously the latter makes a more egalitarian statement, as suggesting courtesy between persons more nearly equal), implies a degree of social leveling that might accompany the trend toward expertise (and in some sense, meritocracy) and away from birth and seniority as career determinants. The nerve of the villager in 9:2 (criticizing the well-born Confucius) and the assertiveness of the courtier in 9:3 (acknowledging the ruler only when he is on a level with him) can be seen as specimens of the same antitraditional movement.

Reasoning in this way, we can see the three sayings 9:1–3 as in the following diagram, taking for the moment only the first half of 9:3 for comparison:

9:1 Short.	Description, not quotation.	Things the Master rarely spoke of.
9:2 Medium.	Extended quotation.	The Master satirizes the abandonment of a tradition.
9:3 Long.	Extended quotation.	The Master condones the replacement of a tradition.

Taking this structure as intentional, and reading the passages in accordance with it, 9:2 and 9:3 *together* might mean something like this: in matters of inward culture, the Master is conservative, but in matters of mere outward form, the Master is flexible. That is, culture is more than competence in specific new skills, but it is also not mere retention of older usages.[23] The two sayings interlock to give an impression of mixed resistance to and flexibility toward social change, and the second part of 9:3 rounds off the pair by reaffirming that in questions of inner respect rather than outward detail, the old ways are indeed to be preserved.

It is worth pausing to notice that the opinion of Confucius as represented by

9:2–3 taken together is more subtle than we would suspect from reading either saying, even 9:3 with its balancing clause, in isolation. How much subtlety are we entitled to assume was originally expected of the hearers of these sayings? There has always been a problem with a saying such as 5:9, where Dž-gùng admits that on hearing one thing he can find out only two more, whereas Hwéı can find out ten more. *Where are they finding out these things from?* Don't the students just memorize what they are told, and then put it into practice? Apparently not; this and other passages make no sense unless some process of active intellection is involved. One possible object of such intellection is to compare single sayings and reflect on their joint implications, thus arriving at a more nuanced understanding of Confucius's mind than if they were holding isolated single sayings separately in memory. Then the pairing structure of 9:2/3[24] may be intended to provoke this process of reflection by providing, in the juxtaposition, a suggestive but not wholly resolved contrast; what the Zen masters would later call a kōan. If so, then in Dž-gùng's terms our reflections on two sayings (both specific) have led us to an additional one (more general). It is not Yén Hwéı, but it is at least a start in behaving in the way that the *Analects* describes Confucius's own disciples as behaving.

The device of suggestive pairing is also readily visible elsewhere in the *Analects*. One place that few readers or commentators have missed is 14:16/17, of which the first admits Gwǎn Jùng's political achievements but laments his lack of rŕn,[25] and the second concedes Gwǎn Jùng's small shortcomings but emphasizes the immense importance of his uniting the entire Chinese culture area against the threat of the non-Chinese culture areas to the north; it ridicules the idea that petty considerations apply in such a case. Of these seemingly opposite sayings, which is right? And whichever is right, what do we do about the other? Our answer would be that, much as in 9:2/3, the verdict is not for either Gwǎn Jùng or the conventional loyalty claims of rŕn, but for a more complex view that recognizes extraordinary achievement without abandoning its adherence to the rŕn ideal. Just as 9:2/3 leads to a reasonable flexibility in matters of cultural change, so 14:16/17 leads to a realistic balance in matters of political accomplishment. To harmonize the two, to conclude that Gwǎn Jùng actually conformed to rŕn while achieving what he did, fails to protect the concept of rŕn, and it also fails to preserve the tension between the two estimates of Gwǎn Jùng. The real point of 14:16/17 may be not to convey information about Gwǎn Jùng, for which the double structure is at best ambivalent, but to furnish *precisely that ambivalence* for extended reflection. One *Analects* name for the mental discipline of adjudicating ambivalence is *byèn hwò* 辨惑, which is mentioned in 12:10 and again in 12:21. Both passages give examples of ambivalence, but neither hints at the process by which ambivalence is to be resolved. That technique remains part of the implicit mental equipment of the *Analects* student.

Two other passages which can cause trouble for a reader are 4:3/4. The first (唯仁者能好人，能惡人) says that only the rŕn man can love others or hate others; the second (苟志於仁矣，無惡也) says that if you just set your mind on rŕn, you will be without hatred. So which are we to believe? That only the rv́n can hate, or that the rv́n never hate? Waley adjudicates this particular ambivalence by interpreting the first as an outside maxim on which Confucius comments in the second; thus, only the second represents Confucius's own views. This certainly brings the two into line with the general image of the Nice Confucius. There is, however, nothing to justify this treatment; as far as the text informs us, 4:3 and 4:4 are equally sayings of the Master. And the Confucius of the *Analects* is not necessarily nice. At a certain level, 14:16/17 go out of their way to praise a statesman who cut every moral corner in the book. 14:34 rejects the principle of returning good for evil, and advocates a firmer response. The famous 17:16 expresses hatred (wù 惡) of cultural vulgarization ("The purple encroaching on the crimson"). 17:22 contains not one but two catalogs of things the gentleman hates. We can hardly reject 4:3 on niceness grounds without getting rid of these other unpleasant sayings also. But if we keep 4:3, what are we to make of it? On the model of the above examples, the question is more precisely: what are we to make of it in the light of 4:4? Due reflection will register the insight that hatred is part of the gentleman's tool kit, but that the *steady practice* of hatred is incompatible with the gentleman's ethos. This is somewhat reminiscent of the familiar Western dictum that power can be safely exercised only by those who do not want power. It is a much more subtle thought than is either of its constituents in isolation.

If we stop here, we have some perhaps interesting annotations for a handful of *Analects* passages, plus a perhaps suggestive reflection on the expected mental equipment of the audience to whom they were addressed, but that is all. In going beyond this point, we enter essentially new territory.[26]

5. Extension to All of LY 9

We have found that it is fruitful in a few instances to regard pairing of sayings as an intentional structural device: an intentional pedagogical device. We now ask: How extensive is the use of this device in the text?

We may test this question on LY 9 itself. Lau, who among commentators is perhaps unusually attentive to formal features, makes no comment about the close relationship of 9:2/3, or for that matter of 14:16/17 and 4:3/4, analyzed above as functionally parallel. In the rest of LY 9, other than glossing some difficult words, Lau notes only that 9:8 "is exceedingly obscure." But even with no theory of statement pairing in mind, we may easily see that 9:6 (asking why Confucius possesses so many skills) and 9:7 (an explicit variant of that saying, attributed to one Láu 牢) are closely associated; they are offered as two different versions of the same thing. This is different from the interpretatively suggestive pairings we looked at in the previous section, but it is still manifestly a pairing; LY 9:7 is explicitly joined to 9:6 and would be inscrutable if placed anywhere but directly after it. There are also some thematic parallels fairly near the surface in adjacent sayings. 9:19, which insists that the Master will help no one who is not making an effort of his own, and 9:20, which describes Yén Hwéı as "one to whom I could talk without his growing weary," both sound the note of persistent effort. 9:21, lamenting that he "saw [Hwéı] start, but did not see him finish," and 9:22, noting more cryptically that there are "some who sprout but do not flower; who flower but do not fruit," are both about interrupted effort; probably both of them, and not merely the more explicit one, refer to Hwéı's early death.[27] Each of these two pairs is a parallel rather than a complementary statement. But up a notch, at the level of the pair 9:19/20 vis-à-vis the pair 9:21/22, we may notice a complementation between "continuous effort" (9:19/20) and "interrupted effort" (9:21/22). Here, we seem to have not merely pairing of sayings, but pairing of pairs of sayings. Proceeding thus, we find that a good many adjacent sayings in LY 9 can readily be construed as intentionally juxtaposed, either for reinforcement or for contrast, in a way that the reader of the text may well have been expected to notice, and in some cases also probably expected to reflect on.[28]

With this much seeming support from the examination of some adjacent passages, we may more boldly go on to notice some seeming parallels between passages which are non-adjacent in the received text. 9:25 concludes "If you make a mistake, do not hesitate to change it," and 9:27 praises Dž-lù for "not being embarrassed" if wearing a tattered robe and standing by those wearing fox and badger." In the one case, one should not fear to change if one is morally wrong; in the other, one should not fear to persist if one is morally right, in both cases regardless of one's own outward dignity or appearance. Between them comes 9:26, "The Three Armies can be deprived of their leader, but a common man cannot be deprived of his will." The interlock between 9:25/27 is so convincing, especially in view of earlier examples, that we may feel inclined to regard that pairing as original, and suspect 9:26, simply from the fact that it interrupts this close pairing, as being a later interpolation.[29]

A still more widely separated example is 9:8 and 9:11. Lau notes 9:8 as obscure. It is indeed obscure, but it clearly has something to do with "getting to the end of a question" asked by a commoner. 9:11 is a rhapsody by Yén Hwéı on how he never gets to the end of the teaching of the Master: "When I have utterly exhausted my capacity, it still seems that there is something there, towering up majestically, and though I want to go toward it, there is no path to follow." We may note that jyé 竭, here "exhaust [one's capacity], reach the end of," also appears in the final line of 9:8 我叩其兩端而竭焉 "I knock at it from both its ends and squeeze something out of it."[30] The thematic interlock here seems to be the contrast between getting to the end and following a path that never ends, as well as the contrast between a humble questioner and an elite disciple. The verbal identity reinforces the sense of thematic relation underlying this contrast. It is fair to ask what the juxtaposition of the two would add to the moral message of each, and though it is rash to formulate where the Analects seems to have left only clues to formulation, we might hazard something like "individual inquiries come to their end, but the path of inquiry itself is lifelong" as the thought that is lost if the two components are not brought into relation in the reader's mind. If we accept the idea that the pairing is intentional, it follows that the intervening 9:9 and 9:10, unless they somehow relate to it, are extraneous to it, and can only have been added later. In our view, they do not in any obvious way relate to it: 9:9 is the Master's complaint that "the phoenix does not come," whereas 9:10 describes how the Master showed respect for those in mourning. They do not readily suggest coordination either with 9:8/11 or with each other.

All this may seem to some readers speculative and even frivolous. But there exists objective confirmation that there may be something to it. It is noteworthy that 9:10, one of the passages here suspected as intrusive, is not a quotation, but a third-person description, of Confucius. Such descriptions are exceptional in the *Analects*, whose standard unit is either a quotation or a dialogue, in most cases featuring Confucius, or more rarely a disciple, as the chief speaker. Another case where a descriptive passage was structurally unincorporated with adjacent quotation passages was 9:1–3, where the quotative 9:2/3 were a related pair, but the descriptive 9:1 had nothing to do thematically with either of them. It turns out that there are three merely descriptive passages in LY 9, the two just mentioned and 9:4, and that *none* of them participates in a plausible pairing pattern. That is to say, the rhetorically anomalous nonquotative passages are *also* anomalous in that they never participate in what seems to be a rather pervasive tendency toward pairing of sayings in the chapter. Whichever of these exceptional traits one happens to notice first is reinforced by the other. The implication that gradually emerges from consideration of these and other details is that pairing is an original structural trait of the chapter, and that the descriptive passages were later added on top of, and in violation of, that original structure. And besides the *descriptive* passages, the pairing pattern suggests that some *sayings* passages, among them 9:9, are intrusive as well.

We are not quite through distinguishing types of passages in LY 9. In addition to the loosely paired 9:7/8, and the more closely interlocked 9:2/3 and 9:8/11, which are all sayings passages, and the thematically extraneous sayings or descriptive passages such as 9:1, there are two passages which seem consistent with the general theme of the preceding material, but for which no convincing pairing pattern exists. These unpaired, and yet not thematically discordant, sayings are 9:5 and 9:30a. 9:5 comes after the 9:2/3 group, Confucius's flexibly conservative attitude toward social and material change; it describes his mandate to preserve Jōu culture. Its cultural *revival* message makes a not unreasonable summary for the preceding lessons on cultural *change*. 9:30a comes after 9:28/29, which in various ways (pine and cypress are the last to fade in 9:28, the wise are without doubt and the brave without fear in 9:29) evoke the theme of constancy in adversity. 9:30a says that not all with whom one associates at one level are suitable company for the *next* level. If we give this a positive expression ("*Some* companions can be retained throughout one's own progress"), the thematic continuity becomes clear. In each of these cases, the *unpaired* saying can be seen as summing up or otherwise completing the general theme of the preceding *paired* sayings. We will call an unpaired passage with this seeming summary function an *envoi*.

9:2/3 plus 9:5 are then a pair plus an envoi, all on the same general theme of culture. 9:28/29 plus 9:30a are also a pair plus an envoi, on the theme of constant versus temporary associates. The fact of thematic continuity over short stretches, and of thematic difference over long stretches, itself has an interesting implication. It implies that in addition to a tendency toward paired sayings as a general texture, the material of the chapter is also organized thematically, *but in more than one group.* Besides these thematic groups at the head and tail of the chapter, how many more might there be? One salient passage for purposes of this question is 9:12, which describes the death of Confucius as taking place in poverty and out of office, but surrounded by devoted disciples. The theme of personal poverty is present also in the previously noted pair 9:6/7, and we have also noted that 9:8/11 give complementary accounts of Confucius's teaching. 9:12 itself, where Confucius dies in poverty, is adjacent to 9:13, where Confucius ruefully notes his failure to find a ministership ("Sell it! Sell it! I am just waiting for a buyer!"); these can be said to represent his unsuccessful political career. 9:15 (his reordering of the court music after returning from Wèi) and 9:16 (where he acknowledges himself perfectly capable of carrying out social and ritual duties) balance this failure image by displaying him as proficient in ceremonial. These eight passages, in four pairs, are all *about Confucius's life,* and together can be seen as giving this summary of it: He was hard up in youth (9:6/7), patiently taught both the ordinary and the elite (9:8/11), and never achieved political power (9:12/13), but did become a recognized expert in ceremonial and deportment (9:15/16). It will be noted that this perfectly coherent series does not end with Confucius's lonely *death* (9:12), but with his courtly *success* (9:15/16). That is, it ends on an upbeat.

The remaining ten sayings, some of which were discussed above, are in the area of the cultivation of personal virtue. They deal in turn with the required continuity, indeed ardor (9:17/18), the need for continued effort (9:19/20), the tragedy of Yén Hwéi, whose pursuit of excellence was interrupted by death (9:21/22), respect for the young (9:23) reinforced by criticism of the experienced who do not use their experience well (9:24), and warnings against denial of error (9:25) and embarrassment at poverty (27), when those feelings interfere with doing, or continuing to do, what is right. Like the biographical group preceding, these passages too may not unreasonably be seen as an extended treatment of a single subject; that is, as a thematic group. There are, then, altogether, four such groups in the chapter.

To take one last step into abstraction, do these four groups themselves constitute a message about Confucius? We would say, not necessarily. The first two sections are about Confucius, whereas the second two focus more on his art of personal development. But if we see that art of personal development as Confucius's chief legacy to his followers in later ages, it may not be overly fanciful to summarize LY 9 in toto somewhat as follows: Confucius was destined to have a role in the development and preservation of culture (9:2–5). In his actual life he failed politically but succeeded as a shaper of culture (9:6–16). His chief lesson is in the assiduousness that the pursuit of virtue requires (9:17–27), which, though he himself never achieved high office, also applies to conduct amid the vicissitudes of office (9:28–30a).

One can easily imagine LY 9 being differently arranged. Another writer might have put Confucius's death at the end of the biographical section[31] or made the death of Yén Hwéi not a parenthesis in the cultivation section, as it seems to be here, but the central tragedy of Confucius's life.[32] But the chapter as we find it makes a certain substantive sense, and it also seems on examination to show a guiding formal hand. The substantive analysis and the formal analysis support one another. This seems sufficient reason to allow the inference that LY 9 is the intentional outcome of a compositional process, in which factors of content and factors of style both played a part.

The entire pattern of the chapter at which we have arrived, both its tetrathematic large structure and its paired-passage fine structure, is displayed in the table opposite, taken from The Original Analects, where it is preceded by a much more terse argument than has been given above. Those passages which have proved on inspection to be formally interruptive, whether quotative or not (the latter including 9:1), have been are eliminated so as this table to display with maximum clarity what our analysis leads us to conclude is the original form. If one accepts the conclusion that Analects chapters have a structure, and that this structure can be recovered by analysis of the received text, new possibilities arise for the understanding of both the original and the interpolated material.

6. Extension to the Entire Analects

Proceeding in approximately this way,[33] we can arrive at comparable analyses of most of the other Analects chapters. The typical Analects chapter has twenty-four sayings, and is organized in four thematic sections,[34] sometimes with a fifth or envoi section, each section being built of pairs of sayings, with an optional final unpaired or envoi saying. Recognition of this form permits the identification of interpolations independently of judgements about the probable age of their content; that is, without the circularity which usually attends such determinations. It also focuses attention on those chapters which turn out to have a different organizing principle. In each case, however, except the seemingly truncated LY 20, some sort of organizing principle exists and can be discovered, and when discovered, it can serve as a formal guide, essentially uncompromised by assumptions about content, in the detection of interpolations.[35]

[A. On Culture]
  2   Culture is **more than** mastery of specific skills
  3   Culture is **not mere** retention of older usages
  5   Confucius has a divine mandate to preserve Jōu culture

[B. Confucius's Life and Teaching]
  6   Confucius stresses his **humble beginnings**
  7   Variant of preceding: **humble circumstances**
  8   **Among beginners**, Confucius will talk with anybody
11   **As an adept**, Yén Hwéı despairs of exhausting Confucius's example
12   Confucius renounces **sham** retinue at death
13   Confucius awaits **proper** office during life
15   Confucius reforms **court poetry** after return from Wèı
16   Confucius satisfied with **court and family** duties

[C. The Pursuit of Virtue]
17   Stream as **model of unremitting progress**
18   Sexual desire as **paradigm of intense concentration**
19   Confucius will help any who **make an effort** on their own
20   Yén Hwéı as an example of **assiduousness** in lessons
21   Confucius **laments** Yén Hwéı's death
22   Confucius **alludes to** Yén Hwéı's death
23   Men deserve no respect **if they fail to realize early promise**
24   Maxims are fine only **if they succeed in inspiring better conduct**
25   **Don't be afraid** to change if you are wrong
27   **Don't be ashamed** of being poorly dressed

[D. Intrigues in Office]
28   Pine as an emblem of **fidelity in hard times**
29   One with true virtue can **withstand adversities and dangers**
30a Distinction among low-level and high-level colleagues

LY 9 Conspectus
Adapted from The Original Analects (Columbia University Press, 1998), p. 129. Copyright © 1998 by
E. Bruce Brooks and A. Taeko Brooks.

With the ground thus cleared, we can review, and perhaps also develop, the
observations of those earlier scholars whose results tend to suggest that different
parts of the *Analects* may be of different ages.

The first of these was Hú Yín 胡寅 (1098–1156), who suggested[36] that the first
ten chapters were earlier than the second ten, a perception still enshrined in the
division into an "upper" (上) and a "lower" (下) *Analects*. Hú was followed by Itō
Jinsai 伊藤仁斎 (1627–1705), who publicized his own version of this view in
Japan, where it still has adherents.[37] The most important work in this area,
however, is that of Tswēi Shù 崔述 (1740–1816),[38] who pointed out that, within
the Hú/Itō late layer LY 11–20, the last five chapters, LY 16–20, were characterized by features that not only distinguished them from the rest of the text, but in
some cases specifically implied a later date. Balancing this suggestion, Arthur Waley
(1889–1966) proposed an earliest zone, consisting of LY 3–9, within the Hú/Itō

early layer LY 1–10. There matters stood, in this line of investigation, until Pokora in 1973 noted[39] that these suggestions can be joined to form a four-layer theory, with Waley's LY 3–9 first, the framing LY 1–2 and LY 10 second (these together constituting the Hú/Itō "upper" group), LY 11–15 third, and then the Tswēi late layer LY 16–20, completing the Hú/Itō "lower" group.[40]

How does all this look from the vantage point of an *Analects* text purged of its many interpolations?[41]

First of all, Tswēi Shù's proposed late layer is unaffected. These chapters being already late, any interpolations in them must be later still; there would seem to be no danger from intrusive *earlier* material. Tswēi's conclusion as to the relative lateness of this group of chapters thus stands. Second, the one passage Waley was inclined to recognize as an interpolation, namely the Syẃndzian LY 13:3 with its "rectification of names" principle and its chain argument, both of which features are unique in the *Analects*, seems indeed to be an interpolation, and in all probability a Syẃndž-influenced one.[42] Third, the remaining material, that is, the sayings which on the formal evidence were original to each separate chapter, tend much more strongly than the received text to suggest the passage of time over the course of the work. That time factor does not, however, suggest a theory which is exactly compatible with the Pokora four-layer one. It suggests instead a slight adjustment and a further refinement.

Commentators since Hàn have noted inconsistencies between the various *Analects* chapters. The usual explanation of this, implicit in Jvng Sywǽn 鄭玄 and repeated with variants down to the present, is that these differences are due to the chapters being the sayings of Confucius *as remembered by different disciples*.[43] This will in principle account for almost any imaginable difference of content, while preserving all the *Analects* material as equally authoritative. But there are at least two exceptions. The multi-disciple theory will not explain internal contradictions, and, as a special case of contradiction, it cannot account for implied development between chapters. That is, it is imaginable that the immediate disciples of Confucius had different interests or different degrees of understanding of Confucius's doctrines, but it is *not* imaginable that those doctrines should themselves be mutually inconsistent as reported by members of the same generation. Again, it is conceivable that the disciples should mention or reflect different aspects of their common historical environment, but not that they should imply historically different environments. Yet the different chapters do conflict with each other doctrinally, and they also imply different stages of external social and material culture.

Taking for the moment only chapters in Waley's proposed early layer LY 3–9, we first note that jr̀ 智, conventionally translated as "wisdom," is bracketed in 9:29 with rʹn 仁, whatever that is, and also with courage (yǔng 勇), as the three principle virtues. But jr̀ is disparaged in 4:2 ("the rʹn are content with rʹn; the knowing [jr̀] turn rʹn to their advantage"). The idea of "selfishly savvy" rather than "morally perceptive" also turns up in 5:18, where a conoisseur is despised ("So how good was his knowledge?") for accumulating tasteful objects to which by rank he had

no right, and in 5:21, where Níng Wǔdž's sacrificially loyal conduct is sardon-
ically praised as "stupid" in contrast to the fair-weather "wisdom" of those who
are smart enough to be loyal in normal times, when loyalty requires no more
than routine accountability. Does jǐ describe the expedient and profit-centered
behavior of the "wiseguy" or the profound insight of the "wise man?" The answer
is that in different chapters it describes both of these things. The same *vocabulary
of approval* thus does not hold across the whole extent of the Waley early chapters.

Again, we may note that LY 3, which is almost all about ritual (lǐ 禮) in one
connection or another, including the theory of sacrifice, contrasts strongly with
LY 4, where ritual is never mentioned, and in which the only appearance of the
character lǐ is in the compound lǐ/ràng 禮讓, which means social deference or
courtesy. On the Jǐng Sywǽn theory, it is imaginable that one student (the source
of LY 3) might be especially well versed in ritual, but if so, all the other students
would certainly still be aware that ritual was an important value in Confucius's
thinking, and their recollections would at least reflect its presence in his discourse.
In LY 4, and for that matter in LY 5 and 6, nothing of the kind occurs. The goal
of all disciples in these chapters is official service, and the quality on which their
fitness for service is evaluated, by themselves, by Confucius, and by prospective
employers, is moral insight cultivated to the level of moral expertise. Dž-gùng,
Rǎn Yǒu, and Dzǎi Wǒ, among others, are judged favorably or otherwise according to their success in meeting this intellectual and moral standard. There is no
hint that they possess, let alone that they are more *employable* for possessing, ritual
expertise. In LY 3, the same three disciples appear as examples of ritual expertise,
and *nothing but* ritual expertise. Not only is the focus of *learning* utterly different
between LY 4–6 and LY 3, but it is in part *the same individuals* in which the contrasting values are exemplified. This disjunction cannot be explained by a theory
of selective but ultimately compatible disciple memories.

Another recurrent emphasis in LY 3, besides ritual, is music. In 3:1 Confucius
is portrayed as viewing a dance performance of a Jōu sacrificial hymn, with the
full royal Jōu complement of eight files of dancers, and disapproving of it as a
usurpation of royal prerogative. That is, he is fully knowledgeable about Jōu music.
In 7:14, on hearing the Sháu music for another royal Jōu dance, he is so overcome with the unexpected beauty of the performance that "for three months he
did not know the taste of meat." Did Confucius, as remembered by the disciples
who presumably tried after his death to get him down in writing, know the Jōu
dances, or did he not?

More simply, what was Confucius's rank? In LY 4 he seems to have none. In
LY 5 and 6 he recommends his students for office (sometimes grudgingly), but
has no other contact with the court. In 9:6 he mentions his early poverty, in 7:33
he says he has never had a chance to prove himself in office, and in 9:12 he dies
without the retinue of lackeys would have been normal for a high minister. In
3:1, however, he ranks high enough to witness the grand ceremonial performance
referred to above; that is, he ranks very high. In both LY 3 and LY 4, he disap-

proves of much that the Lǔ court, or rather the Jì clan who dominated the court in his time, is doing. But was this disapproval that of a minister or an outsider? The different chapters tell different stories. In effect, they report different Confuciuses.

Again, who did Confucius teach? To leave LY 3 for a moment and consider LY 4–6 in a different connection, we find that Confucius's sayings in LY 4 are implicitly directed to the future courtier, and the more fully realized scenes in LY 5 and 6 show several disciples both in and out of office; all three chapters imply the Lǔ capital as their setting and ministership as their goal, and LY 5–6 throng with named disciples. In LY 7, by contrast, only two disciples are named, and Confucius is shown going around the countryside, talking to (but not explicitly teaching) people so questionable that his disciples object to them (7:29). Is this the same man?

LY 3 and 4, which have been contrasted in several aspects above, are especially rich in differences, both in content and literary texture. Here are a few general points: (1) The LY 4 sayings are brief, only Confucius is quoted (no other person is even mentioned), no contexts are given, and no advanced narrative devices are used.[44] The LY 3 sayings include dialogues with disciples and others, reported as well as direct conversations, and descriptions of the speaker's actions as well as words (3:11, "And he pointed to his palm"). (2) In LY 4, Confucius never mentions texts of any kind, and as far as one can tell, he teaches out of his own insights and convictions. In LY 3, he discusses explication of the Shī poems with a disciple, and is presented as having an encyclopedic knowledge of ritual practice and a deep insight into the theory behind ritual practice. (3) In LY 4, rv́n is the central value, figuring in all of the first seven sayings and several later ones; in LY 3 rv́n scarcely appears, and the emphasis, as noted above, is entirely on ritual. In sum, the Confucius of LY 4 and the Confucius of LY 3 have hardly a single trait, doctrinal or biographical, in common. They are not complementary but contradictory. They can be rationalized as being earlier (LY 4) and later (LY 3) stages in the evolution of the Confucius myth, but not as memory portraits of the same person. The multi-disciple theory will not cover this situation. A different theory is required.

So much for mutual inconsistencies. To see whether the inconsistencies make a pattern, that is, whether any long-term changes are reflected in the text, we need to have some idea where the text starts. There are many signs that point to LY 4 as the earliest chapter in the work. We noted above that it patterns frequently with the adjacent LY 5–6 in content but is simpler in form, suggesting that it is earlier. We also noted that LY 4 contrasts with LY 3 in a way that suggests that LY 3 is later. The simplicity of LY 4 contrasts not only with its neighbors on both sides, but with every other chapter in the work. As to content, Tsuda Sōkichi 津田左右 吉, probably the most drastic critic of the authenticity of the *Analects* material, concedes that LY 4 is uniquely free of anachronisms and irregularities.[45] It would be consistent with these indications that LY 4 should have been the earliest chapter;

the nucleus of all that followed. The first presumption, then, is that the work accumulated around that nucleus in two directions, with a few chapters (starting with LY 3) added at the head of the work, and a great many more (starting with LY 5) added at its tail. On the simplest version of this theory, namely, linear addition in both these directions, LY 4–20 will then be in chronological order. Is there any evidence that this is the case?

It is not to be expected that every *Analects* chapter will contain an anachronism pointing to a specific date or event in the real world.[46] Even if, as we suggest, some of the compilers were operating at a period remote from that of Confucius, they would presumably have represented their material as coming from him, and avoided as far as possible any obvious anachronisms that would undercut that representation. Nevertheless, there seem to be a few, and they suggest that LY 4–20 do indeed form a time sequence. This is because the indicators of date, when arranged in the order of the chapters in the LY 4–20 sequence, *are themselves in chronological order.* Thus:

- The unique simplicity of LY 4 would be compatible with a memorial compilation made shortly after Confucius's death; given its reference to Confucius in the third person, it could not be earlier. Confucius died in **0479**.
- LY 6:3 first uses the posthumous epithet (Aī-gūng) of the Lǔ ruler who was alive when Confucius himself died. Aī-gūng died in **0469**, and LY 6 must thus be later than this.
- LY 8:3 portrays the death of Dzv̄ngdž. Dzv̄ngdž died in **0436**, and LY 8 must be later than this.
- LY 9:15 implies court contact, and thus presupposes diplomatic relations, with Wèi, whereas the foreign contact in LY 7 was rather with Chí. Chí invaded the Lǔ border in 0412, 0411, and 0408. Such events were well calculated to induce a diplomatic coolness between Chí and Lǔ. The so-called Byāu Bell inscription records an expedition of Hán 韓 (which in the late 05c occupied most of the territory of the formerly important state Wèi) against Chí. The Bamboo Annals places that expedition in the year 0408, the year of the third and last Chí raid.[47] Such an exploit might well have been a sign of diplomatic warmth toward Lǔ, which (rather than Hán itself) would have been the major beneficiary of a military setback for Chí along the joint Chí/Lǔ border in southwestern Chí. A diplomatic shift of Lǔ from Chí to Hán (presumably for reasons of anachronism avoidance called Wèi in 9:15) in **0408** would be consistent with the evidence. The situation reflected in LY 9 could have existed by 0406.
- LY 12–13 are peppered with near and exact resemblances to phrases in the chapters of the Gwǎndž dated by Rickett to the 04c.[48] The statecraft theory expressed in these passages is very close to that of the interviews of Mencius

as preserved in MC 1.[49] The simpest inference is that LY 12–13 were
composed in Lǔ while Mencius was still associated with the Confucian school
of Lǔ. Lau has shown convincingly that Mencius left Lǔ in **0320**.[50]

- LY 16:1 protests an impending attack on a tiny state by the Jì family of Lǔ.
  The enigmatic curses of 16:2–3, apparently written in retaliation for the
  attack after it had taken place, match the number of generations of Tyén
  rulers of Chí which had elapsed when Chí attacked Lǔ's neighbor Sùng in
  0286. 16:1 is thus probably an allusion to that event,[51] and the aftermath
  passages 16:2–3, as a response to it, are most likely from ca. **0285**.

- LY 19 is ostensibly a set of disciple sayings, an odd feature of which is that
  the disciple featured in each of the first three sections is criticized at the
  beginning of the next. The position held by one of the criticized disciples can
  be seen as a caricature of the doctrines of Syẃndž, who took office in Lán-
  líng, to the south of Lǔ, after Chǔ conquered southern Lǔ in 0255/54. This
  conquest put a rival Confucian in a position of power very close to the Lǔ
  capital. The interpolation *13:3, discussed above, with some other, less
  blatant Syẃndzianisms, might have been added as protective coloration by the
  Lǔ school at this time. LY 19, as a covert satire on the Syẃndzian position
  and (apparently) several other varieties of Confucianism, might date from ca.
  0253.

- LY 20 consists of a long composition in the Shū Jīng style (20:1), followed
  by a conspicuously unpaired long saying (20:2) and a short saying (20:3).
  The material is heterogeneous, its *Analects*-like portion is brief, and none of it
  has begun to be organized into anything resembling any of the other *Analects*
  chapters. It might well represent an interrupted rather than a finished
  compositional process, and since the interruption seems to have brought the
  whole work to an end, it must have been a catastrophic one. The likeliest
  catastrophe is Chǔ's final conquest and extinction of northern Lǔ by a second
  attack in **0249**.

The political events mentioned above are not minor; on the contrary, they
would seem to rank among the landmarks of Lǔ history during the period. If any
outside events left traces in the *Analects*, these are among the most likely candi-
dates. Given that probability, it is then not trivial, but of probable analytical consequence, that these dates, listed above in *chapter* order, also fall in *chronological* order.
This is compatible with the hypothesis that LY 4–20 were added one at a time
over a period of years. It tends to confirm that hypothesis, and it also lets us specify
how many years are involved. The Tswēi Shù theory fails, not indeed of acceptance
(no Sinologist of standing has ever cared to dispute it directly), but of application, precisely because it does not say *how much later* than the rest of the text
it thinks LY 16–20 are. It was thus possible for Hú Shr̀ to rediscover and
champion Tswēi Shù in 1923,[52] and yet in 1933 to rebut Lyàng Chǐ-chāu's asser-

tion that *gūng* 公 "equitable" was an 03c usage by citing its occurrence in LY 20:1 (公則說, Legge "By his justice, all were delighted"). The refutation only works if the entire *Analects*, Tswēi Shù late layer and all, is in Hú's opinion of 04c or earlier date. It fails if the Tswēi Shù layer is in fact, as we have suggested above, the 03c portion of the *Analects*.[53]

The chapters appended not after but in front of LY 4, which on an equally simple first hypothesis were added to the nucleus in parallel with the above sequence, and in the order LY 3–2–1, need to be considered separately. The only readily evident chronological clue is in the protest passages of LY 3, which are ostensibly directed against the Jì usurpation of princely power in Lǔ. But a Jì princely usurpation would not necessarily have involved the royal ceremonies which some of them report and criticize. A better fit with the seeming subject of these passages in LY 3 may be the Chí usurpation of 0342, when the ruler of that state, previously called a Prince (*gūng* 公), began to style himself a King (*wáng* 王), a flagrant appropriation of the title of the Jōu rulers. That Lǔ too had ambitions to occupy a place among the eastern states comparable to that of the culturally influential Jōu in the west is attested by LY 17:4: "If there were one who would use me [in office], could I not make a Jōu in the east?" Lǔ may well have been enraged at seeing that hope anticipated by Chí in 0342, and it is not implausible to assign LY 3 to that date. There are no equally plausible references to outer events in LY 2 or 1, and to place these within the sequence of postposed chapters requires study of their content relations, which we do not attempt to summarize here. At the end, we arrive at this hypothesis for the growth of the *Analects*, the regular chapters being shown in the upper line and the preposed chapters being shown in the lower line, and the dates given being those at or near which the chapters seem to have been written:

LY 4 (0479) 5 6 (0469) 7 8 (0436) 9 (0405) 10 11 12 13 (0320) 14 15 16 (0285) 17 18 19 (0253) 20 (0254)
LY   3 (04342) 2   1

7. Developments within the Analects

The hypothesis above already incorporates a fair amount of observational data. It must, however, additionally meet the test of consistency with all subsequently observed data. This is a very stringent test. Its severest form is the developmental requirement: any indicated differences in doctrine or general culture implied by this material must be orderly and not random, and must all run in the same direction, and that direction must be from left to right on the above diagram. Any significant violation of these expectations will refute the theory; only complete fulfillment of those expectations will sustain it.

A trial inspection seems to suggest that the expectations of the hypothesis are confirmed in a variety of subject categories, ranging from the image of Confucius and the nature of his movement to the large-scale evolutions of society in both peace and war. We may here review a few of the more striking details, concentrating especially on those which put in a larger context the contrasts noted above between LY 4 and its neighbors.[54]

Life. We noted above that the seeming biography in LY 7 and the seeming epitome in LY 9 end in different ways. 7:33–35 make it fairly clear that Confucius has been completely unsuccessful in office (7:33), and perhaps even frustrated in his teaching (7:34), and at the end can offer only his personal conduct to recommend him (7:35). This is extraordinarily touching. Its poignancy is even exceeded by the counterpart death scene 9:12, where Confucius rebukes his disciples for masquerading as the retainers of an important person. But the preceding 9:8/11 contradict 7:34 by making him a success as a teacher, with the general public as well as his own disciples, and 9:15–16 go on to claim a further distinction: not indeed as a minister (that is wryly acknowledged in 9:13), but as a ritual specialist (9:15). The twilight pessimism of LY 7, which essentially ends in failure, is in strong contrast with the assertive optimism of LY 9, which claims success of two kinds, one of them (ritualism) entirely new. Which of these is intrinsically likely to be later? Since the known development of Confucianism is toward the extreme ritualism for which some of its followers are known in Hàn, LY 9 must occupy a later point in the trajectory. Then the order of composition is LY 7 > LY 9, confirming the above general conclusion.

Travel. Here is a larger progression that includes two of the above passages as compatible details. In LY 4 Confucius is apparently out of office, in LY 5–6 he is in contact with the court about the placement of his pupils, in LY 7 we hear for the first time of his traveling outside Lǔ, though he there shows himself unacquainted with ritual, and in LY 9 he is responsible for reforming court music in Lǔ after one such foreign visit and has evidently become an expert in ritual in the interim. Now the official success begins to expand. In LY 11 he occupies a position of sufficient rank that he must follow the great officers of Lǔ in his chariot, in LY 3 (as noted above) he is a privileged, if critical, witness at some solemn state observances, and in 15:1–2 he is equally critical of the policies of foreign heads of state. This seems to define a fairly clear progression in the grandiosity of the Official Confucius persona.

Teaching. Confucius the teacher undergoes a similar process of aggrandizement. In LY 4 he is essentially a mentor for one official at a time, in LY 5–6 an organized school exists in which he can speak to several pupils simultaneously, in LY 7 he is in some way or other proselytizing to strangers and in LY 9 he is claimed as a successful teacher of both disciples and strangers. LY 11:3 lists, as though in a school pantheon, the special accomplishments of ten disciples.[55] Beginning in 12:1 Confucius adopts a much more severe manner with Yén Hwéi, his formerly favored disciple, in 16:1 we see him treating his own son distantly, as just one more student whom he passes in the courtyard, and by 19:23 Confucius's house is described as virtually a palace compound, with its own shrines and acolytes and officials in attendance. The growth in relational formality and architectural scale is unmistakable.

Economics. To leave doctrine for the moment and turn to social developments, the text seems to reflect a declining role for hunting as a source for food or clothing. Landmarks in this process include the wearing of fur robes in 6:4 and 9:27, and the last mention of fur clothing in 10:5a. Wild animals are seen not in the field but in zoos 16:1. We noticed above the indication in 9:2 that silk, a rural labor-intensive product, is replacing other types of fiber. Similarly, the role of grain in the diet and in the state economy seems to grow more prominent: it provides official salaries in 6:4/5,[56] there is a plan to enlarge the government granary in 11:14, the tax rate on grain is increased in 11:17, a further increase is discussed in 12:9, and the existence of state experts in farming is noted (though deplored) in 13:4. The implied development is part of a general evolution from the military elite society with its hunting culture toward an urban/rural polarized society based on increasingly intensive agriculture.[57]

War. At about the same period as the hints of state agricultural management appear (13:4), we see for the first time indications of the jywn 軍, the mass army of maneuver, which at some point must have replaced the smaller, elite chariot force which is called shr 師 in the earlier Analects (and in the earlier Chūn/Chyōu chronicle, which uses only shr). The first Analects signs of the new term (as sān-jywn 三軍 "the Three Armies") are unfortunately in interpolated passages, for whose dating we have no room to argue in this brief discussion,[58] but the commander of such an army is mentioned in 14:19, and its tactics in 15:1. The link between the new army and the new intensive rural society is seen in 13:29/30, which discuss the need to train the people before sending them to war. It is the surplus rural male population created by intensive agriculture that fills the ranks of the mass army, and these new soldiers have to be trained in the elements of military discipline[59] and weapons skills. The old elite warriors (who seem to have survived as the officer corps of the new army) were self-trained all their lives in the difficult arts of chariot driving and archery, as 9:2, which refers to and belittles the old military ethos, reminds us. Here is nothing less than a social revolution.

Linguistics. Though on our hypothesis the material of the Analects accumulated over a 230–year period, from 0479 to 0249, we cannot expect to find many examples of literal linguistic change or vocabulary substitution.[60] There is, however, at least one clear example of meaning change within that time span. This is the word chì 器, which in the early part of the text means a ritual vessel (5:4), or by extension the official capacity of an individual (3:22, 13:25). But beginning with the following chapter, the default meaning of chì changes from a vessel, a thing having volume, to a tool, a thing having an edge; an implement with a special use. Thus 2:12: "A gentleman is not to be used as an implement", but *15:10: "If an artisan wants to do his job well he must first sharpen his tools." Somewhere in the late 04c, then, the word chì, which had earlier denoted a major emblem of the old palace culture, came to refer instead to an appurtenance of the new artisanal high-productivity culture. The simplest explanation of this linguistic shift is that the most commonly encountered product of the bronze workshops, and thus the default meaning of the word for that product, was a vessel in the first phase and an edged tool in the second. That shift in turn suggests a massive redirection of the entire metal industry of Lǔ, and presumably its rival states as well. It suggests a turning of the state economy, not indeed from peace to war, but from intermittent battle to total war. That change is in line with the most important single fact about the period, and indeed the one for which it is named: its warfare. An implied change in the opposite direction would be a setback for our hypothesis. The change we actually observe is to the same extent supportive of that hypothesis.

We might end this series with a glance, not at the content, but at the style of *Analects* thought. The LY 4 maxims are simply maxims; apart from the pairing and thematic sectioning, they do not offer themselves as a system. Some are contrasted, such as hate for the bad and love of the good in 4:3/4, but there is no warrant for assuming that the two between them sum up the full range of desirable qualities. In fact, other qualities such as steadfastness (4:2, 4:5), imperturbability (4:9), judgement (4:10), and dedication (4:14), receive an equally vivid, and equally transitory, prominence. So also with the extended and rather beautiful contrast between rýn and jr̀ in 6:23 (which makes, with 6:22, a pair of sayings on jr̀): it still leaves room for the substance/style opposition in 6:18 (which helps to explain the otherwise cryptic 6:16 with which it is paired) and for the qualities of energy (6:12), scrupulousness (6:14), and common sense (6:26). There is no point in either chapter at which the reader is tempted to feel, Now I know the whole content of Confucius's system. As Yén Hwéi says in 9:11, it keeps going on.

A similar situation obtains with the terms themselves: What do they mean? Rýn is very prominent in LY 4, but at no point is it defined, or even described. Instead, the LY 4 maxims only imply the conduct of the person who is rýn. This can, and in LY 5 it repeatedly does, lead to confusion. Thus in 5:8 the head of the Mv̀ng clan asks Confucius if Dž-lù is rýn; Confucius says he does not know, and proceeds to list various minor skills and presentabilities which Dž-lù has. The hearer will know from the rhetoric of the passage that rýn is something other than these skills, but is not told what it is. Similarly in 5:19b, the behavior of one Master Tswēi is offered as exemplifying rýn, but Confucius withholds that term and allows only that Master Tswēi was uncompromising. Rýn is obviously somewhere else in the universe of good behavior, but exactly where we are not told. The maxims of LY 4 might be said to be addressed to hearers who know what rýn is, and they need only encouragement to live up to it. The questioners in LY 5 appear not to know what it is, and to need to be told what it is, but no plain description of its ethical content is ever given. The most they get is examples of qualifying behavior, or non-qualifying behavior.

This changes perceptibly in LY 10. Accepting the finding of Waley *Analects* 146, that this chapter originally referred to the gentleman officer in general and not to the specific Confucius, we note that it constitutes something like a handbook of behavior in four logical sections (Public Occasions, Clothing and Food, Visits and Gifts, and Private Behavior). No reader will imagine that this Leviticus-like tract covers appropriate behavior in all situations, but then no sensible reader would expect to be prepared for every contingency of battle after reading the Sūndž. LY 10 is at least far more systematic and extended than anything that precedes it. A junior courtier who had mastered it, and reflected on its general tendency, would be in a far better position to learn from, or to improvise appropriately in, new situations than one who had not. This undoubtedly represents progress toward a more systematic preparation for practical life. The point for the present argument is the word "systematic."

In 11:23, Confucius resents a disciple's verbally accurate but situationally inappropriate application of a previously heard saying; he calls it "glib." This is different from the intense attention to previously heard individual sayings that seems to be the expectation over much of LY 4–9, but it is compatible with the seeming expectation of LY 10, in which the maxims are offered not as rules to be pondered, but as samples to be extrapolated.

By LY 3 a further step toward what might be called systematic thought has manifestly been taken. The chapter does not consist of an inventory of procedures in connection with sacrifice, but raises at several points questions about the inner meaning, or the general theory, of sacrifice; the larger understanding that guides extension or application in particular cases. That is, LY 3 directly displays the kind of overall rules that a careful student of LY 10 might formulate, in the protocol area, for himself. In 3:4 a questioner directly asks for a general theory of sacrifice (or more precisely, to judge from the answer, for a set of guidelines in making choices in sacrificial matters) and in 3:8 a disciple asks for the hidden meaning of what seems to be a merely descriptive couplet from the Shr̄. The latter example especially, based not on the practice of ritual but on the text of the Shr̄, shows an advanced technique for extracting guiding principles (ritual rather than moral ones) from seemingly unpromising material. If, as we think, LY 10 is a movement in the direction of completeness of statement, then LY 3 brings in a further movement toward trenchancy and subtlety of summary: a unifying theory to account for and re-simplify the expanding detail.

Yet another kind of rigor appears in LY 12. Lau *Analects* 270 says of it that most of its passages "invariably open with the words 'So-and-so wèn (asked).'" What these people are asking about is rýn (12:1–3), the gentleman (12:4), government (12:7, 11), or even "adjudicating ambiguities" (byèn hwò 辨惑), the technical term referred to above. What they get in response may not be a definition in the modern sense of the term, but it often tends in that direction. Thus Yén Hwéı in 12:1 is told, in Lau's translation, that "To return to the observance of the rites through overcoming the self constitutes benevolence." Yén Hwéı asks for a detailed listing, and is given four parallel statements, beginning with "Do not look at it unless it is in accordance with the rites." This is not far from a definition or primary description followed by an unpacking of that statement into four maxims of behavior. The style of the earlier *Analects* was to give only the maxims of behavior, and even LY 3 induced generalities from, or discovered them in, specifics. Here, teaching begins with a general principle and moves on, if necessary, to more specific and thus more directly implementable rules of behavior.[61] The balance of the discourse has shifted perceptibly from application, behind which a theory may be envisioned, toward theory as the primary statement.

In 13:15 this tendency to theory reaches a political high: the Lŭ Prince asks for a maxim that could compass the rise or fall of a state. "Confucius" politely doubts that any maxim could be that powerful, and then proceeds to give one. It is of no consequence, for our purposes, what that maxim is. What concerns us is simply the fact that it is thought that a single maxim, not a process of teaching involving the inner reconciliation of many diverse maxims or even a general theory extracted from many maxims or practical precepts, can suffice for the most practical of all applications: the success of the state.

Closely allied to this principle of sufficiency is the principle of universality which is embodied in three sayings, unfortunately all interpolations and so not directly datable by their chapter. The first two must at any rate be later than LY 15, the chapter in which they have been placed, and a fortiori definitely after the LY 13 passage above. The third seems to go a step beyond one of these, and so must follow it, probably at no very long interval. The three are: *15:24 (where a disciple asks for a maxim applicable in all circumstances), *15:3 (where it is asserted that Confucius has a linking principle that runs through all his separate sayings), and *4:15 (where the name of that principle is revealed by a senior disciple to a younger colleague).[62] They represent the highpoint of evolution toward what might be called theoretical unification of statement in the *Analects*.

A further wrinkle in the text's search for completeness and systematicity occurs in the Tswēi Shù layer, where, as its discoverer has pointed out, "numerical categories" begin to occur from LY 16 on. LY 16 consists in its middle portion entirely of such statements, which name and list the Three Profitable Kinds of Friendship and so on; in a later chapter comes 17:6 with its Five Things that together constitute the practice of the good ruler. These are not mere sample lists, which might be extended indefinitely, but an attempted systematic inventory. The implication is that the listed items do not exemplify but *exhaust* the named category: these *and only these*.[63]

From this point on, the development goes no further. At points it even seems to subside somewhat. In contrast with the suprasituational *15:24, the later *11:20[64] has "Confucius" insist on the situational relativity of his maxims, each being tailored to the condition of the hearer, and so, precisely, not containing a general rule. In 17:6 (as in 11:23) "Confucius" is uncomfortable at being held to the letter of his own previous remark. Situationality rather than universality is once again the point. We see this change as partly influenced by the strong interest in teaching which LY 17 manifests, but also in part as a retreat from the universality assertion of earlier chapters. This may reflect a certain loss of intellectual tone in the Tswēi Shù chapters. As Tswēi Shù himself observed, their often untidy form, and the presence of such seemingly extraneous passages as the list of terms for the wife of a sovereign in *16:14, imply what one might call a failure of housekeeping. Though there is much in these chapters that compels admiration, a falling off in control is obvious on the formal level, and we see a similar retreat from philosophical grip at the substantive level. We submit these observations as a reminder that morale-dependent developments need not be linear in the same way that material-culture ones can be expected to be. They are instead, by their nature, subject to retrenchment in challenging times.[65] An even more volatile category is the esteem in which certain disciples are held. This too seems to be not a logical development, but one which is continually open to the shifting internal politics and external perils of the ongoing Confucian enterprise.[66]

With these important exceptions, we submit that the discussed above developmental sequences meet the expectations created by the hypothesis. In areas where regularity is to be expected, they do indeed, as required by hypothesis, run from left to right on the diagram above.

8. The Kǔng Family and the School of Confucius

What the accretional theory implies, and what this generally developmental picture so far confirms, is that the *Analects* did not come together all at once, but grew by an orderly process over an extended period, a chapter at a time, maintaining a fairly constant formal and stylistic self-awareness, and what might be called a doctrinal or advocational identity, but continually evolving as a position in its own right, and also continually if incidentally reflecting some of the more dramatic events as well as long-term societal changes in the world outside. This could only have been the case if each successive addition came from a source which itself maintained continuity over this period. For this the obvious candidate is the school of Confucius in Lǔ. It is assumed by tradition that Dž-sẓ 子思, allegedly Confucius's grandson, was the first leader of this school, and it follows that his successors were the later members of that line as they are given, for example, in Shř Jì (SJ) 47, the notice[67] of Confucius. The problem of the Kǔng succession is another scholarly crux which it will be worth our while to solve, and which when solved will make certain strange features of the *Analects* more fully intelligible.

The SJ 47 list gives in most entries only names and ages at death. The first name after that of Confucius is his son Bwó-yẃ, who by early and uncontradicted tradition (LY 11:8) predeceased him. The next is Dž-sẓ. The following persons all have a formal name beginning with the honorific Dž-, until the ninth, Kǔng Fù 孔鮒. He is said to have been an erudite under the briefly successful rebel Chv́n

Shv̀ 陳舍, and to have died at age fifty-seven. This would have been in 0208, when Chv́n Shv̀'s reign of less than a year came to an end with his defeat and death. On the reasonable assumption that Fù perished with him, his lifespan would have been c0265–0208, and by counting back in units of twenty-five years (the standard length of a birth generation) we arrive at a rough estimate for the birth of Dž-sz̄. This turns out to be c0415. Then Dž-sz̄ could not possibly have been the son of Bwó-yv́ (d. c0480), and if he did serve as school head, it would not have been under the reign of Aī-gūng (r. 0494–0469) in the years immediately following the death of Confucius, but must instead have been under the reign of Mù-gūng (0410–0378). This completely contradicts the Kǔng tradition, but surprisingly enough there is early evidence for it. The Mencius text, presumably reflecting Confucian school tradition as it was known to the historical Mencius, includes several stories about Dž-sz̄. Three of these depict him as an advisor to a Lǔ Prince, and that Prince is invariably Mù-gūng.[68]

Here is a dilemma: on the one hand the Mencius anecdotes and the implied dates of the SJ 47 genealogy, which independently place Dž-sz̄'s headship under Lǔ Mù-gūng, and on the other hand the name sequence of the SJ 47 genealogy, which shows nothing between Bwó-yv́ and Dž-sz̄. One of these features must be altered to make a plausible historical picture. The strategy adopted by the Latter Hàn text Kǔng Tsúngdž is to extend Dž-sz̄'s age at death from the SJ figure of sixty-two years to seventy-eight years, and to claim for him a truly remarkable precocity: he is shown conversing with his grandfather Confucius in what can only have been the first year of his life, that is, the year before Confucius's death and the year of his own father's death.[69] This is indeed stretching the human probabilities. Maspero has preferred to work on the dilemma at its other end, by positing that Confucius's death date, as Waley, *Analects*, 79, puts it, "may have been a quarter of a century later than the accepted one."[70] But this would locate Confucius's own last years under Dàu-gūng (r. 0468–0432), and there is not a shred of evidence or tradition to countenance such a proposal.

We find therefore that neither the SJ 47 figure for the age of Dž-sz̄ at death (extended by the Kǔng Tsúngdž to no avail) nor the traditional year of Confucius's death (downdated by Maspero without success) can be altered to advantage. The vulnerable claim, we would suggest, is the implicit SJ 47 one that Dž-sz̄ *directly succeeded Confucius.* Our reasons for doubting this are several. First, in that case, as the ranking male heir, Dž-sz̄ would certainly have been the chief mourner at Confucius's funeral, but the Mencian account of this event (MC 3A4), as well as all later ones of which we are aware, show that the mourning party was led by disciples (Dž-gùng seems to have been the principal figure) and indeed consisted exclusively of disciples. Second, Dž-sz̄ as Confucius's successor would have learned from him in life, but he does not figure in the SJ 67 list of disciples, nor in its Kǔngdž Jyā-yv̌ 38 predecessor.[71] Third, if the school headship was held by Kǔngs from its inception, we cannot readily account for the portrayal of Dzv̄ngdž *in that role* in LY 8:3.[72] If instead we accept the evidence that Confucius's mourning and succession were disciple-dominated rather than Kŭng-dominated, and begin the Kŭng headship period when Mencian tradition and the implications of the SJ 47 list unite in placing it, namely at some time during the reign of Mù-gūng, and accept the idea that the Kŭng line, though in itself correctly reported, errs in juxtaposing Dž-sz̄ with his grandfather Bwó-yẃ, then all contradictions vanish. This is the solution we adopt.

On that understanding, the *Analects* accretion sequence from LY 4 through LY 9 represents the period of disciple headship, and that from LY 10 onward represents the period of Kŭng headship. This immediately makes intelligible the comment in SJ 47 that the last of the Dž- names, Dž-shv̀n 子慎, who on our hypothesis was also the last of the Kŭng school heads, left Lŭ and went to Ngwèi,[73] where he became a minister. By the previous calculation based on the death date of Kŭng Fù, Dž-shv̀n would have been born in c0300, and would thus have been about fifty, just reaching career maturity, at the time of the extinction of Lŭ in 0249. His departure and success elsewhere raise no problems of historical imagination. On the contrary, they support our supposition that the extinction of Lŭ meant the end not only of the *Analects*, but also of the school of Lŭ which had so long sponsored it, with the head of the school leaving the ruins of the state to seek a career as advisor to the ruler of another state.

As to the larger history of the *Analects*, the idea of an 05c disciple-dominated segment, LY 4–9, followed by an 04c and later Kŭng-dominated segment, LY 10–20 (and LY 3–2–1), explains something that is merely puzzling on the usual view of the text. This is the shift in central value from rv́n in the former segment to lĭ in the latter segment. More generally, it is the shift from the outsider culture of the former, with its ceaseless striving, its constant rebuking of laziness, and its equally constant exhortation to effort—typified in the strenuous self-estimate given by Dzv̄ngdž on his deathbed in 8:3 and the assiduous self-description of Yén Hwéi in 9:11, to the successor culture of the latter, with its emphasis on exact performance of rules, on social propriety in general and sacrificial propriety in particular, and its on the filial and even the domestic aspect of virtue. It might very easily represent a shift from *earned qualification* in the disciple period to *inherited position* in the Kŭng period. Against this simple background, the initial Kŭng omission of Dzv̄ngdž, who was evidently the major figure of the early period, from the 11:3 disciple pantheon, and their readmission of him as an emblem of family values in 1:9[74] is not mere caprice. On the contrary, it is entirely orderly and intelligible. It represents first the banishing, and later the reformatting and readmission, of a rival figure.

This division between the 05c and 04c layers of the text also has the merit of harmonizing the view of Fingarette *Sacred*, widely accepted in the West, which argues that lĭ or ritual propriety is the central concept of the work, and the majority Chinese view, which continues to hold that rv́n is central to Confucius's value system. In terms of the present theory, both are right. Rv́n was indeed central to Confucius's own value system, as its frequency and thematic emphasis in LY 4 abundantly attest. And lǐ is indeed the central concept of the majority of the *Analects* chapters, especially those from LY 3 onward. The prominence of lǐ in the period from the mid-04c, when, as we have seen above, the thought-style of the *Analects* itself was reaching something like philosophical maturity, means that the degree of organization in the lǐ-centered chapters, most obviously LY 3 but, as we shall see presently, also LY 12, is for historical reasons much greater than in the rýn-centered chapters, of which the only example is Confucius's own LY 4. That difference has probably counted as an item of convincement for those who accept the Fingarette theory. On the other side of the argument, the elemental character of LY 4 itself tends to exert an impression of literary authenticity, and the master unifying concept of the late 04c, when it is finally introduced in *15:3 and decoded in *4:15, turns out to consist of the old reliability virtue jūng 忠 and the new reciprocal relation shù 恕, the latter of which is easy to see as rýn in a new formulation, but yet still rýn. The placement of the latter in the LY 4 chapter was certainly intended to establish contact with, as well as to reinterpret, this chapter, and that contact has the incidental effect of reanimating LY 4 as a whole. There is a further point: broadly speaking, it is fair to say that rýn bulks larger than lǐ in the theories of the *Mencius*, whereas the opposite is true of the Syẃndž. The canonical status of *Mencius* but not of Syẃndž since the Sùng dynasty has tended to preserve rýn as a virtue in being, despite its more ambiguous treatment in the later *Analects*. All this can make the Fingarette question narrowly balanced for Confucius's world posterity as a whole. It is therefore probably an advantage to have, in stead of the decision crisis which must reject one or the other side of the question, a historical scenario in which both sides find their proper places in the historical development of Confucian thought.[75]

In these and other ways which cannot be explored here, our hypothesis of the *Analects* proves to be consistent with the formal and chronological indications in the data, while hospitable to many of the insights of previous students of the work. It is also able to suggest or permit solutions of various perplexing problems, leaving behind not an inconsistent and unsatisfying *authorial composition*, or its functional equivalent, but instead a fully consistent and intelligible textual and historical *process*.

9. A Proposed Solution of LY 9:1

Meanwhile, our ostensible goal, 9:1, has been floating in limbo ever since our formal examination of LY 9. We had at that time banished it from that chapter as a later interpolation. It is now our task to show that it is possible to locate its date of composition within the time span of the text as we have reconstructed it, and that this placement will somehow make sense of the passage itself: that it will suggest both a meaning and a motive for 9:1.

We think that the answer to the 9:1 riddle is to be sought in a further consideration of the situation just noted: the Analects text is sharply divided into an 05c disciple-dominated segment and an 04c Kŭng-dominated segment, and rı́n, the chief virtue of the former segment, is in the latter segment ousted and replaced by lı̆. This may be seen by looking at the distribution and intensity of the occurrences of rı́n in the Analects. In LY 4, nothing is more important than rı́n. In the chapters that follow, rı́n occurs repeatedly, but often as an object of puzzlement. In 9:29, rı́n appears as only one of three esteemed qualities, one of which, jı̆ "wisdom," was despised as mere cunning (4:2) or expediency (5:21) by Confucius as envisioned by chapters with a strong claim to be earlier in date than LY 9. Even within the disciple portion of the Analects, then, rı́n dwindles markedly from its initial commanding position.

In the first chapters of the Kŭng Analects, rı́n is gone altogether. It is not so much that the behavior guidelines of LY 10 do not mention it, since by virtue of their subject matter they would not be likely to mention rı́n or any other ethical matter. It is rather that their whole atmosphere of diplomatic propriety, of fussiness about whether the color of the mantle may clash with the color of the robe (10:5a), or whether the fish is a little bit spoiled (10:6b), is utterly at variance with the disdain of 4:9 for just these matters: "If an officer is dedicated to the Way, but is ashamed of having bad clothes or bad food, he is not worth taking counsel with." In 11:3, where four categories of excellence are enshrined along with the names of ten disciples who excelled at them, rı́n is not among the categories, nor is it ever mentioned in the less systematic remarks about various disciples which make up the rest of the chapter. In the LY 10–11 span, then, which in our view represents something like fifty years or two generations of Analects history, rı́n simply does not exist. In the ritual theory compendium LY 3, which we conclude follows LY 10–11 in date, rı́n is mentioned only once (in 3:3), and even then as a mere prerequisite for valid ritual practice. It is only in LY 12, later than any of the above chapters, that rı́n can be said to make an appearance, and like Dzv̄ngdž, who reappears in 12:24 and afterward, it reappears in a form quite different from that in the disciple stratum, but comparable to its appearance in 3:3. It is redefined in 12:1–2 essentially as conformity to ritual; that is, it is deprived of any content of its own.[76] In 12:22 it is defined, with reference to the ruler, as the love of the people. This saying, one of the foundation statements of the independent Mencian political philosophy, marks the beginning of the span of Analects chapters within which Legge's translation of rı́n as "benevolence" makes some sense, as it does not in the quite different atmosphere of LY 4 and vicinity. This is the version of the concept that the breakaway Mencian group takes away with them and develops on its own in the sphere of political theory. In the rest of the Analects, rı́n occurs occasionally, never again as an object of intense personal devotion (as in 4:5) or effort (as in 8:3), but simply as one desirable quality, albeit a governmentally exalted one, among several others.

The Kŭng proprietors of the Analects, then, made a clean sweep on their arrival, not only of the Dzv̄ngdž gang, who are humiliated in LY 11, but also of the virtue rv́n which Dzv̄ngdž in 8:3 had kept as his lifelong goal, and which even 9:29 had still bracketed with courage. But what were the Kŭngs to do with 8:3 and 9:29 themselves, and with the entire inherited textual tradition of the school up to that point, which remained intact and available, and by its presence offered some level of dissent from the new lǐ-centered doctrine which they were in the process of erecting? We suggest that they attempted to counteract that presence by inserting, within the disciple stratum, the 9:1 denial that the Master had had much to say about rv́n. This was not, at that time, so preposterous as it has appeared to modern readers of the entire received text. It was, in fact, only in LY 4 that the Master had a great deal to say about rv́n. His reticence (in the face of disciple incomprehension) in LY 5–6 and the greater rarity and reduced relative prominence of rv́n in LY 7–9, must have seemed to create, for an Analects writer working near the date of LY 11, an opportunity for a reorienting statement. We see 9:1 as that reorienting statement.[77]

The tactics of the statement itself may perhaps be plausibly conjectured. Like everything in LY 10, 9:1 is a description rather than a saying, and might have been composed at any time after LY 10 had set that stylistic precedent. We place it in the same period as LY 11, since it is in that chapter that the opposition to former ways, not merely their neglect in favor of newer emphases, becomes explicit. The tactic of partial denial (the use of "rarely" rather than "never" in 9:1, to which we drew attention in §2) is well chosen, as conceding the existence of an unde-niable cluster in LY 4. Its placement in LY 9, a chapter whose use of rv́n can prop-erly be said to be rare, seems also well considered, and its placement at the head of that chapter gives it maximum prominence there.[78] Bracketing rv́n with the clearly disapproved lì "profit" evokes the LY 4 strictures, and the use of the con-junction yw̌ "and" at a time when that structure, as Bodde and Boltz point out, was perhaps already obsolescent, may have been meant to evoke the yw̌ "and" in the eloquent and thus prominent 4:5.[79]

What then of the middle term mìng, over whose value we and previous scholars alike have hesitated? It suffices to note that in the chapters whose perception 9:1 was intended to influence, that is, in LY 4–9, and apart from the neutral sense of "command" in 8:6, mìng occurs only twice, as the "fate" that determines length of lives in 6:3 and 6:10. Of the operations of this "fate" the Master in both these passages openly disapproves. The later, more positive, more numinous, sense of mìng is entirely a creation of the later Kŭng period. The first occurrence of the phrase Tyēn-mìng is in the famous 2:4, from shortly after the LY 12–13 group.[80] In LY 4–9 as they would have appeared to students in the Confucian school at the time when LY 10–11 had just been composed, mìng, like lì, would have been not only rarely, but dis-approvingly, mentioned. This survey of the reconstructed text as it probably existed prior to the composition of 9:1 thus makes it easy to see what the composers of 9:1 had in mind. The first two terms of the triad would have fit the 9:1 statement unproblematically. The intent of that statement was then to maneuver rv́n in the reader's mind so that the LY 5–6 refusals to apply it could be viewed as somehow unfavorable to rýn itself.

The reorientation of values which 9:1 seems to have been intended to bring about ultimately failed.[81] This was probably due in considerable part to the fact that later heads of the Kŭng school saw fit to reintroduce the term as a principle of benevolence, thus creating a new situation, and to the further fact that Mencius and his followers drew on that revived term for their own political theories, which form a highly visible part of later Confucianism. Whether 9:1 achieved its purpose *at the time*, who can say? We find that its probable purposes made tactical sense, and that its wording, including an intentional archaism, made stylistic sense, at the time it was written. It proclaimed: "The Master seldom spoke of profit, or fate, or rýn." For students of the school in about the year 0360, in whose minds the most recent chapters LY 10–11 would have been most prominent, that would quite possibly have been cogent. It would have agreed with the use frequencies in the text which they then possessed, while conceding, in the term "rarely," the existence of a certain cluster of rýn passages in LY 4, and it might well have sufficed to damp any student curiosity about rýn even in the exceptional LY 4. Later, when the reconceptualized rýn was reintroduced into Kŭng doctrine, 9:1 necessarily became somewhat dysfunctional, but there is no reason to think that it was not as effective as intended, at the time it was introduced into LY 9.[82]

10. A Glance at LY 12:1

As a further test of the efficacy of our whole-text approach to single-word problems, we may here briefly consider a second crux, which, like 9:1 though less notoriously, has absorbed considerable scholarly attention, namely 12:1.

That passage begins: 顏淵問仁。子曰，克己復禮為仁, in Lau's version: "Yén Ywæn asked about benevolence. The Master said, To return to the observance of the rites through overcoming the self constitutes benevolence." The rest of the passage, in which Yén Hwéi asks and gets a more detailed set of instructions, does indeed direct him to the systematic suppression of the various sensual distractions; Lau "Do not look at it unless it is in accordance with the rites," and similarly with looking, listening, and speaking. The difficulty that here exercises commentators again turns on the understanding of a single character, in this case kv̀ 克 "overcome."[83]

The Lau translation quoted above reflects the earliest interpretation, that of the Hàn commentator Mǎ Yúng. Another idea, due to the purported Kŭng Añ-gwó commentary, makes kv̀ equal to kv̌ 可 "can; be able to." Such a substitution is undoubtedly valid in some classical instances. Making that substitution here gives essentially Waley's reading: "He who *can* himself submit to ritual is Good." Waley notes that the Dzwǒ Jwàn, under Jāu 12 (ostensibly 0530)[84] quotes this line "as a saying from 'an old record,'" and finds that later readers have failed to appreci-

ate its archaic character, with 克 for 可, thus making "an error fruitful in edifi-
cation." A third suggestion, of Fàn Níng (339–401), takes kằ in a full verbal sense
as "be responsible for," thus reaching the interpretation "to hold oneself responsible to return to lǐ." Kieschnick's final comment is, "The precise intention of the
single individual who first recorded the phrase some time in the [Jōu] dynasty is,
pending the discovery of new material, lost to us."[85] The policy of waiting for
archaeology, which has sunk so deeply into the Sinological soul since the 1930s,
has had its successes. In the meantime, however, *the archaeology of the text*, by which
we mean determining, and basing interpretation on, the stratification of the work
itself, may also have something to offer.

As to the conflicting interpretations of kằ, there is not that much for it to do.
The Mǎ reading of 12:1, like the grammatically normal (if interpretatively problematic) "and" reading of 9:1, is the likely solution, whereas the later suggestions
are ingenuities based on technically possible but contextually awkward constru-
ances of one word. Mǎ's reading makes parallel VO (verb-object) clauses of kằ jǐ
and fù lǐ, and this will strike a practiced reader as not only natural but as having
an appropriate solemnity (quite apart from the pairing of whole passages explored
above, twinning at the phrase and other levels is a constant feature of the elevated
style).[86] These VO clauses in turn are readily felt by a reader as nominalizable for
purposes of a larger sentence structure, thus "to overcome the self . . . *constitutes
benevolence.*" The Kǔng interpretation requires instead that kằ be an auxiliary verb,
and that the following jǐ become an adverb, giving the interpreation "*to be able
of oneself to return to lǐ,*" and the Fàn reading somewhat similarly requires a
governed-verb structure: "*to hold oneself responsible to return to lǐ.*" Neither of these
contravenes any rule for allowable structures in subject clauses, but, subjectively,
they are a little more elaborate than what one usually encounters in that grammatical slot. Both the suggested readings make morally useful points, and in the
Kǔng case at least, the morally useful point, the need for the movement toward lǐ
to come from the self,[87] is actually stated in a later line in the passage: Lau
"However, the practice of benevolence depends on oneself alone, and not on
others." This is in essence also the legitimizing line for the Fàn interpretation. But
both interpretations give the impression of working too hard to plant their point
in the first line of the passage, rather than letting it emerge from a later line, or
for that matter in the subsequent reflection of the reader on the whole passage.
They accelerate the process. They import later knowledge into the first eye contact.
They are sermonizing elaborations, not simple vocabulary glosses, and in that
sense they are typical of the great mass of Hàn and later commentary statements.
We thus, a priori, suspect that the Mǎ reading would have seemed grammatically
more natural to his Hàn contemporaries, and we also suspect that, assuming they
simply kept on reading, the Hàn people were not really in danger of missing the
moral lessons that Kǔng and Fàn are eager to press on them, useful and profitable,
and indeed valid, as those may be.

Thus might run a subjective reaction to the alternatives summarized by

Kieschnick. What does the new hypothesis of the *Analects* have to add? Essentially it adds contextual considerations. First, we may ask, What is the context of 12:1? We find that 12:1, unlike 9:1, is not an interpolation. On the contrary, it has intimate structural parallels with the following 12:2, in which Răn Yŏu also begins by asking about *rʹn*, and concludes with the same formulaic sentence of gratitude for instruction with which Yén Hwéi concluded in 12:1. The fit of both these passages with the above-noted "definitional" cast of LY 12 at large is also obvious. They may thus both be taken as integral to, and not intrusive in, the chapter.[88] As such, they may be validly read in the context of LY 12 and its wider environment, including the Dzwŏ Jwàn, which in our view dates from this period, and in which, as noted above, the opening words of 12:1 also appear. How would a reader of this period have been likely to construe the word *kʹv* 克 in that passage? The *Analects* reader up to 12:1 (our proposed date for it is ca. 0326) had never encountered it; 12:1 is its first occurrence in that text.[89] The Dzwŏ Jwàn (ca. 0312) is the locus classicus of battle descriptions in early literature. *Kʹv* is very frequent in that text, and there it normally means "overcome." There are also places where *kʹv* 克 "overcome" is written for *kě* 可 "can," but the two are generally distinguished, and a Dzwŏ Jwàn sentence like 隨未可克也 "Swéi cannot yet be overcome" is not ambiguous.[90] Slightly later in the *Analects*, at *14:1b, comes what looks like a comment on the earlier 12:1 says: 克伐，怨，欲不行焉，可以為仁乎, which following the vocabulary precedent of the Dzwŏ Jwàn might mean "Overcoming pride, resentment, and desire so that they no longer occur: can this be regarded as *rʹn*?"[91] In 12:1, the suppression of desires (together with a turning to lĭ) was associated with *rʹn*. Here, a wider range of sensory and emotional excesses is kept from occurring, and again that process is linked with *rʹn*. But in this case, unlike 12:1, the Master denies the connection; something more is required. There are a number of *Analects* sayings in which mere restraint, mere scruple, mere outward compliance, are said to be insufficient to earn the name of some virtue. A positive quality, an effort of origination, is also required. That would seem to be the sense here as well.

The diminution of desire, or of sensory and emotional impulses to action in general, is a commonplace of ethical teaching in the *Analects* and elsewhere. It is also a commonplace of meditation discipline; thus Dàu/Dʹv Jīng (DDJ) 19: 少私寡欲 "diminish the self and reduce desires."[92] The association of such inner discipline with rulership is ubiquitous in the DDJ, and a similar connection is made by Mencius in MC 2A2. We thus need not be surprised to find what seem to be desire-suppression techniques mentioned in a statecraft text like the *Analects*, and neither there nor elsewhere in contemporary literature need we be surprised to find that desire-suppression is not an end in itself; in parallel with that reduction process there should be something more expansive taking place.

The reduction process with something else (a turning to lĭ) is called *rʹn* in 12:1, and the reduction process without anything else is denied the name of *rʹn* in 14:1b. The agreement would seem to be complete.

Signs of what look like the concentration of mental attention that is typical of meditation practice go very far back in the *Analects*, and nearly all of them are associated with Yén Hwéi as a practitioner.[93] It is conspicuous that throughout the *Analects*, save for some interpolated passages, Hwéi is never represented as being in conversation or in contact with any other individual except Confucius, and even that relation is rarely portrayed; it is instead reported as an offstage fact by Hwéi himself (9:11) or by Confucius (9:20). Hwéi is the paradigmatic solitary disciple. He is described as living in extreme poverty with minimal food in 6:11, and as able to concentrate on one subject, in fact, on rv́n, for three months in 6:7. He is acknowledged in 5:9 to be by far the most perceptive of the disciples. Confucius in 11:8a describes him as "often empty," the word "empty" (kūng 空) and its synonyms being used in the meditation literature to suggest a state of inner quiescence.[94] He is described by Confucius in 6:3 as the only disciple qualified by love of study for high office, and later by someone questioning *Mencius* (MC 2A2) as the complete disciple, possessing every virtue, and having the same range as Confucius himself. The association of inward completeness and outward comprehensiveness is a theme of the Nèi Yè or Inner Cultivation chapter of the Gwǎndž, another text of approximately this same period.[95] All in all, there are no surprises in the 12:1 conversation of Hwéi and Confucius, except that, apart from some interpolations of intrinsically uncertain date, it is the first such conversation to be directly portrayed, rather than reported, by the *Analects*.

Meditation is not, however, supported by the *Analects* much beyond this point in the text. In 2:15, meditation (sž 思 "reflection") is admitted as coequal to study as a source of moral insight and improvement, but not long afterward, in *15:31, we have "Confucius" saying "I once stayed awake all night in order to reflect (sž 思, meditate), but it was in vain. It is better to study." In the final Tswēi Shù series of chapters, and to a lesser extent in those directly preceding, memorization rather than reflection is increasingly associated with "study," and it is increasingly emphasized: in 16:13 it is the only advice Confucius gives his son. Anything resembling extended or intense reflection is conspicuous by its absence. The meditation tool, we conclude, is in this period ceded to the Dàuist texts, of which the one chiefly parallel to the Tswēi Shù layer of the *Analects* is the Jwāngdž. With that technique goes Yén Hwéi himself, who vanishes completely from LY 15 onward,[96] but turns up as an exemplary, and meditationally adept, figure in the Jwāngdž.[97] As of LY 12:1, then, we are nearing the end of the segment of the text in which meditation as a way of knowledge is acceptable to the Confucians of Lǔ. Within a generation it will be gone altogether.

The histories of rv́n, of meditation techniques, and of Yén Hwéi in the *Analects*, thus converge to some extent in 12:1. Rv́n, having suffered complete eclipse in the early 04c (and having, in 9:1, been denied by the early Kǔng proprietors of the school as having been important even in the 05c), has returned and been rehabilitated, first in 3:3 and now in 12:1, but in both passages in close association with lǐ. Meditation, early associated with Yén Hwéi and in 12:1 associated with him *and* with rv́n, is still valid but will soon vanish from the text as an approved technique (14:1b, which analyzes the 12:1 synthesis and tells us that the meditation component is insufficient by itself, is one more passage that sounds the knell). And Yén Hwéı himself is making his last bow, before he follows meditation out of the text forever.

These large developments, in which 12:1 takes a consecutive place, are part of the dynamic of 12:1, and can help the reader to see it within its *Analects* context. We submit that this whole-text view goes far toward clarifying single passages like *9:1 and 12:1, which, on the record, have proved genuinely perplexing when examined in isolation.[98]

That such large developments also go far toward clarifying the whole text, and recovering its evolving agenda over the more than two centuries of its compilation, is a claim for which we must refer the reader to our extended study, *The Original Analects*. The present, necessarily limited, argument attempts to demonstrate that this solution of the text can accommodate the most insightful of traditional and recent scholarly observations, while at the same time solving recognized problems that are beyond the power of the old explanatory structures, that it reveals the text as possessing an unexpected aesthetic finesse and an unappreciated philosophical and pedagogical subtlety, that it reveals the interplay of rival viewpoints in the formation of opinion and the impingement of life upon thought, and that it meets without internal contradiction the basic tests of textual, institutional, and historical plausibility.

Our final suggestion, in terms of our announced theme, is that the way to understand one word is to keep an eye on the whole text in which that word appears, and ultimately the whole corpus of which that text is in turn a part. Many readers will recognize that this advice is very close to what has always been the traditional Chinese way of working with texts.[99] We are happy, in conclusion, to associate ourselves with that recommendation.

NOTES

Our earliest statement concerning LY 9:1 was contained in the privately circulated Note 36 (8 Sept. 1993), and that concerning LY 12:1 was in Note 37 (9 Sept. 1993). We are grateful to their recipients, the Warring States Working Group as of that period, for their subsequent criticisms and suggestions. We are also grateful to audiences at Harvard University (1995), the University of Massachusetts at Amherst (1995), Indiana University (1996), the University of Pennsylvania (1996), Brown University (1996), Columbia University (1997), and the University of Chicago (1998), where one or both of us presented a version of the present argument, for their comments and questions, from which we have profited in shaping the present exposition, and to the discussion on the Warring States Workshop E-mail network in early 1999 for final input.

Romanization of Chinese words follows the Common Alphabetic system, which is also used in our book-length analysis, E. Bruce Brooks and A. Taeko Brooks, *The Original Analects* (Columbia 1998). The essence of the system is to rely as far as possible on letter values already familiar to users of alphabetic scripts, hence the familiar rule "consonants as in English, vowels as in Italian." For vowels not present in English or without a standard equivalent in English, the conventions are: v [the linguist's inverted v, but *uninverted*] for the vowel of "bug," æ for the vowel of "bag," r as in "fur," z as in "adz," and w for "umlaut u." Tones are represented by contour marks over the main vowel. In the interest of a more culturally inclusive discourse, we use a prefixed 0 to identify dates "BC," whence 0479 for the date of Confucius's death. Centuries are indicated by a postfixed c (as 05c). Short citations in the body of the paper in the form, author's surname, *title keyword*, are expanded in the list of References at the end, as are abbreviations for the names of the Chinese texts frequently mentioned.

Numbering of *Analects* passages is that of the Harvard-Yenching (1929) concordance; it differs slightly from the numbering in Legge and other translations, which at some points also diverge from each other. Passages thought to be interpolated have an asterisk prefixed to the citation number (as *13:3). The authors are grateful to the National Endowment for the Humanities for the 1996–97 Fellowship under which part of the research reflected in this paper was carried out.

1. For examples of Western text-filiation technique as applied to Chinese texts, see Thompson, *Shen*, and Roth, *Textual*. These studies are indeed exemplary, but neither of them spends much time on how the text in question came into being. They concentrate instead on how the text can be recovered from its divergent extant copies. On the Chinese side, it is generally recognized that the crowning achievement of Chǐng philology was the discovery that the so-called Gǔ-wv́n Shàng-shū 古文尚書 were a forgery; see Shaughnessy, "Shang Shu," 384f, and Elman, *Classicism*, 103–6. The latter account emphasizes that there were limits on how far, within traditional Chinese scholarly discourse, the philology of a question could affect the orthodox position on that question.

2. In Chinese, Lún Yw̌ 論語; in citations of specific passages LY. This and other text abbreviations are expanded in the concluding list of References.

3. Two concluding sections, briefly arguing that the ultimate context in which the *Analects* must be read is the entire Warring States corpus, and pointing out that the recently discovered Gwōdyèn text of the Dàu/Dv́ Jīng confirms a crucial detail of our reconstruction of the chronological relations within that corpus, have been eliminated at the request of the present editor. They are nevertheless an important part of the argument. Readers of the Dàu/Dv́ Jīng theory advanced in Brooks, "Prospects," 63–68 and 70–73 (which predicted that a text of early 03c date would comprise approximately DDJ 1–65) will recognize that it agrees well with the truncated early 03c text found at Gwōdyèn (whose range was DDJ 2–66). Neither theory of the text advocated by the scholars gathered at the Dartmouth Conference of 1998 (see Harrington, "Laozi") is confirmed; on the contrary, both are refuted, by that archaeological result. It may thus be said that, quite apart from any intrinsic attractiveness of the view of the *Analects* which is arrived at in the following pages, that view agrees with archaeology much more closely than do any rival theories of the relevant parts of the Warring States corpus which have so far been put forward. See further below, n. 53.

4. "And" is the first meaning given for yw̌ 與 in Dobson, *Particles*, 813, and is there supported by examples from other early texts. In sentences with a negative or negatively implicational verb, in either Chinese or English, a compound object tends to acquire the sense "neither/nor" rather than "both/and," hence the "[or]" in the translation of the second example.

5. That is, 108 exclusive of the present instance. To put this figure in perspective, there are, according to the Hong Kong concordance, only 15,935 words in the *Analects*. Rv́n 仁 is the twenty-seventh most common word in the text. The only higher-ranking words that

are not particles, function words, or pronouns (such as the pause-marker yě 也, the universal coverb yẃ 於 "in relation to," or the pronoun wú 吾 "I") are the following content words: rv́n 人 "man," yǒu 有 "have," wéi 為 "do," jyw̄n 君 "ruler," largely in the compound jyw̄ndž 君子 "gentleman," the auxiliary verb kv̌ 可 "can," rú 如 "be like," yẃ 與 "be with," yén 言 "say," wú 無 "have not," wv̀n 問 "ask," and jī 知 "know." These are all the stuff of ordinary Warring States prose of any doctrinal stripe or persuasion. Except for rú and wv̀n, for instance (and even they are in the top 160), they all rank in the top fifty on the frequency curve of the eclectic Lv̌-shř Chūn/Chyōu 呂氏春秋, a text 20 times the size of the Analects. That rv́n 仁 should occur in the basic-usage stratum of Analects vocabulary makes it not merely common, but more exactly constitutive, for the text as a whole.

6. Unless otherwise credited, Analects translations in this paper are based on Brooks, Original; and translations from other texts are our own.

7. The following extended survey of the 9:1 problem as seen by traditional philology was added to the present paper at the suggestion of the volume editor, a suggestion for which we are grateful. However, readers who are prepared to take it as given that a problem exists, and that traditional philology has been unable to resolve it, may skip that demonstration and proceed directly to §3.

8. This is the traditional view of the passage, with which alone we are here concerned. Beyond referring to the suggestive study Schumacher, Nützlichen, we resist the temptation to take up the question of the role of lì 利 in Mencius.

9. For the following summary, we rely largely on Bodde, "Perplexing," and Boltz, "Word."

10. Durrant, "Translating" 112, following Yáng Bwó-jyv̀n 楊伯峻.

11. Bodde, "Perplexing," 385.

12. Waley, Analects, 74.

13. Bodde, Essays, 28. For yẃ in the sense "than," see also the discussion of Malmqvist, below.

14. Boltz, "Word," 264; the following is generally based on Boltz's treatment. Dobson, Particles, 813, is sufficiently influenced by the idea of "together with" that he gives it along with "and" as a primary meaning of yẃ as a "syntagmatic conjunction," but none of his examples in that section require, or receive, a translation other than "and." See further below.

15. Even the common sense "with" ("alternating with") is precluded here by the following text, in which Confucius complains, "he never disagrees with me; he seems to be stupid." That is, Hwéi does not hold up his end as he is expected to do, by raising objections or asking clarifications. It is an intended two-way conversation which has become by default a one-way discourse. (It turns out in the end that Hwéi has internalized everything, and can manifest it in his conduct; Hwéi is not really stupid). But the idea of an interactive conversation in 2:9, with each party "joining in contributing to a common discourse" is just as thoroughly ruled out as is the idea of a joint discourse. The sense "to" of yẃ when used in such conversational situations is noticed by Dobson, Particles, 814, where such examples are given a separate section under the rubric "Directive Particle."

16. Dobson's examples of "and" for yẃ (Particles, 813) include Shī 31 (and identically Shī 82) 與子偕老, Dobson "[I] and you, sir, will grow old together." But the idea of "together" here is carried by jyē 偕, leaving yẃ to provide only the "and" portion of the meaning. That a semantic migration from one element to the other might occur over the course of frequent repetitions of such statements is perfectly plausible, but the presence of the "together" element jyē (or bìng) in these examples is evidence that the transfer has not yet reached the point where yẃ can represent that meaning on its own.

17. Dobson, Particles, 815, recognizes a "rather" meaning for yẃ, under the rubric of

Disjunctive Conjunction, but explicitly refers it to *yǔ* in a particular sentence form. His statement of the form is 與。。。不如/若 "rather than ... better to. ..." His two cited examples have not merely 與, but 與其. The 不如/若 "not as good as" in the consequent clause of these examples is functionally equivalent to *níng* 寧 "would rather" in our example above. In none of these cases can the 與其 of the antecedent clause be assigned more than the meaning "as compared to," the preferred alternative being always expressed in the consequent clause.

18. Legge (1861, rev. 1893) "profitableness, and also the appointments [of Heaven], and perfect virtue," Giles (1907) "of money-making, or the laws of Providence, or of moral virtue," Soothill (1910) "on profit, on the orderings of Providence, and on perfection," Wilhelm (1921) "der Lohn, der Wille Gottes, die Sittlichkeit," Pound (1950) "profits, destiny, and total manhood," Leslie (1962) "du gain, de la destinée ou du bien," Lau (1979) "profit, Destiny, and benevolence," Dawson (1993) "profit and fate and humaneness," Leys (1997) "profit, or fate, or humanity," Huang (1997) "profit, nor the decree of Heaven, nor humanity," Cai (1998) "the benefit, the fate, and the Heaven's benevolence." The sole exception among translations we have consulted is Ware (1955), whose version follows the spirit of Shř Shvng-dzǔ (or Bodde) in reading "The Master rarely spoke of profit; his attachment was to fate and to Manhood-at-its-best."

19. Waley, *Analects*, 138. It would be merely a distraction to point out that Waley here ignores the definition of *rvn* as "loving others" (愛人) in 12:22. We are concerned only with the strategy of his comment on 9:1.

20. For these and others see Boltz, *Word*, 261–62.

21. Nán, Byé-tsái, 1/431 大家可以從論語全書中，自己拔出答案.

22. As a matter of historical veracity, we should perhaps note that this is not the path we actually followed in arriving at our theory of the *Analects*, nor is either of the two possible approaches outlined in Brooks, *Original*, appendix 1. There are some 530 sayings in the *Analects*, and probably as many interesting circumstantial facts about the text, and it would not be an exaggeration to say that there are a thousand points from which a reader might find a way from the surface of the received text to the structure which we believe underlies it.

23. This last formulation of the contrast is the one given in Brooks, *Original*, 219; a similar process of abstraction should be imagined to lie also behind the rest of that summary, and of the other summaries in Appendix 1.

24. In this and later citation formulas, the slash rather than the hyphen between two numbers indicates that those passages are considered as a pair, and not as two consecutive but unrelated sayings.

25. Reading, with Waley, the end of 14:16, with its suggestive repetition (如其仁，如其仁), as disapproving rather than enthusiastic. The "enthusiastic" reading, going back to the commentary attributed to Kǔng Añ-gwó, harmonizes the two and eliminates the problem; thus (among translators) Legge, Soothill, Wilhelm, Ware, Lau, Huang, Leys, and Cai. We follow Waley (and Dawson) in thinking that there is a problem. Renditions of the "enthusiastic" interpretation take various grammatical forms: the interrogative "Whose beneficence was like his?" (Legge), the exclamatory "Wie [hoch steht] seine Sittlichkeit!" (Wilhelm), and even the indicative "It was his humanity" (Cai). None of them seems to us to be strictly justified by the original, which is reminiscent of the generally disapprobatory idiom *rú* X *hv* "What is to be done about X?"

26. A similar point was reached in a different line of argument in Brooks, *Original*, 207 n. 25. Our approach makes much more systematic use of formal and compositional features in the text than does the work of our predecessors.

27. Alleged early death. We argue in Brooks, *Original*, 293, that Hwéi outlived

Confucius. For present purposes, it will suffice to ignore this and many other fine points and simply take the text as it initially presents itself to us.

28. We should here repeat, and emphasize, our finding that some pairs are merely parallels, not complementary or intentionally ambivalent statements. Some of the pairings, especially in what we will presently identify as the earlier *Analects* chapters, are primarily aesthetic, or even verbally perfunctory. *Analects* rhetoric is a fascinating but complex subject, which, apart from hints in Brooks, *Original*, we have not yet had a suitable occasion to expound in the detail it deserves.

29. It terms of the theory of the text which has not been fully expounded at this point, it turns out that 9:26 also contains anachronisms, supporting the present suggestion that it may be interpolated. See Brooks, *Original*, 106.

30. We agree with Lau that the *metaphor* here is obscure, but the *meaning* is plain enough: the Master does not know the answers in advance, but will investigate particular cases on request, even the request of humble persons.

31. Confucius's death *does* come near the end of LY 7, or at the very end if interpolations are removed by an argument like the one here applied to LY 9. That whole chapter can be seen as a consecutive account of Confucius's life and career. By contrast, the second section of LY 9 is an interpretative epitome. It would be premature to speculate here on which of these "biographies" of Confucius represents the earlier tradition, but we will return to the question in §7, below.

32. Every *Analects* reader will remember that this is exactly how it is treated in 11:8–11.

33. We regret the need to compress the exposition from this point onward. For an admittedly brief outline of the argument for the other *Analects* chapters, the reader may consult Brooks, *Original*, appendix 1. Readers of that necessarily terse exposition are invited to see behind it at all points a much more extended investigation, such as has just been suggested for LY 9.

34. The credit for first recognizing thematic grouping within *Analects* chapters seems to belong to Lau, who noticed it in LY 4 (*Analects*, 269f); similar local observations may have been implied by the remarks of earlier commentators. We believe we are the first to recognize that thematic grouping (tetrathematicity), as well as pairing of sayings, is a ubiquitous, not a sporadic, feature of *Analects* structure. Lau's own perception of *Analects* chapters is that many of them are monothematic, not tetrathematic; he considers all of LY 1–15 *except* 1–2 and 8 to be significantly monothematic (*Analects*, 269–71, 273). With no more exceptions than he allows in these cases, one might argue that LY 16 (predominantly numbered-set sayings) and 19 (exclusively disciple sayings) are monothematic (in the same way as LY 12, which Lau sees as consisting of a series of questions); LY 17, though sometimes cryptic, centers on the general ideas of culture and education. Monothematicity, as the term is employed by Lau, is thus characteristic of most of the *Analects* material. Our tetrathematic analysis is a refinement rather than a refutation of this position; we recognize as exceptions some of the chapters which Lau finds escape his definition also. In our view LY 4 is a partial exception; it was originally tetrathematic but consisted only of sixteen, not 24, sayings. Readers hesitating between the monothematic and tetrathematic models may wish to consider our analysis of the early chapter sequence LY 4–6, where the last or D section in each chapter is a variant of the idea of self-cultivation or preparation for office. That degree of *lateral* agreement is not explainable on the theory that the only dimension of content organization is *vertical*, that is, within the chapter. Ultimately, tetrathematicity is not at odds with a perception of monothematicity. A chapter may have an internal structure and also an overall coherence.

35. For example, we find LY 1 to be palindromic in structure, and LY 8 to consist of a four-saying kernel, the sayings being all by Dzvngdž, around which two concentric layers

of additions, both dealing with ancient traditions but not identical with each other in specific content, were later added. We differ from Lau in finding that LY 2 actually fits our version of the standard LY chapter paradigm.

36. In a now lost commentary; see Brooks, *Original*, 201 n. 5.

37. See for example, from the year 1957, Yang, "Note," 313–14, and note Yang's acknowledgement of the power of the Itō theory to rationalize his data on the term jywndž in the *Analects*.

38. See the recent studies by Shao Dongfang.

39. Pokora, "Pre-Han," 30.

40. There are other theories of the text that are not compatible with these, among them perhaps most notably those of Tsuda Sōkichi, Takeuchi Yoshio, and Kimura Eiichi.

41. We find in all 388 original passages and 142 interpolations (total 530), or almost one interpolation for every three original passages. This heavy overlay of later material, whenever and for whatever reason it was added, must to some extent have obscured the original character of almost all the *Analects* chapters. It follows that the chapters without those additions will much more clearly display any evolutionary character which they originally had.

42. LY 13:1/2 pair as disciple questions about government, and 13:4/5 pair as contrasting the lowly skill of husbandry with the elite accomplishment of mastery of the Shr̄, leaving 13:3 outside the structure and thus presumptively interpolated. This argument from form is completely independent of, but also in agreement with, Waley's argument from content and rhetoric (*Analects*, 21f, 172 n. 1), which many scholars have found convincing; the measured dissent in Makeham, *Name*, appendix C is testimony to the strength of that opinion. The concurrence of our formal argument with this widely accepted substantive argument tends to ratify the formal argument. If instead the formal argument had indicated that 13:3 was original, the formal argument would be in big trouble.

43. The three proposed by Jv̀ng Sywǽn were Rǎn Yūng, Dž-yóu, and Dž-syà. Modern versions of the Jv̀ng theory rarely take the risk of specifying which disciple is supposed to be responsible for which series of chapters, and several versions assume an intervening period in which the text was either held in memory or orally transmitted, in order to account for some of the anachronisms which we shall presently notice.

44. As noted above, the disciple sayings *4:15 and *4:26, the former with a two-scene narrative structure, are here presumed to have been eliminated at an earlier stage of the analysis by the fact that they fail to find a place in the parallelism of the chapter. Note that the pair 4:14/16, which are juxtaposed when *4:15 is removed, are both concerned with career calculations (Brooks, *Original*, 16).

45. Tsuda, *Rongo*, 272f. It is also relevant that LY 4 shows some apparent archaisms of usage. We should add that though we cite Tsuda here, we do not in the end agree entirely with him. We find on continued scrutiny of the evidence that the genuine portion of LY 4 amounts to only sixteen of its present twenty-six sayings, and that the disciple sayings *4:15 and *4:26, for instance, are manifest intrusions. The case is parallel to Yang's approval of Itō (n. 37, above): the earlier opinion clarifies things in the right general direction, but it still remains capable of further refinement.

46. We agree with some reviewers that it would be nice if the compilers had been more careless. It is nevertheless a great advantage in what follows that the previous argument has eliminated what we have reason to believe are not only some, but all, of the later interpolated passages. What is left is a series of presumptive compositional wholes, and under those circumstances, any anachronism in one of its passages fairly implicates the whole chapter.

47. The dating of Karlgren, "Piao," 145f has now been replaced by one agreeing with

the Bamboo Annals entry; see for example von Falkenhausen, *Suspended*, 184f, where this date is assumed as a matter of course.

48. For individual citations of relevant Gwǎndž passages and also for Rickett's conclusions about their date, see Brooks, *Original* ad loc; also Appendix 3.

49. Brooks, *Original*, 97 contains a list of the passages in MC 1 which we conclude go back to the historic Mencius. For the Mencius theory itself, see Brooks, *Nature*. We regret that the present discussion should so quickly lead to questions about the date and authenticity of other Warring States texts, but the fact is that all these texts form a single corpus and thus ultimately a single problem, and that a solution which covered only one text without accounting consistently for the others would hardly deserve the reader's attention.

50. For this classic demonstration see Lau, *Mencius*, Appendix 1.

51. Objection has been raised (Allen, "Confucius," 82) to our seeming freedom to reassign battles in the text, and present readers may be inclined to concur. Taking 16:1 as the chief battle mentioned in the text, we may thus ask: Why could it not simply refer to the event in Confucius's own lifetime which it mentions? The answers are three. (1) LY 16:1 is literarily "hot." It is one of the longest pieces in the book, and by far the longest consecutive speech. In a text whose basic mode of historical disapproval is the wry exit line (see for example 7:31 or 15:1), this extreme tension of language invites explanation. (2) The impending "event" to which 16:1 ostensibly refers, the Jì family attack on Jwān-yẃ, never occurred. No text mentions it, including the Dzwǒ Jwàn, which might be expected to have done so mentions it. Even some very doubtful events in which Confucius is supposed to have participated are lavishly developed in later myth and allusion, but never this one. As Legge notes, commentators cannot even fit 16:1 into the standard construct of Confucius's official career; among other problems, the two disciples scolded in 16:1 are not supposed to have been in the service of the Jì family at the same time. Where the most devoted efforts of scholars and hagiographers have failed to find a place for the Outrage on Jwān-yẃ in the record, what modern onlooker would dare to try? We can only conclude that the Outrage was an invented story, and would have been recognized by its first *audience* as an invented story. The question then becomes askable: For what real event is this emblematic event substituting? (3) The answer seems to be provided by the following passages, 16:2–3, whose calculations fit, not the Jì family, but the Tyén ruling house of Chí. They pronounce a doom on that house. It is quite possible that they did so with the knowledge that the King of Chí who invaded Sùng was soon expelled from his conquest, and driven from his state, by a coalition of rival states who were concerned at this expansion of Chí's territorial base; he died in exile in 0284. When one egregiously prominent denunciation passage ostensibly about a transparently mythical event raises the question of what it is *really* referring to, and two following imprecation passages together provide a key to the answer, we as text philologists feel indisposed to argue. LY 16:1, then, is probably directed not at Rǎn Yǒu and Dž-lù, but at their contemporary counterparts, the Confucians of Chí in the early 0280's, who did nothing to restrain the monstrous appetite of their master the King of Chí, and thereby brought into peril not only the entire balance of power in that period, but the ancestral home of their movement, Lǔ, which as a result of the Sùng conquest was almost entirely surrounded by Chí territory, and could have been easily absorbed by Chí at any desired time in the future. The magnitude of this outrage, and this threat, seem sufficient to account for the literarily extreme qualities of 16:1. We don't see a case, either in fact or fancy, for a literal Jwān-yẃ.

52. Hummel, *Eminent*, 2/776.

53. See Hu, "Recent." The Lyáng/Hú argument, which concerned the date of the Dàu/Dǚ Jīng 道德經, still divided international and Chinese Sinology as late as 1998, when

an international conference at Dartmouth College, on the 1993 archaeological discovery of three sets of DDJ extracts in a Chǔ tomb called Gwōdyèn 1, found itself deadlocked on what this find implied about the composition date of the DDJ. International scholars held out for Lyáng's 03c date (the Gwōdyèn extracts being assumed to have been drawn from a body of orally circulating sayings not yet coalesced into a text), while Chinese scholars were equally firm on Hú's 06c date (the Gwōdyèn extracts being seen as drawn from a long since coalesced text). The Gwōdyèn texts, which contain only DDJ material (and so cannot have been drawn from a cloud of miscellaneous oral traditions), but imply a truncated version of that material (and so cannot have been drawn from a complete text dating from some three centuries earlier), actually refute both hypotheses. A fuller statement of the postion, complete with a statistical analysis of the implications of the Gwōdyèn florilegia, is available at http://www.umass.edu/wsp (see the Site Index at "Dau/Dv Jing in the Light of Gwodyen 1.") See also n. 3, above.

54. What follows is in part abridged from Brooks, *Original*, Appendix 3.

55. Speaking of internal contradictions, some of these listings are violently in conflict with the behavior of the same disciples in LY 5–6. Compare for instance Dzǎi Wǒ in 11:3 ("Language") and as the lazy punster of 6:3.

56. This is an especially obvious pair of sayings concerning official salary: the wrong of accepting it (6:4) and the wrong of refusing it (6:5). As often in these thought pairings, it is the second member that provokes reflection.

57. Against this line of argument, it has been objected that "China has been an agricultural society since Shāng." But there are distinguishable degrees of agricultural development. The Chūn/Chyōu chronicle shows a progressive loss of hunting land to farming land, over the course of the 08th through 06th centuries, with even elite hunting increasingly confined to game preserves. Within the Warring States, both the Gwǎndž and the Mencius attest the systematic conversion of wetlands to agricultural use, one consequence of which was the eventual loss of even fish protein in the rural diet. Increasing pressure on the land supply led to overgrazing of uplands, with the result made famous in the Mencian Ox Mountain passage MC 6A8. The indications in the *Analects*, faint and few as they are, fit unproblematically into this longer and reasonably well-documented six-century trend. It is difficult to make these normal, obvious developments seem dramatic; indeed, their whole point as evidence is that they are normal and obvious. What is philologically dramatic is that if this or any other development implied by our chronology of the *Analects* were anything other than normal and obvious, if for example the trajectory here were from intensive agriculture to greater reliance on the hunt, the entire hypothesis would be refuted.

58. See n. 29, above.

59. For a humorous and yet socially suggestive example of the conscript line breaking and fleeing in battle, see MC 1B12.

60. There are few enough examples of linguistic change over the longer course of the Chūn/Chyōu chronicle, and most of these are statistical shifts rather than simple vocabulary substitutions. The intentional maintenance of an established literary style may well play a role in both cases.

61. We will return to 12:1 in §10, below.

62. The last of these is the passage which is taken up for analysis by Bryan Van Norden in this volume. We are pleased to note that he agrees with our conclusion that *4:15 is an interpolation, and that it is closely related to the earlier saying *15:3; see his n. 19 and n. 20 and associated text; also his n. 23.

63. Study of the contemporary texts in which similar numerical categories appear suggests that this device is not original with the Confucians, but was employed first in the rival statecraft texts Gwǎndž and Mwòdž. Its ultimate source may well be the early

Naturalists (for the Threes and Nine of LY 16, these numbers being reminiscent of the theoretical geography attributed, however plausibly, to Dzōu Yěn) and the Cosmologists (note especially the Five of LY 17, which suggests the correlative developments from the astral Five Planets theory). This linkage in mode of thought is further evidence in favor of Tswēi Shù's late date for LY 16–20, and for our more specific early 03c date for LY 16–17.

64. Later, according to our best estimate. As an interpolated single passage, it is intrinsically more difficult to date than an entire chapter or even a pair of sayings. With interpolations as evidence for developments, there is also the complication that these passages often seem to have been designed for placement in a specific earlier chapter, and they may sometimes have imitated details of that earlier environment as a matter of verisimilitude. As the converse of this principle, it seems that the Sywndzian interpolation *13:3 was added not at random, but at the point where the most nearly analogous sayings already existed, and where it would thus be least out of place. This compatible placement is reflected in the comment of F. W. Mote, quoted in Makeham, Name, appendix C (see n. 42, above).

65. A similar discouragement with large unifying assertions, and a compensating emphasis on teaching, including self-discipline, is conspicuous in the parallel chapters of the Mencius. We suspect that this reflects the fact that the Mencian schools geographically close were experiencing a cognate frustration in contending with a stronger political state which was increasingly impervious to their policy persuasions. See Brooks, Nature.

66. It was noted above that the pantheon of 11:3 contrasts violently at several points with the glimpses we have of those disciples in the earlier chapters LY 5–6. The extreme case is Dzvngdž, portrayed as the respected head of the school in 8:3, but omitted altogether from the 11:3 Big Ten and dismissed as "dull" in 11:18a. When he later returns to the text, it is in a domesticated form (12:24, 1:4), from which the Hàn image of Dzvngdž as a paragon of filial piety is a logical further development. For capsule summaries of the fate of the major disciples over the course of the Analects, see Brooks, Original, 288–94. The mutations of Dzvngdž may be affected in part by the formation and evolution of a Dzvngdž movement outside the Analects, a movement whose text was probably the "Dzvngdž" known to the Hàn bibliographers, and apparently still preserved entire in the Dà Dài Lǐ Jì. Literary conjunctions and oppositions also play a role: Dž-gùng and Dž-lù alternate, but never coincide, as the traveling companion and escort of Confucius.

67. Conventionally, but misleadingly, called a "biography." The jwàn 傳 section of the Shř Jì includes notices of foreign peoples as well as individuals.

68. The recently recovered texts from the Gwōdyèn 1 tomb add to this testimony by including one short text in which Dž-sz̄ is portrayed as defending the right of protest before Mù-gūng. The dating of this tomb and the dating of the Mencius text are both controversial; it suffices here to note that both we and the leading Chinese scholars of the subject make the two essentially comparable in date. There is in the Gwōdyèn cache no direct trace of the Mencius text or its most characteristic doctrines, so that this Mù-gūng text represents new and independent evidence for the tradition that Dž-sz̄ had his public career within the reign of Mù-gūng.

69. Ariel, K'ung, 8, 98f.

70. Maspero, Antique, 376 n. 1, and Antiquity, 44 n. 1. This theory has more recently been championed by Riegel, Review, 791. See, on the other side, Creel, Confucius, 296–97.

71. For a discussion of the problems of these two lists, and a reconstruction of their prototype, see Brooks, "Life." An abbreviated version of this analysis appears in Appendix 4 of Brooks, Original.

72. There is always the possibility of interpolation. But interpolation by whom? Interpolation of a Dzvngdž chapter in an otherwise non-Dzvngdzian text implies either the Lǔ

school's absorption of a parallel Dzv̄ngdž group (which had meanwhile preserved Dzv̄ngdž's sayings), or the opposite. The first possibility is refuted by the fact that the parallel Dzv̄ngdž group survived into Hàn with its own text (see n. 66, above), in which *variants of LY 8 sayings, but not the same sayings*, figure. The second is symmetrically refuted by the fact that the Confucian school preserved *its* own text, in fact the *Analects*, also listed in the Hàn bibliography and also still extant today. The other possibility is for one school to get *temporary* access to the other's text: the hostile interpolation theory. Brooks, *Original*, 183, expresses doubts about this theory as it is used by the otherwise sagacious Waley to explain the Jwāngdzian passages in LY 18. Extending the hostile-interpolation theory to the Dzv̄ngdziana in LY 8, the Gwăndž and Mwòdž echoes in LY 12, the Sywńdzian eyesore in *13:3, and the Dàu/Dv́ Jīng refutations passim, would present the spectacle of various text proprietors (including various varieties of Confucians) lining up outside Lǔ Confucian headquarters, interpolations in hand, waiting to get their five minutes alone with the master copy. Such theories simply collapse when visualized.

73. Now pronounced Wèi, but in preference to many merely arbitrary conventions which have been employed for the purpose, we here retain a lost ng- initial to distinguish Ngwèi 魏 from the otherwise homophonous state Wèi 衛.

74. Waley (*Analects*, 20) had already noted the difference between the ethical Dzv̄ngdž of LY 8 and the filial Dzv̄ngdž of LY 1, and made the crucial observation that the latter "[resembles] far more closely the [Dzv̄ngdž] of later tradition." That is, the *direction of historical evolution* of the Dzv̄ngdž persona can only be from LY 8 to LY 1, not the reverse. This evolutionary development has been much more throughly documented in Hsiao, "Role."

75. We might add that the dilemma of whether Confucius was a systematic philosopher, with which Bryan Van Norden concludes his paper in this volume, can also be seen as resolved by this picture of *Analects* evolution. The key passage *4:15 does not belong in LY 4, and thus is not to be attributed to the *historical* Confucius. It does, however, belong to the *institutional* Confucius of the end of the 04c, and there it validly reflects a concern for precision and consistency, which are evidenced at many other places in that portion of the text and which are collectively of interest to modern philosophers. It is the great if unsung merit of Confucius's successors to have kept him or his image so current with the philosophical trends of later centuries that he also registers in the philosophical consciousness of later millennia.

76. We will return to 12:1 in detail, and to the history of rv́n in general, in §10, below.

77. We have been asked, Why did not the later proprietors simply eliminate the rv́n passages from LY 4, or eliminate LY 4 from the previous school text, or for that matter eliminate the entire previous text? In the end, such questions are beyond philology: people simply do what they do, and it is the task of philology to recover what that was. But the matter is perhaps not beyond conjecture, which might run as follows: (1) The authority of the heads of any *Analects* school in Lǔ *among its own followers and students* would quite likely have derived from a claim of a connection going back to Confucius. (2) The claim of blood relationship that the 04c Kǔng proprietors could have relied on might have been contested by other groups of Kǔngs in Lǔ and thus was not unique. (3) The early death of Confucius's son and the supervision of his funeral by disciples were by then too firmly enshrined in the tradition attaching to Confucius to be directly challenged by a claim that *this group* of Kǔngs had been consecutively in charge from the beginning (note that motifs such as Confucius's early hardship are also not obliterated by later myths of his eventual eminence, but continue to exist thematically alongside them). (4) The only thing distinguishing these Kǔngs from other possible Kǔng claimants was their occupying a position among the actual successive heads of the school. Finally, (5) that the text of the *Analects*, as it had accumulated up to that point, was the only hard evidence for that claim of continuity. In such a

situation, the suppression of the text or any part of it would have been likely to compromise the school's authenticity credential. It was their prerogative, as established in the process that had produced the preceding text, to *add material to* the preceding text. To extend this to *adding material within* the preceding text may well have been the most conservative step available to the mid 04c proprietors.

Another question often raised is, Why would the *Analects* proprietors take such pains with the form of a chapter, including its elaborate scheme of thematic sections and parallel passages, only to violate that form by intruding formally discordant material? To this again there might be conjectural answers. One conclusion that emerges from continual study of the character and placement of interpolations is that the interpolators seem sometimes to have taken pains to minimize the formal impact of new passages, for example, contriving a verbal link with the adjacent passage. This is common enough that, to someone studying the text ab initio, a sequence of passages AAB, where *both* of the first two passages have presentable verbal or thematic links to the third, may come to seem an indication that one of the first two is a *counterfeit* parallel, and thus a presumptive interpolation. We might add our impression that, once the practice of interpolation became established, it seems to have offered to the school proprietors a *second level* of literary composition, where the rules, the styles, and the limits on what could and could not be said, were different from those for primary new material. Contemporary scholars will recognize this feeling: there are things that can be said in footnotes but not so readily in the text, and vice versa. Maintaining the respective styles is a condition for preserving that probably useful freedom, just as printing modern footnotes in the same type size as the main text would tend to diminish the useful difference between them.

78. Opinions may differ as to whether the students of the Lǔ school had access to the preceding text by visually consulting it or by verbally committing it to memory. The present statement would work on either presumption, though on the latter, it would seem that new interpolation by the *head* of the school would sooner or later require rememorization by the *members* of the school.

79. That the forger somewhat overdid it, creating a phrase unique in the literature, with *three* elements rather than two, we can only attribute to the excess to which experts, including expert forgers, are always liable.

80. Brooks, *Original*, 129, proposes that the student reader inspect the *Analects* "Heaven" terms as suggestively distinguished in Eno, *Heaven*, 79f, in the light of the present hypothesis. It would lessen the value of our book as a teaching manual to carry out that exercise here, but it will be obvious that this datum is part of the answer.

81. At least with the free-spirited Chinese reader. The perhaps more regimented reader from the industrial West has often proved more susceptible to the persuasions of *9:1, and indeed to the Kǔng agenda generally.

82. The interpretative fruitfulness of relocating an *Analects* saying on formal grounds may also be tested on the pair of sayings, widely separated in the present text, which P. J. Ivanhoe, in his essay in this volume, cites as the only *Analects* mention of the term sy̆ing 性 "[human] nature," namely 5:13 and 17:2. Briefly, 5:13 does not closely relate to the passages which precede it (5:12 on inadequacy sums up 5:10b/11 on good faith and steadfastness) or to those which follow (it offers no obvious common ground with 5:14, and 5:15 on respect for inferiors pairs instead with 5:17 on politeness toward intimates), and so on structural grounds is presumptively an interpolation. Then the sy̆ing concept cannot be attested as near to the time of Confucius as the early LY 5 would suggest. On the other hand, 17:2 is actually a pair in itself (it contains two "The Master said" formulas), and thus is part of the structure of LY 17. The only more or less datable mention of sy̆ing in the *Analects* is thus 17:2, from the Tswéı Shù or late layer of the *Analects*. From the above

argument, this would put it in the early 03c, and thus make it contemporary with the debate on human nature between Syẃndž and the Mencian school. Ivanhoe remarks that we must choose among the commentarial Confuciuses; we would add that there is also a choice among Analectal Confuciuses, and that the "Confucius" who comments on human nature in 17:2a/b is a device for keeping the *Analects* somewhat current with 03c issues, just as the "Confucius" of the adjacent 17:3, with its scene of playing classical music for the masses, may well be commenting, with affection but also with amusement, on the late Mencian attempts to organize schools for the lower orders of society. The location of LY 17 in the early 03c also makes it easier to notice that the following series, 17:8a/b, 17:9/10, and 17:11/12, all touch on topics that were important to Syẃndž. What then of 5:13? As Ivanhoe recounts in detail, later commentators interpret it as indicating an esoteric tradition of Confucius's teachings concerning human nature and the Way of Heaven. This 5:13 claim would in effect reannex the concept into the *Analects* tradition, and identify the Mencians in particular not as developing a new idea, but as expounding an old one which Confucius had taught to a few selected disciples. Putting that claim into LY 5 would give the claim itself an early, that is, an 05c pedigree. Whereas the intent of 9:1 was to neutralize part of the genuine early heritage, that of 5:13 (and that of 4:15, mentioned above) was to insert another part which had not originally been there. Thus did the philosophical home territory of the Lǔ Confucians undergo reconfiguration according to the perceived needs of the school in its later days.

83. The following is based on the discussion in Kieschnick, "Commentarial." Kieschnick himself feels that the solution of the problem really lies in the meaning of rv́n. Our discussion will follow out that possibility, along with several others, in terms of the present accretional hypothesis, that is, the *evolution* of the meaning of rv́n.

84. This is one of the few cases of quotation of an *Analects* saying (even though not under that title; cf. below) in an undeniably Warring States text; in our view, the DJ is a compilation whose final phase was completed in ca. 0312, about fourteen years after LY 12. There is thus no anomaly in the DJ, a text of Confucian persuasion though apparently finalized in Chí, in making use of what was still a recent saying put out by the home school in Lǔ. Two seeming *Analects* echoes appear in the third of four texts, called by their discoverers Yw̌ Tsúng 語叢 "Sayings Collections," found in the Gwōdyèn 1 tomb (see n. 3 and n. 53, above), which we date to ca. 0288. One of the *Analects* sayings in question is LY 7:6 (ca. 0450), which appears exactly in Yw̌ Tsúng 3 except for loss of its Dž ywē formula ("Intent upon the Way, based on virtue, close to rv́n, and acquainted with the arts"). It is probably from the *Analects*, directly or indirectly; its pairing of dàu and dv́ would be calculated to attract the attention of a tutor whose library also contained three sets of extracts from the Dàu/Dv́ Jīng. The other is LY *9:4, which following Lyóu Bǎu-nán we see as related to *18:8b and thus ascribe to c0262. If this is correct, the Yw̌ Tsúng (ca. 0288) cannot be quoting *9:6 (ca. 0262); rather, the quotation must run in the opposite direction. The Yw̌ Tsúng version as before lacks the *Analects* incipit (here, "The Master avoided four things"); a related comment on the lower ends of the bamboo strips has the helpful phrase 至安 "attain peace," in the light of which the four avoidances (which are in part very cryptic as the phrase stands) would seem to be hindrances of will and ego to the inner calm attained through meditation. This makes unproblematic sense of the entire passage. As implicitly ethicized in *Analects* context, it remains difficult to interpret. Then the passage is natural in the Yw̌ Tsúng context and less so in the *Analects* context, and is thus intelligible as a transplant from the Yw̌ Tsúng (or its source) to the *Analects*. This leaves us with two pre-Han quotes from the *Analects*, in addition to the several reactive contacts in both directions which are mentioned elsewhere in this paper. A supposed third pre-Hán quote, of 1:11 (or the identical *4:20) in the Fāng Jì 坊記 (Lǐ Jì 27; see Waley, *Analects*,

22f, where the quote is wrongly identified as 2:11) fails to qualify because of the manifestly Hàn character of the Fāng Jì; it also cites the *Analects* by its title of Lún Yǔ 論語, a name which it cannot presently be proved to have had in the Warring States period.

85. Kieschnick, *Commentarial*, 576.

86. The subject is a vast one. For a suggestive sample analysis of Confucius's own diction, emphasizing how elaborate its parallel structures are, see Brooks, *Original*, 17–18.

87. As Kieschnick, *Commentarial*, 568 notes, the interpretations explore questions of human nature and the inner geometry of the heart. At the root of the problem which they address is that if the self must be overcome before the individual can turn to lǐ, and so qualify as rǐn, where within the self is the will to do this supposed to come from? At a minimum, one must assume that the individual is already *good enough to want to become good*. The emphasis on impulse coming from the self, later in 12:1, spells this out as much as the style of *Analects* discourse requires or allows. The later commentators, who are concerned that the lesson of the passage should not be missed by their pupils, develop implications that would very likely have been uncovered without difficulty by the original readers of the text.

88. Kwong-loi Shun, in this volume (pp. 60–61), points out, without necessarily endorsing their implications, further similarities in 12:1/2. Shun's caution that the *Analects* text as a whole has different origins, and "does not present a single coherent account of the relation between [rǐn] and [lǐ]" (p. 55), though it does not take account of our specific conclusions, also agrees with the thrust of our present study. So does his observation that rǐn has a different hierarchical position in different parts of the text, being one of several parallel virtues including courage in 9:29, but comprising all the virtues, among them courage, in 14:4. The final position to which all such observations ultimately lead is that no one modern statement about rǐn fits all *Analects* statements about rǐn, and that the *Analects* itself is not a philosophical whole but the record of a philosophical process.

89. And *14:1b, which as we shall presently argue is a comment on 12:1, is the *last* appearance of kǐ in the *Analects*. The word cannot be said to be within the normal *Analects* discourse style.

90. DJ Hwán 8:2.

91. The orthodox interpretation makes kǐ a noun like the following three, whence Legge "When the love of superiority, boasting, resentments, and covetousness are repressed, this may be deemed perfect virtue." Most translators follow suit. Merely as an English sentence, this is open to suspicion in a text that is fond of parallelism. Thus the first two traits, superiority and boasting, seem very close together semantically, whereas either of them is well contrasted with resentment and covetousness, and each of those with the other. Further, "are repressed" is a strong reading of 不行 "do not occur; do not emerge into action," and would better fit the normal semantics of kǐ "overcome." The noun meaning assigned to kǐ thus creates uneven contrasts in the series of nouns, and its normal verbal sense would better carry the semantic function assigned to bù-syíng. Both these imperfections result from the meaning assigned to kǐ, and both would be removed if kǐ had its normal, Dzwǒ Jwàn sense. We prefer that less troublesome reading.

92. This is also the reading of the early 03c extracts from the DDJ discovered in the Gwōdyèn 1 tomb; see *Gwōdyèn*, 111. DDJ 19 varies at several points in these texts from the later standard reading, but this particular line is identical. That the line is important in the DDJ passage is shown by the fact that it occupies the climactic last position. That the passage is for some readers salient in the DDJ as a whole is suggested by the fact that DDJ 19 is the first passage in one of the three Gwōdyèn florilegia.

93. Yén Hwéi 顏回 or, to give him his formal name, Yén Ywēn 顏淵. The convention of the period is that the formal name (dz̀ 字) normally has some connection, usually semantic, with the personal name (míng 名). This expectation holds for virtually all the

names on the KZJY 38 disciple list, and is thus highly relevant to the social practice in the circle around Confucius. Yén Hwéı is one conspicuous exception; the word *hwéı* ("revolve, return") has no obvious connection with the word *ywǣn* ("deep, abyss"). Ywǣn, however, in the sense "profound, unfathomable," is one of the adjectives used in DDJ 14 to characterize the indescribable mystical experience.

94. See for example the use of syw̄ 虛 "empty" in DDJ 5 and 16. This the commoner term.

95. GZ 49. For a range of opinions concerning its date, see Rickett, *Guanzi*, 2/32–39.

96. He appears in *15:11, wholly converted to the lǐ value that is after all the Kǔng period trademark, asking about how to manage a state, and being told in reply about "the calendar of Syà, the carriage of Yīn, and the garments of Jōu," all these being matters within the purview of lǐ. He is shown as knowing nothing and having no special acuity of mind, and the answers with which he is content are the standard ABC of the Three Dynasties Usages theory. At the minimum, he seems to be a beginning rather than an advanced student. Of the 05c Hwéı, the lightning inferrer and the indefatigable concentrator, there is no trace.

97. The absence of Yén Hwéı from LY 16–20 is an observation of which we admit we are proud; it is something Tswēı Shù might have seen but did not. We offer it here in homage to him, as further evidence for the distinctive character of these 03c chapters, which he was the first to point out. For Yén Hwéı in the Jwāngdž, see for example JZ 4:1, 6:7, 22:11, and 28:13.

98. We note as a further example of this general proposition that the interpretation of 5:13, surveyed in P. J. Ivanhoe's paper in this volume, is likely to be affected by the fact that it is not an original passage in that chapter, which would have made LY 5 and vicinity the relevant context for its understanding, but rather an interpolation, which we date to the time of LY 17 (ca. 0270). On that understanding, it would belong in the middle of the early 03c, the time of the human nature debates between Syẃndž and the later Mencians, and also the time when the human nature implications of such passages as 12:1 were beginning to be felt, and worked out, by the Warring States thinkers themselves. The close relation between the chief 03c statements on this issue, MC 6A and SZ 23, has been explored in several recent papers presented to the Warring States Working Group conferences by Dan Robins. With attention to their total Warring States context, it may after all be possible to arrive at a "definitive" understanding of these difficult passages in their own time. For the new philosophical developments to which the *Analects* and other classic texts inspired later thinkers in later, Imperial ages, the writings of those later thinkers (often miscalled "commentaries") are, and will always remain, authoritative.

99. Among the most important traditional statements on the importance of context in interpretation are LY 11:20 and MC 5A4. We may claim it as a final merit of our current solution of both texts that it puts these passages close together in time, as they are clearly kindred in intent, LY 11:20 as an interpolation of c0270, and MC 5A4 as an original statement of ca. 0272. We may venture to repeat an observation from n. 75, above: It is the great if unsung merit of Confucius's successors to have kept him or his image so current with the philosophical trends of later centuries that he also registers in the philosophical consciousness of later millennia.

REFERENCES

Text abbreviations and short citation references above are here expanded. Information given is limited to the minimum required for retrieval. Conventional acronyms for journals (TP = T'oung Pao) are used, and X University Press is normally abbreviated as X.

Allen, Charlotte. "Confucius and the Scholars." *Atlantic Monthly* (Apr. 1999).

Ariel, Yoav. *The K'ung Ts'ung-tzu.* Princeton, 1989.

Bodde, Derk. *Essays on Chinese Civilization.* Princeton, 1981.

————. "A Perplexing Passage in the Confucian Analects." *JAOS* 53 (1933); see also in Bodde, *Essays.*

Boltz, William G. "Word and Word History in the *Analects*: The Exegesis of Lun Yü IX.1." *TP* 69 (1983).

Brooks, Bruce E. "The Life and Mentorship of Confucius." *SPP* 72 (1996).

————. "A Not Very Perplexing Passage in LY 9." *WSWG* note 36 (8 Sept. 1993).

————. "A Not Very Perplexing Passage in LY 12 Either." *WSWG*, note 37 (9 Sept. 1993).

————. "The Present State and Future Prospects of Pre-Hàn Text Studies." *SPP* 46 (1994).

Brooks, Bruce E. and A. Taeko Brooks. "The Nature and Historical Context of the *Mencius.* In Chan, *Mencius.* Chan, Alan K. L. Mencius: Contexts and Interpretations. Hawaii, forthcoming.

————. *The Original Analects.* Columbia, 1998.

Cai, Jack J. and Emma Yu. *The Analects of Confucius* (unabridged). PB Americd-rom, 1998.

Creel, Herrlee G. *Confucius.* John Day, 1949.

Dawson, Raymond. *Confucius: The Analects.* Oxford PB, 1993.

DJ = Dzwǒ Jwàn 左傳.

DDJ = Dàu/Dv́ Jīng 道德經.

Dobson, W. A. C. H. *A Dictionary of the Chinese Particles.* Toronto, 1974.

Durrant, Stephen W. "On Translating Lun yü." *CLEAR* 3 (1981).

Elman, Benjamin A. *Classicism, Politics, and Kinship.* California, 1990.

Eno, Robert. *The Confucian Creation of Heaven.* SUNY, 1990.

Fingarette, Herbert. *Confucius—The Secular as Sacred.* Harper PB, 1972.

Giles, Lionel. *The Sayings of Confucius.* John Murray, 1907.

Gwōdyèn Chǔ-mù Jú-jyèn. 郭店楚墓竹簡. Wv́n-wù 1998.

Harrington, Spencer P. M. "Laozi Debate." *Archaeology* Nov./Dec. 1998, 20–21.

Hirth, Friedrich. *Notes on the Chinese Documentary Style.* 2d. ed. Kelly and Walsh, 1909.

Hsiao, Harry Hsin-i. "Problems Concerning Tseng Tzu's Role in the Promotion of Filial Pietism." *Chinese Culture.* 19, 1 (1978).

Hu Shih. "A Criticism of Some Recent Methods Used in Dating Lao Tzu." *HJAS* 3 (1937).

Huang Chichung. *The Analects of Confucius.* Oxford PB, 1997.

Hummel, Arthur W. *Eminent Chinese of the Ch'ing Period.* Library of Congress, 2 vols. 1943.

Jū Syī 朱熹, Lún Yw̌. 論語 (1177). In Jū Jí-jù.

Jū Syī 朱熹, Sz̀-shū Jí-jù. 四書集注 (nd). Jūng-hwá PB, 1973.

JZ = Jwāngdž 莊子.

Karlgren, Bernhard. "On the Date of the Piao Bells." *BMFEA* 6 (1924).

Kieschnick, John. "Analects 12.1 and the Commentarial Tradition." *JAOS* 112 (1992).

Kimura Eiichi 木村英一. Kōshi to Rongo 孔子と論語. Sōbunsha, 1971.

Lau, D. C. *Confucius: The Analects.* Penguin PB 1979; Chinese University Press, 1983.

————. *Mencius.* Penguin PB, 1970.

Laufer, Berthold. "Lun Yü IX," 1. *JAOS* 54 (1934).

Legge, James. *The Chinese Classics.* 7 vols. 1861–72 = Hong Kong, 1960.

————. *Confucian Analects.* See as Legge, *Classics* 1; Dover PB, 1971.

Leslie, Daniel. *Confucius.* Seghers, 1962.

Leslie, Donald D. et al, *Essays on the Sources for Chinese History.* South Carolina, 1973.

Leys, Simon. *The Analects of Confucius*. Norton, 1997.

Loewe, Michael. *Early Chinese Texts*. Society for the Study of Early China, 1993.

LY = Lún Yw̌ 論語 (*Analects*).

Makeham, John. *Name and Actuality in Early Chinese Thought*. SUNY PB, 1994.

Malmqvist, Göran. "What Did the Master Say." In Roy, *Ancient*.

Maspero, Henri. *China in Antiquity*. Massachusetts, 1971.

———. *La Chine Antique*, 2d. ed. Presses Universitaires, 1965.

MC = *Mencius* (Mv̀ngdž 孟子).

Nán Hwái-jǐn 南懷瑾, *Lún Yw̌ Byé-tsái* 論語別裁, Lǎu-gǔ Wv́n-hwà 老古文化 1976.

Pokora, Timoteus. "Pre-Han Literature." In Leslie, *Sources*.

Pound, Ezra. "The Analects" (*Hudson Review*, spring-summer 1950). In Pound, *Confucius*.

———. *Confucius*. New Directions PB, 1969.

Rickett, Allyn W. *Guanzi*. Princeton, 1985, 1998.

Riegel, Jeffrey K. [Review of Maspero, *Antiquity*]. *JAS* 39 (1980).

Robins, Dan. "An Accretional Analysis of SZ 23." *WSWG*, query 96 (3 Sept. 1997).

———. "The Dialogue Between Syw̌ndž and Mencius." *WSWG*, query 122 (24 Apr. 1999).

Roth, Harold D. *The Textual History of the Huai-nan Tzu*. AAS 1992.

Roy, David T. *Ancient China*. Chinese University Press, 1967.

Schumacher, Jörg. *Über den Begriff des Nützlichen bei Mengzi*. Peter Lang, 1993.

Shaughnessy, Edward L. "Shang Shu." In Loewe *Early*.

Shao Dongfang 邵東方. "Authority and Truth." *JCP* vol. 25 no. 3 (Sept. 1998).

Shao Dongfang 邵東方. *Tswēi Shù yw̌ Jūnggwó Syẃshù Shř Jénjyōu* 崔述與中國學術史研究. Rv́nmín 1998.

Shun Kwong-loi. "Jen and Li in the *Analects*." *PEW* 43, 3 (July 1993).

SJ = Shř Jì 史記.

Soothill, William Edward. *The Analects of Confucius*. Oliphant, 1910; Dover PB, 1965.

Takeuchi Yoshio 武內義雄. "Rongo no Kenkyū 論語の研究." In Takeuchi, *Zenshū*.

Takeuchi Yoshio 武內義雄. *Takeuchi Yoshio Zenshū* 武內義雄全集. Kadokawa, 1978.

Thompson, Paul M. *The Shen Tzu Fragments*. Oxford, 1979.

Tsuda Sōkichi 津田左右吉. *Rongo to Kōshi no Shisō* 論語と孔子の思想. Iwanami, 1946.

Tswēi Shù. "Lún Yw̌ Byèn-yí." In Tswēi, *Yí-shū*.

———. *Tswēi Dūng-bì Yi-shū*. Shř-jyè, 1963.

von Falkenhausen, Lothar. *Suspended Music*. California, 1993.

Waley, Arthur. *The Analects of Confucius*. Allen and Unwin, 1938 = Vintage.

Ware, James R. *The Sayings of Confucius*. Mentor PB, 1955.

Wilhelm, Richard. *Kungfutse Gespräche*. Diederichs, 1921.

Yang Lien-sheng. "A Supplementary Note on Mr Chou Fa-kao's Article on the Final Particle 歟." *BIHP* 29 (1957).

9

Unweaving
the "One Thread"
of *Analects* 4:15

BRYAN W. VAN NORDEN

The differences between Confucius and most Western philosophers from at least Socrates onward are numerous and striking. By way of comparision, consider Plato, who recognizes four "cardinal virtues": courage, justice, wisdom, and moderation. He systematically identifies three of these with the proper functioning of the three parts of his "tripartite soul," and identifies the fourth with the proper relationship among these parts. Aristotle's collection of virtues seems less organized, but he does have a challenging division of virtues into those of the intellect (such as the ability to make logical deductions) and those of character (such as the disposition to feel fear neither excessively nor deficiently). In contrast, Confucius never bothers to organize systematically or justify his list of virtues.

Another fascination of Plato and Aristotle that leaves Confucius cold is the effort to justify the virtuous life. Plato argues in the *Republic* that the life of virtue is happier than the vicious life, and even concludes (although his tongue may be in his cheek at this point) that the life of the virtuous person is 729 times happier than that of the vicious person.[1] Aristotle concedes that philosophical arguments are not persuasive to everyone, but the "function argument" in *Nicomachean Ethics*, book 1, chapter 7, seems designed, at least in part, to justify his claim that human flourishing consists in the exercise of certain virtues, rather than in the pursuit of wealth or prestige. Confucius' remarks that "The wise man is attracted to humaneness (rén 仁) because he finds it to his advantage" (Lau 4:2, modified), and that "If you hear the Way in the morning, in the evening it is acceptable to die" (Lau 4:8, modified), do no more than hint that the virtuous life is better than the vicious one. Even when directly asked a question that seems to open an opportunity to discuss the justification or rationale for the rites, Confucius confesses ignorance: "Someone asked about the theory of the tì sacrifice. The Master said, 'It is not something I understand, for whoever understands it will be able to manage the Empire as easily as if he had it here,' pointing to his palm" (Lau 3:11).

So far, I have been focusing on what seems to be lacking in the *Analects* from the perspective of Western philosophy. However, from the perspective of the *Analects*, we might ask a different question: Why have Western philosophers been so obsessed with certain justificational issues in ethics? The views of many Western philosophers on the importance of theoretical knowledge are quite subtle, and are too frequently caricatured, especially in comparative studies. In particular, Plato and Aristotle, at least, are clear in stating that the teaching of ethical theory is insufficient to make a person virtuous. The basis for adult virtue is the development of good habits, especially in youth. Acquiring true meta-ethical knowledge is not even possible without this pretheoretical groundwork. Nonetheless, Plato and Aristotle do think that there is an important role for such knowledge to play. As Aristotle explains, we are more likely to hit the target if we know what it is. However, Confucius seems not to share this confidence in the value of theoretical knowledge of ethics.

A second factor that contributes to Confucius' teaching style is his assumption about his typical audience. In the West, there is an important style of philosophical narrative whose aim is to assume the minimal agreement or consensus between the speaker and her interlocutors. In this respect, René Descartes is paradigmatic. He tries not to assume that his readers have any particular religious, metaphysical, ethical, or scientific beliefs. In addition, Descartes tries to ask no faith (in him, or in anything else) on the part of his readers. Every claim is to be proven. (In these efforts, he fails, but that is another story.) He is motivated to do this because part of the experience of modernity is an awareness of the breakdown in shared beliefs and assumptions. Although most philosophers have given up the effort to base philosophy on the "Archimedean point" of indubitable truths, the intellectual descendants of Descartes who practice philosophy in modern lecture halls attemp to arrive at philosophical conclusions in discussion with thirty or more students who have no faith in the lecturer and share no consensus on anything except about the "fact" that there are no facts. In sharp contrast, Confucius seems to assume a background of at least some shared beliefs and commitments.

I hope that most of what I have had to say so far is not too controversial. However, one claim I have made might have raised a few eyebrows (or even hackles). For I suggested that Confucius does not have a view of the "cardinal virtues," or any systematic view of the kinds or relationships among the virtues in general. But a much-discussed passage, *Analects*, book 4, chapter 15, suggests that Confucius' views were bound together by "one thread" that consists of two strands: the cardinal virtues of zhōng 忠 and shù 恕. However, in this essay I shall argue that this passage does not give us the "one thread" of Confucius' teaching.[2] First, I try to show that 4:15 is an interpolation, planted by followers of Master Zēng 曾子. However, even if 4:15 is an interpolation, the claim expressed by the passage—that zhōng and shù constitute the "one thread" that binds together Confucius' teachings—may nonetheless be true. Consequently, in the second part of this essay, I shall examine what these terms mean in the *Analects*, and argue that they do not function as anything like Confucius' "cardinal virtues."

Thus, methodologically speaking, the first major section of this essay, "Confucius' Comment," deals in detail with grammatical and philological issues raised by the Chinese text of *Analects* 4:15, whereas the second major section, "Zēngzǐ's

Gloss," is a careful examination, using methods familiar to philosophical historians, of the meaning of two key terms.

The Thread

For the benefit of readers with little or no familiarity with Chinese, I shall begin with a transcription of the passage in Chinese, *pinyin* romanization, and word-for-word English. (An English rendering such as this risks being misleading, but it may also help those without knowledge of Chinese to follow some of the grammatical issues.)[3] Next, I will provide a tentative translation of the key passage, trying to stay as neutral as possible on interpretive issues:

子	曰。	參	乎。	吾	道	一	以	貫	之。
Zǐ	yuē:	Shēn	hū!	Wú	dào	yī	yǐ	guàn	zhī.
Master	says:	Shen	[vocative particle]!	My	way	one	by-means-of	threads it.	

曾	子	曰。	唯。
Zēng	zǐ	yuē:	Wéi.
Zeng	Master	says,	"Yes."

子	出。	門	人	問	曰。	何	謂	也。
Zǐ	chū.	Mén	rén	wèn	yuē:	Hé	wèi	yě?
Master	leaves.	Gate people [= disciples]	ask	say,	"What	means	[grammatical particle]?"	

曾	子	曰。	夫 子	之	道，	忠	恕	而 已 矣。
Zēng	zǐ	yuē:	Fūzǐ	zhī	dào,	zhōng	shù	ér yǐ yǐ.
Zeng	Master	say,	"Master	's	Way,	zhōng	shù	and that's all."

The Master said, "Shen! As for my Way, with one thing it binds it together."
Zengzi said, "Yes."
The Master left, and the disciples asked, "What did he mean?"
Zengzi said, "The Way of the Master is *zhōng* (忠) and *shù* (恕), and that is all."

The two most important parts of this passage are what I shall label "Confucius' Comment" ("As for my Way, with one thing it binds it together") and "Zengzi's Gloss" on that comment ("The Way of the Master is *zhōng* (忠) and *shù* (恕), and that is all"). With one important exception (which I shall discuss later), there is a fair amount of agreement among commentators and translators that something like this is the basic sense of the passage. But, as is so often the case, the devil is in the details! The diabolical detail raised by Zengzi's gloss is

(1) What do *zhōng* and *shù* mean?

I shall return to this issue in the second part of my essay. First, I shall examine some problems raised by Confucius' comment. Surprisingly, this comment has received little explicit commentarial discussion. The earliest surviving commentary, by Hé Yàn 何晏 et al., does not even remark on the syntax. I say that this is surprising, because the syntax and semantics of Confucius' comment are actually quite obscure. In particular, his comment raises three major interpretive issues:

(2) In my translation of Confucius' comment, I have supplied two impersonal pronouns. The first "it" does not correspond to any word in the original Chinese. However, there is a transitive verb in the sentence, and it is not clear what the agent of the action is, so I have supplied the pronoun to leave this open. (The "it" may, of course, also be a "he," "she," or "they," for all we know so far.) But as interpreters we must answer the question, What is the agent that does the "binding together"?

(3) The second "it" is a translation of the Chinese pronoun *zhī* 之, which can mean "it," "him," "her," or "them." Whatever this pronoun refers to, it is the object of the transitive verb in the sentence. So what is it that is being bound together?

(4) What is the relationship between the initial noun phrase, *wú dào* 吾道, and the rest of the sentence? Is it a topic on which the rest of the sentence is a comment? Is it the agent of the verb? Or is it a preposed direct object of the verb?[4]

Confucius' Comment

The commentary of the Northern Song dynasty commentator Xíng Bǐng (邢昺) is unusually (and blessedly!) specific about the syntax of Confucius' comment: "Confucius told Zēngzǐ, 'The Way which I practice uses (*yòng* 用) only one principle (*lǐ* 理) in order to (*yǐ* 以) bind together the principles of the myriad affairs of the world.'"[5] At first, Xíng Bǐng's insertion of the character *yòng* before *yī* 一 seems to be a counsel of desperation. However, what Xíng Bǐng is really doing is taking the phrase *yī yǐ* 一以 as an inversion of *yǐ yī* 以一. In addition, Xíng Bǐng takes the agent of the verb to be "my [i.e., Confucius'] Way." More problematic is Xíng Bǐng's suggestion that the final pronoun *zhī* refers to "the principles of the myriad affairs of the world." This is an awful lot of work for one poor little pronoun to do. How could Zengzi, or anyone else, be reaonably expected to know that this was what Confucius meant?

In the Zhūzǐ yǔlèi 朱子語類, Zhū Xī (朱熹) glosses 一以貫之 as "with one heart-mind respond to the myriad affairs."[6] In other words, Zhū Xī agrees with Xíng Bǐng in taking *yī yǐ* 一以 as an inversion of *yǐ yī* 以一; he also essentially agrees with Xíng Bǐng in taking the "myriad affairs" of the world to be the referent of the final pronoun. He seems to differ slightly from Xíng Bǐng in taking the "one" to be one's "heart-mind" (xīn 心). However, remember that Zhū Xī takes the heart-mind, at least in its pure form, to be "principle." This is verified by Zhū Xī's gloss of Confucius' comment in his Sìshū jízhù 四書集注: "The heart-mind of a sage is undifferentiatedly one principle; it responds universally and is appropriate in the minutest details. . . ."[7] I have been unable to tell, from Zhū Xī's comments, exactly what he takes to be the precise grammatical relationship between the intial "my Way" and the rest of the comment. Does he think it is the agent of the verb, or it is a "topic," on which the rest of the sentence "comments?" Perhaps Zhū Xī did not see much difference between "My Way penetrates the myriad things with one heart-mind" and "As for my Way, it is to respond to the myriad things with one heart-mind." Either reading suffers from the same weakness as Xíng Bǐng's, however, because it "overloads" the final pronoun.

James Legge's translation seems, at first, so surprising that we wonder whether the staid Scots missionary dipped too far into his port: "my doctrine is that of an all-pervading unity." However, further consideration suggests that Legge's reading is not indefensible. Indeed, although Legge seems not to have been directly aware of the work of Dài Zhèn 戴震, their interpretations are very similar. Because Dài Zhèn has a bit more to say about the interpretation, I shall let him speak for both of them: "'Is unified, such that it binds it all together' does not mean 'by means of one binds it all together.'[8] . . . 'My Way is unified, such that it binds it al together' means that the Way one "gets through to above" is precisely the Way one 'learns below.'"[9] Dài Zhèn is invoking a common interpretation of Confucius' thought, according to which one can approach it both "from above" (through an understanding of the Way in itself) and "from below" (through the manifestations of the Way in concrete activities), and suggests that the point of 4:15 is that Confucius' Way unifies these two kinds of activities. As Philip J. Ivanhoe points out in his contribution to the present volume, Dài Zhèn rejected the Neo-Confucian uses of concepts like lǐ 理 ("principle"). His interpretation of 4:15 is motivated by this rejection, for he fears that, if people read the text as Zhū Xī does, they will waste their time chasing the chimera of some "one thing," the metaphysical entity lǐ, that allegedly binds together Confucius' Way.

Dài Zhèn is more clear about what he thinks the syntax of Confucius' comment is not than about what he thinks it is. He insists that the word yī 一 is not being grammatically subordinated by the word yǐ 以. This suggests the translation, "As for my Way, it is unified, so as to bind it all together." What is the "it" that is being bound together? Again, Dài Zhèn is not specific, but he does say, "When the heart-mind is perfected in regard to the Way and complete in sagacity and wisdom, there is naturally nothing that it does not penetrate (guàn tōng 貫通)."[10] This explanation suggests that the Way binds "the myriad affairs."[11] Dài Zhèn (and Legge's) interpretation is ingenious and syntactically possible. Ultimately, I think they must be wrong, but in order to see why we have to look at another relevant passage in the *Analects*. So I shall leave this interpretation behind with a promise to return later.

Arthur Waley's translation (which is followed, with minor variations, by D. C. Lau, Wing-tsit Chan, and Ivanhoe) is, "My Way has one (thread) that runs right through it."[12] This avoids the problem that Xíng Bǐng and Zhū Xī faced (of overloading the final pronoun) by finding a referent for it earlier in the sentence: Waley takes the object of the verb to be "my Way" (which is grammatically preposed and then resumed by the pronoun zhī 之).[13] But this raises another question: what is the agent that is doing the "running through"? Given the way he translates the phrase, Waley apparently takes the logical agent of the action to be yī 一. However, this seems to simply ignore the coverb yǐ 以. If Confucius had wished to say what Waley says, why would he not have simply said, 吾道一貫之, or 吾道有一貫之 or possibly 吾道有一以貫之?

Raymond Dawson offers a translation with distinct advantages: "by one single thread is my Way bound together."[14] This follows Xíng Bǐng regarding the relationship of yī 一 and yǐ 以, but it follows Waley's suggestion of taking "my Way" as a preposed direct object resumed by the final zhi 之. Nonetheless, Dawson's clever translation conceals a serious issue. He translates the verb as a passive, but in the original Chinese the verb is clearly active.[15] Dawson is driven to do this, I think, because his interpretation of the syntax leaves us with no obvious agent for the verb. The agent of a transitive verb need not be explicitly stated in Classical Chinese, but it should be clear from the context what it is. In this case, however, all the available nouns are performing other grammatical functions.

The dilemma that the interpretations of Xíng Bǐng and Dawson illustrate is this: if we take the agent of the verb to be "my [that is, Confucius'] Way," then it is not at all clear what the referent of the final pronoun could be. If, on the other hand, we take "my Way" to be a preposed object that is resumed by the final pronoun, then it is not clear what the agent of the verb is.

The difficulty of finding a satisfactory interpretation of Confucius' comment should make us suspicious that something is amiss. This suspicion receives further confirmation when we look again at a passage that has syntax surprisingly similar to that of 4:15, but that does not seem nearly so hard to interpret. *Analects* 15:3 reads,

> The Master said, "Si, do you take me to be one who [simply] studies
> a lot and remembers it?" (賜也。女以予為多學而識之者與。)
> He responded, "That is so. Is that not the case?"
> He said, "It is not. I bind it together with one thing.
> (非也。予一以貫之。)"

("Sì" is the personal name of Confucius' disciple Zǐgòng 子貢.) In Confucius' final comment here, the agent of the verb is clear: it is Confucius (the clear referent of yú 予). And there is a clear antecedent for the final pronoun to refer to:

it is the things, suggested by Confucius' initial question, which Confucius "studies and remembers."

Notice also that this passage makes clear why Dài Zhèn's and Legge's interpretation of 4:15 cannot be correct. The syntax of 4:15 and 15:3 is so close that they must be interpreted in similar ways. However, it is not at all clear how to read 15:3 in the manner that Dài Zhèn and Legge read 4:15. For example, Legge translates Confucius' final statement in 15:3 as, "I seek a unity all-pervading." This is completely consistent with Legge's translation of 4:15, but it makes no sense at all of the Chinese text in 15:3. Dài Zhèn apparently takes Confucius' comment in 15:3 as elliptical for, "As for my studies, they are unified, so as to bind it all together."[16] This interpretation is a little too elliptical for my own taste.

So the syntax of Confucius' comment in 4:15 seems to be very similar to that of 15:3. However, this syntax makes sense in 15:3, but does not in 4:15. After we notice this anomaly, we notice other strange things about 4:15. For example, Confucius addresses Zengzi with the phrase, 參乎 Shēn hū! Nowhere else in the *Analects* is 乎 hū used vocatively like this. Everywhere else, when Confucius directly addresses (or comments on) a disciple, the construction is

> (personal name) + 也 yě

Analects 15:3 provides an example of this usage itself (see the Chinese text above), as does 5:12: 賜也，非爾所及也. ("Si, that is not something that someone like you can come up to!")

There are also anomalies regarding the actual content of 4:15. To begin with, Confucius announces summarily that his Way has "one thread," and when Zēngzǐ concurs, Confucius walks out of the room. Immediately, disciples rush up to ask Zēngzǐ for an interpretation. I find this somewhat odd in itself for a simple reason: Zēngzǐ was not an especially bright guy. Indeed, he is described in 11:18 as "stupid" (lǔ 魯). In general, if we look at passages other than 4:15, Zēngzǐ seems to have a strong personal commitment to the Way, but he never comes across as someone who was particularly acute intellectually. There is never, for example, a passage in which Zēngzǐ is commended by Confucius for his insight, in the manner that Confucius does commend Zǐxià 子夏 (3:8) or Zǐgòng (1:15). Why, then, does Confucius throw something patently cryptic at Zēngzǐ, and then leave the room? And why do the other disciples assume that Zēngzǐ will know what the Master meant?[17]

Finally, note that Confucius says his Way has "*one* thread." However, when asked what Confucius meant, Zengzi mentions *two* things. Interpreters tend to assume that the "one thread" has two aspects, but it is odd that Zengzi never made clear what the "one thread" was.

Such anomalies might encourage us to read 4:15 with a "hermeneutic of suspicion."[18] Reading 4:15 along these lines, we are led to ask, Who would have had some ulterior motive for composing it? Since Master Zēng is favorably depicted in the passage, it is presumably his followers who would have had such a motive.

What motive would they have had? Zēngzǐ did not have a reputation for being particularly astute. What better way to improve his image than by formulating a passage in which he alone, of all Confucius' disciples, understands the "one thread" of the Master's teachings? Thus, my hypothesis is that 4:15 is an interpolation, added to book 4 long after the rest of this section was compiled, by the followers of Master Zeng, who wanted a story that made their Master seem to have a deep insight into Confucius' Way.

An occasion for fabricating such a story was provided by 15:3, which is intriguing yet obscure. So the fabricators based their interpolation on 15:3, but trying to force fit the syntax of 15:3 into another context resulted in obscurity.

When did this interpolation occur? In their challenging book, *The Original Analects*, E. Bruce Brooks and A. Taeko Brooks make a number of intriguing suggestions about the dating of various strata of the *Analects*. I am pleased to see that we are in agreement on several points: they suggest that 4:15 is an interpolation and that 15:3 is actually an earlier text than 4:15, despite being far outside the "core chapters."[19] I am also convinced by their arguments that book 4 contains much material that is historically early.[20] Now, I assume that Zengzi himself did not fabricate this story,[21] so the terminus a quo for the interpolation is Zengzi's death in 436 B.C.E. Because, on my hypothesis, the syntax of 4:15 was suggested by 15:3, 4:15 cannot be any earlier than book 15 (or at least not any earlier than 15:3 itself). Book 15 contains several doctrines that suggest a worldview quite different from that of book 4: in book 15 we find an endorsement of the "Daoist" doctrine of "inaction" (15:5), efforts to bring systematicity to Confucian doctrine (15:24), which may reflect Mohist challenges, and what may be an attack on Mencius (15:31).[22] This all suggests the intellectual environment of the fourth century B.C.E. However, certainty is so difficult on a topic like this that I am comfortable suggesting only that 4:15 is probably at least forty years older than most of book 4, and perhaps even more than a century older.[23]

Whether or not we accept an interpolation hypothesis, the similarity of 15:3 to 4:15 may shed light on how to read the latter passage. Confucius' comment in 15:3 is, "I bind it [that is, what I study] together with one thing." When the last part of this phrase was lifted out of context to be used in 4:15, a subject for the final pronoun had to be supplied. Consequently, the phrase "my Way" was added in front, as a pre-posed object. The problem this creates is that, now, there is no agent for the transitive verb. However, if we read 4:15 in the light of 15:3, the assumed agent must be Confucius himself. Consequently, I would translate, "Shen, I bind my Way together with one thing."[24]

I have argued, on syntactic and historical grounds, that 4:15 is a fabrication. However, even if the incident recorded in 4:15 is apocryphal, this does not, by itself, invalidate interpretations of Confucius' thought that take zhōng and shù to be his "cardinal virtues." Zēngzǐ (or his disciples) may have been correct in thinking that Confucius' Way was "bound together" with zhōng and shù.[25] Consequently, in the second part of this essay, I would like to approach 4:15 again, this time with a "hermeneutic of restoration."[26] Focusing on "Zengzi's gloss," I shall ask what zhōng and shù mean, and whether they can function as the "one thread" of Confucius' teachings.

Zengzi's Gloss

If we allow ourselves the decadent luxury of citing as evidence passages from all over the received text of the *Analects*, we can tell a fairly convincing story about the meaning of shù. In 15:24, Zǐgòng asks, "Is there one phrase that one can act on to the end of one's life?" Confucius responds, "Is it not shù? That which you do not like yourself, do not inflict on others." Although this and Zengzi's comment are the only occurrences of the term "shù" in the *Analects*, the concept is suggested by other passages, such as 6:30, in which Confucius remarks (again in response to a question from Zǐgòng), "As for humaneness (rén 仁), desiring to be established oneself, one establishes others; desiring to succeed oneself, one helps others to succeed. To take what is near as an analogy may be called the method of humaneness." In addition, in 5:12, Zǐgòng proudly announces, "That which I do not desire others to inflict on me, I also desire not to inflict on others," only to have his ego deflated by Confucius' response: "Si, that is not something that someone like you can come up to!" It seems clear from these passages what shù means, and that it is an important concept for Confucius.

What about zhōng? "Loyalty" is one common translation of zhōng (Waley, Dawson), and this interpretation is clearly suggested by 3:19: Duke Ding asks about how a lord should employ his ministers, and how ministers should serve their lord, and Confucius replies, "A lord employs his ministers according to ritual; ministers serve their lord with loyalty (zhōng)." Also revealing is a pregnant comment by Master Zēng. Although not attributed to Confucius himself, it may shed light on the early Confucian understanding of the term (and it is especially important because Zeng is the one who interprets Confucius' comment in 4:15): "Master Zeng said, 'I daily examine myself thrice: In planning [móu 謀] for others have I failed to be loyal (zhōng)? In dealing with my friends have I failed to be faithful (xìn 信)? Have I passed on what I fail to practice?'" (1:4). Notice that the three "examinations" can be put in correspondence with three dimensions of relationships: toward social superiors, equals, and subordinates. "Planning for others" suggests the role of a minister in relation to his lord,[27] and here the relevant virtue is zhōng or loyalty. Among friends, who are on the same level of the social hierarchy, the relevant virtue is xìn or faithfulness. Finally, one's disciples are one's subordinates, and here what is most important is that one practices what one preaches.

Other passages, although not making explicit the meaning of zhōng, suggest that it was an important virtue for Confucius. In 7:25, we are told that the Master taught four subjects: culture, conduct, loyalty (zhōng), and faithfulness (xìn). And in three different passages, Confucius is reported to have said, "Emphasize loyalty and faithfulness" (1:8, 9:25, and 12:10).

So far so good. But a problem arises when we try to apply what we have learned to 4:15. In order to illustrate that problem, let us examine one noteworthy interpretation of zhōng and shù, that of D. C. Lau:

> Having found out what the other person wants or does not want,
> whether we go on to do to him what we believe he wants and refrain
> from doing to him what we believe he does not want must depend on
> something other than shu. As the way of the Master consists of chung and
> shu, in chung we have the other component of benevolence. Chung is the
> doing of one's best and it is through chung that one puts into effect
> what one had found out by the method of shu. (Lau, 16)

Is Lau correct?

Lau cites three passages in support of his interpretation (1:4, 3:19, and 13:19) and remarks, "In all these cases there is no doubt at all that chung means 'doing one's best.'" In fact, it is not obvious in *any* of these passages that chung has this meaning. We have already examined the first two passages that Lau cites and seen that they actually suggest the meaning of "loyalty." In the third passage, Fan Chi asks about humaneness, and Confucius responds, "Courtesy in private life, reverence in handling business, loyalty in relationships with others" (Dawson). Although the use of zhōng is *not* as obviously hierarchical in this passage as it is in the other two, it is *not* obvious that "loyalty" is an incorrect translation.[28]

Lau goes on to remark in a footnote that "Translators tend to use 'loyal' as the sole equivalent for chung even when translating early texts. This mistake is due to a failure to appreciate that the meaning of the word changed in the course of time. In later usage, it is true, chung tended to mean 'loyalty' in the sense of 'blind devotion', but this was not its meaning at the time of Confucius" (Lau, p. 16, n. 6). Lau seems uncharacteristically confused here. It is certainly true that for Confucius zhōng does not mean "blind obedience." (After all, in *Analects* 14:7, Confucius asks the rhetorical questions, "If you love someone, can you fail to make him work? If you are loyal to someone, can you fail to teach him?") But the English "loyalty" (and its Indo-European cognates) need not (and typically does not) mean "blind obedience." As George P. Fletcher has remarked in a recent analysis and defense of the notion of loyalty, "Blind adherence to any object of loyalty— whether friend, lover, or nation—converts loyalty into idolatry."[29]

What leads Lau to give his unusual, and seemingly forced, interpretation of zhōng? Although he does not "flag" this fact, Lau is probably following the interpretation of Zhū Xī (朱熹).[30] "Doing one's best" is one way of interpreting the phrase jìn jǐ 盡己, which Zhū Xī uses in his gloss on 4:15: "Fully realizing the self (jìn jǐ 盡己) is called zhōng; extending the self (tuī jǐ 推己) is called shù. . . . Hence, someone has said that inner disposition (zhōng xīn 中心) is zhōng; congruent disposition (rú xīn 如心) is shù."[31]

But this is not a complete explanation: For neither Zhū Xī nor Lau simply picks a meaning out of thin air. We can honestly pay each the highest compliment a scholar can get: even when wrong, they have reasons for interpreting as they do. The key, I think, is a seemingly innocent phrase in Lau's explanation of his interpretation: "As the way of the Master consists of *chung* and *shu*, in *chung* we have the other component of benevolence." This sentence suggests the key hermeneutic premises of Lau's (and Zhū Xī's) interpretation: (1) *Zhōng* and *shù* together make up Confucius' *dào* 道, and (2) *shù* is explicitly defined as not doing to others what one does not want done to oneself. Given these assumptions, *zhōng* must expand beyond the sense of mere "loyalty," so that it can fill whatever conceptual space is left unoccupied by *shù*.

Lau is not alone in his predicament. Indeed, I want to argue for the following: (1) interpretations of Zengzi's gloss in 4:15, especially over the last few decades, have been driven largely by the effort to find some expansive sense for *zhōng*; (2) these expansive senses of *zhōng* are not supported by other parts of the *Analects*; and (3) this suggests that Master Zeng may simply be wrong in his interpretation of the "one thread."

Let us see if other major interpreters do better in explaining *zhōng* and *shù*. Herbert Fingarette's interpretation of Zengzi's gloss is subtle and complex.[32] In particular, Fingarette makes philosophically challenging observations about the notion of *shù*. He suggests that *shù* suffers from a conceptual problem that afflicts other ethical principles of reciprocity (such as the Golden Rule or Kant's Categorical Imperative). Namely, telling me to treat others as I would wish (or not wish) to be treated seems inadequate as an ethical guide, because my own wishes might be different from yours, or might simply be inappropriate. Should I give you baseball tickets if I am a baseball fan, even if I know that you do not like baseball? Or, if I am a teacher, should I give easy grades because I was always a lazy student myself? Fingarette intriguingly suggests that a principle of reciprocity must always be used in conjunction with some other principle that weeds out illegitimate or irrelevant "wishes" before reciprocity is applied. In the *Analects*, Fingarette suggests, this function is performed by *zhōng*.

It is on Fingarette's interpretation of *zhōng* that I shall focus. At first, Fingarette's understanding of *zhōng* seems very close to the narrow interpretation I offered earlier: "*Chung* is, in a broad sense, equivalent to the English word 'loyalty.'"[33] Fingarette then notes, correctly, that *zhōng* is often paired with *xìn* 信, and that *xìn* "is, generally, good faith. It is to mean the commitments that one purports to mean by one's word or comportment, not to engender deceptive expectations."[34] I think we're all "on the bus" with Fingarette so far, but we might be tempted to part ways with him soon, because he suggests that

> what we have here, in effect, is a single imprecisely defined concept for which neither the ancient Chinese nor modern English has a single word. The concept is applied by using either of two words whose

traditional meanings overlap. . . . Either term alone presents a different emphasis, but both are used together repeatedly. This concept I will hereafter call *chung-hsin*.[35]

Before we have a chance to catch our breath, Fingarette goes on to argue that because "[c]hung-hsin is commitment to preserve integrity," and because "[i]ntegrity is defined ultimately by the *tao*," therefore "the specific content of *chung-hsin* is defined by the *tao*." Furthermore, the *dao* "is socially manifested . . . in the *li*," or rites.[36] Thus, on Fingarette's reading, what Zengzi means by *zhōng* in *Analects* 4:15 is *zhōng-xìn*, and *zhōng-xìn* is

> the set of good faith commitments, rooted in the Way and manifested
> in *li*—in the Prince being a Prince, the minister a minister, the father a
> father, the son a son, and the friend a friend—it is these communally
> defined statuses that define the specific obligations we have on
> particular occasions.[37]

Zengzi certainly seems to have said a lot in a few words!

It is tempting to simply dismiss Fingarette's interpretation as "speculative." But this is not a real objection, because every interpretation that does more than merely restate the evidence is speculative. The only real issue is whether a particular piece of speculation is warranted. In fact, there are several problems with Fingarette's interpretation. First, the very fact that *zhōng-xìn* occurs so often as a phrase suggests that, had Zengzi wished to invoke this particular concept, he would simply have used the complete phrase. Second, as we have seen, passages in the *Analects* that provide some hint about the meaning of *zhōng* (other than 4:15 itself) suggest that it has the narrow sense of "loyalty," not the broader sense that Fingarette attributes to *zhōng-xìn*. Is there any evidence at all for Fingarette's interpretation? It has been suggested that 5:19 provides some evidence for an expansive understanding of *zhōng*:[38]

> Zizhang asked saying: "Chief Minister Ziwen three times held office as
> chief minister, but showed no sign of delight; three times he was
> deposed, but showed no sign of resentment. He always reported to the
> new chief minister on the conduct of government of himself, the
> former chief minister. So what do you think of him?"
> The Master said: "He was loyal [*zhōng*]."
> "Was he humane?" said Zizhang.
> "One cannot know yet," said the Master. "How could he be
> considered humane?"[39] (Dawson, modified slightly).

Arguably, in this passage, Ziwen shows not simple loyalty to the ruler he serves as chief minister, but rather a general commitment to doing what is required by the Way for a person in his situation. However, although this interpretation is possible, I see no particular reason to favor it over an interpretation that sees Ziwen's actions as exemplification of loyalty to his ruler. If the use of *zhōng* in 5:19 is equally consistent with interpreting it as loyalty or with interpreting it as a general commitment to the Way, the passage provides no evidence in favor of the latter interpretation. In addition, the case for understanding zhōng in this passage as the counterpart to shù is weakened by the fact that Zizhang immediately goes on to ask about Chen Wen Zi, who refused to serve an unvirtuous lord. Confucius decrees that Chen Wen Zi is "pure" (qīng 清), but states again that one "cannot yet know" whether he is humane. Chen Wen Zi is also manifesting a general commitment to doing what the Way requires for a person in his situation, but he is described as qīng, rather than as zhōng. If zhōng were being used in this passage in an expansive sense that covered all of the Way except for what is covered by shù, then it should not appear as a virtue coordinate with qīng.

A third and final problem with Fingarette's interpretation is that, in a passage in which zhōng and lǐ are discussed together, rather than treating lǐ as giving the content of zhōng, Confucius distinguishes them, saying that "A lord employs his ministers in accordance with the rites; ministers serve their lords with loyalty" (3:19).[40]

I now turn (briefly) to the interpretation of David S. Nivison. Nivison presented his interpretation as part of a public lecture at Stanford in 1984, entitled "Golden Rule Arguments in Chinese Moral Philosophy." This lecture has been surprisingly influential, despite having remained unpublished until recently. In his essay, Nivison presents an interesting overview of some interpretations of zhōng and shù over several millennia of the Chinese tradition. For my purposes in this essay, though, what is most important is Nivison's own interpretation of these concepts. Nivison notes that, in the definition of shù in 15:24,

> "Do not do to others what you would not want yourself"—the word for "do," shī 施, is normally used of doings that are givings (or inflictings) directed downward toward one's inferiors in status, or at most toward equals. On the other hand, the ordinary meaning of the word zhong is "loyalty"—and the meaning is so ordinary that it would be very strange . . . if its meaning when paired with shu were utterly different; and zhong as "loyalty" is always directed toward superiors, or at most toward equals.[41]

Nivison concludes that shù is, as we had suspected, a principle of reciprocity: we should treat others as we would want to be treated. However, Nivison takes the word to be specifically hierarchical: shù is reciprocity directed toward social equals or subordinates. Zhōng, then, is the corresponding principle of reciprocity directed toward social equals or superiors. This is quite ingenious. There's only one problem: there is no textual evidence to support reading zhōng in this way.[42] However, Nivison has drawn our attention back to the explicitly hierarchical nature of zhōng, and has made an intriguing suggestion about the nature of shù.

The last major interpretation I shall examine is that of P. J. Ivanhoe, who, in a challenging and important article, "Reweaving the 'One Thread' of the *Analects*,"

critically synthesizes the previous work of Fingarette and Nivison. Ivanhoe follows
Fingarette regarding several points, including the suggestion that "reciprocity" by
itself lacks sufficient content to provide a guide to ethical action, and that zhōng
somehow helps to provide the specific context within which shù operates.
However, Ivanhoe criticizes Fingarette's specific interpretation of zhōng-xìn, saying
that

> it suffers from being based on a misunderstanding of the concept of
> chung. [Fingarette] claims that in the *Analects* there is a kind of hybrid
> notion, chung-hsin, which means something like "interpersonal good
> faith." But this interpretation obscures the very specific and clear use of
> the term chung in the *Analects*. Chung always means, "doing one's duty in
> service to another." . . . Hsin has various related meanings. Its root sense
> is to be true to one's word. . . . When the two graphs are combined
> they describe a person who is reliable and worthy of trust. Fingarette
> has conflated these distinct senses and claimed that this is what
> Confucius intended by chung in [passages such as 4:15].[43]

Turning to Nivison, Ivanhoe agrees that zhōng is explicitly hierarchical; it is
something one is in relation to one's social superiors. However, Ivanhoe rejects
Nivison's suggestion that zhōng and shù are both virtues of reciprocity, the former
directed toward superiors and equals, the latter directed toward equals or subordinates.

Ivanhoe's own interpretation is impressive and fertile, but it seems to me that
there is an unresolved tension in his account. At times, Ivanhoe stresses Nivison's
suggestion that zhōng is hierarchical, directed toward one's social superiors: "Chung
is following the rituals *in service to others*. A person can never be chung to a subordinate (just as it would be odd for us to say one is 'loyal' to a subordinate)."[44] This
interpretation brings out nicely the hierarchical nature of zhōng. However, it also
seems to have an odd consequence: because one can be loyal only to superiors,
it seems that Confucius' "one thread" would not regulate our behavior toward
our social subordinates. From what he says in his article, though, it is clear
that Ivanhoe agrees that it makes an ethical difference how one treats one's
subordinates.

So how does zhōng regulate one's actions toward one's subordinates? This leads
us to what I think is a second conception of zhōng in Ivanhoe's paper: "Chung is
one's loyalty to the Way; it is the personal virtue which assures others that one
will do one's duty, as prescribed by the li, in service to others."[45] However, this
broader conception of zhōng seems to me to be fairly close to Fingarette's understanding of zhōng-xìn.[46]

There clearly are significant disagreements between Ivanhoe and Fingarette.
Ivanhoe clearly rejects Fingarette's suggestion that zhōng-xìn is a "single imprecisely
defined concept" in the *Analects*. In addition, Ivanhoe does stress the hierarchical
nature of zhōng in a way that Fingarette does not. However, I do not think that

Ivanhoe disagrees with Fingarette as much as he thinks he does. Indeed, his disagreements could almost be seen as "friendly amendments" to Fingarette's position, in the following manner. One of the weaknesses of Fingarette's interpretation is the questionable and convoluted way he goes from zhōng to zhōng-xìn to a commitment to the Way. Ivanhoe, in contrast, can be understood as starting from the unobjectionable claim that the "focal meaning" of zhong is loyalty to a person who is one's social superior.[47] Confucius emphasizes that this loyalty is not "blind," but is ethically informed by one's commitment to the Way. Ivanhoe suggests, I think, that the use of zhōng in 4:15 is a natural expansion of this earlier sense. Just as I might be loyal to my lord, I am loyal to the Way. Both my lord and the Way are, metaphorically, my "superiors." However, although Ivanhoe takes a different route from Fingarette, they end up at very similar places. For example, Ivanhoe remarks that the two "strands of the 'one thread' which runs through Confucius' Way" are "to be disposed to carry out one's role-specific duties, as prescribed by li [that is, zhōng], but to insure that the performance of one's duties is informed by an overarching concern for others as fellow human beings [that is, shù]."[48] I cannot imagine Fingarette objecting to this formulation at all. But to the extent that Ivanhoe's interpretation is similar to Fingarette's, it shares the weakness of Fingarette's interpretation: there is no real textual evidence, outside of 4:15, for reading zhōng in an expansive sense.

Conclusion

In the first part of this paper, I argued that 4:15 is an interpolation. However, even if Zengzi did not say what he is reported to have said in 4:15, or even if he did not say it in the circumstances described by 4:15, it still might be true that "the Master's Way is zhōng and shù and that is all." An apocryphal story can still be an enlightening story. However, the difficulties we have had in finding support for any interpretation of zhōng in 4:15 suggest that the view of cardinal virtues suggested by this passage is not one shared by Confucius, nor is it supported by the rest of the *Analects*.

Why have scholars been so fascinated with 4:15, and so determined to read the rest of the *Analects* in the light of it? One of the paradigmatic features of philosophy is systematicity. *Analects* 4:15 suggests that there is some systematicity to Confucius' discussion of human virtue. Students of comparative thought, wanting (out of generous motives) to understand Confucius as a philosopher, have therefore pounced on 4:15 as the key to that systematicity.

I am not suggesting that Confucius is completely haphazard in his observations. But there are degrees of systematicity, and—at least in his description of the virtues—Confucius seems to lack the degree of systematicity that we typically associate with philosophers. To say this is not to denigrate, much less to dismiss, Confucius. The *Analects* is like the *Dhammapada* or the Gospel of Matthew.[49] All of these are works of great beauty and ethical insight, and all have helped inspire great philosophy, but none is itself a philosophical work. In short, if literate people around the world find Confucius interesting and challenging—and I think we should—we should do so based on an understanding of what kind of thinker he truly was, rather than what kind of thinker we want to force him to be.

Appendix: Zhū Xī on 4:15

As we have seen, Zhū Xī has had a great influence on later interpreters of *Analects* 4:15. Indeed, Zhū Xī may very well be the person responsible for the emphasis on 4:15 as the key to understanding the *Analects*. In the Zhūzǐ yǔlèi 朱子語類, he is recorded as having said, "If you want to deeply understand, this is the single most important passage in the *Analects*,"[50] and his comments on the passage in that work run to thirty-two full pages. (In comparison, the next longest discussion of any passage from book 4 is only a little over four pages.) Below is a translation of Zhū Xī's comments on 4:15 in one of his most widely read works, the Sìshū jízhù 四書集注, followed by my "subcommentary" on Zhū Xī.

> 參乎 is calling Zengzi by name to tell him something. 貫 means to penetrate. 唯 is answering him quickly and without doubt.

> The heart-mind of a sage is one undifferentiated principle; it responds universally and is appropriate in the minutest details; each of its operations is distinct. Zengzi, in regard to the operations of his own mind, was pretty much already minutely examining and putting it into practice energetically. However, he did not yet realize that its substance is one. The Master recognized that he had "truly piled up effort for a long time,"[51] and must have grasped something [of the truth]. Hence, he called him to tell him. Zengzi was in fact able to silently understand his meaning. This is precisely why he responded quickly and without doubt.

> Fully realizing the self is what is meant by 忠. To extend oneself is what is meant by 恕。而已矣 is a way of saying to exhaust without anything left over.

> The Master's one principle being undifferentiated, responding universally and being appropriate in the minutest detail may be compared to Heaven and Earth's "having supreme integrity without rest,"[52] so that the myriad things "each obtains its proper place."[53] There is no further method beyond this, and there is no need for extension. Zengzi apprehended this, but had trouble expressing it in words. Hence, he borrowed the notion that a student's program is to

fully realize the self and extend oneself, so as to make it clear, desiring others to easily understand it.

Now, "to have supreme integrity without rest" is the substance of the Way. It is that by which there is "one root"[54] beneath the myriad manifestations. For the myriad things to "each obtain its proper place" is the function of the Way.[55] It is that by which there are myriad manifestations of the "one root." If one looks at it like this, one can understand the significance of "penetrates them by one thing."

Hence, some say, "One's inner heart-mind (中心) is 忠 A congruent heart-mind (如心) is 恕." This expresses the same basic idea. . . . [Illustrative quotations from Master Cheng follow.]

When I read Zhū Xī's comments, I cannot help but wonder if his interpretation of the incident recorded in 4:15 was influenced by the model of the Chan Buddhist gōngàn 公案 (that is, Zen kōan).[56] There are many structural similarities between one sort of kōan exchange and the exchange between Confucius and Zēng (as interpreted by Zhū Xī). The disciple works intently and sincerely for a long time at the tasks the Master assigns him (Zēng had "truly piled up effort for a long time"), yet fails to grasp the underlying unity of the world and of the activities of the sages. The Master, sensing that the disciple is at the right stage, surprises him (Confucius calls to Zēng out of the blue) with some cryptic and possibly paradoxical remark intended to shock him into enlightenment. If the disciple achieves enlightenment ("Zengzi was in fact able to silently understand his meaning"), this manifests itself to the Master, not in any verbal analysis the disciple gives of the kōan, but in a subtle yet profound change that the Master can discern in every simple word and gesture of the disciple (hence, Confucius can leave right after he hears Zeng simply say, "Yes"). After enlightenment, the disciple is himself a Master, who will help others to move toward enlightenment, tailoring his own teaching to their level of understanding (thus, Master Zeng, in teaching the other disciples, refers to two things, whereas Confucius had referred to one).

I am not, of course, suggesting that Zhū Xī was a crypto–Buddhist, or that his reading of 4:15 is like a kōan exchange in every respect. However, given the influence of Chan (Zen) in the Tang and Song dynasties, I think it would be surprising if the structural similarities I have noted are purely coincidental.

ACKNOWLEDGMENTS

I would like to thank Anne Birdwhistell, Bruce Brooks, Herman Capellen, Jennifer Church, Mark Csikszentmihalyi, Robert Eno, Paul Rakita Goldin, Philip J. Ivanhoe, Jesse Kalin, Paul Kjellberg, Thornton "Jack" Kline, Michael McCarthy, Mitch Miller, Joel Sahleen, Uma Narayan, Michael Puett, and several anonymous referees for helpful comments on earlier versions of this paper. I would also like to thank Donald Leslie for a talk he gave at Stanford University years ago, which first sparked my interest in the syntactic and interpretive problems raised by *Analects* 4:15.

NOTES

Citations of the *Analects* in this essay are based on the sectioning in the Harvard-Yenching Institute Sinological Index Series edition. Translations are my own unless otherwise indicated. Full citations of translations may be found on p. 29.

1. *Republic*, book 9, Stephanus 587.

2. Another passage from the *Analects* that might suggest Confucius had a view of cardinal virtues is 9:29 (repeated with some modifications in 14:28): "The wise are not in doubt. The humane are not anxious. The courageous are not afraid." I believe that this passage is an interpolation, and does not represent Confucius' own view, for the following reasons: (1) Courage (*yǒng* 勇) is typically denigrated, or at least treated as a "suspect" disposition, rather than regarded as a cardinal virtue, in every other passage in the "core books" (5:7, 8:2, 8:10; see the introduction to this volume on the notion of the "core books"), and even in most of the other books (e.g., 17:21); and (2) *rén* 仁 in the *Analects* is used in both a broad sense, as the culmination of human virtue (e.g., 4:4), and in a narrow sense, as something like benevolence (e.g., 12:22). I believe that the broad sense was earlier, and was the sense used exclusively by Confucius. But if 9:29 and 14:28 are lists of cardinal virtues, they use *rén* in a narrow sense. Hence, they are late. (I am grateful to Jiang Xinyan for bringing 9:29 and 14:28 to my attention.)

3. Those without a command of Chinese should note that Classical Chinese is typically (although not always) monosyllabic.

4. One more, minor interpretive puzzle: Whose disciples question Zengzi after Confucius leaves? Are these other disciples of Confucius, or are they Zengzi's own disciples? Xing Bing thinks that they are Zengzi's disciples, but I do not see how Zengzi could have disciples of his own while he was still studying with Confucius.

5. 我所行之道唯用一理以統天下萬事之理也（孟子正義）。

6. 以一心應萬事 (*Zhūzǐ yǔlèi* [Taibei: Wenjin chubanshe, 1986], vol. 2, p. 669).

7. For the remainder of Zhǔ Xī's comment, see the appendix to this essay.

8. 一以貫之，非言以一貫之。

9. 孟子字義疏證, sec. 41. The other quoted phrases Dài Zhèn uses to gloss 4:15 come from *Analects* 14:35.

10. 心精於道，全乎聖智，自無弗貫通。

11. Legge specifically says that *zhī* 之 refers to "the myriad affairs."

12. Lau: "There is one single thread binding my way together." Ivanhoe: "Shen! My Way has one thread passing through it." (I discuss Lau's and Ivanhoe's interpretations on pp. 225–26 and 228–30, below.) Note that Waley, Lau, and Ivanhoe all supply the word "thread." In this they follow Zhu Xi, who suggests that *yī guàn* 一貫 is like using a single thread to bind together a pile of loose change (*Zhūzǐ yǔlèi*, vol. 2, p. 669 and pp. 673–74). (Recall that traditional Chinese coins had holes in the middle, which allowed them to be strung together.) Interestingly, Legge anticipates Waley's translation in one of his notes: "to myself it occurs to translate, 'my doctrines have one thing which goes through them,' but such an exposition has not been approved by any Chinese writer." (Legge, p. 169, n. 15.) Yoshida Kenkō's (吉田賢抗) Japanese translation is similar (but also shows the influence of "Neo-Confucian" thought): "As for the Way which I discuss and practice, there is a fundamental principle (原理) by which it is always bound into one" (*Rongo* [Tokyo: Meiji Shoin, 1979], p. 94).

13. For more on this type of grammatical construction, see Edwin G. Pulleyblank, *Outline of Classical Chinese Grammar* (Vancouver, Canada: University of British Columbia Press, 1995), pp. 69–71.

14. Kanaya Osamu's (金谷治) Japanese translation is similar: "As for my Way, by means of one thing, it is bound together (*tsuranukarete iru*)" (*Rongo* [Tokyo: Iwanami, 1963], p. 57).

15. The presence of the pronoun *zhī* 之 after the verb renders the construction active. A passive construction would have to read something like the following: 吾道一以貫. For more on passive constructions in Classical Chinese, see Pulleyblank, pp. 27–28 and 35–38.

16. Or, "I unify [the things I study] so as to bind it all together." But this interpretation seems forced to me.

17. As Robert Eno has observed (in conversation), Zengzi was one of the younger of Confucius' disciples, so he is unlikely to have had such a high status among the other disciples. Furthermore, Bruce and Taeko Brooks have made the radical suggestion that Zengzi never even met Confucius (E. Bruce and A. Taeko Brooks, *The Original Analects: Sayings of Confucius and His Successors* [New York: Columbia University Press, 1998], p. 39 and p. 49). It is intriguing that, with the exception of 4:15, there is no passage in the *Analects* that even purports to record a direct conversation between Confucius and Zengzi. (This is another suspiciously anomalous feature of 4:15.) *Analects* 14:26, 19:17, and 19:18 might seem to be exceptions to this generalization, but these passages actually just report Zengzi commenting on things he had heard the Master say—or, perhaps more accurately, heard that the Master said.

18. The phase is from French philosopher Paul Ricoeur. (See his *Freud and Philosophy: An Essay on Interpretation* [New Haven: Yale University Press, 1970), pp. 27–36.) When employing a "hermeneutic of suspicion," one looks for ulterior motives for the composition of a text. (Marx, Freud, Nietzsche, and more recently Foucault are among the greatest advocates of hermeneutics of suspicion.)

19. Brooks and Brooks, p. 136 and p. 149, respectively. On books 3–9 as the "core chapters" of the *Analects*, see the editor's introduction to this volume.

20. Brooks and Brooks, pp. 203–4.

21. The Brookses agree, attributing the interpolation to Zǐgāo 子高. However, their argument is part of their complex general view of the accretion of the *Analects*, whereas I have a simpler (but equally fallible) moral argument. Given Zēngzǐ's high moral character (there is never a hint of impropriety associated with him), it seems unlikely he would simply have lied about the incident reported in 4:15. After his death, however, his followers might have self-consciously produced the anecdote, or simply become convinced that the story of this incident was part of legitimate and accurate oral history.

22. See Brooks and Brooks, p. 138.

23. The Brookses are more daring than I, attaching specific dates to 15:3 (301 or 300 B.C.E.) and 4:15 (294 B.C.E.). As is clear, I greatly admire the Brookses' achievement. However, I do have disagreements with them on some points. In particular, my own view is much closer to what they describe as the "four-stratum theory" (ibid., p. 202).

24. Brooks and Brooks translate as I do, without discussing alternative interpretations (p. 149: "Shvm! My Way: by one thing I link it together").

25. P. J. Ivanhoe has made this point in correspondence.

26. Again, the phrase is from Ricoeur. When employing a hermeneutic of restoration, we have faith in the text. The faith need not, and should not, be a naivete, but rather a belief that the text has a message that we can uncover. (See also Yearley's discussion of alternative interpretive approaches in his contribution to this volume.)

27. Compare "The Master said: 'If one is not in a certain office, one does not plan [*móu* 謀] the governance involved in that office'" (Dawson, 8:14).

28. Perhaps in this passage, as in 1:4, three dimensions of human interaction are suggested: in the home we should be courteous, when serving in official capacity one should be reverent, and in all other contexts that involve interactions with others one should be zhōng. If this is the intention, "loyalty" is still a plausible sense for zhōng. Notice also that zhōng here is clearly only part of one's proper attitude in relation to others. This insight shows that, in this passage at least, zhōng is used more narrowly than Fingarette and Ivanhoe suggest it is in 4:15. (For Fingarette's and Ivanhoe's interpretations, see below.)

29. George P. Fletcher, Loyalty: An Essay on the Morality of Relationships (New York: Oxford University Press, 1993), p. 6.

30. For more on Zhū Xī's interpretation, see the appendix to this chapter.

31. Sishu jizhu, in loc. Cited in David S. Nivison, "Golden Rule Arguments in Chinese Moral Philosophy," in Bryan Van Norden, ed., The Ways of Confucianism (La Salle, Ill: Open Court Press, 1996), p. 68.

32. Herbert Fingarette, "Following the 'One Thread' of the Analects," Journal of the American Academy of Religion Thematic Issue S (Sept. 1980), pp. 373–405.

33. Fingarette, p. 388.

34. Fingarette, p. 389.

35. Fingarette, p. 389.

36. Fingarette, p. 390.

37. Fingarette, p. 392.

38. Nivison (p. 66) and Ivanhoe (in correspondence) have both cited this passage as evidence for their own interpretations, which I shall discuss below.

39. I have modified Dawson's translation of this line. The text reads 未知。 焉得仁。 Dawson gives "I do not yet understand," said the Master, "how he could be considered humane." Lau translates, "He cannot even be said to be wise. How can he be said to be benevolent." Waley suggests, "I am not sure. I see nothing in that to merit the title Good." Legge gives, "I do not know. How can he be pronounced perfectly virtuous?"

40. A defender of Fingarette's interpretation might raise the following challenge, though. Isn't it possible that, in Confucius' time, zhōng had senses other than those evidently suggested by the Analects passages that we have examined? In particular, isn't it possible that zhōng could have been used in an expansive sense to refer to one's general commitment to one's obligations? This is possible. However, this fact actually reveals another weakness of both Lau's and Fingarette's interpretations. It is possible that, despite the absence of direct evience, zhōng sometimes means what Fingarette suggests. However, it is equally possible that zhōng sometimes means what Lau suggests. The fact that both interpretations could be true only demonstates that neither interpretation is supported by any particular evidence. In other words, if we're willing to opt for interpretations that lack direct textual evidence, zhōng might mean anything.

41. Nivison, p. 65.

42. Nivison cites Analects 5:19 as evidence for his interpretation of zhōng (p. 66). However, we saw above that this passage provides no real evidence for an expansive reading of zhōng. (How, on Nivison's reading, is zhōng related to qīng?)

43. Philip J. Ivanhoe, "Reweaving the 'One Thread' of the Analects," Philosophy East and West 40:1 (Jan. 1990), p. 21.

44. Ivanhoe, p. 25. Emphasis in original.

45. Ivanhoe, p. 24.

46. Admittedly, the last part of this phrase, "in service to others," sounds like the earlier, Nivison-esque reading, but most of this quotation is almost a paraphrase of Fingarette.

47. On the use of the notion of "focal meaning" as a tool in comparative studies, see Lee H. Yearley, Mencius and Aquinas (Albany, N.Y.: SUNY Press, 1990), pp. 188–96.

48. Ivanhoe, p. 29.

49. For a powerful defense of the alternative claim that the *Analects* and the *Dhammapada*, at least, *are* works of philosophy, see Joel J. Kupperman, *Learning from Asian Philosophy* (New York: Oxford University Press, 1999), pp. 3–13 and compare pp. 161–63.

50. *Zhuzi yulei*, vol. 2, p. 669.

51. Xúnzǐ 荀子, Quàn xué 勸學.

52. Zhōngyōng 中庸 26.1.

53. This last phrase may be an echo of *Analects* 9:15.

54. Mèngzǐ 孟子 3A5.

55. "Substance" (tǐ 體) and "function" (yòng 用) are technical terms in Neo-Confucian metaphysics. For more, see A. C. Graham, *Two Chinese Philosophers*, reprint (Chicago: Open Court Press, 1992), pp. 39–40 and passim.

56. My discussion of kōans is deeply indebted to Heinrich Dumoulin, *Zen Buddhism: A History: Volume 1: India and China* (New York: Macmillan, 1994), pp. 245–61.

10

I. Introduction

Among the more haunting of the many haunting passages in the *Analects* is the one that begins "The more I strain my gaze towards it, the higher it soars. The deeper I bore down into it, the harder it becomes. I see it in front; but suddenly it is behind" (Waley 9:10). The comment describes, it could be said, not only the Confucian Way but also the figure or, better, figures of Confucius that appear in the text, as well as the text itself, or at least significant parts of it.

A sober, scholarly way to put this is that we face in the *Analects* a classically indeterminate text, a text that can support either no single interpretation or a number of coherent ones. Solid historical reasons explain why the text manifests itself that way: it is, like the New Testament, a text that was composed by different hands with various agendas over the course of many years. (This is a comparsion to which we shall return.) Acknowledging this fact might tempt us to give up the hope of treating the *Analects*, and the figure of Confucius, as a source of guidance and challenge. Nevertheless, I still find the *Analects* to be a text I am drawn to, even fascinated by, as more than an important historical relic. (And this remains true even though I sometimes despair of meeting the challenge of teaching well or writing about this text in an illuminating way.) It is a text that suggests the presence of a seemingly powerful but surely elusive message. I know from the reactions that the *Analects* provokes among my students that I am not alone in this sense.

Moreover, I harbor the suspicion that the most significant reasons for both the sense of importance and the feeling of elusiveness the text provokes are that the crucial subjects of the *Analects* are the figure of Confucius and the topic of virtue. Neither virtues nor significant people, when well treated, lend themselves to clear, much less static pictures. Real virtues, that is, display themselves differently depending on the situation in which they manifest themselves. (The courageous person's courage may lead her either to flee or to stand firm, a difference that arises from the interaction of her character, thought, and the situation.) And virtuous persons share the quality of being unpredictable—a quality more ordinary people are notable for lacking. Furthermore (to make a comment for which I have only an empirical, not a philosophical, defense) the greater the person the more

An Existentialist Reading of Book 4 of the *Analects*

LEE H. YEARLEY

likely that our simple notions of the coherence of personality are inapplicable. The significant actions of such people, to put it one way, cannot be predicted before the fact, but they always seem both in character and appropriate after the fact. This situation helps explain, I believe, my continuing failures to capture the figure of Confucius, a failure illustrated by the following anecdote: Each year (for a very long time) I set myself the task, in a class on Confucianism, of giving a lecture on the figure of Confucius in the *Analects*. Each year I found it so inadequate that it was swiftly deposited in the waste basket.

One can of course decide, out of some combination of pain and humility, to surrender such grand ambitions and turn to the treatment of single passages or apparently closely related sets of passages. In some cases (such as the understanding of Confucius' "one thread" [in 4:15] and thus the interaction of zhōng 忠 and shù 恕) this approach has led to significant philosophical and philological progress.[1] In other cases, we find evocative presentations that also have theoretical content. An example is the statement that "only when the year grows cold do we see that the pine and cypress are the last to fade" (Waley 9:27).[2] The notion so elegantly put here is one we also see in the Aristotelian tradition: virtues often appear clearly only in situations of stress.

Other strategies are, of course, possible, including ones that take the *Analects* as a whole and then examine either all of it or at least general themes in it. Proponents of this strategy usually justify their approach by noting that the book was traditionally read as a unified text—and they often add to this justification from traditional use the commendable idea that, like interpreters in the past, they aim to make the whole work relevant to their own age. In talented hands, this approach unquestionably produces significant results. Nevertheless, this approach is often connected with the rise (which we see in studies of both East Asian and Western texts) of what can be called a "new fundamentalism." That approach, sometimes for sophisticated reasons, simply takes texts as they are and then interprets their message with little regard for issues about their composition, and even at times cultural context.

Despite the fact that all the approaches noted (as well as others) have integrity, I want here to do something quite different. My hope is to combine two sorts of approaches to classic texts that are often viewed (implicitly or explicitly) as in opposition. (These two approaches may be found in the study of the classic texts of many different traditions, including Christianity, Confucianism, and Buddhism, to name just three examples.) On the one hand, there are scholars who attempt to arrive at a scholarly, historically accurate representation of the meaning (or meanings) of the text in particular historical contexts. On the other hand, there are those who attempt to engage a text as a still viable teaching, one with relevance for how we should live our lives today. Those in the former camp sometimes accuse those in the latter of reading the text in a naive and anachronistic way. Those in the latter camp accuse those in the former of approaching the texts with a sort of secular objectivity that robs the letter of life, and is animated only by the desire to "debunk" and "unmask," rather than to respect and venerate, the tradition. Both accusations are sometimes just.

Although these two approaches are now typically seen as in opposition, I think it is possible, and indeed necessary, to combine the two. If we are to live honestly, we must be able to read our classic texts in ways that do justice to them as products of real human history, with all its problems and foibles. On the other hand, if in our search for more accurate scholarship about the historical Confucius (or Jesus, or Buddha), we fail to ethically engage the challenge posed by that particular character for our own contemporary self-understanding, we have lost something very precious, and very important to being a human. My sense that it is both possible and necessary to combine two approaches arises from my understanding of what is probably the most sophisticated of all those critical traditions that have roots in the West's nineteenth century: the modern tradition of scholarship about the New Testament. Let me now try to show why I think that tradition is relevant to the study of the *Analects*.[3]

II. Interpretative Strategies: The New Testament and the *Analects*

I believe the application of this tradition of scholarship to the study of the *Analects* should prove to be useful given that the New Testament and the *Analects* manifest some remarkable structural similarities. Both texts present different views of a figure and his message whom many people took to be of immense importance, but whom no one seems to have been able to capture without remainder, or at least to capture to the satisfaction of other people who also were deeply moved by the figure. Moreover, both texts also bear the marks of different groups, in different times and cultural contexts, that attempted not only to render the figure in a way that they found satisfactory but also in a way that (in many cases at least) would cement their claims to authority. Questions about who wrote what, when, and for what purposes are, then, crucial in both cases, even if many answers to them are bound always to be unconvincing to some seasoned observers. Finally, both texts are ones that not only have oriented people's lives, but that at least some modern interpreters also believe should continue to orient people's live, despite the various difficulties they may present.[4]

A situation like this, almost inevitably it seems, leads many modern people to attempt to find the "real" person behind the various perspectives on that person. Those attempts can be remarkably clumsy, especially if they rest on the idea that we can have something like uninterpreted facts about the significant features of a human being. Other more sophisticated attempts, however, draw on historical, philological, and textual evidence to make judgments about what are the earliest sayings and descriptions of the figure. The results of even the most sophisticated approaches ought not, of course, lead us to think that we have captured the figure's essence, or even, necessarily, have a more accurate understanding. To use a Western example that has Chinese analogues: neither Paul nor Dante knew Jesus as he lived, and yet surely in the first case and arguably in the second, they knew Jesus in a real sense, and perhaps knew him far better than a sophisticated contemporary scholar who has good reasons for believing that she has uncovered the earliest set of sayings or actions by Jesus.[5]

The nontrivial reason this situation is true rests, I believe, on the notion that at least some figures invite or demand a response from us; that is, "knowing" them involves such a response. That notion, as we will see, rests on a subtle, and controversial, view of who humans are and how they perceive and think, one that is usually associated with the early Heidegger, and surely appears in Kierkegaard, where Heidegger probably found it. The New Testament scholar who most skillfully utilized the idea, a person closely associated with the early Heidegger in what was at minimum a reciprocal relationship, is Rudolf Bultmann, and I shall often employ features of his approach. I shall call it an "existentialist" approach for the purposes of easy identification (and examine certain features of it later in this paper), but I hope that the label is not too misleading, given the number of ideas that often gather under that term. I am not, needless to say, claiming that Confucius was an "existentialist" but rather that we can productively use an existentialist approach to interpret the *Analects*.[6]

I am, then, treating the *Analects* as if it is a sacred text about a founder. (If such religious language makes one squeamish, I could replace "sacred text" with "classic" and "founder" with "central dramatic persona," but those replacements lose much of significance.) My examination will consider both how that text can be treated historically and read existentially. That is, I will take account of both the probable time and context of the text, but also argue that we today encounter it (or can encounter it) in a way that makes a difference to our present understanding and life.

The approach can be called experimental, but only if "experiment" is used in a nontechnical sense. That is, I make no claim that the experiment is simply replicable and could produce communal agreement from those able to judge. (I further address certain methodological concerns my approach may raise later in this paper.) It is, then, an experiment in the sense of an inquiry that is worth pursuing and may be of help to others, but it must also inevitably have a tentative quality.

III. The Rationale for My Focus on Book 4 of the *Analects*

I shall focus my attention on book 4 of the *Analects* for several reasons, apart from the judgment that it contains valuable ideas. Four is surely an early book and many now think it has good claim to being the earliest book. In fact, a fascinating if controversial argument (to which we will return) has been made that it not only is the earliest book but even contains the most unvarnished report about, or picture of, Confucius.[7] Moreover, the book has, I believe, a structure that is far from evident but that, once seen, enables us to make better sense not only of the individual, seemingly disparate, passages but also of the book's overall message. Finally, the book also has the advantage of being short, and can therefore be treated with some thoroughness. More important, that brevity means my reader can grasp the book with some ease and therefore understand more easily, and check, what I am doing.

The most significant problem, given my project, with a focus on book 4 is that it apparently lacks those religious or "mythic" elements that appear so prominently elsewhere in the *Analects*. In book 3 (which I think is probably another early book[8]), for example, we have a set of reflections on ritual and sacrifice that involves complex ideas about the need when sacrificing to behave as though the spirit is present (for example, 3:12), as well as several astonishing comments attributed to Confucius. One is his statement (3:11) that an understanding of the dì 禘 sacrifices would allow him to deal with everything (or alternatively govern everything) as easily as one puts one's fingers in one's palm (or alternatively have them in one's palm). A second is that offenses against Heaven leave one with nowhere to turn in one's prayers, or perhaps even with no means of expiation (3:13). The mythic quality of such sayings is all too evident, but I will argue that we find statements in book 4 whose religious content is quite as pronounced, if less evident, and whose mythic frame is almost as noteworthy, even if they appear in a considerably more subtle form. Let us, then, turn to book 4 beginning with the argument that it is the earliest book and contains the most accurate picture of the historical Confucius.

I draw this argument from one aspect of the work of E. Bruce Brooks and A. Taeko Brooks, and the results of their work that are especially relevant to us are, in brief, as follows. Book 4 is the earliest unit in the *Analects*, put together (they think likely) in 479 B.C.E., the year of Confucius' death. Section 15 (the "one thread" zhōng/shù section) and section 26 (a statement by Zǐyóu 子游 that is the book's last section) are seen, for solid reasons, as interpolations from a considerably later time and perspective.[9] The rest of the book, the Brookses believe, consists of sayings on separable topics. They think, moreover, that 1–17 (minus 15) represent one consistent older group and 18–25 another. This judgment is one that I find less secure.

Some of the Brookses' reasons for regarding chapters 18–25 as from a later historical stratum are philological. I am not qualified to evaluate these arguments, but I do know that some qualified people think they are not decisive. If the linguistic arguments are not definitive, we must judge whether 18–25 belong together with 1–14 and 16–17 at least in part on the grounds of their content. In other words, do the concepts, themes, and teachings of 18–25 "fit with" the earlier chapters? One aspect of the present paper, then, contributes to this debate, for I offer an explanation of how 18–25 fit in with the earlier chapters.

The Brookses makes a number of other fascinating and important comments, which I will not engage directly here, about both the contents of the book and its relationships to other sections of the *Analects*. Our agreements and disagreements on the former subject will, I think, be clear to those who compare our accounts, and I will not address at any length the latter subject. Most important here, I accept for the purposes of this inquiry the version of the Brookses' argument that would say the following: We have in book 4 a set of writings that, in Bruce Brooks's phrase, "is unique in the work for the relative shortness of its sayings, its near-absence of proper names or other contextual detail, and a certain austere antiquity of language." Moreover, these sayings differ from at least much else in the *Analects* in ways that make it plausible to see much of the remainder as containing, at minimum, different views. Bruce Brooks himself is willing to say, given this, that we can "then assume that LY 4 [*Lún Yǔ* 論語 Book, 4] are real transcribed Confucian sayings, and that all the rest is addenda. That is, LY 4 *alone directly represents the historical Confucius . . .*" (italics in original). (He puts this even more precisely at another place saying that at least the first 17 [minus section 15] of the 26 sections contain, in his words "the only authentic record of the historical Confucius.")[10] I would be more tentative, for reasons noted earlier, and just say that we see at many places in the *Analects* later developments of ideas about who Confucius was and what he taught. They are the understandable products not only of debates in Warring States China but also of those processes that almost always surround the attempt to understand an extremely significant figure and persuade others of one's own understanding of that person's significance.

Starting from the more minimal of the Brookses' plausible historical surmises, I will then interpret Book Four aiming to uncover the picture of Confucius and his teaching that we find in it. One feature of my interpretative procedure will be to show the productivity of the kind of existentialist approach Bultmann uses. A second, closely related one, will be to focus on what I take to be features of the text that are religious both in subject matter and in what they demand from the reader. A third will be to show how the often apparently discrete, or even contradictory, sections of the book can be said to fit together, or be juxtaposed to each other in a way that allows them to illuminate each other. The dangers, perhaps especially with the last, of preparing a Procrustean bed are evident. The reader must decide whether any light is shed, and whether that light, crudely put, comes from the text or the ingenuity, or speculative fancy, of the interpreter.

IV. A Translation of Book 4

For the convenience of readers, a translation follows of the text of book 4 (minus the phrase "The Master said," which comes at the beginning of every chapter in this book except 26). The translation basically follows D. C. Lau's, probably the most widely used translation, but some modifications have been made and the two interpolations are excised but noted. I have included section headings to indicate the major thematic divisions for which I shall argue below.[11]

ON VIRTUE (RÉN 仁)

1. Of neighborhoods virtue is the most beautiful. If one does not choose to dwell in virtue, how could one be wise?

2. One who is not virtuous cannot remain long in straitened circumstances, nor can he remain long in easy circumstances.

The virtuous are attracted to virtue because they feel at home in it. The wise are attracted to virtue because they find it profitable.

3. It is only the virtuous who are capable of loving or hating others.

4. If one fixes one's intention on virtue, one will be free from evil.

5. Wealth and high station are what people desire, but if I could not do so while following the Way (dào 道) I would not remain in them. Poverty and low station are what people dislike, but if I could not do so while following the Way, I would not try to escape from them.

If nobles (jūnzǐ 君子) forsake virtue, how can they make names for themselves? Nobles never desert virtue, not even for as long as it takes to eat a meal. If they hurry and stumble, one may be sure that it is in virtue that they do so.

6. I have never met anyone who finds virtue attractive or a man who finds the absence of virtue repulsive. A man who finds virtue attractive cannot be surpassed. A man who finds the absence of virtue repulsive can, perhaps, be counted as virtuous, for he would not allow what is not virtuous to contaminate his person.

Is there a man who, for the space of a single day, is able to devote all his strength to virtue? I have not come across a man whose strength proves insufficient for the task. There must be such cases of insufficient strength, only I have not come across them.

7. In their errors people are true to their type. Observe the errors and you will know their virtue.

HOW THE VIRTUOUS PERSON DIFFERS FROM OTHERS

8. If one hears about the Way in the morning, one may die in the evening.

9. There is no point in seeking the views of Nobles (shì 士) who, though they fix their intention upon the Way, are ashamed of poor food and poor clothes.

10. In their dealings with the world nobles are not invariably for or against anything. They are on the side of right (yì 義).

11. While nobles take to heart moral force (dé 德), petty people take to heart land. While nobles take to heart sanctions, petty people take to heart favors.

The Virtuous Person and Governing

12. If one is guided by profit in one's actions, one will incur much resentment.

13. If one is able to govern a state by observing the rites and showing deference, what difficulties will one have? If one is unable to govern a state by observing the rites and showing deference, what good are the rites to one?

14. Do not worry because you have no official position. Worry about the manner in which you get a position. Do not worry because no one appreciates your abilities. Seek to be worthy of appreciation.

15. [Interpolation.]

16. The noble understands what is right (yì 義). The petty person understands what is profitable.

17. When you meet people better than yourself, turn your thoughts to becoming their equal. When you meet people who are not as good as you are, look within and examine your own self.

The Virtuous Person and Filial Piety

18. In serving your father and mother you ought to dissuade them from doing wrong in the gentlest way. If you see your advice being ignored, you should not become disobedient but remain reverent (jìng 敬). You should not become resentful even if in so doing you wear yourself out.

19. While your parents are alive, you should not go too far afield in your travels. If you do, your whereabouts should always be known.

20. If, for three years, one makes no changes to one's father's ways, one can be said to be filial (xiào 孝).

21. One should not be ignorant of the age of one's father and mother. It is a matter, on the one hand, for rejoicing and, on the other, for anxiety.

The Virtuous Person in Relation to Words and Actions

22. In antiquity people were loath to speak. This was because they counted it as shameful if their person failed to keep up with their words.

23. It is rare for one to miss the mark through strictness (yuē 約).

24. The noble desires to be halting in speech but quick in action.

Conclusion

25. Moral force (dé 德) never stands alone. It is bound to have neighbors.

26. [Interpolation.]

V. The Structure of Book 4 and What It Tells Us

I will begin my analysis by discussing the book's overall structure, but before doing so let me say something about why I have translated rén 仁 as "virtue" (or related forms like "virtuous" or "virtuousness"). The oft-discussed issue of how best to render this character in the *Analects* is a paper in itself, but the subject's importance in book 4 and in my analysis demands some comment. The quality noted as rén, at least as discussed in book 4, is a general one that is instantiated, or specified, in different ways in different contexts. Always rendering rén as benevolence (as, for example, Lau does) is therefore problematic, because it leads us to think that one instantiation is the whole. The difference we see between the general concept and its specific instantiations, that is, resembles the common distinction we make between "virtue" and "virtues." (This means, for example, that we could justify Legge's seemingly odd translation of rén as "virtuous manners," in the book's first passage, given that the context is the life of community.)[12]

Other possible general terms such as "goodness" (Waley) or "humaneness" (even if seen, as Dawson does, as full human flourishing and not a specific attitude) are, I believe, less helpful than "virtue." Utilizing "good" or "humaneness" involves understanding the complicated philosophical issues that enable one to recognize, and employ, the related but different references of those two terms. In contrast to our often muddled use of these two terms, especially of the term "good," we have both a long tradition and at least some common usage that enables us to work more accurately and easily with the supple relationships between the concepts of virtue and virtues. (Moreover, "good" and "humaneness" are, in fact, virtual synonyms for "virtue" from say a Thomistic perspective.) The choice of virtue seems, then, to be a good one. And this remains true even if other more technical difficulties are present (including two uses in book 4 of a character [dé 德], which is normally translated as "virtue") and if some modern Western notions of virtue ill fit its use in early Chinese thought.[13]

Let me now turn to an examination of book 4's overall structure, sketching out in some detail my view of the contents of and relationships among what I believe are the book's separate sections. This presentation is dense at places, but it can provide both an overview of the whole book and a content for our later discussion of specific points.

Any notion that the book has sections and a structure may seem odd to some people to whom it appears to contain little more than a set of disconnected ideas and aphorisms. (Honestly admitting, incidentally, just how bewildering—that is foreign or alien—we initially find texts like this to be is, I think, extremely important.) But the book manifests, I believe, a distinctive logic as well as a subtle and challenging perspective, if one that becomes apparent only when we examine it closely. Telegraphically put, the book starts with seven sections on virtue's attributes, and then has nine sections on how perfected people manifest virtue in specific situations. It then ends with two sections that test the previous treatments, four passages on filial piety and three on the relationship between words and deeds, and concludes with a single passage that intensifies the opening passage.[14]

The first seven sections all clearly deal with virtue (rén) (only the seventh being a possible exception depending on how, see Lau [p. 234, n. 1], rén is read). These sections enumerate qualities virtue has, the various ways it can be manifested, and how and why people do and do not possess it. The claims made, as we will discuss, are often striking: for example, if you lack this quality you are unable to dwell well either in adversity or in pleasurable circumstances, and only if you have it can you truly either like or dislike people. The most fundamental kind of human activities depend, then, on the possession of virtue.

Sections 8–17 (excising 15) can be seen as one whole but I will, if tentatively, divide it into two related sections with the last five sharpening, and therefore also narrowing, the focus of the first four. That is, sections 8–11 can be said to provide glosses on the previous seven sections because the subject is not just the character of virtue, but how perfected people manifest virtue in several specific situations and differ, either clearly or implicitly, from those who do not. (Section 8 provides, as we will examine in our last section, an especially important gloss on the first seven sections.)

The crucial, general notion in these sections is that a perfected person has a distinctive equanimity born of virtue. In each of the successive sections, that is, the perfected person is depicted as being correctly related to one of the following: the Way (dào 道, in 8 and 9), the right (yì 義, in 10), and moral force (dé 德, in 11). (The presence of such terms as dào, yì, and dé is remarkable, showing the centrality of these concepts even in the earliest surviving dicta of Confucius.) Each of those separate "objects" is connected to the others, but each also has distinctive differences; the way and the right, for instance, relate closely yet differ substantially. Moreover, each commendable state is also described as contrasting with a state with which the virtuous person feels no concern. That is, in each of these successive sections the virtuous person is depicted as being unconcerned with one of the following: death (in 8), bad food and clothes (in 9), dominant conventional opinions (in 10), and special favors or leniency (in 11). It is, I think, striking that these last four states are ones that most ordinary people either fear or pursue. Indeed, taken together, as we will see, they describe much of what motivates such people.

Sections 12–17 (excising 15) specify these states in terms of their social implications, or even more precisely in terms of the activity of helping or hoping to govern. This is most obviously true in the case of 13 and 14, but I submit that it is also true of 12, 16, and 17. Chapters 12 and 16 emphasize the importance of not focussing on profit (lì 利) in one's actions. Although neither passage might seem at first, to our late-twentieth-century sensibilities, to be about governing, Confucius' audience might have seen such connections. Taking part in government was, for ambitious young men in Confucius' era and long after, one way to make a profit (see *Mengzi* 6A10; *Analects* 8:12). In addition, I do not think it is too far-fetched to suggest that (even long before the official rise of the Mohist school) the issue of whether governing should aim at profit (perhaps the profit of society as a whole) was beginning to be discussed (compare *Analects* 13:9; *Mengzi* 1A1).

What about 4:17? In general, Confucius advocates rule by virtue. This makes his political philosophy "meritocratic," and people in any meritocratic system must make evaluative comparisons (however just or unjust they may be) among the members of the meritocracy. That situation presents the constant danger of generating destructive emotions such as jealousy, envy, snobbery, and resentment. The saying in 4:17 can be understood as Confucius' advice about how a virtuous person can channel the emotions generated by comparisons of quality within a political environment in a less invidious and more productive direction.

Sections 12–14 and 16–17 discuss, then, how those who are virtuous or pursue virtue relate to the holding of position, deal either with those people who pursue profit or those people who are superior in worth to them, and understand the commitment involved in attempting to run a society by means of ritual and the deferential attitudes it induces and relies on. The treatment resembles that in the previous sections, but the context is now more specifically the set of issues involved in any active life in a polity, issues such as the character of "public policy," the pursuit of office, and the great variety of people one will necessarily encounter while governing.

Sections 18–21 clearly concern issues about filial piety. These sections may initially seem not to fit at all or to fit only as an even more specific example of how virtue must operate in a particular social situation. I think, however, the topic appears here because it presents an apparent test case of great importance for what has been treated previously. In 18, for instance, we have ideas that seem to query sharply the notion presented in 17 that a person either, with good people attempts to emulate them, or with bad people examines herself. With one's parents, however, a different response is called for: a response characterized by gentle remonstrance or respectful attention. Similarly, the son's need to make no changes in his father's way for three years, the subject of 20, seems to war with the notion in 10 that one is not invariably for or against anything. The actions filial piety demands, then, seem to present important cases in which the virtuous attitudes previously described are qualified or called in question. (Features of it, moreover, also exemplify the notion of ritual's significance and perplexities, the subject of 13.) The question of why these sections appear in the book and what of significance they tell us, including why they must be demythologized, will be returned to in section eleven of this paper, but let us turn to the next segment, 22–24.

These passages, which again may seem not to fit into the book, present yet another "test case," this one centering on how the virtuous person deals with the general relationship of words and actions. This is clearly the topic in the case of 22 and 24, but 23 requires special comment. Admittedly, if we examine the use of the key term in 23, yuē 約 (which I follow Waley in rendering as "strictness";

Lau originally had "the essentials"; Legge gives "The cautious seldom err" for the whole line), we see that it is not typically limited to care in one's use of language. (See, for example, Waley 6:25: "A gentleman who is widely versed in letters and at the same time knows how to submit his learning to the restraints [yuē] of ritual is not likely, I think, to go far wrong.")[15] However, the placement of 23 between two quotations about language suggests some connection with this topic, and we can certainly see how one manifestation of the virtue of "strictness" (or "caution") would be in one's use of language.[16]

The subject of 22–24, presented in an austerely brief fashion, is a very important one especially if we presume three things. First, words involve both what one says to one's self and what one says to others. (Self-deception is as involved as are verbal accounts that range from moderate embellishment to outright hypocrisy; each involves a misleading that can be more and less intentional.) Second, this subject covers the uses and misuses of rhetoric, rhetoric in public and private arenas being seen as, at the same time, both necessary and dangerous. Third, the movements of shame (22) (and perhaps by implication other emotions) are a crucial indication for the virtuous of whether or not an action is appropriate, and language, and by extension intellectual analysis, must recognize that.

Finally, we end (having excised 26) with a statement that rounds off the whole book: The notion that virtue (dé) as moral force never stands alone but always has neighbors both echoes and deepens the opening comment about the wisdom of living in a virtuous neighborhood. Virtuous people do not just seek a virtuous neighborhood, they create one. Indeed, we can now understand why that is true because of the topics treated in the rest of the book; for instance, the examination of what both virtue and ritual are and of the luminous qualities, such as equanimity, that virtuous people possess. This last section, however, also contains (if implicitly) a challenging message for readers: if one does not have neighbors, people drawn to one, then one is not virtuous. The book, that is, ends with yet another way to examine whether one actually possesses virtue.

Book 4 is, then, a whole in which passages group into separable sections and illuminate each other. Moreover, it presents a set of fascinating and important subjects. Let us now turn to a few especially significant ones, beginning with the general treatment of the figure of Confucius and his message, focusing on how what is missing illuminates what is present.

VI. The Significance of What Is Missing in Book 4

The absence of certain features in the treatment in book 4 is striking, given other parts of or motifs in the *Analects* and many normal understandings of it. Reasoning from absences to conclusions about, say, the "historical Confucius" is (for the reasons noted) a most tricky enterprise. But recognizing that absences can also manifest presences is important. In fact, the absence of one quality does not just make clearer the presence of other qualities, it can also enable us to see the whole in a different way.

Book 4 contains, for example, no references to ancient sages or classics, and just one reference to the past: the cryptic reference to the models people of old provide about the relationship of words and deeds. The notion is absent, then, that a key part of Confucius is that he transmits and does not create (7:1), or that he reanimates the past as a teacher (2:11). Closely related to this is the absence of any notion of a formal set of educational practices, a "curriculum" in the widest sense, that ought to be followed. (None of the "five classics" [wǔ jīng 五經], which later became central to Confucian education, are even mentioned.) Perhaps even more important, this also means we see nothing about how Confucius models his own ideas on the people and society of a past time. Absent, then, is the notion that both his authority and the substance of much of what he says arise from what happened in the past, whether because of (in a debate later Confucians will have) the genius of the sages or the presence of an experiment that worked.[17] Related to all of these absences is the lack of statements that contain one familiar kind of religious reference, a reference (however explicitly noted) to the sacred: that is, to a religio-cultural system in the past that was sacred; or to the notion of sacred texts or figures one must turn to; or the notion of personalized sacred forces, like Heaven, that operate or did operate in the world.[18]

Different from, if related to, these absences is the absence of statements about the exalted stature of the figure Confucius. We lack statements, that is, that portray him as an instrument Heaven will use to wake the world, or as a person of whom there has never been greater, or as one who in old age was attuned to Heaven (tiān 天, for example, 9:5, 19:25, 2:4) The simplest explanation of these absences is that most statements in the book are attributed to Confucius; they are not statements by others about him. Nevertheless, the statements attributed to Confucius, on my reading, share the characteristic of presenting someone who reports about the qualities of the virtuous person but who does not directly claim he always manifests them. A prominent instance is section 8's treatment of hearing about the Way and then dying content. An extremely influential tradition of interpretation presumed that Confucius had, of course, heard the Way, but the statement need not lead to that conclusion. (Soothill can even say "To the unprejudiced the Sage would be ennobled and not degraded by interpreting" the statement with a conditional "if.")[19] Perhaps even more striking than that instance are two other sections. The complex picture of the relationship between the love of virtue, strength or motivation toward it, and actualization of it in section 6 appears to include Confucius in its comments about imperfections. Second, the statement in section 7, whatever its notable ambiguities, seems to imply that in all human states vices and virtues are mixed.

None of these sections, or others like them, need imply that those who saw Confucius might differ from Confucius' own judgments about himself, although too large a discrepancy does seem odd. Nor should we deny that these statements can have a rhetorical, teaching function—Jesus, for instance, is reported as saying that those without sin should cast the first stone but he does not then throw a stone. Nevertheless, the distinction between descriptions of a state of perfected virtue and statements that Confucius actually possessed that state remains significant.

One last kind of absence is worth noting: the absence of certain kinds of generalizations. Statements attributed to Confucius describe general attributes of the virtuous and the vicious, or the gentleman and the small man, but they contain no comments about humanity as a whole. (There is one implied exception: humans are those sorts of beings who operate in different ways depending on whether or not they have those qualities called virtues.) What we see, that is, is an attitude toward generalization that has two characteristics. One is a lack of interest in, perhaps a reasoned antagonism to, general theoretical statements of the sort: "all human beings are X." The other is an interest in, and a desire to make, general statements of the sort: "people of this kind are or manifest X." This does not mean more general statements cannot be developed from the spare resources given—and the tradition surely has done so. Nor does it mean some kinds of general statements are not made or implied, the most significant being, perhaps, the statement about hearing the Way. (Even it, however, rests on the capacity to be able to hear about the Way and there is no necessary implication that everyone either has that capacity or the ability to use it.) The book manifests, then, an agnosticism about many theoretical issues that combines with a willingness to make clear, even dramatic and controversial, statements about some characteristics of the virtuous life and its contraries.

These absences tell us much of importance, I think, but I want to turn now to those statements that fill out our grasp of both the figure of Confucius and the message. Before doing so, however, I should say more about the Bultmannian methodology I shall employ in interpreting what Confucius does say. Then I shall try to clarify my approach by contrasting it with some other important methodologies, and by answering some objections that my methodology is likely to provoke.

VII. The Basic Features, for Our Purposes, of an Existentialist Approach

Bultmann employs what I will call an "existentialist" approach for the purposes of easy identification, recognizing that the label can be misleading given the often very questionable ideas that can be gathered under it. One very problematic kind of existentialism (associated with Sartre and one reading of Heidegger), for example, focuses on ungrounded choice and attacks almost all notions of character or virtue. Its philosophic inadequacies are, to my mind, evident, and any application of it to the *Analects* would, I believe, distort the text.[20] Bultmann, and a more accurate reading of at least the early Heidegger, represent another kind of existentialism.

That kind has close connections, I think, with Aquinas, if not with the Thomistic tradition. (Heidegger, it is worth remembering, not only made an intensive study of Aquinas as a student but also tended to exempt him from many of his criticisms of the Western tradition.) Indeed, some of the existentialist ideas most important to us resemble closely Aquinas's ideas, although obviously there is not equivalence and the differences in many areas are very significant. A crucial resemblance for us, for example, is between an existentialist understanding of the conditions and importance of choice, and a Thomistic understanding of intention and the significance of dispositions and rational freedom. These resemblances explain why, at some points, I will utilize certain ideas from Aquinas to help explain the results of an existentialist reading of the *Analects*. Let us turn now, however, to those features of Bultmann's existentialist position that are most significant for our purposes.

Bultmann is probably most famous for his claim that one must demythologize the New Testament, a claim that, as we will see, is considerably more subtle than it might appear to be. Simply put, however, to demythologize is to assume, first, that religious materials contain meanings that can be separated from their original mythic form and, second, that such a separation clarifies either the material's real meaning or the material's only possible contemporary meaning. To demythologize the story of Jesus walking on water, for example, is to claim that water is a mythic representation of chaos and that the story therefore manifests how Jesus overcame the constantly threatening forces of chaos. Similarly, to demythologize Jesus's resurrection is to re-describe it as a story which affirms that the values and power embodied in his life continue to live among people or at least continue to have a claim on them. Such demythologizing assumes that modern people do not, in fact cannot, believe a person either could literally walk on water or arise from the dead, but that those stories contain viable ideas that can be uncovered when we penetrate their mythic form. Such a penetration is necessary because myths objectify the reality of which they speak; they make it a part of the world, make it fall within the subject-object correlation, and therefore make a qualitative distinction a quantitative one.

Put more abstractly, the project of demythologizing manifests the need for a contemporary interpreter to deal constantly with two demands that initially may appear to be incompatible or even only to generate conflict: what I will call the demands of being both *credible* and *appropriate*. To meet the demand of being credible is to formulate ideas from a sacred text in a way that meets the conditions of plausibility found in an experience informed by modern scientific explanation, historical consciousness, and ideas about the rights of all humans. To meet the demands of appropriateness is to formulate those ideas in a way that shows fidelity to, is appropriate to, their meaning as judged by the most basic norms found in the most fundamental forms of the tradition the text manifests. The two demands stand in a dialectical relationship with each other, but, roughly put, credibility rests on theoretical considerations and appropriateness on historical, textual considerations.[21]

Underlying this whole approach is the notion that the encounter with at least some texts and events must involve a specific type of thinking, an *existentiell* not an *existential* understanding, to use the relevant technical terms. An *existential* understanding is a worked out understanding of the ontological structures of existence. An *existentiell* understanding, in contrast, is the type of thinking that is inseparable from one's most immediate understanding of one's self as a person. It is an act of thinking connected with an act of being, an individual's understanding of his or her own way to be what he or she is. A classic example of the difference, which will be important to us later, is the distinction between seeing death as a part of the ontological structure of human life and facing death as a part of your own grasp of who you are.

The thinking involved in an *existentiell* understanding need not be rational in the strictest sense, but it will often resemble closely the kind of thinking involved in the interpretation of a situation or in the explanation to one's self or another of why one did something: for instance, acted generously or thought a quality, generosity, was valuable. Another, crucial feature of our *existentiell* understandings or interpretations is that they are neither completely pre-established nor firm. We have, that is, the capacity to throw significant parts of our life into a new relief, to shift our perspective, to change the framework or horizon within which we interpret things. Moreover, part of our responsibility as humans, if we are to actualize the capacities we have, is to reflect upon our interpretations and to appropriate those we think most adequate. Crucial, then, is a kind of self-reflexiveness whereby we evaluate how and why we interpret as we do and then choose to be formed by some interpretations. Much stands in the way of such reinterpretations, perhaps most notably the hold on us of conventional thinking and the fear of facing what will occur if we question, much less surrender, such thinking. Nevertheless, the possibility is always present because of our capacity to reinterpret the way in which events, notably the "fact" of death, ingress on our settled interpretations. We must, then, recognize the role our interpretations play in our life and also decide about appropriating an interpretation (that is, claiming a life as our life) if we are to flourish.[22]

This kind of approach to understanding or interpretation produces what can be called an intensified version (one that has deep ethical and religious ramifications) of the operations of the hermeneutical circle. The hermeneutical circle, in its most basic form, refers to the way in which readers initially understand a text in terms of their own world but then have their world changed by the text, a process that continues on in a circle of changing understandings for as long as the work remains a challenging object. Any work (in fact almost any situation) can be part of such a hermeneutical circle. Clearly, however, some genres invite or even demand engagement in a way that others do not. Moreover, either the subject matter of some genres or the approach to them can be such that the issues involved in religion and ethics are paramount. In my view, book 4 (and much of the whole *Analects*) exemplifies such a text.[23] Below, I shall examine that book using features of an existentialist approach. First, however, I want to clarify further what my approach is, and what it is not, by contrasting it with features of two other noteworthy recent interpretations.

VIII. General Methodological Issues That Arise from Contrasts with Two Other Interpreters

One aspect of my approach to the *Analects* that may seem quite wrongheaded is my insistence (which I will develop at even greater length in section 9) that Confucius values a kind of reflexive choice that is formed by dispositions and an interpretative perspective. In particular, this feature of my approach will seem mistaken, for very different reasons, from the perspective of both Herbert Fingarette's *Confucius—the Secular as Sacred* and David Hall and Roger Ames' *Thinking Through Confucius*. Their interpretations respond to genuine and important aspects of the *Analects*, but I offer here an alternative way to interpret some features of the *Analects* that motivate each of their readings.[24]

Fingarette, I think, would say that I have *overestimated*, or simply exaggerated, the extent and importance of choice in the *Analects*. He has argued that the proper metaphor for understanding Confucius is "a way without a crossroads." In contrast with a number of modern Western views (most notably for our purposes Sartean existentialism) there is no radical choice among alternative ways of life in Confucius' vision.

Fingarette does, I think, grasp a genuinely important aspect of Confucius' world view—an aspect that is alien to many contemporary understandings. I believe, however, that it is important to see that a kind of choice does play a crucial role for Confucius. Even though a context for choice is presupposed and, more important, even though there is no "crossroads," in the sense of alternative, equally worthwhile paths, one must nevertheless make a genuine *existentiell* choice or commitment to follow the Confucian Way. This is evident even in the very first passage of book 4, in which Confucius remarks, "If one does not *choose* (zé 擇) to dwell in virtue, how could one be wise?" Similarly, Confucius tells us that we must "Fix our intention upon (zhì yú 志於) virtue" (4:4), and "Fix our attention upon the Way" (4:9). For Confucius, then, we must make a reflexive commitment to the Way if we are to genuinely follow it.

In contrast to Fingarette, Hall and Ames would object that I have *underestimated*, or failed to fully appreciate, the extent and significance of choice in Confucius. Confucius, they note, seems to have a flexibility and an unpredictability in his responses that suggest a lack of interest in fixed, unchanging rules. As I suggested earlier, I think this is an accurate and significant feature of the figure of

Confucius (one we see for example in 4:10). Nevertheless, I also think it important to recognize that, even within book 4, we see certain "fixities" of action that a virtuous person must acknowledge, however flexible and creative she may be: a virtuous person will not be guided by considerations of profit, for example, and she will not become resentful when correcting her parents.

The combination of flexibility and stability that, to my mind, characterizes the Confucian understanding of a virtuous person manifests a larger interpretative (and normative) issue. Hall and Ames tend at times to draw a sharp—and it sometimes appears exhaustive—contrast between thinkers who believe in an objective order grounded in transcendent principles (like Plato) and those who believe in "freely creating" values and order (like the contemporary pragmatist Richard Rorty). I think, however, there is a third option, one exemplified by a virtue ethics of the kind found in the Aristotelian (or more specifically Thomistic) tradition. Advocates of this kind of virtue ethics recognize that creativity and flexibility are required in order to successfully navigate a complex and changeable world. They also hold, however, that there are "right" and "wrong" ways to behave in particular, determinate contexts. I suggest, then, that for all of their genuine and important differences, Confucians and Aristotelians are similar in that they each fit within one, roughly similar, kind of virtue ethics.

My comparison of Confucianism and Aristotelianism (and even more, perhaps, my use of existentialist ideas) can raise the more general objection that I am distorting both Confucianism and the *Analects* by reading Western ideas into them. Allow me to make two brief comments about this very significant objection. First, we must, of course, always read a text in the light of *some* concepts, and these must, in some sense, be *our* concepts. We need not read a text in terms of concepts that we actually share, but we can only read a text in terms of concepts that are accessible to us from our perspective. (That fact is, one might say, the import here of the idea of being "credible" that we discussed earlier.)

One may still object, however, that we cannot successfully apply concepts from our own tradition to these texts. Rather, we must interpret the texts in terms of new sets of concepts that we learn from the texts; we must, as it were, acquire a second conceptual language. At its most sophisticated, this objection grows from the recognition, born of serious study, of the diversity of concepts and beliefs among traditions, and of the way in which that diversity informs the character of even what seem to be even the most basic human experiences such as the desires for food or sex. This diversity is genuine, and it often has not been adequately acknowledged. Nevertheless, I submit that human experience has enough in common for there to be nontrivial similarities in certain experiences, concepts and claims, especially (and most important here) on topics such as the virtues.[25]

This is not a claim that can be justified a priori. (But neither, it is important to recognize, can it be *disproven* a priori.) It can only be substantiated on the basis of detailed, extensive comparisons of alternative traditions. Many scholars, including myself, have begun to undertake that comparison. This chapter is, in part, a contribution to that debate, by seeing whether, and to what extent, certain Western vocabularies give us insight into at least book 4 of the *Analects*. My approach certainly may be mistaken. If it is mistaken, it can only be because my conceptual framework does not, for some reason, do justice to the text of the *Analects* in a way that an alternative framework does.

Having presented at least an initial account of the methodological issues, let us now return to the text of book 4. I will start my analysis by examining issues that appear in two brief passages, 3 and 4, and then turn to several larger ideas, found elsewhere in book 4, that respond to the issues those brief passages raise. I end with comments about the role both of filial piety and of facing death in the whole book. There are, or course, many other fascinating issues in book 4: for example, the portrait of the motivation toward virtue and the description of attitudes about virtue in 6, and the relationship of virtues and vices in 7. Dealing with the questions I have chosen to examine, however, allows us to treat much that is central in the book. Moreover, it allows us to illustrate an approach that reflects key features of the one Bultmann uses.

IX. The Exemplary Treatment of Virtue in Two Brief Passages and the Central Issue It Presents

Sections 3 and 4 are to my mind closely related passages that surely are very brief (the content is carried in seventeen characters, including grammatical ones) and may appear to be relatively insignificant. I think, however, they are very illuminating; they show us how much can come from close attention to the text and enable us to begin to probe a central issue in the book. In section three, Confucius says it is only the virtuous person who is able to, or capable of, liking or disliking other people. In section four he says that if people set their heart on virtue, they will be free from, or without, evil.[26]

These two passages are open to various kinds of glosses. One could, for example, focus on how the passages point to the idea that a "purified" dislike, or even anger, characterizes a virtuous person. (Note, for example, Confucius' outrage at the unethical actions of a former disciple: "He is no disciple of mine. You, my young friends, may attack him openly to the beating of drums.")[27] This idea seems close to notions in the Thomistic tradition about how anger can, even must, serve justice by giving to it the motivation it may lack. I want here, however, to concentrate on a larger and more illuminating issue, one that leads us into some crucial questions about the perspective seen in book 4.

Section 3 parallels the notion in the preceding section (to which we will return) that virtuousness alone allows one to be satisfied, to dwell for a long time, in the apparently opposed states of pleasure and adversity. The claim in section 3, however, is an even more dramatic one about what virtue allows. Liking and disliking, or love and hate, are two of the most fundamental states or movements that characterize humans. (Indeed, if disinterest is added, these three could even be called the most fundamental states.) Love and hate, then, surely appear to be constantly present in human life, but the claim here is that what appears to be love and hate are either not them at all or are just semblances of them. That is, the claim is that only virtue allows one to manifest love and hate in their full or real state.

Interpreted through an existentialist interpretative framework, the point is that what appears as liking and disliking in most people is nothing more than the reflex-like reactions of conventional understanding. (That state is one the later tradition, and one section of the *Analects*, will label the world of the village honest man [xiāng yuán 鄉原] [17:11; compare the more elaborate discussion in *Mengzi* 7B37] and existentialists will call the world of *Das Man*.) These reactions do not arise from any fully appropriated understanding. Rather they arise from, are the epiphenomena of, those conventional attitudes possessed unreflectively by all people insofar as they are part of a society. Moreover, their origin in unappropriated conventional understanding means they finally are of little worth. Even actions and attitudes that appear to be good, such as my inclinations to like justice or a just person and to dislike their contraries, can be of little or no value if they neither express my reflexively appropriated character nor manifest a view of the world that has been fully accepted.[28]

The point here can be put in a more neutral (or at least more traditional) way; that is, we can say that "intentions" are all important, as are those qualities of character from which genuine intentions arise. Seen from this perspective, the next passage, 4, generalizes the message seen in 3. It moves beyond, that is, the specifics of liking and disliking, to claim in the most general terms that if one's heart is set on virtue, one will be without evil. This dramatic claim echoes, despite the difference in the virtues noted, what we also see in 10: the idea that the perfected person is not invariably for or against anything (or alternatively has no antagonisms or enmities, or favoritisms or affections) but is always on the side of the "right" (yì). These passages taken together seem to reflect a world that, in the West, is associated with Abelard or those thinkers who took as their "motto" Augustine's famous notion that one should love and do what one will. They could even be said to reflect the world of that problematic kind of existentialism, associated with Sartre, that I noted earlier.

Nevertheless, other passages in the book present us with classes of action that seem always to show one's lack of virtue, whether they be, say, caring about bad clothes and bad food, 9, or being unfilial, 18–21, or not having acts follow words, 22, 24. The idea that some classes of action are vicious has, of course, its own Western analogs, whether in Aquinas's developments of Abelard and Augustine's ideas, or in those existentialists, like Bultmann, who believe for both ethical and intellectual reasons that choice must presuppose fixed supports like character. The issue or perhaps better conundrum is one, then, that reverberates through many traditions, whether they be Confucian, Christian, or existentialist.

Let us, however, place the issue squarely in the context of book 4. The question there is whether the position seen in the book is that only intentions are crucial (and perhaps also a most minimal class of actions such as the gratuitous injury of the innocent), or whether the position is that intentions are crucial but that the virtuous person always fulfills the demands presented by some significant classes of actions. If the latter is true (the most likely position to my mind, as we will see), what is significant is not the mere setting of an intention, to use the formulation in 4, but also the character of the intention that is set. Seen this way, on the one hand, the book emphasizes the need to appropriate, to choose, certain attitudes and actions in the belief that they direct one toward virtue. But, on the other hand, it also accepts the notion that virtuous humans have qualities (and probably relationships), whatever their origins, that entail some acts and attitudes that will never be chosen and others that will always be chosen.

The ramifications of this issue, much less a clear-cut answer of it, are surely not fully treated in book 4, nor arguably in the whole of the Analects. One might, however, argue book 4's "incompleteness" or "ambiguity" is commendable, given the significance and the complexity of the problem, as well as the tendency of people to focus too exclusively on either "intention" or "conventionally sanctioned action." That is, we could say the pursuit of resolutions in an area like this is far less important than the recognition that one faces what I would call "irresolvable but revelatory and productive" tensions. These tensions arise from two different but related ideas that stand as the irreducible givens on which reflection works. Both sides of the tension must be upheld and therefore any resolution that even diminishes either side must be rejected. Indeed, a final resolution need not even always be sought because seeing both sides is revelatory and productive. Keeping the tension's irresolvability in mind can enable people to better understand reflection's character and clarify their relationship to ethical and religious realities.[29]

That situation does not mean, however, that the issue cannot be approached. In fact, I think we find a set of oblique responses to it in Book Four and examining them leads us into some of the book's central claims. Examples which we will treat include the idea of expressive virtue, the rationale for the apparent indeterminacy of virtuous action, the significance of filial piety, and the understanding of death. Let us then turn to those topics.

X. Central Claims in Book 4 That Reflect the Issues Seen in These Passages: Expressive Virtues and the Indeterminacy of Virtuous Action

One quality that virtuous actions must have in book 4's account of them is to be "expressive." This quality, which arises from correct intention, is probably manifested most clearly in section 2 (to which we will return), and represents, I believe, one of the most crucial notions in the book. To explain what I mean by "expressiveness," however, let me begin by explicating the relevant conceptual framework, one which is drawn from Thomistic virtue theory but has clear analogs in existentialism.

Virtuous behavior, it is argued, has not only acquisitive but also expressive motives. People choose a virtuous action not only because it contributes to goods they want to acquire but also because it expresses their conception of the good. The essential feature of the idea of expressive virtue, then, is the response it contains to one basic question: Why might, or even should, people pursue an activity if they have severe doubts that it will have the kind of effects in the world that they hope it will? The answer is that the best kind of life simply demands such activity. This does not mean such choices are made recklessly, indeed they must be well considered if they are to be fully expressive. Nevertheless, the crucial motivating force is not the good benefits received or given but the good expressed.

Put in the terminology of existentialism, a person appropriates or chooses a way of life (and, thus, a set of personal qualities) that, for her or him, defines the good life and thereby constitutes flourishing. The outline of that way of life might appear to stay stable over time. But the need to reaffirm it, to appropriate it as one's own, remains a continuing demand, and often one whose form changes as circumstances change. That reaffirmation, moreover, will always rest on the good that is expressed, not on the benefits that will or could be produced. Central, then, to the appropriate motivation of truly virtuous action is the desire to manifest or express a valued state. In fact, it is the desire to express this state that makes merely prudential pursuers of virtue doubt the sanity of (to appeal to a Platonic picture) those mad lovers of virtue who aim to express a virtue. This mad love and its apparent imprudence is the critical defining mark of expressive virtues, and we see striking resemblances to it in certain formulations in the *Analects*.[30]

The distinction between acquisitive and expressive virtues is not, however, explicitly employed in book 4 or even in the early Confucian tradition. Indeed, the formulations of Confucian thinkers usually reflect the language of acquisitive virtue; they write in terms of the goods that virtues can produce; they defend them in terms of their beneficial effects on both the world and the agent. (Interestingly enough, such acquisitive formulations are less evident in book 4—or at least are more obviously in tension with other formulations.) Nevertheless, Confucians also speak of how a person can choose an action or way of life because it expresses that person's conception of what is good, and these formulations not only are central to book 4 but also generate one of the most cogent defenses of the ideas found there.

The passage in book 4 that most clearly manifests this distinction is section 2. The placement is propitious because if we bring together sections 1 and 2 we have an opening passage that announces the most challenging general themes in the book: virtue's expressive character and relationships to the general community and the different kinds of people who live in it.

The key notion in section 2 is the idea that the virtuous rest content with virtue, or rest in it, or are at home with it. That situation is juxtaposed with the wise who seek virtue because they derive advantage from it, believe it pays to do so, or find it to their advantage. That is, the wise seek virtue for acquisitive reasons. Their attitude finds its justification in the comment that starts the passage: the notion that people cannot well, or for long, endure either adversity or ease without virtues. Believing that to be true, a wise person would of course seek virtue, but the guiding rationale (even if it might justifiably start a person's pursuit of virtue) differs most significantly from the rationale of someone who finds contentment in virtue. The latter embrace fully the state virtue represents, have no purpose beyond possessing it, and therefore want also to express it.[31]

This passage puts, then, with particular succinctness, clarity, and even poignancy, an idea versions of which appear throughout the book: expressive virtue differs fundamentally from acquisitive virtue and that distinction helps us understand the characteristics of different kinds of people. The lowest levels of people (small people or lesser people) will have virtually no understanding of expressive virtue and will only pursue profit (16), or what is conventionally believed to be beneficial, even if they recognize that this pursuit will generate resentment (12). Higher levels of people, categorized as the wise, will pursue virtue, but because they recognize it is to their advantage to do so (2, and perhaps 14). What distinguishes the virtuous, however, is that they seek virtue as an end in itself, a goal that needs no further justification (2, 5, 14, 16). Moreover, they understand that, in fact, virtue may not produce some benefits, such as position and good food (9, 14), but that finally those benefits do not provide them with fully adequate goals and may even need to be surrendered.[32]

The idea that the truly virtuous dwell in virtue and express it also helps to explain the apparent indeterminacy of the perfected person's actions, the idea noted earlier that a kind of unpredictability defines virtuous people's actions. There are two different, if closely related, ways to understand that unpredictability, and grasping each is important if we are to understand the portrait of the truly virtuous and, implicitly, of Confucius himself. The first concerns a defining characteristic of the virtues or more accurately of the dispositions that underlie them, and a distinction among kinds of dispositions that appears in Thomistic virtue theory but has clear analogs in existentialism is helpful. In that theory virtues are basically dispositions, but only a few, such as the disposition to be punctual, will always manifest themselves in just one kind of action: e.g., arriving on time. Most characteristically human dispositions, such as the disposition to be courageous, will manifest themselves in often substantially different ways depending on the circumstances in which they are exercised and the peculiar mix of dispositions within the agent: that is, the courageous person can stand firm or can flee.

The concern in book 4 is with this second kind of disposition, even if the text lacks the theoretical framework that allows one to pinpoint it abstractly. (It is worth emphasizing again that when we consider the understanding of virtues in book 4 we are dealing with dispositions, not specific, discrete acts or states.) With this second kind of disposition, specific actions are much less important than is the presence of the needed disposition, and the actions produced may not even seem, especially to the untutored eye, to manifest the disposition's basic character. The character of these dispositions differs greatly, then, from the invariant reactions seen in the first kind of dispositions because subtle kinds of thinking inform their activation. To use existentialist terminology, the activity of these dispositions, is guided by interpretations that are reflexively appropriated. The continuing openness and necessary indeterminacy of those interpretations along with the complexity of the activity of appropriation produces, inevitably, a kind of unpredictability.[33]

These features, when seen from another perspective, also inform the second reason for the unpredictability of the virtuous. Virtuous people do not pursue the obvious goals, do not follow the predictable lines of action, that other people do. The difference from "small people" is most striking. That is, the virtuous do not pursue what seems to be profitable, such as a good position and its accoutrements, to a conventional mind. Put in the existentialist terminology we used in treating the subject of ordinary people's lives and dislikes, small people simply reflect the conventional understanding of the general society.

Even the wise will, however, find odd some actions of the virtuous. This occurs especially at those places where the expression of virtue and the advantageousness of virtue come into conflict, and the clearest examples are situations where virtuous behavior seems likely to bring great harm or even death. Myriad less dramatic circumstances also occur, however, as when a teacher forgoes time with her students because of narrowly defined demands of professional achievement. This distinction between the wise and the virtuous is extremely important, and it may be part of what underlies book 4's statements about words and deeds (in 22, 24, and perhaps 23). That is, the wise, unlike the virtuous, can fail to do what they say they will do for two reasons. They either lack full understanding of the demands of expressing virtue or find they cannot express it, that is reflexively appropriate it, when serious adverse consequences might result.

This second explanation for the unpredictability of the virtuous has implications that are far more dramatic than those that follow from the first. It can open up, for example, a gap between ordinary understanding, even the refined kind of ordinary understanding the wise possess, and the understanding and actions of the truly virtuous. Nevertheless, as a Thomistic or existentialist perspective makes clear, this does not necessarily mean that the virtuous must act in ways that differ radically from ordinary people. Rather it means they approach what they do and who they are from a perspective that differs from what is found in ordinary people. (Aquinas and Bultmann, for example, often focus on Paul's statement that one must be "in but not of" the world to underline that point.) This situation helps to explain, I believe, the apparently discordant presence of the passages on filial piety in book 4.

XI. The Issue of Filial Piety in Book 4: The Role of Origins

The passages on filial piety appear to present what I called earlier a "test case." That is, sections 18–21 apparently test what has been presented previously because the actions and attitudes they require differ from those earlier passages have commended. For example, one is not (as in 17) to emulate good people and with bad people examine oneself, but only to remonstrate gently with one's parents (18), and one surely seems called on to manifest some invariable responses (20 versus 10). (Indeed, the claim in 20 that filiality demands leaving unchanged one's father's way for three years recalls the strictures of 1:11, a text that became authoritative for those later people who propounded a stringent, even oppressive view of filial piety.) The situation we see here is a concrete instance of a much more general issue: it reflects in microcosm the question we discussed earlier about the relationship of the claim that intention is the basic value and the claim that some classes of activity are always virtuous or vicious. The rationale provided for filial piety, then, has implications that extend considerably beyond the limited case it presents, and to that rationale we may now turn.[34]

Before doing so, however, we need to consider an alternative explanation for the presence of these texts. One might argue that filial piety was so deeply ingrained a cultural practice in Confucius' China that no thinker could imagine it needed to be rationalized, or even see it as a phenomenon susceptible to deliberative activity.[35] (Its apparently discordant presence in book 4 could even then be taken as further evidence that it was seen as a "natural fact.") If approached this way, filial piety exemplifies what can be called the fallacy of false fixity, the idea that crucial features of the self and its relationships are part of the nature of things. Such false fixities can be seen, in retrospect, to be social myths that protected particular ways of life, but to the participants in a culture they represent fixed features that cannot be other than they are and therefore they set the limits on human deliberation. No sensible people attempts, that is, to deliberate about them; one thinks in terms of them, one does not think about them. Such an explanation for the presence of these texts is, I believe, a possible one, but I think another explanation is more productive. It focuses on filial piety as not only describing a very special class of action, but also as a notion that demands demythologizing.[36]

Filial piety concerns the service in action and attitude owed to parents. It presents, I believe, a unique case of human activity, one that must involve ritual practice and always have mythic overtones. The rationale for filial actions is, then, far from exhausted by simple notions of ethical obligation; indeed it can even be corrupted by them. Let me explain, recognizing that my explanation moves considerably beyond what is clearly evident in book 4 (or even in the *Analects*) and also involves us in the project of demythologizing. Such an interpretative move is needed, however, if we are to provide an adequate, alternative explanation of why these passages appear here. Even more important, that explanation leads us to certain of the most basic religious motifs in the book: the focus here on the topic of "origins" and the focus in the next section, when we treat death, on the topic of "terminations" or endings.

Both motifs deal with the reactions human beings have when they inhabit liminal states, when they face "thresholds," that will engender significant changes in their situation. Such changes are of two kinds. Either people move from one to another state, from being, say, a child who is cared for by a parent to being a child who must care for a parent. Or people respond to events that radically differ from and challenge their ordinary routine, events such as the death of a family member. The most important of these transitional states usually concern origins or terminations. They manifest, that is, what makes possible or ends human life. They force people to encounter the sustaining and destroying boundaries of life.

At the core of the unique case of filial piety, then, is the notion that human life has various origins or sources. Probably the clearest of these sources is parents who both are a biological origin and represent that basic unit, the family, which provides the social organism that generates human beings. Parents provide, then, the fundamental sources and relationships upon which people build and from which they move. (Thus, Mencius would describe one's love for one's parents as the "one root" [yī běn 一本] of human ethics, and criticize those who sought to supplement this root in a way that he felt undermined its fundamental importance.)[37] People respond strongly to such an origin because they recognize that with it unpayable debts have been incurred. In most relationships, that is, people receive and give in a fashion that allows for repayment; equity can be restored. In these relationships, however, people receive so much that there is no way for them to repay what has been given. When debts exist that cannot be repaid, the only appropriate response is gratitude, reverence, and a set of related reactions.

The recognition of such a debt also, however, unleashes other psychological forces because it illuminates our fundamental dependence, and thus our frailty. We must, if we are to flourish, find ways properly to express the emotions that result from this grasping of our frailty, because failures to do so make us fall prey to one or another human deformation. They lead us, that is, to fall under the dark shadow cast by the crippling attitudes of masochistic religion or the uncontrolled reactions of primordial movements.[38]

The practices that constitute filial piety are designed to protect us from these deformations. Those practices, unsurprisingly, have significant ritual forms, and they in turn draw on mythic bases. (A classic mythic defense of the ritualistic three-year mourning period appears, for example, in 17:19.) Filial piety, then, enables people to deal well with a situation constituted by both the presence of unpayable debts and the recognition of human frailty and dependence.

Moreover, the proper attitudes and actions toward parents that constitute filial piety underlie any kind of virtuous activity. They provide people, that is, with both the protective structures and the frameworks (both ritualistic and mythic) that make other kinds of virtuous activity possible. They also provide us with a locale where expressive virtues can operate, where the expression of states like reverence (jìng 敬) is central enough that it makes no sense to speak only of the operation of acquisitive virtues.

We can, of course, question the truthfulness of the many claims contained in the set of ideas that make so important our relationship with the origin that is our parents. Most important here, however, is another issue. Those ideas, after being demythologized, do provide a rationale for why people must follow the activities prescribed by filial piety, and that in turn explains why these sections appear in book 4. That rationale rests on the significance of origins; let us now turn to its opposite, endings or terminations, a topic that appears in the treatment of death in section 8.

XII. The Issue of Facing Death in Book 4: The Role of Endings

Section 8 comes immediately after the seven opening sections on virtue. This position lends, I think, a special weight to the passage; it might even be said to provide the necessary bridge between those opening sections and the topics the remainder of the book covers. The section is brief and spare, by even the high standards book 4 sets (nine characters, including grammatical ones), and any interpretation must grapple with the lack of any scholarly consensus on the question of whether a sophisticated person in Confucius' time would or would not assume that biological death also meant the end either of consciousness or of life in any meaningful sense. Nevertheless, the general sense seems relatively clear: To hear about the dào in the morning leads one to be able to face death in the evening with an attitude that can be described in related but different ways: contentment, or acceptance, or a lack of regret, or a not minding of it, or a knowing that it is all right to die, or perhaps more problematic, a knowing that you have not lived in vain.[39]

With a hesitancy born of the subject's weight, our ignorance, and the line's terseness and placement, I would suggest the following understanding of how it fits into and illuminates the general picture that book 4 presents. My interpretation, which admittedly is speculative, draws on how the idea of death functions in existentialism. I will begin by examining that complicated topic, only mentioning here that there are, again, clear links with a Thomistic perspective.

Existentialists make, as noted earlier, a fundamental distinction between seeing death as a part of the ontological structure of human life and facing death as a part of your own grasp of who you are. Most important to us is their focus on the latter. That is, they argue that truly facing death involves coming to terms with the apparently broken, often fragmentary character of human life and with the fundamental human need to achieve "recognition" (Anerkennung)—to be seen by others as having integrity. Facing death, then, ingresses on how we understand both our projects—our achievements and aspirations—and those recognitions that give our life meaning. This ingression occurs differently depending on whether we face death in its narrowest sense or in its more extended senses. The narrowest sense is the apparent end of the actual physical presence of my self and of the selves that I love most, those people whose recognition I most treasure. The extended sense is the apparent end of those ideas and practices that give meaning to my life. The two senses differ, but both arise from a single source: those experiences in which we directly face the frailty of all we treasure, of all that gives significance to our lives and generates recognition in it.[40]

Such a direct facing of frailty is, for existentialists, especially significant because people's "horizons," their general perspective, determine specific interpretations and thus also form most attitudes and actions. People's perceptions of the salient characteristics of events and people's reactions to them, that is, control people's attitudes and actions, and the former (the perceptions and reactions) are controlled by the framework within which people place those events. A horizon, then, is the general framework that controls the character of perceptions of and reactions to specific events.

Most important here, existentialists also claim that people's normal horizon does not highlight, or often even include, the notion of death. People understand, of course, that they and others will die. (It is relevant, given our earlier treatment of filial piety, that such an understanding is often triggered by another's death, especially if the deceased is a parent, a protective barrier between oneself and one's own mortality.) But they see death only as part of the ontological structure of human life and that understanding has not been grasped in a way that would change their horizon. They have not an *existentiell* but only an *existential* understanding. They have not, in that apparently odd existentialist locution, "chosen to die."

When and if people do truly face death, changes in their horizon are produced, and those changes will, in turn, affect how they see and react to a multitude of specific occurrences. Indeed, the effect will often be especially pronounced when less is at stake—and therefore little conscious reflection occurs—than when more is at stake. The change in horizon can be debilitating, even destructive, or it can be freeing and constructive; it can produce a distorted life or a more flourishing one.

The destructive reactions will all be variations of an unalloyed fear of annihilation or of its surrogate, separation from what we love and honor. What formerly was overlooked, seen as neutral, or thought to be easily surmountable can become, for example, a troubling, even terrifying event. Even more important here, we can begin to doubt the significance of those projects and recognitions that bring meaning to our life. The fear of destruction can, then, generate responses that range from retreat into a self-enclosed world to the submission to external forces that are seen as producing meaning, whether they be those provided by the conventional world of understanding and aspiration or those found in other, far more dangerous kinds of authoritative systems. In each of these responses, we surrender much of what seems valuable in order to preserve an enduring presence. Therefore, each of them also corrupts what is necessary to pursue and actualize virtue.

A change in horizon can also, however, produce an understanding that enables us to live in a new more actualized way; to live, in that often misused existentialist phrase, "a more authentic life." We can, that is, see the frailty of our projects, understand the contingency of what brings recognition, and yet still pursue them because of what they do contain. We can overcome, then, fears of annihilation or its surrogates, fears that generate responses in which we surrender much that is good in order to preserve an illusory but appealing enduring presence. We fully embrace, to use our earlier terminology, the demand to see true virtue as expressive. Moreover, we realize that only such an understanding can provide the proper motivation for virtuous action. Indeed, to face death truly is to see that any form of acquisitive virtue may fail to bring temporary satisfaction and surely will bring no ultimate satisfaction.

This kind of existentialist perspective allows us, I think, to grasp what is at stake in section 8 of book 4 and to see why that passage can serve as a bridge between the opening section's treatments of virtue and the contents of the remainder of the book. The passage itself has features that make it more like a myth than a propositional statement. It has, for example, the narrative form so characteristic of myths: an event at one time, in the morning, leads to a resolution at another time, in the evening. Moreover, the process occurs in a circumstance, a classically mythic "timeless time," that is both removed from ordinary processes and yet also fundamentally relevant to them. Finally, the narrative concerns someone who is an "every person," or better, an "any person," a paradigmatic figure whose specific characteristics are far less significant than is the figure's general import.

I am, in fact, tempted to say that the passage presents a demythologized account of a much more elaborate myth, an account that I in turn will demythologize yet again. Whatever the truth in that idea, the passage clearly says that hearing about the dào (which I take to be grasping its significance) allows us both to face death and to be content about it. The dào, then, is something that, at minimum, relates positively to that idea of virtue the first seven sections have described and the remainder of the book will turn over in different contexts. (Only if the dào were hostile to, or negatively related to the virtuous life would such a validation be missing.) Hearing the dào and facing death, that is, generate the kind of confidence that enables virtuous people both to see clearly the frailty of what they are about, those practices that generate recognition, and yet also to continue to embrace the significance they do have. Virtuous people can, with this understanding, live fully from expressive, not acquisitive, virtue. They can be fully engaged "in" the world and yet not be "of it" because they grasp the world's contingent, and thus problematic character, and yet also grasp the significance both of virtue and of the pursuit of virtue.[41]

This kind of understanding of death and the *dào*, then, undergirds the virtuous person's character and aspirations. It validates the necessarily contingent but still completely satisfying character of the virtuous life. Moreover, understanding that character both allows virtuous people to possess in full measure the qualities they have and gives them the ethical force that means, as the book's end has it, they will neither be alone nor without beneficial influence. The treatment of the relationship between hearing the *dào* and being content with death, then, concludes in most fitting fashion the initial treatment of virtue and points ahead to the full treatment of the subject that book 4 provides. Or at least that seems to be the result of working through my proposal to present an existentialist reading of what may be the earliest book in the *Analects*.

ACKNOWLEDGMENTS

I am indebted to Thornton "Jack" Kline for insightful and extensive comments on an earlier draft of this paper, as well as to the editor of this volume; his aid far exceeded what the role demanded of him.

NOTES

Citations of the *Analects* in this essay follow the sectioning in the Harvard-Yenching concordance, unless otherwise noted. Complete citations for translations referenced in this essay may be found on p. 29, or in the Annotated Bibliography at the end of this volume.

1. For examples of approaches that focus on particular passages, see the essays by P. J. Ivanhoe, "Whose Confucius? Which *Analects*? (on 5:13), Bryan W. Van Norden, "Unweaving the 'One Thread' of *Analects* 4:15," and Bruce Brooks and Taeko Brooks, "Word Philology and Text Philology in *Analects* 9:1," all in this volume.

2. Literary style in evocative sections like this one is, I believe, important because we are not just dealing with the shadowgraphs of ideas; see Yearley, 1999, pp. 145–49. This is one reason, among others, why Waley's translation is always worth consulting. On this passage for example, Lau's rendition is: "Only when the cold season comes is the point brought home that the pine and the cypress are the last to lose their leaves."

The importance of style helps explain, incidentally, why consulting Ezra Pound's version can be worthwhile, despite the fact that its connection with the Chinese is so slight in many cases that it cannot be taken seriously. In other cases, however, we see the hand of both one of the century's great poets, and one of its most thoughtful and reflective translators of, say, Italian texts. An example is 4:12: Dawson's translation is solid and clear, "If one acts with a view to profit, there will be much resentment." But here is Pound's: "Always on the make: many complaints." In discussing matters like this I do not, I should stress, speak with the particular kind of authority that comes from having real expertise in classical Chinese.

3. See Yearley, 1999, pp. 127–33, 149–53, for a lengthy treatment of certain facets of this notion.

4. For an excellent treatment of the current scholarly situation in regard to historical treatments of the figure of Jesus, see Sanders; for a fine analysis of the development of modern biblical criticism see Harvey; for a fascinating work that queries the whole idea of a historical understanding of the Bible, see Frei.

In these footnotes I will, as in the preceding paragraph, refer to a few significant works on subjects outside Chinese thought to give guidance to those people who might wish to evaluate the possible usefulness of those works to the treatment of topics within Chinese thought. I will also (if with trepidation) refer extensively to my own work because it contains analyses that may be helpful to readers who either want to evaluate my more telegraphic comments or to see which scholars I rely on. I make, however, few references to other works that deal with the *Analects*, and therefore do not attempt really to enter the often heated debates that surround the interpretation of the book.

5. A second comparison may also illustrate my point. Compare two twentieth-century translations of Dante's *Inferno*: one by the poet Robert Pinsky, the other by Charles Singleton. Singleton is without question the finer Dante scholar, but one can at places get a better sense for what Dante is about from Pinsky's translation. That poetry is being translated in Dante's case, to my mind, makes the comparison more, not less, relevant.

6. Questions about the exact sources of Heidegger's work and the character of his relationship with Bultmann are, it needs to be said, much debated, as is the question of how the early and the late Heidegger differ.

Let me also note that the account given here also uses neo-Aristotelian, or more accurately Thomistic, ideas. As we will see, (see, e.g., sections VII, IX, and X, as well as notes 20, 22, and 40) I believe some of those ideas also "parallel" crucial aspects of the kind of existentialist approach I will use despite the noteworthy differences between the two approaches. The most sophisticated theoretical attempt to relate these two traditions appears in the work of Karl Rahner, a Roman Catholic theologian who was deeply influenced by Heidegger; see Rahner and see Yearley, 1970.

7. See Brooks, especially pp. 31–40, and Brooks and Brooks, pp. 13–18, 114–15, 149, 202–3, and 208–9. The Brookess' work concerns, it needs to be said, far more than just book 4 or even the *Analects*. I make no attempt here to query the exact philological or historical grounds on which the Brookses base their argument, having neither the inclination nor, in almost all cases, the expertise to do so. Nevertheless, until shown otherwise, I think the general direction of those philological and historical arguments is sound, whatever problems may arise with the details of the account.

8. The Brookses disagree, suggesting that book 3 is later even than book 10. The issues involved in our differences are too complex to examine here, but let me note that I think their dating is based in part on an assumption I do not share about the incompatibility of a focus on ritual with some aspects of the earlier *Analects*. (For more on how ritual and, say, self-cultivation might be reconciled, see Kwong-loi Shun, "*Ren* and *Li* in the *Analects*," in this volume.) The issue of whether statements about ritual can, or should be, demythologized is also relevant.

9. See, again, Van Norden, in this volume, on 4:15.

10. The first two quotes are from Brooks, p. 31, the last from p. 34.

11. The editor's aid was very substantial in considering modifications to Lau, but he is not, of course, responsible for my interpretations. Let me emphasize that this translation is for the reader's convenience and almost no attempt is made here to consider the range of questions that a more definitive translation would have to consider. (A few of those issues are treated at more length elsewhere in this chapter, for examples see notes 26 and 39.) For that reason specific issues and possible alternative are not noted; e.g., at the end of the third sentence in 4.5, also possible is "how can they live up to the name [of 'noble']?"

12. A brief note on what I mean by virtue, given how significant the idea is here and in what follows. (For more detailed discussions of the idea of virtue, see Yearley, 1990a, especially pp. 6–17, 53–58; Nivison, "'Virtue' in Bone and Bronze," in Nivison, 1996,

pp. 17–30; also note Yearley 1990b, 1993b, and 1994a and b.) A virtue is a disposition to act, desire, and feel that involves the exercise of judgment. The judgments may not be clearly present to my consciousness, much less the result of sustained reflection. At minimum, I must be able to explain (at some point, in some fashion) to myself or another person why I did something; e.g. why I was generous. This requirement may seem too "intellectualistic," but the sort of account or explanation that I have in mind need not be highly theoretical. For example: "Why did you loan your friend Susan $20?" "She is a graduate student with kids on a tight budget, and although she's generally prudent with money, some unexpected expenses made her a little short this week, so. . . ." "But then why did you *refuse* to loan $20 to your friend Bill?" "Bill is a compulsive gambler who has fallen off the wagon, so. . . ." That virtuous individuals were expected (at least soon after Confucius) to give explanations for their (or other virtuous people's) actions is clear from texts like *Analects* 11:20 and most of book 5 of the *Mencius*.

Virtuous activity also involves choosing virtue for itself. I possess not the virtue of generosity, but a semblance—or even counterfeit—if I act because of some ulterior motive such as helping specific people so they will think well of me. Finally, virtuous activity involves choosing specific virtues in light of some justifiable life plan. I believe, for instance, the best kind of human life involves generosity, not selfishness. I have, that is, a general view, and good reasons for it, that lead me to think that kind of life is better than one that lacks generosity.

13. The character *dé* 德 "virtue" is used in 4:11 and 4:25, but arguably in these cases something like Waley's moral force is appropriate. (As Waley correctly notes *dé* often corresponds closely to the Latin *virtus*; 33; and see Yearley, 1990a, pp. 53–57, and David S. Nivison, "'Virtue' in Bone and Bronze," in Nivison, 1996, pp. 17–30, on this whole subject.) A very different kind of difficulty is that the word "virtue" for many today either has very narrow connotations or generates understandable suspicions because it often seems to function as the rhetorical adjunct to one or another dubious political agenda. A sophisticated understanding of the concept does not, however, have such references. (Moreover, there is no reason not to pair "vice" with "virtue" [given a sophisticated understanding of vice] save for the resonances the word has for some people.) On the issue of the different but related meanings of the good see the two pieces by Hampshire; on the question of the relationship of the concepts of virtue and virtues and related issues see Yearley 1990a, pp. 11–17, 40–44, 182–87.

14. There is general agreement that sections 1–7 of book 4 deal with *rén* (but see Lau, p. 228 and p. 234, n. 1, on 4:7), and that 18–21 deal with filial piety (*xiao*). Beyond that, however, there is disagreement, even among those who think that book 4 has significant internal structure. Lau remarks (p. 228) that "IV.8 and IV.9 deal with the Way, IV.10 to IV.17 deal with the gentleman and the small man . . . while the last few chapters [22–26] seem to deal with the way the gentleman should conduct himself."

Brooks and Brooks (p. 209) think the book is divided into discussions of "The Cardinal Virtue [Rén]," 1–7; "The Public Context: [Dào]," 8–10; "The Gentleman and His Opposite," 11–13; "Preparation for Office," 14–17 (minus the interpolated 15); "Filial Duty," 18–21; "Keeping One's Word," 22–24; and a "Chapter Envoi," 25 (with 26 an interpolation). The Brookses' division is driven, in part, by their hypothesis that sayings in the *Analects* are frequently grouped in pairs, often with a third "capping" quotation that follows the pair (p. 207). I worry that this sometimes leads them to force the sense of a section to fit the pairing schema.

15. On the other hand, *yuē* 約 later (in the Warring States Period) came to have the sense of "oral agreement" or even "contract." (See Lewis, 1990, pp. 67–80.) I wonder whether this later usage suggests a meaning liminally available in even the earlier uses of the term.

16. The Brookses remark of 4:23 that it "contrasts the loose modern practice with the ancient scruple of 4:22" (Brooks and Brooks, p. 115).

17. On debates among later Confucians, see Ivanhoe, 1993.

18. The absence of references to Heaven is striking, and could lead to the supposition, supported by other evidence, that the notion of Heaven is intimately connected with the idea of a past perfected society; on a related topic see Yearley, 1985.

19. Soothill, p. 226; also note Legge's treatment of the differences between Mencius and Confucius on the issue of "humility," discussed in Yearley, 1990a, pp. 85–86. Many modern translations either add the "If" (Dawson) or make the statement more general and impersonal (e.g. Waley, Lau, and interestingly enough, Soothill's actual translation). This passage will be treated at length in our last section.

20. Charles Taylor has been a profound and, I think, decisive critic of this kind of existentialism. See, for example, Taylor, 1991. For critiques of efforts to apply existentialist concepts to other figures from Chinese philosophy, see David S. Nivison, "Moral Decision in Wang Yangming: The Problem of Chinese 'Existentialism,'" in Nivison, 1996, pp. 233–47, and Philip J. Ivanhoe, "'Existentialism' in the School of Wang Yangming," in Ivanhoe, 1996, pp. 250–64.

21. For an excellent treatment of what is involved in the notions of the credible and appropriate see Ogden, 1982, pp, 4–6, 89–105. Yearley, 1995, 1999, and forthcoming treats in a Chinese context issues about "developing" ideas to make them credible. It is worth emphasizing that development might so change the original ideas that a disinterested observer could well wonder what role the traditional ideas played. The ideas might seem to be only a device to jog the interpreters's reflections or, worse, to give them an authority they otherwise would not have.

22. Numerous theoretical questions swirl around this account, of course, but I will just note that Bultmann's use of these ideas does not, I think, suffer from the obvious problems found in almost any reading of the early Heidegger's account, much less in the position of Sartre: e.g., questions about the absolute primacy of choice, the vacuity of the idea of authenticity, the apparent lack of any ethical content, and the absence of even a minimal account of many seemingly evident human qualities. (Rahner, to my mind, presents the most sophisticated theological attempt to treat these problems, but unlike Bultmann he was not a New Testament scholar and his work usually seems forbiding to those untrained in the traditions on which he draws.) The account of "thinking"—and thus of the notions of interpretation, choice, appropriation, and dispositions—are especially important to us, and to those who find existentialist terminology uncongenial or worse, I recommend Hampshire's 1989 account of thinking: he often makes similar points in a very different vocabulary.

For representative works, for our purposes, by Bultmann, see the works cited; note especially, 1960, pp. 58–91, 147–57, 183–225 and 1984, 1–43, 95–130. An accessible and reliable treatment of Bultmann is found in Perrin. For more complex treatments that also contain criticisms see Ogden, 1991, and Jones.

23. For treatment of this subject see Yearley, 1999, pp. 135–37, 145–46. This approach resembles features of that process of self-cultivation that Neo-Confucians called a "strenuous spiritual effort," a *gōngfu* 功夫, or sustained effort of both self-understanding and self-cultivation that focuses on examining one's reactions to concrete events. It also resembles the method used for over a millennium in Christianity, in which a four-fold method of interpretation operates, with the tropological mode being most prominent.

24. For a further treatment of Fingarette, 1972, and Hall and Ames, 1984, see Stephen Wilson's contribution to this volume.

25. The use of any Western categories, much less modern ones, in the interpretation of early Chinese texts presents, of course, more complex issues than I can adequately treat

here. Issues about the categories of "the individual" and "choice" are perhaps most difficult, but one could query many others, including the concept of "dispositions." On this
topic see Yearley, 1990a, pp. 4–7, 110–11, 175–82, 196–99; Nussbaum, 1988 and 1993;
and Yearley 1993a.

26. My paraphrase follows both Dawson and Lau, but Waley combines the two passages into one, seeing the first notion as an adage and the second as a commentary on it.
He then translates "evil" as "will dislike no one." (The actual character for "to dislike" and
"evil" are the same: 惡 , read wù in the former sense and è in the latter.) The reading is,
I believe, a possible one, and if we think disliking no one and being free from evil are not
roughly equivalent, conclusions follow that seem to contrast with much else in the book.
(They do, that is, unless the reference is to a special kind of general judgment that differs
from all judgments about specific failings; e.g., the kind of charitable love of people that,
for Aquinas, can combine with severe judgments about an individual.) I have with these
passages, and elsewhere, changed "man" and related forms to gender neutral terms; often
that change, in book 4 at least, is easy to accomplish but in this case a price is paid.

27. Lau 11:17. This is from a "later" book, but it illustrates, I am suggesting, a conception of righteous anger present in book 4. Incidentally, Chad Hansen has suggested that
4:3 is "jarring"—"as if Confucius' highest virtue is one that generates hatred." (Hansen,
1993, p. 58.) I would propose that an examination of kinds of anger, such as that found
in Aquinas, can both illuminate the passage and illustrate how the comparative study of
Chinese and Thomistic ethics opens up productive interpretive possibilities.

28. The idea of semblances and counterfeits of virtue in Mencius addresses this issue,
but the most thorough response in early Confucian thought is Xunzi's. Not only does he
clearly rank people's achievements, but he also argues that practices like ritual can affect
people even if they do understand them. The cogency of especially this last claim is, of
course, questionable. On Mencius treatment see Yearley, 1990a, pp. 67–72; on Xunzi see
Yearley, 1980 and 1996a.

29. On the general idea that much religious thought deals with "irresolvable but revealing and productive tensions," see Yearley, 1975b, but also note 1975a; 1994a, p. 713; and
forthcoming. The issue examined here remains, I think, one of the crucial questions in the
Confucian tradition even if, unsurprisingly, much of the tradition will emphasize "good"
actions over good intentions in a way that at least book 4 does not. Put more dramatically,
we can too easily forget the antinomian side of the Confucian tradition, and it is beneficial to remember that it may be present in one of the tradition's earliest texts.

30. See, for example, 11:24 and 17:11. For a more extensive treatment of this distinction see Yearley, 1990a, pp. 20–23; that analysis draws on Irwin's treatment and also
uses Williams's analysis of the difference between first person statements and third person
descriptions when virtue is the subject. If this distinction is seen as simply descriptive then
any expressive motivation is acceptable. The category, that is, is simply formal and therefore also amoral, a feature that is prominent in some existentialist analogs to the idea. (On
this issue, see the analysis in Scott of Heidegger.) In traditional Western accounts, however,
evaluative elements are always prominent; for examples see Yearley, 1990a, pp. 129–43;
154–68. A muted version of this distinction always, of course, informs ethical action
because we never know for sure that our actions will generate the results we desire.
Nevertheless, the uncertainty is much greater in paradigmatic cases of expressive virtues
because the final outcome is very uncertain and a full knowledge of that uncertainty
informs a person's motivation.

31. Waley presents the initial notion in section 2 as a couplet, presumably a traditional
saying that will be commented on; if that is true the differentiation between the virtuous
and the wise would make even more sense.

The subject of the relationship between the acquisitive virtuousness of the wise and the expressive virtuousness of perfected people is an important topic in early Confucian thought. Treatments range from Xunzi's examination of why the unvirtuous might pursue virtue to Mencius' combination of acquisitive and expressive language in his attempt both to criticize and to "use" Mohist ideas of profit or utility (lì 利). (Zhū Xī 朱熹, interestingly enough, draws on Mencius' paradigmatic treatment of expressive virtue in 6A10 in his comments on 4:16, and 6A10 draws on 4:10.) The different renditions noted in the text are from, in order, Dawson, Waley, Legge, and Lau.

32. My treatment here raises complex issues about the relationship between wisdom (zhì 知) and "virtue" (rén 仁) that I can only gesture toward here. In particular, my analysis seems to significantly subordinate wisdom to rén. How does this fit in, for example, both with the apparent commendation of wisdom in 4:1, and with the fact that in the later Confucian tradition (e.g., Mencius), wisdom became a cardinal virtue? The general theoretical issue involved here is the problem of the unity or connectedness of virtues, and it is a complex and vexing one. (See Yearley, 1998.) In this context, I believe it most likely that Confucius sees wisdom as a subordinate "part" of full virtue. As a part, it is present in the fully virtuous individual, but in the absence of other parts its value is limited.

33. For a more detailed account of four different kinds of dispositions and their use when examining early Confucian thought, see Yearley, 1990a, 106–11. I now think that account does not, however, adequately address all the significant issues an existentialist perspective presents. The unpredictability of Confucius' actions, incidentally, is one of the hallmarks of some portraits of him in the Analects, the most famous probably being 11:20.

34. These sections also are important because features of filial piety fit within the idea of ritual and therefore can cast light on the rather mysterious treatment of ritual in 4:13, with its focus on the yielding or deferential attitude that underlies ritual. This emphasis raises the interesting possibility (which I first encountered when prodded by the editor of this volume in another context) that yielding is an unnamed virtue that corresponds to the activities needed in a specific but variegated sphere of existence; see Yearley, 1993a, and note 1990a, p. 37.

35. The fact that filial piety was frequently violated in Confucius' China (as evidenced by texts like the Zuo zhuan) is no argument that it was not seen as a fixity. The occurrence of some kinds of violation can even provide us with evidence that a fixity is present.

36. On the idea of "false fixities" see Yearley, 1995, p. 13, which draws on the development of this notion in Hampshire's 1989 analysis (In support of this reading it is worth remembering that even one of the more radical parts of the Zhuangzi exempts filial piety from criticism; see Yearley, 1996c.)

37. See Mencius 3A5, and David S. Nivison, "Two Roots or One?" in Nivison, 1996, pp. 133–48.

38. For an analysis of a later Confucian's, Xunzi's, treatment of the notion of origins and the primordial, see Yearley, 1996a, pp. 10–15. One cannot, of course, assume that the two treatments are equivalent, or even that one is an appropriate development of the other. The subject of filial piety is infrequently treated in the Analects, most references coming in book 2, and that makes even more significant its appearance in a book as brief and early as 4.

39. Each of the seven translators I note has surrendered to the need, not just the temptation, to read something into kě yǐ 可矣. Allowing for changes in grammatical form, "contentment" is Soothill and Waley, "with acceptance" is Ivanhoe, 1993, "without regret" is Legge, "a not minding of it" is from the Brookses, "a knowing that it is all right" is Dawson, and "a knowing that you have not lived in vain" is Lau. Specifying this final state involves serious theoretical issues; e.g., does "knowing that it is all right to die" necessarily, in and

of itself, involve contentment or even acceptance. (The general subject of treatments in the *Analects* of one's own possible death or the death of others is examined in Ivanhoe, forthcoming.)

40. For an excellent example of a treatment of this subject that combines existentialist and Thomistic ideas see Rahner, and note Yearley, 1970. (Despite its many conceptual problems, Becker also represents an extraordinary attempt to develop an existential perspective on the facing of death.) For a brief treatment of some of the many complexities in the Hegelian idea of "recognition" see Yearley, 1995, especially page 14; for the operation of those horizons, which include facing death, Yearley, 1990a, pp. 132–34; for the relationship of the idea of the primordial to death, see Yearley, 1996a, particularly pages 14–15 and Yearley, 1985; for the relationship of death and notions of expressive or heroic virtue, see Yearley, 1996b, 1998, and forthcoming.

41. The exact meaning of the "*dào*" in this passage must, I believe, remain fundamentally mysterious given the lack of context and the fact that it surely cannot mean, given the rest of book 4, the Way of the Ancients as it can be reconstructed. *Dào* may not even mean the ideal course of a political organization. In the *Analects*, it often does refer to the ideal course of conduct for an individual, and only once (5:13) is conjoined with Heaven. (See Philip J. Ivanhoe's "Whose Confucius? Which *Analects*?" in this volume, for more on 5:13.) The most I think one can say here is that the *dào* has a positive rather than negative or neutral relationship with the ideas of virtue that book 4 discusses.

REFERENCES

Becker, Carl. 1973. *The Denial of Death*. New York: Free Press.

Brooks, E. Bruce. 1994. "Review Article: The Present State and Future Prospect of Pre-Han Text Studies." *Sino-Platonic Papers* 46 (July): 1–74.

Brooks, E. Bruce, and A. Taeko. 1998. *The Original Analects: Sayings of Confucius and His Successors*. New York: Columbia University Press.

Bultmann, Rudolf. 1951. *Theology of the New Testament*. I. Translated by K. Grobel. New York: Charles Scribner and Sons.

———. 1960. *Existence and Faith: Shorter Writing of Rudolf Bultmann*. Selected, edited, and translated by Schubert Ogden. New York: Meridian Books.

———. 1984. *New Testament and Mythology and Other Basic Writings*. Selected, edited, and translated by Schubert Ogden. Philadelphia: Fortress Press.

Fingarette, Herbert. 1972. *Confucius: The Secular as Sacred*. New York: Harper and Row.

Frei, Hans. 1974. *The Eclipse of Biblical Narrative. A Study in Eighteenth and Nineteenth Century Hermeneutics*. New Haven: Yale University Press.

Hall, David and Roger Ames. 1984. *Thinking Through Confucius*. Albany, N.Y.: SUNY Press.

Hampshire, Stuart. 1971. "Ethics: A Defense of Aristotle." *Freedom of Mind and Other Essays*. Princeton: Princeton University Press. 63–87. (Originally published 1967.)

———. 1989. *Innocence and Experience*. Cambridge, Mass.: Harvard University Press.

Hansen, Chad. 1993. "Term-Belief in Action: Sentences and Terms in Early Chinese Philosophy," in Hans Lenk and Gregor Paul, eds., *Epistemological Issues in Classical Chinese Philosophy*. Albany, N.Y.: SUNY Press.

Harvey, Van Austin. 1966. *The Historian and the Believer. The Morality of Historical Knowledge and Christian Belief*. Philadelphia: Westminster Press.

Irwin, Terence. 1977. *Plato's Moral Theory: The Early and Middle Dialogues*. Oxford: Clarendon Press.

Ivanhoe, Philip J. 1993. *Confucian Moral Self Cultivation*. New York: Peter Lang.

———. 1996. *Chinese Language, Thought, and Culture: Nivison and His Critics.* Chicago: Open Court Press.

———. Forthcoming. "Death and Dying in the *Analects*," in Mary Evelyn Tucker and Tu Weiming, eds., *Confucian Spirituality.* Volume 11, *World Spirituality: An Encyclopedia History of the Religious Quest.* New York: Crossroads Publishing.

Jones, Gareth. 1991. *Bultmann, Towards a Critical Theology.* Cambridge, Eng.: Polity Press.

Lewis, Mark Edward. 1990. *Sanctioned Violence in Early China.* Albany, N.Y.: SUNY Press.

Nivison, David S. 1996. *The Ways of Confucianism: Investigations in Chinese Philosophy.* Chicago: Open Court Press.

Nussbaum, Martha. 1988. "Non-Relative Virtues: An Aristotelian Approach," in Peter A. French, Theodore K. Uehling, and Howard K. Wettstein, eds., *Midwest Studies in Philosophy: Volume XIII: Ethical Theory: Character and Virtue,* pp. 32–53. Notre Dame, Ind.: University of Notre Dame Press.

———. 1993. "Comparing Virtues." Book Discussion: *Mencius and Aquinas* by Lee H. Yearley. *Journal of Religious Ethics* 21, 2: 345–67.

Ogden, Schubert M. 1982. *The Point of Christology.* San Francisco: Harper and Row.

———. 1991. *Christ Without Myth, A Study Based on the Theology of Rudolf Bultmann.* Dallas: Southern Methodist University Press. (Originally published 1961.)

Perrin, Norman. 1969. *The Promise of Bultmann.* Philadelphia: Fortress Press.

Pinksy, Robert. 1996. *The Inferno of Dante: A New Verse Translation.* Noonday Press.

Rahner, Karl. 1961. *On the Theology of Death.* Translated by C. H. Henkey. New York: Herder and Herder.

Sanders, E. P. 1993. *The Historical Figure of Jesus.* Harmondsworth, Eng.: Allen Lane, Penguin Press.

Scott, Charles. 1990. *The Question of Ethics, Nietzsche, Foucault, Heidegger.* Bloomington: Indiana University Press.

Singleton, Charles. 1980. *The Divine Comedy: Inferno.* Princeton: Princeton University Press.

Taylor, Charles. 1991. *The Ethics of Authenticity.* Cambridge, Mass.: Harvard University Press.

Williams, Bernard. 1985. *Ethics and the Limits of Philosophy.* Cambridge, Mass.: Harvard University Press.

Yearley, Lee H. 1970. "Karl Rahner on the Relation of Nature and Grace." *Canadian Journal of Theology.* 16, 3 and 4: 219–31.

———. 1975a. "Mencius on Human Nature: The Forms of His Religious Thought." *Journal of the American Academy of Religion* 43, 2: 185–98.

———. 1975b. "Toward a Typology of Religious Thought: A Chinese Example." *The Journal of Religion* 55, 4: 426–43.

———. 1980. "Hsun Tzu on the Mind: His Attempted Synthesis of Confucianism and Taoism." *Journal of Asian Studies* 39, 3: 465–80.

———. 1985. "Freud as Creator and Critic of Cosmogonies and Their Ethics," in *Cosmogony and Ethical Order,* ed. R. Lovin and F. Reynolds, 381–413. Chicago: University of Chicago Press.

———. 1990a. *Mencius and Aquinas: Theories of Virtue and Conceptions of Courage.* Albany, N.Y.: SUNY Press.

———. 1990b. "Recent Work on Virtue," *Religious Studies Review* 16, 1: 1–9.

———. 1993a. "The Author Replies." Book Discussion: *Mencius and Aquinas* by Lee H. Yearley. *Journal of Religious Ethics* 21, 2: 385–95.

———. 1993b. "Conflicts among Ideals of Human Flourishing," in *Prospects for a Common Morality,* ed. G. Outka and J. J. Reeder, 233–53. Princeton: Princeton University Press.

———. 1994a. "New Religious Virtues and the Study of Religion." *Fifteenth Annual University Lecture in Religion at Arizona State University.* Distributed by the Department of Religious

Studies: 1–26. [A publication sent in autumn 1994 to members of the American Academy of Religion.]

————. 1994b. "Theories, Virtues, and the Comparative Philosophy of Human Flourishings: A Response to Professor Allan." *Philosophy East and West* 44, 4: 711–20.

————. 1995. "Taoist Wandering and the Adventure of Religious Ethics." The William James Lecture, 1994. *Harvard Divinity Bulletin* 24, 2: 11–15.

————. 1996a. "Facing Our Frailty: Comparative Religious Ethics and the Confucian Death Rituals." *Gross Memorial Lecture, 1995, Valparaiso University*. Valparaiso, Ind.: Valparaiso University Press. [A publication sent in spring of 1996 to members of the Counsel on the Study of Religion.]

————. 1996b. "Heroic Virtue in America: Aristotle, Aquinas, and Melville's *Billy Budd*," in *The Greeks and Us: Essays in Honor of Arthur W. H. Adkins*, ed. R. B. Louden and P. Schollmeier, 66–92. Chicago: University of Chicago Press.

————. 1996c. "Zhuangzi's Understanding of the Skillfulness and the Ultimate Spiritual State," in *Essays on Skepticism, Relativism, and Ethics in the Zhuangzi*, ed. P. Kjellberg and P. J. Ivanhoe, 152–82. Albany, N.Y.: SUNY Press.

————. 1998. "The Ascetic Grounds of Goodness: William James's Case for the Virtue of Voluntary Poverty." *Journal of Religious Ethics* 26, 1 (spring): 105–35.

————. 1999. "Selves, Virtues, Odd Genres, and Alien Guides: An Approach to Religious Ethics." *Journal of Religious Ethics* 25, 3 (twenty-fifth anniversary supplement): 125–55.

————. Forthcoming. "Xunzi: Ritualization as Humanization," in T. C. Kline, ed., *Ritual and Religion in the Xunzi*. New York: Seven Bridges Press.

11

A Woman Who Understood the Rites

LISA A. RAPHALS

THERE IS LITTLE DISCUSSION OF WOMEN in the *Analects*. In other texts that purport to transmit remarks of Confucius, he is said to comment on the behavior, ethics, and knowledge of several women. He repeatedly praises "the woman of the Jì" elsewhere referred to as "the mother of Wénbó" and as Jìng Jiāng of the Jì of Lǔ 魯季敬姜 (henceforward Jìng Jiāng or Jìng Jiāng of Lǔ).[1] To judge by the frequency of stories about her in other Warring States texts, he was not alone in his good opinion of her. She was the wife of one official, the mother of another, and the grandaunt of yetanother. Despite an apparent paradigm for female virtue in which woman never comment on politics, she admonished her son and nephew on important matters and negotiated some tricky ritual situations herself. Her arguments stress the "separate spheres" of men and women, but her obvious erudition and savoir faire raise questions about whether "men's" education was available to at least some women.

Confucius' comments about her appear in the *Liènǚ zhuàn* 列女傳 or *Collected Life Stories of Women*, where she is one of two women he praises.[2] He praises her for understanding the rites and the distinctions between men and women and between superior and inferior. Similar praise appears in the *Lǐ jì*, and her expertise is used for a different set of rhetorical purposes in the *Zhànguó cè*. Who was she, and what did Confucius (and so many others) see in her? In the first section I take up the traditions that emphasize her expertise in politics and ritual. Next I consider Confucius' comment about her and traditions that bear on the question of his teaching interactions with women. In the last section, I turn to textual traditions that stress her apparent approval of "separate spheres," including appropriations of Jìng Jiāng of Lǔ in Song and Ming texts.

I. A Woman of Expertise

The life story of Jìng Jiāng of Lǔ is the longest and most detailed life story in the *Liènǚ zhuàn*. The *Guó yǔ* contains eight separate stories about her, all in the second book of Lǔ. She also appears in the *Hán Shì wàizhuàn*, *Zhànguó cè*, and *Lǐ jì*. These narratives portray her as a woman of considerable expertise, who operates within (and appears to approve of) the gender codes of her society, but with no loss of acumen in expressing her views on both state and domestic affairs to her male relatives. She delivers extensive speeches on weaving and statecraft, rebukes her male relatives on several accounts, arranges her son's marriage, and directs his household after his death.

According to the *Liènǔ zhuàn*, Jìng Jiāng was the wife of Gōngfǔ Mùbó 公夫穆伯, the mother of Gōngfǔ Wénbó 公夫文伯, and the paternal grandaunt of Jì Kāngzǐ 季康子. Widowed young, she raised her son and instructed him, his concubines, and her paternal grandnephew. Within the *Liènǔ zhuàn*, her life story (LNZ 1.9) appears in the chapter titled "Maternal Rectitude" (*mǔ yí* 母儀), and contains five narrative elements, in some cases of several parts each.[3] (Correlations between the narrative elements in the *Liènǔ zhuàn* and other texts appear in table 11.1).

The first narrative element describes the early death of Gōngfǔ Mùbó and Jìng Jiāng's raising and reprimanding her young son Wénbó with examples of illustrious men of past dynasties. It closely corresponds to the account in the *Guó yǔ*. The second narrative consists of two discourses on weaving. The third describes

TABLE 11.1
NARRATIVE ELEMENTS

NARRATIVE ELEMENT	GY:LU (−5/−3C)	LY (−3/−1C)	LJ (−2C/−1C)	ZGC (−1C)	LNZ (−1/1C)	KZJY (−1/3C)	HSWZ (2C)
Her instructions to Wénbó							
her genealogy					1:6a		
Wénbó's youth					1:6b		
on weaving and statecraft					1:7a		
Her knowledge of ritual							
a feast of undersized turtles	5.11				1:8b		
plans for Wénbó's marriage	5.15						
instructions to Wénbó's concubines	5.16				1:8b	10:44:8b	
dry eyes at Wénbó's funeral			3,9:24b	20:692			1.1
the funeral of Jì Kāngzǐ's mother			3, 9:24b				
Confucius praises her discourse							
to Jì Kāngzǐ on humility [Zi Xia]	5.10						
to Jì Kāngzǐ on inner and outer court	5:12				1:9a		
to Wénbó on work and self-indulgence	5.13				1:7b	9:41:13a	
to Jì Kāngzǐ on li of men and women	5.14				1:9a		
to concubines of Wénbó on mourning	5.17		3, 924b		1:9a	10:42:3b	
Wénbó as a student of Confucius							1.19

Note: Numbers in parentheses indicate compilation date of text.

her admonitions to the adult Gōngfū Wénbó for a lapse in propriety in the treatment of a guest, and the fourth, her admonitions to Wénbó's concubines after his
death. The fifth, which has three parts, indicates her understanding of and propriety in the performance of ritual, especially her understanding of the separation of men and women. All these narratives take the form of admonitions: to
her son (elements 1, 2, and 3), to his concubines (element 4), and to Jì Kāngzǐ
(element 5). The second narrative element consists of two discourses in which
she draws an analogy between weaving and government. Because of the importance of these analogies, I translate and discuss them at length.

1. WEAVING AND GOVERNMENT

A striking example of her style of instruction to her grown son is a detailed
analogy between government office and the apparatus of weaving. Unlike most of
the narratives about Jìng Jiāng, this story appears only in the Liènǚ zhuàn:

> When Wénbó was minister in Lu, Jìng Jiāng said to him: I will inform
> you about what is important in governing a country; it is entirely in
> the warp (jīng 經). The selvedge [the straight border of woven cloth]
> (fú 幅) is the means by which you straighten what is twisted and
> crooked. It must be strong, therefore the selvedge can be considered as
> the General (jiàng 將). The pattern (huà 畫) evens what is uneven and
> reconciles what is not adjusted. Therefore the pattern can be the
> Director (zhèng 正).⁴ Now the realization (wù zhě 物者) [of the pattern]
> is the means by which you rule tendrils and align cords (chí wú yǔ mò
> 治蕪與莫). Therefore the realization can be Prefect of the Capital (dū dàifū
> 都大夫) The thing that can pass firmly from hand to hand without loss
> and go in and out without interruption is the shuttle (kǔn 捆). The
> shuttle can be Director of Messengers (dà xíng 大行). That which you
> push when you make it go and pull when you make it come is the
> heddles (zòng 綜). The heddles can be the Regional Mentor of Guan Nei
> (guān nèi zhī shī 關內之師). The one that regulates the numbers of great
> and small is the reed comb (jūn 均). The reed comb can be the Royal
> Annalist (nèi shǐ 內史). The one who can fill an important office, travel a
> long road, and is upright, genuine and firm is the axle (zhú 軸). The
> axle can be deemed Minister (xiàng 相). The one that is inexhaustible in
> unfolding is the warp beam (zhāi 摘). The warp beam can be the Three
> Dukes (san gong). Wénbó bowed to her repeatedly and received her
> instruction. (LNZ 1:7a-b)

This passage makes an analogy between eight offices and eight parts of a loom.
The analogy is detailed and coherent. It begins with the General, who determines
the edge and shape of the fabric, and keeps it in formation. The Director sets the
overall shape of the weaving. The analogy is to a pattern or painted design that is
copied onto the cloth; this pattern determines the design even if the weaver does

not know it.[5] The Prefect of the Capital imposes order on disorder, and governs "wild" areas, as well as the city.[6] The Director of Messengers sends his envoys back and forth, without interruption or damage, like the shuttle. The Regional Mentor of Guan Nei, a liaison officer, ensures that the way is clear, like the heddles, which separates the sections of the warp through which the shuttle will pass.[7] The Royal Annalist, like the impartial and evenly ordered teeth of the reed comb, makes accurate discriminations in the sorting of information—an interesting tacit comparison of weaving and text—and "combs" the silk of the warp, thus keeping it straight and untangled. In the same way, the Royal Annalist, by recording events from year to year, orders events. His judgments of what is worthy of inclusion are like the number of teeth in the reed comb, which determines the density of thread in the weave.[8] The Minister, like the axle, is responsible, enduring, upright and firm, and guides the kingdom by these qualities. This was Wénbó's own position at the time. The Three Dukes, like the warp beam, are endless in their virtue and ability. The warp beam gathers up the unused warp and holds it evenly in place.[9]

Jìng Jiāng claims an analogy between government and weaving on two bases. One is a correspondence between the importance of government for men and of weaving for women. The other is that government and weaving each consists of component functions, all of which must be performed adequately and correctly for the activity to succeed. The requisites for each component are particular and specialized. For cloth to be woven effectively, the component parts of the loom must be adequate to their various functions, which differ from each other, and demand different qualities. For example, the reed comb must be notched finely enough to separate hundreds of threads; the warp beam must be strong enough to bear the tension of all of them wound around it. A reed comb would make a terrible warp beam, and vice versa. Similarly, if a state is to be governed effectively, the component offices must be staffed by men whose excellences are those required by the specialized tasks of the offices.

Jìng Jiāng is claiming that her son does not understand government and that she herself is competent to instruct him in the appointment of officials. When Wénbó bows and accepts her teaching, he also presumably accepts her premises. It is noteworthy that neither the text nor its various commentaries remark on where she learned to understand the analogy in detail.

2. Weaving and Work

The second part of the second narrative element is an admonition to Wénbó when he urges her to desist from personally performing the labor of spinning and weaving, as beneath her. She upbraids him with the examples of the illustrious queens of the past, in the following terms. Jìng Jiāng predicts that Lǔ will perish because mere children who have never heard of the Way serve in office. She explains that the sage kings were able to rule for long periods because they, their wives, and their people were all hardworking. According to her argument, the kings lodged their people on hard land and tired them out; tired people are reflective (on their burdens), and as a result, their people grew good hearts. By contrast, farmers of rich lands live in luxury, become licentious, forget good, and grow evil hearts. Barren lands make people hardworking and righteous. The ancient kings worked hard, as did their feudal lords, ministers, and retainers, and the commoners in their realms. Similarly, their queens and the wives of their feudal lords, ministers, and retainers also worked hard at their proper work. They made caps, belts, and clothing for court use and sacrifice, and the commoners' wives clothed their husbands. Thus, men and women each had duties. Jìng Jiāng reprimands her son for suggesting that she abandon labor and live in luxury; such a suggestion shows that he is careless of his ancestors and will certainly be the end of his family line.

These stories appear to contradict statements in the Lǐ jì that call for the strict separation of the affairs of men and women: "Men must not speak of internal affairs; women must not speak of external matters. . . . What is said in the inner quarters does not emerge from them; what is said in the outside world does not enter them."[10] Yet the discourses on weaving end by stating that Confucius heard of her conduct and commented to his disciples about it:

> When Zhong Ni heard of it, he said: Disciples, note! The woman of the
> Ji was not licentious. The Odes' saying
>> Women have no public charge,
>> but tend their silkworms and their looms
> means that a woman has public charge by virtue of her weaving and
> spinning. If she leaves them, she contravenes the rites.[11]

This section corresponds to the Guó yǔ story "Gongfu Wenbo's Mother Discourses on Work and Self-indulgence," and to a passage in the Kǒngzǐ jiāyǔ.[12] The Guó yǔ and Kǒngzǐ jiāyǔ versions include the comment of Confucius, but not his quotation from the Odes. The story also has distinct affinities with the story of Meng mu, the mother of Mengzi, whose admonition to her young son is also based on the premise that women and men have distinctly separate, but exactly analogous, duties, and obligations.[13]

The next broad area of praise for Jìng Jiāng of Lǔ is in her knowledge of various forms of ritual, including the treatment of guests, marriage, mourning, and the separation of men and women.

3. GUEST RITUAL

In the third narrative of the Liènǚ zhuàn, Jìng Jiāng upbraids Wénbó for merely adhering to the letter, and not the full performance, of correct treatment of a guest.

> Gongfu Wenbo feasted Nangong Jingshu with drink; and Lu Dufu was
> a guest. He [Wénbó] provided a tortoise, but it was small. Dufu

became angry, and when they were going to eat the tortoise, he declined, saying: "I'll eat the tortoise after you make it grow larger" and departed. When Wenbo's mother heard about it, she grew angry and said: "I have heard my ancestor say: 'In making sacrifice you provide for the dead; at a banquet you provide for the head guest.' What's all this about tortoises? And now you have made him angry." And she drove him away. Five days later, the Lu minister intervened and she called him back.[14]

This story appears in the *Guó yǔ* as "Gongfu Wenbo Feasts Nangong Jingshu with Wine."[15] It stands in considerable contradiction to passages in the *Lǐ jì*, suggesting that men made judgments on the basis of merit, whereas women were governed by emotion and affection: "Here now is the affection of a father for his sons;—he loves the worthy among them and places on a lower level those who do not show ability; but that of a mother for them is such, that while she loves the worthy, she pities those who do not show ability:—the mother deals with them on the ground of affection and not of showing them honour; the father, on the ground of showing them honour and not of affection."[16]

One way to reconcile this apparent divergence is to view Jìng Jiāng's admonition as a substitute for that of an absent father. Nevertheless, her capacity to make judgments on the basis of merit remains unexplained.

4. MARRIAGE

The *Guó yǔ* story "Gongfu Wenbo's Mother Plans a Marriage for Wenbo" (which does not occur in the *Liènǚ zhuàn*) attests to the nature and scope of her abilities, underscores her expertise in ritual and poetic quotation, and shows her ability to use both effectively without violating propriety: "Gongfu Wenbo's mother wanted to find a wife for Wénbó. She feasted the clan elders, and recited the third line of the 'Luyi' fu. The elders requested the diviners to prognosticate the [prospective] wife's clan. When Shi Hai heard about it he said 'Ah! In a feast of men and women, she did not remain with the clan officials; in planning a marriage for the clan, she never went beyond the clan. She planned, but did not transgress; she was subtle, but made matters clear. The poem was the means by which she unified their intentions."[17]

This story attests to her literary education, her skill in poetic quotation, and her ability to act effectively to achieve her ends without violating the proprieties of clan life. Indeed, she is praised for doing so. In several other accounts, Jìng Jiāng admonishes others who act as moral agents. This story is of particular interest because it portrays Jìng Jiāng herself as an active moral agent. It shows her using poetic quotation, both to express her own views and to unify the intentions of others, a mode of behavior frequently used by ministers to put their views forward to a superior.[18] The story is also an unusual case of a woman being able to affect the marriage of a son or daughter. Although women in Warring States and Han times frequently had a say in the marriage of grandchildren, they rarely had the ability to determine the marriage of their immediate progeny.[19]

This anecdote also provides an interesting reflection on the Lǐ jì account of the education of boys and girls: "At six years [children] were taught the names of the numbers and the cardinal points. At seven years boys and girls did not [sit on] the same mat or eat together. At eight years when they go in and out of doors and gates, proceed to their mats, and eat and drink, they must follow behind their elders. This is the beginning of instruction in deference (rang). At nine, they were taught the numbering of the days. At ten they go out to an outside master, and stay with him and sleep outside [the home]. They study writing and calculation."[20]

The passage describes instruction in reading, polite conversation, music, the Odes, dancing, archery, and charioteering. It presumably applies to boys, but there is no such specification. The Rites does specify that: "As for girls, at ten they do not go out. Governesses teach them to be docile and obedient," to handle hemp, silkworms, women's work, weaving, the preparation of foods, and to assist at sacrifices.[21] This passage specifies the skills that girls were required to learn. The Lǐ jì describes the proper ages for particular instructions, but does not explicitly restrict education according to gender, or explicitly restrict education and literacy to boys.

5. MOURNING

Three narratives about Jìng Jiāng's knowledge of mourning involve the death of her son Wénbó; three others involve her nephew Jì Kāngzǐ. Various accounts of her behavior after the death of Wénbó appear in a number of Warring States and Han compendia. The Liènǚ zhuàn, Guó yǔ, Lǐ jì, Hán Shì wàizhuàn, and Kǒngzǐ jiāyǔ all describe versions of her unusual conduct after Wénbó's death, but with differing emphases.

Several texts present versions of Jìng Jiāng's instructions to Wénbó's concubines after his death.[22] According to the Liènǚ zhuàn, "I have heard that if a man is too fond of the inner [his wives] he dies for women, and if he is too fond of the outer [affairs of state], he dies for scholars (shi). Now my son has died young, and I would hate it to be said of him that he was too fond of the inner." She urges them to mourn, but not excessively, and ends by saying that they can best illuminate the reputation of her son by following the rites and being calm.

So far, all the versions of the narrative agree. They diverge when they come to Confucius' comment on her behavior. In the Liènǚ zhuàn and Kǒngzǐ jiāyǔ versions, when Confucius hears her mourning instructions to Wénbó's concubines he remarks, "A girl never understands as much as a woman; a youth never understands as much as a man; the wisdom of Gongfu's wife was none other than this! She wishes to brighten her son's bright virtue."[23]

In these versions, the referent of the "this" is ambiguous because the terms of the analogy are unclear. One possibility is simple analogy based on age (with the implication of maturity and marriage). An adult (woman or man) knows more than a child (boy or girl); Gōngfū's wife is like an adult. The other possibility is a two-step analogy based on age and gender. A girl knows less than a woman; a woman knows less than a man; Gōngfū's wife is like a man in her knowledge.

There is no ambiguity in the Guó yǔ narrative "Gongfu Wenbo's Mother Admonishes His Concubines after His Death": "A girl never understands as much as a woman; a youth never understands as much as a man; *the knowledge of Gongfu's wife is that of a man!* She wishes to make bright her son's bright virtue [italics added]."[24] The Guó yǔ passage probably predates not only the Liènǚ zhuàn and Kǒngzǐ jiāyǔ versions, but also the Lunyu itself. We can only speculate on the reasons for diluting the force of the analogy in the later accounts of the incident versions. It is interesting that the Guó yǔ version is so clear on this point.

Another version of these events appears in the Lǐ jì, which describes the actual mourning for Wénbó. In this account, during the mourning, Jìng Jiāng touched the couch where his body lay, but did not weep, and remarked that, although she had never seen his conduct at court, she knew it must be wanting, because the ministers did not weep for him, whereas his women cried their voices away.[25] An unrelated passage in the Lǐ jì also attests to Jìng Jiāng's keen eye for ritual decorum. The story describes an incident at the funeral of Jì Kāngzǐ's mother. It attests to Jìng Jiāng's expertise in mourning ritual, not, perhaps, without some sarcasm: "When Ji Kangzi's mother died, her underclothes were visible. Jing Jiang said: 'If a wife is not adorned [properly clothed], she does not dare be seen by her husband's parents. There will be guests coming from all four quarters; why are her underclothes showing?' Whereupon she gave orders that they be removed [from sight]."[26]

Another narrative about the style of her mourning for Wénbó in the years after his death is also framed by a remark of Confucius. In the Liènǚ zhuàn version, when he heard that, living in mourning, she mourned her late husband in the morning and her dead son in the evening, Confucius declared that she knew the lǐ and the separation of higher and lower.[27]

II. Confucius on Women Who Understood the Rites

The story of Jìng Jiāng is one of two in the Liènǚ zhuàn in which Confucius comments on the behavior of a woman as "understanding the rites." The stories differ considerably in the status of the woman, Confucius' presumed acquaintance with her, and how the text refers to him. Before turning to the question of Confucius' praise of her, it is worth noting that one version of the "Mourning" narrative centers on Jìng Jiāng's praise of Confucius, and corresponding dis-praise of her own son. She is also one of several specifically didactic mothers in the Liènǚ zhuàn.

Clearly legendary examples include Jiang Yuan the mother of Hou Ji, Jian Di the mother of Xie, the Tu Shan girl, You Shen the wife of King Tang, and Tai Si the wife of King Wu, who trained her ten sons during their youth. Jìng Jiāng, like Mèng Mŭ, was a "didactic widow," a woman widowed at a young age who took on the didactic "male" role and excelled in the education of her son.

1. JÌNG JIĀNG ON CONFUCIUS

The Hán Shì wàizhuàn elaborates the story of Jìng Jiāng's failure to mourn for Wénbó in a different way, one that suggests a direct connection between her and Confucius. In this version, after Wénbó's death, someone noticed that Wénbó's mother did not weep. Because she was known to be a virtuous woman, he concluded that Wénbó must have been at fault somehow, and sent to ask her about it. This account provides a fairly unusual instance of a woman being asked directly to explain her own conduct. She precedes her explanation with the following remarks: "Formerly I had this son of mine serve Zhòng Nĭ. When Zhòng Nĭ left Lŭ, my son did not go beyond the suburbs of the capital in sending him off; in making him presents, he did not give him the family's precious objects."[28] In this version we learn three things: that Wénbó was a student of Confucius (he does not appear in the Analects), that he was sent to Confucius by his mother, and that he was less than wholehearted in his behavior toward his teacher.

This implicit criticism of Wénbó also appears in the Zhànguó cè, where "the story of Wenbo's mother" is used as a rhetorical trope, to show how the attitudes of listeners depend on their assessment of the speaker. Here, Lou Huan of Qin uses the story to avoid giving advice to the King of Zhao on Zhao's prospects after a defeat by Qin. In this version, Wénbó's (former) wet nurse asks Jìng Jiāng how she can forebear to mourn for her son. Her response is to criticize Wénbó in the strongest terms. "Confucius was a sage, and when he was driven from Lu this man did not follow him. Now he is dead and sixteen women of his household have killed themselves to honour him. If this is the way it is, then he must have treated worthy men lightly but treated his women well."[29] Lou Huan ends by remarking that these words sound righteous when spoken by a mother, but would seem mere jealousy if spoken by a wife: "In truth the words would be the same but when the speaker is different, the attitude of the listener is changed. Now I have just come from Qin, but if I say, 'don't give the towns' it would be no plan at all; yet if I say, 'give the towns,' I am afraid your majesty will say I am doing it for Qin. This is why I said I dare not answer you."[30]

The Zhànguó cè version, which has little to do with the actual story of Jìng Jiāng of Lŭ, emphasizes the different roles of mother and wife: a mother's admonitions bear the stamp of propriety, a wife's merely of jealousy. It also shows that she could and did assess her son, not on the "feminine" basis of affection (implicit, for example, in the wet nurse's question in the Zhànguó cè version), but on the basis of his merit. It is of some interest that the story represents her, a woman, as knowing of Confucius and assessing him as a sage, presumably during his own lifetime.

The good opinion is also clearly mutual. In these narratives, Confucius praises "the woman of the Ji" for admonishing Wénbó (the discourse on weaving) during his life, for "brightening" his virtue by refusing to mourn him at the time of his death, and for understanding of ritual and hierarchy by mourning both husband and son continually after their deaths (see table 11.1). At the heart of all this praise is Jìng Jiāng's unremitting, indeed relentless, efforts at "improvement." Several things about this "improvement" are noteworthy. In his admonitions to his disciples and in his statements about himself, Confucius constantly emphasizes that self-cultivation is a necessary prerequisite to the instruction of others. In the case of Jìng Jiāng, however, Confucius shows no explicit interest in any effort she may have made at cultivating herself; his praise is confined entirely to her instruction of her son. The implication is that at least women, presumably mothers, are capable of effective teaching without explicit self-cultivation! An extraordinary gendering of virtue!

Any number of Warring States and Han narratives portray Confucius or his disciples commenting favorably on Jìng Jiāng's actions and expertise. Why does she receive so much attention in these texts? Her husband and father are not widely attested as important personages. I speculate that one reason is the quite direct association with Confucius and his disciples. Several accounts specify contact between him and Wénbó, possibly at her instigation. Thus, when Confucius is said to have "heard of her conduct," it was probably at no great remove. Confucius seems to express strong approval of her conduct as a combination of efficacy and propriety. Confucius, like Jìng Jiāng herself, seems to describe women's work—weaving and sericulture—as equivalent to public affairs. Yet given the context, it is noteworthy that his comment does not suggest that women should be ignorant of statecraft. Indeed, his praise reflects the propriety of the manner in which she deployed her knowledge.

The life story of Jìng Jiāng never explicitly states that she was taught to read, to recite fu, to master the principles that underlie statecraft or ritual propriety, but the details of the stories about her—and even Confucius' praise of her—attest to the mastery of all these skills. Stories in four Warring States texts provide a variety of details about her life, yet all agree on the kind of expertise they portray.

2. THE GIRL OF AGU

The other woman praised by Confucius as "understanding the rites" in the Lienü zhuàn is "The Girl of Agu" 阿谷處女 (LNZ 6.6). Whereas Jìng Jiāng of Lǔ is a "Righteous Mother," the girl of Agu exemplifies "Skill in Argument" (LNZ 6) in a chapter that includes several cases of skillful arguments by commoners, both in the form of persuasions made to rulers and in arguments made within the course of their own quotidian interactions. Here, Confucius notices a washerwoman on the road to Agu, and remarks to Zigong that she is capable with words (kě yǔ yán 可與言). He suggests that they observe her intentions (guàn qí zhì 觀其志), and gives Zigong a cup (to ask for water), a lute (to drive away pigs), and linen cloth (as a betrothal gift). When Zigong asks her for water, she conforms to the prescriptions of the Lǐ jì by placing it on the ground, rather than handing it to him directly. When he asks her to tune the lute, she claims not to know the five tones. When he tries to woo her, she refuses him politely. After the encounter, Confucius describes her to Zigong as "penetrating about human affairs" (dá yú rén qíng 達於人情) and "understanding the rites" (zhī lǐ 知禮).[31] This story also occurs in the Hán Shì wàizhuàn (1:3) and Kǒng cóngzǐ.

3. CONFUCIUS AND FEMALE EDUCATION

In the story of the girl at Agu, Confucius already has the accoutrements of a teacher, if not a sage. He is referred to by the honorific title of Kǒngzǐ 孔子, and is accompanied by a disciple. It is Zigong, rather than Confucius, who speaks with the girl, and it is Zigong, rather than the girl, who is the object of instruction. Both men are clearly her social and hierarchical superiors. (Once again, the story does not occur in the Analects.)

Defenders of Confucius against charges of elitism have often pointed out that Confucius had students who were poor, most notably Yan Hui, and his inclusion of poor, but worthy, men among his students certainly suggests that he thought any man could practice self-cultivation. These narratives show a more ambiguous record in the case of women. In these accounts, Jìng Jiāng of Lǔ and the girl of Agu are clear cases of women of whose behavior, and whose understanding, Confucius clearly approves, albeit in different contexts and for different reasons. On this score, we might be tempted to extend his "spiritual" openhandedness to women. Yet it is noteworthy that, although Confucius approves of both women, he treats them as objects, rather than subjects of instruction. (He does not "objectify" them insofar as he considers them moral agents, but he does use then as "object lessons" for his male disciples.) His remarks are addressed to his students, not to the women whose examples he uses for their instruction.

Does propriety prevent his instructing women? I argue that it does not. The Lǐ jì notwithstanding, Warring States texts show many cases of instruction, admonition, and argument between unrelated men and women, and Confucius shows no reticence in having Zigong speak directly with the girl at Agu. In these instances, it is to his male students that Confucius stands in a benefactor/beneficiary relation, and in his interactions with women Confucius is a superior, but not a benefactor.[32] Although these instances are two few to provide any certainty, they do provide the uncomfortable suggestion that Confucius' views on human perfectibility and self-cultivation may have spanned social class, but not gender.

In both these stories, Confucius has sufficient respect for the understanding of Jìng Jiāng and the girl of Agu to use their examples as models for the instruction of his male disciples. In Jìng Jiāng's case, he hears of her by reputation, and, as I argue below, may have direct acquaintance with her. In the case of the girl of Agu, he is already on his travels, and perceives her virtues in a direct encounter.

4. CONFUCIUS AND THE JI LINEAGE

It is well known that Confucius was used as a mouthpiece for a range of late Warring States and Han dynasty views, for example in the *Zhuangzi* and *Hanfeizi*. These accounts of Confucius' praise of a virtuous female aristocrat, Jìng Jiāng of Lǔ, and a virtuous female commoner, the girl of Agu, raise questions of historicity that revolve around two issues. One objection to their historical veracity is textual. If Wénbó had been a disciple of Confucius, we would expect him to be mentioned in the *Analects*, and he is not. Second, the accounts of Confucius' praise of Jìng Jiāng refer to him by his style as Zhòng Ní 仲尼, suggesting a relatively late date. By contrast, in the story of the lower-class washerwoman of Agu, he is referred to by the honorific title "Kǒngzǐ," but later collectors and commentators question the attribution of this incident to Confucius. In a passage in the *Kong congzi*, the Prince of Pingyuan asks Zigao about the tradition that Confucius had had words with a washerwoman. Zigao replies that "the Agu story is of recent origin, probably concocted by those who use that sort of thing to give currency to their ideas."[33]

The Jìng Jiāng of Lǔ stories are less easily dismissed, for several reasons. They appear repeatedly in the *Guó yǔ*, a text that probably predates the *Analects* in compilation.[34] Despite the silence of the *Analects*, other accounts suggest that Wénbó was an unsuccessful student of Confucius, before he was driven out of Lǔ. How historically plausible is the claim that there was a direct connection between Confucius and Jìng Jiāng? Given a number of significant interactions with the Ji lineage in the received accounts of the life of Confucius, I speculate that there may have been a very direct connection between Jìng Jiāng and Confucius, which appears only indirectly in the *Analects* through its accounts of his interactions with male members of the Ji lineage. I further speculate that Confucius's praise of her may reflect his changing attitudes toward the Ji lineage and his relations with two ministers of Lǔ, father and son, Ji Huanzi and Ji Kangzi. The *Analects*, *Mengzi*, and *Zuo zhuan* present several incidents, early in Confucius' career, in which he comments negatively on the Ji lineage, on the behavior of Ji Huanzi as minister of Lǔ, and on Yang Hu, a close associate of the Ji lineage. The *Analects* also presents any number of accounts of more positive conversations between Confucius and Ji Huanzi's son Ji Kangzi, who became Minister of Lǔ in 494 B.C.E., with the accession of Duke Ai. These events are summarized in table 11.2.[35]

The Ji lineage was one of three (the Ji, Shu, and Meng) that maintained close connections to the ducal house, and were able to hold the rulers of the state of Lu in some degree of dependency. In the *Analects* (3.1–2), Confucius condemns both the Ji family and the Three Families as usurpers of authority. Nonetheless,

TABLE 11.2
CONFUCIUS AND THE JI LINEAGE

DUKE	MINISTER	DATE	INCIDENT	TEXTUAL SOURCES
Zhao	[Ji Daozi]	541–509		
	Ji Pingzi	529	Jì Píngzǐ becomes head of Ji lineage	Zuo, Zhao 12
		517	Confucius criticizes the Ji	LY 3:1–2, 6, 10–11
		516–510	Three families seize power in Lǔ	
		516	Duke Zhao flees to Qi, as does Confucius	
		515	Confucius returns to Lǔ, without office	
		510	death of Duke Zhao, heir bypassed	
Ding		509	Ding, a member of ducal house, named Duke	
		505	death of Jì Píngzǐ	Zuo, Ding 5
			Yang Hu imprisons Jì Huánzǐ and usurps power	LY 17:1
			in Lǔ, criticized by Confucius	Meng 3B7
	Ji Huanzi	505–492		
		501	victory of Three Families, Yang Hu flees to Qi, invites Confucius to join him Confucius appointed sikou in Lǔ	LY 17.5 Zuo Ding 1 Meng 5B4, 6B6
		500	disagreement with Jì Huánzǐ over criminal case	
			Zilu and Ziyu enter service of the Ji	
			Jì Huángzǐ	
		497	Confucius leaves Lǔ for Wei after present of girls to Jì Huánzǐ	LY 17:4 Meng 6B6
Ai	Ji Kangzi	494		
		484	Confucius returns to Lǔ Jì Kāngzǐ consults him on taxation	LY 11:17 Meng 4A14 ZuoZS 58:27a–b
		484–479	conversations with Jì Kāngzǐ	LY 6:8 10:16 11:7 12:17 12:18 12:19
		479	death of Confucius	

Confucius himself seems to have been a dependent of the Ji. In 517 B.C.E., during the reign of Duke Zhao, he criticized the Ji family after the performance of the di sacrifice in the temple of Duke Xiang. As the three powerful families of Ji, Shu, and Meng gained power, he fled Lu for Qi, along with Duke Zhao. He returned the following year, but held no office during the reign, first of the Ji family, and then of Yang Hu, who was forced to flee to Qi in 502. By this time, Duke Ding had succeeded to the throne of Lu, and Ji Huanzi was minister in Lu. Confucius assumed the office of *sikou* under Ji Huanzi, and, according to tradition, came into a difference of opinion with him over a legal case and left Lǔ as a result Ji Huanzi's conduct.[36] Thus Confucius' initial interactions with the Ji family seem to have been critical.

In 494, Duke Ai acceded to the throne of Lu and Ji Kangzi succeeded his father Ji Huanzi as minister of Lǔ. The *Analects* and *Mengzi* present a number of accounts of conversations between Confucius, Duke Ai, and Ji Kangzi, all of which presumably occurred between Confucius' return to Lǔ in 484, ten years after Ji Kangzi's ministry, and his death in 479. These conversations between Confucius and Ji Kangzi are far friendlier in tone. According to the *Analects*, Ji Kangzi consulted Confucius on the qualifications of the officials Zhong You and [Ran] Qiu (6:8), made him a gift of medicine (10:16), asked him about learning and his disciples (11:7, a discussion of Yan Hui), about thieves (12:18), and about government (12:17, 19). The latter is the famous statement that "the virtue of the gentleman is like wind; the virtue of the small man is like grass. Let the wind blow over the grass and it is sure to bend."[37]

In summary, Confucius was, to some degree, a contemporary of several generations of the Ji lineage. He was born shortly after the death of Jì Wénzǐ 季文子 (Jìsūn Hángfù 季孫行父, d. 566). His life spanned those of Jì Wǔzǐ 季武子 (Jìsūn Sù 季孫宿, d. 534), his son Jì Dàozǐ 季悼子 (d. 529), his son Jì Píngzǐ 季平子 (Jìsūn Yìrú 季孫意如 or Yǐnrú 隱如, d. 504), his son Jì Huánzǐ 季桓子 (Jìsūn Sī 季孫斯, d. 491), and his son Jì Kāngzǐ 季康子 (Jìsūn 季孫, d. 467).[38] We know him to be a direct acquaintance of both Jì Huánzǐ and Jì Kāngzǐ.

According to the *Liènǚ zhuàn*, Jìng Jiāng was the wife of the younger brother of Jì Kāngzǐ's paternal grandfather (his *zòngzǔ shúmǔ* 從組叔母.)[39] Gōngfù Mùbó thus would be a younger brother of Jì Píngzǐ (d. 505 B.C.E.), the son of Jì Dàozǐ. This genealogy would make Jì Dàozǐ the grandfather of Wénbó and the great-grandfather of Jì Kāngzǐ. It is consistent with commentaries that refer to Jì Daòzǐ as Jìng Jiāng's father-in-law and Jì Kāngzǐ's great-grandfather.[40] Thus, we might estimate her birth as circa 540 B.C.E., and the birth of Wénbó some time between 525 and 515. These dates are consistent with Wénbó being a student of Confucius for a brief period between 501 and 497, when he left Lǔ for Wèi. By this reckoning, the story of Jìng Jiāng's sending her son to Confucius as a student is historically credible. Given Confucius' brief tutelage of Wénbó and the latter's lackluster record and early departure, it is no surprise that he does not appear in the *Analects*. Further, if Jì Kāngzǐ was an associate of both Confucius and Jìng Jiāng, it is plausible that Confucius might have met her, or at least heard of her exploits in detail, from a great-nephew who clearly held a great deal of respect (and fear) for her.

The *Gúo yǔ*, *Liènǚ zhuàn*, and *Hán Shì wàizhuàn* all support this dating of Jìng Jiāng as a contemporary of Confucius. The *Zuo zhuan* contains a separate account of a Mùbó of Lǔ, who marries a woman named Dài Jǐ 戴己 of Jǔ 莒 , whose son Wénbó succeeded Mùbó in office in Lǔ. These details all appear in the Lìènǚ zhuàn life story of Jìng Jiāng, but the events described in the Zuo zhuan take place between 640 and 612 B.C.E, some one hundred and fifty years before the life of Jì Kāngzǐ. Closer examination reveals that the Zuǒ zhuàn and Gúo yǔ (and later) narratives refer to different sets of individuals. Nevertheless, the similarities in names and places provide interesting insights into how the Lìènǚ zhuàn life story may have been constructed. That information is discussed in the appendix, below.

The foregoing account of Confucius' association with Jìng Jiāng also sheds light on his changing relations with the Ji family. His initial criticisms of Ji Huanzi and Yang Hu have now mellowed into a far more positive attitude toward Jì Kāngzǐ, and, perhaps, through him, for the entire family. In this light, Confucius' repeated praise of "the woman of the Ji" (Jì shì zhī fù 季氏之婦) is all the more striking, in that it exemplifies this new attitude. His respect for the Ji family is now so great that he uses Jìng Jiāng as an example to instruct his disciples![41]

III. Later Lives of Jìng Jiāng

Confucius praises Jìng Jiāng (and the girl of Agu) for knowledge of the rites. These narratives show a tension between Jìng Jiāng's unmistakable expertise in learning, politics, and ritual, and Confucius's praise of her, which is directed toward her knowledge of ritual and cultivation of her son, but not of herself. Confucius' good opinion seems to ignore striking aspects of her actual talents and behavior: her expertise in argument and analogy. This aspect of Jìng Jiāng's virtue all but disappears in later depictions of her in Song Neo-Confucian texts and Ming illustrated editions of the Lìènǚ zhuàn. In the next section I explore a second range of narratives that clearly portray Jìng Jiāng as an expert participant in the delineation of the separate spheres of men and women.

1. THE SEPARATION OF MEN AND WOMEN

The last two sections of the Lìènǚ zhuàn narrative describe admonitions to Jì Kāngzǐ after Wénbó's death, when Jìng Jiāng had remained with the Ji family. These narratives specifically stress her understanding of the "separate spheres" of men and women. In the first, Jì Kāngzǐ repeatedly tried to speak with her, first at court, then at the gate of her house. She entered without speaking to him, and he followed her and asked how he had offended her. She replies,

> Have you not heard? The son of Heaven and the assembled princes
> manage the affairs of the people in the [outer court and manage the
> affairs of the spirits in the] inner court. From the prime minister
> down, official matters are deliberated in the outer court and domestic
> matters are served in the inner court. Within the household gates,
> women rule and hold office; high and low are alike in this. In the outer

court, you attend to the responsibilities of lords and officials; in the inner court, you attend to the business of the Ji. Of these things it is not for me to venture to speak.[42]

Jìng Jiāng emphasizes that women govern and hold office within the household. Her account breaks down government functions to an outer and an inner sphere: the outer sets the duties of state officials; the inner administers the Ji family. When Jì Kāngzǐ follows her to her door and attempts to visit her, she speaks to him but does not allow him past the threshold. She performs sacrifices for Jì Dàozǐ (her father-in-law), and Jì Kāngzǐ assists. She does not personally receive the sacrificial meats or stay for the feast, and would only sacrifice if all the clan officials were present. Confucius described her as knowing how to distinguish the lǐ of women from the lǐ of men.[43]

Both Jìng Jiāng's account of the lǐ of men and women and Confucius' praise of her for it raise questions about the extent to which such separations were maintained during Warring States and early Han times, even by conservative "Confucians." For all her defense of the gender system, many of her actions seem to break down the very gender separations her words advocate. For example, Jìng Jiāng personally offers sacrifice when mourning her son Wénbó. Other Liènǚ zhuàn accounts show women as active in sacrifice and divination, performing sacrifice directly or supervising it.[44]

Despite Lǐ jì prescriptions that the concerns and activities of men and women should differ, there is considerable evidence that the activities of women of all classes overlapped considerably with those of their male relatives. Weaving, the paradigmatic women's work, was typically done within the home for use within the home; even aristocratic women such as Jìng Jiāng wove and spun. Widows and other women also engaged in weaving and the care of silkworms as a livelihood.[45] Women engaged in other occupations outside the home; they worked in the fields with their husbands, and were expert at the occupations of their husbands or fathers.[46] Erudite and expert women gave instruction outside their homes and were recognized for their wisdom, technical expertise and erudition. They participated in political life, both by actual presence at court and by indirect influence. Other accounts of female expertise include agriculture, archery, astronomy, divination, ferrying, funerary rites, and physiognomy, as well as general skills of prediction, interpretation, the quotation of poetry, knowledge of ritual, and the composition of eulogies and petitions.[47]

In sum, Jìng Jiāng is portrayed as an exemplary woman whose words seem to uphold the gender system of separation of men and women, but whose actions undermine traditional prohibitions against women's concern with politics or matters external to the home. Warring States and Han accounts of her preserve this tension. Jìng Jiāng is a prominent figure in Song and Ming accounts of women's virtue. They portray her entirely as an exemplar of the gender system, and completely de-emphasize her intellectual acumen and decisiveness.

2. NEO-CONFUCIAN VIEWS ON FEMALE EDUCATION

Zhū Xī emphasized intellectual aspects of the separation, stressing the dangers of women's participation in political life, and stressing that women should "never initiate affairs or take action on their own."[48] He encouraged education for women, within the proper limits of moral tracts and directed toward the proper goals of assisting a husband.[49] Zhū Xī's (1130–1200) Xiǎo xué 小學 or Elementary Learning articulated what was to become a standard position on women: "A wife is one who bends to the will of another and so her rectitude lies in not following her own will."[50] This work draws extensively on the "Nei ze" or "Domestic Regulations" chapter of the Lǐ jì.[51] It is organized by life cycle, not by virtues. Its instructions to girls, wives, and mothers draw heavily on the Lǐ jì, and emphasize prohibitions against remarriage, the importance of the physical separation of men and women, and filiality to mothers-in-law.[52] It quotes the Liènǚ zhuàn to emphasize the importance of instruction, including prenatal instruction, and the maintenance of separate spheres: the physical, social, and intellectual separation of men and women. Zhū Xī includes the examples of the mothers of King Wen and Mengzi as examples of the instruction of sons. He uses Jìng Jiāng, whom he calls "the aunt of Jì Kāngzǐ," as a model of separate spheres.[53] Zhū Xī emphasizes the need to keep women away from political life, and criticizes self-willed women.[54] Although he stresses the importance of women as teachers, this stress on moral education was in the interest of filiality, including the submission of wife to husband.[55]

3. MING EDITIONS

The Liènǚ zhuàn style of narrative was adopted and transformed on a wide scale. Beginning with the Standard History of the Later Han, a chapter of exemplary biographies of women (liènǚ 列女) began to appear in the "Collected Biographies" sections of dynastic histories. These works, however, varied considerably in their definitions of virtue and the kind of women they selected for their exemplary biographies. It was also a popular subject for illustration from an early period. Pictorial work based upon it ranged from scrolls, screens, and illustrated books to wall and tomb decorations.[56]

Over time, however, the original arguments for the importance of women and some of the most important original criteria for deeming them exemplary were lost or transformed. Starting with the Later Han, collected biographies of virtuous women (liènǚ 列女) were included in dynastic histories. Over the course of time, the criteria for this official recognition of female virtue changed considerably. The liènǚ of the dynastic history of the Later Han resembled those of the Liènǚ zhuàn, but the self-sacrificing, chastity obsessed, and apolitical liènǚ of the Ming dynasty were all but unrecognizable from their earlier predecessors.[57] These new

editions reflected a Ming cultural vocabulary, in which the husband-wife relationship was moved to the foreground. The result was a considerable increase in
numbers of suicides in Ming writings, and a corresponding diminution of "no-
nonsense girls who argued with kings; in their place is a repertoire of expressions
of fidelity to the husband's lineage (widow suicide, widow fidelity, heroic service
to parents-in-law), and (through resistance to rape by invaders) fidelity to the
empire, the family writ large. The strong-minded women in these Ming expan-
sions are now likely to be mothers, who bring sons, rather than rulers, to their
senses, and reprove them for any hint of venality or immorality."[58]

A brief survey of the portrayal of Jìng Jiāng in four illustrated editions shows
important contrasts between (Ming redactions of) Song dynasty editions, and
Ming appropriations of the story of Jìng Jiāng.[59] The *Wénxuǎnlóu* and *Sìbù cóngkān*
editions, which, for purposes of this discussion, I call Han-Song editions, are
organized in chapters titled by six virtues.[60] To these I contrast two Ming dynasty
editions: Lǚ Kun's *Gūi fàn* (1618) and the *Huìtú liènǚ zhuàn*, published during the
Wanli reign (1610–20). Both were Huizhou editions, produced by individual
publishers whose sponsors employed the best illustrators and engravers of the
period.

All four editions show Wénbó bowing before a seated Jìng Jiāng (figures 1–4).
They vary as to Wénbó's age and size, the location of the interview, and what she
is doing. In the *Wénxuǎnlóu* and *Sìbù cóngkān* editions, the illustrations are clearly secondary to the content of the stories themselves. They are small (half the page or
less) and follow the action of the story closely. They emphasize the text and the
human actors over architectural detail and elaborate furnishings of the Huizhou
editions.

The Huizhou editions use elaborate one- or two-page illustrations. In the *Huìtú*
Liènǚ zhuàn, stories appear in a different order and with no conceptual structure
whatever. In the *Gūi fàn*, the stories have been reclassified, both in chapter and
within the chapters; here Jìng Jiāng is classified under the "All Virtues" subhead-
ing of "Wives."

All four editions show Wénbó in a subordinate role, but the Han-Song
editions (*Wénxuǎnlóu* and *Sìbù cóngkān*) reinforce Jìng Jiāng's superiority, whereas the
Ming Huizhou editions (*Gūi fàn* and *Huìtú liènǚ zhuàn*) minimize it. In the Han-Song
editions, Wénbó is noticeably smaller than his mother; the *Sibu congkan* edition in
fact transforms him into a child. The *Gūi fàn* and *Huìtú liènǚ zhuàn* lessen his subordination by showing him as adult, equal to his mother in size, and in elaborate
dress.

IV. Conclusions

Warring States and Han texts portray Jìng Jiāng as a decisive and powerful woman
who did not hesitate to intervene in either family matters or affairs of state, yet

FIGURE 1
The *Wénxuǎnlóu* edition

FIGURE 2
The *Sìbù cóngkān* edition

who was repeatedly praised by Confucius as "understanding the rites" in various contexts. Is this understanding a mode of knowledge equally available to—if not prevalent among—women and men, or does it have some special connotation when used of women? Let me argue in conclusion that, like wisdom, benevolence and the other virtues praised by Confucius are not gendered. The "rites" that Jìng Jiāng understands span much of the range of private and official ritual activity. At the level of family and private conduct, she is expert in the rites of hospitality, marriage, and mourning. She was able to exert influence with family

FIGURE 3
The Gūi fàn edition

FIGURE 4
The Hùitú Liènǔ zhuàn edition

elders without violating proprieties, including skill at apt use of poetic quotation, as, for example, with her arrangement of Wénbó's marriage. She also had a keen sense of the spirit with which rites should be conducted in particular circumstances, as seen in her instructions to Wénbó's concubines. In addition, she had understanding of high state ritual, as shown in her account of the complementary activities of men and women in its preparation and performance. In short, there is nothing restricted, "feminine," or "gendered" about her degree or kind of understanding, nor does Confucius remark on her being a woman as in any way unusual or special.

Yet before using the case of Jìng Jiāng to argue for the moral or epistemological status of women in the earliest layers of "Confucian" thought, we would do well to reflect on the extent to which the recognition of her admittedly unusual abilities may have been a product of her circumstances. As the young widow of a high official, she was in an unusual (but not unique) position to take on the social roles of both father and mother. To this extent, she may have been able to achieve far more of the learning and status of a jūnzǐ 君子 than would normally have been permitted to, or recognized in, a woman.[61] In this sense, her preeminence was far too particular to be indicative of early Confucian views of the status or potential of women. It does suggest a degree of flexibility (especially in the treatment of elite women) that was to be lost or de-emphasized in later Classical Confucian and Neo-Confucian views of women.

V. APPENDIX: MUBO, DAN JI, AND WENBO IN THE ZUO ZHUAN

The *Guó yǔ*, *Liènǚ zhuàn*, *Chūnqiū* and *Zuo zhuan* all contain detailed references to a Mùbó of Lǔ who marries a woman named Dài Jǐ 戴己 of Jǔ 莒 and whose son Wénbó succeed Mùbó in office in Lǔ. The *Guó yǔ* and *Liènǚ zhuàn* accounts center on Jìng Jiāng and her instructions to Wénbó and Jì Kāngzǐ. The *Zuo zhuan* narratives center entirely on Mùbó. They are summarized in table 11.3.

Three significant inconsistencies make it clear that these narratives refer to different sets of individuals. In the first place, the name Mùbó of Lǔ occurs only in the *Zuo zhuan*; the *Chūnqiū* refers to him as Gōngsūn Ào 公孫敖, and once as Mèng Mùbó 孟穆伯. The latter name clearly identifies him as a member of the Meng lineage and rules out any possible relation to the Jì Kāngzǐ of the *Guó yǔ* and later narratives.

The second inconsistency concerns the life spans of Mùbó and Dài Jǐ. In the *Guó yǔ* and *Liènǚ zhuàn* narratives, Mùbó dies young and Jìng Jiāng raises and instructs Wénbó alone. In the *Chūnqiū* and *Zuǒ zhuàn*, Dài Jǐ dies before Mùbó, Mùbó returns to Jǔ in search of another wife, flees Lǔ for Jǔ, and is succeeded in Lǔ by Wénbó. In each narrative, the early death of one spouse is a crucial element in the events that follow. In the *Guó yǔ* and *Liènǚ zhuàn*, it is Mùbó's early death that forces Jìng Jiāng to take on the "paternal" role of instructing her son about

TABLE 11.3
GONGSUN MUBO IN THE ZUO ZHUAN

CHUNQIU	ZUO ZHUAN	NAME	YEAR	EVENT
	Xi 15.1	Mèng Mùbó		led a force in aid of Xu
Xi 15.3		Gōngsūn Ào	643	comes to the aid of Xu
	Wen 1.1	Gōngsūn Ào		receives prognostication that he would be fed by Wénbó and buried by Hui Shu, and that Wénbó would bear progeny in Lǔ
Wen 1.9		Gōngsūn Ào	625	meets with Marquis of Jin
	Wen 1.6	Gōngsūn Ào		meets with Marquis of Jin
Wen 1.11		Gōngsūn Ào		enters Qi
	Wen 1.8	Mùbó		enters Qi
Wen 2.4		Gōngsūn Ào	624	meets with Duke of Song
	Wen 2.4	Mùbó		meets with princes
Wen 5.4		Gōngsūn Ào	621	enters Jin
Wen 7.10		Gōngsūn Ào	619	goes to Jǔ to superintend a covenant
	Wen 7.7	Mùbó	[c.640]	marries Dài Jí of Jǔ, who gives birth to Wénbó. Her younger sister Sheng Ji gives birth to Huì Shú 惠叔. After her death, returns to Jǔ and attempts to marry Lady Sì 巳
	Wen 7.7	Gōngsūn Ào		advised to send Lady Sì back to Jǔ
Wen 8.6		Gōngsūn Ào	618	leaves for the capital, retraces his steps, and flees to Jǔ
	Wen 8.5			enters Zhou bearing mourning gifts, does not arrive there, flees to Jǔ to follow Lady Sì
Wen 14.8		Gōngsūn Ào	612	dies in Qi
	Wen 14.11	Mùbó		After Mùbó's flight, Wénbó established in office in Lǔ. Mùbó bears two sons in Jǔ and seeks Wénbó's help to return. He returns only to flee back to Jǔ. Wénbó falls ill, dies and is succeeded by Hui Shu. Mùbó asks Hui Shu's help to return to Lǔ. He dies before he can return.
Wen 15.4		Gōngsūn Ào	611	his coffin sent back to Luby people of Qi
	Wen 15.4	Mèng		coffin returned after earlier
		Gōngsūn Ào		objections by Duke and buried with honors by Hui Shu. [His mother] Sheng Ji does not attend. Later, Mùbó's sons from Jǔ come to Lǔ and are received with affection by Wénbó's son Mèng Xiànzǐ 孟獻子

Notes: Dài Jí and Shēng Jí 聲巳 are posthumous titles. Wénbó's date of birth is estimated at twenty years before his assumption of office in Lǔ. Section numbering is taken from the Yang Bojun edition of the Zuo zhuan.

government. In the Zuǒ zhuàn, it is the early death of Dai Ji that impels Mùbó to return to Jǔ and eventually flee Lǔ in pursuit of another wife.

Finally, in the Guó yǔ and Liènǚ zhuàn narratives, Wénbó holds office in Lǔ many years after his father Mùbó's death. In the Zuǒ zhuàn, Wénbó attains office at the time of his father's flight to Ju, and dies before Mùbó, who intercedes first with him, and later with his half brother Hui Shu, in order to return to Lǔ from Ju.

The names Mùbó and Wénbó are generic enough that their recurrence is unremarkable; the duplication of a woman's name is more surprising. However, the name Dài Jǐ occurs only in the Liènǚ zhuàn and there only once in the first lines of the life story. The Guó yǔ, Hán Shì wàizhuàn, and Zhànguó cè all call her "the mother of Gongfu Wenbo"; the Lǐ jì and Liènǚ zhuàn call her Jìng Jiāng, and in remarks attributed to Confucius, she is always "the woman of the Ji." Nor does the Zuo zhuan narrative ascribe any particular virtues to Dài Jǐ. It seems most likely that, somehow, during the compilation of the Liènǚ zhuàn the name Dài Jǐ was added to the otherwise consistent life story of Jìng Jiāng, the mother of Gōngfū Wénbó of Lǔ, the woman praised by Confucius.

NOTES

1. Lǔ and Jì are her husband's state and clan. Jìng Jiāng can be construed either as an honorary title or as the woman's personal name and natal family name (xìng 姓). Either is consistent with the typology of women's names in Liu 1990.

2. The Liènǚ zhuàn is a compendium of 125 life stories of women from legendary times to the Han dynasty, mostly of consorts of rulers, but also of commoners. Many of the same narratives appear in other Warring States and Han texts. In the Liènǚ zhuàn the stories are arranged to exemplify the specific virtues that title its chapters. It is conventionally attributed to Liu Xiang and dated approximately 25 B.C.E. For discussion of several problems that surround this dating and attribution see Raphals 1998, chap. 4. For translation see O'Hara 1971.

3. Each woman is praised for one virtue. The other chapters are (2) xián míng 賢明, sage intelligence, (3) rén zhì 仁智, benevolent wisdom, (4) zhēn shùn 貞順, purity and obedience, (5) jié yì 節義 chastity and righteousness, and (6) biàn tōng 辯通, skill in argument. Liènǚ zhuàn narratives within these chapters have a consistent structure. Each story has at least three components. The first is an introduction that consists of genealogical information, a brief statement of virtues or accomplishments, and/or a brief assessment of abilities or virtues. This introduction may be distinct from, or may blend into the second element: one or more life-story narratives that describe meritorious action(s). Each account ends with an assessment of the life-story example, prefaced by the phrase "the lord says" (jūnzǐ yuē 君子曰) and/or one or more apt quotations from the Shi jing. The third is a eulogy or sòng 頌, which summarizes her virtuous deeds and lists her virtues. It may recapitulate the contents of the introductory summary. Most Liènǚ zhuàn life stories have only one narrative element. Four stories are longer, with two to five narrative elements; of these, the story of Jìng Jiāng is the longest. It consists of five elements, several of which are of considerable length. The other long Liènǚ zhuàn narratives are: Ding Jiang of Wei (LNZ 1.7, four elements), the mother of Mencius (1.11, four elements), Queen Deng Man of Chu (LNZ 3.2, two elements) and Yang Shuji of Jin (LNZ 3.10, three elements). For discussion see Raphals 1998, chap. 1.

4. For *zhèng* see Bielenstein 1980:38–39. Titles are taken from Bielenstein (1980) and Hucker (1985).

5. This section refers to a pattern or painted design, copied onto the cloth. According to the *Works of Nature and Man* or *Tiāngōng kāiwù* 天工開物, a seventeenth-century work on technology: "The mental calculations (*xīn jì* 心計) of the artisan who makes the figure design are of the greatest ingenuity (*jīng qiǎo* 精巧). An artist first paints the design and color onto a paper. The artisan follows the painted design (*hua*) in silk and translates it into a pattern, which is hung in the figure tower" (*huà lóu* 花樓, TGKW 64, trans. Zen, Sun, and Sun 1966:56).

6. I am indebted to John Major for this interpretation of *hua* and *wù* (物), which improves the coherence of the analogy. According to the commentary for this passage, the "marking" (*wù* 物) was one *zhāng* 章 of ink. The reference is to an inked string used for measurement. The "weeds" (*wú* 蕪) refer to the "wild" silk that comes from wild silkworms whose silk cannot be reeled, but only cut. The compound "weeds and tendons" (*wu yu mo*) refers to the kinds of fibers from which all clothing is made. According to the *Tiāngōng kāiwù*, the fibers from which all clothing is made come equally from plant and animal sources: "Therefore Nature has provided the materials (*wù* 物) for clothing. Of these the vegetable ones are cotton [hemp] (*xǐ* 枲), hemp (*má* 麻), *meng* hemp (*méng* 苘), and creeper hemp (*gé* 葛); those derived from birds, animals, and insects are furs, woolens, silk (*sī* 絲), and spun silk (*mián* 綿). All the clothing materials [in the world] are about equally divided between vegetable and animal origins" (TGKW 45, trans. Zen, Sun, and Sun 1966:35).

7. This title may refer to the *guan nei hou* or Marquis of Guan Nei, the nineteenth of twenty (second highest) titles of nobility awarded to exceptionally meritorious individuals. See Hucker 1985:286, 421.

8. The commentary indicates that the *jūn* refers to the teeth of the comb. According to Sun Yutang, the term *jūn* 均 in the *Liènǚ zhuàn* is equivalent to "reed" (*gou* 筬) in the *Tiangong kaiwu* (Sun 1963:152). Similarly, the *Tiangong kaiwu* states that the reed comb regulates the breadth and density of the cloth (TGKW 62). The reed consists of eight hundred teeth for gauge and twelve hundred for damask or pongee. Each tooth has a hole or eyelet that holds four unsized threads (or four sized threads combined into two warp yarns), the comb of a draw loom regulates the breadth and density of the cloth. See Zen, Sun, and Sun 1966:53.

9. Liang Duan's commentary adds that the warp beam is *shèng* 勝, victorious, and that being able to unfold (stretch) without limit is an example of the virtue (*dào dé* 道德) of the *san gong*. For description of the drawloom see Sun 1963:155, TGKW 63–64, (trans. Zen, Sun, and Sun 1966:55).

10. LJ 12, 27:8a, trans. Legge 1:454.

11. LNZ 1:8b, quoting *Zhanhan* (Mao 264).

12. GY 5.13 (Lu 2) pp. 205–9, JY 9:41:13a–14a.

13. For Meng Mu's admonition, see LNZ 1.11, HSWZ 9.1 and 9.17, and *Mengzi* 1A12.

14. LNZ 1:8b. Nángōng Jìngshú 南宮敬叔 and Lù Dǔfù 露堵父 both held the office of *daifu* in Lǔ. Nángōng Jìngshú was the son of Mèng Xīzǐ 孟僖子. Jìng Jiāng quotes the words of Jì Dàozǐ 季悼子, her father-in-law.

15. GY 5.11 (Lu 2), pp. 202–3.

16. LJ 32, 54:15a–b, trans. Legge 2:341.

17. GY 5.15 (Lu 2), p. 210. Shī Hài 師亥 was a music master from Lǔ.

18. For discussion of analogies between the behavior of *Liènǚ zhuàn* wives and ministers see Gipoulon (1997) and chapter 1 of Raphals (1998).

19. See Thatcher (1991) and Holmgren (1991).

20. LJ 12, 28:20a. For a different translation see Legge 1:478.

21. 姆教婉娩聽從 LJ 12, 28:21a–b (Legge 1:479).

22. For women's ability to manage their own homes after the death of their husbands see Thatcher (1991) and Raphals (1998), chap. 9.

23. LNZ 1:9a, JY 10:44:8b–9a.

24. 公父氏之婦智也夫 GY 5.16 (Lu 2) p. 211. The note to this passage reiterates that her understanding is 丈夫之智 (p. 212 n. 8).

25. LJ 3, 9:24b–25a. For a different translations see Legge 1:176.

26. LJ 3, 9:25b. For another translation see Legge 1:176.

27. LNZ, GY 5.17 (Lu 2), p. 212.

28. HSWZ 1.19, pp. 6b–7a, trans. modified from Hightower 26.

29. ZGC 20 (Zhao 3) pp. 692–99, trans. Crump 338.

30. ZGC 20 (Zhao 3) pp. 692–99, trans. Crump 339.

31. LNZ 6:5b.

32. I owe this formulation of "superior/inferior" as "benfactor/beneficiary" to Henry Rosemont.

33. Kǒng cóngzǐ 孔叢子, trans. Hightower 14 n. 16.

34. For the dating of these texts see Loewe 1993.

35. I draw upon the standard accounts of the life of Confucius by D. C. Lau, James Legge, and SJ 47. For more recent, and more controversial, accounts see Jensen (1997) and Brooks and Brooks (1998).

36. An account of a disagreement between Confucius and Jì Kāngzǐ (possibly Ji Huanzi) appears in the Han Shi waizhuan (HSWZ 3.22), Shuo yuan (SY 7:3b–4a) and Kongzi jiayu (KZJY 1:5b–6a) All three texts name Jì Kāngzǐ as Confucius's antagonist, but the event seems to have occurred during the ministry of Ji Huanzi.

37. Analects, Lau trans., 115–16.

38. This genealogy is based on Zuo zhuan references to Ji Wenzi (Wen 6 to Xiang 5), Ji Wuzi (Xiang 6 to Zhao 7.7), Ji Daozi (Zhao 12.8), Ji Pingzi (Zhao 9.5 to Ding 5.4), Ji Huanzi (Ding 5 to Ai 3), and Jì Kāngzǐ (Ai 7 to 27).

39. LNZ 1:6b. For kinship terminology, see Feng 1967.

40. For example, LNZ 1:8b and, GY Lu 5.10 (p. 202 n. 1) and 5.14 (p. 210 n. 4).

41. LNZ 1:8b.

42. LNZ 1:9a. The passage corresponds identically to the Gúo yǔ story "Gongfu Wenbo's Mother Discourses on the Inner and Outer Court" (GY 5.12 [Lu 2] pp. 203–4).

43. This passage corresponds to the Gúo yǔ story "Gongfu Wenbo's Mother on the Separation of Men and Women in the Rites" (GY 5.14 [Lu 2] p. 209). Another Gúo yǔ story "Gongfu Wenbo's Mother replies to Jì Kāngzǐ," which does not occur in the Liènǚ zhuàn, describes another admonition to Jì Kāngzǐ. When he asks whether Gōngfū Wénbó ever speaks of him, Jìng Jiāng responds that, according to her mother-in-law, a gentleman who can be humble may enjoy long posterity (GY 5.10 [Lu 2] p. 202).

44. Jiang Yuan divined and personally performed a sacrifice in an attempt to avoid her strange pregnancy (LNZ 1.2); the mother-teacher of Lǔ returned to her parents' home to oversee the ancestral sacrifices (LNZ 1.12); and the filial widow of Liang offered sacrifices for her mother-in-law (LNZ 4.15).

45. For example, Meng Mu (LNZ 1.11), the widow of Duke Bai of Chu (LNZ 4.11), Tao Ying of Lǔ (LNZ 4.13), and the filial widow of Chen (LNZ 4.15). Xuwu of Qi and the women in her association also engaged in weaving and spinning outside the home (LNZ 6.14). Women who engaged in sericulture included the wife of Qiu Huzi of Lu (LNZ 5.9) and "Su of the Goitre" of Qi (LNZ 6.11).

46. Women who worked in the fields with their husbands included the wives of Shun

(LNZ 1.1), Jiang Yuan (LNZ 1.2), and the wives of Lao Lai (LNZ 2.14) and Yue Ling (LNZ 2.15); the wife of Jieyu of Chu went to market (LNZ 2.13), the wife of the bowmaker of Jin instructed Duke Ping in archery (LNZ 6.3), the washerwoman at Agu discoursed with Confucius and his disciple (LNZ 6.6), and the daughter of the ferry officer of Zhao took her father's place as ferryman (LNZ 6.7).

47. For example, Ding Jiang of Wei successfully averted an invasion by Jin (LNZ 1.7). Duke Wen of Jin regained his throne through the efforts of his wife (LNZ 2.3). Zhongzi, the wife of Duke Ling of Qi, remonstrated unsuccessfully with her husband regarding the succession (Zuo, Xiang 19, trans. Legge 483, and LNZ 3.8). Guan Zhong of Qi consulted his concubine on affairs of state (LNZ 6.1); his patron Duke Huan of Qi discussed military campaigns with his wife (LNZ 2.2), as did King Wu of Chu with his (LNZ 3.2). Wives (and sisters) advised their husbands (or brothers) on accepting office (LNZ 2.13, 2.14, 2.15, and 3.12); the woman from Qi Shi in Lu was intensely aware of the political situation of her state (LNZ 3.13). Huai Ying of Yu of Jin resolved a conflict between duty to her state and to her husband (LNZ 5.3). The daughter of Ji Zhong resolved a conflict of loyalty to her father and to her husband. On the advice of her mother, she warned her father, who killed her husband. (The Earl of Zheng, who had plotted to use her husband to kill her father, responded that her husband deserved to die because he took counsel with his wife [Zuo, Huan 15, trans. Legge 64].)

48. Zhū Xī, *Xiǎoxué jíjiě* 5:118 and 2:35 as cited in Ebrey 1993:24. For discussion of the class basis of constructions of virtue in upper-class Song families, see Ebrey 1993:23–25.

49. Zhū Xī, *Zhūzǐ yǔlèi* 7:127 as cited in Ebrey 1993:124.

50. XX 2:66.

51. The *Nèi zé* 內則 or "Domestic Regulations" chapter of the *Lǐ jì* (LJ 11), gives detailed rules for the management of families, including rules that specify and limit contact between the sexes.

52. XX 2:61 and 5:44 (monogamy); 2:64 (seclusion); and 6:14, 27, and 30 (filiality to mothers-in-law).

53. XX 4:1–2 and 4:28.

54. XX 5:45. Zhū Xī quotes the *Yan Family Instructions* to this effect. In his critique of the inadequacies of Ban Zhao's *Nü jie*, Zhu Xi suggested eight chapter headings of his own, which emphasize familial roles over intellectual and moral judgment: propriety, subordination, filiality, harmony, diligence, frugality, generosity, and learning. See Chan 1989:542 and 546 n. 37.

55. Birge 1989:340–41.

56. Wu 1989.

57. See Raphals 1998, chap. 5 and 10, for further discussion of these differences.

58. Carlitz 1991:122.

59. See WXL 1.9, SBCK 1.9, HTLNZ 2.6 (p. 168), all cited by book and story number, and GF 3.1.2 (cited by book, section, and story number). For discussion of these see Carlitz 1991:134–35.

60. The *Wénxuánlóu* edition of 1881 was based on the Southern Song Jian'an Yu family edition, the oldest known edition of the *Liènü zhuàn*. The *Sìbù cóngkān* edition was based on the Ming Changsha Yeshiguan edition of a Song original.

61. By contrast, consider Xunzi's view of the relative capabilities of fathers and mothers: "A father can beget them [children] but cannot suckle them; a mother can feed [suckle] them but cannot instruct or correct them. A junzi not only can feed them [his people], but can instruct and correct them as well" (X 75/19/110). Almost all references to the term "mother" in the *Xúnzǐ* are within the compound "fathers and mothers." For further discussion see Raphals 1998, chap. 1.

REFERENCES

Bielenstein, Hans. 1980. *The Bureaucracy of Han Times*. Cambridge Studies in Chinese History, Literature, and Institutions. Cambridge, Eng., and New York: Cambridge University Press.

Birge, Bettine. 1989. "Chu Hsi and Women's Education." In *Neo-Confucian Education: The Formative Stage*, ed. William Theodore de Bary and John W. Chaffee. Berkeley: University of California Press.

Brooks, E. Bruce Brooks, and A. Taeko Brooks. 1998. *The Original Analects: Sayings of Confucius and His Successors*. New York: Columbia University Press.

Carlitz, Katherine. 1991. "The Social Uses of Female Virtue in Late Ming Editions of Lienu Zhuan." *Late Imperial China* 12.2 (Dec. 1991): 117–52.

Chan, Wing-tsit. 1989. *Chu Hsi: New Studies*. Honolulu: University of Hawaii Press. Chūnqiū Zuǒ zhuàn zhù (Zuo) 春秋左傳注. 1991. Edited by Yang Bojun 楊伯峻. Gaoxiong: Fuwen tushu chubanshe.

Crump, James Irving, trans. 1970. *Chan-kuo ts'e*. Oxford: Clarendon Press.

Ebrey, Patricia Buckley. 1993. *The Inner Quarters: Marriage and the Lives of Chinese Women in the Sung Period*. Berkeley: University of California Press.

Feng, Han-yi. 1967. *The Chinese Kinship System*. Harvard-Yenching Institute Studies 22. Cambridge, Mass.: Harvard University Press.

Gipoulon, Catherine. 1997. "L'image de l'épouse dans le Lienüzhuan." In *En suivant la voie royale: Mélanges offerts à Léon Vandermeersch*, eds. J. Gernet and M. Kalinowski. Paris: École Française d'Extrême-Orient.

Gǔ Liènǚ zhuàn (GLNZ) 古列女傳.

[Xīn biān] Gǔ Liènǚ zhuàn 新編古列女傳 (WXL). Wénxuǎnlóu 文選樓 ed. Wénxuǎnlóu cóngshū 文選樓叢書.

Guī fàn (GF) 閨範. 1618. By Lǚ Kūn 呂坤 (1536–1618). Xin'an (Huizhou): She Yongning. Facsimile ed. in Harvard-Yenching Library.

Gúo yǔ (GY) 國語. Shanghai: Guji chubanshe, 1988.

Hán Shì wàizhuàn (HSWZ) 韓氏外傳. SBCK.

Hàn shū (HS) 漢書. 1962. Beijing: Zhonghua shuju.

Hightower, James R., trans. 1952. *Han Shih Wai Chuan, Han Ying's Illustration of the Didactic Application of the Classic of Songs*. Cambridge Mass.: Harvard University Press.

Holmgren, Jennifer. 1991. "Imperial Marriage in the Native Chinese and Non-Han State, Han to Ming." In *Marriage and Inequality in Chinese Society*, ed. Rubie Watson and Patricia Buckley Ebrey. Berkeley: University of California Press.

Hucker, Charles O. 1985. *A Dictionary of Official titles in Imperial China*. Stanford, Calif.: Stanford University Press.

Hùitú liènǚ zhuàn (HTLNZ) 繪圖列女傳. [Illustrated life stories of women]. Taibei: Zhengzhong shuju, 1971. Reprint of 1779 Zhibuzu zhai ed., 16 juan, similar to Ming edition of 1610–20.

Jensen, Lionel M. 1997. *Manufacturing Confucianism: Chinese Traditions and Universal Civilization*. Durham, N.C.: Duke University Press.

Kǒngzǐ jiāyǔ (JY) 孔子家語. SBBY.

Kǒngzǐ jiāyǔ zhúzì suǒyǐn 孔子家語逐字索引. By D. C. Lau. ICS Ancient Chinese Text Concordance Series. Hong Kong: Commercial Press, 1994.

Legge, James. 1885. *Li chi: Book of Rites*. *Sacred Books of the East*, vols. 27 and 28. London: Oxford University Press; reprint, New York: University Books, 1967.

———. trans. 1872. *V. The Ch'un Ts'ew with the Tso Chuen*. In *The Chinese Classics*, vol. 5. Reprint, Hong Kong: Hong Kong University Press, 1960.

Lǐ jì (LJ) 禮記. Shisanjing zhushu.

Liènǔ zhuàn jiàozhù (LNZ) 列女傳 • 校注. Attributed to Liú Xiàng 劉向. Edited by Liáng Duān 梁端 (ca.1793–1825). SBBY.

Liú Déhàn 劉德漢. 1990. *Dōng Zhōu fùnǔ wèntí yánjiù* 東周婦女問題研究 [Research on the problem of women in the eastern zhou]. Taibei: Taiwan xuesheng shudian.

Loewe, Michael A. N., ed. 1993. *Early Chinese Texts: A Bibliographic Guide*. Berkeley: Society for the Study of Early China and The Institute of East Asian Studies, University of California, Berkeley.

O'Hara, Albert Richard. 1971. *The Position of Women in Early China According to Lieh nu chuan*. Taipei: Mei Ya.

Raphals, Lisa. 1998. *Sharing the Light: Representations of Women and Virtue in Early China*. Albany, N.Y.: SUNY Press.

Shǐ jì (SJ) 史記. 1959. Beijing: Zhonghua shuju.

Shūo yuàn 說苑 (SY) SBBY.

Sūn Yùtáng 孫毓棠. 1963. "*Zhàngúo Qín-Hàn shídài fǎngzhīyè jìshù de bèngbù*" 戰國秦漢時代紡織業技術的進步 *Lìshǐ yánjiù* 歷史研究 3:143–73.

Tàipíng yùlàn (TPYL) 太平御覽. 1960; reprint, 1983. Beijing: Zhonghua shuju.

Thatcher, Melvin P. 1991. "Marriages of the Ruling Elite in the Spring and Autumn Period." In *Marriage and Inequality in Chinese Society*, ed. Rubie Watson and Patricia Buckley Ebrey. Berkeley: University of California Press.

Tiāngōng kāiwù (TGKW) 天工開物. By Sòng Yīngxīng 宋應星. Taibei: Zhonghua, 1955.

Wu Hong. 1989. *The Wu Liang Shrine: The Ideology of Early Chinese Pictorial Art*. Stanford Calif.: Stanford University Press.

Xúnzǐ yǐndé (X) 荀子引得. 1986. Shanghai: Guji chubanshe.

Yán Shì jiāxùn (YSJX) 顏氏家訓. By Yan Zhitui 顏之推 (531–91). ZZJC.

Zen Sun, E-tu, and Shiou-Chuan Sun, trans. *Sung Ying-hsing. Chinese Technology in the Seventeenth Century* [*Tiāngōng Kāiwù*]. University Park: Pennsylvania State University Press, 1966; reprint, Dover Publications, 1997.

Zhàngúo cè (ZGC) 戰國策. 1985. Attributed to Liú Xiàng 劉向. Shanghai: Guji chubanshe.

Zhū Xī 朱熹 (1130–1200). *Xiǎoxué jíjiě* (XX) 小學集解. Edited by Zhāng Bóxíng 張伯行 (1651–1725). Congshu jicheng.

———. *Zhūzǐ yǔleì* 朱子語類. 1986. Beijing: Zhonghua shuju.

An Annotated Bibliography of Works on Confucius and the *Analects*

JOEL SAHLEEN

THE AMOUNT OF MATERIAL WRITTEN about Confucius and the *Analects* is truly enormous. A complete listing of all such works would require a separate volume (or even volumes) of its own. The current bibliography has been designed to provide the reader with a fairly comprehensive (through 1998) survey of scholarly works in English, along with selected works in French, German, Chinese, and Japanese. It does not contain references to any traditional (that is, pre-1911) Chinese scholarship. Scholars interested in those texts are encouraged to look in *Wu ch'iu pei chai Lun yü chi ch'eng* 無求備齋論語集成, published in Taipei in 1966, and compiled under the direction of Yen Ling-fung 嚴靈峰. This 408-volume collection contains most (if not all) of the extant traditional editions of and works on the *Analects*, plus several noteworthy Japanese and modern Chinese commentaries. For a more complete discussion of traditional Chinese scholarship on the *Analects*, please see Henderson (1991), Cheng (1993), and Ivanhoe (this volume). Because the space available for this bibliography is limited, I have chosen not to include any references to individual articles or essays published in Chinese or Japanese language serials. The following bibliography does, however, contain several collections of essays, as well as a few excellent bibliographical materials that can be used to find these essays and articles. Although the *pinyin* romanization system has been used in the rest of this volume, I have elected to use the Wade-Giles system employed by most library catalogs. For the English, French, and German works, I have used the romanization found in the original publication.

Allinson, Robert E. 1982. "On the Negative Version of the Golden Rule as Formulated by Confucius." *New Asia Academic Bulletin* 3: 223–31.

———. 1985. "The Confucian Golden Rule: A Negative Formulation." *Journal of Chinese Philosophy* 12.3: 305–15.

———. 1988. "The Golden Rule in Confucianism and Christianity." *Asian Culture Quarterly* 16.4: 1–15.

———. 1992. "The Golden Rule as the Core Value in Confucianism and Christianity: Ethical Similarities and Differences." *Asian Philosophy* 2.2: 173–85.

Ames, Roger T. 1981. "A Response to Fingarette on Ideal Authority in the Analects." *Journal of Chinese Philosophy* 8.1: 51–7. [Response to Fingarette's article in ibid., 29–50.]

Ames, Roger T. 1984. "On the Contingency of Confucius' Emergent *Tao.*" *Philosophical Review* 7: 117–39.

———. 1988. "Confucius and the Ontology of Knowing." In G. Larson and E. Deutsch, eds. *Interpreting Across Boundaries.* Princeton, N.J.: Princeton University Press. 265–79.

———. 1988. "Rites as Rights: The Confucian Alternative." In Leroy S. Rouner, ed. *Human Rights and the World's Religions.* Notre Dame, Ind.: University of Notre Dame Press. 199–216.

———. 1991. "Reflections on the Confucian Self: A Response to Fingarette." In Mary Bochover, ed. *Rules, Rituals, and Responsibility: Essays Dedicated to Herbert Fingarette.* LaSalle, Ill.: Open Court. 103–14.

———. 1994. "The Focus-Field Self in Classical Confucianism." In Roger T. Ames, ed. *Self as Person in Asian Theory and Practice.* Albany, N.Y.: SUNY Press. 187–212.

Ames, Roger T., and Henry Rosemont Jr., trans. 1998. *The Analects of Confucius: A Philosophical Translation.* New York: Ballantine. xv + 327 pp. [First English translation informed by the partial text of the *Analects* discovered in 1973 in the Dingzhou prefecture 定州 of modern-day Hebei province. Introduction includes discussion of the historical, textual, philosophic, and linguistic background of the text, as well as a "Chinese lexicon" of important terms. Translation is followed by two appendixes: "The Dingzhou Analects" and "Further Remarks on Language, Translation, and Interpretation."]

Arbuckle, Gary. 1993. "An Unnoticed Religious Metaphor in the *Analects?*" *Journal of Chinese Religions* 20 (fall): 1–9.

Bahm, Archie J. 1969. *The Heart of Confucius.* New York: Wetherhill. 159 pp. [A very free interpretation of the *Analects* based on the translations of Legge, Collier, Lin, and others. Designed for the general reader.]

Beattie, Paul H. 1988. "The Religion of Confucius: The First Humanist." *Religious Humanism* 22.1: 11–17.

Behuniak, Jim P. 1998. "Poem as Proposition in the *Analects*: A Whiteheadian Reading of a Confucian Sensibility." *Asian Philosophy* 8.3: 191–202.

Bloom, Irene T. 1997. "The *Analects* of Confucius: Then and Now." In Ainslie T. Embree and Carol Gluck, eds. *Asia in Western and World History: A Guide for Teaching.* Armonk, N.Y.: M. E. Sharpe. 295–308.

Bodde, Derk. 1933. "A Perplexing Passage in the Confucian *Analects.*" *Journal of the American Oriental Society* 53: 347–51.

Boltz, William G. 1983. "Word and Word History in the *Analects*: The Exegesis of Lun Yü IX.1." *T'oung Pao* 69.4–5: 261–71.

Bresciani, Umberto. 1986. "The Religious Thought of Confucius." *Ching Feng* 29.2/3: 129–44.

Brooks, E. Bruce. 1996. "The Life and Mentorship of Confucius." *Sino-Platonic Papers,* no. 72.

Brooks, E. Bruce, and A. Taeko Brooks. 1998. *The Original Analects: Sayings of Confucius and His Successors.* New York: Columbia University Press. x + 342 pp. [Offers a novel, though highly controversial, interpretation of the chronology and composition of the *Analects,* which maintains that the text developed gradually through a process of accretion over a period of 230 years. Includes introduction, translation (reordered by proposed dates), and several appendixes on the methodology and historical significance of the project.]

Bui, Duc Tin. 1989. *Essai sur le "Luan Ngu" ou "Entretiens" de Confucius.* Paris: Sudestasie. viii + 121 pp.

Buri, Fritz. 1985. "Die Gespräche des Konfuzius und Gotthelfs Bernerkalender." *Zeitschrift für Religions- und Geistesgeschichte* 37.3: 216–52.

Callahan, William A. 1994. "Resisting the Norm: Ironic Images of Marx and Confucius." *Philosophy East and West* 44.2: 279–301.

Casey, E. S. 1984. "Commemoration and Perdurance in the *Analects,* Books I and II." *Philosophy East and West* 34.4: 389–99.

Chan, Alan. 1984. "Philosophical Hermeneutics and the *Analects*: The Paradigm of Tradition." *Philosophy East and West* 34.4: 421–36.

Chan, Charles Wing-Hoi. 1996. "Confucius and Political Loyalism: The Dilemma." *Monumenta Serica* 44: 25.

Chan, Wing-tsit. 1955. "The Evolution of the Confucian Concept of *Jen*." *Philosophy East and West* 4: 295–319. [See esp. 295–301.]

————, trans. 1969. "The Humanism of Confucius." In Wing-tsit Chan, ed. *A Sourcebook in Chinese Philosophy*. London: Oxford University Press. 14–48. [Translation of selected passages with commentary and an introductory essay.]

Chang, Chi-yun 張其昀 (trans. by Shih Chao-yin). 1954. *A Life of Confucius*. Taipei: China Culture Publishing Foundation. 113 pp.

————(trans. by Tsao Wen-yen). 1974. "Confucius' Contribution to World Civilization." *Chinese Culture* 15.3: 1–8.

————. 1975. "Emerson and Confucius." *Sino-American Relations* 1.3: 54–60.

————(trans. by Orient Lee). 1980. "A System of Cardinal Values for Ideal Personality and Ideal Society." *Chinese Culture* 21.3: 39–70. [Similar title in *Asian and Pacific Quarterly of Cultural and Social Affairs* 14.1 (1982) 1–23.]

————(trans. by Orient Lee). 1980–83. *Confucianism: A New Interpretation*. Published serially in *Chinese Culture*. Chapter 1, "The Great Confucius," 21.2 (1980) 1–56; chapter 2, "Confucius' Philosophy of Life," 21.3 (1980) 1–36; chapter 3, "Confucius' Philosophy of Education," 21.4 (1980) 21–56; chapter 4, "Confucius' Political Philosophy," 22.1 (1981) 1–31; chapter 5, "Confucius' Philosophy of Law," 22.3 (1981) 1–21; chapter 6, "Confucius Philosophy of Art," 22.4 (1981) 73–94; chapter 7, "Confucius' Philosophy of Change and of History," 23.1 (1982) 1–31; chapter 8, "Confucius' Military Philosophy," 23.2 (1982) 1–19; chaper 9, "Confucius' Religious Philosophy," 23.4 (1982) 39–63; chapter 10, "The Model Types of Man by Confucian Standards," 24.1 (1983) 1–17; chapter 11, "The Disciples of Confucius," 24.2 (1983) 1–25. [Translation of the author's *K'ung hsüeh chin i* 孔學今義.]

Chang, T'ai-yen 章太炎. 1986. "Kuang Lun yü p'ien chih." 廣論語駢枝. In *Chang T'ai-yen chüan chi* 章太炎全集. Shanghai: Shanghai jen min ch'u pan she. 6. [Originally published in *Chung fa ta hsüeh yueh k'an* 中法大學月刊 2.2 (1932) 1–18.]

Chao, Chi-pin 趙紀彬. 1972–73. "The Origin of Confucius' Ideology of Harmony but not Equality and the Logical Goal of His Theory of Reconcilling Contradictions." *Chinese Studies in Philosophy* 4.1–2: 100–164.

————. 1976. *Lun yü hsin tan* 論語新探. Beijing: Jen min ch'u pan she. 419 pp. [Originally published in 1959 by Jen min ch'u pan she, Beijing (172 pp.); see the author's "Lun yü hsin t'an tao yen" 論語新探導言, in *Chung-kuo che hsüeh* 中國哲學 10 (1983) 49–62, and the review essay by Rongen (1978).]

Chao, Ts'ung 趙聰. 1975. *Lun yü hsiang shih* 論語詳釋. Taipei: Hua lien ch'u pan she. 443 pp. [Originally published in 1967 as *Lun yü i chu* 論語譯註. Hong Kong: Yu lien ch'u pan she.]

Ch'e, Ming-shen 車銘深. 1938. *Lun yü yü ju chia ssu hsiang* 論語與儒家思想. Ch'ang-sha: Shang wu yin shu kuan. 106 pp.

Chen, Ellen. 1988. "Confucius, Aristotle, and Contemporary Revolutions." In George F. McLean, ed. *Person and Society*. Lanham, Md.: University Press of America. 17–24.

Chen, Huan-Chang. 1911. *The Economic Principles of Confucius and His School*. New York: Columbia University Press. xv + 756 pp. [See pp. 73–138.]

Chen, Jun-min. 1987. "Clarifications on Confucius' Confucianism: Concerning the Rise of Confucianists in the Confucian School Founded by Confucius and its Historical Position." *Journal of Chinese Philosophy* 14.1: 91–95.

Chen, N. 1997. "Confucius' View of Fate (ming)." *Journal of Chinese Philosophy* 24.3: 323–59.

Ch'en, Ching-p'an. 1993. *Confucius as a Teacher*. Petaling Jaya: Delta. 522 pp. [Originally published in 1990 by Foreign Languages Press, Beijing.]

Ch'en, Li-fu. 1976. *Why Confucius has been Regarded as the Model Teacher of All Ages*. Jamaica, N.Y.: St. John's University Press. vi + 126 pp.

————(trans. by Shih-shun Liu). 1986. *The Confucian Way: A New and Systematic Study of the 'Four Books.'* New York: KPI. xxvi + 614 pp. [Translation of Ch'en. 1967. *Ssu shu tao kuan* 四書道貫. Taipei: Shih chieh shu chu. 2 vols. 796 pp.]

Ch'en, Ta-ch'i 陳大齊. 1968. *Lun yü i chieh* 論語臆解. Taipei: Taiwan shang wu yin shu kuan. 306 pp.

————. 1979. *K'ung-tzu hsüeh shuo* 孔子學説. Taipei: Cheng chung shu chu. 327 pp.

————. 1987. *K'ung-tzu yen lun kuan t'ung chi* 孔子言論貫通集. Taipei: Hsüeh sheng shu chu. 139 pp.

Cheng, Anne, trans. 1981. *Entretiens de Confucius*. Paris: Éditions du Seuil. 153 pp. [Reviewed by F. Aubin in *Archives de Sciences Sociales des Religions* 28.56 (1983) 240.]

————. 1993. "Lun yü." In Michael Loewe, ed. *Early Chinese Texts: A Bibliographical Guide*. Berkeley: Society for the Study of Early China, Institute of East Asian Studies, University of California, Berkeley. 313–23. [Provides an excellent introduction to the history and authorship of the text, followed by bibliographical references to: (1) modern annotated editions, (2) traditional, modern, and Japanese secondary studies, (3) Western language translations, (4) Japanese kambun editions, and (5) indexes.]

Cheng, Chung-ying. 1977. "Some Responses to Creel's 'Comments on Harmony and Conflict.'" *Journal of Chinese Philosophy* 4: 279–86. [Response to Creel's article in ibid., 271–77. On the relationship between the philosophy of Confucius and the "Ten Wings" of the I Ching.]

————. 1983. "On Timeliness (Shih-Chung) in the *Analects* and I Ching: An Inquiry into the Philosophical Relationship Between Confucius and the I Ching." *PICS: Thought and Philosophy* 1: 277–338.

————. 1987. "Confucius, Heidegger, and the Philosophy of the I Ching: A Comparative Inquiry into the Truth of Human Being." *Philosophy East and West* 37.1: 51–70.

Cheng, Hsüeh-li. 1987. "Confucius and Ayer on the Logic of Morals." *Bulletin of the College of Liberal Arts, National Taiwan University* 35: 309–25.

Cheng, T'ien-hsi. 1950. "Confucius: The Man and His Teachings." *Asiatic Review* (Jan.): n.p.

Ch'eng, Shih-chüan 程石泉. 1981. *Lun yü tu hsün chieh ku* 論語讀訓解故. Taipei: Hsien chih ch'u pan she. 372 pp. [First published in 1972 by Yu lien ch'u pan she, Hong Kong.]

Ch'eng, Shu-te 程樹德. 1973. *Lun yü chi shih* 論語集釋. Taipei: Ting wen shu chu. 2 vols. [First published in 1943 by Hua pei p'ien i kuan, Beijing. Probably the most complete modern edition of the *Analects*.]

Chien, Ch'ao-liang 簡朝亮. 1973. *Lun yü chi chu pu cheng shu shu* 論語集注補正述疏. Taipei: Ting wen shu chu. 641 pp. [First published in 1917.]

Ch'ien, Mu 錢穆. 1918. *Lun yü wen chieh* 論語文解. Shanghai: Shang wu yin shu kuan. 2 vols.

————. 1962. *Lun yü yao lüeh* 論語要略. Taipei: Taiwan shang wu yin shu kuan. 162 pp. [First published in 1925 by Shang wu yin shu kuan, Shanghai.]

————. 1985. *Lun yü hsin chieh* 論語新解. Sichuan: Pa shu shu she. 482 pp. [First published (as an independent volume) in 1963 by Hsin ya yen chiu suo, Hong Kong (687 pp.). See also the Taiwan edition published in 1965 by San min shu chu, Taipei (687 pp.).]

————. 1994. *K'ung-tzu yü Lun yü; K'ung-tzu chuan* 孔子與論語；孔子傳. Taipei: Lien ching ch'u pan she. 465 and 254 pp. [Originally published separately.]

Chin ssu shih nien lai K'ung-tzu yen chiu lun wen hsüan pien 近四十年來孔子 研究論文選編. 1987. Chi-nan: Chi Lu shu she. 661 pp.

Ching hsüeh yen chiu lun chu mu lu, 1912–1987 經學研究論著目錄 1912–1987. 1994. Han hsüeh *yen chiu chung hsin ts'ung kan: Mu lu lei*. No. 9. Taipei: Han hsüeh yen chiu chung hsin. 2 vols. vi + 26 + 1003 pp. [Lin Ch'ing-chang 林慶彰, senior ed.; a comprehensive bibliography of Chinese books and articles written on each of the thirteen classics. For works on the *Analects*, see vol. 2, 638–721.]

Chiu, Chen-ching 邱鎮京. 1977. *Lun yü ssu hsiang t'i hsi* 論語思想體系. Taipei: Wen chin ch'u pan she. 195 pp.

Chong, Chong Kim. 1998. "Confucius's Virtue Ethics. Li, yi, wen and chih in the *Analects.*" *Journal of Chinese Philosophy* 25.1: 101–30.

Chou, Chung 周中. 1967. *Lun yü tsung ho yen chiu* 論語綜合研究. Nan-t'uo hsien: Ji hsin wen hua ch'u pan she. 148 pp.

Chung, Chao-p'eng 鍾肇鵬. 1983. *K'ung-tzu yen chiu* 孔子研究. Taipei: Shu hsin chu pan she. 367 pp. [Mainland edition published by Chung-kuo she hui k'o hsüeh ch'u pan she in 1990.]

Cleary, Thomas F., trans. 1992. *The Essential Confucius*. San Francisco: Harper. xii + 179 pp.

Cohen, Maurice. 1976. "Confucius and Socrates." *Journal of Chinese Philosophy* 3.2: 159–68.

Cohen, Stanley G. 1983. "The Religiousness of K'ung-Fu-Tzu (Confucius)." *Zeitschrift für Religions- und Geistesgeschichte* 35.1: 34–49.

Couvreur, Séraphin, trans. 1930. *Entretiens de Confucius*. In *Les Quatre Livres*. Sien Hsien: Mission Catholique. vii + 748 pp. [Chinese text; translation in Latin and French.]

Creel, Herrlee Glessner. 1932. "Confucius and Hsün-tzu." *Journal of the American Oriental Society* 51: 23–32. [On Confucius' and Hsün-tzu's theories of human nature.]

———. 1932. "Was Confucius Agnostic?" *T'oung Pao* 29: 55–99.

———. 1953. *Chinese Thought from Confucius to Mao Tse-tung*. Chicago: University of Chicago Press. ix + 292 pp. [See pp. 25–46.]

———. 1960. *Confucius and the Chinese Way*. New York: Harper. 363 pp. [Previously published as *Confucius, the Man and the Myth* (New York: John Day, 1949).]

———. 1977. "Comments on Harmony and Conflict." *Journal of Chinese Philosophy* 4: 271–77. [See response by Cheng Chung-ying in ibid., 279–86.]

———. 1979. "Discussion of Professor Fingarette on Confucius." In Henry Rosemont Jr. and Benjamin I. Schwarz, eds. *Studies in Classical Chinese Thought. Journal of the American Academy of Religion*. Special Thematic Issue 47.3: 407–16.

Creel, Lorraine 1943. *The Concept of Social Order in Early Confucianism*. Ph.D. dissertation, University of Chicago. 140 pp. [See pp. 5–52.]

Crow, Carl. 1938. *Master Kung: The Story of Confucius*. New York and London: Harper. 347 pp.

Cua, Antonio S. 1977. "The Concept of Paradigmatic Individuals in the Ethics of Confucius." *Inquiry* 14.1/2: 41–55.

———. 1984. "Confucian Vision and Human Community." *Journal of Chinese Philosophy* 11.3: 227–38.

Danton, George H. 1943. "Schiller and Confucius." *German Quarterly* 16: 173–87.

Dawson, Raymond. 1982. *Confucius*. Oxford: Oxford University Press. viii + 95 pp.

———, trans. 1993. *Confucius: The Analects*. Oxford and New York: Oxford University Press. xxxiv + 110 pp.

de Bary, William Theodore. 1989. *Confucius as a Noble Man. Occasional Paper and Monograph Series.* No. 14. Singapore: Institute of East Asian Philosophies. 24 pp.

———. 1989. *The Noble Man in the Analects. Occasional Paper and Monograph Series.* no. 17. Singapore: Institute of East Asian Philosophies. 23 pp.

———. 1990. "The Prophetic Voice in the Confucian Nobleman." *Ching Feng* 33.1: 3–19.

———. 1991. *The Trouble with Confucianism*. Cambridge: Harvard University Press. 132 pp. [A more extensive treatment of the issues covered in de Bary. 1989. *The Trouble with*

Confucianism. Occasional Paper and Monograph Series. No. 13. Singapore: Institute of East Asian Philosophies. 20 pp.]

Ding, Wangdao. 1997. *Understanding Confucius.* Beijing: Chinese Literature Press. 250 pp.

Do-Dinh, Pierre (trans. by Carles Lam Markmann). 1969. *Confucius and Chinese Humanism.* New York: Funk and Wagnalls. 217 pp.

Drengson, Alan R. 1983. "Being a Mountain, Astride a Horse, The Warlord Faces South: Reflection on the Art of Ruling." *Philosophy East and West* 33: 35–48. [A comparison of Confucius' and Kagemusha's notions of the ideal ruler.]

Dubs, Homer H. 1928. "Did Confucius Study the Book of Changes?" *T'oung Pao* 25: 82–90.

———. 1930. "'Nature' in the Teaching of Confucius." *Journal of the American Oriental Society* 50: 233–37.

———. 1946. "The Political Career of Confucius." *Journal of the American Oriental Society* 66: 273–89.

———. 1949–52. "The Date of Confucius' Birth." *Asia Major* n.s. 1–2: 139–46.

———. 1951. "Confucius: His Life and Teaching." *Philosophy* 26: 307–27.

Durrant, Stephen W. 1981. "On Translating Lun Yü." *CLEAR* 3.1: 109–19.

Ebhard, Wolfram. 1971. "Confucius as a Revolutionist and a Critic of Morals." In Wolfram Ebhard, ed. *Moral and Social Values of the Chinese: Collected Essays.* Taipei: Cheng-wen Publishing. 401–11. [Originally published as "Konfuzius als Revolutionär und Sittenkritiker." *Der Weltkreis* 3 (1993) 1–7.]

Englert, Siegfried, and Roderich Ptak. 1986. "Nan-Tzu, or Why Heaven Did Not Crush Confucius." *Journal of the American Oriental Society* 106.4: 679–86. [On the wife of Duke Ling of Wei and traditional Confucian attitudes toward women.]

Eno, Robert. 1990. "Two Levels of Meaning: The Role of T'ien in the *Analects.*" In Eno's *The Confucian Creation of Heaven: Philosophy and the Defense of Ritual Mastery.* Albany, N.Y.: SUNY Press. 79–98. [Entire book reviewed by Philip J. Ivanhoe in *Journal of Asian Studies* 50.4 (1991a) 907–8; Kwong-loi Shun in *Harvard Journal of Asiatic Studies* 52.2 (1992) 739–56; Mark Csikszentmihalyi in *Journal of the American Oriental Society* 112 (1992) 681–2; and Kidder Smith in *Journal of Ritual Studies* 7.1 (1993) 192–93.]

Eoyang, Eugene. 1988. "Waley or Pound? The Dynamics of Genre in Translation." *Tamkang Review* 19: 441–65. [On translating the *Analects.*]

Étiemble, René. 1958. *Confucius.* Paris: Gallimard. viii + 314 pp.

Fan, Wen-lan. 1975–76. "Confucius and the Confucian Theories He Created." *Chinese Law and Government* 8.3: 11–22.

Fingarette, Herbert. 1966. "Human Community as Holy Rite: An Interpretation of Confucius' *Analects.*" *Harvard Theological Review* 59.1: 53–67.

———. 1972. *Confucius: The Secular as Sacred.* New York: Harper and Row. xi + 84 pp. [Reviewed by Frederick Sontag in *Religious Studies* 10 (1974) 245–46; Henry Rosemont Jr. in *Philosophy East and West* 26.4 (1976) 463–77; Chad Hansen in *Journal of Chinese Philosophy* 3.2 (1976) 197–204. For other discussions of Fingarette's interpretation, see Fu (1978), Creel (1979), Schwarz (1985), Graham (1989), Hwang (1990), Ivanhoe (1990), Shun (1993), and Wilson (1995).]

———. 1978. "Comments on Charles Fu's Discussion of *Confucius: The Secular as Sacred.*" *Philosophy East and West* 28.2: 223–26. [Response to Fu's article in ibid., 181–98.]

———. 1979. "Following the 'One Thread' of the *Analects.*" *Studies in Classical Chinese Thought. Journal of the American Academy of Religion* Special Thematic Issue, vol. 47.3: 373–406. [On this topic see also Ivanhoe (1990) and Van Norden (this volume).]

———. 1979. "The Problem of the Self in the *Analects.*" *Philosophy East and West* 29.2: 129–40.

———. 1981. "How the *Analects* Portrays the Ideal of Efficacious Authority." *Journal of Chinese Philosophy* 8.1: 29–50. [See Response by Roger T. Ames in ibid., 51–57.]

———. 1983. "The Music of Humanity in the *Conversations* (*Analects*) of Confucius." *Journal of Chinese Philosophy* 10.4: 331–56.

———. 1991. "Reason, Spontaneity, and the li—A Confucian Critique of Graham's Solution to the Problem of Fact and Value." In Henry Rosemont Jr., ed. *Chinese Texts and Philosophical Contexts: Essays Dedicated to Angus C. Graham*. La Salle, Ill.: Open Court. 209–25. [See also Graham's response, pp. 297–308.]

Fu, Charles Wei-hsun. 1978. "Fingarette and Munro on Early Confucianism: A Methodological Examination." *Philosophy East and West* 28.2: 181–98. [On Fingarette (1972) and Munro (1969). See response by Fingarette in ibid., 223–26.]

Fu, Yunlung. 1981. "Studies on Confucius Since Construction (Since 1949)." *Chinese Studies in Philosophy* 12.2: 25–51.

Fung, Yu-lan. 1957. "Problems in the Study of Confucius." *People's China* 1: 21–2, 27–31.

———. 1978. "On Confucius." *Chinese Studies in Philosophy* 9.3/4: 3–135.

———(trans. by Derk Bodde). 1952–53. "Confucius and the Rise of Confucianism." In Fung's *A History of Chinese Philosophy*. Princeton, N.J.: Princeton University Press. vol. 1, 43–75. [Entire book reviewed by J. K. Shyrock in *Journal of the American Oriental Society* 58 (1938) 488; Peter A. Boodberg in *Journal of Asian Studies* 12.4 (1953) 419; H. G. Creel in *Journal of Religion* 33 (1953) 303; Wing-tsit Chan in *Philosophy East and West* 4:1 (1954) 73; and Homer H. Dubs in *Mind* n.s. 66 (1957) 280.]

Gassmann, Robert H. 1988. *Cheng ming, Richtigstellung der Bezeichnungen: Zu den Quellen eines Philosophens im antiken China: Ein Beitrag zur Konfuzius-Forschung*. Bern and New York: Peter Lang. 382 pp.

Gen, Lewis. 1961. "What Legge Thinks of Confucius." *Eastern Horizon* 1.12: 44–46.

Gier, Nicholas. 1993. "On the Deification of Confucius." *Asian Philosophy* 3.1: 43–54.

Giles, L., trans. 1961. *The Sayings of Confucius*. New York: Grove Press. 132 pp.

Graham, A. C. 1989. "A Conservative Reaction: Confucius." In Graham's *Disputers of the Tao: Philosophical Argument in Ancient China*. Chicago and La Salle, Ill: Open Court. 9–33. [Entire book reviewed by Joseph M. Kitagawa in *History of Religions* 31.2 (1991) 181–209; John Knoblock in *Journal of Asian Studies* 50.2 (1991) 385–87; Heiner Roetz in *Bulletin of the School of Oriental and African Studies* 54.2 (1991) 410–14; Jesse Fleming in *Journal of Chinese Philosophy* 19.1 (1992) 109–15; Jay Sailey in *Journal of the American Oriental Society* 112.1 (1992) 42–54; and Benjamin I. Schwarz in *Philosophy East and West* 42.1 (1992) 3–15. (See Graham's response in ibid., 17–19).]

Grange, J. 1996. "The Disappearance of the Public Good: Confucius, Dewey, Rorty." *Philosophy East and West* 46.3: 351–66.

Grimm, Tilemann. 1976. *Meister Kung: Zur Geschichte der Wirkungen des Konfuzius*. Rheinisch-Westfälische Akademie der Wissenschaften. G216. Voträge: 44 pp.

Gripekoven, Jeanne. 1955. *Confucius et son temps*. Bruxelles: Office de publicité. 111 pp.

Gurdak, Thaddeus J. 1980. "Benevolence: Confucian Ethics and Ecstasy." In James Gaffney, ed. *Essays in Morality and Ethics*. New York: Paulist Press. 76–84. [Uses Paul Tillich's definition of ecstasy to reexamine the passages that concern Yen Hui in the *Analects*.]

Hall, David L. 1994. "Confucian Friendship: The Road to Religiousness." In Leroy S. Rouner, ed. *The Changing Face of Friendship*. Notre Dame, Ind.: University of Notre Dame Press. 77–94.

———. 1999. *The Democracy of the Dead: Dewey, Confucius, and the Hope for Democracy in China*. Chicago: Open Court. xii + 267 pp.

Hall, David L., and Roger T. Ames. 1984. "Getting It Right: On Saving Confucius from the Confucians." *Philosophy East and West* 34.1: 3–23. [On the significance of the term 義 (yi) in the philosophy of Confucius.]

———. 1987. *Thinking through Confucius*. Albany, N.Y.: SUNY Press. xxii + 393 pp. [Reviewed by A. C. Graham in *Bulletin of the School of Oriental and African Studies* 51.P3 (1988) 591–92; Chad Hansen in *Journal of Asian Studies* 47.4 (1988) 852–53; Joel J. Kupperman in *Harvard Journal of Asiatic Studies* 49.1 (1989) 251–59; Daniel D. Leslie in *Pacific Affairs* 62.1 (1989) 89–90; R. P. Peerenboom in *Chinese Culture* 30.4 (1989) 71–3; Michael Martin in *Journal of Chinese Philosophy* 17.4 (1990) 495–503 (see response); and Philip J. Ivanhoe in *Philosophy East and West* 41.2 (1991) 241–54. See also the discussion of Hall's and Ames's interpretation in Gregor Paul (1991).]

———. 1991. "Against the Graying of Confucius: Responses to Gregor Paul and Michael Martin." *Journal of Chinese Philosophy* 18.3: 333–47. [Responses to Paul (1991) and Martin (1990).]

Hamburger, Max. 1956. "Aristotle and Confucius: A Study in Comparative Philosophy." *Philosophy* 31: 324–57.

———. 1959. "Aristotle and Confucius: A Comparison." *Journal of the History of Ideas* 20: 236–49.

Hansen, Chad. 1992. "The Positive Dao Period: Confucius: The Baseline." In Hansen's *A Daoist Theory of Chinese Thought: A Philosophical Interpretation*. New York and Oxford: Oxford University Press. 57–94.

Harbsmeier, Christoph. 1978. *Konfuzius und der Raüber Zhi: Neue Bildergeschichten und alte Anekdoten aus China*. Frankfurt: Insel. 165 pp.

———. 1990. "Confucius-Ridens, Humor in the *Analects*." *Harvard Journal of Asiatic Studies* 50.1: 131–61.

Hattori, Unokichi. 1936. "Confucius' Conviction of His Heavenly Mission." *Harvard Journal of Asiatic Studies* 1: 96–108.

Hauser, Philip M. 1967. "Lao-Tze, Confucius, and the Conservative-Liberal Debate." *Proceedings of the American Philosophical Society* 111.5: 259–67.

Henderson, John B. 1991. *Scripture, Canon, and Commentary: A Comparison of Confucian and Western Exegesis*. Princeton, N.J.: Princeton University Press. 247 pp. [On the commentarial tradition.]

Hess, L. E. 1993. "The Manchu Exegesis of the Lunyu." *Journal of the American Oriental Society* 113.3: 402–17.

Hinton, David, trans. 1998. *The Analects*. Washington, D.C.: Counterpoint. xxxv + 252 pp.

Holz, Harald. 1987. "Transferability of Ethical Ideals: Aristotle's and Confucius' 'Ideal Man' in Comparison: Methodological Reflections." *Confucianism and Modernization: A Symposium*. Taipei: Freedom Council. 121–48.

———. 1988. "Confucius, Mencius and the Stoic Panaitios on the Goodness of Human Nature: Can Their Ideas Serve as a Pattern for a New Anthropology of Mankind?" *International Symposium on Confucianism and the Modern World: Proceedings*. Taipei: Kuo chi K'ung hsüeh hui i ta hui mi shu chu. 1235–75.

Holzman, Donald. 1978. "Confucius and Ancient Chinese Literary Criticism." In Adele Austin Rickett, ed. *Chinese Approaches to Literature from Confucius to Liang Ch'i-Ch'ao*. Princeton, N.J.: Princeton University Press. 21–41.

Hsiao, Harry Hsin-i. 1978. "Problems Concerning Tseng Tzu's Role in the Promotion of Filial Pietism." *Chinese Culture* 19:1.

Hsiao, Kung-chuan (trans. by F. W. Mote). 1979. "Confucius." In Hsiao's *A History of Chinese Political Thought. Volume One: From the Beginnings to the Sixth Century A.D.* Princeton, N.J.: Princeton University Press. 79–142. [Entire book reviewed by L. S. Chang and Young-oak Kim in *Philosophy East and West* 31.3 (1981) 355–75; A. C. Graham in *Bulletin of the School of Oriental and African Studies* 44 (1981) 400–103; Benjamin E. Wallacker in *Journal of Asian History* 14 (1980) 173–74; and Hsu Cho-yun in *Journal of the American Oriental Society* 102 (1982) 426–7.]

Hsieh, Teh-yi. 1954. *Konfuzius: Eine Einführung in das Leben und Wirken des Weisen und eine Auswahl seiner Gespräche und Gedanken.* Zurich: W. Claasen. 78 pp.

Hsin, Kwan-chue. 1970. "Confucius on Art and Poetry." *ASPAC Quarterly of Cultural and Social Affairs* 2.2: 26–53. [Reprinted in *Chinese Culture* 16.3 (1975) 31–62.]

Hsü, Dau-lin. 1970–71. "The Myth of the 'Five Human Relations' of Confucius." *Monumenta Serica* 29: 27–37.

Hsü, Leonard Shih-lien. 1932. *The Political Philosophy of Confucianism.* London: G. Routledge. xxii + 257 pp.

Hsüeh, Chün-chang 薛春章. 1978. *K'ung-tzu yü Lun yü t'an wei* 孔子與論語探微. Chia-i: Chia-i wen hua ch'u pan she. 165 pp.

Hu, Shih. 1928. *The Development of the Logical Method in Ancient China.* Shanghai: Oriental Book. 187 pp. [See pp. 22–7, 46–52.]

———(trans. by Franke von Wolfgang). 1935–36. "Der Ursprung der Ju und ihre Beziehung zu Konfuzius und Lao-dsi." *Sinica Sonderausgabe* (1935) 141–71; (1936) 1–42.

Huang, Chi-chung. 1997. *The Analects of Confucius.* New York: Oxford University Press. viii + 216 pp. [Reviewed by Stephen Owen in *New Republic* 216.18 (1997) 36–39; G. Hardy in *Journal of Chinese Philosophy* 25.2 (1998) 273–80; and Philip J. Ivanhoe in *Journal of Chinese Religions* 26 (1998) forthcoming.]

Huang, Siu-chi. 1963. "Musical Art in Early Confucian Philosophy." *Philosophy East and West* 13: 49–59.

Hwang, Philip H. 1980. "A New Interpretation of Confucius." *Philosophy East and West* 30.1: 45–55. [Same title in *Journal of Chinese Philosophy* 8.1 (1981) 87–95.]

———. 1990. "Fingarette's Interpretation of Confucius' View of Ritual." *Dialogue and Alliance* 23.3: 22–31.

Imamichi, Tomonobu. 1986. "Mimesis and Expression: A Comparative Study in Aesthetics." In Marinus C. Doeser, ed. *Facts and Values: Philosophical Reflections from Western and Non-Western Perspectives.* Dordrecht: Nijhoff. 139–47. [On Confucius' and Plato's aesthetics.]

Ishizuka, Harumichi. 1981. "The Texts of the Lun-yü 論語, with Commentaries by Cheng Hsuan 鄭玄, Discovered in Tunhuang and Turfan." *Journal Asiatique* 269: 101–8.

Ito, Tomonobu, et al. 1971. "Symposium: The Logic of "ji-sho-yi" (time, place, and human relations): (1) The Logic of "ji-sho-yi" in the *Analect* [sic] of Confucius." *East and West: The Studies of History of Ideas* [sic] 2: 1–8.

Ivanhoe, Philip J. 1990. "Reweaving the One Thread of the *Analects.*" *Philosophy East and West* 40.1: 17–33.

———. 1990. "Thinking and Learning in Early Confucianism." *Journal of Chinese Philosophy* 17.4: 473–93.

———. 1991. "Character Consequentialism: An Early Confucian Contribution to Contemporary Ethical Theory." *Journal of Religious Ethics* 19.1: 55–70.

———. 1993. "Confucius." In Ivanhoe's *Confucian Moral Self Cultivation.* New York: Peter Lang. 9–21.

Jennings, William, trans. 1982. *The Wisdom of Confucius.* New York: Avenel Books. 226 pp. ["Critical and Biographical Sketches by Epiphanus Wilson." Originally published in 1900.]

Jensen, Lionel M. 1993. "The Invention of Confucius and His Chinese Other 'Kong Fuzi.'" *Positions* 1.2: 414–59.

———. 1995. "Wise Man of the Wilds: Fatherlessness, Fertility, and the Mythic Exemplar, Kongzi." *Early China* 20: 407–37.

———. 1997. *Manufacturing Confucianism: Chinese Traditions and Universal Civilization.* Durham, N.C.: Duke University Press. xv + 444 pp.

Jih pen yen chiu ching hsüeh lun chu mu lu 1900–1992 日本研究經學論著目錄 1900–1992. 1994.
T'u shu wen hsien chuan k'an. No. 1. Taipei: Chung yang yen chiu yuan chung-kuo wen che
yen chiu so ch'o pei ch'u. xxii + 878 pp. [Lin Ch'ing-chang 林慶彰, senior ed. For
works on Confucius and the *Analects,* see 419–620. This is the bibliographical resource
for Japanese works on Confucius and the *Analects.*]

Jin, J. F. 1981. "On the Question of Methodology in the Study of Confucius." *Chinese Studies
in Philosophy* 12.2: 68–75.

Joblin, Kingsley J. 1971. "The Humanistic Faith of Confucius." *Chinese Culture* 12.3: 1–8.

Jones, D. 1995. "Straight as an Arrow: Reading Confucius Archetypally." *Journal of Chinese
Philosophy* 22.4: 465–85. [On Confucius and the ancient Chinese mythical figure Yü.]

Kaizuka, Shigeki 貝塚茂樹, trans. 1973. *Rongo* 論語. Tokyo: Chuo Koron-sha. 571 pp.

———(trans. by Geoffrey Bownas). 1956. *Confucius.* London: Allen and Unwin. 191 pp.
[Translation of Kaizuka. 1951. *Kōshi* 孔子. Tokyo: Iwanami. ii + 204 pp.]

Kanaya, Osamu 金谷治, trans. 1963. *Rongo* 論語. Tokyo: Iwanami. xxii + 280 pp.

———. 1990. *Kōshi* 孔子. Tokyo: Kodansha. 428 pp.

———. 1996. "The Mean in Original Confucianism." In Philip J. Ivanhoe, ed. *Language,
Thought, and Culture: Nivison and His Critics.* Chicago and La Salle Ill.: Open Court. 83–93.
[See also Nivison's response, pp. 289–92.]

Kang, Thomas H. 1997. *Confucius and Confucianism: Questions and Answers.* Washington, D.C.:
Confucian Publications. xxx + 246 pp.

K'ang, Yu-wei 康有為. 1984. *Lun yü chu* 論語注. Beijing: Chung hua shu chu. 305 pp. [Textual
arrangement by Lo Yü-lieh 樓宇烈. Originally published in 1917.]

Kao, Ming 高明, and Ta-ch'i Ch'en 陳大齊. 1983. *K'ung-tzu ssu hsiang yen chiu lun chi* 孔子思想
研究論集. Taipei: Li ming wen hua shih yeh kung ssu. 2 vols.

Kelen, Betty. 1971. *Confucius: In Life and Legend.* New York: T. Nelson. 160 pp.

Ketcham, Ralph. 1985. "Aristotle, Confucius, and Jefferson on the Problem of Good
Government." *Journal of East West Studies* 14.2: 127–42.

Kieschnick, John. 1992. "*Analects* 12.1 and the Commentarial Tradition." *Journal of the
American Oriental Society* 112.4: 567–76.

Kimura, Eiichi 木村英一. 1971. *Kōshi to Rongo* 孔子と論語. Tokyo: Sobunsha. 484 pp.

Koo, Bon Myung. 1975. "Thorough Comparative Studies on the Morality of Confucius and
Socrates." *Journal of East and West Studies* 4.2: 3–25.

Kramers, R. P. 1979. *Konfuzius, Chinas entthronter Heiliger?* Bern: Peter Lang. 136 pp. [On the
re-evaluations of Confucius in modern China; Serbo-Croation article by the same title
in *Filozof Istraz* 29.2 (1989) 569–73.]

———. 1990. "Konfuzius als Scharfrichter: Eine legalistiche Fiktion?" In Peter M. Kufus,
ed. *China: Dimensionen der Geschichte: Festschrift für Tilemann Grimm anlässlich seiner Emeritierung.*
Tübingen: Attempto. 121–32.

K'uang, Ya-ming 匡亞明. 1985. *K'ung-tzu p'ing chuan* 孔子評傳. Chi-nan: Ch'i Lu shu she. 408 pp.

K'ung, Ch'uan-sheng 孔傳生. 1982. *Lun yü hsin t'an* 論語新探. Taipei: Wu ling ch'u pan she.
215 pp.

K'ung, Teh-cheng. 1977. "Confucius' Political Philosophy and World Peace." *Asian Culture
Quarterly* 5.1: 41–45.

K'ung-tzu chiao yü ssu hsiang lun wen hsuan: 1949–1980 孔子教育思想論文選 1949–1980. 1981.
Beijing: Chiao yu k'o hsueh ch'u pan she. 256 pp.

K'ung-tzu chiao yü ssu hsiang lun wen chi 孔子教育思想論文集. 1985. Chang-sha: Hu-nan chiao yü
ch'u pan she. 315 pp.

K'ung-tzu chiao yü ssu hsiang yen chiu 孔子教育思想研究. 1985. Beijing: Jen min chiao yü ch'u
pan she. 286 pp.

K'ung-tzu ssu hsiang yen chiu wen chi 孔子思想研究文集. 1988. T'ai-yuan: Shan-hsi jen min ch'u
pan she. 417 pp.

K'ung-tzu yen chiu lun wen chi 孔子研究論文集. 1987. Beijing: Chiao yü k'o hsueh ch'u pan she. 462 pp.

K'ung-tzu yen chiu lun wen chu tso mu lu 1949–1986 孔子研究論文著作目錄 1949–1986. 1987. Chi-nan: Ch'i lu shu she. 267 pp.

Kupperman, Joel J. 1968. "Confucius and the Problem of Naturalness." *Philosophy East and West* 18.3: 17–85.

———. 1971. "Confucius and the Nature of Religious Ethics." *Philosophy East and West* 21.2: 189–94.

———. 1989. "Confucius, Mencius, Hume, and Kant on Reason and Choice." In Schlomo Biderman and Ben-Ami Scharfstein, eds. *Rationality in Question: Eastern and Western Views of Rationality.* New York: E. J. Brill. 119–39.

Lai, Whalen W. 1990. "Rectifying the Theory of 'Rectifying Names:' Humanism and Ethical Religion in China. *Journal of Humanism and Religion* 3.3: 124–40.

Lau, D. C., trans. 1979. *Confucius: The Analects.* Harmondsworth, Eng.: Penguin Books. 249 pp. [Reprinted, with Chinese text, by Chinese University Press (Hong Kong, 1979). Revised edition reviewed by Roger T. Ames in *China Review International* 1.2 (1994) 170–73.]

Laufer, Berthold. 1934. "Lun Yu IX, i." *Journal of the American Oriental Society* 54: 83.

Lauridsen, Kristen Ronbol. 1988. "Long Live Confucius: Some Remarks on Creel, Confucius, and Humanistic Values." In Lief Littrup, ed. *Analecta Hafniensia: Twenty-Five Years of East Asian Studies in Copenhagen.* London: Curzon. 78–81.

Lee, Orient. 1988. "The Real Confucius: What Did He Do?" *International Symposium on Confucianism and the Modern World: Proceedings.* Taipei: Kuo chi K'ung hsüeh hui i ta hui mi shu chu. 277–97.

Legge, James. 1887. *The Life and Teaching of Confucius, with Explanatory Notes.* London: N. Trubner. 338 pp.

———, trans. 1893. *Confucian Analects, the Great Learning, and the Doctrine of the Mean.* In *The Chinese Classics.* Vol. 1. Oxford: Clarendon Press. xv + 503 pp. [Interpretation follows that of Zhu Xi. Contains introductory essays, numerous annotations, bibliographical materials, and a Chinese character index. Can also be found in James Legge, trans., *The Four Books* (various printings and reprintings).]

Leslie, Daniel. 1956. "Notes on the *Analects:* Appendixed by a Select Bibliography for the *Analects.*" *T'oung Pao* 49: 1–63.

———. 1962. *Confucius.* Paris: Editions Seghers. 222 pp.

Leung, Y. S. 1982. "The Golden Past Revisited: A Reappraisal of the Views of Confucius and Mencius on History." *Chinese Culture* 23.4: 65–73.

Lévy, André, trans. 1994. *Entretiens de Confucius et des ses Disciples.* Paris: Flammarion. 256 pp.

———. 1994. "A propos de quatre mots des *Entretiens de Confucius et ses disciples.*" *Études Chinoises* 13.1–2: 285–93.

Leys, Simon [Pierre Ryckmans]. 1997. *The Analects of Confucius.* New York and London: W. W. Norton xxxii + 224 pp. [Reviewed by Stephen Owen in *New Republic* 216.18 (1997) 36–39, and Jonathan Spence in *New York Review of Books* 44.6 (1997) 8+.]

Li, Ming 李鳴. 1972. *Lun yü yen chiu* 論語研究. Taipei: Ta hsüeh t'u shu ch'u pan she. 685 pp.

Li, Qiqian. 1991. "A Survey of Confucius Studies in China Today." *Copenhagen Papers in East and Southeast Asian Studies* 6: 7–28.

Li, Zehou. 1980. "A Re-Evaluation of Confucius." *Social Sciences in China* 1.2: 99–127. [Same title in Anna-Teresa Tymieniecka, ed. 1984. *Phenomenology of Life in a Dialogue between Chinese and Occidental Philosophy.* Dordrecht: Reidel.]

Liang, Ch'i-ch'ao 梁啟超. 1962. *K'ung-tzu* 孔子. Taipei: Chung hua shu chu. 69 pp. [Originally published in 1936.]

———(trans. by L. T. Ch'en). 1930. *History of Chinese Political Thought During the Early Tsin Period.*

London: Kegan Paul. 210 pp. [Translation of Liang. 1925 *Hsien-Ch'in cheng-chih ssu-hsiang shih* 先秦政治思想史. Shanghai: Shang wu yin shu kuan. 217 pp. See 38–52.]

Lin, I-cheng 林義正. 1987. *K'ung-tzu hsüeh shuo t'an wei* 孔子學說探微. Taipei: Tung ta t'u shu kung ssu. 285 pp.

Lin, Shuen-fu. 1987–88. "Confucius in the 'Inner Chapters' of the Chuang Tzu." *Tamkang Review* 18.1–4: 379–401.

Lin, T. M. 1988. "Thought and Action in Confucius." *Religious Humanism* 22.1: 7–10.

Lin, Yu-sheng. 1974–75. "The Evolution of the Pre-Confucian Meaning of Jen (仁) and the Confucian Concept of Moral Autonomy." *Monumenta Serica* 31: 172–204.

Lin, Yutang. 1943. *The Wisdom of Confucius*. New York: The Modern Library. xvii + 265 pp.

Liu, Hsin-han. 1988. "Confucius' Educational Thought." *International Symposium on Confucianism and the Modern World: Proceedings*. Taipei: Kuo chi K'ung hsüeh hui i ta hui mi shu chu. 357–98.

Liu, Hsin-shu. 1988. "On the Confucian Ideal of Sageliness Within and Kingliness Without." *International Symposium on Confucianism and the Modern World: Proceedings*. Taipei: Kuo chi K'ung hsüeh hui i ta hui mi shu chu. 401–22.

Liu, Shu-hsien. 1991. "On Confucius' Attitude Toward Gods, Sacrifice, and Heaven." *Ching Feng* 34: 16–27.

Liu, W. H. 1986. "The Methodological Question in the Study of Confucius." *Chinese Studies in Philosophy* 17.3: 78–101.

Liu, Wu-chi. 1956. *Confucius: His Life and Times*. New York: Philosophical Library. 189 pp.

Lo, Hsiang-lin. 1976. "An Inquiry into the Doctrinal System of Confucius from the Lun-yü." *Chinese Studies in Philosophy* 8.1: 57–76.

Lo, Meng-ts'e 羅夢冊. 1982. *K'ung-tzu wei wang er wang lun* 孔子未王而王論. Taipei: Taiwan hsüeh sheng shu chu. 299 pp.

Lu, Martin. 1983. "Was Mencius a True Successor of Confucius?" *Philosophy East and West* 33.1: 79–86.

———. 1988. "The Theory and Practice of Confucius." *International Symposium on Confucianism and the Modern World: Proceedings*. Taipei: Kuo chi K'ung hsüeh hui i ta hui mi shu chu. 437–61.

———. 1990. "Jen (humanity) as the Good in the *Analects*: A Confucian Solution to Contemporary Value Confusion." *World Academic Conference of the Seoul Olympiad, Seoul 1988. The World Community in Post-Industrial Society, 3: The Confusion of Ethics and Values in Contemporary Society and Possible Approaches to Redefinitions*. Seoul: Wooseok Publishing. 229–45.

Lun yü chu tzu so yin 論語逐字索引 [A concordance to the Lunyu]. 1994. *Institute of Chinese Studies Ancient Chinese Text Concordance Series*. No. 14. Hong Kong: Commercial Press. iv + 200 pp. [Senior eds. D. C. Lau and Chen Fong Ching.]

Lun yü yin te 論語引得. 1940. Harvard Yenching Institute Sinological Index Series. No. 16. Beijing: Harvard Yenching Institute. xix + 190 pp. [Chief editor William Hung.]

Lyall, Leonard A., trans. 1925. *The Analects of Confucius*. New York: Allen and Unwin. xii + 112 pp.

Mahood, George H. 1971. "Socrates and Confucius: Moral Agents or Moral Philosophers." *Philosophy East and West* 21.2: 177–88.

———. 1974. "Human Nature and the Virtues in Confucius and Aristotle." *Journal of Chinese Philosophy* 1.3–4: 295–312.

———. 1977. "Interpersonal Values in the Teaching of Philosophy." *Philosophy East and West* 27.1: 23–34. [On the philosophy of education in Plato and the *Analects*.]

Makeham, John. 1988. "Rectifying Confucius' Zheng-Ming." *Papers on Far Eastern History* 38 (Sept.) 1–24.

———. 1993. "The *Analects* and Reputation: A Note on *Analects* 15.18 and 15.19." *Bulletin of the School of Oriental and African Studies, University of London* 56.P3: 582–86.

———. 1996. "The Formation of Lunyu as a Book." *Monumenta Serica* 44: 1–24.

———. 1997. "The Earliest Extant Commentary on the Lunyu: Lunyu Zheng zhi zhu." *T'oung Pao* 83: 260–99.

———. 1998. "Between Chen and Cai: *Zhuangzi and the Analects*." In Roger T. Ames, ed. *Wandering at Ease in the Zhuangzi*. Albany, N.Y.: SUNY Press. 75–100.

Malmqvist, Göran. 1978. "What Did the Master Say?" In David T. Roy and Tsien Tsuen-hsuin, eds. *Ancient China: Studies in Early Civilization*. Hong Kong: Chinese University of Hong Kong Press. 137–55.

Martin, Michael R. 1991. "Against the Graying of Confucius: A Rejoinder to Hall and Ames." *Journal of Chinese Philosophy* 18.4: 489–93. [Rejoinder to Hall and Ames' criticisms of Martin's review in ibid., 18.3 (1991) 333–47.]

———. 1995. "Ritual Action (Li) in Confucius and Hsun-Tzu." *Australasian Journal of Philosophy* 73.1: 13–30.

McCarthy, Maureen. 1974. "Community from the Perspective of Confucius and Teilhard." *Second Order* 3: 92–94.

Mercado, Leonardo N. 1989. "The Holy in the Analects of Confucius." *Sophia* 19.2: 26–36.

Miyazaki, Ichisada 宮崎市定. 1974. *Rongo no shinkenkyū* 論語の 新研究. Tokyo: Iwanami Shoten. 388 pp.

———, trans. 1993. *Rongo* 論語. Tokyo: Iwanami Shoten. 443 pp.

Mizoguchi, Yūzō 溝口雄三. 1996. *Kōshi* 孔子. Tokyo: Sanseido. iv + 111 pp.

Mollgaard, Eske J. 1993. "Negation, Poetry, and Philosophy: Moments Between the *Feng* and the Lunyu." *Philosophy East and West* 43.4: 715–36.

Moritz, Ralph, trans. 1982. *Konfuzius Gespräche*. Leipzig: Pahl-Rugenstein.

Morohashi, Tetsuji 諸橋轍次. 1973. *Rongo no kōgi* 論語の 講義. Tokyo: Taishūkan Shoten. 527 pp.

Morton, Scott W. 1964. *The Chün tzu, Ideal Man, in the Analects of Confucius Compared to the Greek and Christian Concepts*. Edinburgh: University of Edinburgh. 162 pp.

———. 1971. "The Confucian Concept of Man: The Original Formulation." *Philosophy East and West* 21.1: 69—77.

Munro, Donald J. 1969. *The Concept of Man in Early China*. Stanford, Calif.: Stanford University Press. xi + 256 pp. [See esp. chaps. 3–4, 49–116.]

Nan, Huai-chin 南懷瑾, and Ts'e Ts'ai 蔡策. 1986. *Lun yü pieh ts'ai* 論語別裁. Taipei: Lao ku wen hua shih yeh kung ssu. 955 pp. [First published in *Jen wen shih chieh* 仁文世界 4.3–6.2 (1974–76).]

Nieh, T'ao 聶濤. 1963. *K'ung-tzu yü Lun yü* 孔子與論語. Taipei: Taiwan chung hua shu chu. 85 pp.

Nikkilä, Pertti. 1982. *Early Confucianism and Inherited Thought in Light of Some Key Terms of the Confucian Analects. I. The Terms in Shuching and Shihching*. Studia Orientalia. 53. Helsinki: Finnish Oriental Society. 275 pp.

———. 1997. *Preference and Choice in the Analects by Pertti Nikkilä:* Helsinki: Finish Oriental Society. vii + 177 pp.

Nivison, David S. 1996. "Golden Rule Arguments in Chinese Philosophy." In Bryan W. Van Norden, ed. *The Ways of Confucianism*. Chicago: Open Court. 59–76.

Ogyu, Sorai 荻生祖來 (1666–1728), and Tamaki Ogawa 小川環樹. 1994. *Rongo chō* 論語注. Tokyo: Heibonsha. 2 vols.

Opitz, Peter J. 1990. "Konfuzius." In S. Krieger and R. Truazettel, eds. *Konfuzian-ismus und die Modernisierung Chinas*. Mainz: v. Hase and Köhler. 506–34.

Park, Y. H. 1997. " 'Rationality' and 'Human Dignity'—Confucius, Kant, and Scheffler on the Ultimate Aim of Education." *Studies in the Philosophy of Education* 16.1–2: 7–18.

Paul, Gregor. 1990. *Aspects of Confucianism: A Study of the Relationship Between Rationality and Humaneness*. Frankfurt: Peter Lang. 203 pp. [See espp. 43–55.]

Paul, Gregor. 1991. "Reflection of the Usage of the Terms 'Logic' and 'Logical.'" *Journal of Chinese Philosophy* 18.1: 73–87. [On Hall and Ames (1987); see Hall and Ames' response in ibid., 18.3 (1991) 333–47.]

———. 1992. "Against Wanton Distortion: A Rejoinder to David Hall and Roger Ames' Criticism of My Reflections on Logic and Confucius." *Journal of Chinese Philosophy* 19.1: 119–22. [Response to Hall and Ames' criticisms in ibid., 18.3 (1991) 333–47.]

Pfister, Lauren. 1986. "Considerations for the Contemporary Revitalization of Confucianism: Meditations on *Te* in the *Analects*." *Journal of Chinese Philosophy* 13.2: 239–65.

Phelps, D. L. 1928. "The Place of Music in the Platonic and Confucian Systems of Moral Education." *Journal of the North China Branch of the Royal Asiatic Society* 59: 128–45.

Porter, Lucius C. 1951. "A Conversation with Confucius." *Philosophy East and West* 1: 67–70.

Pound, Ezra, trans. 1956. *Confucian Analects*. London: P. Owen. 136 pp.

Radcliffe, R. J. 1989. "Confucius and John Dewey." *Religious Education* 84.2: 215–31.

Rembert, Ron B. 1983. "The Golden Rule: Two Versions and Two Views." *Journal of Moral Education* 12: 100–103.

Riegel, Jeffrey K. 1986. "Poetry and the Legend of Confucius' Exile." *Journal of the American Oriental Society* 106.1: 13–22.

Roberts, Moss P. 1966. *The Metaphysical Context of the Analects and the Metaphysical Theme in Later Chou Confucianism*. New York: Columbia University Press. 150 pp. [On relationship of the *Analects* to the *Doctrine of the Mean, Mencius, and the Book of Changes*.]

———. 1968. "Li, Yi, and Jen in the Lun Yü: Three Philosophical Definitions." *Journal of the American Oriental Society* 88: 765–71.

Roetz, Heiner. 1993. *Confucian Ethics of the Axial Age*. Albany, N.Y.: SUNY Press. xiii + 373 pp.

Rongen, Ole Bjorn. 1978. "A Chinese Marxist Study of the *Analects*." *Bulletin of Concerned Asian Scholars* 10.1: 53–62. [Review article on Chao Chi-pin's Lun yü hsin t'an 論語新探.]

Rosemont, Henry Jr. 1976. "Notes from a Confucian Perspective: Which Acts are Moral Acts." *International Philosophical Quarterly* 16.1: 49–61.

———. 1986. "Kierkegaard and Confucius: On Finding the Way." *Philosophy East and West* 36.3: 201–12. [Same title in *China Notes* 25.1 (1986–87) 429–33.]

———. 1988. "Why Take Rights Seriously? A Confucian Critique." In Leroy S. Rouner, ed. *Human Rights and the World's Religions*. Notre Dame, Ind.: University of Notre Dame Press. 167–82.

———. Forthcoming. "Tracing a Path of Spiritual Progress in the *Analects*." In Tu Wei-ming and Mary Evelyn Tucker, eds. *Confucian Spirituality*. New York: Crossroads Press.

Rousselle, E. 1954. "Konfuzius und das archaische Weltbild der chinesischen Frühzeit." *Saeculum* 5: 1–33.

Rubin, Vitaly A. (trans. by Steven I. Levine). 1976. "Tradition and Human Personality: Confucius and Early Confucianism." In Rubin's *Individual and State in Ancient China: Essays of Four Chinese Philosophers*. New York: Columbia University Press. 1–32.

Rule, Paul. 1986. *K'ung-tzu or Confucius? The Jesuit Interpretation of Confucianism*. Sydney and Boston: Allen and Unwin. xiii + 303 pp.

———. 1990–91. "Was Confucius a Taoist?" *Journal of the Oriental Society of Australia* 22–23: 146–55.

Ruskola, T. H. 1992. "Moral Choice in the *Analects*: A Way Without a Crossroads." *Journal of Chinese Philosophy* 19.3: 285–96.

Ryckmans, Pierre, trans. 1987. *Les Entretiens de Confucius*. Paris: Gallimard. ix + 168 pp. [Reviewed by M. Adam in *Revue Philosophique de la France et de l'Etranger* 121.1 (1996) 150–51; A. Comtesponville in *Critique* 44.491 (1998) 350–51; J. L. Gautier in *Nouvelle Revue Francaise* 422 (1988) 83–84; and F. Han in *Europe-Revue Litteraire Mensuelle* 66.707 (1988) 218–19.]

de Saint-Ina, Marie. 1963. "Confucius: Witness to Being." *International Philosophical Quarterly* 3.4: 537–53.

Sartwell, C. 1993. "Confucius and Country Music." *Philosophy East and West* 43.2: 243–54.

Schneider, Laurence A., trans. 1965. "A Translation of Ku Chieh-Kang's Essay 'The Confucius of the Spring and Autumn Era and the Confucius of the Han Era.' " *Phi Theta Papers*; 105–47.

Schrecker, J. 1997. "Filial Piety as a Basis for Human Rights in Confucius and Mencius." *Journal of Chinese Philosophy* 24.3: 401–12.

Schwarz, Benjamin I. 1959. "Some Polarities in Confucian Thought." In David S. Nivison and Arther F. Wright, eds. *Confucianism in Action*. Stanford, lalif.: Stanford University Press. 50–62. [Reprinted in Arthur F. Wright, ed. 1964. *Confucianism in Chinese Civilization*. New York: Antheneum. 1–15.]

———. 1985. "Confucius: The Vision of the *Analects*." In Schwarz's *The World of Thought in Ancient China*. Cambridge, Mass.: Harvard University Press. 56–134. [Entire book reviewed by Benjamin Wallacker in *Journal of the American Oriental Society* 106.3 (1986) 609–11; Thomas A. Metzger in *The American Asian Review* 4.2 (1986) 68–116; Robert B. Crawford in *American Historical Review* 92.3 (1987) 720–21; Robert E. Hegel in *CLEAR* 9.1–2 (1987) 161; T. H. Barrett in *Bulletion of the School of Oriental and African Studies* 51.2 (1988) 370–71; Jean Lévi in *T'oung Pao* 74.4–5 (1988) 305–108; David S. Nivison in *Philosophy East and West* 38.3–4 (1988) 411–20; Henry Rosemont Jr. in *Journal of Asian Studies* 47.3 (1988) 621–23; Wong Yuk in *The Journal of the Institute of Chinese Studies of the Chinese University of Hong Kong* 19 (1988) 423–31; and Frederick W. Mote in *Harvard Journal of Asiatic Studies* 50.1 (1990) 384–402.]

Seo, Kunio 瀨尾邦雄. 1992. *Kōshi, Moshi ni kansuru bunken mokuroku* 孔子、孟子に關する文獻目録. Tokyo: Hakuteisha. 245 pp. [Covers works written between 1882 and 1992.]

Shih, Joseph. 1970. "The Place of Confucius in the History of Chinese Religion." *Gregorianum* 51: 485–507.

Shirakawa, Shizuka 白川靜. 1972. *Kōshi den* 孔子伝. Tokyo: Chuyo Koron sha. 317 pp.

Shryock, John Knight. 1966. *The Origin and Development of the State Cult of Confucius*. New York: Paragon Book Reprint. 298 pp.

Shun, Kwong-loi. 1993. "The Concepts of Jen and Li in the *Analects*." *Philosophy East and West* 43.3: 457–79.

Sims, Bennet B. 1968. *Confucius*. New York: F. Watts. 139 pp.

Slingerland, Ted. 1996. "The Conception of 'Ming' in Early Confucian Thought." *Philosophy East and West* 46.4: 567–81.

Smith, David Howard. 1973. *Confucius*. New York: Scribner. 240 pp.

Soles, D. E. 1995. "Confucius and the Role of Reason." *Journal of Chinese Philosophy* 22.3: 249–61.

Sontag, Frederick. 1990. "The *Analects* of Confucius: The Universal Man." *Journal of Chinese Philosophy* 17.4: 427–38.

Soothill, William, trans. 1995. *The Analects of Confucius*. Mineola, N.Y.: Dover Publications. xii + 128 pp. [Originally published in Shansi in 1910.]

Steinkraus, Warren E. 1980. "Socrates, Confucius, and the Rectification of Names." *Philosophy East and West* 30.2: 261–64.

Su, Hsin-wu. 1983. *The Importance of Economic Thought in Confucius' Philosophy*. Singapore: National University of Singapore. 30 pp.

Sunoo, Harold Hakwon. 1985. *China of Confucius: A Critical Interpretation*. Virginia Beach, Va.: Heritage Research House. xii + 201 pp. [Reviewed by J. D. Schmidt in *Pacific Affairs* 61.1 (1988) 147–49.]

Taam, Cheuk-woon. 1953. "On Studies of Confucius." *Philosophy East and West* 3: 147–65.

Tai, Chao-fu 戴朝福. 1993. *Ju chia ti sheng ming ch'ing tiao: Lun yü i li lun ts'ung* 儒家的生命情調：論語義理論叢. Taipei: Taiwan hsüeh sheng shu chu. x + 326 pp.

Takeuchi, Teruo. 1966. "A Study of the Meaning of *Jen* Advocated by Confucius." *Acta Asiatica* 9: 57–77.

Takeuchi, Yoshio 武內義雄. 1972. *Rongo no kenkyu* 論語の研究. Tokyo: Iwanami. 362 pp.

Tam, Kwok-kan. 1987–88. "Sir Philip Sidney's An Apology for Poetry in the Light of Confucian Analects." *Tamkang Review* 18.1–4: 423–33.

T'ang Hua 唐華. 1977. *K'ung tzu che hsüeh ssu hsiang yüan liu* 孔子哲學思想源流. Taipei: Cheng chung shu chu. 857 pp.

T'ang, Lan (trans. by Elma E. Kopetsky). 1975–76. "Discussing Confucius Should Begin with a Clear Understanding of the Nature of the Society in which Confucius Lived." *Chinese Law and Government* 8.3: 34–55.

Tazaki, Masayoshi 田崎仁義. 1944. *Kōshi to ōdō no seijikeizai* 孔子と王道の政治經濟. Tokyo: Sanseido. 317 pp.

Tillman, Hoyt Cleveland. 1981. "The Development of the Tension Between Virtue and Achievement in Early Confucianism." *Philosophy East and West* 31: 17–28. [On the different attitudes toward Kuan Chung found in the *Analects*, the *Mencius*, and the *Hsun-tzu*.]

Tōjō, Itsudō 東條一堂. 1965. *Rongo chigen* 論語知言. Tokyo: Shoseki Bunbutsu Ryutsukai. 765 pp.

Tran, Van Doan. 1988. "Harmony and Consensus: Confucius and Habermas on Politics." *International Symposium on Confucianism and the Modern World: Proceedings*. Taipei: Kuo chi K'ung hsüeh hui i ta hui mi shu chu. 1507–44.

Ts'ai, Shang-ssu 蔡尚思. 1982. *K'ung-tzu ssu hsiang t'i hsi* 孔子思想體系. Shanghai: Shanghai jen min ch'u pan she. 293 pp.

Tsuda, Sōkichi 津田左右吉. 1946. *Rongo to Kōshi no shisō* 論語と孔子の思想. Tokyo: Iwanami. 545 pp.

Tu, Wei-ming. 1968. "The Creative Tension between *Jen* and *Li*." *Philosophy East and West* 18.1/2: 29–39. [Reprinted in Tu, Wei-ming. 1979. *Humanity and Self-Cultivation: Essays in Confucian Thought*. Berkeley: University. of California Press. 5–16]

————. 1972. "*Li* as a Process of Humanization." *Philosophy East and West* 22.2: 187–201. [Reprinted in Tu. 1979. *Humanity and Self-Cultivation: Essays in Confucian Thought*. Berkeley: University of California Press.]

————. 1973. "On the Spiritual Development of Confucius' Personality." *Ssu yü yen: Thought and Word* 11.3: 29–37.

————. 1976. "The Confucian Perception of Adulthood." *Daedalus* 105.2: 109–23.

————. 1979. "The Value of the Human in Classical Confucian Thought." *Humanities* 15.2: 161–76 [Reprinted in Tu Wei-ming. 1985. *Confucian Thought: Selfhood as Creative Transformation*. Albany, N.Y.: SUNY Press. 67–80.]

————. 1981. "*Jen* as a Living Metaphor in the Confucian *Analects*." *Philosophy East and West* 31.1: 45–54.

————. 1984. "A Confucian Perspective on Learning to be Human." In Frank Whaling, ed. *The World's Religious Traditions*. Edinburgh: T. and T. Clark. 55–71. [Reprinted in Tu Wei-ming. 1985. *Confucian Thought: Selfhood as Creative Transformation*. Albany, N.Y.: SUNY Press. 51–65.]

————. 1985. "Selfhood and Otherness: The Father-Son Relationship in Confucian Thought." In Anthony Marsella et al., eds. *Culture and Self*. London: Tavistock Publications. 113–30.

————. 1987. "The Confucian Sage: Exemplar of Personal Knowledge." In John S. Hawley, ed. *Saints and Virtues*. Berkeley: University of California Press. 73–86.

————. 1987. "Confucian Studies in the People's Republic." *Humanities* 8.14–16: 34–35.

Tung, Nai-ch'iang 董乃強. 1988. K'ung-tzu yen chiu lun chu so yin, 1900–1983.6 孔子研究論著索引 1900–1983.6. Hong Kong: n.p. ii + 210 pp. [Reprint of the 1984 edition published by Pei-ching shih fan ta hsüeh li shih hsi.]

Unger, Ulrich. n.d. "Der Familienname des Konfuzius." Ch'ien-yüeh chi (Universität Tübingen) 2: 303–24.

Van Zoeren, Steven. 1991. Poetry and Personality: Reading, Exegesis, and Hermeneutics in Traditional China. Stanford, Calif.: Stanford University Press. [On the various interpretations and usages of passages from the Book of Poetry in traditional Chinese culture. See esp. 43–44.]

Versfeld, M. 1983. "Plato and Confucius." South African Journal of Philosophy 2.1: 20–25.

Waley, Arthur, trans. 1989. The Analects of Confucius. New York: Vintage Books. 257 pp. [Originally published in 1938 by Allen and Unwin, London.]

Wallacker, Benjamin E. 1978. "Han Confucianism and Confucius In the Han." In David T. Roy and Tsien Tsuen-hsuin, eds. Ancient China: Studies in Early Civilizaion. Hong Kong: Chinese University of Hong Kong Press. 215–28.

Wang, Hsian-jung 王向榮. 1939. Lun yü yao i 論語要義. K'un-ming: Chung hua shu chu. 79 pp.

———. 1958. Lun yü er shih chiang 論語二十講. Taipei: Taiwan chung hua shu chu. 509 pp. [First published in 1937.]

Wang, Hsi-yuan 王熙元. 1981. Lun yü t'ung shih 論語通釋. Taipei: Taiwan hsüeh sheng shu chu. 1220 pp.

Wang, Shu-lin 王書林. 1982. Lun yü i chu chi i wen chiao k'an chi 論語議注及異文校勘記. Taipei: Taiwan shang wu yin shu kuan. 497 pp.

Wang, Su-ts'un 王素存. 1966. Lun yü pien sung 論語辨訟. Taipei: Taiwan shang wu yin shu kuan. 1580 pp.

Ware, James R., trans. 1955. The Sayings of Confucius. New York: New American Library. 212 pp.

Watanabe, Suego 渡辺末吾. 1964. Rongo shūchū 論吾集注. Tokyo: Musashino Shoin. viii + 212 pp.

Wawrytko, Sandra A. 1982. "Confucius and Kant: The Ethics of Respect." Philosophy East and West 32.3: 237–57.

Wei, Tat. 1968. "Confucius and the I-Ching." Chinese Culture 9: 1–9.

Wen, Yü-min 溫裕民. 1930. Lun yü yen chiu 論語研究. Shanghai: Shanghai yin shu kuan. 115 pp.

West, Stephen H. 1988. "A Forgotten Classicist Looks at the Analects: Wang Jo-hsu's Lun-yü pien-huo." International Symposium on Confucianism and the Modern World: Proceedings. Taipei: Kuo chi K'ung hsüeh hui i ta hui mi shu chu. 993–1023.

Whitlock, G. 1994. "Concealing the Misconduct of One's Own Father: Confucius and Plato on a Question of Filial Piety." Journal of Chinese Philosophy 21.2: 113–37.

Wickert, Erwin. 1990. "The Relations Between the Ruler and the People According to Confucius and his Early Followers." ASIEN 34: 76–81.

Wilhelm, Richard, trans. 1923. Kungfutse: Gespräche. Jena: E. Diederichs. p. [Originally published in 1910. Reviewed by S. Behrsig in Orientalistische Literaturzeitung 77 (1982) 600.]

———. 1931. Confucius and Confucianism. London: K. Paul, Trench, Trubner. x + 181 pp.

Williams, J. N. 1988. "Confucius, Mencius, and the Notion of True Succession." Philosophy East and West 38.2: 157–71.

Williams, Jay G. 1991. "On Reading a Confucian Classic: The Rhetoric of the Lun yu." Journal of Chinese Religions 19 (autumn): 105–11.

Wilson, Stephen A. 1995. "Conformity, Individuality, and the Nature of Virtue: A Classical Confucian Contribution to Contemporary Ethical Reflection." Journal of Religious Ethics 23.2: 263–89. [A critical analysis of several previous interpretations of the Analects followed by the author's own analysis of the text. Reprinted in this volume.]

Wisman, Jon D. 1988. "The Dominance of Consensual over Technical Rationality in Confucius' Socio-Economic Thought." *International Journal of Social Economics* 15.1: 58–67.

Wong, M. "A Comparison between the Philosophies of Confucius and Plato as Applied to Music Education." *Journal of Aesthetic Education* 32.3: 109–12.

Wu, Chin-an 吳進安. 1993. *K'ung-tzu chih jen yu Mo-tzu chien ai pi chiao yen chiu* 孔子之仁與墨子之兼愛比較研究. Taipei: Wen shih che ch'u pan she. 228 pp.

Wu, Ching-hsiung. 1976. "The Thought of Confucius and Chinese Culture." *Chinese Studies in Philosophy* 8.3: 77–88.

Wu ch'iu pei chai Lun yü chi ch'eng 無求備齊論語集成. 1966. Taipei: I wen yin shu kuan. Fourhundred and eight vols. [Yen, Ling-feng 嚴靈峰, senior ed. By far the most convenient resource for traditional editions, commentaries, and studies.]

Wu, John C. H. 1935. "The Real Confucius." *T'ien Hsia Monthly*. 1: 11–20, 180–89.

———. 1962. "Chinese Legal and Political Philosophy." In Charles A. Moore, ed. *Philosophy and Culture—East and West*. Honolulu: University of Hawaii Press. 611–30. [See 613–18. Reprinted in Charles A. Moore, ed. 1967. *The Chinese Mind: Essentials of Chinese Philosophy and Culture*. Honolulu: University of Hawaii Press.]

Wu, K'ang 吳康. 1987. *K'ung, Meng, Hsün che hsüeh* 孔、孟、荀哲學. Taipei: Taiwan shang wu yin shu kuan. 2 vols. [Originally published in 1967.]

Wu, Te-yao. 1978. *Confucius' and Plato's Ideas of a Republic*. Singapore: Institute of Humanities and Social Sciences, College of Graduate Studies, Nanyang University. 72 pp.

Xu, Y. 1993. "Confucius: An Educationalist of Aesthetics in Ancient China." *Journal of Popular Culture* 27.2: 121–28.

Yang, Ching-fan 楊景凡, and Jung-ken Yu 俞榮根. 1984. *K'ung-tzu ti fa lu ssu hsiang* 孔子的法律思想. Beijing: Ch'un chung ch'u pan she. 190 pp.

Yang, Po-chun 楊伯峻. 1986. *Lun yü i chu* 論語議注. Taipei: Hua cheng shu chu. 324 pp. [First published in 1958 by Ku chi ch'u pan she, Beijing.]

Yang, Shu-ta 楊樹達. 1986. *Lun yü shu cheng* 論語疏證. Shanghai: Shanghai ku chi ch'u pan she. 521 pp. [First published in 1955 by K'e hsüeh ch'u pan she, Beijing.]

Yen, Joseph C. Y. 1972. "The Interpretations of the Character *TAO* in the Confucian Analects." *Chinese Culture* 13.3: 17–34.

Yen, Ling-feng 嚴靈峰. 1963. *Lun yü chiang i* 論語講義. Hong Kong: Chiu-wu pei chai: 1 vol. (various pagings).

———. 1983. *Lun yü chang chu hsin p'ien* 論語章句新篇. Taipei: Chung hua ts'ung shu p'ien fan wei yüan hui. 608 pp. [First published in 1968 by Shui niu ch'u pan she, Taipei (465 pp.).]

Yen, T'ao 延濤. 1994. *K'ung-tzu yü ju chia* 孔子與儒家. Taipei: T'ai-wan shang wu yin shu kuan. iv, ii + 148 pp.

Yeo, Khiok-Khng. 1990. "Amos (4:4–5) and Confucius: The Will (Ming) of God (Thien)." *The Asia Journal of Theology, Singapore* 4.2: 472–88.

Yoshida, Kenkō 吉田賢抗, trans. 1979. *Rongo* 論語. Tokyo: Meiji Shoin. 464 pp.

Yoshikawa, Kōjirō 吉川幸次郎, trans. 1959. *Rongo* 論語. Tokyo: Asahi Shinbunsha. 338 pp.

Youn, Laurent Eulsu. 1943. *Confucius, sa vie, son oeuvre, sa doctrine*. Paris: Adrien Maisonneuve. 126 pp.

Yu, Chin-sei. 1977. "The Quest for Sagehood in Confucius." *Korea Journal* 17.9: 33–41.

Yu, J. Y. 1998. "Virtue: Confucius and Aristotle." *Philosophy East and West* 48.2: 323–47.

Zau, Sinmay. 1938. "Confucius on Poetry." *T'ien Hsia Monthly* 7: 137–50.

Zhang, Hengshou. 1981. "Theories of Humaneness in the Spring and Autumn Era and Confucius' Concept of Humaneness." *Chinese Studies in Philosophy* 12.4: 3–36.

Conversion Charts

FOLLOWING ARE ROMANIZATION conversion charts. Pinyin has become the standard system, and is used in most of the essays in this volume. Wade-Giles is an older system still used in many texts. Common Alphabetic (CA) is the system developed and used by Bruce and Taeko Brooks.

PINYIN TO WADE-GILES

PINYIN	WADE-GILES	PINYIN	WADE-GILES
-a	-a	k-	k'-
-ai	-ai	l-	l-
-an	-an	li	li
-ang	-ang	m-	m-
-ao	-ao	mi	mi
b-	p-	n-	n-
bi	pi	ni	ni
c-	ts'-	-o	-o
ch-, q-	ch'-	-ong	-ung
chi	ch'ih	-ou	-ou, -u
ci	tz'ǔ, ts'ǔ	p-	p'-
d-	t-	pi	p'i
di	ti	q-, ch-	ch'-
-e	ê, o	qi	ch'i
-ei	-ei	r-	j-
-en	-ên	ri	jih
-eng	-êng	s-	s-
er	ěrh	sh-, x-	sh-
f-	f-	shi	shih
g-	k-	si	szǔ, ssǔ
h-	h-	t-	t'-
-i	-i, -ih, ǔ	ti	t'i
-ia	-ia	-u, -ü	-u, -ü
-ian	-ien	-ua	-ua
-iang	-iang	-uai	-uai
-iao	-iao	-uan	-uan
-ie	-ieh	-uang	-uang
-in	-in	-ue, -üe	-üeh
-ing	-ing	-ui	-ui
-iong	-iung	-un	-un
-iu	-iu	-uo	-o
j-, zh-	ch-	w-	w-
ji	chi	wu	wu

PINYIN TO WADE-GILES

PINYIN	WADE-GILES	PINYIN	WADE-GILES
x-, sh-	hs-	z-	ts-
xi	hsi	zh-, j-	ch-
y-	y-	zhi	chih
yi	yi	zi	tzŭ, tsŭ

WADE-GILES TO PINYIN

WADE-GILES	PINYIN	WADE-GILES	PINYIN
-a	-a	m-	m-
-ai	-ai	mi	mi
-an	-an	n-	n-
-ang	-ang	ni	ni
-ao	-ao	-o	-o
ch-	j-, zh-	-ou, -u	-ou
chi	ji	p-	b-
chih	zhi	pi	bi
ch'-	ch-, q-	p'-	p-
ch'i	qi	p'i	pi
ch'ih	chi	s-	s-
-ê, o	-e	sh-	sh-, x-
-ei	-ei	shih	shi
-ên	-en	szŭ, ssŭ	si
-êng	-eng	t-	d-
ěrh	er	ti	di
f-	f-	t'-	t-
h-	h-	t'i	ti
hs-, sh-	x-, sh-	ts-	z-
hsi	xi	tzŭ, tsŭ	zi
-i, -ih, ŭ	-i	ts'-	c-
-ia	-ia	tz'ŭ, ts'ŭ	ci
-ien	-ian	-u, -ü	-u, -ü
-iang	-iang	-ua	-ua
-iao	-iao	-uai	-uai
-ieh	-ie	-uan	-uan
-in	-in	-uang	-uang
-ing	-ing	-üeh	-ue, -üe
-iung	-iong	-ui	-ui
-iu	-iu	-un	-un
j-	r-	-ung	-ong
jih	ri	w-	w-
k-	g-	wu	wu
k'-	k-	y-	y-
l-	l-	yi	yi
li	li		

COMMON ALPHABETIC TO PINYIN

CA	PY	CA	PY
a	a	fan	fan
ai	ai	fang	fang
an	an	fei	fei
ang	ang	fou	fou
ar	er	fu	fu
au	ao	fvn	fen
ba	ba	fvng	feng
bai	bai	fwo	fo
ban	ban	gai	gai
bang	bang	gan	gan
bau	bao	gang	gang
bei	bei	gau	gao
bi	bi	gei	gei
bin	bin	gou	gou
bing	bing	gu	gu
bu	bu	gun	gun
bvn	ben	gung	gong
bvng	beng	gv	ge
bwo	bo	gvn	gen
byau	biao	gvng	geng
bye	bie	gwa	gua
byen	bian	gwai	guai
cha	cha	gwan	guan
chai	chai	gwang	guang
chan	chan	gwei	gui
chang	chang	gwo	guo
chau	chao	ha	ha
chi	qi	hai	hai
chin	qin	han	han
ching	qing	hang	hang
chou	chou	hau	hao
chr	chi	hei	hei
chu	chu	hou	hou
chun	chun	hu	hu
chung	chong	hun	hun
chv	che	hung	hong
chvn	chen	hv	he
chvng	cheng	hvn	hen
chwai	chuai	hvng	heng
chwan	chuan	hwa	hua
chwang	chuang	hwai	huai
chwei	chui	hwan	huan
dzu	zu	hwang	huang
dzun	zun	hwei	hui
dzung	zong	hwo	huo
dzv	ze	ja	zha
dzvn	zen	jai	zhai
dzvng	zeng	jan	zhan
dzwan	zuan	jang	zhang
dzwei	zui	jau	zhao
dzwo	zuo	jei	zhei
fa	fa	ji	ji

COMMON ALPHABETIC TO PINYIN

CA	PY	CA	PY
jin	jin	lin	lin
jing	jing	ling	ling
jou	zhou	lou	lou
jr	zhi	lu	lu
ju	zhu	lun	lun
jun	zhun	lung	long
jung	zhong	lv	le
jv	zhe	lvng	leng
jvn	zhen	lw	lyu
jvng	zheng	lwan	luan
jwa	zhua	lwo	luo
jwai	zhuai	lya	lia
jwan	zhuan	lyang	liang
jwang	zhuang	lyau	liao
jwei	zhui	lye	lie
jwo	zhuo	lyen	lian
jya	jia	lyou	liu
jyang	jiang	lywe	lüe
jyau	jiao	ma	ma
jye	jie	mai	mai
jyen	jian	man	man
jyou	jiu	mang	mang
jyung	jiong	mau	mao
jyw	ju	mei	mei
jywæn	juan	mi	mi
jywe	jue	min	min
jywn	jun	ming	ming
ka	ka	mou	mou
kai	kai	mu	mu
kan	kan	mvn	men
kang	kang	mvng	meng
kau	kao	mwo	mo
kou	kou	myau	miao
ku	ku	mye	mie
kun	kun	myen	mian
kung	kong	myou	miu
kv	ke	na	na
kvn	ken	nai	nai
kvng	keng	nan	nan
kwa	kua	nang	nang
kwai	kuai	nau	nao
kwan	kuan	nei	nei
kwang	kuang	ni	ni
kwei	kui	nin	nin
kwo	kuo	ning	ning
la	la	nou	nou
lai	lai	nu	nu
lan	lan	nun	nun
lang	lang	nung	nong
lau	lao	nv	ne
lei	lei	nvn	nen
li	li	nvng	neng

COMMON ALPHABETIC TO PINYIN

CA	PY	CA	PY
nw	nyu	shei	shei
nwan	nuan	shou	shou
nwo	nuo	shr	shi
nyang	niang	shu	shu
nyau	niao	shun	shun
nye	nie	shv	she
nyen	nian	shvn	shen
nyou	niu	shvng	sheng
nywe	nüe	shwa	shua
ou	ou	shwai	shuai
pa	pa	shwan	shuan
pai	pai	shwang	shuang
pan	pan	shwei	shui
pang	pang	shwo	shuo
pau	pao	sou	sou
pei	pei	su	su
pi	pi	sun	sun
pin	pin	sung	song
ping	ping	sv	se
pou	pou	svn	sen
pu	pu	svng	seng
pvn	pen	swan	suan
pvng	peng	swei	sui
pwo	po	swo	suo
pyau	piao	sya	xia
pye	pie	syang	xiang
pyen	pian	syau	xiao
r	ri	sye	xie
ran	ran	syen	xian
rang	rang	syi	xi
rau	rao	syin	xin
rou	rou	sying	xing
ru	ru	syou	xiu
run	run	syung	xiong
rung	rong	syw	xu
rv	re	sywæn	xuan
rvn	ren	sywe	xue
rvng	reng	sywn	xun
rwa	rua	sz	si
rwan	ruan	ta	ta
rwei	rui	tai	tai
rwo	ruo	tan	tan
sa	sa	tang	tang
sai	sai	tau	tao
san	san	ti	ti
sang	sang	ting	ting
sau	sao	tou	tou
sha	sha	tsa	ca
shai	shai	tsai	cai
shan	shan	tsan	can
shang	shang	tsang	cang
shau	shao	tsau	cao

COMMON ALPHABETIC TO PINYIN

CA	PY	CA	PY
tsou	cou	vng	eng
tsu	cu	wa	wa
tsun	cun	wai	wai
tsung	cong	wan	wan
tsv	ce	wang	wang
tsvn	cen	wei	wei
tsvng	ceng	wo	wo
tswan	cuan	wu	wu
tswei	cui	wvn	wen
tswo	cuo	wvng	weng
tsz	ci	ya	ya
tu	tu	yang	yang
tun	tun	yau	yao
tung	tong	ye	ye
tv	te	yen	yan
tvng	teng	yi	yi
twan	tuan	yin	yin
twei	tui	ying	ying
two	tuo	you	you
tyau	tiao	yung	yong
tye	tie	yw	yu
tyen	tian	ywæn	yuan
v	e	ywe	yue
vn	en	ywn	yun

Index Locorum

This index lists citations of passages from the *Four Books*: the *Analects*, *Mengzi* (*Mencius*), *Great Learning*, and *Doctrine of the Mean*. Citations of the former two follow the sectioning in the Harvard-Yenching concordance (HY). Citations of the latter two follow the sectioning in James Legge's translations. For the convenience of those who do not read Chinese, I have identified the corresponding sectioning in D. C. Lau's translation of the *Analects* and the *Mengzi* where it differs from that in the Harvard-Yenching text, in parentheses *after the Harvard-Yenching section heading*. Finally, since contributors were free to use whichever edition they preferred, I have identified in parentheses *after a page reference* if it is cited on that page according to a different section number from the Harvard-Yenching text. So a citation might be of the form "HY (Lau): page (cited as)." For example, if you look up a reference to *Analects* 10:3 below, you will find under the heading for Book 10 "3 (4): 44 (4)," which means that Harvard-Yenching section number 3 corresponds to Lau's section number 4 and is cited on p. 44 of this book, where the author identifies it (following Soothill in this case) as section 4. (Fortunately, most references are not this complicated.) I have also provided references for discussions of entire books in the *Analects*, but only when three or fewer books are discussed at one time. Thus, a reference to books 1–3 of the *Analects* is noted under the headings for books 1, 2, and 3, but a reference to books 16–20 as a whole is not noted in the list below.

Analects

Book 1: 14, 184, 204n. 34, 209n. 74
2: 61
4: 208n. 66, 224, 225, 235n. 28
7: 10
8: 225
9: 192
11: 10, 34n. 67, 211–12n. 84, 261
12: 42–46, 51, 103
13: 27
15: 104, 222

Book 2: 14, 180–96 passim, 204n. 34, 205n. 35, 271n. 38
1: 21, 24, 50, 91n. 37, 103
3: 19, 54, 59, 146
4: 79, 92n. 42, 112n. 9, 165, 195, 249
5: 61
6: 10
7: 104
8: 48

9: 168, 202n. 15
11: 3, 212n. 84, 249
12: 186
15: 199
16: 51
23: 59
24: 18, 27

Book 3: 14, 18, 144, 180–96 passim, 241, 267n. 8
1: 9, 61, 180, 286, 287
2: 9, 286, 287
3: 59, 71nn. 15, 20–21; 194, 199
4: 54, 60, 156n. 39, 169, 188
6: 9, 287
8: 188, 222
9: 59, 127, 133n. 37
10: 287
11: 19, 181, 216, 241, 287
12: 241
13: 78, 241
14: 59, 61

The Great Learning

no citations

Mengzi (Mencius)

Doctrine of the Mean

General Index